TEACHER'S EDITION

Houghton
Mifflin
Harcourt

JOURNEYS
COMMON CORE

Unit
3

LESSON 11

LESSON 12

LESSON 13

LESSON 14

LESSON 15

Printed in China

ISBN   978-0-547-97543-6

7 8 9 10   0940   21 20 19 18 17 16 15 14 13

4500433803   C D E F G

Houghton
Mifflin
Harcourt

JOURNEYS
COMMON CORE

Grade 1

TEACHER'S EDITION

Program Authors

James F. Baumann · David J. Chard · Jamal Cooks
J. David Cooper · Russell Gersten · Marjorie Lipson
Lesley Mandel Morrow · John J. Pikulski · Shane Templeton
Sheila W. Valencia · Catherine Valentino · MaryEllen Vogt

Consulting Author

Irene Fountas

Common Core Consultants

Carol Jago · J. Helen Perkins

PROGRAM AUTHORS

David J. Chard
Leon Simmons Endowed Chair
Southern Methodist University
Dallas, Texas

RESEARCH CONTRIBUTIONS:
Reading interventions, direct instruction of comprehension, alphabetic principle on the reading development of first graders

Marjorie Lipson
Professor Emerita, Principal Investigator, Vermont Reads Institute, University of Vermont
Burlington, Vermont

RESEARCH CONTRIBUTIONS:
Struggling readers and reading disabilities, reading comprehension, school change and literacy improvement

John J. Pikulski
Professor Emeritus, School of Education, University of Delaware
Newark, Delaware

RESEARCH CONTRIBUTIONS:
Early intervention to prevent reading difficulties, teaching and developing vocabulary

James F. Baumann
Wyoming Excellence Chair of Literacy Education
University of Wyoming, Laramie, Wyoming

RESEARCH CONTRIBUTIONS:
Reading teacher effectiveness, national trends in elementary reading instruction

Jamal Cooks
Associate Professor, San Francisco State University, San Francisco, California

RESEARCH CONTRIBUTIONS:
Urban education; language, literacy, and culture; popular culture in the classroom

J. David Cooper
Professor of Education, Retired
Ball State University, Muncie, Indiana

RESEARCH CONTRIBUTIONS:
Classroom instruction, classroom management, development of programs for Response to Intervention

CONSULTING AUTHOR

Irene Fountas
Professor of Education
Lesley University
Cambridge, Massachusetts

RESEARCH CONTRIBUTIONS:
Leveled texts, readers' and writers' workshop, assessment, classroom management and professional development

COMMON CORE CONSULTANTS

Carol Jago
Teacher of English, Santa Monica High School, Santa Monica, California; Past President, National Council of Teachers of English; Editor, California Association of Teachers of English journal, *California English*; Planning Committee Participant, 2009 NAEP Framework and 2011 NAEP Writing Framework

J. Helen Perkins, Ed. D.
Associate Professor of Reading & Urban Literacy; Coordinator, Reading Program; Board of Directors, Association of Literacy Educators & Researchers (ALER), The University of Memphis, Memphis, Tennessee

Russell Gersten
Professor Emeritus, College of Education
University of Oregon, Eugene, Oregon

RESEARCH CONTRIBUTIONS:
English language learners, studies of implementation, measurement of classroom instruction, reading comprehension

Shane Templeton
Foundation Professor of Literacy Studies, The University of Nevada, Reno, Reno, Nevada

RESEARCH CONTRIBUTIONS:
Morphological knowledge in vocabulary and spelling development; integrated word study in the development of phonics, spelling, and vocabulary

Sheila W. Valencia
Professor, Curriculum and Instruction, University of Washington, Seattle, Washington

RESEARCH CONTRIBUTIONS:
Literacy assessment, reading and writing instruction, teacher development

MaryEllen Vogt
Distinguished Professor Emerita, College of Education
California State University, Long Beach, Long Beach, California

RESEARCH CONTRIBUTIONS:
English language learners, Sheltered Instruction Observation Protocol Model for teaching English-language arts to English language learners

Lesley Mandel Morrow
Professor of Literacy, Graduate School of Education, Rutgers University, The State University of New Jersey, New Brunswick, New Jersey

RESEARCH CONTRIBUTIONS:
Early literacy development, organization and management of language arts programs

Catherine Valentino
Author-in-Residence, Houghton Mifflin Harcourt
West Kingston, Rhode Island

RESEARCH CONTRIBUTIONS:
Inquiry-based learning in reading and writing, motivating reluctant learners, literacy through early childhood problem-solving projects

Journeys Reviewers

Sheliah Cosby
Forge Ridge Elementary
Harrogate, TN

Kelly Guiliano
Fulton Elementary School
Lancaster, PA

Amy Gullion
Stewarts Creek Elementary
School
Smyrna, TN

Gina Hipsher
Joppa Elementary School
Rutledge, TN

Jennifer Lingenfelter
Twin Lakes School District
Monticello, IN

Sara Maloney
Greater Clark County School
District
Jeffersonville, IN

Jill Martin
Fulton Elementary School
Lancaster, PA

Brenda Marty
Fort Wayne Community Schools
Fort Wayne, IN

Sherri Mitchell
School Town of Highland
Highland, IN

Katie Pattullo
Metro Nashville School District
Nashville, TN

Matthew Portell
Cole Elementary School
Antioch, TN

Betty Salvatore
Fayetteville, WV

Stacey Schmidt
Valparaiso Community Schools
Valparaiso, IN

Brandi Self
Moreland Heights Elementary
School
Knoxville, TN

Vicki Weber
School Town of Highland
Highland, IN

Student Book

Common Core State Standards shown at point of use

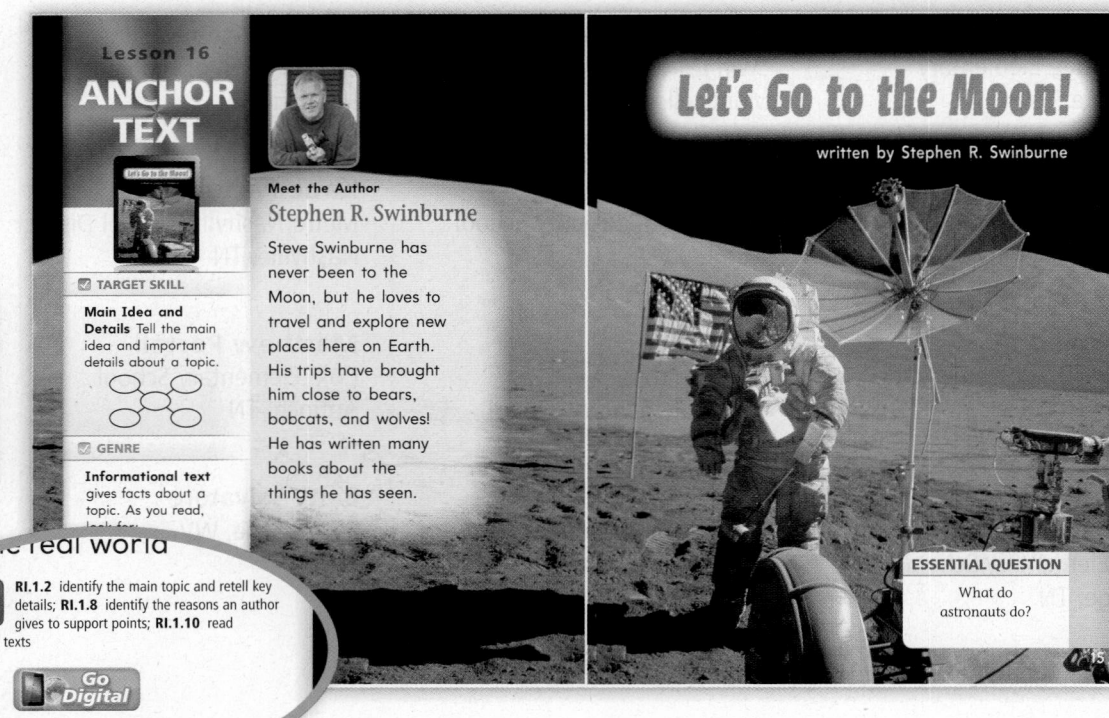

Weekly Focus Wall

Weekly lesson at a glance

Available online and as a Classroom Poster

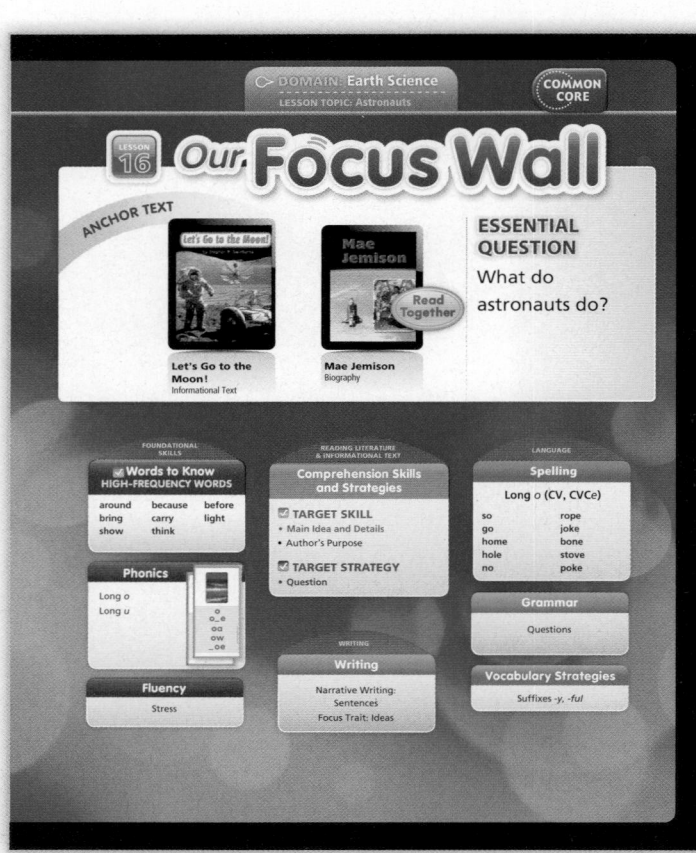

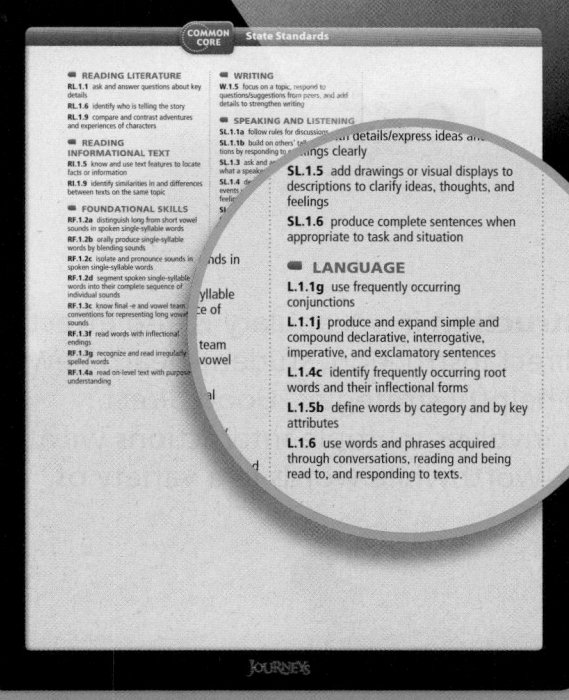

Lesson Tabs
- Weekly **Common Core State Standards coverage** at a glance

for Teachers

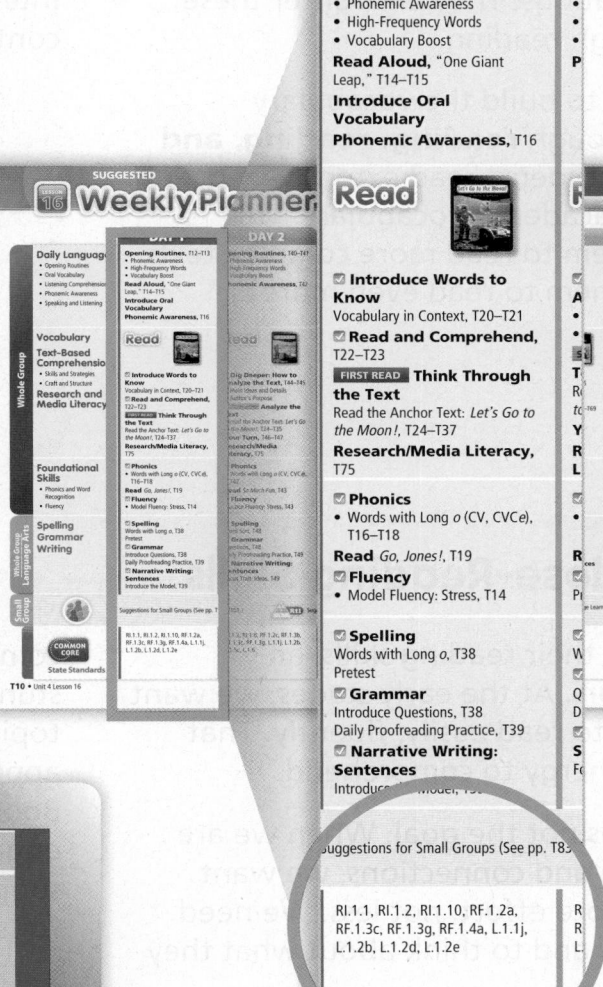

DAY 1

Opening Routines, T12–T13
- Phonemic Awareness
- High-Frequency Words
- Vocabulary Boost

Read Aloud, "One Giant Leap," T14–T15

Introduce Oral Vocabulary

Phonemic Awareness, T16

Read

☑ **Introduce Words to Know**
Vocabulary in Context, T20–T21

☑ **Read and Comprehend,** T22–T23

FIRST READ Think Through the Text
Read the Anchor Text: *Let's Go to the Moon!*, T24–T37

Research/Media Literacy, T75

☑ **Phonics**
- Words with Long *o* (CV, CVC*e*), T16–T18

Read *Go, Jones!*, T19

☑ **Fluency**
- Model Fluency: Stress, T14

☑ **Spelling**
Words with Long *o*, T38
Pretest

☑ **Grammar**
Introduce Questions, T38
Daily Proofreading Practice, T39

☑ **Narrative Writing: Sentences**
Introduce the Model, T39

Suggestions for Small Groups (See pp. T8...)

RI.1.1, RI.1.2, RI.1.10, RF.1.2a, RF.1.3c, RF.1.3g, RF.1.4a, L.1.1j, L.1.2b, L.1.2d, L.1.2e

Online Planning: *my*SmartPlanner
Online planning for *Journeys, Go Math!,* and *Science Fusion* in one location

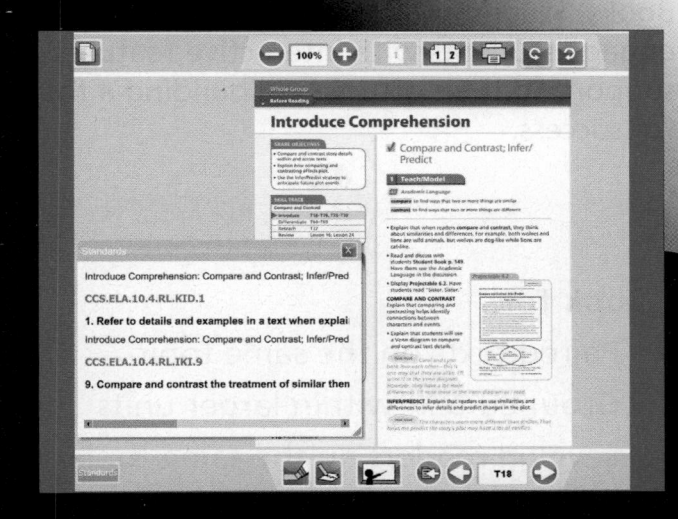

COMMON CORE Daily **Common Core State Standards** planning support

The Challenge of Complex Text

Developing Academic Vocabulary

Academic vocabulary is the vocabulary of schools and books—vocabulary that is used across many domains and topics by mature language users. Students do not learn academic vocabulary in everyday social situations. They encounter these words mostly through reading.

Therefore, one way to build the vocabulary students need is through **reading, reading, and more reading**. As students read extensively over time, they develop academic vocabulary. This vocabulary helps them to read more complex texts, and that prepares them to read even more complex texts.

Direct instruction in vocabulary is also effective. Through direct instruction, students learn new words and helpful strategies. Good direct instruction involves multiple interactions with interesting, worthwhile words in a variety of contexts.

Look for:
- Multiple texts with the same target vocabulary
- Multiple interactions with vocabulary
- Instruction in vocabulary strategies

Developing Close-Reading Skills

As students grow in their reading skills, an important shift occurs. At the early stages, we want students to be able to read easily, fluently. That leaves them more energy to comprehend.

Later, easy reading is not the goal. When we are building knowledge and connections, we want students to make more effort, not less. We need them to read closely and to think about what they read.

Close reading pays off in the end, but motivation and a feeling of success are key. That is why *Journeys* includes accessible texts as well as more complex ones. *Journeys* also motivates with stunning photographs and illustrations, as well as topics and authors that are chosen for student appeal. In addition, *Journeys* eBooks—Student Books, Student Magazines, and Write-in Readers—engage students with interactive features while supporting their efforts and building a foundation for success.

Look for:
- Paired texts on the same topic
- Grouped text within larger units
- Leveled readers on the same topic
- Opportunities for structured research
- Media literacy instruction

As students move up the grades, one of their most important challenges is learning from and about complex texts. To prepare students for this challenge, Journeys focuses on repeated reading of complex texts.

WHAT IS COMPLEX ABOUT COMPLEX TEXTS?

The Common Core State Standards Initiative uses a triangle model to categorize the many aspects of text complexity:

QUALITATIVE aspects include the style, structure, and purpose of the text.

QUANTITATIVE aspects include word length, word frequency, and sentence length measured by Lexile or Guided Reading Level.

READER AND TASK considerations require teacher judgment. What will motivate your students? What do you want them to learn?

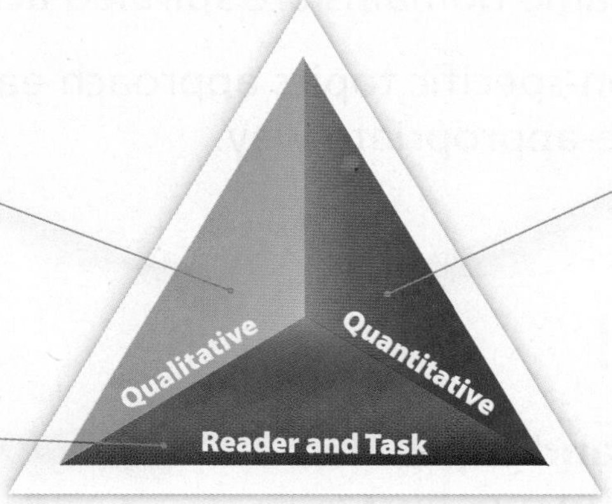

Qualitative

Quantitative

Reader and Task

THE *JOURNEYS* TEXT COMPLEXITY RUBRIC

To help teachers assess text complexity at a glance, *Journeys* provides a rubric in every lesson. Look for rubrics like the example shown below.

- **Qualitative measures** shown on a 4-point continuum
- Text-specific rationales

Quantitative measures

Title of **Anchor Text**

Title of **related paired text**

Overall text complexity labels: Accessible, Complex, or More Complex

TEXT COMPLEXITY RUBRIC

Overall Text Complexity		Ecology for Kids INFORMATIONAL TEXT	Wonderful Weather POETRY
		COMPLEX	**MORE COMPLEX**
Quantitative Measures	Lexile	770	NP
	Guided Reading Level	S	R
Qualitative Measures	Text Structure	organization of main ideas and details may be complex, but is clearly stated and generally sequential	somewhat complex poetic structure
	Language Conventionality and Clarity	some unfamiliar or academic words	some figurative language
	Knowledge Demands	specialized knowledge required	everyday knowledge (familiarity with genre conventions) required
	Purpose/Levels of Meaning	implied, but easy to infer	multiple levels of meaning (multiple themes)

Support for **Reader and Task Considerations** appears with each Anchor Text. Look for suggestions to Motivate, Access, Knowledge, and Experiences, Increase Scaffolding, and Foster Independence so that students will read and comprehend the text successfully.

Journeys Common Core
DOMAINS and TOPICS

Journeys **builds a deep understanding** of key domains and topics within a single lesson, across a grade, and across the program. Each lesson features a domain and topic that tie the week's two text selections together.

☞ The same domains are spiraled across the grades.

☞ Lesson-specific topics approach each domain in a grade-appropriate way.

At the Lesson Level

Within a lesson, the domain and topic are

- Introduced just before reading the lesson's anchor text
- Supported across the lesson through cross-curricular teaching notes at point of use during the reading
- Expanded on later in the week using another text that complements the anchor text
- Extended with domain-specific vocabulary and through text-based Research and Speaking & Listening activities

Across a Grade

Journeys **student texts and Teacher's Editions**

- Provide exposure to a wide range of domains and topics through high-quality texts and focused instruction
- Incorporate text-based scaffolding so that students learn to read complex texts independently

Across the Program

Journeys **student texts and instructional support**

- Prepare students to read complex informational texts
- Build a rich bank of domain-specific vocabulary for college and career readiness

◗ DOMAIN: Life Science

The diagram below shows how animal-related topics in the Life Science domain are developed and reviewed across *Journeys*.

Kindergarten

Lesson 6:   Using Our Senses
Lesson 8:   Ways to Move
Lesson 13: Animal Bodies
Lesson 14: Animal Homes
Lesson 22: Growing Up
Lesson 24: Animal Colors

Grade 1

Lesson 7:   Animal Communication
Lesson 11: Marine Habitats
Lesson 12: Jungle Animals
Lesson 15: Animals
Lesson 22: Animals
Lesson 24: Life Cycles
Lesson 29: Insects

Grade 2

Lesson 1:   Animal Traits
Lesson 3:   Animal Traits
Lesson 6:   Animal Homes
Lesson 10: Ocean Life
Lesson 21: Animal Development
Lesson 26: Life Cycles

Grade 3

Lesson 6:   Mammals
Lesson 18: Life Cycles
Lesson 22: Animal Migration

Grade 4

Lesson 13: Interdependence
Lesson 14: Insects
Lesson 23: Life Cycles
Lesson 24: Animal Behavior
Lesson 26: Spiders
Lesson 27: Amphibians

Grade 5

Lesson 6:   Wild Animals
Lesson 10: Animal Behavior
Lesson 20: Human-Animal Interaction
Lesson 26: Adaptations and Instincts

Grade 6

Lesson 9: Island Ecosystems

◗ Additional Domains Explored in *Journeys*

American History

The Arts

Civics

Communication

Community

Cultures

Earth Science

General Science

Health and Safety

Math

Media

Physical Science

Recreation and Travel

Social Relationships

Technology and Innovation

Values

Supporting the Common Core *through* Extended Reading

Exemplar Texts

Rich, high-quality literature gives students the opportunity for close reading and analysis using full-length trade books.

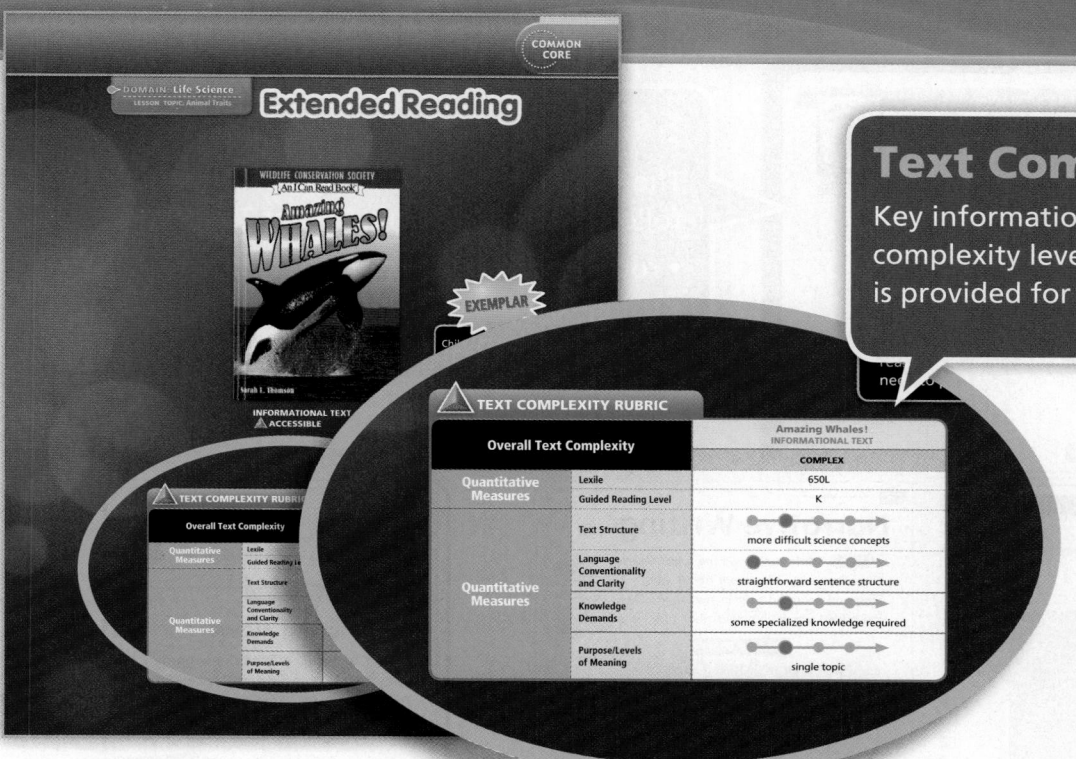

Text Complexity Rubrics

Key information and details about text complexity levels, including Lexile scores, is provided for each trade book.

for Teachers

TEXT COMPLEXITY RUBRIC

Overall Text Complexity		Amazing Whales! INFORMATIONAL TEXT
		COMPLEX
Quantitative Measures	Lexile	650L
	Guided Reading Level	K
Quantitative Measures	Text Structure	more difficult science concepts
	Language Conventionality and Clarity	straightforward sentence structure
	Knowledge Demands	some specialized knowledge required
	Purpose/Levels of Meaning	single topic

Analyze the Text

Opportunities for close reading with each text segment

Performance Task

Measure both understanding and progress

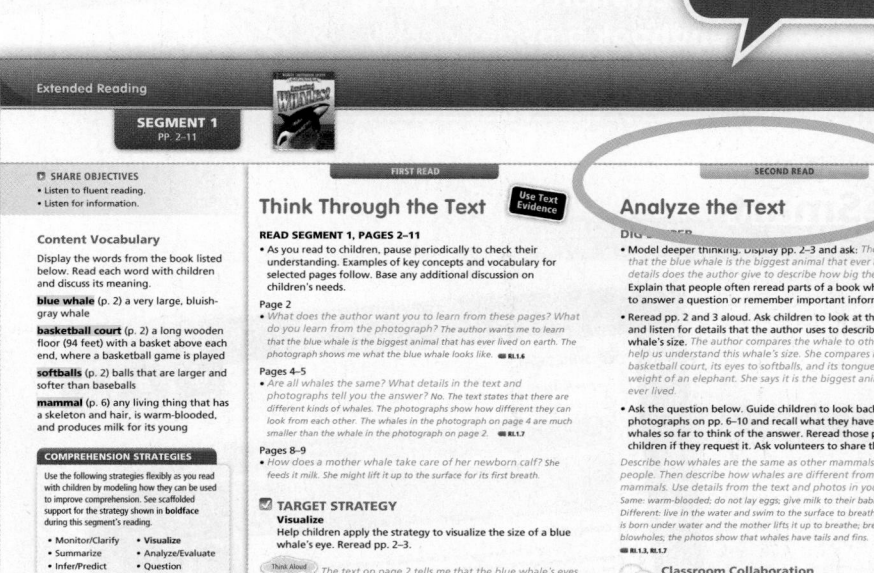

Common Core Writing and Performance Tasks

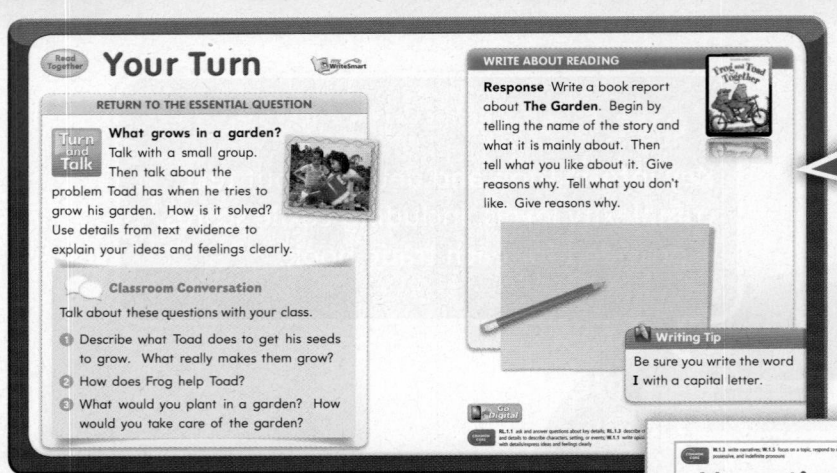

Student Book: Your Turn

The **Write About Reading** performance task following each lesson's Anchor Text promotes

- routine writing in response to texts
- using text evidence to support ideas
- using the conventions of standard English

Student Book: Writing Traits and Process

Weekly writing instruction models the writing process, from prewriting through publishing, and the importance of the traits of good writing. A wide range of text types and writing purposes are shown, giving students clear expectations about their performance tasks.

The **Common Core Writing Handbook** provides weekly writing support and resources.

Student Online!

*my*WriteSmart

- Variety of digital tools to produce and publish writing
- Multiple opportunities for peer collaboration
- Opportunities to create multimedia visual displays in presentations.
- Research projects of varying lengths build knowledge about a topic.

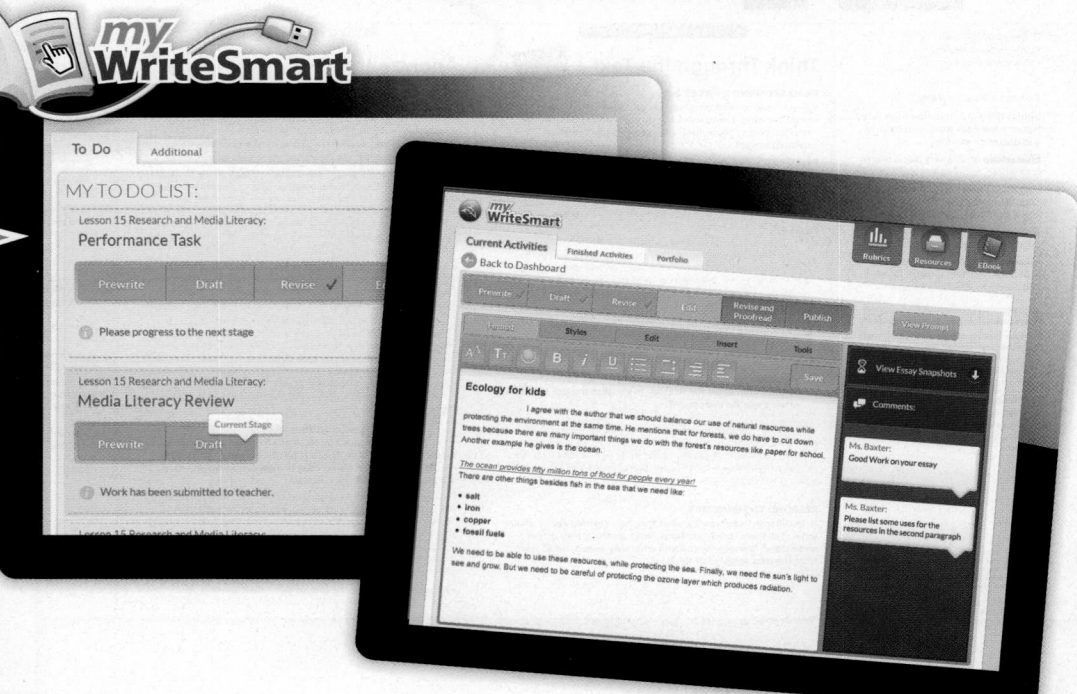

for Teachers

Teacher's Edition

Five days of Narrative, Informative, and Opinion Writing lessons connect to the Common Core Standards, to the Anchor Text, and to Writing Rubrics.

Teacher Online!

*my*WriteSmart is an interactive online writing and Performance Assessment tool.

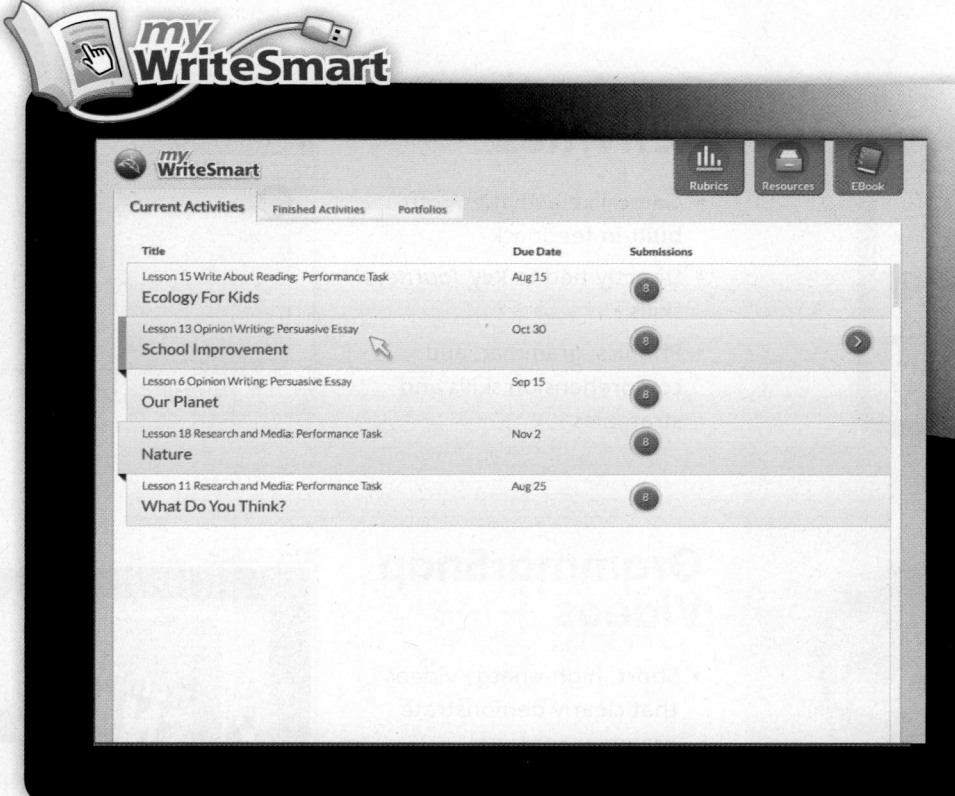

Go Digital

Through the DIGITAL Gateway

1 PLAN

*my*SmartPlanner

- Totally integrated lesson plans for *GoMath!, Science Fusion,* and *Journeys*

Through the DIGITAL Gateway

- Your personal gateway to customized instruction
- View online activities and lessons and assign to students
- Lessons, tests, and management tools at your fingertips

Interactive Focus Wall

- Key skills and concepts at a glance
- Quick links to online instruction and practice

Journeys Online Teacher's Edition

- Instant access to all *Teacher's Editions*
- *Teacher's Edition* and resources also available on the Teacher One-Stop DVD

2 ENGAGE

*my*WriteSmart

- Performance Tasks and Assessment
- Interactive writing support
- Connected to the *Student Book*

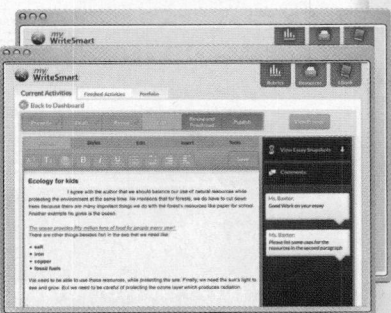

Interactive Whiteboard Lessons

- Grab and hold students' interest
- Weekly lessons in grammar or phonics, text analysis, vocabulary strategies, and writing

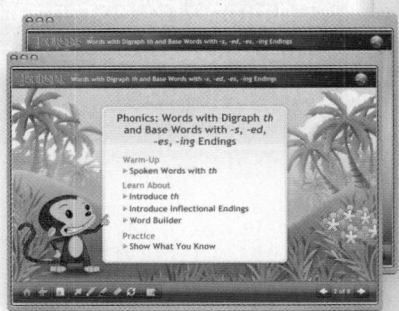

Destination Reading Activities

- Game-like activities with built-in feedback
- Directly tied to key *Journeys* skills
- Phonics, grammar, and comprehension skills and strategies

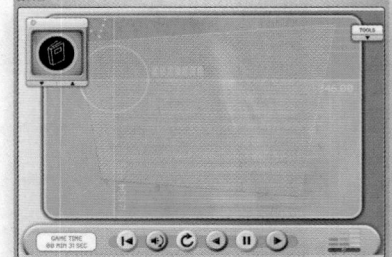

GrammarSnap Videos

- Short, high-energy videos that clearly demonstrate grammar concepts

3 TEACH

Student eBook

- Whiteboard-friendly navigation tools
- Audio for all selections and skills
- Destination Reading activities linked to key skills

 RtI Write-in Reader eBook

- eBook for Tier II Intervention
- Dual-speed audio: fluent and emergent
- Follow-Text feature for text tracking
- Whiteboard-friendly navigation tools

Online Leveled Readers

- Full audio text
- Online *Teacher's Guides*

Decodable Readers

- Provide opportunities for students to apply knowledge of *Journeys* phonics instruction in connected text

4 ASSESS

 Online Assessment System

- Weekly Tests
- Benchmark and Unit Tests
- Test Power
- Automatic scoring and reporting
- Correlated to Common Core State Standards
- Prescriptions for reteaching to meet Common Core State Standards
- Student Profile System to track student growth
- Reports for teachers, administrators, and parents

 EXAMVIEW® ASSESSMENT SUITE

- Weekly Tests
- Benchmark and Unit Tests
- Test Power
- Build your own tests

Printable PDFs

- Benchmark and Unit Tests
- Weekly Tests
- Test Power
- Cold Reads
- Progress Monitoring Assessments (Tier II Intervention)
- Literacy Kit Assessments (Tier III Intervention)

Journeys Assessment

Entry-Level

Emerging Literacy Survey

- Individually administered tests
- Diagnosis of phonemic awareness and basic reading skills, plus passages for reading in context

Diagnostic Assessment

- Individually-administered tests
- Diagnosis of basic reading skills, plus passages for reading in context
- Results provide targeted suggestions to inform instruction for grouping

Weekly

Weekly Tests in

- Group-administered tests
- State Test Formats
- Assess the Common Core State Standards
- Weekly assessment of Target Vocabulary, Vocabulary Strategies, Comprehension, Decoding, and Grammar
- Indicates need for reteaching, differentiated instruction

Assessment book in

- Observation Checklists
- Periodic Assessments

Test Power

- Prepare students for Common Core State Standards assessments
- Reading Complex Texts
- Performance Tasks

Ongoing Assessment

Diagnostic Assessment

- Monitor progress in key skills
- Identify focused instruction to meet students' needs

Assessment book in

- Periodic Assessments

The assessments in Journeys provide you with the data you need to make informed instructional decisions and guide students on the path to success. Use these assessments to determine which Common Core State Standards students have mastered and which require additional instruction.

COMMON CORE

End of Unit

Test Power in the Student Book

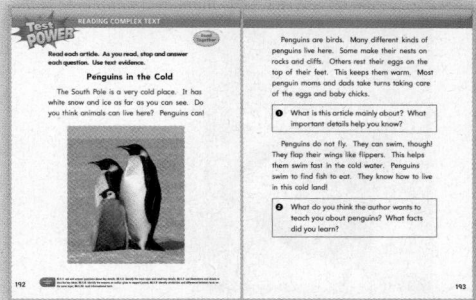

■ **Prepare students for the Common Core Assessment**
  ■ Performance Tasks

Benchmark and Unit Tests

■ **Prepare students for the Common Core Assessment**
  ■ Reading Complex Texts
  ■ Performance Tasks
  ■ Comprehensive Assessment of Common Core State Standards

Assessment Book in

- Periodic Assessments
- Units 2, 4, 6 Fluency Tests

Online **Assessment System**

- Weekly Tests
- Benchmark and Unit Tests
- Test Power
- Automatic scoring and reporting
- Correlated to Common Core State Standards
- Prescriptions for reteaching to meet Common Core State Standards
- Student Profile System to track student growth
- Reports for teachers, administrators, and parents

EXAMVIEW®
ASSESSMENT SUITE

- Weekly Tests
- Benchmark and Unit Tests
- Test Power
- Build your own tests

Cold Reads
- Increasingly difficult passages with comprehension questions

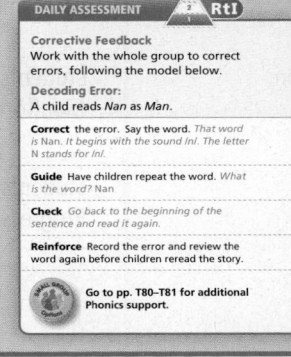

DAILY ASSESSMENT RtI

Corrective Feedback
Work with the whole group to correct errors, following the model below.

Decoding Error:
A child reads *Nan* as *Man.*

Correct the error. Say the word. *That word is Nan. It begins with the sound /n/. The letter N stands for /n/.*

Guide Have children repeat the word. *What is the word?* Nan

Check *Go back to the beginning of the sentence and read it again.*

Reinforce Record the error and review the word again before children reread the story.

Go to pp. T80–T81 for additional Phonics support.

Daily Assessment in the Teacher's Edition

my **WriteSmart**

- Performance Tasks

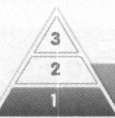 **RtI** Response to Intervention

Tier I Core Program

Teach

- Research-Based Core Instruction
- Built on Common Core State Standards
- Includes Scaffolds for Reading Complex Text
- Includes Differentiated Instruction

Assess

Weekly Tests
Group-administered
assessment of

- High-Frequency Words
- Phonics
- Comprehension
- Vocabulary Strategies

- Entry-Level Assessments (Emerging Literacy Survey,
- Benchmark and Unit Tests

Benchmark and Unit Tests

Tier II Core Program + Strategic Intervention

Write-In Reader

- Research-Based Strategic Intervention
- Extra Support for Common Core State Standards
- Accessible Text to Build Student Independence

Progress-Monitoring Assessments

- Core Assessments
- Progress Monitoring Assessments

Adjust

IF...	THEN...
students perform on-target on core assessments,	maintain challenging core instruction.
students do not perform on-target on core assessments,	add strategic intervention.

IF...	THEN...
students perform on-target on core assessments,	consider exiting them from strategic intervention.
students make progress on Progress Monitoring Assessments,	maintain strategic intervention.
students do not make progress on Progress Monitoring assessments,	add intensive intervention.

Tier III

Core Program + Strategic Intervention + Intensive Intervention

Reading Tool Kit

- Research-Based Intensive Intervention
- Intensive Support for Common Core State Standards
- Targeted Lessons to Bridge Learning Gaps

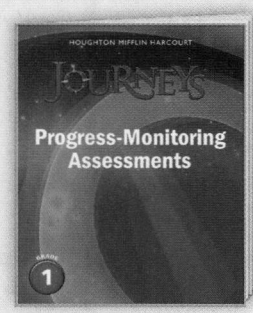

JOURNEYS

Progress-Monitoring Assessments

GRADE 1

- Core Assessments
- Progress Monitoring Assessments
- Diagnostic Assessment (as needed)
- Emerging Literacy Survey (as needed)

IF...	THEN...
students make progress on Progress Monitoring Assessments,	consider exiting them from intensive intervention; maintain strategic intervention.
students do not make progress on Progress Monitoring Assessments,	use Diagnostic Assessment or Emerging Literacy Survey to gain more information about individual needs.

Go Digital

Online Assessment System

- Online Tests with automatic scoring and reporting
- Correlated to Common Core State Standards
- Prescriptions for reteaching to meet Common Core State Standards
- Student Profile System to track student growth
- Reports for teachers, administrators, and parents

Tips

- Consider multiple measures of student performance.
- Use Tier II and Tier III intervention in addition to Tier I, not as a substitute.
- Provide all students with opportunities to engage with complex text and interact with peers.
- Keep family members informed and involved.

Unit 3 Planning for English Language Development ELL

Lesson 11
At Home in the Ocean

Lesson 12
How Leopard Got His Spots

Lesson 13
Seasons

Begin with High-Utility Words
Tier 1 Words
* = Spanish cognates

Lesson 11

High-Utility Words *animals*, home, lots, swim, ocean*, turtle*
- Language Support Card 11
- Building Background Videos
- Teacher's Edition p. E2
- Oral Language Chant, Blackline Master ELL11.5

Lesson 12

High-Utility Words *black, spot, stripe, fur, grass*
- Language Support Card 12
- Building Background Videos
- Teacher's Edition p. E12
- Oral Language Chant, Blackline Master ELL12.5

Lesson 13

High-Utility Words *ends, hot, spring, sun, wet, snow, tree*
- Language Support Card 13
- Building Background Videos
- Teacher's Edition p. E22
- Oral Language Chant, Blackline Master ELL13.5

Move on to Developing Vocabulary
Tier 2 & 3 Words
* = Spanish cognates

Lesson 11

Words to Know *cold, where, blue, live, far, their, little, water*
- Vocabulary in Context Cards

Reading/Language Arts Terms
consonant*, informational text*, analyze*, evaluate*, author's purpose*, topic, classify*, category*, base word, proper noun*, capital letter, title*, sentence, information*, verb*, adverb*, period
- Teacher's Edition pp. E2, E4, E6, E8, E10

Lesson 12

Words to Know *brown, own, very, off, never, know, out, been*
- Vocabulary in Context Cards

Reading/Language Arts Terms
consonant*, folktale, question, sequence of events, homophone*, apostrophe*, possessive*, informational text*, command, instructions*, letter
- Teacher's Edition pp. E12, E14, E16, E18, E20

Lesson 13

Words to Know *green, yellow, grow, open, fall, new, down, goes*
- Vocabulary in Context Cards

Reading/Language Arts Terms
consonant*, informational text*, visualize*, cause*, effect*, present tense*, past tense*, contraction*, apostrophe*, poetry*, subject*, verb*, sentence, inform*, facts, topic, main idea*
- Teacher's Edition pp. E22, E24, E26, E28, E30

Scaffolding Comprehension

Lesson 11

Build Background
- Language Support Card 11
- Building Background Videos
- Selection Blackline Master, ELL11.6

Comprehension
- Teacher's Edition pp. E3, E4, E5, E8, E10

Author's Purpose
- Teacher's Edition pp. E3, E5, E10

Lesson 12

Build Background
- Language Support Card 12
- Building Background Videos
- Selection Blackline Master, ELL12.6

Comprehension
- Teacher's Edition pp. E13, E14, E15, E18, E20

Sequence of Events
- Teacher's Edition pp. E13, E15, E20

Lesson 13

Build Background
- Language Support Card 13
- Building Background Videos
- Selection Blackline Master, ELL13.6

Comprehension
- Teacher's Edition pp. E23, E24, E25, E28, E30

Cause and Effect
- Teacher's Edition pp. E23, E25, E30

Scaffolding Writing

Lesson 11

Informative Writing
Sentences That Inform pp. T74–T75
- Teacher's Edition p. E11
- Common Core Writing Handbook: Sentences That Inform

Lesson 12

Informative Writing
Instructions in a Letter pp. T174–T175
- Teacher's Edition p. E21
- Common Core Writing Handbook: Instructions in a Letter

Lesson 13

Informative Writing
Sentences That Inform pp. T278–T279
- Teacher's Edition p. E31
- Common Core Writing Handbook: Sentences That Inform

Scaffolding Grammar

Lesson 11

Grammar: Proper Nouns pp. T72–T73
- Teacher's Edition p. E9
    Language Transfer Issue: Using Capital Letters
- Language Support Card 11: Questions with *What*

Lesson 12

Grammar: Commands pp. T172–T173
- Teacher's Edition p. E19
    Language Transfer Issue: Commands
- Language Support Card 12: Adverbs of Time

Lesson 13

Grammar: Subjects and Verbs pp. T276–T277
- Teacher's Edition p. E29
    Language Transfer Issue: Subject-Verb Inversion
- Language Support Card 13: Verb Forms and Complex Sentences with *Because*

COMMON CORE

Lesson 14
The Big Race

High-Utility Words *chase, hop, race, trip, win, lizard, snake*
- Language Support Card 14
- Building Background Videos
- Teacher's Edition p. E32
- Oral Language Chant, Blackline Master ELL14.5

Words to Know *two, into, three, starts, over, four, five, watch*
- Vocabulary in Context Cards

Reading/Language Arts Terms
vowel, fantasy*, infer*, predict*, conclusion*, classify*, category*, informational text*, consonant*, verb*, present tense*, past tense*, report, facts, topic, inform*
- Teacher's Edition pp. E32, E34, E36, E38, E40

Build Background
- Language Support Card 14
- Building Background Videos
- Selection Blackline Master, ELL14.6

Comprehension
- Teacher's Edition pp. E33, E34, E35, E38, E40

Conclusions
- Teacher's Edition pp. E33, E35, E40

Informative Writing
Report pp. T380–T381
- Teacher's Edition p. E41
- Common Core Writing Handbook: Report

Grammar: Verbs and Time pp. T378–T379
- Teacher's Edition p. E39
  Language Transfer Issue: Verb Tense
- Language Support Card 14: Simple Present Verbs

Lesson 15
Animal Groups

High-Utility Words *body, hair, shape, size, skin, cat, frog*
- Language Support Card 15
- Building Background Videos
- Teacher's Edition p. E42
- Oral Language Chant, Blackline Master ELL15.5

Words to Know *bird, fly, both, long, eyes, or, those, walk*
- Vocabulary in Context Cards

Reading/Language Arts Terms
vowel, consonant*, informational text*, monitor, clarify*, compare*, contrast*, suffix*, play, verb*, present tense*, past tense*, report, facts, inform*, topic
- Teacher's Edition pp. E42, E44, E46, E48, E50

Build Background
- Language Support Card 15
- Building Background Videos
- Selection Blackline Master, ELL15.6

Comprehension
- Teacher's Edition pp. E43, E44, E45, E48, E50

Compare and Contrast
- Teacher's Edition pp. E43, E45, E50

Informative Writing
Report pp. T480–T481
- Teacher's Edition p. E51
- Common Core Writing Handbook: Report

Grammar: The Verb *be* pp. T478–T479
- Teacher's Edition p. E49
  Language Transfer Issue: Verb Tense
- Language Support Card 15: Conjunctions and Complex Sentences

Go Digital

ELD Station
- Picture Card Bank Online
- Multimedia Grammar Glossary
- Language Support Posters Online
- Cross-Curricular Activity Bank
- eGlossary

Word Study Online
- Teacher's Guide Online
- Leveled Word Lists in Literacy and Language Guide

ADDITIONAL RESOURCES

ELL Teacher's Handbook
- ELLs Today
- Instructional Strategies
- Assessment
- Classroom Resources

Small Group Instruction
- ELL Leveled Readers
- ELL Leveled Reader Teacher Guides
- ELL Blackline Masters

Support for Newcomers
- ELL Newcomer Teacher's Guide
- Vocabulary and Concepts Posters
- Newcomer Audio

School-Home Connections
My Journey Home: Family Connections

		Lesson 11	**Lesson 12**	**Lesson 13**
	ESSENTIAL QUESTION	*What kinds of plants and animals would you find in the ocean?*	*How are jungle animals different from animals on a farm?*	*What changes do the different seasons cause?*
Whole Group	**Oral Language**	**Teacher Read Aloud** "The Piano Lessons" pp. T14–T15	**Teacher Read Aloud** "Turtle, Frog, and Rat" pp. T112–T113	**Teacher Read Aloud** "The Prickly Pride of Texas" pp. T212–T213
	Vocabulary	Oral Vocabulary Classify and Categorize Words	Oral Vocabulary Homophones	Oral Vocabulary Word Endings -ed, -ing, or -s
	Text-Based Comprehension • Skills and Strategies • Craft and Structure	**Target Skill** Author's Purpose **Target Strategy** Analyze/Evaluate **Anchor Text** *At Home in the Ocean* **Connect to the Topic** *Water*	**Target Skill** Sequence of Events **Target Strategy** Question **Anchor Text** *How Leopard Got His Spots* **Connect to the Topic** *The Rain Forest*	**Target Skill** Cause and Effect **Target Strategy** Visualize **Anchor Text** *Seasons* **Connect to the Topic** *Four Seasons for Animals*
	Research and Media Literacy Speaking/ Listening	Facts About an Ocean Animal and Its Habitat	Giving Clear Descriptions	Discuss Informational Text: Compare and Contrast
	Foundational Skills • Fluency • Phonemic Awareness • Phonics	**Fluency** Phrasing: Punctuation **Phonics** Digraph *th*; Base Words and -s, -es, -ed, -ing Endings	**Fluency** Rate **Phonics** Digraphs *ch, tch*; Possessives with *'s*; Phonogram -atch	**Fluency** Accuracy: Word Recognition **Phonics** Digraphs *sh, wh, ph*; Contractions with *'s, n't*
Whole Group Language Arts	**Spelling Grammar Writing**	**Spelling** Words with *th* **Grammar** Proper Nouns **Writing** Informative: Sentences That Inform	**Spelling** Words with *ch, tch* **Grammar** Commands **Writing** Informative: Instructions	**Spelling** Words with *sh, wh, ph* **Grammar** Subjects and Verbs **Writing** Informative: Sentences That Inform
Small Group	**Vocabulary Reader**	Differentiate *Shark*	Differentiate *Spots*	Differentiate *Ducks*
	Leveled Readers	● *In the Sea* ▲ *Coral Reefs* ■ *The Amazing Octopus* ◆ *Life in the Coral Reefs*	● *Giraffe's Neck* ▲ *Bear's Tail* ■ *Peacock's Tail* ◆ *Bear's Long, Brown Tail*	● *Winter* ▲ *Fall Changes* ■ *Seasons Around the World* ◆ *In the Fall*
	Differentiate Instruction	Phonics, Words to Know, Fluency, Comprehension, Vocabulary Strategies	Phonics, Words to Know, Fluency, Comprehension, Vocabulary Strategies	Phonics, Words to Know, Fluency, Comprehension, Vocabulary Strategies

Key ● Struggling Readers ▲ On-Level Readers ■ Advanced Readers ◆ English Language Learners

RESEARCH and MEDIA PERFORMANCE TASK

Multimedia Profiles
Children will use research tools to learn about how some animals live.

Checkpoints
☐ Create a list of animals and generate questions.
☐ Research factual sources. Write facts that answer the questions.
☐ Post the answers and present the findings to the class.
☐ Discuss what can be learned through research.

COMMON CORE

Lesson 14

Why is it important to have rules?

Teacher Read Aloud
"The Tortoise and the Hare" pp. T316–T317

Oral Vocabulary
Shades of Meaning

Target Skill Conclusions
Target Strategy Infer/Predict
Anchor Text *The Big Race*
Connect to the Topic *Rules and Laws*

Speaking About a Topic

Fluency Expression
Phonics Long *a* (CVCe); Phonogram *-ake*; Soft *c*, *g*, *dge*; Phonogram *-ace*

Spelling Words with Long *a*
Grammar Verbs and Time
Writing Informative: Report

Differentiate *Desert Animals*

● *Izzy's Move*
▲ *The Treasure Map*
■ *Cam the Camel*
◆ *The Map and the Treasure*

Phonics, Words to Know, Fluency, Comprehension, Vocabulary Strategies

Lesson 15

What makes birds different from mammals?

Teacher Read Aloud
"The Dancing Wolves" pp. T418–T419

Oral Vocabulary
Suffixes *-er*, *-est*

Target Skill Compare and Contrast
Target Strategy Monitor/Clarify
Anchor Text *Animal Groups*
Connect to the Topic *Animal Picnic*

Ask and Answer Questions:
Using Information from Media

Fluency Intonation
Phonics Long *i* (CVCe); Digraphs *kn*, *wr*, *gn*, *mb*; Phonograms *-ine*, *-ite*

Spelling Words with Long *i*
Grammar The Verb *be*
Writing Informative: Report

Differentiate *Animals*

● *Making a Home*
▲ *All About Bats*
■ *Bald Eagles*
◆ *Many Kinds of Bats*

Phonics, Words to Know, Fluency, Comprehension, Vocabulary Strategies

Go Digital

FOR STUDENTS

my WriteSmart

- Student eBook
- Write-In Reader eBook
- GrammarSnap Videos
- Destination Reading
- Context Cards

FOR TEACHERS

- *Journeys* Digital Gateway
- Interactive Focus Wall
- Teacher One-Stop Lesson Planning
- Interactive Whiteboard Lessons
- Literacy and Language Guide

Online Assessment System

- Benchmark and Unit Tests

For daily **ELL** and **Intervention** lessons, see the tabs at the back of this *Teacher's Edition*.

Read *Vulture View*

INTRODUCE Display the cover. Track the print as you read aloud the title. Identify the author and the illustrator and review their roles. Turn to the title page and read the text. Review how the title page is like the cover.

BACKGROUND Lead children to use the title and the illustrations to predict whether the book is a fantasy or gives information. Discuss what children already know about vultures. Explain that the vulture in the book is called a turkey vulture. ▬ RI.1.7

READ ALOUD For the first reading, focus on enjoyment and gaining familiarity with the book. Pause occasionally to allow reactions to the information and the rhyme and rhythm of the language. Point out that the text gives clues about what turkey vultures will not eat until the reader can figure out what they do eat. Save pp. 30–31 for a second reading. ▬ RI.1.10

RESPOND After reading, discuss general questions such as: *What do you like about this book? What did you learn about vultures? Would you like to read this book again? Why?* Encourage volunteers to point to pages to discuss their ideas. ▬ RI.1.1, RI.1.2, RI.1.7

Reread *Vulture View*

DEVELOP CONCEPTS AND SKILLS Revisit the **Big Book** from time to time, prompting children to join in the reading. Use the book to develop various concepts and skills. For example:
▬ RI.1.1, RI.1.2, RI.1.4, RF.1.1a, RF.1.4b

- Understanding concepts of print, such as directionality and punctuation (including the ellipses on p. 12 and what they lead to on p. 13).

Big Book

- Identifying and producing rhyming words.
- Appreciating information given in illustrations.
- Using context, in language and in illustrations, to determine word meanings.

DEVELOP COMPREHENSION After another reading of the **Big Book**, ask the following questions:
▬ RI.1.1, RI.1.2, RI.1.7, RI.1.10

1 *What do turkey vultures eat? Vultures eat dead animals.*

2 *How do turkey vultures find food? They use their senses of sight and smell.*

3 *What do turkey vultures do after the sun goes down? They stop flying, perch together on trees, and sleep.*

4 *Why do you think the author and the illustrator created this book?* Accept all reasonable answers. If necessary, lead children to conclude that they wanted to teach about vultures and help people appreciate these birds.

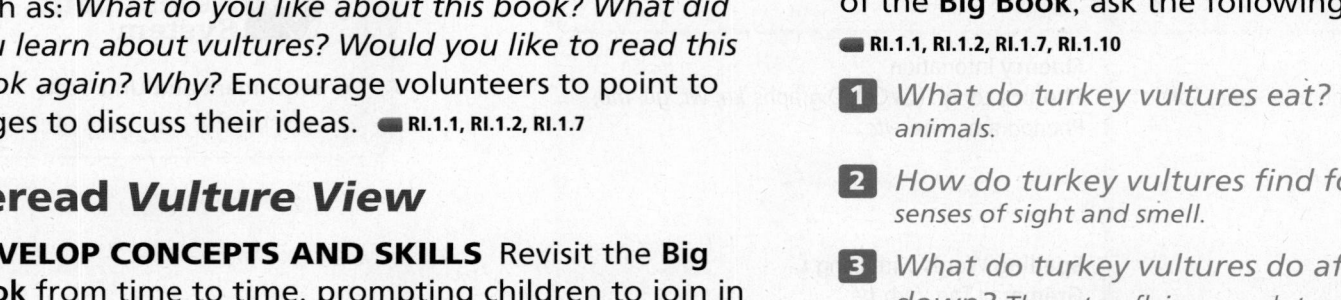

RL.1.5 explain major differences between story books and informational books; **RI.1.1** ask and answer questions about key details; **RI.1.2** identify the main topic and retell key details; **RI.1.4** ask and answer questions to help determine or clarify the meaning of words and phrases in a text; **RI.1.7** use illustrations and details to describe key ideas; **RI.1.10** read informational texts; **RF.1.1a** recognize the features of a sentence; **RF.1.4b** read on-level text orally with accuracy, appropriate rate, and expression; **SL.1.4** describe people, places, things, and events with details/express ideas and feelings clearly; **L.1.1f** use frequently occurring adjectives

Read *Beetle Bop*

INTRODUCE Discuss the cover, tracking the print as you read aloud the title and the name of the author/illustrator. Thumb through pp. 1–5 to glance at the illustrations with children. Track the print as you read aloud the information on the title page.

BACKGROUND Discuss the illustrations on the cover and on pp. 1–5. Lead children to use the title and the illustrations to discuss what the book might be about and whether it is a fantasy story or gives information. Accept responses children can justify. 🔲 RL.1.5, RI.1.7

READ ALOUD For the first reading, focus on enjoyment and gaining familiarity with the book. Track the print as you read, pausing occasionally to allow children to react to the text and the illustrations. Pause after p. 11 and ask again whether the book is fantasy or informational. Have children explain how they can tell. If necessary, point out that the beetles are not characters in a make-believe story, and the book gives information about many different kinds of beetles. Include p. 32 in the first reading and briefly discuss the additional information. 🔲 RL.1.5, RI.1.7

RESPOND After reading, discuss general questions such as: *What did you learn? What surprised you? What do you think of the illustrations? Why do you think the author used the title* Beetle Bop? Allow volunteers to point to pages to discuss their ideas. 🔲 RI.1.2, RI.1.7

Reread *Beetle Bop*

DEVELOP CONCEPTS AND SKILLS Revisit the **Big Book** from time to time for various purposes, such as: 🔲 RI.1.1, RI.1.10, SL.1.4, L.1.1f

- To reinforce concepts of print regarding directionality and the use of letters and words as decorative elements.

- To identify and discuss the meanings of describing words and to use them to describe things orally with details, expressing ideas and feelings clearly.

Big Book

- To identify and discuss the meanings of action verbs.

- To use library and computer resources to find out the names of and information about beetles in the book.

DEVELOP COMPREHENSION After rereading the **Big Book**, ask the following questions: 🔲 RF.1.4b, SL.1.4

1 *How is information given in the text and in the illustrations in this book?* The text uses rhythm and rhyme to tell information about various beetles. The illustrations show information about the beetles.

2 *Do you think this is a good way to learn information about beetles? Why or why not?* Accept all reasonable responses. Sample: The language and the illustrations make learning about beetles fun.

3 *How did you feel about beetles before you read this book? Do you feel differently now? Why or why not?* Accept all responses children can justify. If necessary, ask additional questions to help children elaborate on their ideas.

Research Animals

Several selections in this unit are about animals. In the unit project, children use research tools to find answers to questions about the way some animals live.

▶ SHARE OBJECTIVES
- Write informative texts.
- Generate research topics and questions.
- Gather information from relevant sources to answer questions.
- Participate in shared research and writing projects.

DEVELOP BACKGROUNDS

- Define and discuss **research**.
- Tell children that they can find facts about many topics by doing research.
- Make sure children understand that research is a way to find information in nonfiction books, on the Internet, and from newspapers or magazines to answer questions they have about a topic.

Materials

- nonfiction books or articles about animals
- index cards
- construction paper
- crayons
- bulletin board

Step 1

Plan and Gather Brainstorm with children a list of animals they are interested in. Write the list on the board.

a Discuss what children know about the animals.

b Write questions children have about the way the animals live. For example: *What food does the animal eat? Does it live in warm or cold places? How does the animal move from place to place? Do people affect the way the animal lives?*

W.1.2 write informative/explanatory texts; **W.1.7** participate in shared research and writing projects; **W.1.8** recall information from experiences or gather information from sources to answer a question

Research Skills

For instruction in the following applicable skills, see the lessons in the **Resources** section, pp. R2–R3.

Unit 3 Research Skills

p. R2	• Library Research: Find a Book
p. R2	• Parts of a Book
p. R3	• Distinguish Nonfiction from Fiction

PROJECT ASSESSMENT

Assess children's work on the project by reviewing multiple factors:

☑ **Speaking and Listening:** Do children follow rules of discussion when working together in groups? Do they speak clearly and audibly when sharing their research findings?

☑ **Writing:** Do children write the answers to their research questions clearly?

☑ **Language:** Do children use end punctuation for sentences and attempt correct spellings?

Step 2

Organize Have small groups choose an animal to research.

a Guide groups to write questions they have about their animal.

b Provide nonfiction books, children's magazines, picture dictionaries, Internet sites, and other factual sources about animals. To determine the relevance of a source, guide children to skim the Table of Contents and look at the photographs. Tell groups to find and write facts on index cards to answer their questions and make a picture of their animal.

c Have group members ask each other questions about the information they find, such as *Does this fact help answer our question?* and *How do you know _____?* Help groups adjust their topics as they find answers. They can add new questions or delete irrelevant ones. Remind children to revise their writing to correct any errors, and to use the language skills they are learning in this unit.

Step 3

Complete and Present

a Post the fact cards and animal pictures on the bulletin board. Arrange them by the animal, or by the type of question the card answers. Have each group present its research findings to the rest of the class. Remind children to speak clearly as they present their research facts.

b Ask children what they have learned about doing research and how to find out what they want to know.

 **ENGLISH LANGUAGE LEARNERS**

Comprehensible Input

Beginning Children say missing facts in statements you provide orally, such as, *Bears use _____ to catch fish.* Use gestures to help elicit the correct answer.

High Intermediate Children can use words and gestures to act out the facts found in small group research.

Low Intermediate Guide children to find an animal in a picture dictionary and read about it.

Proficient Have pairs take turns asking a question and reading a fact card to answer it.

Have children record progress of their **Research and Media Performance Task** in *my*WriteSmart.

Research and Media Performance Task • **xxvii**

Contents

Unit 3

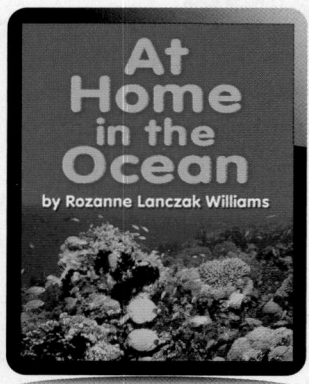

Lesson 11

Contents

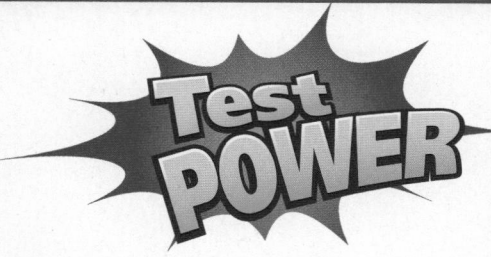 T485

WRITING & LANGUAGE

ENGLISH LANGUAGE LEARNERS

RESOURCES

Journeys

LESSON
11

Go Digital

See pages xvi-xvii in this Teacher's Edition for the full digital offering.

*my*SmartPlanner

Plan Across Disciplines, Schedule, Organize

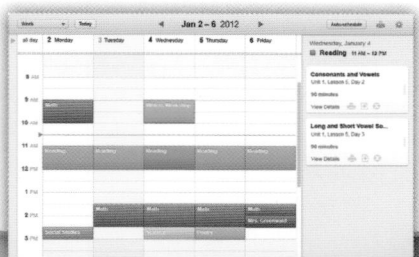

my WriteSmart

Write, Collaborate, Respond

Online Assessment

Assess, Prescribe, Remediate, Report

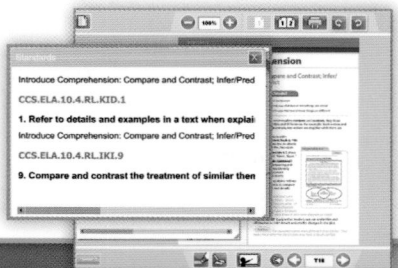

CHALLENGE

Research Oceans

After reading the selection "At Home in the Ocean," ask children to research the oceans of the world.

- Ask children to name as many oceans as they can. Help children find the five oceans on a globe and tell the name of each.
- Give children access to books or an online resource to research the oceans of the world. Ask: *Which ocean is the largest? What animals live in the ocean? What countries border the oceans?*
- Have children make posters and use pictures and captions to tell what they learned.

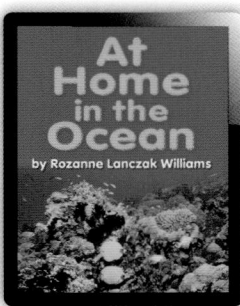

Informational Text

SCIENCE

Connection to Informational Text

ANIMALS AROUND US "At Home in the Ocean" tells about the amazing plants and animals that live in and around the sea. As a class, come up with a list of animals found in your state or region. Have children say whether the animals live in water or on land or both. Have children work in small groups to find out more about one of the listed animals. Have them answer these questions: *Where does the animal live? What does it eat? How is it important?* Ask each group to design a display about their chosen animal. Invite groups to draw, print, or cut out out pictures of the animal. Have them write a few facts about the animal next to each picture. **Common Core, *English Language Arts:* W.1.7** participate in shared research and writing projects

---

JOURNEYS

READING
INFORMATIONAL TEXT

RI.1.1 ask and answer questions about key details

RI.1.3 describe the connection between individuals, events, ideas or information in a text

RI.1.5 know and use text features to locate facts or information

RI.1.8 identify the reasons an author gives to support points

RI.1.9 identify similarities in and differences between texts on the same topic

RI.1.10 read informational texts

FOUNDATIONAL SKILLS

RF.1.2b orally produce single-syllable words by blending sounds

RF.1.2d segment spoken single-syllable words into their complete sequence of individual sounds

RF.1.3a know the spelling-sound correspondences for common consonant digraphs

RF.1.4a read on-level text with purpose and understanding

WRITING

W.1.2 write informative/explanatory texts

W.1.7 participate in shared research and writing projects

W.1.8 recall information from experiences or gather information from sources to answer a question

SPEAKING AND LISTENING

SL.1.1a follow rules for discussions

SL.1.1b build on others' talk in conversations by responding to others' comments

SL.1.1c ask question to clear up confusion about topics and texts under discussion

SL.1.4 describe people, places, things, and events with details/express ideas and feelings clearly

SL.1.5 add drawings or visual displays to descriptions to clarify ideas, thoughts, and feelings

SL.1.6 produce complete sentences when appropriate to task and situation

LANGUAGE

L.1.1a print upper- and lowercase letters

L.1.1b use common, proper, and possessive nouns

L.1.2a capitalize dates and names of people

L.1.5a sort words into categories to gain a sense of concepts the categories represent

LESSON 11 Our Focus Wall

ANCHOR TEXT

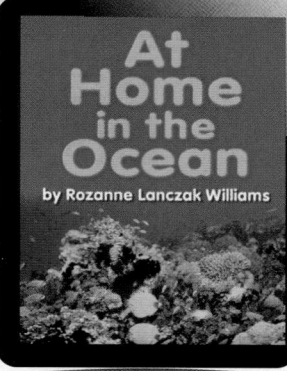

At Home in the Ocean
Informational Text

Read Together

Water
Informational Text

ESSENTIAL QUESTION

What kinds of plants and animals would you find in the ocean?

FOUNDATIONAL SKILLS

☑ Words to Know
HIGH-FREQUENCY WORDS

blue	cold	far
little	live	their
water	where	

Phonics

Digraph *th*
Base Words
and *-s, -es,
-ed, -ing* Endings

th

Fluency

Phrasing: Punctuation

READING LITERATURE & INFORMATIONAL TEXT

Comprehension Skills and Strategies

☑ TARGET SKILL
• Author's Purpose
• Details

☑ TARGET STRATEGY
• Analyze/Evaluate

WRITING

Writing

Informative Writing:
Sentences

Focus Trait: Sentence Fluency

LANGUAGE

Spelling

Digraph *th*

that	them
then	with
this	bath

Grammar

Proper Nouns

Vocabulary Strategies

Classify and Categorize Words

WHOLE GROUP

⌄ Reading

ANCHOR TEXT

DOMAIN: **Life Science**
LESSON TOPIC: Marine Habitats

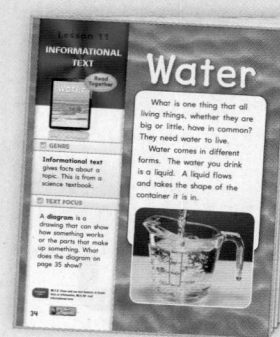

At Home in the Ocean
Informational Text

Children will read *At Home in the Ocean* to

- understand an author's purpose for writing.
- observe details to learn more about a text's topic.

Water
Informational Text

Children will read *Water* to

- learn about the different forms of water.
- gain information from a diagram.

⌄ Language Arts

○ Grammar

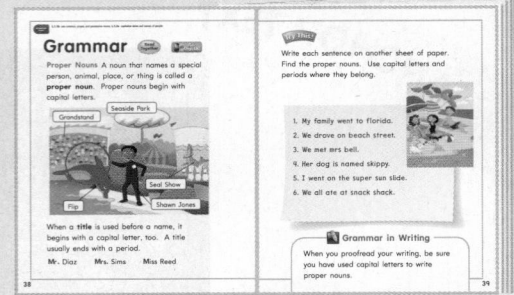

Children learn about proper nouns through writing sentences that relate to people, animals, places, or things at the ocean.

○ Writing

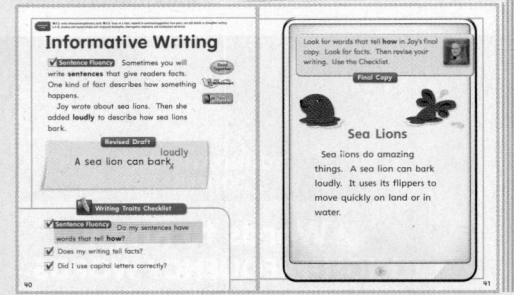

Children write sentences that inform using *At Home in the Ocean* as a model for writing about animals.

◭ TEXT COMPLEXITY RUBRIC

Overall Text Complexity		At Home in the Ocean INFORMATIONAL TEXT	Water INFORMATIONAL TEXT
		COMPLEX	MORE COMPLEX
Quantitative Measures	Lexile	400	460
	Guided Reading Level	G	H
Qualitative Measures	Text Structure	Genre traits common to informational text	More difficult science concepts
	Language Conventionality and Clarity	Longer descriptions	More complex sentence structure
	Knowledge Demands	Some specialized knowledge required	Specialized knowledge required
	Purpose/Levels of Meaning	Single topic	Single topic

⌄ Additional Whole Group Resources

● Decodable Readers

Seth and Beth
by Anna Guzman
Illustrated by Piero Corva

Seth and Beth met at the path.
Beth has a big map. It can help.
They will go and see Bob Frog.

- *Seth and Beth,* pp. 3–8
- *Zeb Yak,* pp. 9–14
- *The Duck Nest,* pp. 15–20
- *Animal Moms,* pp. 21–26

● Progress Monitoring

Assess and monitor children's progress to determine who is on track and who needs help. Clear prescriptions identify targeted instruction to address children's needs and get them back on track.

Respond to Assessment
- ☑ Vocabulary, p. T76
- ☑ Phonics, p. T76
- ☑ Comprehension, p. T77
- ☑ Language Arts, p. T77
- ☑ Fluency, p. T77

Lesson resources organized by week.

● Lesson 11 Blackline Masters
- Home Letter 11.1
- Weekly To-Do List 11.2
- Vocabulary Word Cards 11.3
- Words to Know 11.4
- Leveled Reader Graphic Organizers 11.5–11.8
- Leveled Practice for Words to Know and Phonics SR11.1–SR11.4, A11.1–A11.4, ELL11.1–ELL11.4
- Weekly Tests 11.1–11.14

● Assessment
- Weekly Tests Answer Key
- Observation Checklists
- Fluency Tests
- Periodic Assessments

● Additional Resources
- Reading Log
- Vocabulary Log
- Listening Log
- Proofreading Checklist
- Writing Conference Form
- Writing Checklist
- Instructional Routines
- Graphic Organizer Blackline Masters
- Handwriting Models

FOR STUDENTS

- my WriteSmart
- eBook
- GrammarSnap Videos
- Destination Reading
- Context Cards

FOR TEACHERS
- Teacher One-Stop
- Interactive Whiteboard Lessons
- Literacy and Language Guide

- Lesson 11 Blackline Masters
- Additional Resources
- Assessment

Small Group *At a Glance*

SMALL GROUP

Weekly Leveled Readers

Struggling Readers

Guided Reading Level: D
Lexile: 360
DRA: 6

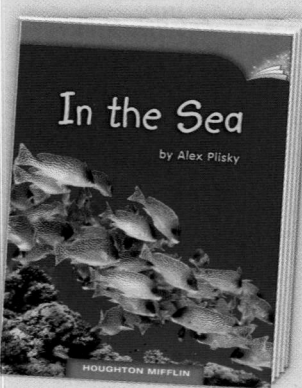

In the Sea
by Alex Pilsky

HOUGHTON MIFFLIN

On Level

Guided Reading Level: H
Lexile: 570
DRA: 14

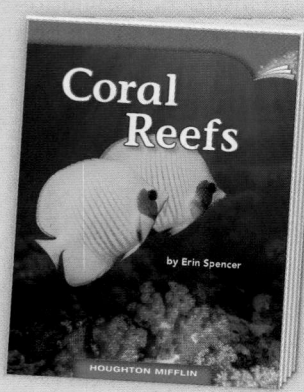

Coral Reefs
by Erin Spencer

HOUGHTON MIFFLIN

Advanced

Guided Reading Level: L
Lexile: 520
DRA: 24

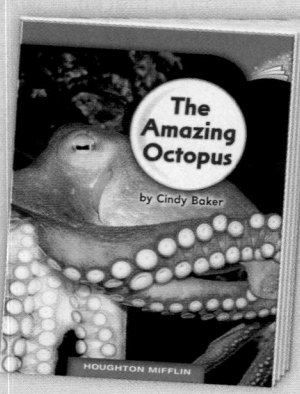

The Amazing Octopus
by Cindy Baker

HOUGHTON MIFFLIN

English Language Learners

Guided Reading Level: G
Lexile: 430
DRA: 12

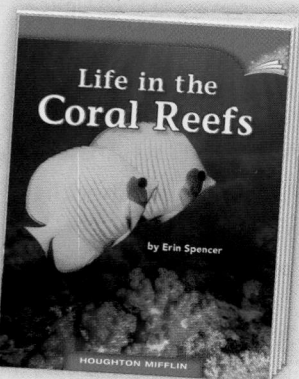

Life in the Coral Reefs
by Erin Spencer

HOUGHTON MIFFLIN

Vocabulary Reader

for all levels

Guided Reading Level: D
Lexile: 20
DRA: 6

Shark
by Anita Sanders

HOUGHTON MIFFLIN

Leveled Reader Teacher's Guides

8-page lessons for each book support instruction in guided reading groups

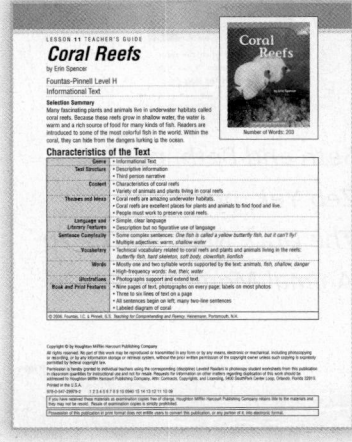

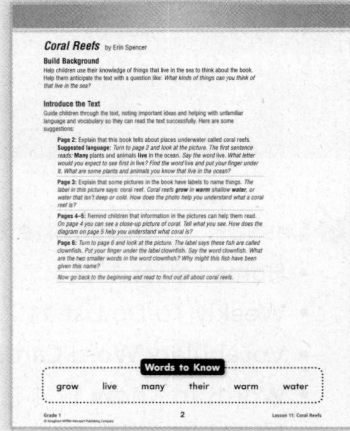

What My Other Students Are Doing

my WriteSmart — Performance Task

- Write About Reading
- Informative Writing
- Research and Media Literacy
- Unit Performance Assessment, Task 1 of 5

Literacy Centers

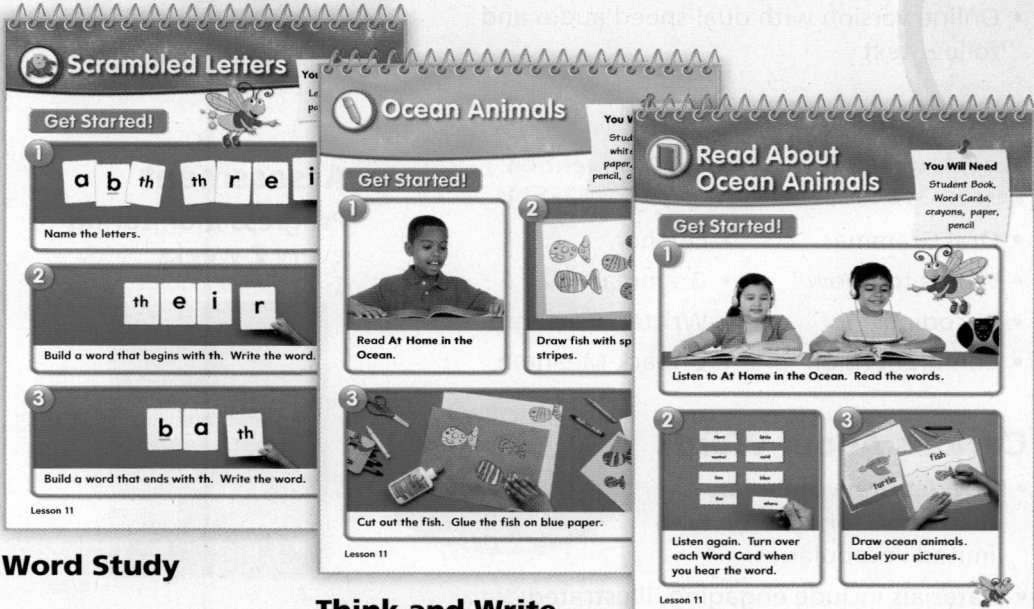

Scrambled Letters

Get Started!

1. a b th th r e i
   Name the letters.

2. th e i r
   Build a word that begins with th. Write the word.

3. b a th
   Build a word that ends with th. Write the word.

Lesson 11

Word Study

Ocean Animals

Get Started!

1. Read At Home in the Ocean.
2. Draw fish with stripes.
3. Cut out the fish. Glue the fish on blue paper.

Lesson 11

Think and Write

Read About Ocean Animals

You Will Need
Student Book, Word Cards, crayons, paper, pencil

Get Started!

1. Listen to At Home in the Ocean. Read the words.
2. Listen again. Turn over each Word Card when you hear the word.
3. Draw ocean animals. Label your pictures.

Lesson 11

Comprehension and Fluency

Reader's Notebook

Includes practice for:

- Text analysis and citing text evidence
- Words to Know
- Phonics
- Spelling
- Grammar
- Writing Traits

HOUGHTON MIFFLIN HARCOURT
JOURNEYS
COMMON CORE
Reader's Notebook
GRADE 1
Volume 1

Go Digital

FOR STUDENTS
- Leveled Readers Online
- Vocabulary Reader Online

FOR TEACHERS
- Teacher One-Stop
- Literacy and Language Guide
- Leveled Readers Database
- Leveled Reader Teacher's Guides

Grab-and-Go!

- Lesson 11 Blackline Masters
- Additional Resources
- Assessment

Go Digital

FOR STUDENTS
- Write-in Reader eBook
- Vocabulary Reader Online
- Struggling Readers Leveled Reader Online

FOR TEACHERS
- Leveled Reader Teacher's Guide

Grab-and-Go!

- Struggling Readers Blackline Masters

RtI INTERVENTION

∨ Strategic Intervention: TIER II

Use these materials to provide additional targeted instruction for children who need Tier II strategic intervention.

● Write-In Reader:
Pup's Bath

- Engaging selection connects to main topic
- Interactive worktext reinforces this week's vocabulary and comprehension
- Opportunities for student interaction
- Builds the foundational skills for reading more complex texts
- Online version with dual-speed audio and follow-text

● Daily Lessons

For this week's daily Strategic Intervention Lesson, see Teacher's Edition pages S2–S11:

- Oral Grammar
- Words to Know
- Decoding
- Comprehension
- Fluency
- Grammar
- Written Response
- Unpack Meaning

Curious About Words

- Provides oral vocabulary instruction for children with limited vocabularies.
- Materials include engaging, illustrated Read Alouds with Teacher Manual.
- Teaches high-utility, research-based words, including academic vocabulary.
- Assessment includes weekly pretests and posttests.

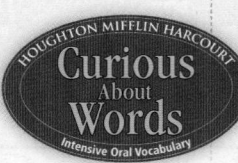

● Assessment
Progress monitoring every 2 weeks.

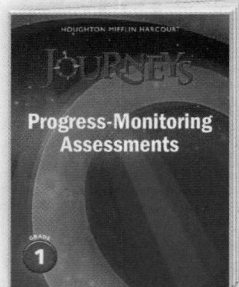

∨ Intensive Intervention: TIER III

● Interactive lessons provide support for

- **Phonics and Word Study Skills**
- **Vocabulary**
- **Comprehension**
- **Fluency**

- Lesson cards for small-group or individual instruction
- Blackline masters for additional practice

- Leveled books for additional reading and skill application
- Lesson assessments evaluate the effectiveness of the intervention

English Language Learners *At a Glance*

 **ELL**

ENGLISH LANGUAGE LEARNERS

⌄ Whole Group

Use these resources to help English Language Learners access the core content with the whole group.

● Point-of-Use Scaffolded Support

- Use Visuals
- Use Gestures
- Comprehensible Input
- Peer-Supported Learning
- Language Issues
- Idiomatic Language
- Use Sentence Frames
- Expand Language Production

● Vocabulary in Context Cards

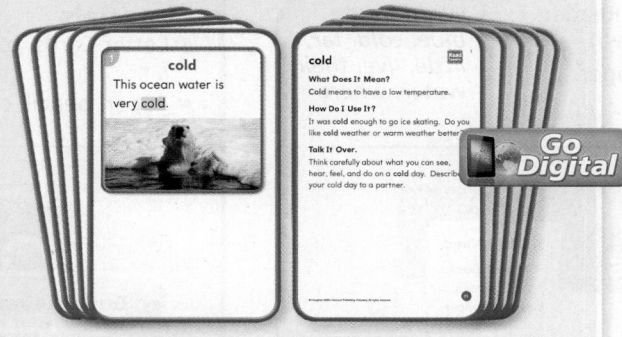

cold
This ocean water is very cold.

cold
What Does It Mean?
Cold means to have a low temperature.
How Do I Use It?
It was cold enough to go ice skating. Do you like cold weather or warm weather better?
Talk It Over.
Think carefully about what you can see, hear, feel, and do on a cold day. Describe your cold day to a partner.

Go Digital

front   back

⌄ Small Group

Use these resources to help English Language Learners access the core content with a smaller group.

● ELL Leveled Reader

- Contains the same content as the On-Level Reader but uses more accessible language
- ELL Leveled Reader Lesson Plan
- ELL Blackline Masters

Life in the Coral Reefs
by Erin Spencer
HOUGHTON MIFFLIN

⌄ ELL Extra Support

Use these additional resources to support English Language Learners as needed.

● ELL Lesson 11 Resources

- Daily Lessons to support the core
- Language Support Card 11
- ELL Blackline Masters
- ELL Teacher's Handbook
  Professional Development
  Peer Conferences Forms
  Cooperative Learning Guidelines

At Home in the Ocean   Language Support Card
Lesson 11
ocean   turtle

● Building Background

Video Clip for Lesson 11:
Snorkeling

 **Go Digital**

FOR STUDENTS

- ELL Leveled Reader Online
- Vocabulary Reader Online
- Cross-Curricular Activity Bank
- Multimedia Grammar Glossary
- Picture Card Bank Online

FOR TEACHERS

- ELD Station Online
- Leveled Readers Database
- Leveled Reader Teacher's Guide

 **Grab-and-Go!**

- ELL Blackline Masters

Comprehension and Fluency

Materials
- Student Book and Audio: *At Home in the Ocean*
- Decodable Reader: *Seth and Beth*
- Crayons, paper, pencil
- Word Cards: *blue, cold, far, little, live, their, water, where*

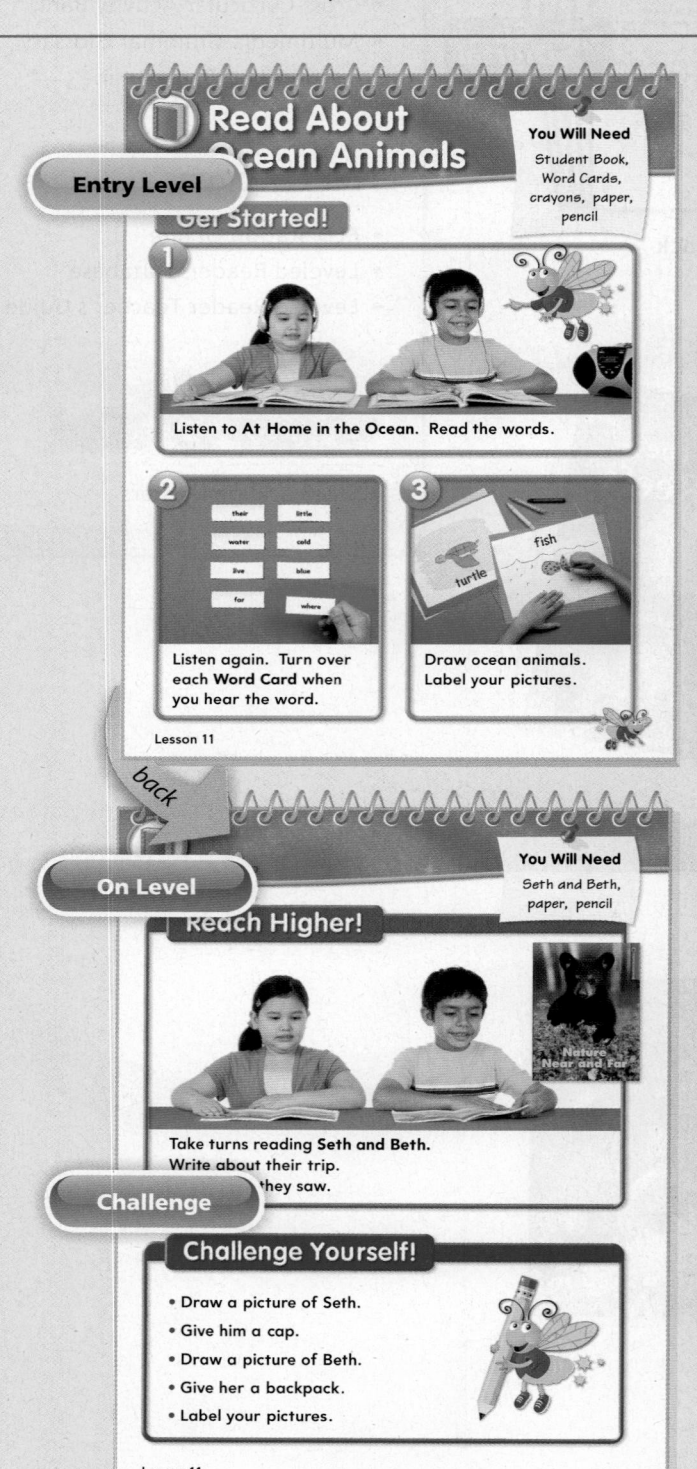

Read About Ocean Animals

Entry Level

Get Started!

You Will Need
Student Book, Word Cards, crayons, paper, pencil

1. Listen to **At Home in the Ocean**. Read the words.

2. Listen again. Turn over each **Word Card** when you hear the word.

3. Draw ocean animals. Label your pictures.

Lesson 11

back

On Level

You Will Need
Seth and Beth, paper, pencil

Reach Higher!

Take turns reading **Seth and Beth**. Write about their trip. [...] they saw.

Challenge

Challenge Yourself!
- Draw a picture of Seth.
- Give him a cap.
- Draw a picture of Beth.
- Give her a backpack.
- Label your pictures.

Lesson 11

Word Study

Materials
- Letter Cards: *b, a, th, e, i, r*
- Paper, pencil, crayons
- Word Cards: *moth, mouth, thorn, thumb, tooth*
- Picture Cards: *moth, mouth, thorn, thumb, tooth*

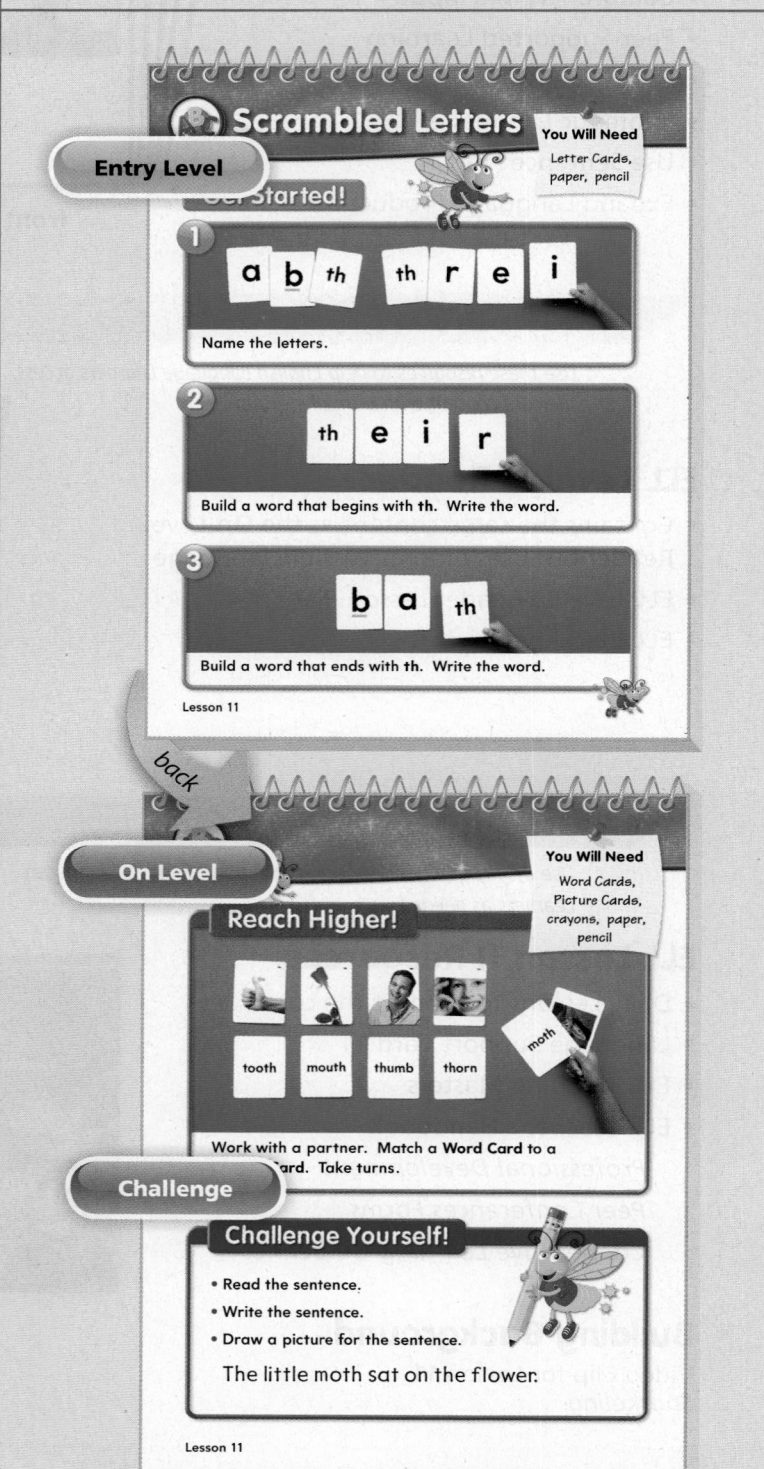

Scrambled Letters

Entry Level

Get Started!

You Will Need
Letter Cards, paper, pencil

1. a b *th*   *th* r e i
   Name the letters.

2. *th* e i r
   Build a word that begins with **th**. Write the word.

3. b a *th*
   Build a word that ends with **th**. Write the word.

Lesson 11

back

On Level

You Will Need
Word Cards, Picture Cards, crayons, paper, pencil

Reach Higher!

tooth   mouth   thumb   thorn   moth

Work with a partner. Match a **Word Card** to a [...] Card. Take turns.

Challenge

Challenge Yourself!
- Read the sentence.
- Write the sentence.
- Draw a picture for the sentence.

The little moth sat on the flower.

Lesson 11

Use Literacy Centers to support this week's Common Core focus. Each center contains three activities. Children who experience success with the entry-level activity move on to the on-level and challenge activities, as time permits.

Think and Write

Materials
- Student Book
- Crayons
- White and blue paper
- Scissors
- Glue
- Pencil

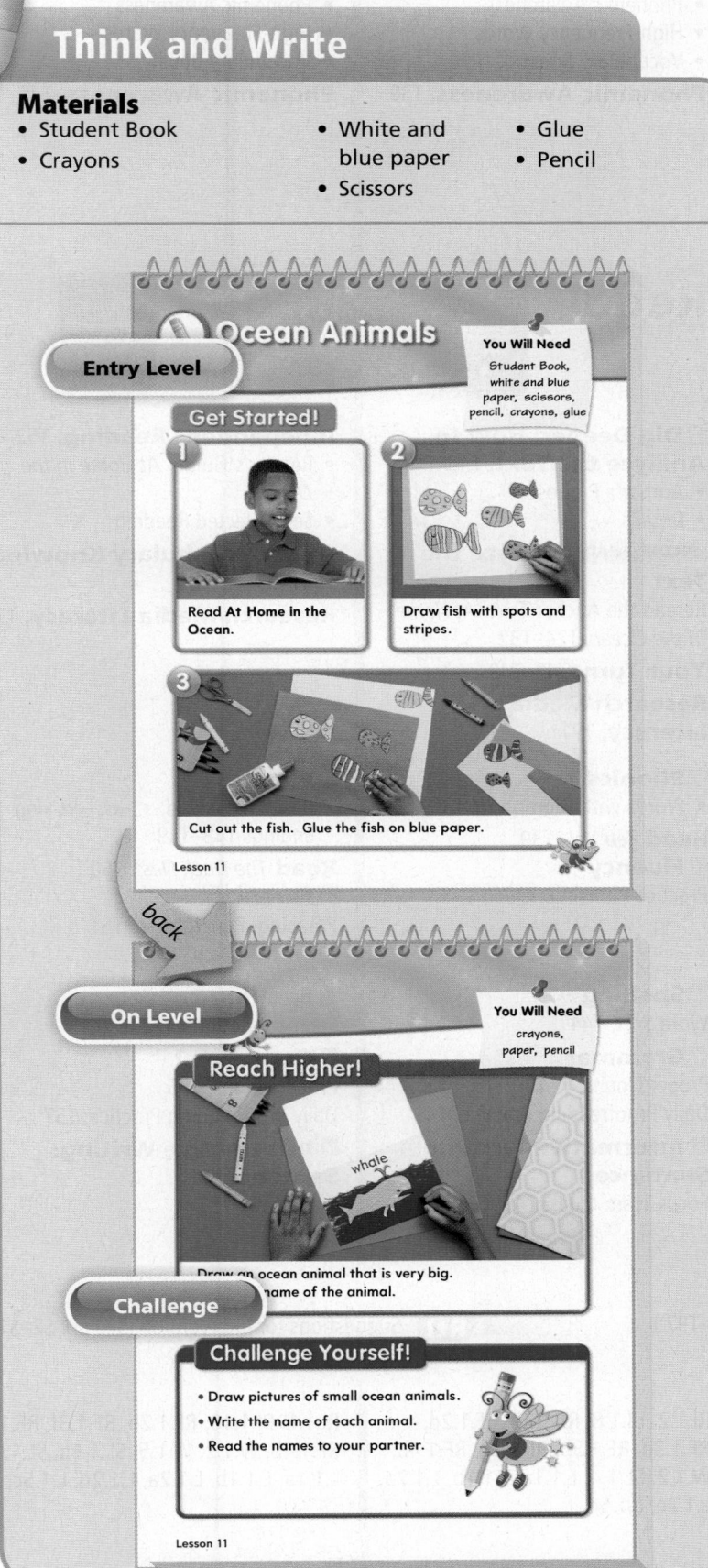

Ocean Animals

Entry Level

You Will Need
Student Book, white and blue paper, scissors, pencil, crayons, glue

Get Started!

1. Read At Home in the Ocean.

2. Draw fish with spots and stripes.

3. Cut out the fish. Glue the fish on blue paper.

Lesson 11

back

On Level

You Will Need
crayons, paper, pencil

Reach Higher!

whale

Draw an ocean animal that is very big. ... name of the animal.

Challenge

Challenge Yourself!
- Draw pictures of small ocean animals.
- Write the name of each animal.
- Read the names to your partner.

Lesson 11

Go Digital

FOR STUDENTS

my WriteSmart

Children complete performance tasks related to the week's instruction.

eBook
Children read and listen to *At Home in the Ocean* and *Water*, generate questions about ocean life, and reread the texts to deepen their knowledge.

Leveled Readers Online
Children read and listen to **Leveled Readers,** reinforcing lesson's Target Vocabulary, Target Skill, and Target Strategy.

Destination Reading
Children practice and apply key lesson skills through gamelike activities.

GrammarSnap Videos
Children practice and apply understanding of proper nouns.

Read

Independent Reading

Have children read daily from a self-selected trade book and record their progress in their Reading Log.

See p. T53 for support in guiding children to select an appropriate book.

LESSON 11 WeeklyPlanner

	DAY 1	DAY 2	DAY 3
Whole Group			
Daily Language • Opening Routines • Oral Vocabulary • Listening Comprehension • Phonemic Awareness • Speaking and Listening	**Opening Routines,** T12–T13 • Phonemic Awareness • High-Frequency Words • Vocabulary Boost **Read Aloud,** "The Piano Lessons," T14–T15 **Introduce Oral Vocabulary** **Phonemic Awareness,** T16	**Opening Routines,** T36–T37 • Phonemic Awareness • High-Frequency Words • Vocabulary Boost **Phonemic Awareness,** T38	**Opening Routines,** T46–T47 • Phonemic Awareness • High-Frequency Words • Vocabulary Boost **Phonemic Awareness,** T48
Vocabulary **Text-Based Comprehension** • Skills and Strategies • Craft and Structure **Research and Media Literacy**	**Read**  ☑ **Introduce Words to Know** High-Frequency Words, T20–T21 ☑ **Read and Comprehend,** T22–T23 **FIRST READ** **Think Through the Text** Read the Anchor Text: *At Home in the Ocean,* T24–T33 **Research/Media Literacy,** T71	**Read**  ☑ **Dig Deeper: How to Analyze the Text,** T40–T41 • Author's Purpose • Details **SECOND READ** **Analyze the Text** Reread the Anchor Text: *At Home in the Ocean,* T24–T32 **Your Turn,** T42–T43 **Research/Media Literacy,** T71	**Read** **Independent Reading,** T52–T53 • Reader's Guide: *At Home in the Ocean* • Self-Selected Reading **Apply Vocabulary Knowledge,** T54–T55 **Research/Media Literacy,** T71
Foundational Skills • Phonics and Word Recognition • Fluency	☑ **Phonics** • Words with Digraph *th*, T16–T18 **Read** *Seth and Beth,* T19 ☑ **Fluency** Model Phrasing, T14	☑ **Phonics** • Words with Digraph *th*, T38 **Read** *Zeb Yak,* T39 ☑ **Fluency** Practice Phrasing, T39	☑ **Phonics** • Base Words and *-s, -es, -ed, -ing* Endings T48–T49 **Read** *The Duck Nest,* T50 ☑ **Fluency** Phrasing: Punctuation, T51
Whole Group Language Arts			
Spelling Grammar Writing	☑ **Spelling** Words with *th*, T34 Pretest ☑ **Grammar** Introduce Proper Nouns, T34 Daily Proofreading Practice, T35 ☑ **Informative Writing: Sentences** Introduce the Model, T35	☑ **Spelling** Word Sort, T44 ☑ **Grammar** Proper Nouns, T44 Daily Proofreading Practice, T45 ☑ **Informative Writing: Sentences** Focus Trait: Ideas, T45	☑ **Spelling** Segment Sounds, T56 ☑ **Grammar** Proper Nouns, T56 Daily Proofreading Practice, T57 ☑ **Informative Writing: Sentences** Prewriting, T57

Small Group

 Suggestions for Small Groups (See pp. T79–T97.)    **RtI** Suggestions for Intervention (See pp. S2–S11.)

 **COMMON CORE**
State Standards

RI.1.1, RI.1.8, RI.1.10, RF.1.2b, RF.1.3a, RF.1.3b, RF.1.4b, RF.1.3g, SL.1.1a, SL.1.1b, SL.1.2, SL.1.3, L.1.1b, L.1.2a, L.1.2d, L.1.6	RI.1.2, RI.1.8, RF.1.2b, RF.1.2d, RF.1.3a, RF.1.3b, RF.1.3g, RF.1.4b, W.1.2, SL.1.4, L.1.1a, L.1.1b, L.1.2a, L.1.2e, L.1.5c	RI.1.1, RI.1.10, RF.1.2b, RF.1.3f, RF.1.4a, RF.1.4b, W.1.2, W.1.5, SL.1.1a, SL.1.1b, L.1.1a, L.1.1b, L.1.2a, L.1.2d, L.1.5c, L.1.6

DAY 4

Opening Routines, T58–T59
• Phonemic Awareness
• High-Frequency Words
• Vocabulary Boost
Phonemic Awareness, T60

Connect to the Topic
• Read Informational Text: *Water*, T62
• Think Through the Text, T62
☑ **Compare Texts,** T63
☑ **Vocabulary Strategies**
Classify and Catagorize Words, T64–T65
Research/Media Literacy, T71

☑ **Phonics**
• Words with Digraph *th*, T60
• Base Words and -*s, -es, -ed, -ing* Endings, T60
Read *Animal Moms*, T61
☑ **Fluency**
Phrasing: Punctuation, T51

☑ **Spelling**
Connect to Writing, T66
☑ **Grammar**
Spiral Review: Possessives, T66
Daily Proofreading Practice, T67
☑ **Informative Writing: Sentences**
Drafting, T67

 Suggestions for English Language Learners
(See pp. E2–E11.)

RI.1.3, RI.1.5, RI.1.10, RF.1.2b, RF.1.2d,
RF.1.3a, RF.1.3f, RF.1.3g, RF.1.4b, W.1.5,
SL.1.1a, SL.1.5, L.1.1b, L.1.5a, L.1.5c

DAY 5

Opening Routines, T68–T69
• Phonemic Awareness
• High-Frequency Words
• Vocabulary Boost
Phonemic Awareness, T69

Extend the Topic
• Domain-Specific Vocabulary, T70
• Research Skills: Facts About an Ocean Animal and Its Habitat, T71
• Optional Second Read: *Water*, T62

☑ **Phonics**
• Words with Digraph *th*, T76
• Base Words and -*s, -es, -ed, -ing* Endings, T76
☑ **Fluency**
Phrasing: Punctuation, T51

☑ **Spelling**
Assess, T72
☑ **Grammar**
Weekly Review: Proper Nouns, T72–T73
Daily Proofreading Practice, T74
☑ **Informative Writing: Sentences**
Revising and Proofreading, T74–T75

RF.1.2b, RF.1.2d, RF.1.3g, W.1.2, W.1.5, W.1.6,
W.1.7, W.1.8, L.1.1b, L.1.1j, L.1.2a, L.1.2d,
L.1.6

FOR STUDENTS

my WriteSmart

• eBook
• GrammarSnap Videos
• Destination Reading
• Context Cards

FOR TEACHERS

• Teacher One-Stop
• Interactive Whiteboard Lessons
• Literacy and Language Guide

• Lesson 11 Blackline Masters
• Additional Resources
• Assessment

DAY 1

Today's Goals

Vocabulary & Oral Language
- **Teacher Read Aloud:** "The Piano Lessons"
- **Oral Vocabulary**
- **Listening Comprehension**
- **Model Fluency**

Phonemic Awareness
- **Blend Phonemes**
- **Segment Phonemes**

Phonics & Fluency
- **Words with Digraph** *th*
- **Read Decodable Reader:** *Seth and Beth*
- **Fluency:** Phrasing

☑ **WORDS TO KNOW**

blue	live
cold	their
far	water
little	where

Text-Based Comprehension
- **Read and Comprehend**
- **Read the Anchor Text:** *At Home in the Ocean*

Grammar & Writing
- **Proper Nouns**
- ✏ **Informative Writing:** Sentences That Inform

Spelling
- **Words with** *th*

COMMON CORE

RF.1.2b orally produce single-syllable words by blending sounds; **RF.1.3g** recognize and read irregularly spelled words; **SL.1.1a** follow rules for discussions; **L.1.5c** identify real-life connections between words and their use; **L.1.6** use words and phrases acquired through conversations, reading and being read to, and responding to texts

Opening Routines

Warm Up with Wordplay

How Do They Go Together?

Display and read aloud the following:

fish	**dolphins**	**seals**

Have children discuss how these words belong together. As children compare their answers, remind them to follow good discussion rules, such as listening carefully and taking turns. Then reveal the correct answer: *These words name animals that live in the water.*

Encourage children to come up with more words that name animals that live in the water. Write down the responses and say them aloud with children. Tell children that this week they will read selections about animals and water. ⬤ **SL.1.1a**

Daily Phonemic Awareness

Blend Phonemes

- *I'm going to say the sounds in a word and blend them. Then you say the word. I'll do the first one. Listen: /b/ /ă/ /th/. What is the word? bath*

- Have children repeat with you, then by themselves.

- Continue with the following words:

/j/ /ŭ/ /m/ /p/ *jump*	/f/ /ă/ /s/ /t/ *fast*	/th/ /ĕ/ /n/ *then*
/th/ /ĭ/ /s/ *this*	/w/ /ĕ/ /n/ /t/ *went*	/m/ /ă/ /th/ *math*
/ă/ /s/ /k/ *ask*	/s/ /ĭ/ /k/ *sick*	/th/ /ă/ /t/ *that* ▬ **RF.1.2b**

Corrective Feedback

- If a child misses a word, say the correct word and model the task. *The word is ask. Listen: /ă/ /s/ /k/. What is the word? ask*

- Then have children do it with you before doing it on their own.

- Back up several words and continue the activity.

Daily High-Frequency Words

Introduce

- Point to the Words to Know on the Focus Wall. *Our Words to Know for this week are* blue, cold, far, little, live, their, water, *and* where. *You are going to see these words in your reading.*

- Use **Instructional Routine 10** and the **High-Frequency Word Card** to introduce the word *blue*.

- Repeat the procedure with the words *cold, far, little, live, their, water,* and *where.* ▬ **RF.1.3g**

Corrective Feedback

- Say the correct word and have children repeat it. Blue. *What is the word? blue*

- Have children spell the word. *b-l-u-e How do we say this word? blue*

- Have children reread all of the cards in random order.

Daily Vocabulary Boost

- Have children think about a time when they had to do something they did not want to do. Encourage children to make real-life connections between words and their use. Guide them to interact with the oral vocabulary from previous weeks by asking the following questions. Remind them to speak clearly when participating in a discussion.

What has someone told you that you must *do?*

Did you wonder *why you had to do it?*

Did you think about how to sneak *out of doing it? Explain.*

How did you ease *into doing it?*

- Have children work together to explain *must, wonder, sneak,* and *eases* in their own words. ▬ **L.1.5c, L.1.6**

 **Oral Vocabulary**

must

wonder

sneak

eases

DAY 1

Teacher Read Aloud

▶ **SHARE OBJECTIVES**
- Listen for natural pauses.
- Answer questions about a text read aloud.
- Participate in a classroom conversation.

Model Fluency

- Explain to children that good readers use correct phrasing. That is, they pause at the right places, such as between phrases and at commas. *As you read aloud, pause between groups of words that go together and at commas. Taking a short break at those places will make your reading sound more natural.*

- Read the first two sentences of the story "The Piano Lessons" aloud. Ask children to raise their hands when they hear you pause.

- *When did you hear me pause? How did the pauses help you understand what I was reading?*

- Read the entire story aloud. Ask children to listen carefully to find out how the two girls are the same and different.

COMMON CORE **RL.1.2** retell stories and demonstrate understanding of the message or lesson; **SL.1.1b** build on others' talk in conversations by responding to others' comments; **SL.1.1c** ask questions to clear up confusion about topics and texts under discussion; **SL.1.2** ask and answer questions about details in a text read aloud, information presented orally, or through other media; **SL.1.3** ask and answer questions about what a speaker says

The Piano Lessons

The sign above the door simply read, "Mrs. Johnson's Music School." It was small, neat, and simple, just like Mrs. Johnson.

What the sign didn't say was that Mrs. Johnson was a **strict** teacher. Everyone knew that she was the best music teacher around, but also the toughest. She had certain rules, and she made her students stick to them.

1 "All my students must **practice** every day," she cried at the end of each class. "One hour, or more!"

Kim and Kayla were two of Mrs. Johnson's regular students. They had been **companions** since they met in art class at age 5. Then they had ballet together at age 6, soccer camp at age 7, and now piano lessons.

Both girls liked the lessons. They were filled with loud music, laughter, and Mrs. Johnson banging her cane to keep time. But practicing at home was different. Kayla didn't mind so much, but Kim hated it.

Kim didn't like sitting alone at the big piano. *Plink, plunk, thud,* went the piano, as Kim just pounded random keys. "This is *soooo* boring," she groaned to anyone who would listen. Kim sat on the piano bench for an hour every day, but she didn't even try to learn the music.

Introduce Oral Vocabulary

Use **Instructional Routine 16** to define each highlighted oral vocabulary word.

- For additional support and reinforcement, have children look up each word in a children's dictionary.

strict having firm rules • *What the sign didn't say was that Mrs. Johnson was a strict teacher.*

practice doing something over and over to get better at it • *"All my students must practice every day," she cried at the end of each class.*

companions people who spend time together • *They had been companions since they met in art class at age 5.*

Each week, the girls and the other students would return to Mrs. Johnson's school to show what they had learned. The students who practiced would play **gracefully**, but Kim was terrible. She would have nothing to play and Mrs. Johnson would cry, "You must practice every day! One hour, or more!" **2**

This went on week after week. Kayla would play her piece and do pretty well. Then Kim would get up in front of the group, **exchange** a look with Kayla, and play horribly. Mrs. Johnson knew that Kim had not practiced. She would cry, "You must practice every day! One hour, or more!"

Then one day, strict Mrs. Johnson surprised Kim by bending her rules just a little. "Kim," she said in a low voice. "When I was your age, I didn't like to practice either. It was dull and lonely for me, too. I have an idea. I know that you and Kayla are friends, so the two of you will practice together. One hour or more, of course!"

After that, Kim and Kayla sat together at the piano bench every day after school. Kayla showed Kim how she made her practice fun by playing **portions** of the music really loudly. They played songs where Kayla was the left hand and Kim was the right one. They learned a lot of duets, so that they each played one part of the song.

Kim started playing really well in class. It made her even more willing to practice. Soon she found that an hour started to go by really fast. Kim didn't like to admit it at first, but sometimes she even practiced for more! **3**

gracefully in a skilled and elegant way • *The students who practiced would play gracefully, but Kim was terrible.*

exchange to give one thing and receive another • *Then Kim would get up in front of the group, exchange a look with Kayla, and play horribly.*

portions parts of something • *Kayla showed Kim how she made her practice fun by playing portions of the music really loudly.*

Listening Comprehension

Read aloud the story. Pause at the numbered stopping points to ask children the questions below. Discuss the meanings of the highlighted words, as needed, to support the discussion.
RL.1.2, SL.1.2

1 *What are some words that tell about Mrs. Johnson?* Sample answers: piano teacher, strict, small, neat, simple, tough **CHARACTER TRAITS**

2 *What problem does Kim have?* Sample answer: She does not like to practice, and she is a terrible piano player. **IDENTIFY STORY STRUCTURE**

3 *Retell the story in your own words. What lessons does the author want us to think about?* Sample answer: People can change, and they can surprise us by showing another side of themselves. **THEME**

Classroom Collaboration

Have children participate in a classroom conversation about the characters in "The Piano Lessons." Guide them to ask and answer questions about the text or about comments made during discussion. Remind children to build on each others' comments to further the discussion.
SL.1.1b, SL.1.1c, SL.1.3

Whole Group

DAY 1

Go Digital • Interactive Whiteboard Lesson

JOURNEYS Phonics

Interactive Whiteboard Lesson:
Words with Digraph *th*

Phonemic Awareness/Phonics

▶ SHARE OBJECTIVES

- Blend and segment spoken words with digraph *th*.
- Learn the sound-spelling correspondence for digraph *th*.
- Blend and decode regularly spelled one-syllable words with digraph *th*.

▶ SKILLS TRACE

Words with Digraph *th*	
Introduce	**T16–T17**
Differentiate	T82
Reteach	T96
Review	T38, T60
Assess	Weekly Tests, Lesson 11

ELL ENGLISH LANGUAGE LEARNERS
Use Visuals

Beginning Show the *Sound/Spelling Card* for *thumb*. Review the sound /th/ and have children say the word *thumb*.

Low Intermediate Write *th* on the board. Model the sound as you point to the letters. Say *thumb, thank, think,* and have children repeat.

High Intermediate Have children use letter cards to build *thin, think,* and *thank*. Then have them read each word.

Proficient Have children use letter cards to build *tin, hen, link,* and *tank*. Have them read each word. Then have them change the first letter of each word to *th* and read the words.

See ELL Lesson 11, p. E3, for scaffolded support.

COMMON CORE

RF.1.2b orally produce single-syllable words by blending sounds; **RF.1.2d** segment spoken single-syllable words into their complete sequence of individual sounds; **RF.1.3a** know the spelling-sound correspondences for common consonant digraphs; **RF.1.3b** decode regularly spelled one-syllable words; **RF.1.3g** recognize and read irregularly spelled words; **SL.1.6** produce complete sentences when appropriate to task and situation

Words with Digraph *th*

PHONEMIC AWARENESS WARM-UP Guide children to listen for the sound /th/ in words. *Listen as I blend some sounds to say a word: /th/ /ă/ /t/. The word is* that. *Listen again: /p/ /ă/ /th/. The word is* path.

Now let's do it together. Listen. Blend the sounds: /th/ /ĭ/ /n/. What is the word? thin *Now you listen, blend the sounds, and tell me each word. /b/ /ă/ /th/* bath, */m/ /ă/ /th/* math, */th/ /ŭ/ /m/* thumb.

Reverse the process, segmenting instead of blending. Use the same words but in random order.

Then guide children to blend longer words. *Say the sounds after me and then blend them to say the word: /b/ /ă/ /th/–/t/ /ŭ/ /b/,* bathtub; */p/ /ă/ /th/–/w/ /ā/,* pathway; */th/ /ŭ/ /m/–/p/ /r/ /ĭ/ /n/ /t/,* thumbprint. ◼ **RF.1.2b, RF.1.2d**

1 Teach/Model

SOUND/SPELLING CARD Display the card for *thumb*. Name the picture and say the sound. Have children repeat after you. *Listen:* thumb, */th/. Now you say it.*

- **Say the sound and give the spelling.** Thumb *begins with the sound /th/. The letters* th *stand for the sound /th/ at the beginning, middle, or end of a word.*

- **Write and read *thin*.** *This is the word* thin. *The letters* th *stand for the beginning sound /th/. The letter* i *stands for the middle sound /ĭ/. The letter* n *stands for the sound /n/ at the end. Read with me: /th/ /ĭ/ /n/,* thin.

- **Write and read *math*.** *This is the word* math. *The letter* m *stands for the beginning sound /m/. The letter* a *stands for the sound /ă/ in the middle. The letters* t *and* h *together stand for the sound /th/ at the end. Read with me: /m/ /ă/ /th/,* math. **Repeat with the words** *path* **and** *thump*.

2 Guided Practice

CONTINUOUS BLENDING ROUTINE Use **Instructional Routine 3** to model blending *thin*. Write the word *thin* on the board.
RF.1.2b, RF.1.3a, RF.1.3b

- Point to **Sound/Spelling Card** *thumb* and remind children that knowing the sound/spelling *th* can help them read words.

- Display **Letter Cards** *th, i,* and *n*.

- Blend the sounds. *Listen: /th/ /ĭ/ /n/.* Have children blend with you. *Now you blend the sounds: /th/ /ĭ/ /n/. /th/ /ĭ/ /n/*

- Repeat the routine with **Letter Cards** *w, i,* and *th*.

REPEAT CONTINUOUS BLENDING ROUTINE with the words in Row 1 below. Then write the words in Rows 1–3 and have children read them. Use the **Corrective Feedback** steps if children need additional help.

- Repeat until children are reading at a rate of three seconds per word.

DECODING Call on individuals to blend one or more words and to read the sentences. RF.1.3a, RF.1.3b, RF.1.3g

1. math	bath	with	them	than
2. jump	drill	Beth	dress	path
3. scrap	frog	thump	tack	thin

I <u>like</u> <u>to</u> <u>do</u> math.
<u>My</u> dog <u>was</u> in <u>the</u> bath.

3 Apply

Hands-on Practice

Have partners use letter cards to take turns building and reading words with digraph *th*. After reading a word, each partner should use the word in a sentence. RF.1.3a, RF.1.3b, SL.1.6

Corrective Feedback Work with the whole group to correct errors, following the model below.

Phonics Error:
A child reads *thin* as *tin*.

Correct the error. Review the **Sound/Spelling Card.** Say the word and the sound. *The word is* thin. *The letters* th *stand for the sound /th/.*

Model as you touch the letters. *I'll blend: /th/ /ĭ/ /n/. What is the word?* thin

Guide *Let's blend together: /th/ /ĭ/ /n/. What is the word?* thin

Check *You blend: /th/ /ĭ/ /n/. What is the word?* thin

Reinforce Go back three or four words and have children continue reading. Make note of errors and review those words during tomorrow's lesson.

SMALL GROUP Options Go to p. T82 for additional phonics support.

Reader's Notebook Vol. 1 p. 150
See Grab-and-Go™ Resources for additional leveled practice.

Phonics/Spelling

▶ SHARE OBJECTIVES

- Write words with consonant digraph *th*.
- Read decodable text with regularly spelled one-syllable words and irregularly spelled high-frequency words.
- Practice reading fluently, paying attention to commas.
- Read on-level text with purpose and understanding.

▶ DICTATION SENTENCES

- **thin.** Seth is **thin**.
- **than.** A dog is bigger **than** a bug.
- **math.** We learn to add in **math**.
- **path.** Dan walks on the **path**.
- **thud.** The book fell with a **thud**.
- **fifth.** She is the **fifth** girl in line.

Write Words with Digraph *th*

1 Teach/Model

CONNECT SOUNDS TO SPELLING Review **Sound/Spelling Card** *thumb*. Tell children that they will write words with the sound /th/.

Use **Instructional Routine 6** to dictate, using the first sentence at the left. *Listen as I say each word and use it in a sentence.*

- Model how to spell the word *thin*. Point to *th* on the **Sound/Spelling Card**. *What sound do the letters* th *stand for?* /th/ *I remember that when the letters* th *are side by side, they make the /th/ sound. I will write* th *at the beginning of the word. I will write* i *for the middle sound and* n *for the end sound. Then I'll reread to check the whole word:* thin.

2 Guided Practice

CONNECT SOUNDS TO WRITING Continue the dictation, using the sentences at the left. ▬ L.1.2d, L.1.2e

- Have children say each word aloud after you. Then have them identify the sounds they hear at the beginning, middle, and end of each word and write the letters that stand for each sound.
- Remind children to write only the dictation word.

3 Apply

- Read aloud the following decodable sentence for children to write.

> Seth will <u>play</u> with Beth <u>today</u>.

- Remind children that *play* and *today* are Words to Know that they learned in previous lessons.
- Print the dictation words and the sentence for children to check their work. ▬ L.1.2d

COMMON CORE **RF.1.3a** know the spelling-sound correspondences for common consonant digraphs; **RF.1.3b** decode regularly spelled one-syllable words; **RF.1.3g** recognize and read irregularly spelled words; **RF.1.4a** read on-level text with purpose and understanding; **RF.1.4b** read on-level text orally with accuracy, appropriate rate, and expression; **L.1.2d** use conventional spelling for words with common spelling patterns and for frequently occurring irregular words **L.1.2e** spell untaught words phonetically, drawing on phonemic awareness and spelling conventions

Decodable Reader

Go Digital

Read *Seth and Beth*

**Decodable Reader,
Unit 3, pp. 3–8**

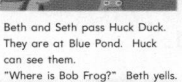

Seth and Beth
by Anna Guzman
illustrated by Piero Corva

Seth and Beth met at the path. Beth has a big map. It can help. They will go and see Bob Frog. 3

This trip is far. Seth and Beth pass Ben. Ben can see them. Seth tips his cap. Then Ben tips his cap. 4

This trip is far. Beth and Seth pass Sam. Sam can see them. Seth and Sam tip their hats. 5

Beth and Seth pass Huck Duck. They are at Blue Pond. Huck can see them. "Where is Bob Frog?" Beth yells. 6

"Does Bob Frog live here?" Seth asks. "Bob Frog is in this pond," Huck quacks. 7

"Get up, Bob Frog!" Seth and Beth call. "Play with us! This is fun! It is fun." 8

REVIEW /th/ AND WORDS TO KNOW Tell children that many words in this story have the letters *th,* which stand for /th/. Point out that children have learned the following words, which they will also read in the story: *blue, far, live, their, where.*

PREVIEW Have children preview pages 3–5 and predict what the story is about. Ask volunteers to tell about the farthest place from home they have ever been.

MODEL FLUENCY AND PHRASING Read aloud page 7 as children follow along. Point out how you paused when you came to the comma after *pond*. Lead children in choral reading the page with fluency and appropriate phrasing.

READ Remind children to read from left to right and when they come to the end of a line, to continue reading at the beginning of the next line. Have children read independently for a sustained period of time. Have them read to find out what happens on Seth and Beth's trip. RF.1.3a, RF.1.3b, RF.1.3g, RF.1.4a

RESPONDING Ask children which page they used to identify the title, the author, and the illustrator of this story. Then ask them to tell what other information about this story they learned from that page. Ask partners to retell the story to each other.

DAILY ASSESSMENT
RtI

Corrective Feedback Work with the whole group to correct errors, following the model below.

Decoding Error:
A child reads *Seth* as *set*.

Correct the error. Say the word. *That word is* Seth. *It ends with the sound /th/. The letters* th *stand for /th/.*

Guide Have children repeat the word. *What is the word?* Seth

Check *Go back to the beginning of the sentence and read it again.*

Reinforce Record the error and review the word again before children reread the story.

SMALL GROUP Options

Go to p. T82 for additional phonics support.

Reread for Fluency/ Develop Automaticity

READ WITH A PARTNER Have partners reread *Seth and Beth* three or four times, taking turns reading aloud each page. Remind them to read words correctly and to read smoothly. Visit partners to listen to them read. Give feedback about reading accurately, at an appropriate rate, and with expression, and provide guidance for improving fluency. RF.1.4b

Whole Group

DAY 1

Go Digital
• eBook
• Context Cards
• Vocabulary Reader

Introduce Words to Know

▷ SHARE OBJECTIVE
- Recognize and read irregularly spelled words.

Teach

Display and discuss the **Vocabulary in Context Cards,** using the routine below. See also **Instructional Routine 15.**

1. **Read and pronounce the word.** Read the word once alone and then together.

2. **Explain the word.** Read aloud the explanation under *What Does It Mean?*

3. **Discuss vocabulary in context.** Together, read aloud the sentence on the front of the card. Help children explain and use the word in new sentences.

4. **Engage with the word.** Ask and discuss *How Do I Use It?*

Practice/Apply

Give partners or small groups one or two **Vocabulary in Context Cards.** Help children complete the *Talk It Over* activities for each card. ▱ **RF.1.3g**

COMMON CORE · **RF.1.3g** recognize and read irregularly spelled words

---

Lesson 11

At Home in the Ocean
by Rozanne Lanczak Williams

Water

✓ WORDS TO KNOW
High-Frequency Words

cold
where
blue
live
far
their
little
water

Vocabulary Reader   Context Cards

COMMON CORE · **RF.1.3g** recognize and read irregularly spelled words

10   Go Digital

Words to Know

▶ **Read each Context Card.**

▶ **Make up a new sentence that uses a blue word.**

1 cold

This ocean water is very cold.

2 where

Sharks live where the ocean is deep.

ELL ENGLISH LANGUAGE LEARNERS
Comprehensible Input

Beginning Point to the classroom and say, *We are in the classroom.* Then ask, *Where are we?* Have children answer, *In the classroom.*

High Intermediate Have partners ask each other where they like to play the most. One child should ask the question using *where,* and the other child should answer. Then they should switch roles.

Low Intermediate Use online **Picture Cards** or classroom illustrations to ask where things are. *Where is the dog?* Have children answer, *In the park.* Then have children ask the question *Where is _____?*

Proficient Have partners talk about where they like to perform certain activities, such as playing, painting, or reading. Have them explain why they prefer those places using *where.*

See ELL Lesson 11, p. E2, for vocabulary support.

3 blue

Today the ocean water looks blue.

4 live

Whales live in all the oceans of the world.

5 far

Squid swim far below the ocean's surface.

6 their

Their home is by the ocean.

7 little

Many little fish live in the ocean.

8 water

Some people take photos in the water.

11

VOCABULARY IN CONTEXT CARDS 61–68

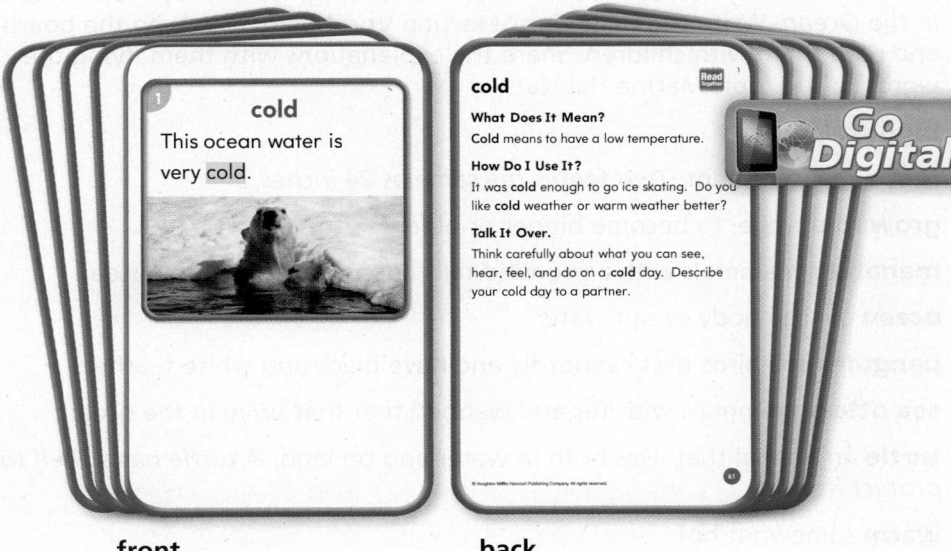

front

back

1 cold

This ocean water is very cold.

cold

What Does It Mean?
Cold means to have a low temperature.

How Do I Use It?
It was cold enough to go ice skating. Do you like cold weather or warm weather better?

Talk It Over.
Think carefully about what you can see, hear, feel, and do on a cold day. Describe your cold day to a partner.

Go Digital

DAILY ASSESSMENT **RtI**

Are children able to understand and use the Words to Know?

IF...	THEN...
children have difficulty understanding and using Words to Know,	▶ use **Vocabulary in Context Cards** and the Struggling Readers activity, p. T84. *See also Intervention Lesson 11, pp. S2–S11.*
children can understand and use most Words to Know,	▶ use **Vocabulary in Context Cards** and the On Level activity, p. T84.
children can understand and use all Words to Know,	▶ use the Advanced activity, p. T85.

SMALL GROUP Options

Vocabulary Reader pp. T84–T85
Provide support for English Language Learners according to language proficiency. See also Differentiate Words to Know, p. T83.

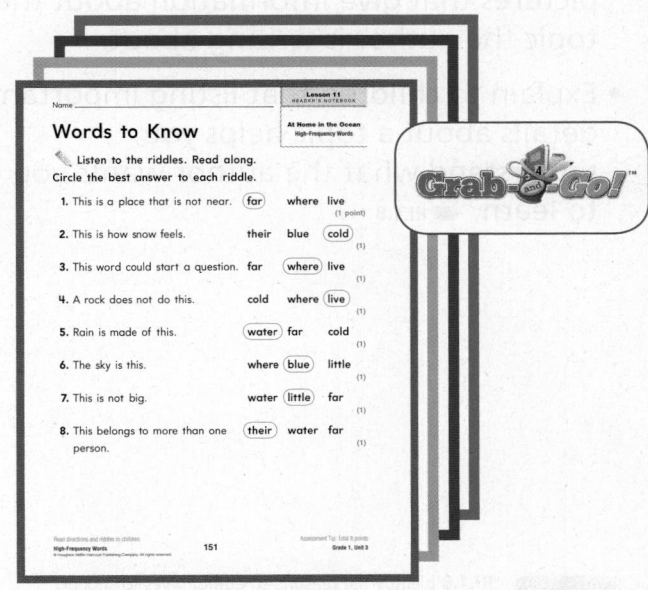

Grab-and-Go!

Reader's Notebook Vol. 1 p. 151
See Grab-and-Go™ Resources for additional leveled practice.

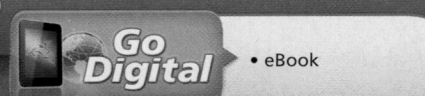
Read and Comprehend

- Identify author's purpose and the reasons an author gives to support points.
- Analyze and evaluate text to aid comprehension.

☑ **TARGET SKILL**

Author's Purpose

- Read the top section of **Student Book** p. 12 with children.
- Tell children that the reason an author writes is called the *author's purpose*.
- Then ask children if the *author's purpose* in an informational text is to give information about a topic or to make them laugh. *to give information*

  🔖 **RI.1.8**

- Draw children's attention to the graphic organizer on **Student Book** p. 12. Tell children that as they read they can use a graphic organizer like this one, adding details they find from the words and pictures that give information about the topic the author is writing about.

- Explain to children that listing important details about a topic helps you understand what the author wants you to learn. 🔖 **RI.1.8**

 **RI.1.8** identify the reasons an author gives to support points

---

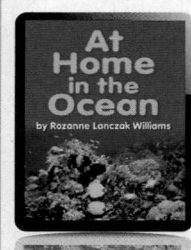
At Home in the Ocean
by Rozanne Lanczak Williams

Read and Comprehend

 Read Together

 Go Digital

☑ **TARGET SKILL**

Author's Purpose Authors may write to make you laugh or to give information. The reason an author writes is called the **author's purpose**. In informational texts, the author's purpose is to give information about a topic. As you read, think about what the author wants you to learn. List details that explain the author's purpose.

☑ **TARGET STRATEGY**

Analyze/Evaluate Tell what you think and how you feel about the selection. Tell why.

12 COMMON CORE **RI.1.8** identify the reasons an author gives to support points

---

SELECTION VOCABULARY

Tell children they may see words they do not recognize as they read *At Home in the Ocean*. Write the following Selection Vocabulary words on the board, and read them with children. Share the explanations with them, tying the words to the topic Marine Habitats.

biggest largest

feet a measurement; *Two **feet** is the same as 24 inches.*

grow to change; to become bigger or older

manatees mammals with a rounded tail flipper that live in the ocean

ocean a large body of salt water

penguins sea birds that cannot fly and have black and white feathers

sea otters mammals with fur and webbed feet that swim in the ocean

turtle an animal that lives both in water and on land; *A **turtle** has a shell to protect its body.*

warm somewhat hot

whales large mammals that live in the ocean; ***Whales** breathe through a blowhole at the top of their heads.*

COMMON CORE

DAY 1

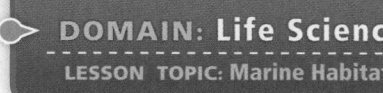

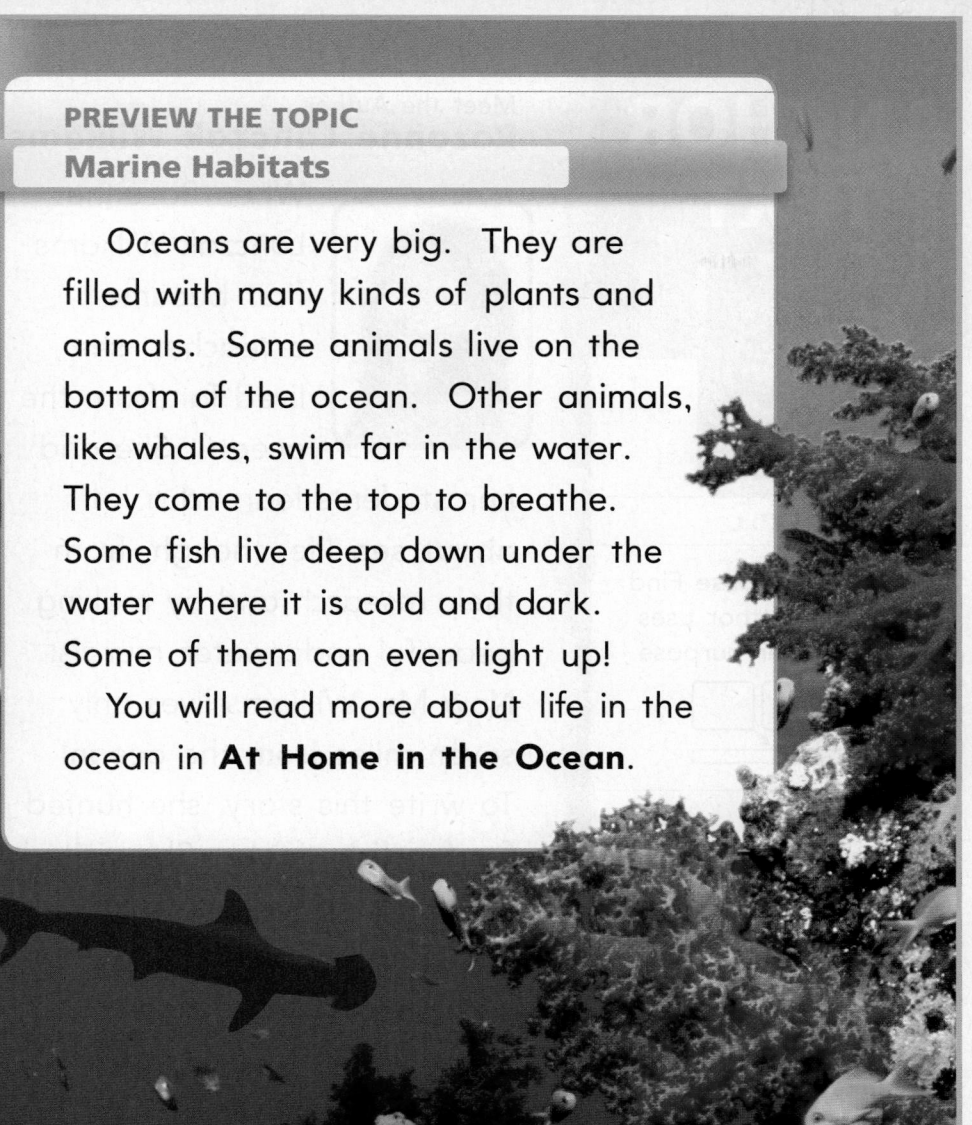

Oceans are very big. They are filled with many kinds of plants and animals. Some animals live on the bottom of the ocean. Other animals, like whales, swim far in the water. They come to the top to breathe. Some fish live deep down under the water where it is cold and dark. Some of them can even light up!

You will read more about life in the ocean in **At Home in the Ocean**.

13

COMPREHENSION STRATEGIES

Use the following strategies flexibly as you read with children by modeling how they can be used to improve comprehension. See scaffolded support for the strategy shown in boldface during this week's reading.

- Monitor/Clarify
- **Analyze/Evaluate**
- Summarize
- Question
- Infer/Predict
- Phonics/Decoding
- Visualize

Use the Strategy Projectables, S1–S8, for additional support.

○ DOMAIN: **Life Science**
LESSON TOPIC: Marine Habitats

☑ TARGET STRATEGY
Analyze/Evaluate

- Read the bottom section of **Student Book** p. 12 with children.

- Explain that good readers **analyze,** or think hard about, a selection. They find clues in the words and photos to help them understand the information.

- Tell them that good readers also **evaluate,** or tell what they think and how they feel about the selection. They may or may not think the information is interesting. They may or may not think the author explained it well.

- Tell children that good readers look for text evidence to help them give reasons for why they think and feel as they do about the selection.

- Explain that you will show them how to use the Analyze/Evaluate strategy when you read together.

Preview the Topic: Marine Habitats

- Tell children that they will read a selection titled *At Home in the Ocean*.

- Read the information on **Student Book** p. 13 with children. Prompt them to identify and describe ocean animals and plants and the places in the ocean where they live.

- Then display a globe and help children identify the areas of water and land. Through discussion and using the globe, guide children to recognize that the Earth's surface has many things on it, such as oceans, lakes, rivers, rocks, soil, mountains, people, animals, and plants. Help them understand that more of the Earth is covered by oceans than by land, and that the oceans are filled with many different kinds of plants and animals.

Read the Anchor Text

☑ **TARGET SKILL**

Author's Purpose

- Point out to children the graphic organizer on **Student Book** p. 14.

- Tell children it will help them list the important information the author tells about the topic she is giving information about.

☑ **GENRE Informational Text**

- Read the genre information on **Student Book** p. 14 with children.

- Preview the selection with children, and model identifying the characteristics of informational text.

Think Aloud *An Informational text gives facts about a topic. It uses details to support the main idea. The title of this selection is* At Home in the Ocean. *From the title and the photos, I think I will be getting facts and details about animals that live in the ocean. So this must be an informational text.*

- As you preview, ask children to identify other features of informational text, such as photographs and labels.

 **RI.1.10** read informational texts; **RF.1.4a** read on-level text with purpose and understanding

---

Lesson 11

ANCHOR TEXT

 At Home in the Ocean
by Rozanne Lanczak Williams

☑ **TARGET SKILL**

Author's Purpose Find details the author uses to explain her purpose.

☑ **GENRE**

Informational text gives facts about a topic. Look for:
- ▸ information and facts in the words
- ▸ photos that show the real world
- ▸ labels for photos

COMMON CORE **RI.1.2** identify the main topic and retell key details; **RI.1.8** identify the reasons an author gives to support points; **RI.1.10** read informational texts

14 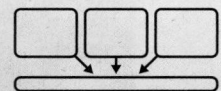 Go Digital

---

Meet the Author
Rozanne Lanczak Williams

When Rozanne Lanczak Williams first became a teacher, she lived far from the ocean. She and her students learned a lot about sea life, though, from their research and by making beautiful underwater murals. Now Ms. Williams lives only seven miles from the ocean! To write this story, she hunted for fun fishy facts. She visited a big aquarium, the library, a bookstore, a friend's classroom library—and the ocean!

 **RI.1.10**

Scaffold Close Reading

Think Through the Text	Analyze the Text	Independent Reading
FIRST READ	**SECOND READ**	
Develop comprehension through • Guided Questioning • Target Strategy: Analyze/Evaluate • Vocabulary in Context **IF** children demonstrate understanding of what the selection is mostly about, **THEN** provide additional challenge using the questions labeled A Closer Look.	Support analyzing short sections of text: • Author's Purpose • Details Use directed note-taking by working with children to complete a graphic organizer during reading. Distribute copies of Graphic Organizer 7.	• Children analyze the text independently, using the Reader's Guide on pp. 157–158 of the **Reader's Notebook**. (See p. T52 for instructional support.) • Children read independently in a self-selected trade book.

At Home in the Ocean

by Rozanne Lanczak Williams

ESSENTIAL QUESTION

What kinds of plants and animals would you find in the ocean?

15

ESSENTIAL QUESTION

• Read aloud the Essential Question on **Student Book** p. 15: *What kinds of plants and animals would you find in the ocean?* Then tell children to think about this question as they read *At Home in the Ocean.*

Predictive Writing

• Write the Essential Question on the board.

• Explain that together you will write about what they expect *At Home in the Ocean* to be about. Ask children to think about how the Essential Question relates to what they noticed while previewing the selection or what they already know about the Essential Question from their own experiences or past readings.

• Ask children to think about the genre of the selection as they offer ideas.

Set Purpose

• Tell children that good readers set a purpose for reading, based on their preview of the selection, what they know about the genre, and what they want to learn from the selection.

• Model setting a reading purpose.

Think Aloud *I know that lots of fish live in the ocean. There are other animals and plants that live there, too, but I don't know much about them. I will read to learn about those animals and plants.*

• Have children set their own purpose for reading. Ask several volunteers to share their purpose for reading. Then have children read the selection.

RI.1.10, RF.1.4a

READER AND TASK CONSIDERATIONS

Determine the level of additional support your children will need to read and comprehend *At Home in the Ocean* successfully.

READERS

• **Motivate** Ask children to tell about their favorite animal that lives in the ocean.

• **Access Knowledge and Experiences** Remind children of the Preview the Topic information on Student Book p. 13. Ask them to share with a partner what they recall, and if possible, share one other thing they know about animals or plants that live in the ocean.

TASKS

• **Increase Scaffolding** Stop periodically as you read to have children recall the topic and retell key details from the text and photographs.

• **Foster Independence** Have children read the selection in small groups. Tell them to pause throughout the selection to ask any questions they have about the information. Have them look together for text evidence in the words and photographs to help them answer the questions.

The ocean is big!
It is big and blue as far as you can see.

16

It is home to many plants and animals.

17

ELL ENGLISH LANGUAGE LEARNERS

Comprehensible Input

Beginning Ask children *yes/no* questions about the photos, such as *Is this selection funny? Does it give information?*

Intermediate Ask children questions about the photos, such as *Is this selection true or make-believe?*

Advanced Write action verbs such as *jump* and *swim* on the board. Ask children to use the words to describe an animal in the photos.

Advanced High Work with children to describe the animals in the photos. Prompt them to use color words and the names of body parts, such as *fins*, *tail*, and *gills*.

 **RI.1.1** ask and answer questions about key details; **RI.1.2** identify the main topic and retell key details; **RI.1.5** know and use text features to locate facts or information; **RI.1.7** use illustrations and details to describe key ideas; **RI.1.8** identify the reasons an author gives to support points

---

FIRST READ

Use Text Evidence

Think Through the Text

1 *Describe what you see in the photograph on p. 16. Two dolphins are leaping into the air. Their tails are above the water.*
🔲 **RI.3.7**

☑ TARGET STRATEGY: Analyze/Evaluate

After reading **Student Book** pp. 16–17 with children, display **Projectable S7**. Help children use the Analyze/Evaluate strategy by analyzing details about the animals and the ocean.

Think Aloud *I can see that the ocean is large and wide open and that large animals live here. I think that there is room for many plants and animals to live in such a large place. I think this selection will give information about many kind of things that live in the big, blue sea.*

KEY: ☑ **WORDS TO KNOW**
High-Frequency Words ▭
Decodable Words with ▁
Digraph *th*

COMMON
CORE

DAY 1

The biggest animals in the ocean are blue whales. They eat little animals called krill.

krill

blue whale ③

18

19

② *How is the photograph on p. 17 different from the one on p. 16?* The dolphins are leaping out of the water. Sharks and smaller fish are swimming under the water.
▬ **RI.3.7**

③ *What important information do the labels and sentences on pp. 18–19 give?* The first label tells that the large animal in the photograph is a blue whale. The second label tells that the little animals are krill. The sentences tell that blue whales are the biggest animals in the ocean and they eat krill. ▬ **RI.1.1, RI.2.5**

 A Closer Look

The sentence on p. 16 says that the ocean is "big and blue as far as you can see." What does that mean? When you look at the ocean, you cannot see the other side. As far as you can see, everything looks blue. ▬ **RI.1.1, RI.1.2**

ANALYZE THE TEXT

11.2 **Author's Purpose** Display **Projectable 11.2,** and distribute **Graphic Organizer 7.** Discuss: *What important information about whales do you learn from the words and photos? How do these details help you understand the author's purpose? How do the details help you understand why the whale is at home in the ocean?*

Tell children they will find facts that give reasons why the animals and plants have a good home in the ocean. Continue to work with children to record details on the graphic organizer and to state the author's purpose, such as *to give information about animals and plants that have a good home in the ocean.*
▬ **RI.1.1, RI.1.8**

penguins ⑤

Many animals live in cold water. Brrr! ④

Penguins swim fast! They flap their wings to zip, zip, zip in the water.

20

21

ELL **ENGLISH LANGUAGE LEARNERS**

Review Key Understandings

Beginning Make gestures to show climate on pages 20 and 22. Have children repeat as you say the words *cold* and *warm*.

Low Intermediate Ask children to act out fast and slow to help them visualize how penguins and manatees move.

High Intermediate Have children complete sentence frames, such as: *Penguins live where it is ___. Manatees live where it is ___.*

Proficient Have children tell facts about where penguins and manatees live and how they move.

FIRST READ

Use Text Evidence

Think Through the Text

④ *What facts about oceans do you learn from the words on p. 20?* The water in the ocean can be cold. Many animals can live in cold water. ⬛ **RI.1.1, RI.1.2**

⑤ *Why do you think the author put two different photographs of penguins on p. 21?* The author wants to show that penguins can live in and out of the water. The photographs also give details about how penguins are birds that use their wings to dive and to swim. ⬛ **RI.1.7, RI.1.8**

COMMON CORE **RI.1.1** ask and answer questions about key details; **RI.1.2** identify the main topic and retell key details; **RI.1.7** use illustrations and details to describe key ideas; **RI.1.8** identify the reasons an author gives to support points; **RF.1.3b** decode regularly spelled one-syllable words; **RF.1.3g** recognize and read irregularly spelled words

KEY: ☑ **WORDS TO KNOW**
High-Frequency Words
Decodable Words with
Digraph *th*

COMMON CORE

DAY 1

Manatees live **where** the water is warm. ⑥
They do not swim fast.

manatees

Manatees eat lots and lots of plants.
Then they rest.

22   23

⑥ *Why does the author write that manatees live in
water that is warm? The author wants us to know that
ocean water is not always cold. Some parts of the ocean are
warm.* ▬ **RI.1.1, RI.1.2, RI.1.8**

> ## A Closer Look

*What do you think the author's purpose is in putting
manatees in the selection right after the penguins?
Penguins swim fast in cold water. Manatees swim slowly in warm
water. The author wants to show that many different kinds of
animals live in different places in the ocean.* ▬ **RI.1.8**

SECOND READ   DAY 2

ANALYZE THE TEXT

Details Review with children the
characteristics of informational text. Have
children state the topic of the selection in their
own words. *life in the ocean*

Discuss questions like these to guide children
to retell key details about the topic: *What
words in* At Home in the Ocean *tell important
facts about the topic? Which photos show
what life in the ocean is really like? What
information do you learn from the photos?
What do you learn from the labels?*
▬ **RI.1.1, RI.1.2, RI.1.7**

This turtle swims far!

It digs in the sand and lays its eggs.

Then it swims back to its ocean home. **7**

eggs

turtle

8

24

25

⟜ **DOMAIN: Life Science**

LESSON TOPIC: Marine Habitats

Cross-Curricular Connection Tell children that most of the earth is covered by ocean. Ask them what else is found on the earth's surface, such as rocks, soil, people, plants, and animals. Explain that the plants that live in the ocean give people the oxygen they need to breathe. Explain how the water in the ocean is a part of a cycle that involves evaporation and rain. Discuss with children the reasons why people, animals, and plants need water.

COMMON CORE **RI.1.1** ask and answer questions about key details; **RI.1.2** identify the main topic and retell key details; **RI.1.6** distinguish between information provided by pictures and words; **RI.1.8** identify the reasons an author gives to support points; **RF.1.3b** decode regularly spelled one-syllable words

FIRST READ

Think Through the Text

☑ Phonics/Decoding Strategy:

Use **Projectable S1** and help children apply the Phonics/ Decoding strategy while reading p. 24. Review the digraph *th* sound, /th/, with children. Then have them point to the word *This*. Model blending the sounds: th/ĭ/s. Have children repeat. Ask them to read the sentence to make sure that *this* makes sense. Then have them do the same with *Then*. ▬**RF.1.3b**

7 *What facts about turtles do you learn from the words on pp. 24–25? Turtles can swim far. Turtles dig in the sand and lay their eggs there. Turtles leave their eggs in the sand and return to the ocean where they live.* ▬**RI.1.1, RI.1.2**

KEY: ✓ **WORDS TO KNOW**
High-Frequency Words
Decodable Words with
Digraph *th*

COMMON
CORE

DAY 1

kelp

sea otter

Kelp is the biggest plant in the ocean.
It can grow fast.

Kelp can grow two feet in a day!
Sea otters can get lots of food here. **9**

26

27

8 *What different information about turtles do you learn
from the photographs on pp. 24–25?* Turtles use their flippers
to swim. A turtle lays many eggs at once. Baby turtles break out of
their eggs. Baby turtles have flippers. ▬ **RI.1.2, RI.2.6**

9 *What reasons does the author give for why the ocean is a
good place for kelp and sea otters to live? Use your own
ideas, too.* Kelp grows fast and is the biggest plant in the ocean. It
needs lots of room to grow. The ocean is very big, so kelp has a good
place to live and grow. Sea otters live in the ocean because they can
find lots of food there. ▬ **RI.1.1, RI.1.8**

Lots of plants and animals, big and little, live in the ocean.
The ocean is their home.

28

29

DAILY ASSESSMENT — **RtI**

3
2
1

Analyze/Evaluate IF children have difficulty applying the Analyze/Evaluate strategy, **THEN** use this model:

Think Aloud *The words say that the ocean is home to many plants and animals and that some are big and some are little. The photos show these ideas, too. I'll think about what I learned and decide what I think of the selection and the reasons why.*

Have children reread the text and look at the photographs and then use the strategy to explain what they think and feel about what they learned about ocean life.

RI.1.2 identify the main topic and retell key details

FIRST READ

Use Text Evidence

Think Through the Text

☑ TARGET STRATEGY: Analyze/Evaluate

Guide children to practice the Analyze/Evaluate strategy as they read **Student Book** p. 28 to themselves. Ask several children to point out where they used the strategy to help them understand the information and figure out what they think of *At Home in the Ocean.*

Think Aloud *The last page makes me think about all of the animals in the selection. I think about the facts I learned about each animal. I think that the author included many kinds of plants and animals to show that the ocean is a big place with room for all different kinds of life. I liked reading about the interesting animals and plants.*

Guided Summary

Oral Language Use the prompts on the Retelling Cards to guide children to identify the main topic and retell key details as they summarize the selection.

▬ RI.1.2

front

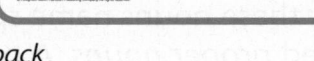

back

front

back

front

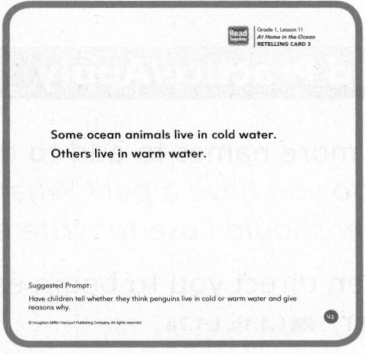

back

front

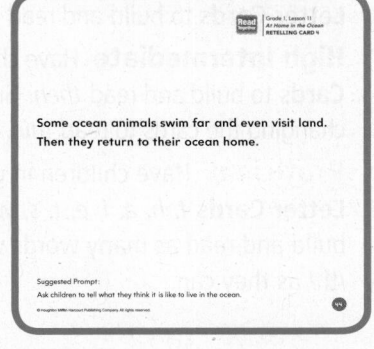

back

	SUMMARIZING RUBRIC	
4	**Highly Effective**	The child restates the main idea; identifies the important facts or details; retells the order of events by referring to the words and/or illustrations; requires little or no prompting.
3	**Generally Effective**	The child restates the main idea; identifies some important facts or details; retells the order of most events and may refer to the words and/or illustrations; may require some prompting.
2	**Somewhat Effective**	The child may restate the main idea; identifies some facts or details; retells the order of some events with some omissions or errors; requires some prompting.
1	**Ineffective**	The child is unable to restate the main idea; identifies some facts or details, possibly with errors; is unable to retell the order of events; is unable to summarize without prompting.

Go Digital
- *my*WriteSmart
- eBook
- GrammarSnap Videos
- Literacy and Language Guide

Grammar Introduce Proper Nouns

▶ SHARE OBJECTIVES

- **Grammar** Identify and use proper nouns that name people and animals.
- **Spelling** Spell words with *th* using conventional spelling patterns.
- **Writing** Write sentences that inform as a class.

ELL ENGLISH LANGUAGE LEARNERS
Language Transfer

Beginning Display the words *mouth, that, with, thick*. Read them aloud. Have children clap every time they hear the /th/ sound.

Low Intermediate Have children use **Letter Cards** to build and read *with, then, bath*.

High Intermediate Have children use **Letter Cards** to build and read *then*. Guide them in changing the cards to read *thin, this, that*.

Proficient Have children in groups use **Letter Cards** *t, h, a, i, e, t, s, w, n, b, m* to build and read as many words with the sound /th/ as they can.

1 Teach/Model

- Display a picture of Gus from *Gus Takes the Train* from Lesson 5. *What is the name of this animal? Gus*

- Explain that people and some animals have names. Ask children to tell you names of pets that they have or know about.

- Write children's responses on a chart. In the first column, write the name of the child, in the second column write the name of his or her pet.

My Name	Name of Pet
Jeff Nadler	Pokey
Carlos Sanchez	Whiskers

- Point out that these nouns name special people and animals. These are called *proper nouns*. A proper noun always begins with a capital letter.

2 Guided Practice/Apply

- Brainstorm more names to add to the chart. Ask questions such as: *Bobby, do you have a pet? What is your pet's name? What kind of letter should I use to write each name?*

- Have children direct you to begin each name you add with a capital letter. ▬ **L.1.1b, L.1.2a**

Spelling Words with *th*

SPELLING WORDS AND SENTENCES

BASIC

1. **that** *That* is my hat.
2. **then** Come to my house and *then* we will bake cookies.
3. **this** *This* is my bed.
4. **them** Please tell *them* to go slowly.
5. **with** Alex will go *with* you to the store.
6. **bath** I take a *bath* every night.

CHALLENGE

7. **thick** The sauce was *thick* and creamy.
8. **tenth** I was *tenth* in line because nine people were ahead of me.

Administer the Pretest

Say the first word and read the sentence. Have children spell untaught words phonetically. Repeat the word as children write it. Write the word on the board and have children correct their spelling if needed. Repeat the procedure for words 2–8. Tell children that they can use their list to practice at home. ▬ **L.1.2d, L.1.2e**

Teach the Principle

Review **Sound/Spelling Card** *thumb*. Write *that*, underlining *th*. Read the word aloud. Explain that the letters *th* stand for /th/.

COMMON CORE **W.1.2** write informative/explanatory texts; **W.1.5** focus on a topic, respond to questions/suggestions from peers, and add details to strengthen writing; **SL.1.6** produce complete sentences when appropriate to task and situation; **L.1.1b** use common, proper, and possessive nouns; **L.1.1e** use verbs to convey sense of past, present, and future; **L.1.2a** capitalize dates and names of people; **L.1.2d** use conventional spelling for words with common

Informative Writing Introduce the Model

1 Teach/Model

- Explain that some sentences give information. These sentences tell facts, or information that is true. They do not give opinions, or what people think. Writers use sentences that inform so they can share what they know.

- Display **Projectable 11.1**.

- Read and discuss the model. Use the Talk About It questions.

- Sum up by reviewing the Writer's Checklist about sentences that inform.

2 Shared Writing

- Help the class choose an animal to write about. Explain that the class will work together to write sentences that inform readers about this animal.

- Have partners tell each other a fact about the animal. Have partners ask each other questions about their facts and make suggestions for improvement. Have children use the ideas from their partner to improve their statements. Have them use words or pictures to record the facts.

- Then help the class create a topic sentence. Add detail sentences based on children's suggestions. Ask children to be sure that each sentence tells a fact, not an opinion.

- Provide support with prompts like these: *What color is the animal? How big is it? Where does it live? What does it eat? How does it move?* ▬ **W.1.2, W.1.5, SL.1.6**

Oral Language Conventions

Verbs Remind children that some words tell what someone or something does. These are called *action words,* or *verbs*. Then remind children that a complete sentence must have a verb in it. Have children orally identify the verbs they used in the sentences created during Shared Writing. ▬ **L.1.1e**

Projectable 11.1

Projectable 11.1

At Home in the Ocean **Writing** Informative Writing

Writing Model

Sentences That Inform

The topic sentence tells what all the sentences are about.	→	**Penguins**
		· Penguins are unusual birds.
Detail sentences tell facts, things that are true.	→	· Most penguins are black and white.
		Penguins walk slowly.
		Penguins can't fly but they are good swimmers.

Talk About It

1. What kind of writing is this? How do you know?
   it gives information; the sentences tell facts
2. What is the job of the topic sentence?
   to tell what all the sentences are about
3. What facts do the detail sentences tell about penguins?
   they are black and white; they walk slowly; they can't fly; they are good swimmers
4. Which word tells *how* penguins walk? slowly

Writing
© Houghton Mifflin Harcourt Publishing Company. All rights reserved.

Grade 1, Unit 3

Daily Proofreading Practice

    seals
Two seal jump.
       ^

    children
Many child watch them.
       ^

Writer's Checklist

What Makes Great Sentences That Inform?

- The **topic sentence** tells what all the sentences are about.

- **Detail sentences** tell facts, not opinions.

- Some details describe how something happens.

Performance Task

 Have children complete the writing assignment through *my*WriteSmart. Children will read the prompt and have access to multiple writing resources.

Additional support for Informative Writing appears in the **Common Core Writing Handbook,** Lesson 11.

---

spelling patterns and for frequently occurring irregular words; **L.1.2e** spell untaught words phonetically, drawing on phonemic awareness and spelling conventions

DAY 2

Today's Goals

Vocabulary & Oral Language
• Oral Vocabulary

Phonemic Awareness
• Segment Phonemes
• Blend Phonemes

Phonics & Fluency
• Words with Digraph *th*
• Read Decodable Reader: *Zeb Yak*
• Fluency: Phrasing

☑ **WORDS TO KNOW**

blue	live
cold	their
far	water
little	where

Text-Based Comprehension
• Dig Deeper: How to Analyze the Text
• Author's Purpose
• Details
• Reread the Anchor Text: *At Home in the Ocean*

Grammar & Writing
• Proper Nouns
👉 Informative Writing: Sentences That Inform
Focus Trait: Ideas

Spelling
• Words with *th*

 **COMMON CORE** **RF.1.2d** segment spoken single-syllable words into their complete sequence of individual sounds; **RF.1.3g** recognize and read irregularly spelled words; **L.1.5c** identify real-life connections between words and their use

Opening Routines

Warm Up with Wordplay

Share a Rhyme

Display and read the following rhyme:

> Jack and Jill went up the hill
> To fetch a pail of water.
> Jack fell down, and
> broke his crown,
> And Jill came tumbling after.

Have children name the rhyming words they hear. Underline each word as children suggest it. Then ask children to tell which words in the rhyme are proper nouns. Have them explain how they know. Reread the rhyme with children.

Daily Phonemic Awareness

Segment Phonemes

- *I'm going to say a word. Then I'll take it apart and say each sound in the word, one by one. Listen to the word:* pick. *I hear three sounds in that word:* /p/ /ĭ/ /k/, pick. *Join me as I do it again.*

- Have children repeat with you, then say the word by themselves.

- Continue with the following words:

shed /sh/ /ĕ/ /d/	*grin* /g/ /r/ /ĭ/ /n/	*black* /b/ /l/ /ă/ /k/
stop /s/ /t/ /ŏ/ /p/	*clock* /k/ /l/ /ŏ/ /k/	*six* /s/ /ĭ/ /ks/
thumb /th/ /ŭ/ /m/	*faith* /f/ /ā/ /th/	*those* /th/ /ō/ /z/  **RF.1.2d**

Corrective Feedback

- Model the task. *Listen:* clock. *I'll say each sound in the word, one-by-one:* /k/ /l/ /ŏ/ /k/, clock. *How many sounds are in the word* clock? four, /k/ /l/ /ŏ/ /k/

- Have children repeat once with you before doing it on their own. Then back up a few words and continue.

Daily High-Frequency Words

Introduce

- Point to the **High-Frequency Word Card** *cold.*

- *Say the word.* cold *Spell the word.* c, o, l, d *Write the word. Check the word.*

- Repeat the procedure with the words *blue, far, little, live, their, water,* and *where.* **RF.1.3g**

Robot Game

- Call on volunteers to demonstrate a "robot" voice and body movements. Then point to a High-Frequency Word on the Words to Know board.

- Have the children spell the word aloud with you, chanting each letter in a robotic voice, and swinging their arms back and forth like a robot.

- Continue in the same way for the remaining High-Frequency Words.

Corrective Feedback

- Say the correct word and have children repeat it. Cold. *What is the word?* cold

- Have children spell the word. *c, o, l, d How do we say this word?* cold

- Have children reread all of the cards in random order.

Daily Vocabulary Boost

- Review the Oral Vocabulary words and their definitions with children. (See pp. T14–T15.) Remind children that they heard these words in the Read-Aloud "The Piano Lessons."

- Recall with children the story events and then guide them to interact with each word's meaning.

  They had been companions since they met in art class at age 5. *Who are some of your oldest* companions?

  The students who practiced would play gracefully, but Kim was terrible. *What does it look like when someone dances or plays soccer* gracefully?

- Continue in the same manner with *exchange, portions, practice,* and *strict.* **L.1.5c**

☑ **Oral Vocabulary**

companions
exchange
gracefully
portions
practice
strict

Go Digital
• Interactive Whiteboard Lesson
• Decodable Reader

JOURNEYS Phonics

Interactive Whiteboard Lesson:
Words with Digraph *th*

Phonemic Awareness/Phonics

▶ SHARE OBJECTIVES

- Blend, build, and decode regularly spelled one-syllable words with consonant digraph *th*.
- Read text with consonant digraph *th* and high-frequency words.
- Read on-level text with purpose and understanding.

▶ SKILLS TRACE

Words with Digraph *th*	
Introduce	T16–T17
Differentiate	T82
Reteach	T96
Review	**T38, T60**
Assess	Weekly Tests, Lesson 11

Reader's Notebook Vol. 1 p. 152
See Grab-and-Go™ Resources for additional leveled practice.

COMMON CORE **RL.1.3** describe characters, settings, and major events; **RF.1.2b** orally produce single-syllable words by blending sounds; **RF.1.3a** know the spelling-sound correspondences for common consonant digraphs; **RF.1.3b** decode regularly spelled one-syllable words; **RF.1.3g** recognize and read irregularly spelled words; **RF.1.4a** read on-level text with purpose and understanding; **RF.1.4b** read on-level text orally with accuracy, appropriate rate, and expression; **L.1.2e** spell untaught words phonetically, drawing on phonemic awareness and spelling conventions

Words with Digraph *th*

PHONEMIC AWARENESS WARM-UP *I'll say each sound in a word. You blend the sounds to say the word. Listen: /th/ /ŭ/ /d/. thud* Repeat with these: *bath, this, then, that.* 🔲 **RF.1.2b**

1 Teach/Model

Review the **Sound/Spelling Card** *thumb*.

CONTINUOUS BLENDING ROUTINE Use **Instructional Routine 3** to model blending *thump*, displaying **Letter Cards** *th, u, m,* and *p*. Repeat the routine with the words in Row 1 below.

Write the words and sentence shown below. Call on individuals to blend and read one or more words and to read the sentence.

1.	this	that	thin	path	math
2.	Seth	miss	Beth	them	grab
3.	than	then	drop	bath	prop

Seth will <u>go</u> <u>far</u> on that path.

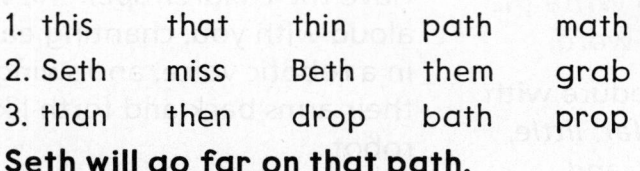

2 Guided Practice

BUILD WORDS Model how to spell *that*. *The letters* th *stand for the first sound, /th/. The next sound is /ă/. I know the letter* a *stands for /ă/. The last sound is /t/. The letter* t *stands for /t/.*

- Guide children to identify sounds and spell the words *than, click, then, stop, with, thin.* 🔲 **L.1.2e**
- Call on individuals to spell the words with **Letter Cards** while other children check their work.

3 Apply

Hands-on Practice

Have partners use letter cards to take turns building and reading words with digraph *th*. 🔲 **RF.1.3a, RF.1.3b**

Decodable Reader

Read *Zeb Yak*

**Decodable Reader,
Unit 3, pp. 9–14**

REVIEW /th/ AND WORDS TO KNOW Tell children that many words in this story have the letters *th,* which stand for /th/. Point out that children have learned the following words, which they will also read in the story: *blue, cold, little, live.*

PREVIEW Have children preview pages 9–11 and predict what the story is about. Ask volunteers to name some things they hope to do when they grow up that they cannot do now.

MODEL FLUENCY AND PHRASING Read aloud page 10 as children follow along. Point out how you paused when you came to the commas in "thud, thud, thud." Lead children in choral reading the page with fluency and appropriate phrasing.

READ Remind children to track the words from left to right and when they come to the end of a line, to sweep their hand down to the beginning of the next line and continue reading. Have children read each page silently and then choral read it. Have them read to find out about Zeb and where he lives.
🔲 RF.1.3a, RF.1.3b, RF.1.3g, RF.1.4a

RESPONDING Have children work in pairs to describe the characters using details from the story. 🔲 RL.1.3

DAILY ASSESSMENT

Corrective Feedback Work with the whole group to correct errors, following the model below.

Decoding Error:
A child reads *path* as *past.*

Correct the error. Say the word. *That word is* path. *It has the sound /th/. The letters* th *stand for /th/.*

Guide Have children repeat the word. *What is the word? path*

Check *Go back to the beginning of the sentence and read it again.*

Reinforce Record the error and review the word again before children reread the story.

Reread for Fluency/ Develop Automaticity

READ WITH A PARTNER Have partners reread *Zeb Yak* three or four times, taking turns reading aloud each page. Remind them to read words correctly and to read smoothly. Visit partners to listen to them read. Give feedback about reading accurately, at an appropriate rate, and with expression and provide guidance for improving fluency. 🔲 RF.1.4b

Dig Deeper: How to Analyze the Text

SHARE OBJECTIVES

- Understand the author's purpose and the reasons the author gives to support points.
- Identify details that support the topic.

 **ENGLISH LANGUAGE LEARNERS**

Expand Language Production

Beginning Point to photographs from the selection, and have children identify the animals. Expand by saying, *Yes, this animal is a ___.*

Low Intermediate Have children identify animals in the photographs. Provide a sentence frame to help children use complete sentences to describe what they see. *This animal is a ___.*

High Intermediate Have children identify animals in the photographs. Tell them to answer in complete sentences to describe what they see.

Proficient Ask a question about a photograph and have children answer in complete sentences. *What bird zips through the water? A penguin zips through the water.*

 **RI.1.2** identify the main topic and retell key details; **RI.1.7** use illustrations and details to describe key ideas; **RI.1.8** identify the reasons an author gives to support points

Text-Based Comprehension

1 Teach/Model

Terms About Informational Text

author a person who writes a story

author's purpose the reason an author writes a selection

details facts and other bits of information about a topic

- Remind children that they have just read *At Home in the Ocean,* an informational text the **author** wrote about the topic of animals and plants that make their home in the ocean.

- Read and discuss **Student Book** p. 30 with children. Remind them that you can find important details in a selection that can help explain the **author's purpose**, or reason for writing about the topic. Discuss the inference map using this model.

Think Aloud *This graphic organizer can show details that help explain the author's purpose. Information from the words and photos in the selection can be listed on it. I read an important fact that gives a good reason why blue whales are at home in the ocean: Blue whales eat krill, so I know they have food to eat in the ocean. I will write this under* Detail *since it is an important piece of information about the topic. I have read about many other things that seem to belong living in the ocean. I think that the author's purpose is to give information. What do you think the author wants to give information about? I will write about that under* Author's Purpose.

- Next, read and discuss **Student Book** p. 31 with children. Explain that **details** are facts and other bits of information about a topic.

- Have children discuss what the details in the words and pictures in *At Home in the Ocean* taught them about ocean life.

- Tell children to use details from *At Home in the Ocean* to explain what the ocean is like. *big and blue (p. 16); cold (p. 20); warm (p. 22)*

- Have children review the selection to look for examples of details that support the topic. Ask children to tell what they have learned about *At Home in the Ocean* in their own words.

COMPREHENSION

Dig Deeper

Read Together

How to Analyze the Text
Use these pages to learn about
Author's Purpose and Details. Then
read **At Home in the Ocean** again.

Author's Purpose

Authors write for many different reasons.
Why do you think the author wrote **At
Home in the Ocean**? What topic does
she want you to learn about? You can find
important details in the selection that help
explain the author's topic. Use a chart to
list the details and the author's purpose.

Detail | Detail | Detail

Author's Purpose

COMMON CORE

RI.1.2 identify the main topic and retell key details; RI.1.8 identify the reasons an author gives to support points

30

Go Digital

Details

Details are facts and other bits of
information. They tell more about a topic.
A detail you learned in **At Home in the
Ocean** is that manatees eat lots of plants.

What other details from this selection
teach you about life in the ocean? You
can find important details in the words
and pictures.

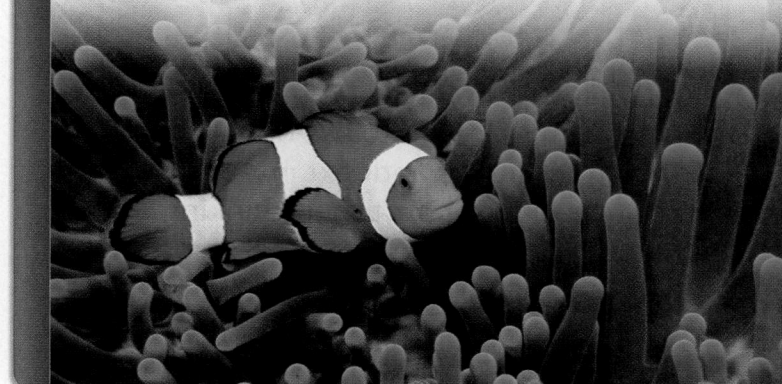

31

SECOND READ

2 Guided Practice/Apply

READ FOR TEXT EVIDENCE Begin a second read of *At
Home in the Ocean* with children. Use the instructional
support to guide children to analyze the text:

• Author's Purpose, p. T27 RI.1.8

• Details, p. T29 RI.1.2, RI.1.7

DIRECTED NOTE-TAKING The graphic organizer will
be completed with children during the second read
on p. T27.

DAILY ASSESSMENT

3 2 1 RtI

*Can children understand the author's
purpose for writing a selection?*

IF...	THEN...
children have difficulty understanding the author's purpose,	use **Differentiate Comprehension** for Struggling Readers, p. T86. *See also Intervention Lesson 11, pp. S2–S11.*
children can understand in part the author's purpose,	use **Differentiate Comprehension** for On Level Readers, p. T86.
children can understand the author's purpose and reasons given to support points,	use **Differentiate Comprehension** for Advanced Readers, p. T87.

SMALL GROUP Options

Differentiate Comprehension,
pp. T86–T87
*Group English Language Learners according to
language proficiency. See also ELL Lesson 11,
pp. E5, for scaffolded support.*

Go Digital
• *my*WriteSmart
• eBook

SECOND READ

Your Turn
Use Text Evidence

▶ SHARE OBJECTIVES
• Understand the author's purpose.
• Have a discussion about the selection.
• Write facts about ocean life.

RETURN TO THE ESSENTIAL QUESTION

As small groups discuss the Essential Question, tell them to use details from the photographs and text in *At Home in the Ocean* to support their thinking. Remind children to listen to each other and add their ideas to what others say during the discussion. Help children to build on others' talk in conversations by coaching them to have multiple exchanges with classmates, responding appropriately to the comments of others. ▬ **RI.1.7, RI.1.8, SL.1.1b**

 Classroom Conversation Have the class continue the discussion about the plants and animals in *At Home in the Ocean*. Ask children what details helped them better understand life in the ocean. Guide them to describe in detail an animal or plant they learned about. Ask children to explain what is the same about all of the animals in the selection. Then have them identify an animal they would like to learn more about and give reasons why.
▬ **RI.1.2, RI.3.8, SL.2.4**

COMMON CORE

RI.1.2 identify the main topic and retell key details; **RI.1.7** use illustrations and details to describe key ideas; **RI.1.8** identify the reasons an author gives to support points; **W.1.2** write informative/explanatory texts; **W.1.5** focus on a topic, respond to questions/suggestions from peers, and add details to strengthen writing; **SL.1.1b** build on others' talk in conversations by responding to others' comments; **SL.1.4** describe people, places, things, and events with details/express ideas and feelings clearly

---

Read Together
Your Turn
 *my*WriteSmart

RETURN TO THE ESSENTIAL QUESTION

Turn and Talk **What kinds of plants and animals would you find in the ocean?** Talk with a small group about what you learned. Use details from **At Home in the Ocean** to answer. Listen. Add your ideas to what others say.

Classroom Conversation

Talk about these questions with your class.

1 Describe an animal or plant you learned about. Use details to tell more.

2 How are all the animals the same?

3 Which animal or plant would you like to learn more about? Why?

32

ELL **ENGLISH LANGUAGE LEARNERS**
Language Transfer

Beginning Tell children that the English and Spanish words for *detail* are similar. Point out that *detalle* sounds like *detail*. Have children say both words aloud.

High Intermediate Have children use sentences to talk about what a detail is. Prompt them to give details about an animal in the selection.

Low Intermediate Have children use the word *detail* to complete a sentence frame. *One detail about turtles is they can _____. swim.*

Proficient Have children discuss how details tell more about a topic. Ask children why they think the detail about manatees eating a lot of plants is important.

See ELL Lesson 11, p. E4, for further comprehension support.

WRITE ABOUT READING

Response Write two facts that you learned from **At Home in the Ocean**. Find text evidence in the words and photos to get ideas. Use your own words when you write your facts.

Writing Tip

Add details that give more information about your topic.

 **Go Digital**

 COMMON CORE **RI.1.7** use illustrations and details to describe key ideas; **RI.1.8** identify the reasons an author gives to support points; **W.1.2** write informative/explanatory texts; **SL.1.1b** build on others' talk in conversations by responding to others' comments; **SL.1.4** describe people, places, things, and events with details/express ideas and feelings clearly

33

WRITE ABOUT READING — Performance Task

Tell children they will write two facts that they learned from *At Home in the Ocean*. Have children look back at the words and photos in the selection for ideas. Remind them to use their own words when they write. ▬ **RI.1.7, W.1.2**

Discuss points like the following to guide children in organizing and writing their responses:

• What photo shows the animal or plant you are writing about? What important information does it show?

• What facts do you read in the words?

• What other words can you use to describe the animal or plant clearly?

After children have drafted their two facts, have them read them to a partner. Have partners ask questions if something is not clear and make suggestions for improvements. Then have children revise their facts, make a final copy, illustrate the facts, and share them in small groups. ▬ **W.1.2, W.1.5**

WRITING TIP Read the Writing Tip with children before they begin writing. Guide them to add describing words, exact nouns and verbs, and other details to give more information about their topic.

 **Go Digital** **my WriteSmart**

Have children complete the Write About Reading activity through *my*WriteSmart. Children will read the prompt within *my*WriteSmart and have access to multiple writing resources, including the Student eBook, Writing Rubrics, and Graphic Organizers.

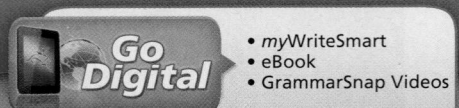

- *my*WriteSmart
- eBook
- GrammarSnap Videos

Grammar Proper Nouns

▶ SHARE OBJECTIVES

- **Grammar** Identify and use proper nouns that name people, animals, places, and things.
- **Spelling** Spell words with *th* using conventional spelling patterns.
- **Handwriting** Print the spelling words.
- **Writing** Write sentences that inform with details that tell how.

ELL ENGLISH LANGUAGE LEARNERS

Language Transfer

All Proficiencies Display the examples from Projectable 11.3. Point to the proper nouns and explain that proper nouns are always capitalized. Have children write their own names, and the names of two of their classmates, being sure to capitalize each name.

1 Teach/Model

NAMES FOR PEOPLE, ANIMALS, PLACES, AND THINGS Display **Projectable 11.3**.

- Review that some *proper nouns* name a special person or animal. Tell children that proper nouns can also name special places and things, such as their school.

- Review that proper nouns begin with a capital letter. Explain that when a proper noun contains more than one word, such as a person's first and last name, each word begins with a capital letter.

- Discuss the example at the top of the **Projectable**.

> **Think Aloud** *In the first sentence,* Wendy Waters *is the name of a person.* Wendy *is her first name, and* Waters *is her last name. Each word begins with a capital letter.* Elm Street *is the name of the street where* Wendy *lives. Each word begins with a capital letter.*

2 Guided Practice/Apply

- Work together to complete **Projectable 11.3**.

- Ask children to explain how they identified each proper noun. Then have them use the proper nouns in new sentences.
  📰 **L.1.1b, L.1.2a**

Spelling Words with *th*

SPELLING WORDS

BASIC	
that	them
then	with
this	bath
CHALLENGE	
thick	tenth

Word Sort

- Review **Sound/Spelling Card** *thumb*. *What sound do you hear at the beginning of* thumb? *th The letters* t *and* h *stand for* /th/.

- Draw two columns. Write *Start* in one, and *End* in the other. Have children sort the spelling words by where they hear /th/.

- For additional practice, distribute **Reader's Notebook** Vol. 1, p. 153.
  📰 **L.1.2d, L.1.2e**

Handwriting

Model how to form the basic words *that*, *then*, and *this*. Have children use their best handwriting to print the spelling words, forming the lowercase letters correctly. Ball-and-stick and continuous stroke handwriting models are available on the **Handwriting Models Blackline Masters**, pp. R12–R17. 📰 **L.1.1a**

COMMON CORE **W.1.2** write informative/explanatory texts; **SL.1.6** produce complete sentences when appropriate to task and situation; **L.1.1a** print upper- and lowercase letters; **L.1.1b** use common, proper, and possessive nouns; **L.1.2a** capitalize dates and names of people; **L.1.2d** use conventional spelling for words with common spelling patterns and for frequently occurring irregular words; **L.1.2e** spell untaught words phonetically, drawing on phonemic awareness and spelling conventions

T44 • Unit 3 Lesson 11

Informative Writing Focus Trait: Ideas

1 Teach/Model

WORDS THAT TELL HOW Tell children that some words tell how things happen. Explain that these words are called *adverbs*, and that many of these words end with the letters *-ly*.

- Write the words *softly* and *quickly* on the board. Read them aloud and use them in sentences with children. Have children brainstorm other *-ly* words, such as *helpfully* and *happily*.

- Discuss how the author of *At Home in the Ocean* uses words that tell how things happen.

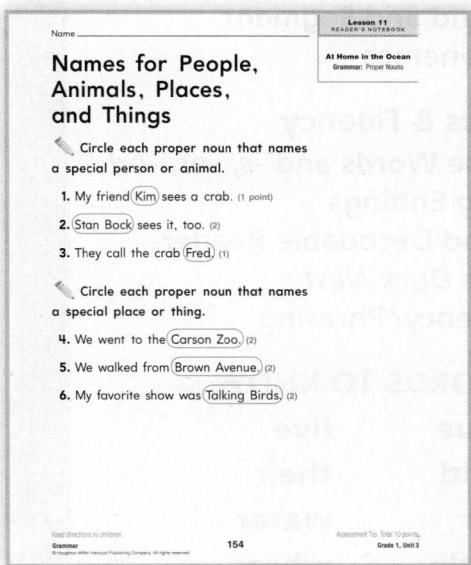

Connect to *At Home in the Ocean*	
Instead of this...	**...the author wrote this.**
Penguins can swim.	Penguins swim fast!

- *How does the word* fast *help you understand more about the animal?* It helps create a picture in your mind by telling how the animal moves.

- Display **Projectable 11.4**. Choose several animals from *At Home in the Ocean*. Model using the frames to write informational sentences with words that tell how.

2 Guided Writing

- Guide children to choose an animal described in *At Home in the Ocean*. Have them draw a picture of the animal.

- Then ask children how their animals move, eat, sleep, or hunt. Guide them to name action verbs and adverbs that tell how.

- Then have children construct factual sentences that tell how these animals do things. Remind them that a complete sentence must include a subject, or who or what does something, and a predicate, or what that thing or person does. Have children check that the sentences are complete and tell how to fix the ones that are not. **W.1.2, SL.1.6**

Daily Proofreading Practice

My friend joe simon has a ~~litle~~ little fish.

He named his fish betty.

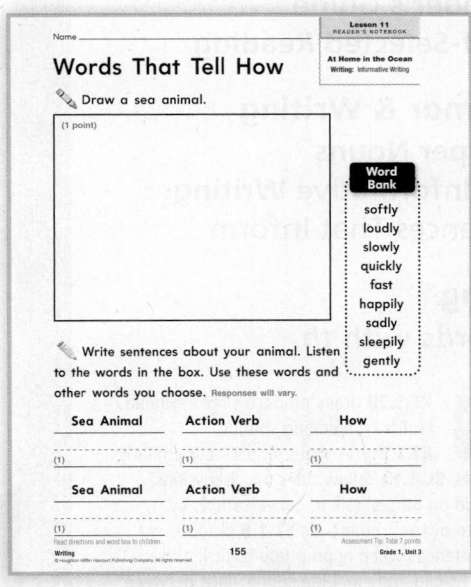

Reader's Notebook Vol. 1 p. 154

Reader's Notebook Vol. 1 p. 155

DAY 3

Today's Goals

Vocabulary & Oral Language
- Apply Vocabulary Knowledge

Phonemic Awareness
- Blend and Segment Phonemes

Phonics & Fluency
- Base Words and *-s, -es, -ed, -ing* Endings
- Read Decodable Reader: *The Duck Nest*
- Fluency: Phrasing

 WORDS TO KNOW

blue	live
cold	their
far	water
little	where

Text-Based Comprehension
Independent Reading
- Reader's Guide
- Self-Selected Reading

Grammar & Writing
- Proper Nouns
- Informative Writing: Sentences That Inform

Spelling
- Words with *th*

COMMON CORE **RF.1.2b** orally produce single-syllable words by blending sounds; **RF.1.3g** recognize and read irregularly spelled words; **SL.1.1a** follow rules for discussions; **SL.1.1b** build on others' talk in conversations by responding to others' comments; **SL.1.6** produce complete sentences when appropriate to task and situation; **L.1.5c** identify real-life connections between words and their use; **L.1.6** use words and phrases acquired through conversations, reading and being read to, and responding to texts

Opening Routines

Warm Up with Wordplay

The Never-Ending Story

This week children are reading about animals and water. Tell children that today they will help you write a story about animals that live in the water. Display and read aloud the following:

> # First I saw a dolphin jump out of the ocean. And then . . .

Prompt children to continue the story by asking: *And then what happened?* Have volunteers continue the story line by line. Encourage children to use one of the week's high-frequency words. Have children continue adding to the story until all the high-frequency words have been used. As children speak, record the story and then read it aloud with children. **SL.1.1b, SL.1.6**

Daily Phonemic Awareness

Blend Phonemes

- *I'm going to say the sounds in a word and blend them. Then you say the word. I'll do the first one. Listen: /th/ /ē/ /f/. What is the word? thief*

- Have children repeat with you, then by themselves.

- Continue with the following words:

/b/ /ĕ/ /th/ *Beth*	/t/ /ē/ /th/ *teeth*	/th/ /ē/ /z/ *these*
/p/ /ă/ /th/ *path*	/w/ /ē/ /k/ *week*	/d/ /ī/ /v/ *dive*
/d/ /ŭ/ /n/ *done*	/g/ /ā/ /m/ *game*	/th/ /ĕ/ /n/ *then* **RF.1.2b**

Corrective Feedback

- If a child misses a word, say the correct word and model the task. *The word is game. Listen: /g/ /ā/ /m/. What is the word? game*

- Have children do it with you before doing it on their own.

- Back up several words and continue the game.

Daily High-Frequency Words

Introduce

- Point to the **High-Frequency Word Card** *far*.

- *Say the word. far Spell the word. f, a, r Write the word. Check the word.*

- Repeat the procedure with the words *blue, cold, little, live, their, water,* and *where*.   **RF.1.3g**

Raise the Roof Game

- Choose one of this week's High-Frequency Words.

- As you point to each letter in the word, have the children name it with you and push up toward the ceiling, one push for each letter.

- Repeat the procedure for the remaining High-Frequency Words.

Corrective Feedback

- Say the correct word and have children repeat it. *Far. What is the word? far*

- Have children spell the word. *f, a, r How do we say this word? far*

- Have children reread all of the cards in random order.

Daily Vocabulary Boost

- Guide children to interact with the Oral Vocabulary words by asking the following questions. Remind them to speak clearly when participating in a discussion.

  What are some qualities of good companions?

  What might people say when they exchange *greetings?*

  Which of these animals do you think is most graceful: *a deer, an elephant, or a toad?*

- Ask children to work with a partner to explain *companions, exchange,* and *gracefully* in their own words. Remind them to pay attention to what their partner says. Make sure children follow appropriate rules for discussion such as listening to speakers, taking turns, and staying on topic.
    SL.1.1a, L.1.5c, L.1.6

 **Oral Vocabulary**

companions
exchange
gracefully
portions
practice
strict

Phonemic Awareness/Phonics

▶ SHARE OBJECTIVES

- Blend and decode words with inflectional endings -*s*, -*es*, -*ed*, and -*ing*.
- Recognize that the inflectional ending -*ed* stands for different end sounds.

▶ SKILL TRACE

Base Words and -*s*, -*es*, -*ed*, -*ing*	
Introduce	T48–T49
Differentiate	T88
Reteach	T96
Review	T60
Assess	Weekly Tests, Lesson 11

ELL ENGLISH LANGUAGE LEARNERS
Comprehensible Input

Beginning Tell children to listen for ending sound /s/ as you say *packs, claps, jumps, kicks*. Repeat with words with /z/: *runs, plays, falls*. Have them repeat each word.

Low Intermediate Say *packs, runs, claps, jumps, plays*, stressing ending sounds. Have children repeat and tell whether the final sound is /z/ or /s/.

High Intermediate Write *jumps, fishes, misses, packs, pitches*. Have volunteers read the words and underline the endings.

Proficient Write *jump* on the board. Have children write *jumps, jumped, jumping*, and then read the new words with a partner.

See ELL Lesson 11, p. E7, for scaffolded support.

COMMON CORE **RF.1.2b** orally produce single-syllable words by blending sounds; **RF.1.2d** segment spoken single-syllable words into their complete sequence of individual sounds; **RF.1.3b** decode regularly spelled one-syllable words; **RF.1.3f** read words with inflectional endings; **RF.1.3g** recognize and read irregularly spelled words; **L.1.2e** spell untaught words phonetically, drawing on phonemic awareness and spelling conventions

Base Words and -*s*, -*es*, -*ed*, -*ing* Endings

PHONEMIC AWARENESS WARM-UP *Listen as I blend some sounds to say a word: /r/ /ŭ/ /n/ /z/,* runs. *I'll do another one. Listen: /j/ /ŭ/ /m/ /p/ /t/,* jumped. *Let's do one together. Listen to tell what word I get when I blend the sounds: /r/ /ĕ/ /n/ /t/ /s/.* rents

Reverse the process to segment phonemes. *Listen to tell me the sounds that make the word* fished. *They are: /f/ /ĭ/ /sh/ /t/. Now you try. Tell me the sounds in* claps. */k/ /l/ /ă/ /p/ /s/.* ◼ **RF.1.2b, RF.1.2d**

1 Teach/Model

INTRODUCE VERB ENDINGS Explain that sometimes action words, or verbs, have letters added to them at the end. The added letters tell when the action happens.

- Display **Letter Cards** *j, u, m, p*. Read the word: *jump*. Now add **Letter Card** *s*. Read the word: *jumps*. Have children repeat it. Use *jumps* in a sentence: *Jan jumps up and down.*

j	u	m	p	s

- Replace **Letter Card** *s* with *e, d*. Blend the new word. Have children repeat it. Use *jumped* in a sentence: *Jan jumped up and down.*

- Replace the -*ed* ending with **Letter Cards** *i, n, g*. Repeat the exercise. *Jan is jumping up and down.*

- Repeat the routine with **Letter Cards** to build the words *miss, missed, missing*, and *misses*.

2 Guided Practice

CONTINUOUS BLENDING ROUTINE Use **Instructional Routine 3** to model blending *pack* with different endings.
▬ RF.1.2b, RF.1.3b, RF.1.3f

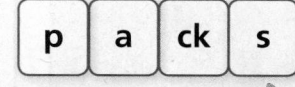

- Display **Letter Cards** *p, a, ck, s*. Blend *pack* and *packs*, sweeping your hand under the letters. Blend and say each word. *Listen:* /p/ /ă/ /k/, pack; /p/ /ă/ /k/ /s/, packs. Remind children that the letters *ck* can stand for /k/. Blend once more with children.

- Now model how to blend *packed*. Tell children that *-ed*, added to an action word, can stand for /t/, /d/, or /Ǝd/. Blend *packed*. Demonstrate that /t/ is the correct sound for *-ed* in this word. Repeat the process to blend *packing*.

REPEAT CONTINUOUS BLENDING ROUTINE with the words in Row 1 below. Use the **Corrective Feedback** steps if children need additional help.

DECODING Call on individuals to blend one or more words and to read the sentence. ▬ RF.1.3b, RF.1.3f, RF.1.3g

1. clicks	thumped	telling	missed	bumps
2. ticking	sits	asked	this	fill
3. selling	that	cracking	then	gets

<u>My friend</u> is packing <u>a</u> big red bag.

3 Apply

Use **Instructional Routine 6** and the sentences shown to connect sounds to writing. Have children repeat each word after you. Then have them identify the sounds and write the letters that stand for each sound. Print the words so children can check their work.
▬ RF.1.3b, RF.1.3f, L.1.2e

- **tack**   I will <u>tack</u> up the pictures.
- **misses**   Matt <u>misses</u> his friend Pat.
- **ticking** The clock is <u>ticking</u>.

Corrective Feedback Work with the whole group to correct errors, following the model below.

Phonics Error:
A child reads the *-ed* in *asked* as /ĕ/ /d/.

Correct the error. Say the word and the sound. *The word is* asked. *The letters* ed *stand for the sound* /t/ *in this word.*

Model by asking children what sound is at the end of *asked*. Say the word, emphasizing the end sound /t/. *What is the word?* asked

Guide *Let's read the word together. The word is* asked.

Check *You read* ask-ed. *What is the correct word?* asked

Reinforce Go back three or four words and have children continue reading. Make note of errors and review those words during tomorrow's lesson.

 **Go to pp. T88 for additional Phonics support.**

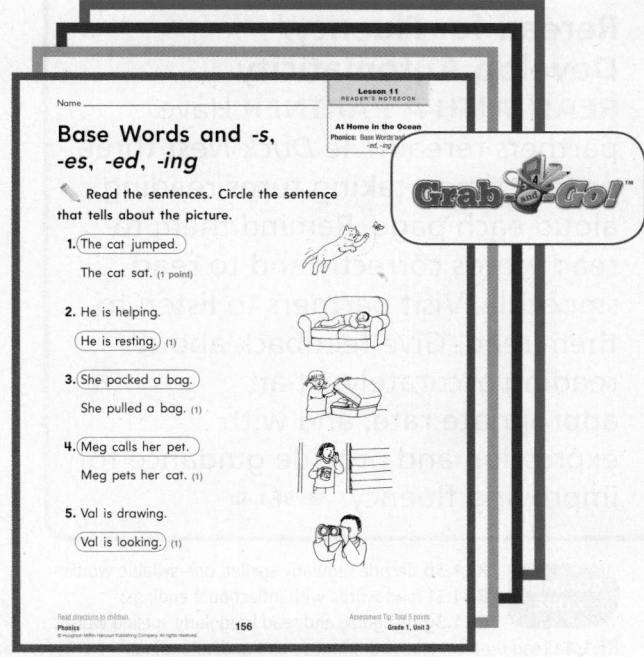

Reader's Notebook Vol. 1 p. 156
See Grab-and-Go™ Resources for additional leveled practice.

• Decodable Reader
• Cold Reads Online

Decodable Reader

▶ SHARE OBJECTIVES

• Read text with regularly spelled one-syllable words and irregularly spelled High-Frequency Words.

DAILY ASSESSMENT 3 2 1 **RtI**

Corrective Feedback Work with the whole group to correct errors.

Decoding Error:
A child reads *jumped* as *jump*.

Correct the error. Say the word. *That word is* jumped. *Remember that the ending -ed can be added to a word to make a new word.*

Guide Review the sound/spelling. Have children blend and read the word.

Check *Read the sentence again.*

Reinforce Review the word again before children reread the story.

Go to p. T88 for additional phonics support.

Reread for Fluency/ Develop Automaticity

READ WITH A PARTNER Have partners reread *The Duck Nest* three or four times, taking turns reading aloud each page. Remind them to read words correctly and to read smoothly. Visit partners to listen to them read. Give feedback about reading accurately, at an appropriate rate, and with expression and provide guidance for improving fluency. 🔲 RF.1.4b

COMMON CORE
RF.1.3b decode regularly spelled one-syllable words;
RF.1.3f read words with inflectional endings;
RF.1.3g recognize and read irregularly spelled words;
RF.1.4a read on-level text with purpose and understanding;
RF.1.4b read on-level text orally with accuracy, appropriate rate, and expression

Read *The Duck Nest*

Decodable Reader, Unit 3, pp. 15–20

REVIEW BASE WORDS AND *-s, -es, -ed, -ing* **AND WORDS TO KNOW** Tell children that many words in this story end with *-s, -es, -ed,* or *-ing.* Review with them the following Words to Know, which children will also read in the story: *far, little,* and *where.*

PREVIEW Have children preview pages 15–17 and predict what they think the story is about. Ask what they know about nests and about nests they have seen. Tell children they are going to read what happens when Beth Ann and Gram find a duck's nest.

MODEL FLUENCY AND PHRASING Have children follow along as you read page 17 aloud, not stopping to pause after "Gram." Tell children that you made a mistake by not pausing when you came to the comma. Read the sentences again, pausing after each comma and at the end of each sentence. Lead children in a choral reading, reading fluently and with appropriate phrasing.

READ Remind children to track words from left to right and when they come to the end of a line, to continue reading at the beginning of the next line. Have children read each page silently and then choral-read aloud. Coach them to read fluently, and to pause when they come to a comma or end mark.
🔲 RF.1.3b, RF.1.3f, RF.1.3g, RF.1.4a

RESPONDING Make sure children understand the story events. *What kind of egg do Gram and Beth Ann find? What do they do after the the duck hatches? Where was Mom Duck?*

Fluency

Phrasing: Punctuation (Comma)

1 Teach/Model

Explain that good readers read with feeling. Tell children that punctuation can help them read more naturally. Display **Projectable 11.5**. First, read sentence 1 by modeling how to pause after the comma. Point to the comma, tell children the name of this mark, and have them repeat. Then read the sentence incorrectly, with no pauses. Explain that the sentence sounded better when you paid attention to the comma. It sounded more like speaking. Repeat with sentence 2.

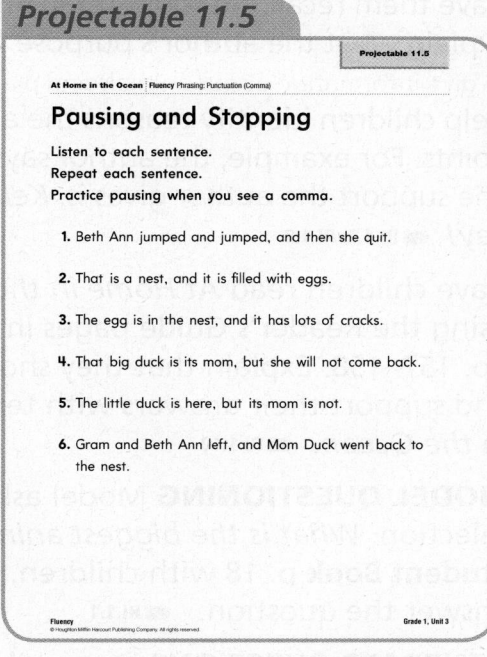

Projectable 11.5

At Home in the Ocean | Fluency Phrasing: Punctuation (Comma)

Pausing and Stopping

Listen to each sentence.
Repeat each sentence.
Practice pausing when you see a comma.

1. Beth Ann jumped and jumped, and then she quit.
2. That is a nest, and it is filled with eggs.
3. The egg is in the nest, and it has lots of cracks.
4. That big duck is its mom, but she will not come back.
5. The little duck is here, but its mom is not.
6. Gram and Beth Ann left, and Mom Duck went back to the nest.

2 Guided Practice

Read sentence 3 as you point to and pause at the comma. Have children echo read. Repeat with sentence 4. Then have children choral read sentences 5 and 6 as you point to the comma in each sentence.

3 Apply

Have pairs practice reading *At Home in the Ocean*. Remind them to pause at the commas and stop at the end marks. Coach children to connect words to read them smoothly and accurately. Have volunteers read each page aloud with accuracy, appropriate rate, and expression. **RF.1.4b**

▶ SHARE OBJECTIVE

• Read on-level text fluently with accuracy and understanding by learning to pause after phrases with commas.

Go to p. T89 for additional fluency support.

HOUGHTON MIFFLIN HARCOURT

JOURNEYS

Cold Reads

GRADE 1

Cold Reads: Support for fluent reading and comprehension

Independent Reading

▶ **SHARE OBJECTIVES**

- Read and comprehend informational text.
- Ask and answer questions about key details.
- Read independently from a "just right" book.
- Read fluently with appropriate phrasing.

ELL **ENGLISH LANGUAGE LEARNERS**

Comprehensible Input

Beginning Ask children *yes/no* questions about animals and plants in the selection.

Low Intermediate Ask children about details about the selection and have them answer with words or phrases, such as *What are the biggest animals in the ocean? What do manatees eat?*

High Intermediate Have children tell a fact about each animal and plant they learned about.

Proficient Have partners choose one animal from the selection, display the photo that shows it, and tell a partner facts about it.

COMMON CORE **RI.1.1** ask and answer questions about key details; **RI.1.2** identify the main topic and retell key details; **RI.1.8** identify the reasons an author gives to support points; **RI.1.10** read informational texts; **RF.1.4b** read on-level text orally with accuracy, appropriate rate, and expression; **SL.1.1c** ask questions to clear up confusion about topics and texts under discussion; **SL.1.6** produce complete sentences when appropriate to task and situation

Reader's Guide

Revisit the Anchor Text

Lead children in a brief discussion about *At Home in the Ocean*. Have them recall the topic, retell important details, and explain what the author's purpose was in writing the selection. to give information about animals and plants that are at home in the ocean Help children identify reasons the author gives to support her points. For example, the author says that kelp can grow fast. The support the author gives is: *Kelp can grow two feet in a day!* **RI.1.2, RI.1.8**

Have children read *At Home in the Ocean* on their own, using the Reader's Guide pages in their **Reader's Notebook**, pp. 157–158. Explain that they should answer the questions and support their answers with text evidence from *At Home in the Ocean*. **RI.1.10**

MODEL QUESTIONING Model asking a question about the selection: *What is the biggest animal in the ocean?* Reread **Student Book** p. 18 with children, and work together to answer the question. **RI.1.1**

GENERATE QUESTIONS Have children generate questions about things that are unclear to them from *At Home in the Ocean*. Discuss questions children have in common or that are most significant to their understanding of the selection. Have them work together to answer the questions, using complete sentences. **RI.1.1, SL.1.1c, SL.1.6**

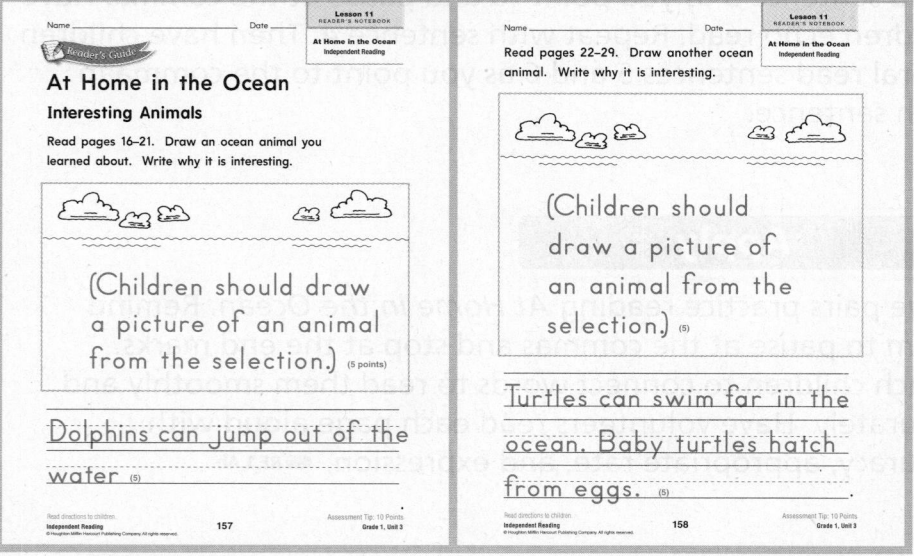

Reader's Notebook pp. 157–158

Self-Selected Reading

Topics of Interest

Guide children to think about topics of interest and select a book to read independently. Discuss the following with them:

• Ask yourself: *What would I like to learn more about?* Maybe there is something interesting that you have read or heard about recently, and you would like to know more.

• Make a list of topics you like the most, such as *turtles, whales, dogs,* and *friends.*

• Look at books in the classroom or at the library that match your topic of interest.

Tell children that once they have selected a book, they should open it and read one or two pages to be sure it is "just right." Tell children that if they lose interest in the first few pages, they should try another book.

Self-Correction Strategies

Read for Fluency and Appropriate Phrasing

Tell children that reading smoothly and understanding what they read takes practice. Tell children that as they read their independent reading books, they will pay attention to reading groups of words that go together so that their reading sounds natural, like the way people speak. Explain that some sentences have commas separating groups of words that will help them know where to pause briefly while reading. Model pausing at commas using this sentence from *At Home in the Ocean: Lots of plants and animals, big and little, live in the ocean.* Read the sentence two times, once with, and once without pausing for the commas. As a class, discuss how appropriate phrasing can help readers understand what they are reading.

Have partners practice reading aloud to each other from their self-selected books. When one child has finished reading, his or her partner should provide feedback, using appropriate phrasing. Each partner should read more than once to improve his or her accuracy, rate, expression, and use of appropriate phrasing.

▬ RF.1.4b

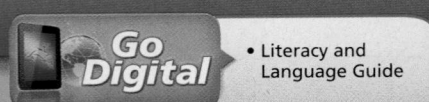

Apply Vocabulary Knowledge

▶ SHARE OBJECTIVES

- Use words and phrases acquired through conversations, reading and being read to, and responding to texts.
- Identify real-life connections between words and their use.
- Learn how to use a print and online dictionary.

ELL ENGLISH LANGUAGE LEARNERS

Comprehensible Input

Beginning Discuss the words *adapt* and *change*. Explain that these words mean about the same thing.

Low Intermediate Have children say other words that mean the same thing as *extraordinary*.

High Intermediate Have children complete this sentence frame: *I think _____ is extraordinary.*

Proficient Have children tell how an animal or plant might *adapt* to a new home. Have them use complete sentences.

See ELL Lesson 11, p. E6, for further vocabulary support.

COMMON CORE **RI.1.5** know and use text features to locate facts or information; **L.1.5c** identify real-life connections between words and their use; **L.1.6** use words and phrases acquired through conversations, reading and being read to, and responding to texts

---

☑ SELECTION VOCABULARY >> Review

Review with children the Selection Vocabulary words on p. T22. Call on children to explain how the words were used in *At Home in the Ocean.*

ENRICH VOCABULARY Write the following Related Words on the board. Read each word aloud, and have children repeat after you. Then read the student-friendly explanation for each word. Connect each word's meaning to the selection *At Home in the Ocean* by writing the context sentences on the board and reading them aloud.

---

classify: when you classify something, you put it into a group with other things like it. *You can classify the animals in the selection as Animals that Live in the Ocean.*

extraordinary: Something extraordinary is something that is very unusual or remarkable. *Kelp is an extraordinary plant.*

adapt: If an animal adapts to a place, it has body parts or ways of acting that help it live there. *Many sea animals have to adapt to live in cold water.*

MAKE CONNECTIONS Discuss all of the words using the items below to help children make connections between vocabulary words and their use. **L.1.5c**

- Tell about a time you went to the **ocean**.
- What is the **biggest** animal you have ever seen? Tell about it.
- Show how **penguins** move through the water. Show how a **turtle** moves on the land.
- Which items of clothing help keep you **warm**?
- How do you think an animal might **adapt** to living in cold weather?
- Tell how you would **classify** these animals: **whales**, **manatees**, fish.
- How would you look if you saw something **extraordinary**?
- How much do you think you might **grow** in a year?
- Which of these animals have feet: eels, sea gulls, **sea otters**, starfish?

Dictionary Skills

DISCUSS USING A DICTIONARY Using a beginning dictionary, discuss with children how to look up a word. Guide children to notice that the entries are in A, B, C order. Have them explain how this can help them find words. Then tell how the guide words at the top of the page can be used to locate words.

The words at the top of the page tell us what word begins the page and what word ends the page. We have to use our alphabetical order skills to know if the word we are looking for is between those two words.

Guide children to look up the Lesson 11 Selection Vocabulary words *penguins* and *manatees* in a print dictionary. As a class, discuss how you look up the singular form of the words, when you want to find the plural form. Then, show children how to look up the same words in an online dictionary. Point out the search fields and submit buttons.

Have partners work together to look up the new word *adapt* in a print dictionary and an online dictionary. Discuss Internet safety rules before children use the computer. Ask volunteers to read aloud the definitions. As a class talk about how the definitions are the same and how they are different. ⬤ RI.1.5

Literacy and Language Guide
Additional Lesson 11 vocabulary lessons appear in the Literacy and Language Guide.

QUICKWRITE

Have children write about life in the ocean. Write the new vocabulary words on the board: *classify, extraordinary, adapt.* Tell children to include these new words in their writing. ⬤ L.1.6

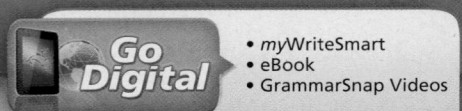

Go Digital
• *my*WriteSmart
• eBook
• GrammarSnap Videos

Grammar Proper Nouns

▶ SHARE OBJECTIVES

- **Grammar** Identify and capitalize titles for people.
- **Spelling** Spell words with *th* using conventional spelling patterns.
- **Writing** Choose a topic and use a graphic organizer to plan sentences that inform.

ELL ENGLISH LANGUAGE LEARNERS
Language Transfer

All Proficiencies Display on the board, *Mr. Diaz, Mrs. Sims, Miss Reed.* Tell children that these are proper nouns with titles, and that every title except *Miss* ends in a period. Help children write the names of three teachers in the school, spelling their titles correctly.

1 Teach/Model

11.6

TITLES FOR PEOPLE Display and read aloud the top of **Projectable 11.6.** Use the boxed words to model identifying titles and the proper nouns that name people.

- Point out that some names for special people include titles. A title comes before a person's name and begins with a capital letter. Titles usually end with a period because they are shortened forms of words. Ask children to say *Mr.* and point out that it is a shortened form for *Mister*. Explain that *Miss Black* does not have a period because it is not a shortened form.

Think Aloud *All the titles, except* Miss, *begin with a capital letter and end with a period. Each title goes before a person's name. The first letter of the person's name also begins with a capital letter.*

2 Guided Practice/Apply

- Work together to complete **Projectable 11.6.** Pronounce each title. Then have children write their first and last names with a title. Have them form the capital letters correctly and keep a space between the names.
- For additional practice, distribute **Reader's Notebook** Vol. 1 page 160.

▭ L.1.1b, L.1.2a

Spelling Words with *th*

SPELLING WORDS

BASIC	
that	them
then	with
this	bath

CHALLENGE	
thick	tenth

Segment Sounds

- Model segmenting sounds. *Listen as I say* that: /th/ /ă/ /t/. *Repeat after me:* /th/ /ă/ /t/.
- Repeat the procedure with *then* and *this*. Tell children that saying the sounds in a word will help them to spell the word.

▭ RF.1.2d

Build Words

- Model building the word *that*. Have children write and read the word.
- Have partners use **Letter Cards** to build *th* words. Have partners read and spell one of the words they built.
- For additional practice, distribute **Reader's Notebook** Vol. 1 p. 159.

▭ L.1.2d, L.1.2e

COMMON CORE **RF.1.2d** segment spoken single-syllable words into their complete sequence of individual sounds; **W.1.2** write informative/explanatory texts; **W.1.5** focus on a topic, respond to questions/suggestions from peers, and add details to strengthen writing; **L.1.1b** use common, proper, and possessive nouns; **L.1.2a** capitalize dates and names of people; **L.1.2d** use conventional spelling for words with common spelling patterns and for frequently occurring irregular words; **L.1.2e** spell untaught words phonetically, drawing on phonemic awareness and spelling conventions

Informative Writing Prewriting

1 Teach/Model

AUTHOR'S PURPOSE Remind children that the purpose of informational sentences is to tell facts.

- Display **Projectable 11.7**. Explain that this kind of chart can help writers prepare to write sentences that inform.
- Read the prompt aloud. Then fill in the graphic organizer to model the process.

> **Think Aloud** *I want to tell what I know about crabs. So my topic will be crabs. My purpose is to tell facts about crabs, so I'll think of two things I know about crabs and write them in the other boxes.*

- Ask children to help you choose facts about crabs.
- Save the completed chart for Day 4.

2 Independent Writing

- Write the prompt on the board and read it aloud with children.
- Help children choose a sea animal to write about. Help them brainstorm a list of animals if they have trouble finding a topic.
- Have children complete a graphic organizer such as the one from **Projectable 11.7.** Remind them to list things that they know are true about their chosen animals.
- Have children work with partners to ask each other questions about their animals and make suggestions for improving their writing. ▬ W.1.2, W.1.5

Oral Language Conventions

Adverbs Remind children that some words tell how someone does something. These words often end in *-ly*. Provide examples such as *slowly, quickly,* and *happily*. Ask children to suggest *-ly* words that they could use to describe how the animals they chose to write about move or make sounds.

Daily Proofreading Practice

live
Sharks ~~life~~ in the sea.
   ^

                                    them
My teacher Ms. Allen told us about ~~tem~~.
                   ^   ^

Projectable 11.7

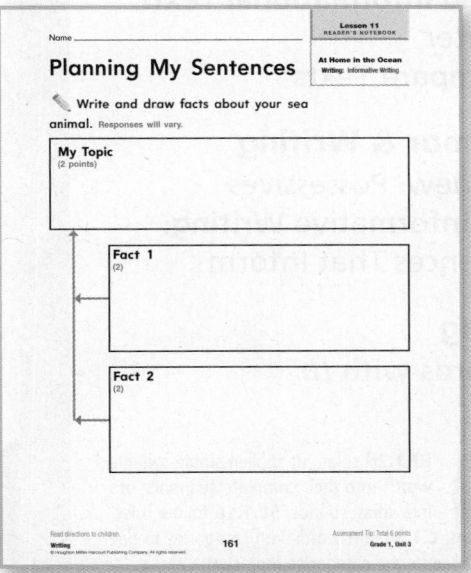

Reader's Notebook Vol. 1 p. 161

DAY 4

Today's Goals

Vocabulary & Oral Language
- **Vocabulary Strategies:** Classify and Categorize Words

Phonemic Awareness
- **Segment Phonemes**
- **Blend Phonemes**

Phonics & Fluency
- **Words with Digraph** *th*
- **Base Words with** *-s, -es, -ed, -ing* **Endings**
- **Read Decodable Reader:** *Animal Moms*

☑ **WORDS TO KNOW**

blue	live
cold	their
far	water
little	where

Text-Based Comprehension
Connect to the Topic
- **Read Informational Text:** *Water*
- **Compare Texts**

Grammar & Writing
- **Review:** Possessives
- ⬤➤ **Informative Writing:** Sentences That Inform

Spelling
- **Words with** *th*

 **COMMON CORE** **RF.1.2d** segment spoken single-syllable words into their complete sequence of individual sounds; **SL.1.1a** follow rules for discussions; **L.1.5a** sort words into categories to gain a sense of concepts the categories represent; **L.1.5c** identify real-life connections between words and their use

Opening Routines

Warm Up with Wordplay

Two Words

Remind children that they have been reading about animals and the ocean. Tell children they will each think of two words that name things they might see in the ocean. Give examples such as *plants* or *sand*.

rocks	**fish**
crabs	**eggs**
dolphin	**kelp**

Ask children to help you identify the longest word, the shortest word, and the most unusual word. Then have children sort the words into categories. Write headings on the board such as *Animals, Plants, Other*. Guide children to sort each word into the appropriate category. Record the sort and reread all the words with children.

⬛ L.1.5a

Daily Phonemic Awareness

Segment Phonemes

- *I'm going to say a word. Then I'll take it apart and say each sound, one by one. Listen to the word:* thick. *I hear three sounds:* /th/ /ĭ/ /k/, thick. *Join me as I do it again.*

- Have children repeat with you, then do it by themselves.

- Continue with the following words:

luck /l/ /ŭ/ /k/   *thin* /th/ /ĭ/ /n/
drain /d/ /r/ /ā/ /n/   *club* /k/ /l/ /ŭ/ /b/
thud /th/ /ŭ/ /d/   *pane* /p/ /ā/ /n/ ◼ **RF.1.2d**

Corrective Feedback

- *Model the task. Listen:* thin. *I'll say each sound in the word, one by one:* /th/ /ĭ/ /n/, thin. *How many sounds are in the word* thin? *three,* /th/ /ĭ/ /n/

- Have children repeat once with you before doing it on their own. Then back up several words and continue the game.

Daily High-Frequency Words

Introduce

- Point to the **High-Frequency Word Card** *little.*

- *Say the word.* little *Spell the word.* l, i, t, t, l, e *Write the word. Check the word.*

- Repeat the procedure with the words *blue, cold, far, live, their, water,* and *where.*

Squeaky Mouse Game

- Have children take turns being the "mouse leader" in a spelling game.

- Children curl their hands up by their faces, pretending to be mice.

- The leader points to a High-Frequency Word and leads the class in spelling it letter by letter in a squeaky voice.

- Continue the procedure with different leaders for the remaining High-Frequency Words.

Corrective Feedback

- Say the correct word and have children repeat it. Little. *What is the word?* little

- Have children spell the word. *l, i, t, t, l, e How do we say this word?* little

- Have children reread all of the cards in random order.

Daily Vocabulary Boost

- Guide children to interact with the Oral Vocabulary words by asking the following questions. Tell them to think about something they have seen or done as they answer. Remind children to speak clearly when participating in a discussion.

  If you eat a portion of your food, how much do you eat?

  When have you practiced doing something?

  Why are there strict rules to follow during a fire drill?

- Ask children to work with a partner to explain *portions, practice,* and *strict* in their own words. Remind them to pay attention to what their partner says. Make sure children follow appropriate rules for discussion such as listening to speakers, taking turns, and staying on topic. ◼ **SL.1.1a, L.1.5c**

☑ **Oral Vocabulary**

companions
exchange
gracefully
portions
practice
strict

Whole Group

DAY 4

Go Digital
• Interactive Whiteboard Lesson
• Decodable Reader

JOURNEYS
Phonics

Interactive Whiteboard Lesson: Words with Digraph *th* and Base Words with *-s, -ed, -es, -ing* Endings

Phonemic Awareness/Phonics

▶ SHARE OBJECTIVES

- Blend, build, and decode words with inflectional endings *-s, -es, -ed,* and *-ing.*
- Review and sort words with short *u* and digraph *th.*
- Read on-level text with fluency and appropriate phrasing.

▶ SKILLS TRACE

Digraph *th*	
Introduce	T16–T17
Differentiate	T82
Reteach	T96
▶ **Review**	**T38, T60**
Assess	Weekly Tests, Lesson 11

▶ SKILLS TRACE

Base Words and *-s, -es, -ed, -ing*	
Introduce	T48–T49
Differentiate	T88
Reteach	T96
▶ **Review**	**T60**
Assess	Weekly Tests, Lesson 11

COMMON CORE

RI.1.2 identify the main topic and retell key details; **RF.1.2b** orally produce single-syllable words by blending sounds; **RF.1.2c** isolate and pronounce sounds in spoken single-syllable words; **RF.1.2d** segment spoken single-syllable words into their complete sequence of individual sounds; **RF.1.3b** decode regularly spelled one-syllable words; **RF.1.3f** read words with inflectional endings; **RF.1.3g** recognize and read irregularly spelled words; **RF.1.4a** read on-level text with purpose and understanding; **RF.1.4b** read on-level text orally with accuracy, appropriate rate, and expression

Review Digraph *th*; Base Words with *-s, -es, -ed, -ing* Endings

PHONEMIC AWARENESS WARM-UP Model how to blend sounds to make a word. *Listen as I say sounds to make a word: /p/ /ĭ/ /k/ /t/. The word is* picked. *Now you do it with me.* Repeat the process. *Let's do the opposite. Let's separate the sounds we hear in* picked: */p/ /ĭ/ /k/ /t/.* Continue having children segment sounds with the words *hunts* and *ticking.* 🔲 **RF.1.2b, RF.1.2d**

MAKE AND READ WORDS On the board, copy the words and sentences shown below. Have children use what they know about blending words with endings to read the words. Then ask children to read each sentence and choose a word from the top to complete it. 🔲 **RF.1.3b, RF.1.3f, RF.1.3g**

> **hunted camping ticked jumped**
>
> 1. My little frog _____ up.
> 2. She is _____ at the pond.
> 3. The clock _____ and tocked.
> 4. I _____ for my missing socks.

GROUPING WORDS BY SOUND Display the **Sound/Spelling Cards** for *umbrella* and *thumb* and review short *u* and digraph *th.* Then make a two-column chart on the board, using the cards as headings. Say the word *then.* Have children identify its beginning sound and vowel sound. Then ask children under which card you should write the word. Continue sorting words: *then, run, that, bump, this, thin, cluck, drum.*

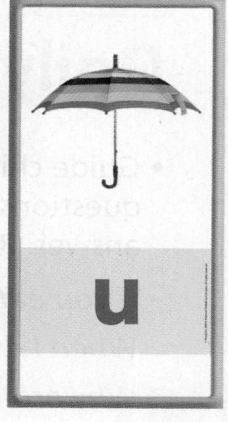

Have children copy the completed chart. Then ask them to work with partners to underline the vowel in each word. Review their work. 🔲 **RF.1.2c**

Decodable Reader

Go Digital

Read *Animal Moms*

Decodable Reader, Unit 3, pp. 21–26

REVIEW WORDS WITH -s, -es, -ed, -ing AND WORDS TO KNOW
Tell children that many words in this selection have the endings -s, -es, -ed, and -ing. Point out that children have learned the following words, which they will read in the selection: *cold, little, their, water*.

PREVIEW Have children preview pages 21–23 and predict what the selection is about. Ask volunteers to tell any names they know for baby animals. For example, tell them a baby dog is a puppy.

MODEL FLUENCY AND PHRASING Read aloud page 21 as children follow along. Point out how you paused when you came to the comma after *rest*. Lead children in choral reading the page with fluency and appropriate phrasing.

READ Remind children to track the words from left to right and when they come to the end of a line, to sweep their hand down to the beginning of the next line and continue reading. Have children read each page silently and then choral read it. Have them read to find out what the animal moms do. ◼ RF.1.3b, RF.1.3f, RF.1.3g, RF.1.4a

RESPONDING Ask children what important facts they learned in *Animal Moms*. Then have each child choose two animals they read about and talk with a partner about how the animals they chose are the same and different. Check that children are sharing accurate facts and details from the story. ◼ RI.1.2

DAILY ASSESSMENT ▲3 2 1 **RtI**

Corrective Feedback Work with the whole group to correct errors, following the model below.

Decoding Error:
A child reads *filled* as *filling*.

Correct the error. Say the word. *That word is* filled. *It ends with the /d/ sound. The letters* ed *stand for /d/.*

Guide Have children repeat the word. *What is the word?* filled

Check *Go back to the beginning of the sentence and read it again.*

Reinforce Record the error and review the word again before children reread the story.

Reread for Fluency/ Develop Automaticity

READ WITH A PARTNER Have partners reread *Animal Moms* three or four times, taking turns reading aloud each page. Remind them to read words correctly and to read smoothly. Visit partners to listen to them read. Give feedback about reading accurately, at an appropriate rate, and with expression and provide guidance for improving fluency. ◼ RF.1.4b

Lesson 11

INFORMATIONAL TEXT

Water

Read Together

☑ **GENRE**

Informational text gives facts about a topic. This is from a science textbook.

☑ **TEXT FOCUS**

A **diagram** is a drawing that can show how something works or the parts that make up something. What does the diagram on page 35 show?

 **RI.1.5** know and use text features to locate facts or information; **RI.1.10** read informational texts

34 Go Digital

Water

What is one thing that all living things, whether they are big or little, have in common? They need water to live.

Water comes in different forms. The water you drink is a liquid. A liquid flows and takes the shape of the container it is in.

ice
water
snow

Water can freeze into ice or snow. Frozen water is a solid. A solid has its own shape.

What is ice? Ice is water that has frozen. It is hard and cold.

Where does snow come from? Snow is tiny pieces of frozen water that fall from the clouds.

35

DOMAIN: Life Science

LESSON TOPIC: Marine Habitats

Cross-Curricular Connection Tell children about the water cycle. Explain how water from oceans evaporates into the sky, forms clouds, and later falls as rain. Discuss bodies of water children have seen, such as oceans, lakes, and rivers. Guide children to recognize that people, animals, and plants need water. Have them describe reasons why.

 **RI.1.3** describe the connection between individuals, events, ideas, or information in a text; **RI.1.5** know and use text features to locate facts or information; **RI.1.10** read informational texts; **SL.1.5** add drawings or visual displays to descriptions to clarify ideas, thoughts, and feelings

Connect to the Topic
Informational Text

Introduce Genre and Text Focus

• Read with children the genre and text focus information on **Student Book** p. 34. Tell children that writers use a **diagram** to show information in a clear way. Readers can use a diagram to find out facts and to find the sentences that will tell more about it. Have children tell the information about water they learn from the diagram. ▬ **RI.1.3, RI.1.5**

• Read the selection with children. Then ask them to describe the forms water can take, such as liquid water, solid ice, and snow, and how water turns into these forms. Have children describe other forms of water they have seen, such as fog, steam, hail, or slush. ▬ **RI.1.3, RI.1.10**

• Ask children to tell how the photos and the diagram help them find information in the selection. Have them retell important facts they learned. ▬ **RI.1.5**

Ice and snow are found in many places around the world. The North Pole is one of these places. There is cold, blue water all around it. People cannot live that far north for very long, but some animals make their homes near the North Pole.

36

Compare Texts

Read Together

TEXT TO TEXT

Compare Animals Use text evidence to compare the polar bear with an animal from **At Home in the Ocean**. How are they alike and different?

TEXT TO SELF

Describe It Find the photo of your favorite animal from either selection. How does it look? What does it do? Use the photo to help describe it.

TEXT TO WORLD

Use a Globe Use a globe to find two different oceans. Draw and label animals that you think might live in each ocean.

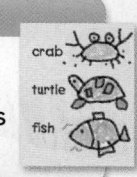
crab
turtle
fish

Go Digital

COMMON CORE **RI.1.3** describe the connection between individuals, events, ideas, or information in a text; **RI.1.7** use illustrations and details to describe key ideas; **RI.1.9** identify similarities in and differences between texts on the same topic; **SL.1.4** describe people, places, things, and events with details/express ideas and feelings clearly; **SL.1.5** add drawings or visual displays to descriptions to clarify ideas, thoughts, and feelings

37

Compare Texts

TEXT TO TEXT

Compare Animals Have children decide how a polar bear compares with one of the animals from *At Home in the Ocean*. Have children look for text evidence in the words and photos to help them tell how the two animals are alike and different. Have children share in small groups how these animals are alike and different.

RI.1.3, RI.1.7, RI.1.9

TEXT TO SELF

Describe It Hold up a photo of your favorite animal from the selections. Model for children how to use it to help make your ideas, thoughts, and feelings about the animal clear, such as pointing out details. Explain that using a picture can help make a description clearer. Have children use photos as visual aids, as you did, as they describe in detail an animal from the selections.

SL.1.4, SL.1.5

TEXT TO WORLD

Use a Globe Display a globe. Explain its purposes and features. Explain that the Poles are very cold and the Equator is warm. Have children identify land and water. Guide them to recognize that the surface of the Earth has water, rocks, soil, and living things. Then have children use a globe to find two different oceans. Tell them to draw and label animals that might live there, based on the selections and their locations.

Whole Group

DAY 4

Go Digital
• Interactive Whiteboard Lesson
• Literacy and Language Guide

JOURNEYS Vocabulary Strategies

Interactive Whiteboard Lesson:
Classify and Categorize Color Words

Vocabulary Strategies

▶ SHARE OBJECTIVES
- Sort words into categories.
- Understand the concepts represented by categories.

▶ SKILLS TRACE

Classify and Categorize Words	
Introduce	Unit 1 T62–T63
Differentiate	T94–T95
Reteach	T97
▶ Review	T64–T65; Unit 6 T166–T167
Assess	Weekly Tests, Lesson 11

ELL ENGLISH LANGUAGE LEARNERS
Comprehensible Input

Beginning Write on the board, *pigs, cows, apple, orange, sheep, strawberry.* Ask, *If you had to put these words into groups, how many groups would you make? two* Help children name the groups as *animals* and *fruits.*

Low Intermediate On the blackboard, write, *pigs, cows, apple, orange, sheep, strawberry.* Ask, *If you had to put these words into groups, how many groups would you make? two How would you identify those groups? animals and fruits.*

High Intermediate Have children dictate the name of different classroom objects. Write the names on the board. Then have children tell you how they could organize those things into groups. Ask them to name the groups and the items in each of them.

Proficient Have partners classify and sort classroom objects.

See ELL Lesson 11, p. E7, for further support.

COMMON CORE **L.1.5a** sort words into categories (e.g., colors, clothing) to gain a sense of the concepts the categories represent

Classify and Categorize Words

1 Teach/Model

Terms About Language

classify to place similar things in a group

categorize to name a group of similar things

- Explain to children that to *classify* is to put similar things in a group, or category. Explain that when children name a group, they are *categorizing*.

- Explain that sorting words into groups and naming the groups is a good way to understand the meanings of the words. In order to place words in categories, children have to think about why they belong in one category and not another. And to name a category, they must think about what is common to all the words in it.

- Model classifying and categorizing words. Write the following sentences on the board, underlining the adjectives. Read the sentences aloud.

> The fish had <u>big</u> <u>blue</u> spots.
> We saw a bird with a <u>long</u> <u>brown</u> tail.

Think Aloud *I can classify and categorize the underlined words. That will help me understand what kind of words they are. I know that blue and brown are colors, so I can put them in the same group. I'll call it Color Words. Big and long describe size. So I'll put them in a group. I'll call it Size Words.*

Literacy and Language Guide
Additional Lesson 11 vocabulary lessons appear in the Literacy and Language Guide.

2 Guided Practice

- Display the story at the top of **Projectable 11.8**. Read the story aloud. Point to the boldfaced words and re-read them. Explain that you want to sort the words into groups and name the groups.

- Display the rest of **Projectable 11.8**. Point out that the chart has three columns and that the first column already has a name, Color.

- Ask a volunteer to read the story until he or she comes to a color word. Write *yellow* in the chart.

Projectable 11.8

Projectable 11.8

At Home in the Ocean · Vocabulary Strategies · Classify and Categorize Words

Classify and Categorize Words

Pam **woke** early. **Yellow** sunshine **filled** her room. She **pulled** on her old **blue jeans**. She **put** on a **green shirt**. She **laced** up her favorite **sneakers**, the **black** ones. It was a warm day, so she didn't need a **hat**. She didn't need a **sweater**. Spring vacation—no school! Pam was going to **play** all day. She **grabbed** a **red** ball and **ran** outside.

Color	Clothing	Actions
yellow	jeans	woke
blue	shirt	filled
green	sneakers	pulled
black	hat	put
red	sweater	laced
		play
		grabbed
		ran

Vocabulary Strategies
© Houghton Mifflin Harcourt Publishing Company. All rights reserved.

Grade 1, Unit 3

3 Apply

- Have children discuss the rest of the boldfaced words. Which words have something in common and could be placed in a group together?

- Point out that some words have already been sorted in the chart. Ask children what they might name the group that includes *jeans* and *shirt*. Write *Clothing* at the top of the second column. Ask children what they might name the group that includes *woke* and *filled*. Write *Actions* at the top of the third column.

- Have children read the story until they come to a boldfaced word that hasn't been classified yet. Ask a volunteer to state which category the word should be put in—Colors, Clothing, or Actions. Write the word in the appropriate column of the chart.

L.1.5a

DAILY ASSESSMENT　RtI

Are children able to sort words into categories and understand the categories?

IF...	THEN...
children have difficulty sorting words into categories and understanding the categories,	▶ **Use Differentiate Vocabulary Strategies** for Struggling Readers, p. T94
children can sort most words into categories and understand most categories,	▶ **Use Differentiate Vocabulary Strategies** for On-Level Readers, p. T94
children can easily sort words into categories and understand the categories,	▶ **Use Differentiate Vocabulary Strategies** for Advanced Readers, p. T95

Differentiate Vocabulary Strategies: pp. T94–T95.

Group English Language Learners according to academic ability and language proficiency. See also ELL Lesson 11, p. E7, for scaffolded support.

SMALL GROUP Options

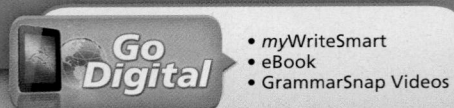

Grammar Spiral Review: Possessives

▶ SHARE OBJECTIVES

- **Grammar** Review possessive nouns.
- **Spelling** Spell words with *th* using conventional spelling patterns.
- **Handwriting** Print the spelling words.
- **Writing** Draft sentences that inform.

ENGLISH LANGUAGE LEARNERS

Language Transfer

All Proficiencies Display the frame _____ *'s chair.* Have children complete the frame with the name of someone else in the class.

See ELL Lesson 11, p. E9, for scaffolded support.

1 Teach/Model

POSSESSIVE NOUNS Have children look at the picture of a dolphin on p. 16 of *At Home in the Ocean*. Point out the dorsal fin and say: *This is the dolphin's fin.* Write the example on the board.

- Review that a singular possessive noun can show that one person or animal has or owns something. Singular possessive nouns usually ends in *'s*.

- Have children look through the rest of *At Home in the Ocean*. Have them find other examples of items they can describe using singular possessive nouns. Add their examples on the board.

2 Guided Practice/Apply

- Point to an item that belongs to a specific child. Say, for example: *This is Shawn's backpack.* Write *Shawn's backpack* on the board. Discuss the capital letter at the beginning of *Shawn's* and the *'s* at the end. Add another example using your own title and name.

- Have children use possessive proper nouns to give other examples of items owned by individual people in the class. Record their examples on the board and have children add the capital letters as needed. 🔲 **L.1.1b, L.1.2a**

Spelling Words with *th*

SPELLING WORDS

BASIC

that	them
then	with
this	bath

CHALLENGE

thick	tenth

Connect to Writing

- Remind children that they have been learning how to write using proper nouns.

- Have children use the spelling words to write sentences that contain proper nouns. Then invite volunteers to read their sentences aloud.

- Practice spelling the words as a class. Say each word and spell it aloud. 🔲 **L.1.1b, L.1.2d**

Handwriting

Model how to form the basic words *them*, *with*, and *bath*. Have children use their best handwriting to print the spelling words. Ball-and-stick and continuous stroke handwriting models are available on the **Handwriting Models Blackline Masters**.

COMMON CORE **W.1.2** write informative/explanatory texts; **W.1.5** focus on a topic, respond to questions/suggestions from peers, and add details to strengthen writing; **L.1.1b** use common, proper, and possessive nouns; **L.1.1j** produce and expand simple and compound declarative, interrogative, imperative, and exclamatory sentences; **L.1.2a** capitalize dates and names of people; **L.1.2d** use conventional spelling for words with common spelling patterns and for frequently occurring irregular words

Informative Writing Drafting

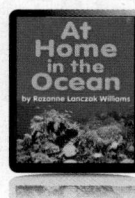

1 Teach/Model

CAPITAL LETTERS Remind children that sentences always begin with capital letters.

> Connect to *At Home in the Ocean*
>
> **Many** animals live in cold water.

- *Which word begins with a capital letter? Why?* Many *because it's the first word in the sentence*

- Display **Projectable 11.7** from Day 3. Review the topic and facts you wrote on the graphic organizer.

 Then display **Projectable 11.9**. Model how to draft sentences that inform.

Think Aloud *I'll turn these ideas into sentences with a capital letter at the beginning. I'll also use words that tell how something happens. I'll write this detail sentence: Crabs can safely live in water or on land.*

- As you draft, ask children to help you turn the information on the graphic organizer into sentences.

2 Independent Writing

- Ask children to share the facts on their completed graphic organizers from Day 3 with a partner.

- Have children draft their own sentences that inform, referring to their graphic organizer and the Focus Wall.

- Then have children work with their partner and read their writing to each other. Have them ask and answer questions about it and tell how to make the writing better. Tell children to use some of the ideas to make changes to make their writing better. ▬ W.1.2, W.1.5, L.1.1j

Daily Proofreading Practice

I see dr. Key with a ~~bigg~~ big book.

It tells about animals that live in ~~kold~~ cold water.

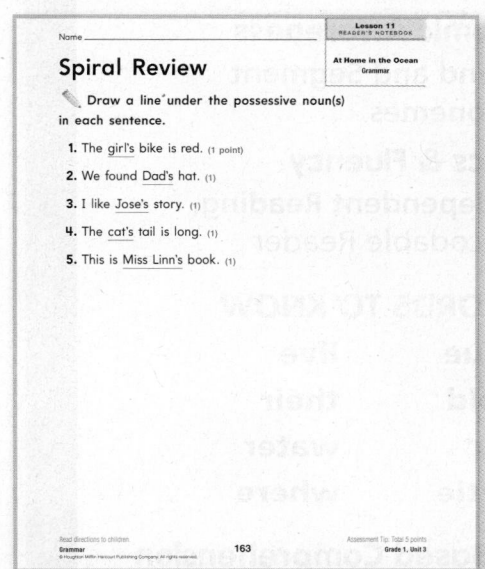

Reader's Notebook Vol. 1 p. 163

Reader's Notebook Vol. 1 p. 162

DAY 5

Today's Goals

Vocabulary & Oral Language
- Domain-Specific Vocabulary
- Speaking & Listening

Phonemic Awareness
- Blend and Segment Phonemes

Phonics & Fluency
- Independent Reading: Decodable Reader

☑ **WORDS TO KNOW**

blue	live
cold	their
far	water
little	where

Text-Based Comprehension
Extend the Topic
- Research & Media Literacy: Facts About an Ocean Animal and Its Habitat

Assess & Reteach
- Assess Skills
- Respond to Assessment

Grammar & Writing
- Proper Nouns
- ➡ Informative Writing: Sentences That Inform

Spelling
- Words with *th*

 **COMMON CORE** **RF.1.2b** orally produce single-syllable words by blending sounds; **RF.1.2d** segment spoken single-syllable words into their complete sequence of individual sounds; **L.1.3g** recognize and read irregularly spelled words; **SL.1.6** produce complete sentences when appropriate to task and situation; **L.1.5c** identify real-life connections between words and their use; **L.1.6** use words and phrases acquired through conversations, reading and being read to, and responding to texts

Opening Routines

Warm Up with Wordplay

Use New Vocabulary

Have children review and work with the new vocabulary words they learned on Day 3. Write the words, and read them aloud with children.

> classify
> extraordinary
> adapt

Guide children to work together to say a few sentences about animals that live in different environments. Tell them to use each new vocabulary word. You may wish to prompt children with questions, such as *What animals live in the desert? What does a jellyfish look like?* ⬛ **SL.1.6, L.1.5c**

Daily Phonemic Awareness

Blend and Segment Phonemes

- *I'm going to say the sounds in a word and blend them. Then you say the word. Ready? Here we go. Listen /k/ /ă/ /t/, cat.*
- Have children repeat the following words with you and then by themselves.

  /j/ /ĕ/ /t/ *jet* /h/ /ĭ/ /m/ *him* /y/ /ĕ/ /s/ *yes*

  /k/ /l/ /ĭ/ /k/ *click* /th/ /ă/ /t/ *that* /k/ /r/ /ā/ /t/ *crate*

  /b/ /ō/ /th/ *both* /p/ /r/ /ī/ /d/ *pride* /th/ /ā/ *they*

- Reverse the process. Say each word below and have children repeat it. *How many sounds are in* jet? *three Say the first sound. /j/ Say the middle sound. /ĕ/ Say the last sound. /t/*

  jet   him   yes   that   both

  ◼ RF.1.2b, RF.1.2d

Corrective Feedback

- Model the task. *The word is* both. *Listen: /b/ /ō/ /th/. What is the word?* both
- Have children do the blending with you before doing it on their own.
- Back up several words and continue the game.

Daily High-Frequency Words

Introduce

- Point to the **High-Frequency Word Card** *water*.
- *Say the word. water Spell the word. w, a, t, e, r Write the word. Check the word.*
- Repeat the procedure with the words from this week (*blue, cold, far, little, live, their, where*) and last week (*eat, give, one, put, small, take*). ◼ RF.1.3g

Throwing Letters

- Choose a High-Frequency Word from this week or the previous week.
- As you point to each letter in the word, have children name it and "throw it" into the air as they would throw a ball.
- Choose a child to lead for the remaining words.

Corrective Feedback

- Say the correct word and have children repeat it. Water. *What is the word?* water
- Have children spell the word. *w, a, t, e, r How do we say this word?* water
- Have children reread all of the cards in random order.

Daily Vocabulary Boost

- Reread "The Piano Lessons" aloud to children. (See pp. T14–T15.)
- As you read each Oral Vocabulary word in the selection, have a volunteer explain or describe its meaning. Call on each child to make a sentence out of the Oral Vocabulary words. Repeat the list until each child has made a sentence.
- After reading, review the Oral Vocabulary words and their definitions. Challenge children to use the words in their everyday speech and encourage them to relate the words to their own experiences ("I *practice* the piano because I want to play well."). ◼ L.1.5c, L.1.6

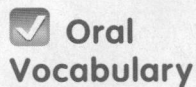

☑ Oral Vocabulary

companions
exchange
gracefully
portions
practice
strict

DAY 5

DOMAIN: **Life Science**
LESSON TOPIC: Marine Habitats

Extend the Topic

SHARE OBJECTIVES

- Acquire and use domain-specific vocabulary.
- Participate in conversations about a topic.
- Write informative texts in which children name a topic, supply facts about the topic, and provide a sense of closure.
- Participate in shared research and writing projects.

Words About the Topic: Marine Habitats

- **arctic** very cold and wintry
- **current** the flow of water in a river or the ocean
- **tidal** related to ocean tides

Domain-Specific Vocabulary

INTRODUCE WORDS ABOUT THE TOPIC Remind children that this week's topic is Marine Habitats. Display the words shown at the left. Tell children that these are words that can help them learn more about the topic. Read aloud the meaning of each word, and have children respond to the following prompts. **L.1.5c, L.1.6**

- *Alaska is the northernmost state in the USA. It is cold and has a lot of snow, so it is an _____ place.* arctic
- *Why is it easier to row a boat one way on a river than the other way?* The current flows one way. If you row with it, it pushes you forward. If you row against it, it pushes against you.
- *When it's high tide, the ocean reaches farther up a beach. When it's low tide, it reaches less far. Many kinds of animals live in these _____ areas, such as crabs, clams, and small fish.* tidal

INTERACT WITH THE WORDS Have children work in small groups to create Four-Square Maps. For each of the domain-specific words, children should fold a blank sheet of paper into four equal sections. Work with them to follow the steps below for each word. As needed, display the meanings of the words on the board. Ask individual children to use the words in a sentence orally. Then write the sentence on the board for other children to refer to for ideas.

1. In the first corner, draw a picture for the word.
2. In the second corner, write the meaning of the word.
3. In the third corner, write a sentence using the word.
4. In the fourth corner, write the word.

When groups have finished, have them share their Four-Square Maps with the class. **L.1.5c, L.1.6**

COMMON CORE
W.1.2 write informative/explanatory texts; **W.1.7** participate in shared research and writing projects; **W.1.8** recall information from experiences or gather information from sources to answer a question; **SL.1.1.c** ask questions to clear up confusion about topics and texts under discussion; **L.1.5.c** identify real-life connections between words and their use; **L.1.6** use words and phrases acquired through conversations, reading and being read to, and responding to texts

Research and Media Literacy

Facts About an Ocean Animal and Its Habitat

CHOOSE RESEARCH TOPIC AND QUESTION Review *At Home in the Ocean*. Brainstorm a list of other animals that live in the ocean. Organize children into small groups and have each choose an animal. Explain that they will work together to write a report on that animal and its habitat.

Tell each group to write a research question by discussing what they would like to know about their animal. Explain that their report will answer the question that they all agree to research.

EXPLORE AND CHOOSE RESOURCES Tell the class that they are going to begin their research by exploring books and other media to find the best information on their topic. Provide books and access to approved sites on the Internet. Each group should choose at least three sources. As children work, circulate to help them locate facts and details that help to answer the group's research question.
🔲 W.1.7, W.1.8

TAKE NOTES AND ORGANIZE THEM Give children time to research. Tell them to take notes as they read. Tell them taking notes means writing facts they find so they can remember them later when they begin to write. When they have enough information, children can organize their notes on note cards or in a graphic organizer.
🔲 W.1.7, W.1.8

WRITE THE REPORT Guide children to select information from their research and write sentences about each fact. Guide them to put together the sentences to write their reports. Help them to include:
🔲 W.1.2

• a title

• a topic sentence that tells the main idea

• facts that explain the main idea

• a closing sentence

ILLUSTRATE AND SHARE When each group has completed its report, have children draw illustrations. Give each group an opportunity to present its report to the class. Encourage children to ask and answer questions to clear up confusion and to get additional information. 🔲 SL.1.1c

> **DAY 1 Choose a topic.**
>
> **DAY 2 Explore and choose resources.**
>
> **DAY 3 Take and organize notes.**
>
> **DAY 4 Write the report.**
>
> **DAY 5 Illustrate and share.**

Performance Task

 Have children complete the Research and Media Literacy task through *my*WriteSmart. Children will read a prompt within *my*WriteSmart and have access to multiple writing resources, including the Student eBook, a Writing Checklist, and Graphic Organizers.

Grammar Weekly Review: Proper Nouns

▶ SHARE OBJECTIVES

- **Grammar** Review proper nouns.
- **Spelling** Spell words with *th* using conventional spelling patterns.

ELL ENGLISH LANGUAGE LEARNERS
Language Transfer

Beginning Display the words *bath, this, earth, than*. Read them aloud. Have children clap every time they hear the /th/ sound.

Low Intermediate Have children use **Letter Cards** to build and read *this, them, math*.

High Intermediate Have children use **Letter Cards** to build and read *bath*. Guide them in changing the cards to read *math, path, that*.

Proficient Have children in groups use **Letter Cards** *t, h, a, i, e, t, s, w, n, b, m* to build and read as many words with the sound /th/ as they can.

1 Review/Practice

- Together with children, read the text at the top of **Student Book** p. 38. Discuss the definition of proper nouns. Then discuss the examples in the middle of **Student Book** p. 38 and the titles at the bottom of the page.

- Direct children's attention to the Try This! activity on **Student Book** p. 39. Have children share their completed sentences with a partner and discuss where they used capital letters and periods.
  📖 **L.1.1b, L.1.2a**

2 Connect to Writing

- Write the following statements on the board. Ask children to identify the mistakes orally.

  That penguin is named ollie. I see mr. Bell swim.

- Model using proofreading marks to correct the first sentence. Ask a volunteer to correct the errors in the second sentence. Then have children write their own sentences using proper nouns for a place, a person, an animal, and a thing.
  📖 **L.1.1b, L.1.2a**

Spelling Words with *th*

SPELLING WORDS AND SENTENCES

BASIC

1. *that* *That* is my hat.
2. *then* Come to my house and *then* we will bake cookies.
3. *this* *This* is my bed.
4. *them* Please tell *them* to go slow.
5. *with* Alex will go *with* you to the store.

6. *bath* I take a *bath* every night.

CHALLENGE

7. *thick* The sauce was *thick* and creamy.
8. *tenth* I was *tenth* in line because nine people were ahead of me.

Assess

Say each spelling word, read the sentence, and then repeat the word. Have children write the word.
📖 **L.1.2d**

Corrective Feedback

Review any words that children misspell.

COMMON CORE **L.1.1b** use common, proper, and possessive nouns; **L.1.2a** capitalize dates and names of people; **L.1.2d** use conventional spelling for words with common spelling patterns and for frequently occurring irregular words; **L.1.2e** spell untaught words phonetically, drawing o phonemic awareness and spelling conventions.

L.1.1b use common, proper, and possessive nouns; L.1.2a capitalize dates and names of people

Grammar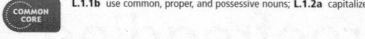

Proper Nouns A noun that names a special person, animal, place, or thing is called a **proper noun**. Proper nouns begin with capital letters.

Grandstand

Seaside Park

Flip

Seal Show

Shawn Jones

When a **title** is used before a name, it begins with a capital letter, too. A title usually ends with a period.

Mr. Diaz   **Mrs.** Sims   **Miss** Reed

38

Write each sentence on another sheet of paper. Find the proper nouns. Use capital letters and periods where they belong.

1. My family went to florida.

2. We drove on beach street.

3. We met mrs bell.

4. Her dog is named skippy.

5. I went on the super sun slide.

6. We all ate at snack shack.

Grammar in Writing

When you proofread your writing, be sure you have used capital letters to write proper nouns.

39

Try This!

1. **My family went to Florida.**

2. **We drove on Beach Street.**

3. **We met Mrs. Bell.**

4. **Her dog is named Skippy.**

5. **I went on the Super Sun Slide.**

6. **We all ate at Snack Shack.**

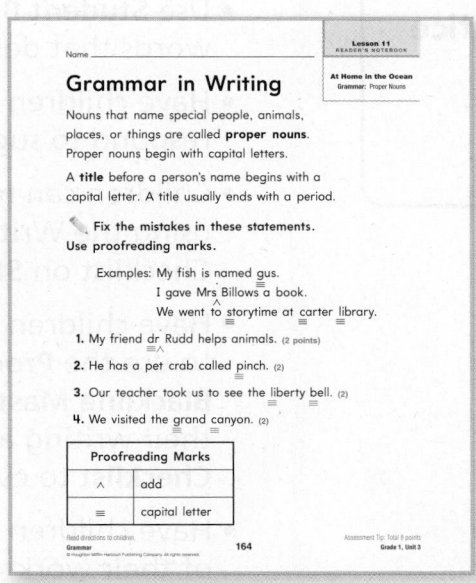

Reader's Notebook Vol. 1 p. 164

Go Digital
• myWriteSmart
• eBook

Informative Writing Revising and Proofreading

SHARE OBJECTIVE
• Revise and proofread sentences that inform.

ELL ENGLISH LANGUAGE LEARNERS
Comprehensible Input

Beginning Write a list of common *-ly* adverbs children can use as they revise their drafts. Discuss each adverb.

Low Intermediate Write a list of adverbs children can use as they revise. Have each child act one out and incorporate it into his or her draft.

High Intermediate Have children work with partners to check their sentences for correct end marks and capitalization.

Proficient Have children proofread partners' drafts to suggest edits.

See ELL Lesson 11, p. E11, for scaffolded support.

Daily Proofreading Practice

I see mrs. Lang go to the sea.

The water looks b̶l̶u̶. ^blue

COMMON CORE
W.1.2 write informative/explanatory texts; **W.1.5** focus on a topic, respond to questions/suggestions from peers, and add details to strengthen writing; **W.1.6** use digital tools to produce and publish writing; **L.1.1j** produce and expand simple and compound declarative, interrogative, imperative, and exclamatory sentences

1 Teach/Model

• Display **Projectable 11.10**.

• Explain that a first grader named Joy wrote these sentences that inform.

• Review what revision is. *Revising means making your draft better. One way to revise is to use words that are clearer or more interesting.*

• Use the Talk About It questions to guide an analysis of the draft.

• Have children suggest revisions. Remind them to listen as their classmates speak and to wait to speak until they are recognized.

• Model revising the draft.

Projectable 11.10

Projectable 11.10

At Home in the Ocean Writing Informative Writing

Revising Joy's Draft
Read Joy's draft. Then help Joy think of ways to make her sentences better.

Sea Lions
Sea lions do amazing things.
loudly
A sea lion can bark. ^
It uses its flippers to move
quickly
on land or in water.

Talk About It
☐ Do Joy's sentences have words that tell how?
☐ Did Joy write a topic sentence?
☐ Did Joy use capital letters correctly?

Writing   Grade 1, Unit 3

---

2 Independent Writing

• Use **Student Book** pp. 40–41 to review the Focus Skill, using words that describe by telling how.

• Have children ask and answer questions with their partners and respond to suggestions to improve their writing.

• Children can revise their work using the Writing Traits Checklist on **Student Book** p. 40.

• Have children work with a partner to use the **Proofreading Checklist Blackline Master** to proofread their writing and the **Writing Checklist** to evaluate their drafts.

• Have children make a clean copy of their work. Guide them to publish their work using classroom computers or tablets. Have children share their writing.
  ▬ W.1.2, W.1.5, W.1.6, L.1.1j

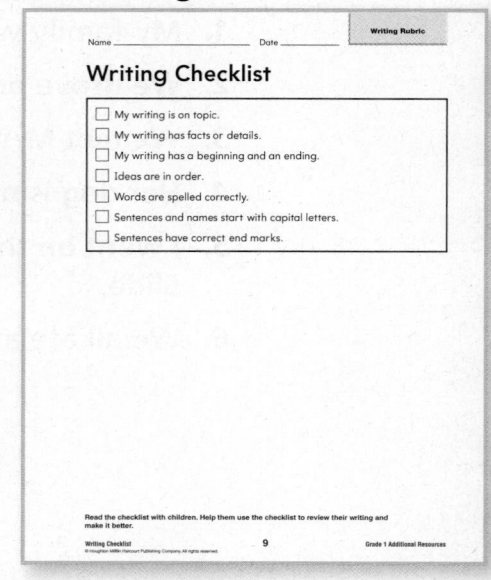

Name _____ Date _____   Writing Rubric

Writing Checklist

☐ My writing is on topic.
☐ My writing has facts or details.
☐ My writing has a beginning and an ending.
☐ Ideas are in order.
☐ Words are spelled correctly.
☐ Sentences and names start with capital letters.
☐ Sentences have correct end marks.

Read the checklist with children. Help them use the checklist to review their writing and make it better.
Writing Checklist   9   Grade 1 Additional Resources

Writing Checklist

 W.1.2 write informative/explanatory texts; **W.1.5** focus on a topic, respond to questions/suggestions from peers, and add details to strengthen writing; **L.1.1j** produce and expand simple and compound declarative, interrogative, imperative, and exclamatory sentences

Informative Writing

 **Ideas** Sometimes you will write **sentences** that give readers facts. One kind of fact describes how something happens. Joy wrote about sea lions. Then she added **loudly** to describe how sea lions bark.

 Read Together

 my WriteSmart

Go Digital

Revised Draft

loudly

A sea lion can bark.
^

Writing Traits Checklist

 **Ideas** Do my sentences have words that tell **how**?

☑ Does my writing tell facts?

☑ Did I use capital letters correctly?

40

Look for words that tell **how** in Joy's final copy. Look for facts. Then revise your writing. Use the Checklist.

Final Copy

Sea Lions

Sea lions do amazing things. A sea lion can bark loudly. It uses its flippers to move quickly on land or in water.

41

---

*See also the **Writing Checklist Blackline Master** on Teacher's Edition p. R11.*

WRITING TRAITS SCORING RUBRIC

	Focus/Support	Organization	Word Choice/Voice	Conventions/Sentence Fluency
6	Develops topic or events with relevant facts or details.	Introduces topic or situation clearly, organizes ideas to support purpose, has relevant conclusion.	Links ideas with words, phrases. Uses specific language. Connects with reader in unique way.	Demonstrates exemplary command of conventions of standard written English. Includes variety of complete sentences that flow smoothly, naturally.
5	Mostly develops topic or events with relevant facts or details.	Introduces topic or situation, mostly organizes ideas to support purpose, has mostly relevant conclusion.	Links most ideas with words, phrases. Uses specific language. Connects with reader.	Demonstrates good command of conventions of standard written English. Includes some variety of complete sentences that flow smoothly, naturally.
4	Adequately develops topic or events with relevant facts or details.	Introduces topic or situation, adequately organizes ideas to support purpose, has adequate conclusion.	Links some ideas with words, phrases. Uses some specific language. Connects with reader.	Demonstrates adequate command of conventions of standard written English. Includes some variety of complete sentences. Some flow smoothly, naturally.
3	Develops topic or events with some relevant facts or details.	Introduces topic or situation, organizes some ideas to support purpose, has somewhat relevant conclusion.	Links some ideas with words, phrases. May use some specific language. May connect with reader.	Demonstrates command of some conventions of standard written English. Includes little variety of complete sentences. Few flow smoothly, naturally.
2	Develops topic or events with few relevant facts or details.	May introduce topic or situation, organizes few ideas to support purpose, may have somewhat relevant conclusion.	Attempts to link ideas with words. Rarely uses specific language. May not connect with reader.	Demonstrates little command of conventions of standard written English. Includes little sentence variety. Incomplete sentences hinder meaning.
1	May not develop topic or events with relevant facts or details.	May attempt to introduce topic or situation, may not organize ideas to support purpose, may not have relevant conclusion.	May not link ideas with words. Does not use specific language or connect with reader.	Demonstrates little or no command of conventions of standard written English. Sentences do not vary. Incomplete sentences hinder meaning.

Progress Monitoring

Assess

- **Weekly Tests**
- **Periodic Assessments**

COMMON CORE

Respond to Assessment

☑ Vocabulary

High-Frequency Words
Strategies: Classify and Categorize Color Words

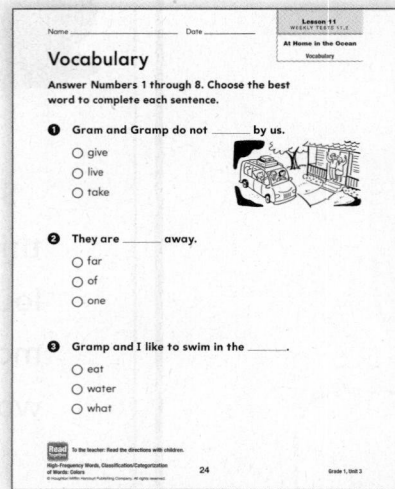

Weekly Tests 11.2–11.4

RF.1.3g recognize and read irregularly spelled words; **L.1.5a** sort words into categories to gain a sense of concepts the categories represent

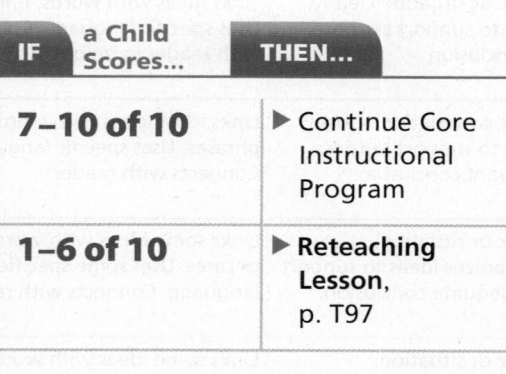

IF a Child Scores...	THEN...
7–10 of 10	▶ Continue Core Instructional Program
1–6 of 10	▶ Reteaching Lesson, p. T97

If a child scores below target on two or more tests, then consider using Diagnostic Assessment to pinpoint the child's instructional needs. The child may need systematic intervention.

☑ Phonics/Decoding

Words with Digraph *th*
Base Words and *-s, -es, -ed, -ing* Endings

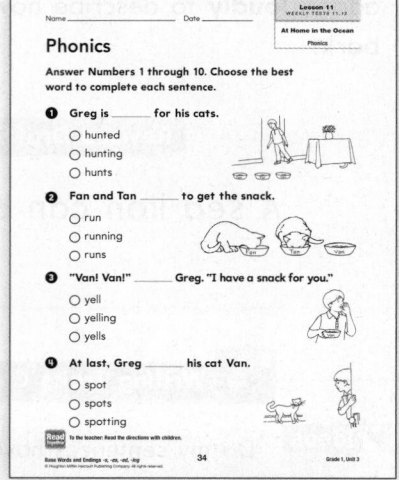

Weekly Tests 11.9–11.14
Phonemic Awareness
See Observation Checklist *in Grab-and-Go™ Resources.*

RF.1.3a know the spelling-sound correspondences for common consonant digraphs; **RF.1.3f** read words with inflectional endings

IF a Child Scores...	THEN...
7–10 of 10	▶ Continue Core Instructional Program
1–6 of 10	▶ Reteaching Lesson, p. T96

If a child scores below target on two or more tests, then consider using Diagnostic Assessment to pinpoint the child's instructional needs. The child may need systematic intervention.

Go Digital
- Grab-and-Go Weekly Tests
- Online Assessment System
- Cold Reads Online
- ExamView Banks

COMMON CORE

☑ Comprehension

Author's Purpose
Details

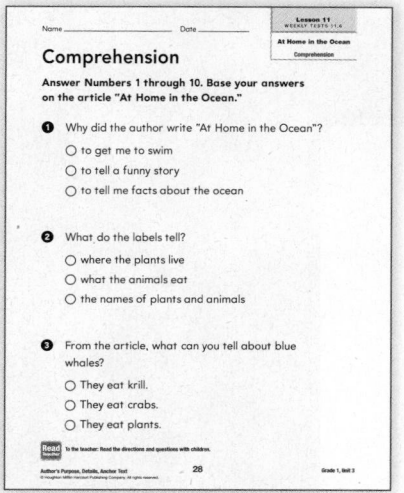

Weekly Tests 11.5–11.8

🔲 **RI.1.2** identify the main topic and retell key details; **RI.1.8** identify the reasons an author gives to support points

IF a Child Scores...	THEN...
7–10 of 10	▶ Continue Core Instructional Program
1–6 of 10	▶ **Reteaching Lesson,** p. T97

If a child scores below target on two or more tests, then consider using Diagnostic Assessment to pinpoint the child's instructional needs. The child may need systematic intervention.

☑ Language Arts

Grammar: Proper Nouns

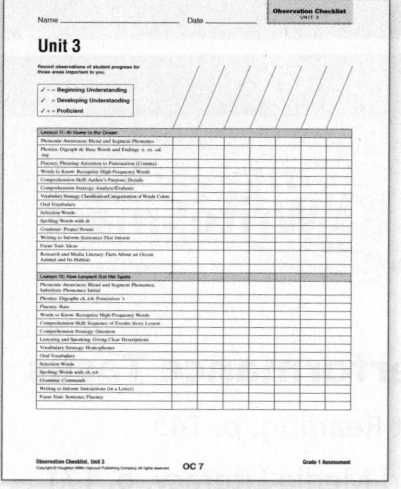

Observation Checklist, *Assessment,* **p. OC7**

🔲 **L.1.1b** use common, proper, and possessive nouns; **L.1.2a** capitalize dates and names of people

IF a Child Scores...	THEN...
Proficient	▶ Continue Core Instructional Program
Developing	▶ **Review Instruction,** p. T44, T56, T72–T73
Beginning	▶ **Intervention** Lesson 11, pp. S2–S11

If a child scores below target on two or more tests, then consider using Diagnostic Assessment to pinpoint the child's instructional needs. The child may need systematic intervention.

☑ FLUENCY

Fluency Plan Assess one group per week. Use the suggested plan below.

● **Struggling Readers**	**Weeks 1, 3, 5**
▲ **On Level**	**Week 2**
■ **Advanced**	**Week 4**

Fluency Scoring Rubrics
See *Grab-and-Go™ Resources Assessment* for help in measuring progress.

Oral Reading Practice
Use the **Student Book,** the **Leveled Readers,** or other reading materials in this unit to help children improve fluency.

☑ COLD READS

Cold Reads *are leveled passages that can be used to practice and monitor fluency and comprehension.*

LESSON 11

Performance Tasks

Lesson Performance Tasks

- Write About Reading, p. T43

- Research and Media Literacy, p. T71

- Informative Writing: Sentences That Inform, pp. T74–T75

- Cumulative Performance Assessment: Task 1 of 5

Unit-Level Performance Tasks

- Research and Media Performance Task, pp. xxvi–xxvii

- Cumulative Performance Assessment

  Task 1: complete after Lesson 11

  Task 2: complete after Lesson 12

  Task 3: complete after Lesson 13

  Task 4: complete after Lesson 14

  Task 5: complete after Lesson 15

Weekly
Small Group Instruction  Go Digital

DAY 1

Differentiate
Phonics & Words to Know
- Digraph *th*
- *blue, cold, far, little, live, their, water, where*

Vocabulary Reader
- *Shark*

Vocabulary Reader

DAY 2

Differentiate Comprehension
- Author's Purpose
- Analyze/Evaluate

DAY 3

Differentiate
Phonics & Fluency
- Base Words and *-s, -es, -ed, -ing*
- Phrasing: Punctuation (Comma)

Leveled Readers
- ⬤ *In the Sea*
- ▲ *Coral Reefs*
- ■ *The Amazing Octopus*
- ◆ *Life in the Coral Reefs*

Leveled Readers

DAY 4

Differentiate
Vocabulary Strategies
- Classify and Categorize Color Words

DAY 5

Options for Reteaching
- Phonics
- Vocabulary Strategies
- Comprehension

Literacy Centers

Independent Practice
- Word Study, T8
- Think and Write, T9
- Comprehension and Fluency, T8
- Digital Center, T9

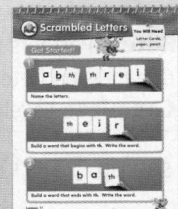

Word Study   **Think and Write**   **Comprehension and Fluency**

Suggested
Small Group Plan
Differentiated Instruction

		DAY 1	DAY 2	DAY 3
Teacher-Led	**Struggling Readers**	**Vocabulary Reader** *Shark*, Differentiated Instruction, p. T84 **Differentiate Phonics:** Digraph *th*, T82	**Differentiate Comprehension:** Author's Purpose; Analyze/Evaluate Strategy, p. T86 **Reread** *Zeb Yak*, p. T39	**Leveled Reader** *In the Sea*, p. T90 **Differentiate Phonics:** Base Words and *-s, -es, -ed, -ing*, p. T88
	On Level	**Vocabulary Reader** *Shark*, Differentiated Instruction, p. T84	**Differentiate Comprehension:** Author's Purpose; Analyze/Evaluate Strategy, p. T86 **Reread** *Zeb Yak*, p. T39	**Leveled Reader** *Coral Reefs*, p. T91 **Differentiate Fluency:** Phrasing: Punctuation, p. T89
	Advanced	**Vocabulary Reader** *Shark*, Differentiated Instruction, p. T85	**Differentiate Comprehension:** Author's Purpose; Analyze/Evaluate Strategy, p. T87	**Leveled Reader** *The Amazing Octopus*, p. T92 **Differentiate Fluency:** Phrasing: Punctuation, p. T89
	English Language Learners	**Vocabulary Reader** *Shark*, Differentiated Instruction, p. T85 **Differentiate Words to Know** Using Context Cards, p. T83	**Differentiate Comprehension:** Author's Purpose; Analyze/Evaluate Strategy, p. T87 **Reread** *Zeb Yak*, p. T39	**Leveled Reader** *Life in the Coral Reefs*, p. T93 **Differentiate Fluency:** Phrasing: Punctuation, p. T89
What are my other kids doing?	**Struggling Readers**	**Word Building:** Build and read Spelling Words using Letter Cards **Complete** Leveled Practice, SR11.1–SR11.2	**Words to Know:** Partners practice reading Context Cards **Reread** *Seth and Beth* and *Zeb Yak* **Complete** Leveled Practice, SR11.3	**Reread:** Partners read *In the Sea* **Complete** Leveled Practice, SR11.4
	On Level	**Word Building:** Build and read Words to Know using Letter Cards	**Words to Know:** Practice reading Context Cards **Reread** *Seth and Beth* and *Zeb Yak*	**Reread:** Partners read *Coral Reefs*
	Advanced	**Context Cards** Assign Talk It Over activities **Complete** Leveled Practice, A11.1–A11.2	**Reread:** Partners read *At Home in the Ocean* **Complete** Leveled Practice, A11.3	**Reread** *The Amazing Octopus* **Complete** Leveled Practice, A11.4
	English Language Learners	**Listen** to Audio of *At Home in the Ocean* **Complete** Leveled Practice, ELL11.1–ELL11.2	**Listen:** Follow along with Audio of *At Home in the Ocean* **Retell:** Partners retell *At Home in the Ocean* using Retelling Cards **Complete** Leveled Practice, ELL11.3	**Reread:** Partners read *Life in the Coral Reefs* **Listen** to Audio of *Water* **Complete** Leveled Practice, ELL11.4

For Strategic Intervention for this lesson, see pp. S2–S11.

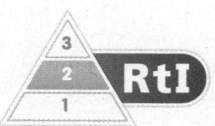

DAY 4 	DAY 5 
Differentiate Vocabulary Strategies: Classify and Categorize Color Words, p. T94 **Reread** *Animal Moms*, p. T61	**Options for Reteaching,** pp. T96–T97 **Reread** one of this week's Decodable Reader selections.
Differentiate Vocabulary Strategies: Classify and Categorize Color Words, p. T94 **Reread** *Animal Moms*, p. T61	**Options for Reteaching,** pp. T96–T97 **Reread** one of this week's Decodable Reader selections.
Differentiate Vocabulary Strategies: Classify and Categorize Color Words, p. T95	**Options for Reteaching,** pp. T96–T97 **Reread** one of this week's Decodable Reader selections.
Differentiate Vocabulary Strategies: Classify and Categorize Color Words, p. T95 **Reread** *Animal Moms*, p. T61	**Options for Reteaching,** pp. T96–T97 **Reread** one of this week's Decodable Reader selections.

Reread: Partners read *Animal Moms* **Listen** to Audio of *Water*	**Reread:** Choose among this week's stories • Complete and share Literacy Center activities
Reread *Animal Moms*	**Reread:** Choose among this week's stories • Complete and share Literacy Center activities
Reread: Partners read *Water*	**Reread:** Choose among this week's stories • Complete and share Literacy Center activities
Listen to Audio of *Water* **Reread:** Partners read *The Duck Nest*	**Reread:** Choose among this week's stories • Complete and share Literacy Center activities

Weekly To-Do List

This Weekly To-Do List helps children see their own progress and move on to additional activities independently.

Differentiate Phonics and Words to Know

Struggling Readers

Phonemic Awareness/Phonics

Digraph *th*

I DO IT

- Show **Picture Card** *thorn*. Name the picture, emphasizing the /th/ sound.

Use **Instructional Routine 2** to model how to blend *thorn*.

- Write and underline *t, h*. *These letters stand for the sound /th/.* Continue for the remaining letters in *thorn*.

- Repeat the procedure with *tooth*, pointing out the *th* at the end.

- Repeat with words with *th* in the **Decodable Reader** selection *Seth and Beth*.

WE DO IT

- Review the *th* spelling on the **Sound/Spelling Card** *thumb*.

- Ask children to shout /th/ each time they hear a word with the sound. Say the following words: *think, both, bat, this, mouth, tell*.

- Help children blend the sounds to read the words below. Use the **Corrective Feedback** if children need additional help.

that	bath	with	than
them	math	this	path

- Discuss the meaning of the words.

YOU DO IT

- Distribute **Letter Cards** to pairs of children so they can make *th* words.

- Have children make a list of their words and then read them with the class.

DAILY ASSESSMENT

Corrective Feedback Work with children to correct errors, following the model below.

Phonics Error:
A child reads *bath* as *bat*.

Correct the error. Say the word and the final sound. *The word is* bath. *The letters* th *stand for the sound /th/.*

Model as you touch the letters. *I'll blend /b/ /ă/ /th/. What is the word?* bath

Guide *Let's blend together: /b/ /ă/ /th/. What is the word?* bath

Check *You blend. /b/ /ă/ /th/ What is the word?* bath

Reinforce Have children continue reading. Make note of errors and review those words during tomorrow's lesson.

ELL **English Language Learners**

Words to Know

- Write this week's Words to Know on the board and read them aloud.
- Use the backs of the **Vocabulary in Context Cards** to review the explanations of the words.
- Tell children that they will see these words in this week's reading selections.
- Have children look for the words in the selection *At Home in the Ocean*.

☑ **WORDS TO KNOW**

blue	live
cold	their
far	water
little	where

Vocabulary in Context Cards

Beginning
- Point to each word on a **Vocabulary in Context Card** as you read it. Have children repeat after you. Then display the pictures as you have children echo-read each word after you.

Low Intermediate
- Display the **Vocabulary in Context Card** pictures, then the words. Have children echo-read each word as you point to it. Have children work with partners to repeat the activity.

High Intermediate
- Have children read each word aloud as you point to it. Encourage volunteers to use each word in a sentence of their own.

Proficient
- Have children work with a partner. One child uses a word from the cards to ask a question. The other child answers, using the word in a sentence. Have children switch roles.

On Level

See Literacy Center Practice—Unit 3 Lesson 11 Word Study

Have partners show each other the **Vocabulary in Context Cards** for this week's words and use each word in an oral sentence.

Advanced

See Literacy Center Practice—Unit 3 Lesson 11 Word Study

Have partners use the **Vocabulary in Context Cards** for this week's words to give clues about each word for the other to guess. Ask them to write each word they guess correctly.

Vocabulary Reader
Shark

Shark
by Anita Sanders

HOUGHTON MIFFLIN

Summary

This book explores a white shark's body—its back, fins, mouth, nose, belly, and scary teeth.

☑ **WORDS TO KNOW**

blue	live
cold	their
far	water
little	where

Struggling Readers

- Display a photograph of a shark. Ask children to tell where sharks live.

- Preview the selection by taking a picture walk. Ask them to describe what they see on each page. When they use Words to Know, write the responses on the board and circle the words.

- Read the selection aloud. Point out how the first sentence on most of the pages begins with *A shark has*. Then have children take turns reading the selection aloud. Guide them to use context clues when they come to an unfamiliar word (or phrase).

- Have partners work together to complete the Responding page. Read aloud the directions on **Blackline Master 11.4** and guide children to complete it.

On Level

- Ask children to tell what they know about sharks. Use the Words to Know in questions, such as *Where do sharks live? What do their heads look like?*

- Remind children that context clues can help them figure out unfamiliar words (or phrases) in a sentence.

- Read the selection aloud, leaving off the last word of each sentence. Have children say the missing word. Then ask children to read the book to a partner. Remind them to use context clues when they come to an unfamiliar word (or phrase).

- Have children read the Words to Know. Then assign the Responding page and **Blackline Master 11.4**. Review the directions with children and have them discuss their responses with a partner.

Advanced

- Ask children to share what they know about sharks. Then have them preview the selection and make predictions about what they will read.

- Remind children to use context clues to help them determine the meaning of unknown words (or phrases). Ask them to point out the repeating words in the selection.

- Ask children to take turns reading pages of the selection aloud with a partner. Have them use context clues as necessary to read unfamiliar words (or phrases).

- Review the Words to Know and have children use them to discuss the selection. Then assign the Responding page and **Blackline Master 11.4**.

ELL English Language Learners

Beginning

Draw a picture of a shark on butcher paper. Then have children look in the selection and find all the different parts of the shark's body. Help them label the picture with the different body parts.

High Intermediate

Have children innovate on the book. Have the group choose another animal they like and use the sentence frames *A _____ has teeth. I see the teeth.* Then have one child choose one pair of sentences to write and illustrate. Bind their pages into a book and title it with the animal's name.

Low Intermediate

Draw a picture of a shark and a person on the board. Have children label the teeth, back, belly, mouth, and nose on each drawing. Then have children compare and contrast a shark body with a human one.

Proficient

Have children use the Words to Know to write sentences about sharks. Encourage them to illustrate their sentences.

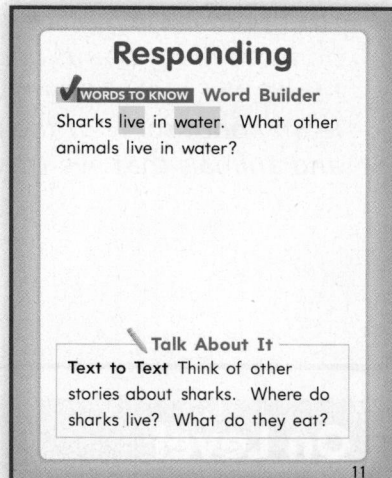

Responding

✓ WORDS TO KNOW Word Builder

Sharks live in water. What other animals live in water?

Talk About It
Text to Text Think of other stories about sharks. Where do sharks live? What do they eat?

11

Shark, p. 11

Name _____

Words to Know

Lesson 11
BLACKLINE MASTER 11.4
Shark
Words to Know

Listen to the words. Draw lines to match the words that go together.

Word Bank
blue   far   live   water
cold   little   their   where

1. blue — alive
2. cold — place
3. far — belongs to them
4. little — rain
5. live — small
6. their — sky
7. water — snow
8. where — not close

Words to Know   6   Grade 1, Unit 3

Blackline Master 11.4

Differentiate Comprehension

Author's Purpose; Analyze/Evaluate

Struggling Readers

I DO IT

- Read aloud **Student Book** pp.15–17, and model identifying the author's purpose. Then explain that the author wants you to learn about life in the ocean.

  Think Aloud *The author says that the ocean is a big place that is home to many plants and animals. I think the author wants us to learn about some of the plants and animals that live there.*

WE DO IT

- Have children read **Student Book** pp.15–27. Have them restate the main topic in the story.

- Help children identify details that support the main topic. For example, *The author explains that the ocean is a big place that is home to many animals. We learned that sharks, blue whales, and krill are some of the animals that live there.*

- Have volunteers list plants and animals from the story, and write them on the board.

YOU DO IT

- Have children review **Student Book** pp.15–29. Have them complete an Inference Map to help them analyze and evaluate the details of the story.

- Help children write a title or topic for their chart, such as *Animals in the Ocean*. Then help them list three details from the story. For example, *Blue whales are big.*

- Have volunteers read aloud the details on their charts.

On Level

I DO IT

- Read aloud **Student Book** pp. 15–17. Model identifying the author's purpose.

  Think Aloud *The title tells us what the author wants us to learn. The words "At Home in the Ocean" tell us that we will find out about things that live in the ocean.*

WE DO IT

- Have children read aloud pp.18–27. Have a volunteer identify what the author wants us to learn.

- Work together to identify details that support the main topic. For example, say, *The author says that the ocean is home to many plants and animals. We can see some of these plants and animals in the photographs. We can use these illustrations to help us make our list.*

- Have volunteers help write on the board a list of plants and animals that live in the ocean.

YOU DO IT

- Have children review **Student Book** pp.15–29. Have them complete an Inference Map to help them analyze and evaluate the details of the story.

- Have children write a title or topic for their chart. Then have them list three details from the story.

- Explain that a reader analyzes the details of a story and evaluates the meaning. Help children write an inference about the three details on their chart. For example, *Many different animals live in the ocean.*

Advanced

I DO IT	**WE** DO IT	**YOU** DO IT
• Read aloud **Student Book** pp.15–17.	• Have children read **Student Book** pp. 20–29.	• Have children review **Student Book** pp.15–29. Have them complete an Inference Map to help them analyze and evaluate the details of the story.
• Point out that using the title and illustrations in a text helps readers identify the author's purpose for writing the story.	• Have children discuss details that help us identify the author's purpose.	• Have children write a title or topic for their chart. Then have them list three details from the story.
• Demonstrate how to preview the illustrations on pp.15–17. Emphasize how the photographs of marine life relate to the title, *At Home in the Ocean*.	• Have partners write lists of marine plants and animals from the story.	• Review that a reader analyzes the details of a story and evaluates the meaning. Have children write an inference about the three details on their chart.

ELL English Language Learners

Use **Projectable S7** to review the **Analyze/Evaluate Strategy**. Explain that good readers examine the information in a story and decide how these details help them better understand the story. Then use the following activities with children according to their level of English proficiency.

Beginning	**Low Intermediate**	**High Intermediate**	**Proficient**
Read aloud **Student Book** pp.15–17. Name animals that appear in the story, and have children point out the corresponding photographs.	Read aloud **Student Book** pp.15–17. Have children read after you. Then ask them to name the marine animals they see in the photographs.	Have children draw a picture of one of the marine animals in the story. Tell them to use the name of this animal in the following sentence frame. *A _____ lives in the ocean.* Have children write this frame at the bottom of their paper. Have them read aloud their sentence.	Have children identify a marine animal from the story. Have them draw a picture of the animal. Then ask them to write a sentence about their animal. For example, *Penguins swim fast.* Have children read aloud their sentence.

Differentiate Phonics and Fluency

Struggling Readers

Phonics

Base Words and -s, -es, -ed, -ing

I DO IT

- Write *pumps* on the board. Read it aloud for children. Underline the base word *pump* and read it. Then point to and circle the *s* and explain that it is an ending added to an action verb.

- Use **Instructional Routine 2** to model how to blend *pumps*. /p/ /ŭ/ /m/ /p/ /s/, pumps Emphasize the last sound /s/ to differentiate *pumps* from *pump*.

- Repeat with *pumped* and *pumping*.

- Use all three words with endings in oral sentences.

- Preview base words with *-s, -es, -ed,* and *-ing* in the **Decodable Reader** selection *Animal Moms*.

WE DO IT

- Write *gulped* on the board.

- Have children use **Letter Cards** to build *gulped*.

- Ask children to identify the letter or letters that stand for each sound: /g/ *g;* /ŭ/ *u;* /l/ *l;* /p/ *p;* /t/ *ed.*

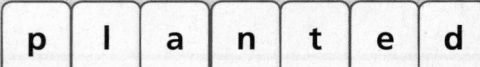

YOU DO IT

- Have children build *gulps, gulping* and *plants, planted* and *planting*.

- Have partners explain the difference in the sounds and the spellings of the words. Then have the partners use the words in oral sentences.

- Offer **Corrective Feedback** as needed.

DAILY ASSESSMENT ▲ 3 2 1 **RtI**

Corrective Feedback

If children lose track of individual sounds as they are blending the longer words with endings, repeat each individual sound, gathering each new one as it is added. Pay particular attention to children's pronunciation of the *-ed* ending. Help them decide which pronunciation is correct by trying each one.

All Levels

Fluency

Phrasing: Punctuation (Comma)

I DO IT

- Write *Far at the bottom of the sea, the water is cold and blue.*

- Model reading the sentence with appropriate phrasing.

- Use a Think Aloud as you insert a slash in the sentence to model separating phrases while reading.

Think Aloud *I see that there is a comma in the sentence. The comma will help me know what words to group together as I read. Far at the bottom is a phrase. I'll put a slash mark between it and of the sea, which is another phrase. The comma tells me to pause before the water is cold, and I'll put a slash after that, before and blue.*

WE DO IT

- On the board, write three sentences with commas from each **Leveled Reader**.

- Look at the first sentence with children. Ask them what the comma tells them. Guide children to understand that it sets off phrases in sentences.

- Have children help you read the sentences with correct phrasing by telling you where to insert slashes to indicate phrases. Provide **Corrective Feedback** as needed.

YOU DO IT

- Have children write the other two sentences in their notebooks. Have them work alone to insert slashes where appropriate. Then partners can offer peer assessment.

- Remind children to pay attention to the commas and the phrasing of each sentence.

- Monitor and provide **Corrective Feedback** as needed.

DAILY ASSESSMENT

Corrective Feedback
Help children with correct phrasing. Remind them to look for commas. Provide a correct answer to an example. *I'll mark up slashes to show where phrases are. Then I'll read groups of words that go together.* **Guide children to repeat the correct phrasing. Then have them read on their own.**

✓ TARGET SKILL
Author's Purpose

✓ TARGET STRATEGY
Analyze/Evaluate

✓ WORDS TO KNOW

blue	live
cold	their
far	water
little	where

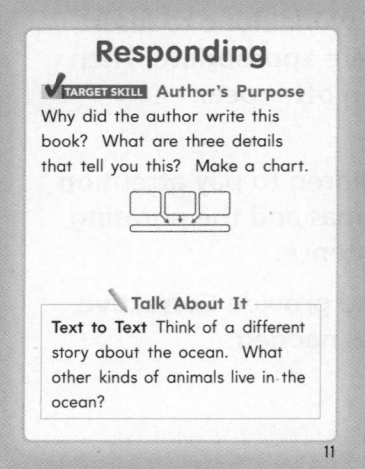

In the Sea, p. 11

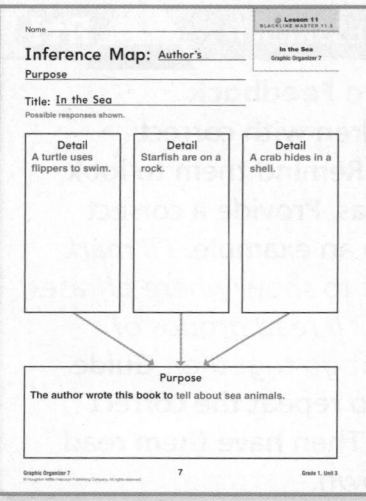

Blackline Master 11.5

Leveled Readers

Struggling Readers

 ### *In the Sea*

SUMMARY A diver explores the sea, both on the top and the bottom to find all kinds of fish and sea creatures.

GENRE: INFORMATIONAL TEXT

Introducing the Text

• Review and discuss this week's Words to Know.

• Preview the photographs and have children talk about the different animals they see. Also have children identify any words on the page they recognize.

• Review that an author has a purpose when writing a book. Remind them that an Inference Map can help them determine the author's purpose.

Supporting the Reading

• **pp. 6–7** *What does the author want you to know about what lives on the floor of the sea? Sample answers: A starfish and crab live on the bottom of the sea. A crab hides in a shell. A starfish clings to a rock.*

• **p. 9** *Why would a diver want to go under the water and look at things? Sample answers: The diver can see things up close and see what kinds of creatures live in the sea. This is the only place to see sea creatures up close.*

Discussing and Revisiting the Text

CRITICAL THINKING Read aloud the top half of Responding p. 11 in *In the Sea*.

• Have partners list facts they learned in *In the Sea*.

• Show children how to list information they learned about sea animals in the top boxes of **Blackline Master 11.5**. Then help them figure out what the author wanted them to learn in *In the Sea*.

FLUENCY: PHRASING Explain that readers pause after a period or comma and read a sentence ending with an exclamation point with excitement. Read aloud pp. 9–10 to model for children.

On Level

Coral Reefs

SUMMARY This book explores a coral reef and the many different fish that live in and around it.

GENRE: INFORMATIONAL TEXT

Introducing the Text

- Review and discuss this week's Words to Know.

- Read the title of *Coral Reefs* and preview the photographs with children. Have them point to the different animals they see that live in a coral reef and help them identify each one.

- Review that an author can write a book to give information. Remind children that an Inference Map can help them determine the author's purpose.

Supporting the Reading

- **p. 6** *What does the author want you to learn on this page? The colorful fish that live in coral reefs like the warm shallow water because they can hide from danger.*

- **p. 10** *Why do we need to save coral reefs? Sample answers: Many different fish live there and we need to protect them. If the reefs die, then the fish that live there will not have a place to be safe and find food.*

Discussing and Revisiting the Text

CRITICAL THINKING Read aloud the top half of Responding p. 11 in *Coral Reefs*.

- Have partners share details they learned in *Coral Reefs*.

- Show children how to list information they learned about coral reefs in the top boxes of **Blackline Master 11.6**. Then help them figure out what the author wanted them to know about coral reefs and record that in the bottom box.

FLUENCY: PHRASING Explain that you pause only slightly after a comma, and you pause a little longer after a period at the end of a sentence. Read aloud p. 10 to model for children.

Responding

✓ **TARGET SKILL** **Author's Purpose** Why did the author write this book? What are three details that tell you this? Make a chart.

▸ **Write About It**
Text to Text Think of another story about the ocean. What did the story tell you about the plants and animals that live in the ocean? Write two sentences with facts you learned.

11

Coral Reefs, p. 11

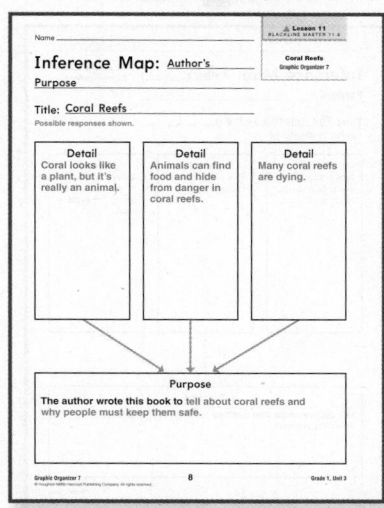

Blackline Master 11.6

TARGET SKILL
Author's Purpose

TARGET STRATEGY
Analyze/Evaluate

WORDS TO KNOW

blue	live
cold	their
far	water
little	where

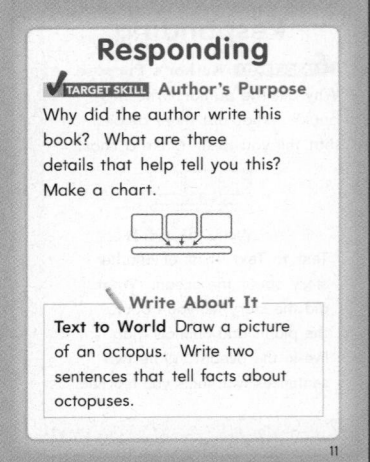

Responding

TARGET SKILL Author's Purpose
Why did the author write this book? What are three details that help tell you this? Make a chart.

Write About It
Text to World Draw a picture of an octopus. Write two sentences that tell facts about octopuses.

11

The Amazing Octopus, p. 11

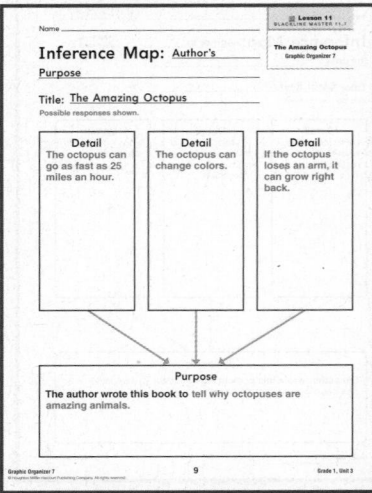

Blackline Master 11.7

Leveled Readers

Advanced

■ *The Amazing Octopus*

SUMMARY This book explores how an octopus moves, what it eats, where it lives, how it protects itself, and what it looks like.

GENRE: INFORMATIONAL TEXT

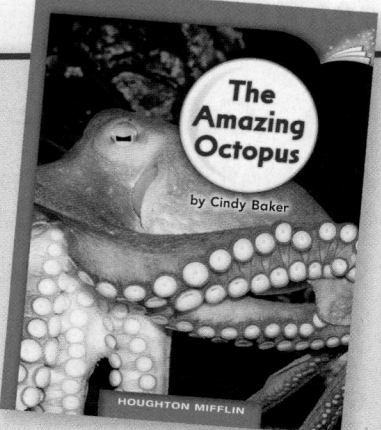

Introducing the Text

• Review and discuss this week's Words to Know.

• Display the cover of *The Amazing Octopus* and read the title. Explain to children that they will learn more about this amazing animal in the book.

• As they read, have children think about why they think the author wrote *The Amazing Octopus*.

Supporting the Reading

• **p. 3** *What does the author want you to learn on these pages? The octopus fills its body with water and pushes it out to go very fast.*

• **pp. 3, 7, 9** *What makes the octopus so amazing? Sample answers: The octopus doesn't look like any other animal. It can change colors. It uses ink to get away from its enemies.*

Discussing and Revisiting the Text

CRITICAL THINKING Have children read the top half of Responding p. 11 in *The Amazing Octopus*.

• Have partners talk about the details the author includes about the octopus.

• Have children list the details and why the author wrote this book on **Blackline Master 11.7**.

FLUENCY: PHRASING Invite children to choose a page to read aloud. Remind them to pause after punctuation and read with expression.

 **English Language Learners**

 ## Life in the Coral Reefs

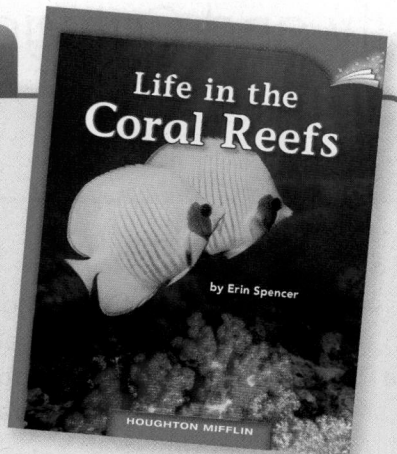

SUMMARY This book explores a coral reef and the many different fish that live in and around it.

GENRE: INFORMATIONAL TEXT

Introducing the Text

• Review and discuss this week's Words to Know.

• Take a picture walk through *Life in the Coral Reefs*. Work with children to identify the fish and other things they see in the selection. Then label the pictures in English.

• Remind children that an author has a purpose for writing. In this book, the author wants to share information.

Supporting the Reading

• **p. 6** *What details do you learn about fish in coral reefs? They like warm water and can hide from danger in the coral.*

• **p. 10** *Why do we need to save coral reefs? They are a place where fish live, and we should work to keep them a long time.*

Discussing and Revisiting the Text

CRITICAL THINKING Help children read the top half of Responding p. 11 in *Life in the Coral Reefs*.

• Have partners share details they learned about coral reefs.

• Ask children to list these details on **Blackline Master 11.8** and write the author's purpose.

FLUENCY: PHRASING Model pausing after periods and commas by reading p. 10 of *Life in the Coral Reefs*. Have children echo-read the page with you.

For more reading options, see ELL Lesson 11, pp. E2–E11.

Responding

✓ **TARGET SKILL** **Author's Purpose**
Why did the author write this book? What are three details that tell you this? Make a chart.

✏ **Write About It**
Text to Text Think of a different story about the ocean. What did the story tell you about the plants and animals that live in the ocean? Write two sentences with facts you learned.

11

Life in the Coral Reefs, p. 11

Name _____

Inference Map: Author's Purpose

Lesson 11
BLACKLINE MASTER 11.8
Life in the Coral Reefs
Graphic Organizer 7

Title: Life in the Coral Reefs
Possible responses shown.

Detail	Detail	Detail
Coral is many small animals that live together.	Many animals can find food and a safe home in coral reefs.	People need to keep coral reefs safe.

Purpose
The author wrote this book to tell about coral reefs.

Graphic Organizer 7   10   Grade 1, Unit 3

Blackline Master 11.8

Differentiate Vocabulary Strategies
Classify and Categorize Color Words

Struggling Readers

I DO IT

- Explain that to *classify* is to put similar things in a group, or category. When children name a group, they are *categorizing*.
- Explain that sorting words into groups and naming the groups is a good way to understand the meanings of words.
- Write the following sentence on the board: *She put on a blue shirt.* Say, *Blue is a color, so I can put it in a group called* colors. *A shirt can go in a group called* clothing.

WE DO IT

- Write the following sentences on the board: *Where are your green pants? Where is your red sweater?* Underline *green, pants, red*, and *sweater*.
- Have children sort the underlined words into two groups. Ask, *Which words will we put in the group of* color words?
- Ask volunteers to name the second group. Ask, *Which words will we put in the group of* clothing words?

YOU DO IT

- Write the following sentences on the board: *Matt wore his black sneakers. Heather bought some yellow jeans.*
- Have children work with partners to sort words into two groups: *color words, clothing words*.
- Challenge children to name a third category (such as *action words* or *people words*) and to place words in it.

On Level

I DO IT

- Explain that to *classify* is to put similar things in a group, or category. Explain that when children name a group, they are *categorizing*.
- Explain that sorting words into groups and naming the groups is a good way to understand the meanings of words. Remind children that they'll need to think about why a word belongs in one group and not in another.

WE DO IT

- Write the following sentences on the board: *A black dog ran to the gate. Three white cats stood on the fence.* Underline *black, dog, white*, and *cats*.
- Say, *I want to categorize these words. I can think of a category for some of them:* animals. Have children name a category for the other underlined words (*colors*).
- Have children sort the four underlined words into the two categories.

YOU DO IT

- Write the following sentences on the board: *Bob grabbed his yellow soccer ball. Sue kicked the ball on the green grass.* Underline the verbs and adjectives.
- Have children work with partners to sort the underlined words into two groups: *colors, actions*.
- Challenge children to name a third category (such as *people* or *things*) and to place words in it.

Advanced

I DO IT

- Remind children that to *classify* is to put similar things in a group, or category. Remind children that when they name a group, they are *categorizing*.

- Explain that sorting words into groups and naming the groups is a good way to understand the meanings of words. Remind children that they should think about why a word belongs in one group and not in another.

WE DO IT

- Write the following sentences on the board: *It was a deep lake. The water was clear and cold.* Underline *lake, water,* and the adjectives.

- Say, *I want to categorize these words. I can think of a category for some of them:* things. Have children name a category for the other underlined words (*description words,* or *adjectives*).

- Have children sort the underlined words into the two categories.

YOU DO IT

- Write several categories on the board, such as *actions, adjectives, animals, places.*

- Have each child write two sentences that include words in one or more of the categories.

- Have children exchange sentences with their partners. They should classify as many words in their partners' sentences as they can, placing the words in the correct categories from the board.

ELL English Language Learners

Group English Language Learners according to language proficiency.

Beginning

- Explain that to *classify* is to put similar things in a group, or category. Explain that when children name a group, they are *categorizing*.

- Say, *Listen to this list: white shirt, green skirt, red socks.*

- Say, *I can make a group of color words. What other group can we make?* clothing

Low Intermediate

- Complete the practice for beginners. Then say, *It was a deep lake. The water was clear and cold.* Underline *lake, water,* and the adjectives.

- Have children classify the words into two groups. Have them describe what they did.

High Intermediate

- Complete the previous practice. Then write on the board: *Tom saw tiny fish, colorful birds, and playful puppies in the pet shop.*

- Underline *fish, birds,* and *puppies.* Ask children to think of a category for these words. Then ask them what other category they could create and name the words from the sentence they would include in it.

Proficient

- Provide children with index cards with the names of different fruits written on it, one per card, and a similar number of index cards with color words, one per card.

- Have children work in pairs to organize the words into two groups. Then have them combine the name of a fruit with a color word.

Options for Reteaching

Reteach Phonics

Digraph *th*

I DO IT
- Tell children that you will review some words that will help them read the **Decodable Reader** selection *Animal Moms* on their own.
- Review **Instructional Routine 2.** Remind children that they have been reading *th* words this week.
- Review this week's Words to Know: *blue, cold, far, little, live, their, water,* and *where.*
- Have children open to p. 21 of *Animal Moms.*

WE DO IT
- Write *This* on the board.
- Help children find the word *This* on the page.
- Model how to decode *This* step by step.

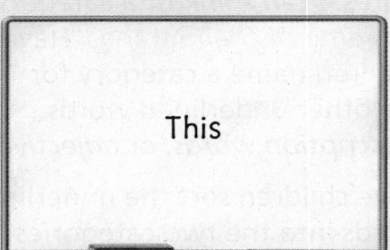

This

YOU DO IT
- Have partners work together to read *Animal Moms.*
- Use the **Corrective Feedback** on p. T82 if children need additional help.

Animal Moms
by James Wong

This mom has pups. She is resting on the rocks with them. Rest, pups. Rest, mom.
21

Reteach Phonics

Base Words and *-s, -es, -ed, -ing*

I DO IT
- Tell children that you will review some words that will help them read **Decodable Reader** selection *Animal Moms* on their own.
- Review **Instructional Routine 2.** Remind children that they have been reading base words with endings *-s, -es, -ed, -ing* this week.
- Review Words to Know *blue, cold, far, little, live, their, water, where.*
- Have children open to p. 21 of *Animal Moms.*

WE DO IT
- Write *pups* on the board.
- Help children find the word *pups* on the page.
- Model how to decode *pups* step by step.

pups

YOU DO IT
- Have partners work together to read *Animal Moms.*
- Use the **Corrective Feedback** on p. T88 if children need additional help.

Animal Moms
by James Wong

This mom has pups. She is resting on the rocks with them. Rest, pups. Rest, mom.
21

Reteach Vocabulary Strategies

Classify and Categorize Color Words

I DO IT

- Remind children that to *classify* is to put similar things in a group or category. Remind children that when they name a group, they are *categorizing*.

- Remind children that sorting words into groups and naming the groups is a good way to understand the meanings of the words.

WE DO IT

- Display **Projectable 11.8**. Read the story aloud.

- Point to the boldface words and have children read them aloud.

Think Aloud *I know some of these words are colors. But a word like* woke *isn't a color. Pam woke early. It's something that Pam did. When a person wakes, she opens her eyes and gets up. That's an action. So I'll name one category Action Words, or just Actions.*

- Have children discuss the third category of words and name it (Clothing, or Clothing words).

YOU DO IT

- Have children work with their partners to classify all the boldface words in **Projectable 11.8**.

- Challenge children to name categories of words that some of the other words could be sorted into (for example, Things, Places, Description Words).

Reteach Comprehension Skill

Author's Purpose

I DO IT

- Remind children that the author is the person who wrote the selection. The author's purpose is the person's reason for writing the selection.

WE DO IT

- Have children read aloud **Student Book** pp. 16–19.

- Model how to identify the author and infer the author's purpose.

Think Aloud *On the first page, I see the title,* At Home in the Ocean, *and the words "by Rozanne Lanczak Williams." The word* by *tells me that name is the author. The photographs and words in the selection are about different animals that live in the sea. I think the author's purpose is to teach about sea animals.*

- Help volunteers infer the author's purpose for writing *At Home in the Ocean*.

YOU DO IT

- Distribute **Graphic Organizer 7: Inference Map**.

- Have children fill in the author's purpose and details that support it. *Details: photographs of sea animals; tells kinds of animals; tells what animals do. Purpose: teach about sea animals.*

- Have children work in pairs to complete the graphic organizer.

- Review the completed graphic organizers together.

 **Journeys**

 **Go Digital**

See pages xvi-xvii in this Teacher's Edition for the full digital offering.

*my*SmartPlanner
Plan Across Disciplines, Schedule, Organize

 **my WriteSmart**

Write, Collaborate, Respond

Online Assessment
Assess, Prescribe, Remediate, Report

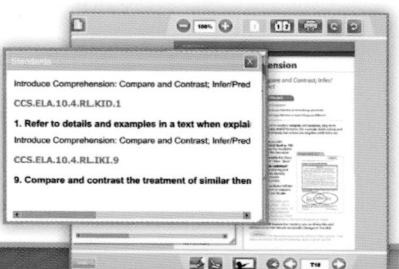

CHALLENGE

Research Rain Forests

After reading the selection "How Leopard Got His Spots," ask children to research rain forests.

- Ask children what they know about rain forests. Help them create a word web as they brainstorm ideas related to rain forests, such as parrots, trees, and snakes. Ask them to choose one of the ideas to research.
- Give children access to books or an online resource to research their ideas. Tell them to include descriptions to make their writing clear.
- Ask children to write and draw pictures to show what they learned. Guide them to collect their papers into one book called "All About Rain Forests."

Folktale

SCIENCE

Connection to Informational Text

SPOTTED OR STRIPED? "How Leopard Got His Spots" explains how animals got their stripes and spots. Ask: *Do you know any striped or spotted animals that live in the state?* Help children use books or online resources to find names and pictures of animals in your state or region that have stripes or spots. Ask children to look for as many different kinds of animals as they can. Ask: *Are there any striped or spotted bugs, birds, fish, mammals, or reptiles?* Draw a two-column chart on the board and fill it out with the names of the animals children found. List spotted animals in one column and striped animals in the other column.
Common Core, *English Language Arts:* W.1.7
participate in shared research and writing projects

 **JOURNEYS**

READING LITERATURE

RL.1.1 ask and answer questions about key details

RL.1.2 retell stories and demonstrate understanding of the message or lesson

READING INFORMATIONAL TEXT

RI.1.5 know and use text features to locate facts or information

RI.1.9 identify similarities in and differences between texts on the same topic

FOUNDATIONAL SKILLS

RF.1.2b orally produce single-syllable words by blending sounds

RF.1.2c isolate and pronounce sounds in spoken single-syllable words

RF.1.2d segment spoken single-syllable words into their complete sequence of individual sounds

RF.1.3a know the spelling-sound correspondences for common consonant digraphs

RF.1.3g recognize and read irregularly spelled words

RF.1.4a read on-level text with purpose and understanding

RF.1.4b read on-level text orally with accuracy, appropriate rate, and expression

WRITING

W.1.2 write informative/explanatory texts

SPEAKING AND LISTENING

SL.1.1c ask question to clear up confusion about topics and texts under discussion

SL.1.4 describe people, places, things, and events with details/express ideas and feelings clearly

LANGUAGE

L.1.1h use determiners

L.1.1j produce and expand simple and compound declarative, interrogative, imperative, and exclamatory sentences

L.1.1a print upper- and lowercase letters

L.1.2d use conventional spelling for words with common spelling patterns and for frequently occurring irregular words

L.1.2e spell untaught words phonetically, drawing on phonemic awareness and spelling conventions

L.1.4a use sentence-level context as a clue to the meaning of a word or phrase

L.1.5b define words by category and by key attributes

LESSON 12

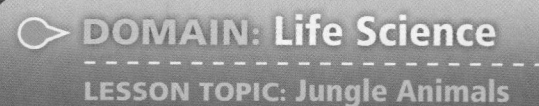 **Our Focus Wall**

ANCHOR TEXT

How Leopard Got His Spots
Folktale

Read Together

The Rain Forest
Informational Text

ESSENTIAL QUESTION

How are jungle animals different from animals on a farm?

FOUNDATIONAL SKILLS

☑ Words to Know
HIGH-FREQUENCY WORDS

been	brown	know
never	off	out
own	very	

Phonics

Digraphs *ch*, *tch*

Possessives with *'s*
Phonogram -*atch*

ch
_tch

Fluency

Rate

READING LITERATURE & INFORMATIONAL TEXT

Comprehension Skills and Strategies

☑ **TARGET SKILL**
- Sequence of Events
- Story Lesson

☑ **TARGET STRATEGY**
- Question

WRITING

Writing

Informative Writing: Instructions

Focus Trait: Sentence Fluency

LANGUAGE

Spelling

Digraphs *ch tch*

chin	chip
chop	rich
much	chick

Grammar

Commands

Vocabulary Strategies

Homophones

WHOLE GROUP

∨ Reading

ANCHOR TEXT

🕊 **DOMAIN: Life Science**

LESSON TOPIC: Jungle Animals

How Leopard Got His Spots
Folktale

Children will read *How Leopard Got His Spots* to
- review events in order.
- discuss the aspects of a folktale, including its origins as an oral tradition.

The Rain Forest
Informational Text

Children will read *The Rain Forest* to
- learn about the ecosystem of the rain forest.
- understand how to use a map.

∨ Language Arts

⦿ Grammar

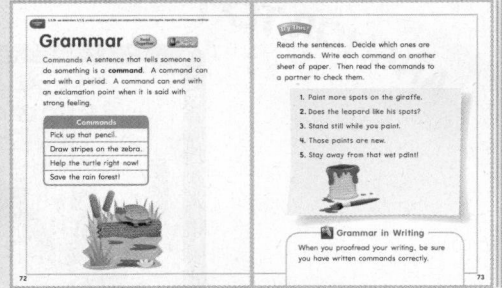

Children learn about imperative sentences through reading and writing commands.

⦿ Writing

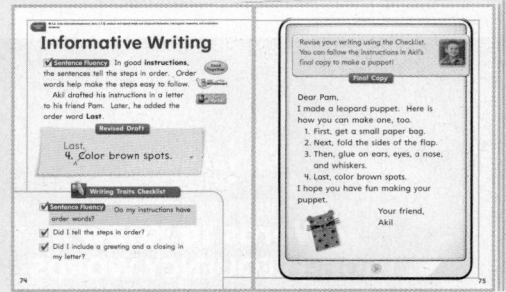

Children write instructions in a letter using *How Leopard Got His Spots* as a model for sequencing correctly.

⚠ TEXT COMPLEXITY RUBRIC

Overall Text Complexity		How Leopard Got His Spots **FOLKTALE**	The Rain Forest **INFORMATIONAL TEXT**
		ACCESSIBLE	**MORE COMPLEX**
Quantitative Measures	Lexile	390	550
	Guided Reading Level	F	I
Qualitative Measures	Text Structure	Less familiar story concepts	Somewhat complex science concepts
	Language Conventionality and Clarity	Some natural dialogue	Increased unfamiliar or academic words
	Knowledge Demands	Some cultural and literary knowledge useful	Specialized knowledge required
	Purpose/Levels of Meaning	Single level of meaning	Implied, but easy to identify from context

∨ Additional Whole Group Resources

○ Decodable Readers

Scratch, Chomp
by Edward Bonfant
Illustrated by Rick Brown

Chuck and his dad went off on a trip. At Finch Pond, Chuck and his dad played catch. Chuck has a fast pitch.

27

- *Scratch, Chomp*, pp. 27–32
- *Rich Gets a Dog*, pp. 33–38
- *Champs*, pp. 39–44
- *Kits, Chicks, and Pups*, pp. 45–50

○ Progress Monitoring

Assess and monitor children's progress to determine who is on track and who needs help. Clear prescriptions identify targeted instruction to address children's needs and get them back on track.

Respond to Assessment
- ☑ Vocabulary, p. T176
- ☑ Phonics, T176
- ☑ Comprehension, p. T177
- ☑ Language Arts, p. T177
- ☑ Fluency, p. T177

Lesson resources organized by week.

○ Lesson 12 Blackline Masters
- Home Letter 12.1
- Weekly To-Do List 12.2
- Vocabulary Word Cards 12.3
- Words to Know 12.4
- Leveled Reader Graphic Organizers 12.5–12.8
- Leveled Practice for Words to Know and Phonics SR12.1–SR12.4, A12.1–A12.4, ELL12.1–ELL12.4
- Weekly Tests 12.1–12.14

○ Assessment
- Weekly Tests Answer Key
- Observation Checklists
- Fluency Tests
- Periodic Assessments

○ Additional Resources
- Reading Log
- Vocabulary Log
- Listening Log
- Proofreading Checklist
- Writing Conference Form
- Writing Checklist
- Instructional Routines
- Graphic Organizer Blackline Masters
- Handwriting Models

Go Digital

FOR STUDENTS

my WriteSmart

- eBook
- GrammarSnap Videos
- Destination Reading
- Context Cards

FOR TEACHERS

- Teacher One-Stop
- Interactive Whiteboard Lessons
- Literacy and Language Guide

- Lesson 12 Blackline Masters
- Additional Resources
- Assessment

SMALL GROUP

▼ Weekly Leveled Readers

 **Struggling Readers**

Guided Reading Level: E
Lexile: 310
DRA: 8

Giraffe's Neck
by Denise Carter
illustrated by Timothy Banks
HOUGHTON MIFFLIN

 **On Level**

Guided Reading Level: H
Lexile: 480
DRA: 14

Bear's Tail
by Dermot McManus
illustrated by
Eileen Hine
HOUGHTON MIFFLIN

 **Advanced**

Guided Reading Level: L
Lexile: 530
DRA: 24

Peacock's Tail
by Patrick Doherty
illustrated by Stephan Daigle
HOUGHTON MIFFLIN

 **English Language Learners**

Guided Reading Level: H
Lexile: 250
DRA: 14

Bear's Long, Brown Tail
by Dermot McManus
illustrated by
Eileen Hine
HOUGHTON MIFFLIN

Leveled Reader Teacher's Guides

8-page lessons for each book support instruction in guided reading groups

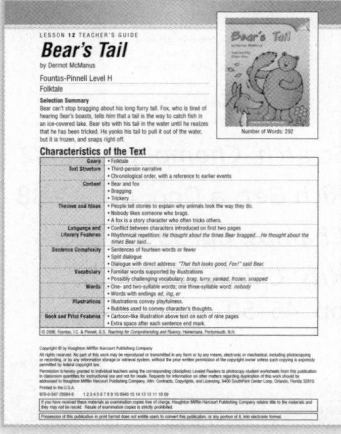

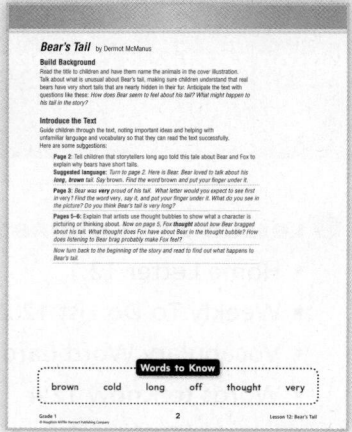

Vocabulary Reader
for all levels

Guided Reading Level: D
Lexile: 90
DRA: 6

Spots
by Heather Gray
HOUGHTON MIFFLIN

What My Other Students Are Doing

my WriteSmart — Performance Task

- Write About Reading
- Informative Writing
- Research and Media Literacy
- Unit Performance Assessment, Task 2 of 5

Literacy Centers

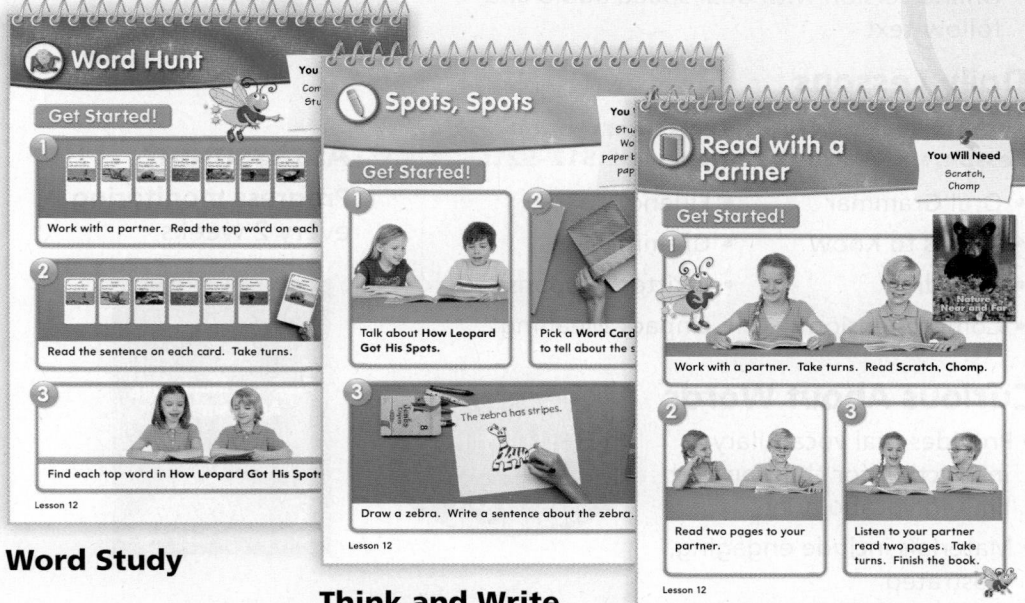

Word Hunt

Get Started!

1. Work with a partner. Read the top word on each

2. Read the sentence on each card. Take turns.

3. Find each top word in How Leopard Got His Spots.

Lesson 12

Word Study

Spots, Spots

Get Started!

1. Talk about How Leopard Got His Spots.

2. Pick a Word Card to tell about the s

3. The zebra has stripes. Draw a zebra. Write a sentence about the zebra.

Lesson 12

Think and Write

Read with a Partner

You Will Need
Scratch, Chomp

Get Started!

1. Work with a partner. Take turns. Read Scratch, Chomp.

2. Read two pages to your partner.

3. Listen to your partner read two pages. Take turns. Finish the book.

Lesson 12

Comprehension and Fluency

Reader's Notebook

Includes practice for:

- Text analysis and citing text evidence
- Words to Know
- Phonics
- Spelling
- Grammar
- Writing Traits

HOUGHTON MIFFLIN HARCOURT

JOURNEYS
COMMON CORE
Reader's Notebook

GRADE 1
Volume 1

Go Digital

FOR STUDENTS

- Leveled Readers Online
- Vocabulary Reader Online

FOR TEACHERS

- Teacher One-Stop
- Literacy and Language Guide
- Leveled Readers Database
- Leveled Reader Teacher's Guides

Grab-and-Go!

- Lesson 12 Blackline Masters
- Additional Resources
- Assessment

Go Digital

FOR STUDENTS

- Write-in Reader eBook
- Vocabulary Reader Online
- Struggling Readers Leveled Reader Online

FOR TEACHERS

- Leveled Reader Teacher's Guide

Grab-and-Go!

- Struggling Readers Blackline Masters

RtI INTERVENTION

Strategic Intervention: TIER II

Use these materials to provide additional targeted instruction for children who need Tier II strategic intervention.

Write-In Reader:
Al and Lop

- Engaging selection connects to main topic
- Interactive worktext reinforces this week's vocabulary and comprehension
- Opportunities for student interaction
- Builds the foundational skills for reading more complex texts
- Online version with dual-speed audio and follow-text

Daily Lessons

For this week's daily Strategic Intervention Lesson, see Teacher's Edition pages S12–S21:

- Oral Grammar
- Words to Know
- Decoding
- Comprehension
- Fluency
- Grammar
- Written Response
- Unpack Meaning

Assessment

Progress monitoring every 2 weeks.

Curious About Words

- Provides oral vocabulary instruction for children with limited vocabularies.
- Materials include engaging, illustrated Read Alouds with Teacher Manual.
- Teaches high-utility, research-based words, including academic vocabulary.
- Assessment includes weekly pretests and posttests.

Intensive Intervention: TIER III

Interactive lessons provide support for

- Phonics and Word Study Skills
- Vocabulary
- Comprehension
- Fluency

- Lesson cards for small-group or individual instruction
- Blackline masters for additional practice

- Leveled books for additional reading and skill application
- Lesson assessments evaluate the effectiveness of the intervention

English Language Learners *At a Glance*

 **ENGLISH LANGUAGE LEARNERS**

⌄ Whole Group

Use these resources to help English Language Learners access the core content with the whole group.

 **Go Digital**

Point-of-Use Scaffolded Support

- Use Visuals
- Use Gestures
- Comprehensible Input
- Peer-Supported Learning
- Language Issues
- Idiomatic Language
- Use Sentence Frames
- Expand Language Production

Vocabulary in Context Cards

brown
Some hyenas have brown fur.

brown

What Does It Mean?
Brown is a color. Tree bark and mud are brown.

How Do I Use It?
The cow is white and brown. What brown things do you see in your classroom?

Talk It Over.
Think about animals you know that are brown. Make a list of five brown animals. Talk about your list with a partner.

Go Digital

front   back

FOR STUDENTS

- ELL Leveled Reader Online
- Vocabulary Reader Online
- Cross-Curricular Activity Bank
- Multimedia Grammar Glossary
- Picture Card Bank Online

FOR TEACHERS

- ELD Station Online
- Leveled Readers Database
- Leveled Reader Teacher's Guide

 **Grab-and-Go!**

- ELL Blackline Masters

⌄ Small Group

Use these resources to help English Language Learners access the core content with a smaller group.

ELL Leveled Reader

- Contains the same content as the On-Level Reader but uses more accessible language
- ELL Leveled Reader Lesson Plan
- ELL Blackline Masters

Bear's Long, Brown Tail
by Dermot McManus
illustrated by Eileen Hine
HOUGHTON MIFFLIN

⌄ ELL Extra Support

Use these additional resources to support English Language Learners as needed.

ELL Lesson 12 Resources

- Daily Lessons to support the core
- Language Support Card 12
- ELL Blackline Masters
- ELL Teacher's Handbook
    Professional Development
    Peer Conferences Forms
    Cooperative Learning Guidelines

How Leopard Got His Spots   Language Support Card — Lesson 12

Building Background

Video Clip for Lesson 12:
Rainforest Animals

LESSON 12 Literacy Centers

 **COMMON CORE** Managing Independent Activities

Comprehension and Fluency

Materials

- Decodable Reader: *Scratch, Chomp*
- Student Book and Audio: *How Leopard Got His Spots*
- Crayons, paper, pencil

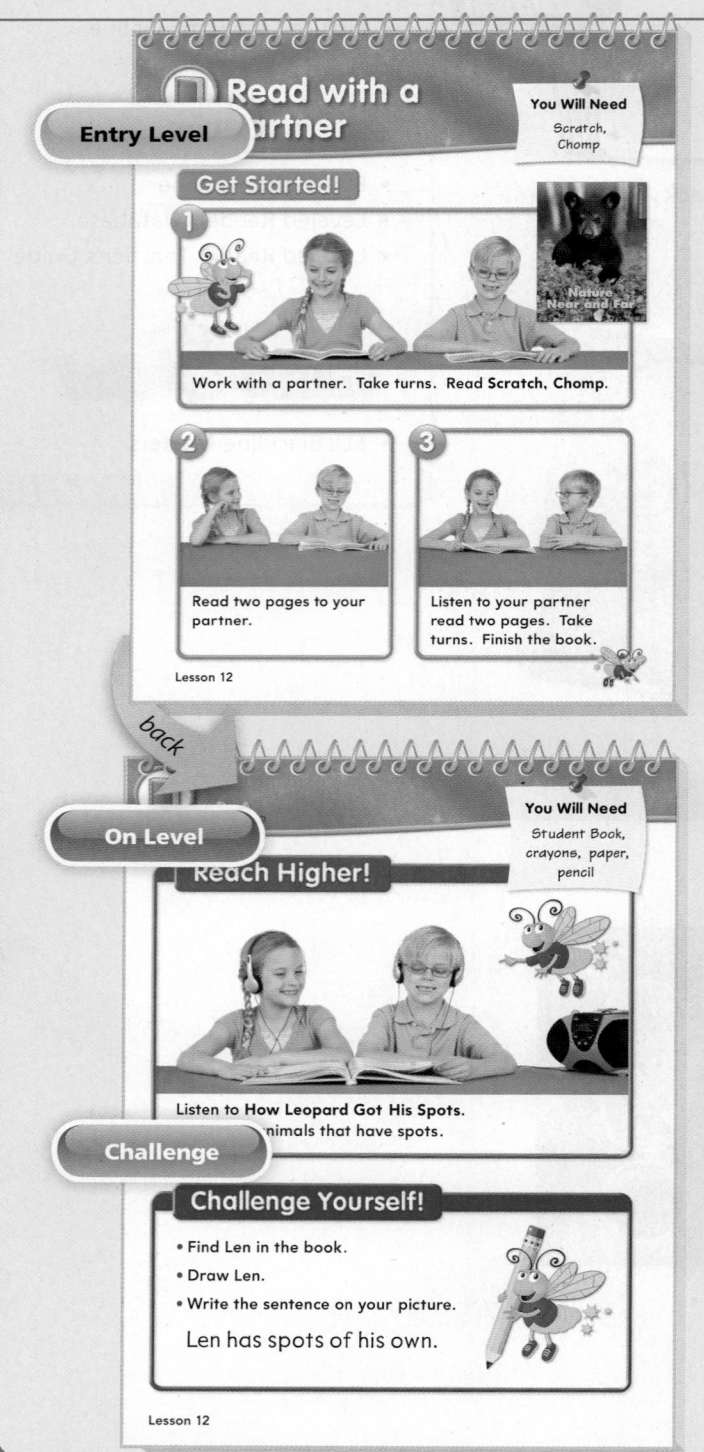

Read with a Partner

Entry Level

You Will Need
Scratch, Chomp

Get Started!

1. Work with a partner. Take turns. Read **Scratch, Chomp**.
2. Read two pages to your partner.
3. Listen to your partner read two pages. Take turns. Finish the book.

Lesson 12

back

On Level

You Will Need
Student Book, crayons, paper, pencil

Reach Higher!

Listen to **How Leopard Got His Spots**. ... animals that have spots.

Challenge

Challenge Yourself!

- Find Len in the book.
- Draw Len.
- Write the sentence on your picture.

Len has spots of his own.

Lesson 12

Word Study

Materials

- Context Cards: *been, brown, know, never, off, out, own, very*
- High-Frequency Word Cards: *been, brown, know, never, off, out, own, very*
- Student Book
- Crayons, pencil, paper

Word Hunt

Entry Level

You Will Need
Context Cards, Student Book

Get Started!

1. Work with a partner. Read the top word on each card.
2. Read the sentence on each card. Take turns.
3. Find each top word in **How Leopard Got His Spots**.

Lesson 12

back

On Level

You Will Need
Word Cards, crayons, paper, pencil

Reach Higher!

Work with a partner. Pick up two cards. Use both words in a sentence. ...ards back. Take turns.

Challenge

Challenge Yourself!

- Write the question.
- Write and finish the answer.

What animal has spots?

A _____ has spots.

Lesson 12

Use Literacy Centers to support this week's Common Core focus. Each center contains three activities. Children who experience success with the entry-level activity move on to the on-level and challenge activities, as time permits.

Think and Write

Materials
- Student Book
- Paper bag
- Crayons

- High-Frequency Word Cards: *been, brown, know, never, off, out, own, very*

- Paper
- Pencil

Spots, Spots

Entry Level

You Will Need
Student Book, Word Cards, paper bag, crayons, paper, pencil

Get Started!

1 Talk about **How Leopard Got His Spots.**

2 Pick a **Word Card.** Use it to tell about the story.

3 The zebra has stripes.

Draw a zebra. Write a sentence about the zebra.

Lesson 12

On Level

You Will Need
crayons, paper, pencil

Reach Higher!

giraffe

leopard

Draw a picture of an animal that has big spots. Draw a picture of an animal that has ___. Label your pictures.

Challenge

Challenge Yourself!

- Look at your pictures.
- Write a sentence about each picture you drew.

Lesson 12

Go Digital

FOR STUDENTS

my WriteSmart

Children complete performance tasks related to the week's instruction.

eBook
Children read and listen to *How Leopard Got His Spots* and *The Rain Forest,* generate questions about jungle animals, and reread the texts to enjoy a folktale and to deepen their knowledge.

Leveled Readers Online
Children read and listen to **Leveled Readers,** reinforcing lesson's Target Vocabulary, Target Skill, and Target Strategy.

Destination Reading
Children practice and apply key lesson skills through gamelike activities.

GrammarSnap Videos
Children practice and apply understanding of commands.

Read

Independent Reading

Have children read daily from a self-selected trade book and record their progress in their Reading Log.

See p. T153 for support in guiding children to select an appropriate book.

Whole Group

		DAY 1	**DAY 2**	**DAY 3**
Daily Language	• Opening Routines • Oral Vocabulary • Listening Comprehension • Phonemic Awareness • Speaking and Listening	**Opening Routines,** T110–T111 • Phonemic Awareness • High-Frequency Words • Vocabulary Boost **Read Aloud,** "Turtle, Frog, and Rat," T112–T113 **Introduce Oral Vocabulary** **Phonemic Awareness,** T114	**Opening Routines,** T136–T137 • Phonemic Awareness • High-Frequency Words • Vocabulary Boost **Phonemic Awareness,** T138	**Opening Routines,** T146–T147 • Phonemic Awareness • High-Frequency Words • Vocabulary Boost **Phonemic Awareness,** T148
Vocabulary **Text-Based Comprehension** • Skills and Strategies • Craft and Structure **Research and Media Literacy**		**Read**  ☑ **Introduce Words to Know** High-Frequency Words, T118–T119 ☑ **Read and Comprehend,** T120–T121 **FIRST READ Think Through the Text** Read the Anchor Text: *How Leopard Got His Spots,* T122–T133	**Read**  ☑ **Dig Deeper: How to Analyze the Text,** T140–T141 • Sequence of Events • Story Lesson **SECOND READ Analyze the Text** Reread the Anchor Text: *How Leopard Got His Spots,* T122–T131 **Your Turn,** T142–T143	**Read**  **Independent Reading,** T152–T153 • Reader's Guide: *How Leopard Got His Spots* • Self-Selected Reading **Apply Vocabulary Knowledge,** T154–T155
Foundational Skills • Phonics and Word Recognition • Fluency		☑ **Phonics** Words with Digraphs *ch, tch,* T114–T116 **Read** *Scratch, Chomp,* T117 ☑ **Fluency** Model Rate, T112	☑ **Phonics** Words wth Digraphs *ch, tch,* T138 **Read** *Rich Gets a Dog,* T139 ☑ **Fluency** Practice Rate, T139	☑ **Phonics** Possessives with *'s,* T148–T149 **Read** *Champs,* T150 ☑ **Fluency** Rate, T151

Whole Group Language Arts

Spelling Grammar Writing		☑ **Spelling** Words with *ch, tch,* T134 Pretest ☑ **Grammar** Introduce Commands, T134 Daily Proofreading Practice, T135 ☑ **Informative Writing: Instructions** Introduce the Model, T135	☑ **Spelling** Word Sort, T144 ☑ **Grammar** Writing Commands, T144 Daily Proofreading Practice, T145 ☑ **Informative Writing: Instructions** Focus Trait: Sentence Fluency, T145	☑ **Spelling** Segment Sounds, T156 ☑ **Grammar** Commands, T156 Daily Proofreading Practice, T157 ☑ **Informative Writing: Instructions** Prewriting, T157

Small Group

Suggestions for Small Groups (See pp. T179–T197.)   **3 2 1 RtI** Suggestions for Intervention (See pp. S12–S21.)

COMMON CORE **State Standards**	RL.1.1, RL.1.5, RL.1.10, RF.1.2b, RF.1.3a, RF.1.3g, RF.1.4b, W.1.2, W.1.5, SL.1.1a, SL.1.2, SL.1.6, L.1.1j, L.1.2e	RL.1.2, RL.1.3, RF.1.2b, RF.1.3a, RF.1.3g, RF.1.4b, W.1.2, SL.1.1b, SL.1.6, L.1.1h, L.1.1j, L.1.2d, L.1.5a	RL.1.1, RL.1.3, RF.1.3b, RF.1.3g, RF.1.4a, RF.1.4b, W.1.2, W.1.5, SL.1.1a, L.1.1h, L.1.1j, L.1.5b, L.1.5c, L.1.6

DAY 4

Opening Routines, T158–T159
- Phonemic Awareness
- High-Frequency Words
- Vocabulary Boost

Phonemic Awareness, T160

Connect to the Topic
- Read Informational Text: *The Rain Forest,* T162
- Think Through the Text, T162
- ☑ **Compare Texts,** T163
- ☑ **Vocabulary Strategies,** T164–T165

☑ **Phonics**
- Words with Digraphs *ch, tch*, T160
- Possessives with *'s*, T160
- Phonogram *-atch*, T160

Read *Kits, Chicks, and Pups,* T161

☑ **Fluency**
Rate, T151

☑ **Spelling**
Connect to Writing, T166

☑ **Grammar**
Spiral Review: Complete Sentences, T166
Daily Proofreading Practice, T167

☑ **Informative Writing: Instructions**
Drafting, T167

 Suggestions for English Language Learners (See pp. E12–E21.)

RI.1.2, RI.1.5, RI.1.10, RF.1.3a, RF.1.3g, RF.1.4b, W.1.2, W.1.5, SL.1.1a, L.1.1c, L.1.1j, L.1.2d, L.1.4a, L.1.6

DAY 5

Opening Routines, T168–T169
- Phonemic Awareness
- High-Frequency Words
- Vocabulary Boost

Phonemic Awareness, T169
Speaking and Listening, T171

Extend the Topic
- Domain-Specific Vocabulary, T170
- Speaking and Listening: Giving Clear Descriptions, T171
- Optional Second Read: *The Rain Forest,* T162

☑ **Phonics**
- Words with Digraphs *ch, tch*, T176
- Possessives with *'s*, T176
- Phonogram *-atch*, T176

☑ **Fluency**
Rate, T151

☑ **Spelling**
Assess, T172

☑ **Grammar**
Weekly Review: Commands, T172–T173
Daily Proofreading Practice, T174

☑ **Informative Writing: Instructions**
Revising and Proofreading, T174–T175

RL.1.3, RF.1.3g, W.1.2, W.1.5, SL.1.1c, SL.1.3, SL.1.4, L.1.1h, L.1.1j, L.1.2d, L.1.6

FOR STUDENTS

- eBook
- GrammarSnap Videos
- Destination Reading
- Context Cards

FOR TEACHERS
- Teacher One-Stop
- Interactive Whiteboard Lessons
- Literacy and Language Guide

- Lesson 12 Blackline Masters
- Additional Resources
- Assessment

DAY 1

Today's Goals

Vocabulary & Oral Language
- Teacher Read Aloud: "Turtle, Frog, and Rat"
- Oral Vocabulary
- Listening Comprehension
- Model Fluency

Phonemic Awareness
- Blend and Segment Phonemes

Phonics & Fluency
- Words with Digraphs *ch, tch*
- Read Decodable Reader: *Scratch, Chomp*
- Fluency: Rate

☑ **WORDS TO KNOW**

been	off
brown	out
know	own
never	very

Text-Based Comprehension
- Read and Comprehend
- Read the Anchor Text: *How Leopard Got His Spots*

Grammar & Writing
- Commands
- ➡ Informative Writing: Instructions

Spelling
- Words with *ch, tch*

 **COMMON CORE**
RF.1.2b orally produce single-syllable words by blending sounds; **RF.1.2d** segment spoken single-syllable words into their complete sequence of individual sounds; **RF.1.3g** recognize and read irregularly spelled words; **SL.1.1a** follow rules for discussions; **SL.1.6** produce complete sentences when appropriate to task and situation; **L.1.6** use words and phrases acquired through conversations, reading and being read to, and responding to texts

Opening Routines

Warm Up with Wordplay

Share a Riddle

Display and read the following riddle:

> ## Why don't leopards play hide-and-seek?

Have children discuss possible responses. Remind children to listen carefully to each other and to build on each others' comments. Then provide the answer: *because they would be spotted!*

Point out that this riddle works because the word *spotted* is used in two ways: it names the markings on a leopard's fur, and it tells about the action of seeing something. Have children use each meaning of *spotted* in a sentence.

▬ SL.1.1a, SL.1.6

Daily Phonemic Awareness

Blend and Segment Phonemes

- *I'm going to say the sounds in a word and blend them. Then you say the word. Ready? Listen: /t/ /ă/ /n/. What is the word? tan Good. Now let's do some more.*

- Have children do the blending with you and then by themselves.

/ch/ /ŏ/ /p/ *chop*	/b/ /ă/ /th/ *bath*	/m/ /ŭ/ ch/ *much*
/r/ /ĭ/ /ch/ *rich*	/th/ /ĕ/ /n/ *then*	/k/ /ă/ /ch/ *catch*
/ch/ /ā/ /n/ *chain*	/d/ /ĭ/ /ch/ *ditch*	/ch/ /ĭ/ /k/ *chick*

- Reverse the process. Say each word below and have children repeat it. *How many sounds are in the word? three Say the first sound. . . . Say the middle sound. . . . Say the last sound.*

chop   bath   much   rich   then   catch   chain   ditch   chick

🔊 **RF.1.2b, RF.1.2d**

Corrective Feedback

- Model the task. *The word is* rich. *Listen: /r/ /ĭ/ /ch/. What is the word?* rich

- Have children do the blending with you before doing it on their own.

- Back up several words and continue the game.

Daily High-Frequency Words

Introduce

- Point to the Words to Know on the Focus Wall. *Our Words to Know for this week are* been, brown, know, never, off, out, own, *and* very. *You are going to see these words in your reading.*

- Use **Instructional Routine 10** and the **High-Frequency Word Card** to introduce the word *been.*

- Repeat the procedure with the words *brown, know, never, off, out, own,* and *very.* 🔊 **RF.1.3g**

Corrective Feedback

- Say the correct word and have children repeat it. Been. *What is the word?* been

- Have children spell the word. *b, e, e, n How do we say this word?* been

- Have children reread all of the cards in random order.

Daily Vocabulary Boost

- Demonstrate fluent reading by reading aloud the **Big Book** *Beetle Bop.* Tell children to listen carefully for the word *beetle.* Then reread the story and ask children to join in. Stop after each page and ask a volunteer to point to the word *beetle.*

- Review words that may be unfamiliar to children. Guide them to determine what words mean from how they are used in a sentence or appear in a picture.

- Have children discuss beetles using previously discussed vocabulary, such as *forests, predators, dashing,* or *beautiful.* Encourage them to talk about beetles they like or any experiences they have had with beetles in nature. Remind them to stay on topic and follow classroom rules for discussion. 🔊 **SL.1.1a, SL.1.6**

Teacher Read Aloud

▶ SHARE OBJECTIVES

- Listen for fast or slow reading.
- Answer questions about a text read aloud.
- Follow rules for discussions.

Model Fluency

- Explain that readers may read at different rates, or speeds. They should read easy, short, and familiar words faster than hard, long, or unfamiliar words. *As you read aloud, you will be able to skim easy and familiar words. You will need more time with new and harder words.*

- Read the sixth paragraph of the story "Turtle, Frog, and Rat" aloud, slowing for long words such as *unfortunate*. Have children put their hands out (as in "slow down") when they hear words read more slowly.

- *When did you hear me read words more slowly? Why did that happen?*

- Read the entire selection aloud. Ask children to listen to find out what happens to Turtle, Frog, and Rat.

COMMON CORE **SL.1.1a** follow rules for discussions; **SL.1.1b** build on others' talk in conversations by responding to others' comments; **SL.1.2** ask and answer questions about details in a text read aloud, information presented orally, or through other media

Turtle, Frog, and Rat

Long ago, Turtle, Frog, and Rat were best friends. They lived together in a lovely house made of woven grasses, with a wide **view** of the ocean. When they felt **frisky**, they would dance and sing or play hide-and-seek with bugs. When they felt relaxed, they would drink tea and talk.

The friends spent many happy evenings complimenting each other.

"You have beautiful flat eyes," Turtle and Rat told Frog.

"No one has a smoother shell than you," Rat and Frog told Turtle.

1 "Your tail is so long and furry," Frog and Turtle told Rat.

One night, after days of rain, the friends had an unfortunate **adventure**. A flood rushed toward their house! Turtle and Frog were strong swimmers, so they were in no danger.

2 Rat did not swim as well as his friends, so he ran to the forest and climbed a tall tree to safety. There, he met a beautiful lady rat. She thought that his furry tail was handsome. They fell in love, married, and built a tree house together.

After the floodwaters went down and some time had passed, Rat went to check on his friends. The grass house had washed away, but Frog and Turtle were living in a fine new house with mud walls and a roof made from a giant leaf.

3 Rat told them, "I made a new home in the forest and now I have a wife. Will you come meet her?"

Introduce Oral Vocabulary

Use **Instructional Routine 16** to define each highlighted oral vocabulary word.

- Discuss the meaning of each word as it is used in the selection.

- For additional support and reinforcement, have children look up each word in a children's dictionary.

view what you can see from a certain place • *They lived together in a lovely house made of woven grasses, with a wide view of the ocean.*

frisky playful and full of energy • *When they felt frisky, they would dance and sing or play hide-and-seek with bugs.*

The friends agreed and went off together.

At Rat's tree, Frog and Turtle realized that it was too high for them. Rat thought for a moment and had an idea.

"You can grab my tail with your jaws," he said to Turtle, "and I will pull you up." Turtle **shivered** with fear, but he agreed and took Rat's tail in his mouth. Rat started to climb.

When they were nearly at the top, Turtle opened his mouth to say hello to Rat's wife. When he did, he lost his grip and **tumbled** down. As he fell, his sharp beak slid along Rat's tail and accidentally pulled off all the hair. When he landed, Turtle's smooth shell cracked all over. Frog **spied** the whole thing. He was so upset by what he saw that his eyes bulged out in alarm.

"I'm not hurt," said Turtle. "But my beautiful shell is ruined. Now it looks cracked!"

"It's not ruined!" said Frog. "Your shell is much more interesting now than when it was smooth. But look what happened to my eyes!"

"I like your bulging eyes," said Rat. "Now you can keep them above the water when you swim. But my tail, just look at my tail!" he wailed. "My wife won't love me without a thick, furry tail!"

"Don't be silly," his wife said. "I love you for who you are, not what you look like."

So Rat, Turtle, and Frog got used to their new looks and stayed friends forever. But to this day, turtles still have shells that look cracked, frogs have bulging eyes, and rats have hairless tails. **4**

adventure an exciting or dangerous experience • *One night, after days of rain, the friends had an unfortunate adventure.*

shivered shook with cold or fear • *Turtle shivered with fear, but he agreed and took Rat's tail in his mouth.*

tumbled fell suddenly • *When he did, he lost his grip and tumbled down.*

spied saw something • *Frog spied the whole thing.*

Listening Comprehension

Read aloud the story. Pause at the numbered stopping points to ask children the questions below. Discuss the meanings of the highlighted words, as needed, to support the discussion.
SL.1.2

1 *At the beginning of the story, what is special about each animal? Sample answer: Turtle has a smooth shell, Frog has flat eyes, and Rat has a furry tail.* **CHARACTER TRAITS**

2 *What was the unfortunate adventure that happened to the three friends? a flood* **IDENTIFY STORY STRUCTURE**

3 *How did life change for each of the three friends after the flood? Sample answer: Rat moved into a tree with his new wife. Frog and Turtle had a fine new house.* **UNDERSTANDING CHARACTERS**

4 *What lesson does the author want us to think about? Sample answer: Although we might compliment our friends' external features, it is really something inside them that we admire.* **THEME**

 Classroom Collaboration

Invite children to talk about how each animal probably felt about each event that took place in the story. Guide children to further the discussion by responding to each others' comments. Remind children to follow good rules for discussion, such as listening carefully and speaking one at a time.
SL.1.1a, SL.1.1b

Phonemic Awareness/Phonics

▶ SHARE OBJECTIVES

- Blend and segment sounds in spoken single-syllable words.
- Learn the sound-spelling correspondences for digraphs *ch, tch*.
- Blend and decode regularly spelled one-syllable words with digraphs *ch, tch*.

▶ SKILLS TRACE

Words with Digraphs *ch, tch*	
Introduce	T114–T115
Differentiate	T182
Reteach	T196
Review	T138, T160
Assess	Weekly Tests, Lesson 12

ELL ENGLISH LANGUAGE LEARNERS
Comprehensible Input

Beginning Write *ch* and *tch* on the board. Model the sounds as you point to each one. Have children repeat.

Low Intermediate Show **Sound/Spelling Card** *chick*. Review the consonant digraphs *ch* and *ck* and have children read the word *chick*.

High Intermediate Build and read these words using letter cards: *hip, hop, pin, nap, mat, Nick*. Have children change the first letter of each word to *ch* and read the new words.

Proficient Have partners use letter cards to build and read as many words as they can that end in *tch*.

ELL Lesson 12, p. E13, for scaffolded support.

COMMON CORE **RF.1.2b** orally produce single-syllable words by blending sounds; **RF.1.2d** segment spoken single-syllable words into their complete sequence of individual sounds; **RF.1.3a** know the spelling-sound correspondences for common consonant digraphs; **RF.1.3b** decode regularly spelled one-syllable words; **RF.1.3g** recognize and read irregularly spelled words; **SL.1.6** produce complete sentences when appropriate to task and situation

Words with Digraphs *ch, tch*

PHONEMIC AWARENESS WARM-UP *Listen as I blend sounds to say a word: /h/ /ĭ/ /p/. I'll say the sounds again.* **Repeat the sounds.** *The word is* hip. *I'll do another one. Listen: /ch/ /ĭ/ /p/. The word is* chip.

Now let's do it together. What word do I get when I blend the sounds? **Say:** */ch/ /ĭ/ /n/. What is the word?* chin **Repeat the process with:** */h/ /ŏ/ /p/* hop, */ch/ /ŏ/ /p/* chop, */p/ /ĭ/ /n/ /ch/* pinch.

Reverse the process, segmenting instead of blending. Use the same words but in random order. 🔲 **RF.1.2b, RF.1.2d**

1 Teach/Model

SOUND/SPELLING CARDS Display the card for *chick*. Name the picture and say the sound. Have children repeat after you. *Listen:* chick, */ch/. Now you say it.*

- Say the sound and give the spelling. *Chick begins with the sound /ch/. The letters* ch *stand for the sound /ch/ at the beginning, middle, or end of a word.*

- Write and read *chin*. *This is the word* chin. *The letters* ch *stand for the sound /ch/ in* chin. *The letter* i *stands for the sound /ĭ/ in* chin. *The letter* n *stands for the sound /n/ in* chin. *Read with me: /ch/ /ĭ/ /n/:* chin.

- Write and read *match*. *This is the word* match. *The letter* m *stands for the beginning sound /m/ in* match. *The letter* a *stands for the sound /ă/ in* match. *The letters* t, c, *and* h *stand for the sound /ch/ at the end of* match. *Read with me: /m/ /ă/ /ch/:* match. **Repeat with the words** *pinch* **and** *hatch*.

ch
_tch

2 Guided Practice

CONTINUOUS BLENDING ROUTINE Use **Instructional Routine 3** to model blending *chin*.

- Point to **Sound/Spelling Card** *chick* and remind children that knowing the sound/spelling *ch* and *tch* can help them when they read.
- Display **Letter Cards** *ch*, *i*, and *n*.
- Blend the sounds. *Listen: /ch/ /ĭ/ /n/.* Have children blend with you. Now you blend the sounds /ch/ /ĭ/ /n/, chin.
- Repeat the routine with **Letter Cards** *p, a*, and *tch*.

ch | i | n

REPEAT CONTINUOUS BLENDING with the words in Row 1 below. Then write the words in Rows 1–3 and have children read them. Use the **Corrective Feedback** steps if children need additional help.

- Repeat until children are reading at a rate of three seconds per word.

DECODING Call on individuals to blend one or more words and to read the sentences. ▬ RF.1.3a, RF.1.3b, RF.1.3g

---

1. chip   chop   chin   match   chick
2. thick   Mitch   thin   dress   with
3. hatch   path   drip   jump   batch

The **brown** **chimp** **is** thin.
We **can** **see** **the** chick hatch.

3 Apply

Hands-on Practice

Have partners use letter cards to take turns building and reading words with *ch* and *tch*. After reading a word, each partner should use the word in a sentence. ▬ RF.1.3a, RF.1.3b, SL.1.6

Corrective Feedback Work with the whole group to correct errors, following the model below.

Phonics Error:
A child reads *patch* as *path*.

Correct the error. Review the **Sound/Spelling Card.** Say the word and the *sound. The word is* patch. *It takes three letters together to spell /ch/ in* patch. *The letters* tch *stand for the sound /ch/.*

Model as you touch the letters. *I'll blend: /p/ /ă/ /ch/.* What is the word? *patch*

Guide *Let's blend together: /p/ /ă/ /ch/. What is the word? patch*

Check *You blend: /p/ /ă/ /ch/. What is the word? patch*

Reinforce Go back three or four words and have children continue reading. Make note of errors and review those words during tomorrow's lesson.

SMALL GROUP Options

Go to p. T182 for additional phonics support.

Reader's Notebook Vol. 1 p. 165
See Grab-and-Go™ Resources for additional leveled practice.

Phonics/Spelling

▶ SHARE OBJECTIVES

- Write words with digraphs *ch* and *tch*.
- Read decodable text with regularly spelled one-syllable words and irregularly spelled high-frequency words.
- Practice reading on-level text fluently and accurately paying attention to rate.

▶ DICTATION SENTENCES

- **check.** I will **check** my homework.
- **hatch.** When will the eggs **hatch?**
- **champ.** He is the **champ** of the game.
- **much.** We have so **much** fun.
- **hitch.** Dad can **hitch** the trailer to the car.
- **chant.** The crowd will **chant** for the team.

COMMON CORE **RF.1.3a** know the spelling-sound correspondences for common consonant digraphs; **RF.1.3b** decode regularly spelled one-syllable words; **RF.1.3g** recognize and read irregularly spelled words; **RF.1.4b** read on-level text orally with accuracy, appropriate rate, and expression; **L.1.2d** use conventional spelling for words with common spelling patterns and for frequently occurring irregular words; **L.1.2e** spell untaught words phonetically, drawing on phonemic awareness and spelling conventions

Write Words with *ch, tch*

1 Teach/Model

CONNECT SOUNDS TO SPELLING Review Sound/Spelling Card *chick*. Tell children that they will write words with the sound /ch/.

Use **Instructional Routine 6** to dictate, using the first sentence at the left. *Listen as I say each word and use it in a sentence.*

- Model how to spell the word *check*. Point to *ch* on the **Sound/Spelling Card.** *What is the sound? /ch/ I remember that when these letters are side by side, they stand for the /ch/ sound. I will write ch at the beginning of the word. I will write e for the middle sound and ck for the end sound. Then I'll reread to check the whole word:* check.

2 Guided Practice

CONNECT SOUNDS TO WRITING Continue the dictation, using the sentences at the left.

- Have children say each word aloud after you. Then have children identify the sounds they hear at the beginning, middle, and end, and write the letters that stand for each sound. ▬ **L.1.2e**
- Remind children to write only the dictation word.

3 Apply

Read aloud the following decodable sentence for children to write.

> Mitch chats with a chum at the ranch.

Remind children that *with* and *the* are Words to Know that they learned in previous lessons.

Print the dictation words and the sentence for children to check their work. ▬ **L.1.2d**

Decodable Reader  Go Digital

Read *Scratch, Chomp*

Decodable Reader, Unit 3, pp. 27–32

REVIEW /ch/ AND WORDS TO KNOW Tell children that many words in this story have the /ch/ sound spelled *ch* or *tch*. Point out that children have learned the following words, which they will also read in the story: *brown, never, off, out.*

PREVIEW Have children preview pages 27–29 and predict what the story is about. Ask volunteers to tell what kinds of animals they might see near a lake or in the woods.

MODEL FLUENCY AND RATE Read aloud page 30 as children follow along. Point out that you read the first two sentences quickly to show excitement about the noise Dad and Chuck hear. Lead children in choral reading the page with fluency and at an appropriate rate.

READ Remind children to track the words from left to right and when they come to the end of a line, to sweep their hand down to the beginning of the next line and continue reading. Have children read each page silently and then choral-read aloud. Listen as children read to make sure they are correctly decoding the words with /ch/ and accurately reading the Words to Know.
RF.1.3a, RF.1.3b, RF.1.3g

RESPONDING Have partners take turns reading one page of the story aloud as the other partner follows along. Then ask them to retell the story to each other.

Reread for Fluency/ Develop Automaticity

READ WITH A PARTNER Have partners reread *Scratch, Chomp* three or four times, taking turns reading aloud each page. Remind them to read words correctly and to read smoothly. Visit partners to listen to them read. Give feedback about reading accurately, at an appropriate rate, and with expression and provide guidance for improving fluency. RF.1.4b

Whole Group

DAY 1

 **Go Digital**
• eBook
• Context Cards
• Vocabulary Reader

Introduce Words to Know

 **Read Together**

Lesson 12

✓ **WORDS TO KNOW**
High-Frequency Words

brown
own
very
off
never
know
out
been

Vocabulary Reader

Context Cards

COMMON CORE **RF.1.3g** recognize and read irregularly spelled words

42  **Go Digital**

Words to Know

▶ **Read each** Context Card.

▶ **Describe a picture, using the blue word.**

1 **brown**
Some hyenas have brown fur.

2 **own**
Zebras know their own mother by her stripes.

▶ SHARE OBJECTIVE
• Recognize and read irregularly spelled words.

Teach

Display and discuss the **Vocabulary in Context Cards,** using the routine below. See also **Instructional Routine 15.**

1 **Read and pronounce the word.** Read the word once alone and then together.

2 **Explain the word.** Read aloud the explanation under *What Does It Mean?*

3 **Discuss vocabulary in context.** Together, read aloud the sentence on the front of the card. Help children explain and use the word in new sentences.

4 **Engage with the word.** Ask and discuss *How Do I Use It?*

Practice/Apply

Give partners or small groups one or two **Vocabulary in Context Cards.** Help children complete the *Talk It Over* activities for each card. ⬤ **RF.1.3g**

 **COMMON CORE** **RF.1.3g** recognize and read irregularly spelled words

ELL **ENGLISH LANGUAGE LEARNERS**

Use Visuals

Beginning Display or point to different objects in the classroom. Ask children questions about these objects, such as: *Is this chalk short? yes* Then point to a shorter one and ask, *Is this one very short? yes*

Low Intermediate Show a classroom object. Ask children simple questions about it, such as: *Is the pencil long or very long?* Help children answer using the sentence frame *It's (very) _____.*

High Intermediate Have children describe objects in the classroom. You may want to provide the sentence frame *This _____ is (very) _____.*

Proficient Tell children they are going to draw a "very very" object. Explain that they have to think of an object that is "very very" beautiful, or big, or small, or long or heavy, and try to draw it. Then have partners describe their objects to each other.

See ELL Lesson 12, p. E12, for scaffolded support.

3 very
The snake in that tree is very long.

4 off
The bird flew off the rock and into the air.

5 never
Rhinos eat plants. They never eat meat.

6 know
Leopards know how to climb trees.

7 out
I called out to Mom, "Look at that turtle!"

8 been
The giraffes have been moving fast.

43

DAILY ASSESSMENT

3
2
1

RtI

Are children able to understand and use the Words to Know?

IF...	THEN...
children have difficulty understanding and using Words to Know,	▶ use **Vocabulary in Context Cards** and the Struggling Readers activity, p. T184. *See also Intervention Lesson 12, pp. S12–S21.*
children can understand and use most Words to Know,	▶ use **Vocabulary in Context Cards** and the On Level activity, p. T184.
children can understand and use all Words to Know,	▶ use the Advanced activity, p. T185.

SMALL GROUP Options

Vocabulary Reader pp. T184–T185
Provide support for English Language Learners according to language proficiency. See also Differentiate Words to Know, p. T183.

VOCABULARY IN CONTEXT CARDS 69–76

front   back

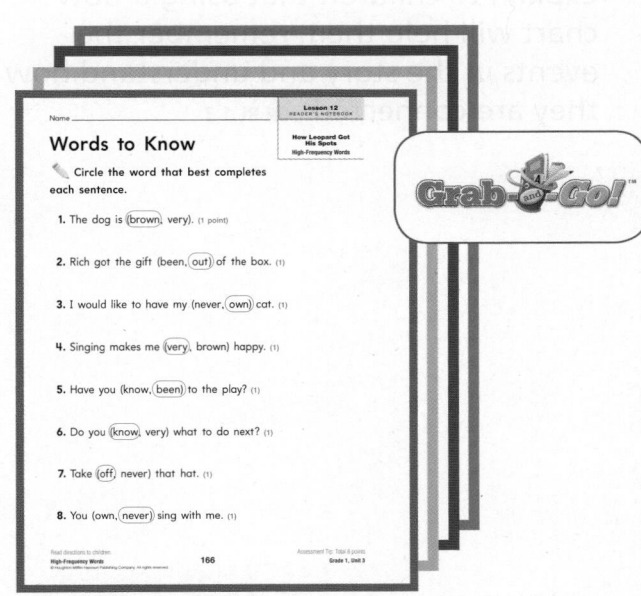

Reader's Notebook Vol. 1 p. 166
See Grab-and-Go™ Resources for additional leveled practice.

Read and Comprehend

 **Read and Comprehend**  Read Together  Go Digital

▶ SHARE OBJECTIVES

- Understand the sequence of events and describe the major events.
- Ask and answer questions about key details while reading.

☑ TARGET SKILL
Sequence of Events

- Read **Student Book** p. 44 with children.

- Explain to children that many stories tell about events in the order in which they happen. Explain that this is called the **sequence of events**.

- Then tell them the sequence of events is what happens first, next, and last.

- Draw children's attention to the graphic organizer on **Student Book** p. 44. Tell them that, as they read, they can use a flow chart like this one to describe the main events that happen. They can add one event in each box of the flow chart.

- Explain to children that using a flow chart will help them remember the events in the story and understand how they are connected. **RL.1.3**

☑ TARGET SKILL

Sequence of Events Most story events are told in time order. This order is called the **sequence of events.** Good readers think about what happens **first, next,** and **last** so that a story makes sense. You can describe the sequence of events in a flow chart like this.

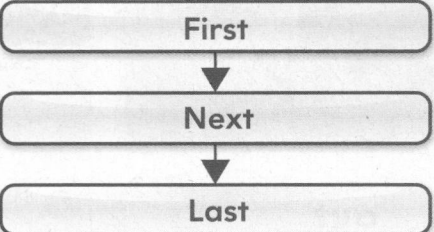

First
↓
Next
↓
Last

☑ TARGET STRATEGY

Question Ask yourself questions as you read. Look for text evidence to answer.

 COMMON CORE **RL.1.1** ask and answer questions about key details; **RL.1.3** describe characters, settings, and major events

44

SELECTION VOCABULARY

Tell children they may see words they do not recognize as they read *How Leopard Got His Spots*. Write the Selection Vocabulary words on the board and read them with children. Share the explanations with them.

danced moved with rhythmic steps, usually in time to music

flowers the parts of a plant that have colorful petals

giraffe a tall, African animal with a very long neck and legs and a tan coat with brown patches

hyena a wild animal of Asia and Africa that looks like a big dog with spots

leopard a large, wild cat that has a light brown coat with black spots

paint to coat or decorate with paint

zebra a wild, African animal that looks like a horse with white and black stripes

---

 **COMMON CORE** **RL.1.1** ask and answer questions about key details; **RL.1.3** describe characters, settings, and major events

T120 • Unit 3 Lesson 12 (SB p. 44)

PREVIEW THE TOPIC
Jungle Animals

Many animals live in the jungle. Monkeys swing on vines. Frogs and snakes hide in the bushes. Birds fly through the trees. Which jungle animal is your favorite? You will read about jungle animals in **How Leopard Got His Spots.**

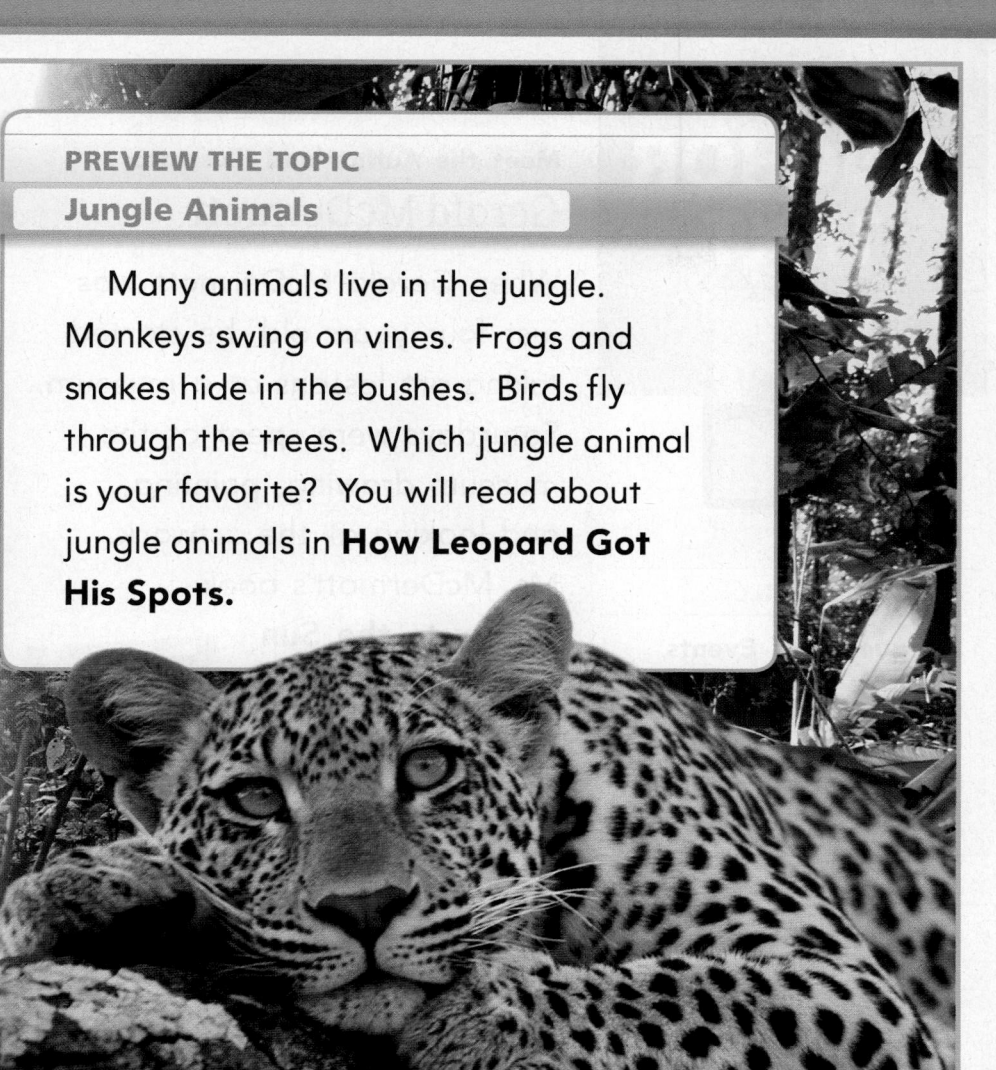

45

COMPREHENSION STRATEGIES

Use the following strategies flexibly as you read with children by modeling how they can be used to improve comprehension. See scaffolded support for the strategy shown in boldface during this week's reading.

- Monitor/Clarify
- Analyze/Evaluate
- Summarize
- **Question**
- Infer/Predict
- Phonics/Decoding
- Visualize

Use the Strategy Projectables, S1–S8, for additional support.

◯ **DOMAIN: Life Science**
LESSON TOPIC: Jungle Animals

☑ **TARGET STRATEGY**
Question

- Read the bottom of **Student Book** p. 44 with children.

- Explain to children that good readers stop periodically to ask themselves questions as they read. Tell them that then they look for text evidence in the story, such as details in the words and pictures, to find the answers to their questions. Tell children that this is a good strategy to use while reading to help them find and remember important information.

- Then explain that you will demonstrate how they should use this strategy when they read *How Leopard Got His Spots* together. ◖ RL.1.1

Preview the Topic: Jungle Animals

- Tell children that today they will begin reading *How Leopard Got His Spots*.

- Read the information on **Student Book** p. 45 with children.

- Then write on the board the word *jungle*. Have children explain their understanding of a jungle and jungle animals, using the information in the text, the photo, and their own experiences.

- Have children describe the photo on **Student Book** p. 45 using the word *jungle*.

Read the Anchor Text

☑ **TARGET SKILL**

Sequence of Events

- Point out the graphic organizer on **Student Book** p. 46 to children.

- Tell children that a flow chart can help them tell about the important events that happen in the story in the correct order.

☑ **GENRE** **Folktale**

- Read the genre information on **Student Book** p. 46 with children.

- Preview the selection with children, and model identifying the characteristics of a folktale.

Think Aloud *A folktale is a story that has been told many times over many years. A folktale might have animals that act like people. The tale may entertain people or explain how something came to be. The title* How Leopard Got His Spots *makes me think the story will explain how leopards got spots. I think this is a folktale.*

- As you preview, ask children to point out other features of folktales, such as the phrase *Once upon a time.*

- Then have children explain the major difference between folktales like *How Leopard Got His spots* and informational texts like *At Home in the Ocean.* ▬ **RL.1.5**

RL.1.5 explain major differences between story books and informational books; **RL.1.10** read prose and poetry; **RF.1.4a** read on-level text with purpose and understanding

---

Lesson 12

ANCHOR TEXT

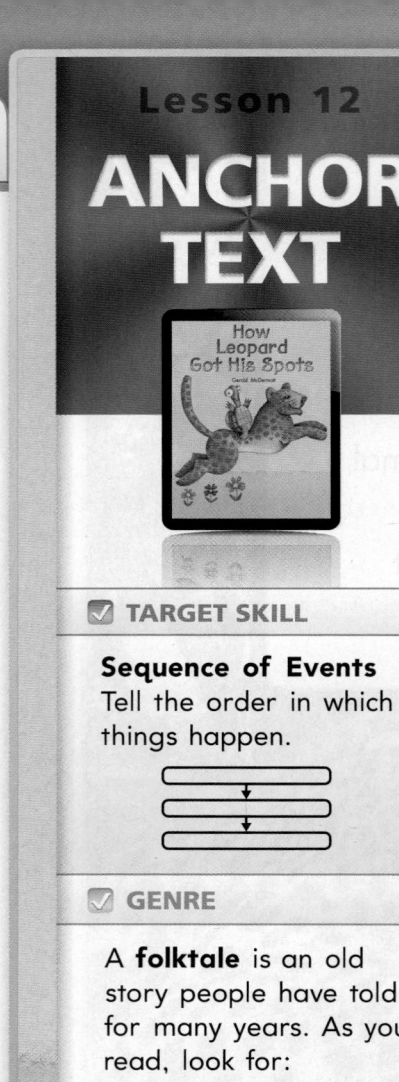

☑ **TARGET SKILL**

Sequence of Events
Tell the order in which things happen.

☑ **GENRE**

A **folktale** is an old story people have told for many years. As you read, look for:

▸ a lesson about life
▸ the words **once upon a time**

COMMON CORE **RL.1.2** retell stories and demonstrate understanding of the message or lesson; **RL.1.3** describe characters, settings, and major events; **RL.1.10** read prose and poetry

46 ▬ Go Digital

Meet the Author and Illustrator

Gerald McDermott

When Gerald McDermott was just four years old, he started taking art lessons at a museum. Saturdays were spent at the museum drawing, painting, and looking at the artwork. Mr. McDermott's book **Arrow to the Sun** won the Caldecott Medal for best illustrations.

▬ **RL.1.10**

Scaffold Close Reading

Think Through the Text	Analyze the Text	Independent Reading
FIRST READ	**SECOND READ**	
Develop comprehension through	Support analyzing short sections of text:	• Children analyze the text independently, using the Reader's Guide on pp. 172–173 of the **Reader's Notebook**. (See p. T152 for instructional support.)
• Guided Questioning	• Sequence of Events	
• Target Strategy: Question	• Story Lesson	
• Vocabulary in Context	Use directed note-taking by working with children to complete a graphic organizer during reading. Distribute copies of Graphic Organizer 6.	• Children read independently in a self-selected trade book.
IF children demonstrate understanding of what the story is mostly about,		
THEN provide additional challenge using the questions labeled A Closer Look.		

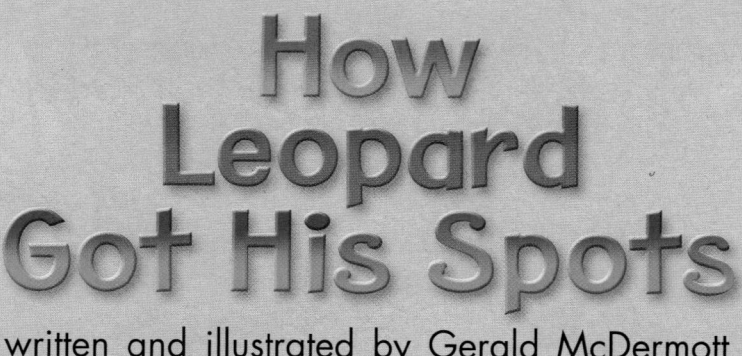

How Leopard Got His Spots

written and illustrated by Gerald McDermott

ESSENTIAL QUESTION

How are jungle animals different from animals on a farm?

47

⚠ READER AND TASK CONSIDERATIONS

Determine the level of additional support your children will need to read and comprehend *How Leopard Got His Spots* successfully.

READERS

- **Motivate** Ask children to name and describe a favorite jungle animal.

- **Access Knowledge and Experiences** Remind children of the Preview the Topic information on **Student Book** p. 45. Ask them to share with a partner what they recall, and if possible, share one other thing they know about jungle animals.

TASKS

- **Increase Scaffolding** Stop periodically as you read to have children retell the main story events in order.

- **Foster Independence** Have children read the story in small groups. Tell them to pause throughout the story to ask any questions they have about the characters, setting, or events. Have them look together for text evidence in the words and pictures to help them answer the questions.

ESSENTIAL QUESTION

- Read aloud and discuss the Essential Question on **Student Book** p. 47: *How are jungle animals different from animals on a farm?* Tell children to think about this question as they read *How Leopard Got His Spots*.

Predictive Writing

- Write the Essential Question on the board.

- Explain that partners will work together to write what they expect *How Leopard Got His Spots* to be about. Tell them to think about how the Essential Question relates to what they noticed while previewing the folktale or what they already know from their own experiences or past readings.

- Guide children to think about the genre as they write. Then discuss their predictions.

Set Purpose

- Tell children that good readers set a purpose for reading. *Look at the pictures in the story. What do you hope to enjoy about this folktale?*

- Model setting a reading purpose.

> **Think Aloud** *From the title, I know that the folktale will tell me how the leopard got his spots. I will read to find out how this happens.*

- Have children set their own purpose for reading. Ask volunteers to share their purposes for reading. Then have children read the story.

🔖 RL.1.10, RF.1.4a

④

Do you know how
Leopard got his spots?

48

Once upon a time, Fred
Turtle was playing catch with
Hal Hyena. Hal tricked Fred.
Then he ran away. ①

49

ELL **ENGLISH LANGUAGE LEARNERS**
Comprehensible Input

Beginning Ask children *yes/no* questions to guide them in understanding the sequence. Ask: *Does Fred get stuck after Hal tricks him? Does Hal get stuck in the plants?*

Low Intermediate Ask children simple questions to guide them in understanding the sequence, such as, *Which happens first, Fred and Hal play catch or Fred gets stuck?*

High Intermediate Have children draw pictures to show what happens first, next, and last, on pp. 49–53.

Proficient Ask children to tell what happens first, next, and last on pp. 49–53, using complete sentences.

COMMON CORE **RL.1.1** ask and answer questions about key details; **RL.1.3** describe characters, settings, and major events; **RL.1.7** use illustrations and details to describe characters, setting, or events; **RF.1.3b** decode regularly spelled one-syllable words; **RF.1.3g** recognize and read irregularly spelled words

FIRST READ

Use Text Evidence

Think Through the Text

① *Describe what happens between Hal Hyena and Fred Turtle.* Hal tricks Fred, and Fred gets stuck in the plants.  **RL.1.3**

② *Describe the character Len Leopard on p. 51. What does he look like? How does he act?* Len Leopard is a big, brown cat. He looks worried. He is leaping through the air to come help Fred. *How is he different from the picture on p. 48?* Len does not have spots on p. 51.  **RL.1.1, RL.1.3, RL.1.7**

▶ A Closer Look

Look at the pictures on pp. 49 and 50, and think about what we've read so far. How do you think Fred feels about Hal playing a trick on him? Fred has hurt feelings and is sad and a little angry that Hal tricked him into falling into the plants. ◼ **RL.1.3**

KEY: ☑ **WORDS TO KNOW**
High-Frequency Words ▬
Decodable Words with —
Digraphs *ch, tch*

COMMON
CORE

DAY 1

Fred felt very sad.
He called out for help.
"Help! I am stuck in
the plants," he yelled.

50

Len Leopard ran to help.

51

☑ TARGET STRATEGY: Question

Reread **Student Book** pp. 49–50 with children. Then model the strategy.

Think Aloud *The words on p. 49 tell me that Hal tricked Fred. How exactly did Hal trick Fred? I'll look for text evidence to help me answer my question. The picture on p. 49 shows that Hal threw the ball close to the plants to get Fred to fall into them. On p. 50, the words tell that Fred is stuck in the plants. From this text evidence, I know the answer to my question: Hal tricked Fred by throwing the ball too close to the plants. Fred fell into the plants and got stuck.*

Tell children to use the Question strategy as they continue reading, such as asking themselves *How will Len Leopard help?* Help them look for evidence in the words and pictures to help them find answers. ◖RL.1.1

Chop! Chop! Chop!
Len cut the plants off and
let Fred out.

52

Fred and Len danced in the sun.
"This is such fun!" they said.

53

LESSON TOPIC: Jungle Animals

Cross-Curricular Connection Tell children that many animals live in jungles and other places in the wild. Recall with them the animals they have read about. *turtle, hyena, leopard, zebra* Work with them to list the animals on a chart under *Wild Animals* and to describe them in terms of size, color, motion, number of legs, and so on. Add a *Farm Animals* column. Ask children to describe ones they know. Add to the chart as children read.

COMMON CORE **RL.1.1** ask and answer questions about key details; **RL.1.2** retell stories and demonstrate understanding of the message or lesson; **RL.1.3** describe characters, settings, and major events; **RL.1.7** use illustrations and details to describe characters, setting, or events; **RF.1.3b** decode regularly spelled one-syllable words

FIRST READ

Use Text Evidence

Think Through the Text

3️⃣ *Describe what Len Leopard does after Fred calls for help.* Len Leopard uses his claws to chop the plants and get Fred out. ▬ **RL.1.1, RL.1.3**

▶ A Closer Look

Why do Fred and Len dance in the sun? They dance because they are happy that Len helped Fred get out of the plants. ▬ **RL.1.1**

KEY: ☑ **WORDS TO KNOW**
High-Frequency Words ▬
Decodable Words with ▬
Digraphs *ch*, *tch*

COMMON CORE

DAY 1

"I have never been this glad,"
said Fred. "I like to paint if I
am glad!"

54

Fred mixed paints from many
flowers. Then he painted
black stripes on Zel Zebra. **4**

55

☑ Phonics/Decoding Strategy

Use **Projectable S1** to help children apply the Phonics/
Decoding strategy. Have children go back to p. 52. Ask
them to point to the first word, *Chop.* Model how to
say each sound and then blend the sounds to read the
word: /ch/ /ŏ/ /p/, *chop.* Have children do the same.
Emphasize that the letters *ch* together stand for one
sound, /ch/. Then have children read aloud p. 52 to
make sure the word *chop* makes sense. Repeat for *such*
on p. 53. ▬ **RF.1.3b**

4 *Describe how Fred's paint changes Zel Zebra.* At
first, Zel Zebra was plain, but now Zel has black stripes all
over. ▬ **RL.1.1, RL.1.3, RL.1.7**

SECOND READ   **DAY 2**

ANALYZE THE TEXT

Sequence of Events Display
Projectable 12.2, and distribute
Graphic Organizer 6.

Tell children they will describe the important
story events in the order that they happened.
Ask children to recall what Hal did to Fred at
the beginning of the story, and record the
event on the flow chart. *First, Hal tricks Fred,
and Fred gets stuck in the plants.* Ask them to
describe what Fred did when he was stuck,
and add the ideas to the top box. *Fred is sad.
He calls out for help.* Have children describe
the next important event that happens when
Len Leopard comes, and add it to the next
box. *Next, Len Leopard chops the plants. Fred
gets out. They are happy.* Continue filling in
the flow chart with children, having them
describe important events in order. ▬ **RL.1.2, RL.1.3**

Fred painted Jill Giraffe next.
"Look at me!" said Jill.
"I have big brown spots now."

56

"I like spots very <u>much</u>.
Can I have spots, too?"
asked Len. **6**

57

ELL ENGLISH LANGUAGE LEARNERS
Comprehensible Input

Beginning Ask children simple questions about the sequence, such as, *Which happens first, does Fred paint Zebra or Giraffe?*

Low Intermediate Have small groups act out what happens *first*, *next*, and *last* in the story.

High Intermediate Have children draw pictures from the story to show the sequence of events. Ask them to talk about their pictures, using the words *first*, *next*, and *last*.

Proficient Ask children to tell what happens *first*, *next*, and *last* in the story, using complete sentences.

COMMON CORE **RL.1.1** ask and answer questions about key details; **RL.1.2** retell stories and demonstrate understanding of the message or lesson; **RL.1.3** describe characters, settings, and major events; **RL.1.7** use illustrations and details to describe characters, setting, or events; **RF.1.3g** recognize and read irregularly spelled words

---

FIRST READ

Use Text Evidence

Think Through the Text

5 *How do the illustration and the words on p. 56 work together to tell what is happening?* The illustration shows Fred painting big spots on Jill. The words say, "Fred painted Jill Giraffe next" and "big brown spots." **RL.1.3, RL.1.7**

6 *What happens next when Len sees Jill's spots?* He asks Fred to paint spots on him, too. **RL.1.1, RL.1.3**

☑ TARGET STRATEGY: Question

Use **Projectable S5** to help children practice the Question strategy as they read pp. 56–59. They should ask themselves a question about the story and then read on to find the answer. Ask children to share the questions they asked themselves and the text evidence they used to find the answers. Guide them to understand that they could ask themselves a question like this to help them understand the story: *Will Fred paint spots on Len?* **RL.1.1**

KEY: ☑ **WORDS TO KNOW**
High-Frequency Words
Decodable Words with
Digraphs *ch, tch*

COMMON CORE

DAY 1

Fred got set to paint Len. **7**

58

Now Len had spots
of his very own. **8**

59

7 *Retell the things Fred does after Len gets him out of the plants.* Fred paints stripes on Zel Zebra and spots on Jill Giraffe and Len Leopard. ⬛ **RL.1.1, RL.1.2**

8 *Why would Fred be glad to paint spots on Len?* Len helped Fred get out of the plants, so he wants to do something nice for Len. *How do you think Len feels about having spots of his very own?* He likes his spots. He looks happy and proud. ⬛ **RL.1.3, RL.1.7**

SECOND READ **DAY 2**

ANALYZE THE TEXT

Story Lesson Review with children that folktales often teach a lesson about life. Have children retell the important events that have happened so far. Then discuss the following to help them determine a lesson that Len Leopard learns. Have children find text evidence in the words and pictures to support their responses: *What does Len Leopard do to help Fred? Why does Fred agree to paint spots on Len? How does this make Len feel? What lesson do you think Len learns from what has happened?* Guide children to state the lesson in their own words. As children continue reading, help them determine the main lesson of the folktale—the lesson that Hal Hyena learns. ⬛ **RL.1.2, RL.1.3**

9 Zel, Jill, and Len had <u>such</u> fun looking at their spots and stripes.
Hal said, "Paint me, too!"

60

But Fred had a trick for Hal. He splashed Hal with brown paint. Hal yelled and ran off.

61

DAILY ASSESSMENT  **RtI**

Question IF children have difficulty applying the Question strategy, **THEN** use this model:

Think Aloud *When Fred is painting his friends, I ask myself, "Do the animals really want to be painted? Will they like the stripes and spots?" I read on and find out they all do.*

Have children ask questions about what will happen to Hal and then read to find out.

T130 • Unit 3 Lesson 12 (SB pp. 60–61)

FIRST READ

Use Text Evidence

Think Through the Text

9 *In what ways do Zel, Jill, and Len look alike?* They all have fur and four legs, and spots or stripes that Fred painted. *In what ways are they different?* They are different kinds of animals. Zel has black stripes. Jill and Len have brown spots. Len's spots are smaller than Jill's spots.  **RL.1.1, RL.1.3, RL.1.7**

10 *What does Fred do after Hal says, "Paint me, too!"?* Fred tricks Hal. He splashes Hal with brown paint. *Which event happens at the very beginning of the story?* Hal tricks Fred. *Which event happens last?* Fred tricks Hal. *How do you think Hal feels now?* I think he is sad that he has messy spots. Maybe he is also a little mad or embarrassed that he got tricked. **RL.1.2, RL.1.3**

Now Fred and Len
are best friends.

62

63

☑ TARGET STRATEGY: Question

Help children apply the Question Strategy after
reading **Student Book** p. 63. Have children tell a
partner what questions they have about Fred, Len, Jill,
Zel, and Hal. Children can use the sequence of events
flow chart to help them generate questions. Point out
how children can reread the story and use the pictures
to help them find answers. Discuss children's questions
and the answers they found. 🔊 **RL.1.1**

Guided Retelling

Oral Language Use the prompts on the **Retelling Cards** to guide children to retell the story, including important details, and to demonstrate understanding of the lesson the story teaches. ⬛ **RL.1.2, RL.1.3, RL.1.7**

front

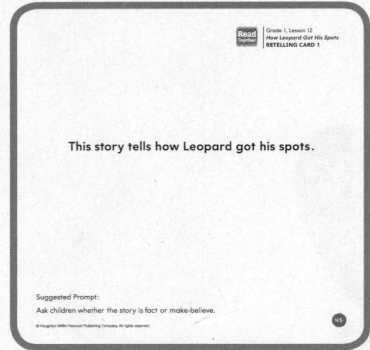

This story tells how Leopard got his spots.

Suggested Prompt:
Ask children whether the story is fact or make-believe.

back

front

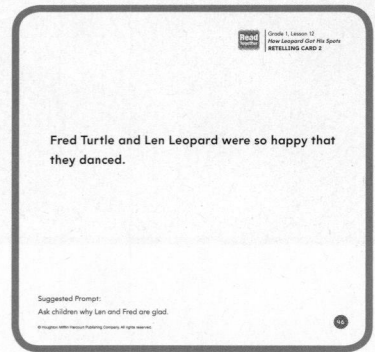

Fred Turtle and Len Leopard were so happy that they danced.

Suggested Prompt:
Ask children why Len and Fred are glad.

back

COMMON CORE **RL.1.2** retell stories and demonstrate understanding of the message or lesson; **RL.1.3** describe characters, settings, and major events; **RL.1.7** use illustrations and details to describe characters, setting, or events

front

Grade 1, Lesson 12
How Leopard Got His Spots
RETELLING CARD 3

Hal Hyena wants Fred to paint him, too.

Suggested Prompt:
Have children explain how Fred changed Len Leopard, Zel Zebra, and Jill Giraffe.
Ask why Fred decides to play a trick on Hal.

© Houghton Mifflin Harcourt Publishing Company. All rights reserved.

back

front

Grade 1, Lesson 12
How Leopard Got His Spots
RETELLING CARD 4

Fred and Len are good friends.

Suggested Prompt:
Ask children to share how Fred and Len showed that they care about each other.

© Houghton Mifflin Harcourt Publishing Company. All rights reserved.

back

RETELLING RUBRIC	
4 Highly Effective	The child describes the plot (problem and solution); retells the beginning, middle, and end, with attention to the sequence of events; describes the characters and the reasons for their actions and feelings; requires little or no prompting.
3 Generally Effective	The child describes most of the plot; retells most of the beginning, middle, and end, with some attention to the sequence of events; describes the characters and may provide some reasons for their actions and feelings; may require some prompting.
2 Somewhat Effective	The child describes some plot details; retells some of the beginning, middle, and end, with some omissions or errors; describes some of the characters; requires some prompting.
1 Ineffective	The child retells few, if any, details about the story elements, possibly with errors; is unable to retell the story without prompting.

- *my*WriteSmart
- eBook
- GrammarSnap Videos
- Literacy and Language Guide

Grammar Introduce Commands

▷ SHARE OBJECTIVES

- **Grammar** Identify and create simple commands.
- **Spelling** Spell words with *ch* and *tch* using conventional spelling patterns.
- **Writing** Name parts of and write together instructions.

 **ENGLISH LANGUAGE LEARNERS**

Language Transfer

Beginning Display the **online Picture Cards** *chair, beach, kitchen*. Read the words aloud and have children clap whenever they hear the /ch/ sound.

Low Intermediate Have children use **Letter Cards** to build and read *chin, match, rich*.

High Intermediate Have children use **Letter Cards** to build and read *chin*. Guide them to change the cards to read *chick, rich, cheer*.

Proficient Have children in groups use **Letter Cards** *t, c, h, a, i, e, t, s, w, r, p, m* to build and read as many words with the sound /ch/ as they can.

1   Teach/Model

- Tell children to listen carefully and do what you tell them to do.

  Examples:

  Sit up straight.
  Put your hands on your desk.
  Raise your left hand.
  Put your hand down.

- Write these commands on the board. Point out that each one starts with a capital letter and ends with a period.

- Explain that you have just given them commands. A sentence that tells someone to do something is called a *command*.

2   Guided Practice

- Have children work with a partner. Have them take turns giving and following simple commands they can do while sitting at their desks. ▬ **L.1.1j**

Spelling Words with *ch* and *tch*

SPELLING WORDS AND SENTENCES

BASIC

1. **chin** A fly was on his *chin*.
2. **chop** *Chop* the apples into small pieces.
3. **much** How *much* does that toy cost?
4. **chip** The cup has a *chip* in it.
5. **rich** He is *rich* and has many things.
6. **chick** The baby *chick* was yellow.

CHALLENGE

7. **match** Find the *match* for each card.
8. **pitch** *Pitch* the ball to me.

Administer the Pretest

Say the first word and read the sentence. Repeat the word as children write it. Write the word on the board and have children check their spelling. Repeat for words 2–8. Guide children to use what they know about letter sounds to spell the words phonetically. ▬ **L.1.2e**

Teach the Principle

Write *chin*, underlining *ch*. Write *match*, underlining *tch*. Say the words. Review that the /ch/ sound can be spelled with the letters *ch* or *tch*.

 **COMMON CORE**

W.1.2 write informative/explanatory texts; **W.1.5** focus on a topic, respond to questions/suggestions from peers, and add details to strengthen writing; **SL.1.6** produce complete sentences when appropriate to task and situation; **L.1.1f** use frequently occurring adjectives; **L.1.1j** produce and expand simple

Informative Writing Introduce the Model

1 Teach/Model

- Remind children that when they write to inform, they write to share information. One way to inform is to write instructions. A letter to a friend may contain instructions.

- Display **Projectable 12.1**. Read aloud and discuss the model with children. Discuss the **Talk About It** questions.

- Sum up by reviewing the **Writer's Checklist** about writing instructions.

2 Shared Writing

- Tell children that today they will work together to write a letter to another class explaining how to dress for a rainy day.

- Have children discuss how they dress when the weather is rainy, such as putting on raincoats and making sure to carry an umbrella. Have them brainstorm the steps they would take to dress for a rainy day, paying attention to the order of steps.

- Guide the whole group to write a letter to another class providing instructions on how to dress for a rainy day. Remind them to name the steps in order and to use complete sentences.

- As needed, prompt children with questions such as: *What would you do first to get dressed? What would you do next? What would you do last?* ▬ **W.1.2, W.1.5, SL.1.6**

Projectable 12.1

Projectable 12.1

How Leopard Got His Spots | Writing | Informative Writing

Writing Model

Topic Sentence and Detail Sentences

A topic sentence tells what the instructions are about.	Dear Lou, You can make a frog puppet. Here is how to do it.
Detail sentences and order words make the steps easy to follow.	1. First, get a paper lunch bag. 2. Next, glue green paper on the front of the bag. 3. Last, draw a face on the green paper. Your friend, Michelle

Talk About It
1. What do the instructions tell how to make? a frog puppet
2. What is the topic sentence? You can make a frog puppet.
3. What order words are used? first, next, last
4. How do you know that the instructions are part of a letter? The instructions are written to someone named Lou and signed by Michelle.

Writing
© Houghton Mifflin Harcourt Publishing Company. All rights reserved.
Grade 1, Unit 3

Oral Language Conventions

Using Adjectives Tell children that when they write an instructional letter, they should use adjectives so their instructions will be specific. Explain that it is more specific to say, "Use brown paper" than to say, "Use paper." The adjective *brown* makes this instruction better. ▬ **L.1.1f**

Daily Proofreading Practice

Ned's   brown
N̶e̶d̶s̶ hat is b̶r̶o̶n̶.
   ^   ^

          never
He n̶e̶v̶u̶r̶ takes it off.
       ^

Writer's Checklist

What Makes Great Instructions?

- **A topic sentence** tells what the instructions are about.

- **Detail sentences** tell what the instructions are about.

- **Order words** help make the steps easy to follow.

Performance Task

my WriteSmart Have children complete the writing assignment through *my*WriteSmart. Children will read the prompt and have access to multiple writing resources.

HOUGHTON MIFFLIN HARCOURT
Common Core Writing Handbook

GRADE 1

Additional support for Informative Writing appears in the **Common Core Writing Handbook,** Lesson 12.

and compound declarative, interrogative, imperative, and exclamatory sentences; **L.1.2e** spell untaught words phonetically, drawing on phonemic awareness and spelling conventions

DAY 2

Today's Goals

Vocabulary & Oral Language
- Oral Vocabulary

Phonemic Awareness
- Blend and Segment Phonemes

Phonics & Fluency
- Words with Digraphs *ch, tch*
- Read Decodable Reader: *Rich Gets a Dog*
- Fluency: Rate

☑ **WORDS TO KNOW**

been	off
brown	out
know	own
never	very

Text-Based Comprehension
- Dig Deeper: How to Analyze the Text
- Sequence of Events
- Story Lesson
- Reread the Anchor Text: *How Leopard Got His Spots*

Grammar & Writing
- Commands
-  **Informative Writing:** Instructions
- Focus Trait: Sentence Fluency

Spelling
- Words with *ch, tch*

COMMON CORE **RF.1.2b** orally produce single-syllable words by blending sounds; **RF.1.2d** segment spoken single-syllable words into their complete sequence of individual sounds; **L.1.2d** use conventional spelling for words with common spelling patterns and for frequently occurring irregular words; **L.1.5a** sort words into categories to gain a sense of concepts the categories represent

Opening Routines

Warm Up with Wordplay

How Do They Go Together?

Display and read aloud the following:

turtle	leopard	zebra

Have children discuss with a partner how these words belong together. Have children compare their answers. Tell them there can be several correct answers, but one is that these words all name animals.

Encourage children to name other animals and write down the responses. Have children work with you to sort the animals into categories. Provide headings, such as *Mammals, Reptiles,* or *Fish.* After all the words have been sorted, reread them aloud with children. **L.1.5a**

Daily Phonemic Awareness

Blend and Segment Phonemes

- *I'm going to say and blend sounds in a word. Then you say the word. Listen: /h/ /ŏ/ /t/. What is the word?* hot *Let's do more.*

- Have children blend with you and then on their own.

  /t/ /ā/ /k/ *take*
  /th/ /ă/ /t/ *that*
  /t/ /r/ /ă/ /p/ *trap*

  /b/ /ĕ/ /s/ /t/ *best*
  /t/ /ā/ /m/ *tame*
  /d/ /ĭ/ /ch/ *ditch*

  /th/ /ĭ/ /s/ *this*
  /s/ /ŭ/ /ch/ *such*
  /ch/ /ā/ /s/ *chase*

- Reverse the process. Say each word below and have children repeat it. *How many sounds are in the word?* three *Say the first sound. . . . Say the middle sound. . . . Say the last sound.*

  take   best   this   that   tame   such   trap   ditch   chase
  📖 **RF.1.2b, RF.1.2d**

Corrective Feedback

- **Model the task.** *The word is* such. *Listen: /s/ /ŭl /ch/. What is the word?* such

- Have children do the blending with you before doing it on their own.

- Back up several words and continue the game.

Daily High-Frequency Words

Introduce

- Point to the **High-Frequency Word Card** *brown.*

- *Say the word.* brown *Spell the word.* b, r, o, w, n *Write the word. Check the word.*

- Repeat the procedure with the words *been, know, never, off, out, own,* and *very.* 📖 **RF.1.3g, L.1.2d**

Cheer It Game

- Choose a child to be the cheerleader and stand in front of the room.

- The cheerleader calls out each letter of a High-Frequency Word. The class responds by repeating it. *Give me a B! B! Give me an R! R! Give me an O! O! Give me a W! W! Give me an N! N! What is the word? BROWN!*

- Choose a different child to be the cheerleader for the remaining words.

Corrective Feedback

- Say the correct word and have children repeat it. Never. *What is the word?* never

- Have children spell the word. *n, e, v, e, r How do we say this word?* never

- Have children reread all of the cards in random order.

Daily Vocabulary Boost

- Review the Oral Vocabulary words and their definitions with children. (See pp. T112–T113.) Remind children that they heard these words in the Read Aloud, "Turtle, Frog, and Rat." Recall with children the story events and then guide them to interact with each word's meaning.

  One night, after days of rain, the friends had an unfortunate adventure. What kind of adventure *would you like to have?*

  They lived together in a lovely house made of woven grasses, with a wide view of the ocean. Where could you go to see a view *of the ocean?*

- Continue in the same manner with *frisky, shiver, spy,* and *tumbles.* 📖 **L.1.6**

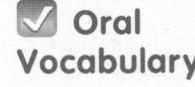
☑ **Oral Vocabulary**

adventure
frisky
shiver
spy
tumbles
view

Whole Group

DAY 2

Go Digital
• Interactive Whiteboard Lesson
• Decodable Reader

JOURNEYS
Phonics

Interactive Whiteboard Lesson:
Words with Digraphs *ch, tch*

Phonemic Awareness/Phonics

▶ SHARE OBJECTIVES

- Blend, build, and decode regularly spelled one-syllable words with digraphs *ch* and *tch*.
- Read on-level text with digraphs *ch, tch* and irregularly spelled high-frequency words.

▶ SKILLS TRACE

Words with Digraphs *ch, tch*	
Introduce	T114–T115
Differentiate	T182
Reteach	T196
▶ Review	**T138, T160**
Assess	Weekly Tests, Lesson 12

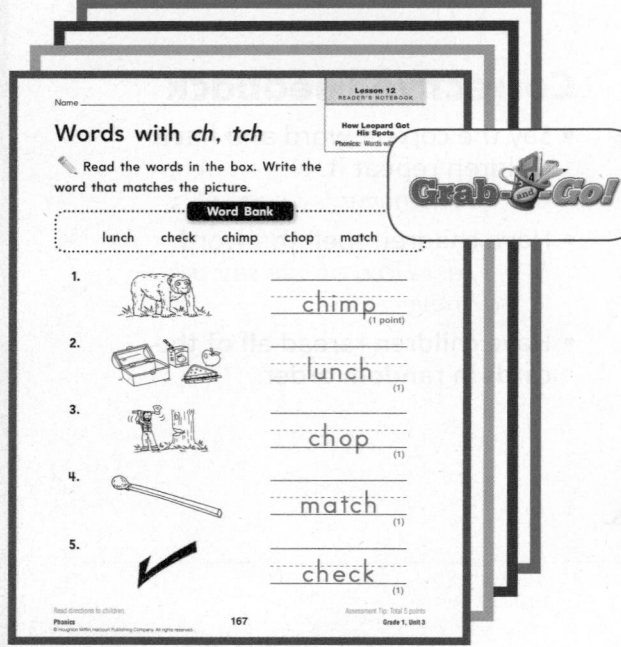

Reader's Notebook Vol. 1 p. 167
See Grab-and-Go™ Resources for additional leveled practice.

COMMON CORE **RF.1.2b** orally produce single-syllable words by blending sounds; **RF.1.3a** know the spelling-sound correspondences for common consonant digraphs; **RF.1.3b** decode regularly spelled one-syllable words; **RF.1.3g** recognize and read irregularly spelled words; **RF.1.4b** read on-level text orally with accuracy, appropriate rate, and expression; **L.1.1.j** produce and expond simple and compound declarative, interrogative, imperative, and exclamatory sentences; **L.1.2d** use conventional spelling for words with common spelling patterns and for frequently occurring irregular words; **L.1.2e** spell untaught words phonetically, drawing on phonemic awareness and spelling conventions

Words with Digraphs *ch, tch*

PHONEMIC AWARENESS WARM-UP *Listen as I blend some sounds to say a word: /ch/ /ĭ/ /p/, chip. Let's do one together. Listen to tell what word I get when I blend the sounds /ch/ /ă/ /t/. chat* 🔊 **RF.1.2b**

1 Teach/Model

Review the **Sound/Spelling Card** *chick*.

CONTINUOUS BLENDING ROUTINE Use **Instructional Routine 3** to model blending *chick*, displaying **Letter Cards** *ch, i,* and *ck*. Repeat the routine with the words in Row 1 below.

Write the words and sentence shown below. Call on individuals to blend and read one or more words and to read the sentence.

ch
_tch

ch | i | ck

> 1. much   chop   patch   chip   chat
> 2. chick   missing   chin   that   grab
> **I can catch <u>the</u> pitch <u>today</u>.**

2 Guided Practice

BUILD WORDS Model how to spell the word *check*. *The letters* ch *stand for the first sound in* check. *The next sound is /ĕ/. The letter* e *stands for /ĕ/. The last sound is /k/. The letters* ck *can stand for /k/.*

- Guide children to identify sounds and spell the words *pitch, click, this, much, with.* 🔊 **L.1.2e**
- Call on individuals to spell the words with **Letter Cards** while other children check their work.

3 Apply

Hands-on Practice

Have partners use letter cards to take turns building and reading words with digraphs *ch, tch*. 🔊 **RF.1.3a, RF.1.3 b, L.1.2d**

Decodable Reader

Read *Rich Gets a Dog*

Decodable Reader, Unit 3, pp. 33–38

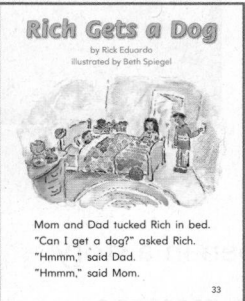

Mom and Dad tucked Rich in bed. "Can I get a dog?" asked Rich. "Hmmm," said Dad. "Hmmm," said Mom. *33*

Then Mom and Dad said yes. Rich sat up in bed. Mom, Dad, and Rich like dogs very much. *34*

Today, Mom and Dad will get Rich a dog. Rich can see dogs, dogs, dogs. Rich can get just one dog. *35*

Here are big dogs and small dogs. Here are fat dogs and thin dogs. Dogs, dogs, dogs! *36*

Rich picks a brown dog called Fletch. Fletch is big and can run fast. Rich has his own dog! *37*

Rich hugs Fletch. Fletch and Rich will be pals. *38*

REVIEW /CH/ AND WORDS TO KNOW Tell children that many words in this story have the sound /ch/ spelled *ch* and *tch*. Point out that children have learned the following words, which they will also read in the story: *brown, own, very.*

PREVIEW Have children preview pages 33–35 and predict what the story is about. Ask volunteers to describe a pet they would like to have and why they would like it.

MODEL FLUENCY AND RATE Read aloud page 33 as children follow along. Point out that you read the last two sentences slowly to show that Mom and Dad were taking their time and thinking. Lead children in choral reading the page with fluency and at an appropriate rate.

READ Remind children to track the words from left to right. Have children read each page silently and then choral read aloud. Listen as children read to make sure they are correctly decoding the words with /ch/ and accurately reading the Words to Know.
■ RF.1.3a, RF.1.3b, RF.1.3g

RESPONDING Guide children to brainstorm different kinds of dogs they have seen, including different types, colors, and sizes. Ask them to draw pictures of the different kinds of dogs, circle the dog they like best, and then write sentences that tell what this dog is like, such as *This dog is _____. This dog has _____.* ■ L.1.1.j

Reread for Fluency/ Develop Automaticity

READ WITH A PARTNER Have partners reread *Rich Gets a Dog* three or four times, taking turns reading aloud each page. Remind them to read words correctly and to read smoothly. Visit partners to listen to them read. Give feedback about reading accurately, at an appropriate rate, and with expression and provide guidance for improving fluency.
■ RF.1.4b

Whole Group

DAY 2

 Go Digital
• eBook
• Interactive Whiteboard Lesson

JOURNEYS Text Analysis

Interactive Whiteboard Lesson:
Text Analysis: Folktale

Dig Deeper: How to Analyze the Text

▶ SHARE OBJECTIVES

• Identify and describe the sequence of events.
• Understand a story's main lesson or message.

 **ELL ENGLISH LANGUAGE LEARNERS**

Use Visuals

Beginning Put three children in a line. Identify them for the class orally and with word cards as *first, next,* and *last.* Have children repeat the words.

Low Intermediate Line up three volunteers. Have children point to who is first, next, and last in line and say the words.

High Intermediate Point to the first child in a line of three. *Is this person first in line? Is she next? Is she last?* Repeat for each child in line.

Proficient Have children identify who is *first, next,* and *last* in a line of three children using complete sentences.

Text-Based Comprehension

1 Teach/Model

Terms About Literature

sequence of events the order that events happen in a story

story lesson the lesson a story teaches; the main message

• Remind children that they have read *How Leopard Got His Spots,* a folktale about how the leopard got his spots. Read and discuss **Student Book** p. 64 with them.

• Explain to children that things characters do, or **events,** happen in a certain order in a story. This is called the **sequence of events.**

• Remind them that a flow chart can help them describe the important events in the correct order. Model:

Think Aloud *You can use a flow chart to describe the important story events in order. What did Hal Hyena do to Fred Turtle at the beginning of the story? I will describe this first story event and write it in the top box:* First, Hal tricks Fred, and Fred gets stuck in the plants. *As we read, we will think about the rest of the important events that happen and add them to the flow chart.*

Read and discuss **Student Book** p. 65 with children. Explain that:

• A folktale is a story that people have told for many years before it was written down. Explain that folktales can teach a lesson about life or explain why something in nature is the way it is, such as how leopards got their spots.

• Recall with children that Hal tricks Fred at the beginning of the story. Ask them what Fred does to Hal at the end. *Fred tricks Hal.* Ask children to tell about the lesson they think Hal learns, supporting their responses with text evidence from the words and pictures in the folktale and from their own experiences.

• Tell children that many characters in *How Leopard Got His Spots* learn something. Then work together to determine the main lesson about life that the folktale is teaching when they reread the folktale.

 **COMMON CORE** **RL.1.2** retell stories and demonstrate understanding of the message or lesson; **RL.1.3** describe characters, settings, and major events; **RL.1.7** use illustrations and details to describe characters, setting, or events

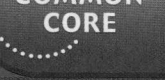

COMPREHENSION

Dig Deeper

 Read Together

How to Analyze the Text

Use these pages to learn more about Sequence of Events and Story Lesson. Then read **How Leopard Got His Spots** again.

Sequence of Events

In **How Leopard Got His Spots,** Fred Turtle helps Len Leopard get his spots. Think about the important events in the story. What happens **first**, **next**, and **last**? This order is called the **sequence of events**. Use a flow chart like this to describe the order of events in the story.

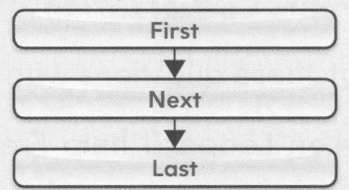

First
↓
Next
↓
Last

COMMON CORE RL.1.2 retell stories and demonstrate understanding of the message or lesson; RL.1.3 describe characters, settings, and major events

64 Go Digital

Story Lesson

How Leopard Got His Spots is a folktale. People told this story for many years before it was written down. Folktales often teach a lesson. What lesson do you learn from Hal Hyena?

Folktales can also tell why something is the way it is. Think about Len Leopard's spots. What does this folktale try to explain?

65

SECOND READ

2 Guided Practice/Apply

READ FOR TEXT EVIDENCE Begin a second read of *How Leopard Got His Spots* with children. Use the instructional support to guide children to analyze the text:

- Sequence of Events, p. T127 ▬ **RL.1.3, RL.1.7**

- Story Lesson, p. T129 ▬ **RL.1.2**

DIRECTED NOTE-TAKING The graphic organizer will be completed with children during the second read on p. T127.

DAILY ASSESSMENT

Are children able to describe the sequence of events?

IF...	THEN...
children have difficulty describing the sequence of events,	use **Differentiate Comprehension** for Struggling Readers, p. T186. See also Intervention Lesson 12, p. S21.
children can describe many of the events in sequence,	use **Differentiate Comprehension** for On Level Readers, p. T186.
children can describe the sequence of events,	use **Differentiate Comprehension** for Advanced Readers, p. T187.

SMALL GROUP Options

Differentiate Comprehension, pp. T186–T187
Group English Language Learners according to language proficiency. See also ELL Lesson 12, p. E15, for scaffolded support.

Whole Group

DAY 2

 Go Digital

• *my*WriteSmart
• eBook

SECOND READ

Your Turn  Use Text Evidence

Your Turn  *my*WriteSmart

▶ SHARE OBJECTIVES

• Discuss the story, using text evidence and drawings to clarify ideas.
• Write the story from another character's point of view as a response to literature.

RETURN TO THE ESSENTIAL QUESTION

Have partners discuss the Essential Question. Have children provide text evidence from the words and pictures in the story to support their discussion. Then, have one partner draw a jungle animal while the other draws a farm animal. Have partners take turns telling how the two animals are different, using the pictures as visual aids to clarify their ideas. ▬ **RL.1.2, RL.1.7, SL.1.5**

 **Classroom Conversation** Have children continue their discussion of the folktale, retelling story events, including key details. Ask children to recall the lesson Hal Hyena learned, and then discuss what they think will happen the next time Hal sees the other animals. Have children follow classroom discussion rules, such as listening carefully to the speaker, waiting their turn to talk, and staying on topic. Help them to build conversations by coaching them to have multiple exchanges with classmates, responding appropriately to others' comments and adding their own ideas. ▬ **RL.1.1, RL.1.2, SL.1.1a, SL.1.1b**

 **COMMON CORE** **RL.1.1** ask and answer questions about key details; **RL.1.2** retell stories and demonstrate understanding of the message or lesson; **RL.1.7** use illustrations and details to describe characters, setting, or events; **W.1.3** write narratives; **SL.1.1a** follow rules for discussions; **SL.1.1b** build on others' talk in conversations by responding to others' comments; **SL.1.5** add drawings or visual displays to descriptions to clarify ideas, thoughts, and feelings

RETURN TO THE ESSENTIAL QUESTION

 **Turn and Talk** **How are jungle animals different from animals on a farm?** Use the words and pictures in the story to describe the jungle animals. Then draw a jungle animal and a farm animal. Take turns telling how the animals are different.

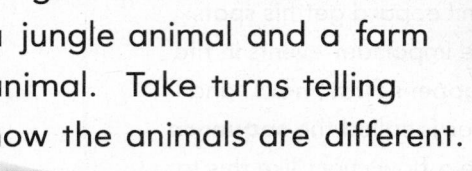

 **Classroom Conversation**

Now talk about these questions with your class.

1 How does Len Leopard help Fred Turtle?

2 Why does Fred splash paint on Hal?

3 What do you think will happen the next time Hal Hyena sees the other animals?

66

ELL ENGLISH LANGUAGE LEARNERS
Comprehensible Input

Beginning Help children review the words *first*, *next*, and *last*. Have them put these words in order and read them aloud.

Low Intermediate Have children draw pictures from *How Leopard Got His Spots* to show the sequence of events in the story. Have them tell what their pictures show.

High Intermediate Reread the story, having children pay attention to the sequence of events. Have them tell what happened first, next, and last.

Proficient Have children use complete sentences to tell the important events that happen in the story, in the correct sequence.

See ELL Lesson 12, p. E14, for further comprehension support.

WRITE ABOUT READING

Response Write the story the way Hal Hyena would tell it. Write sentences to tell what happens in the beginning, middle, and end of the story.

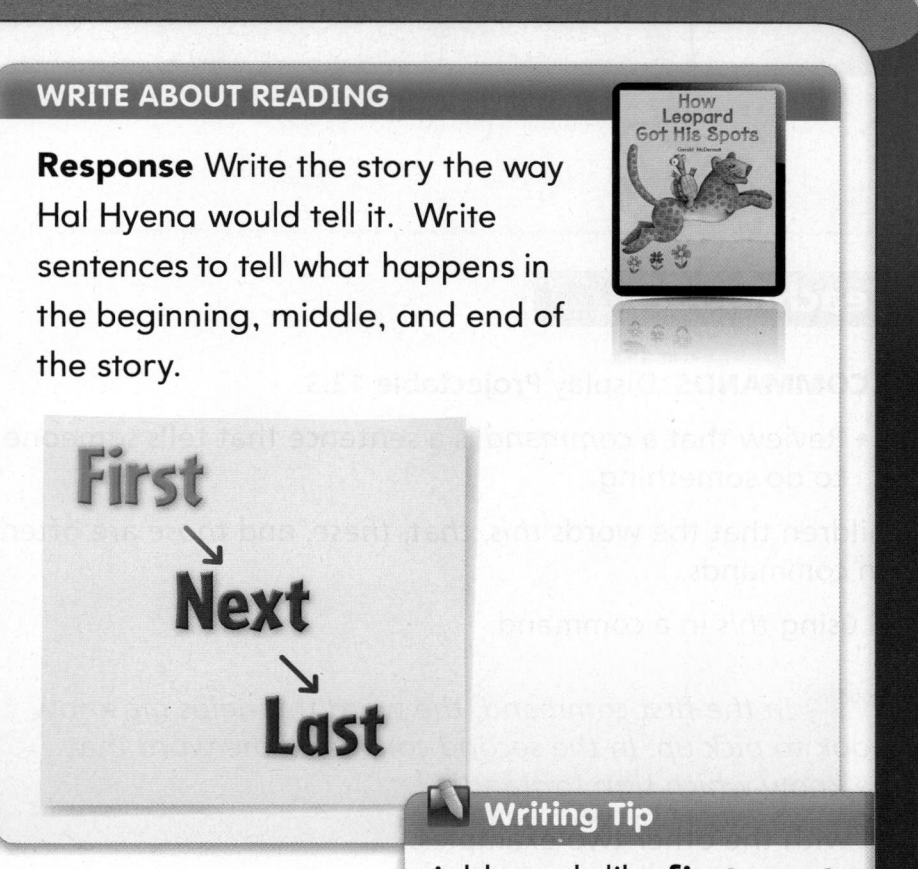

Writing Tip

Add words like **first**, **next**, and **last** to tell the events in order.

Go Digital

COMMON CORE **RL.1.1** ask and answer questions about key details; **RL.1.2** retell stories and demonstrate understanding of the message or lesson; **RL.1.7** use illustrations and details to describe characters, setting, or events; **W.1.3** write narratives; **SL.1.1a** follow rules for discussions

67

WRITE ABOUT READING — Performance Task

Tell children that they will write a story in response to the folktale *How Leopard Got His Spots*.

- Read and discuss **Student Book** p. 67.

- Explain that children will write a story from Hal Hyena's point of view, or what Hal saw, did, and felt during the story.

- Make sure children understand they must tell what happens at the beginning, middle, and end of the story.

- Guide them to write a good ending sentence that provides a sense of closure for their stories.

- Have children draft, revise, illustrate, and then share their stories with classmates.

WRITING TIP Read the Writing Tip with children before they begin writing. Explain to them that using time-order words, such as *first, next,* and *last,* will help make the order of the events clear in their stories. ▬ **W.1.3**

Have children complete the Write About Reading activity through *my*WriteSmart. Children will read the prompt within *my*WriteSmart and have access to multiple writing resources, including the Student eBook, Writing Rubrics, and Graphic Organizers.

Go Digital
• *my*WriteSmart
• eBook
• GrammarSnap Videos

Grammar Commands

▶ SHARE OBJECTIVES

- **Grammar** Identify and use simple commands with *that*, *this*, or *those*.
- **Spelling** Spell words with *ch* and *tch* using conventional spelling patterns.
- **Handwriting** Print the spelling words.
- **Writing** Write instructions using order words.

ELL ENGLISH LANGUAGE LEARNERS
Language Transfer

All Proficiencies Display the line from **Student Book** p. 56 *Look at me!* Have the class repeat the phrase. Explain to them that this is a command because it tells someone to do something. Guide them in finding another command phrase in the text.

1 Teach/Model

COMMANDS Display **Projectable 12.3**.
- Review that a *command* is a sentence that tells someone to do something.
- Tell children that the words *this, that, these,* and *those* are often used in commands.
- Model using *this* in a command.

Think Aloud *In the first command, the word* this *helps me know which book to pick up. In the second command the word* that *helps me know which sign to stand by.*

- Repeat with the other two examples.

2 Guided Practice/Apply

- Work together to complete **Projectable 12.3**.
- Read aloud each sentence and ask volunteers to identify how the word they circled helps make the command clearer.
- Provide sentence starters for children to use to produce commands. Tell them to use *this, that,* or *those.* (Cover up _____; Run down _____; Feed the _____.) ▪ **L.1.1h, L.1.1j**

Spelling Words with *ch* and *tch*

SPELLING WORDS

BASIC	
chin	chop
much	chip
rich	chick

CHALLENGE	
match	pitch

Word Sort

- Review **Sound/Spelling Card** *chick*. *What sound do you hear at the beginning of* chick? *the /ch/ sound*
- Draw a two-column chart on the board. Write *ch* in the left column. Write *tch* in the right column. Model underlining the /ch/ sound in *chin* and putting in the correct column. Have children add spelling words to each column.
- For additional practice, you may want to distribute **Reader's Notebook** Vol. 1 p. 168. ▪ **L.1.2d**

Handwriting

Model how to form *chin, chop,* and *much*. Handwriting models are available on the **Handwriting Models Blackline Masters**.

ch	tch
chin	match
much	pitch
rich	
chop	
chip	
chick	

COMMON CORE **W.1.2** write informative/explanatory text; **SL.1.5** add drawings or visual displays to descriptions to clarify ideas, thoughts, and feelings; **SL.1.6** produce complete sentences when appropriate to task and situation; **L.1.1h** use determiners; **L.1.1j** produce and expand simple and compound declarative, interrogative, imperative, and exclamatory sentences; **L.1.2d** use conventional spelling for words with commands spelling patterns and for frequently occurring irregular words

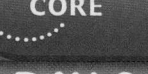

Informative Writing Focus Trait: Sentence Fluency

1 Teach/Model

USING ORDER WORDS Explain to children that some words tell the order in which things happen. Explain that these include words like *first*, *second*, *third*, and *last* as well as *now*, *next*, *then*, and *finally*.

- Write *first*, *next*, and *last* on the board. Read them aloud. Then have three children stand up in succession. Help children use *first*, *next*, and *last* to describe the order in which the children stood.

- Discuss examples of order words used by the author of *How Leopard Got His Spots*.

Connect to *How Leopard Got His Spots*

Instead of this...	...the author wrote this.
Hal tricked Fred. He ran away.	Hal tricked Fred. **Then** he ran away.
Fred painted Jill Giraffe.	Fred painted Jill Giraffe **next**.

What does the word next *tell you about the order in which Fred painted his friends?* He painted somebody before he painted Jill.

- Display **Projectable 12.4**.

- Discuss the pictures and point out that they are in the wrong order. Model using the words *first*, *next*, and *last* to write instructions and list the steps in the proper order.

2 Guided Writing

- Have the whole group work together to draw three steps to doing something simple, such as making a peanut butter sandwich.

- Have each child tell a partner about the three pictures. Have them use order words as they tell about the steps shown.

- Have children work with partners to create instructions to match the pictures. Remind them to use order words as they write or dictate their instructions. ▬ **W.1.2, SL.1.5, SL.1.6**

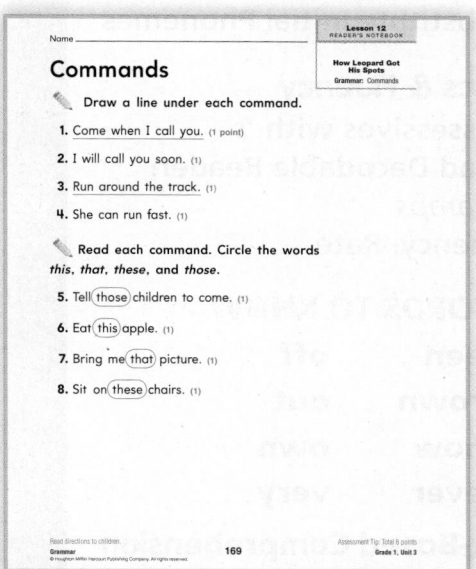

Reader's Notebook Vol. 1 p. 169

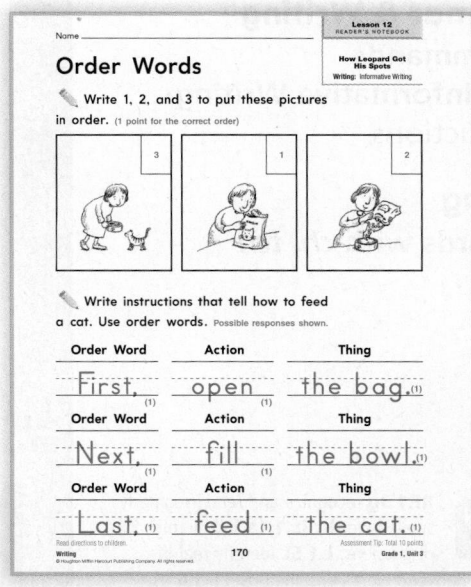

Reader's Notebook Vol. 1 p. 170

DAY 3

Today's Goals

Vocabulary & Oral Language
• Apply Vocabulary Knowledge

Phonemic Awareness
• Substitute Initial Phonemes

Phonics & Fluency
• Possessives with *'s*
• Read Decodable Reader: *Champs*
• Fluency: Rate

☑ **WORDS TO KNOW**

been	off
brown	out
know	own
never	very

Text-Based Comprehension
Independent Reading
• Reader's Guide
• Self-Selected Reading

Grammar & Writing
• Commands
 Informative Writing: Instructions

Spelling
• Words with *ch, tch*

 **COMMON CORE** **RF.1.3g** recognize and read irregularly spelled words; **SL.1.1a** follow rules for discussions; **L.1.5c** identify real-life connections between words and their use; **L.1.6** use words and phrases acquired through conversations, reading and being read to, and responding to texts

Opening Routines

Warm Up with Wordplay

Make a Rhyme

Remind children they have been learning about words that end with /ch/. Display and read the word *match*.

Have children turn and talk to a partner to come up with as many other words in this word family (words that rhyme with *match*) as they can. Call on children to share their words. Record the words and reread them with children. Then have children work together to use as many of the rhyming words as they can to make a poem. Have them take turns adding lines. Write down the poem and read it aloud with the whole class.

batch	hatch
latch	catch
patch	snatch

Daily Phonemic Awareness

Substitute Initial Phonemes

- *Today we're going to change the first sound in a word to make a new word. For example, what do we get if we change the /b/ in* bat *to /s/?* sat *Good! Now let's change the /s/ in* sat *to /m/. What word do we get?* mat *Let's keep going.*

Change the . . .	Result
/r/ in *rich* to /d/	*ditch*
/j/ in *jump* to /l/	*lump*
/h/ in *hat* to /th/	*that*
/m/ in *men* to /th/	*then*
/ch/ in *chain* to /r/	*rain*
/n/ in *neck* to /ch/	*check*
/d/ in *dance* to /ch/	*chance*

Corrective Feedback

- If a child misses a word, say the correct word and model the task. *Listen: hat, /h/ /ă/ /t/. Now change the /h/ to /th/. What is the new word?* that

- Have children do it once with you before doing it on their own. Then back up several words and continue the game.

Daily High-Frequency Words

Introduce

- Point to the **High-Frequency Word Card** *know*.

- *Say the word.* know *Spell the word.* k, n, o, w *Write the word. Check the word.*

- Repeat the procedure with the words *been, brown, never, off, out, own,* and *very.* ◀ RF.1.3g

Throw the Stars Game

- Choose one of this week's High-Frequency Words *(been, brown, know, never, off, out, own,* or *very).*

- As you point to each letter, have children say it with you and throw one hand at a time toward the ceiling as if "throwing a star."

- Repeat the procedure for the remaining High-Frequency Words.

Corrective Feedback

- Say the correct word and have children repeat it. Out. *What is the word?* out

- Have children spell the word. *o, u, t How do we say this word?* out

- Have children reread all of the cards in random order.

Daily Vocabulary Boost

- Guide children to interact with the Oral Vocabulary words by asking the following questions. Remind them to speak clearly when participating in discussion.

  What is your favorite adventure *story or movie?*

  What kind of pet is frisky?

  What are some of the things that make you shiver?

- Ask children to work together to explain *adventure, frisky,* and *shiver* in their own words. Make sure children follow appropriate rules for discussion, such as listening to speakers, taking turns, and staying on topic. ◀ SL.1.1a, L.1.5c, L.1.6

☑ **Oral Vocabulary**

adventure
frisky
shiver
spy
tumbles
view

Whole Group

DAY 3

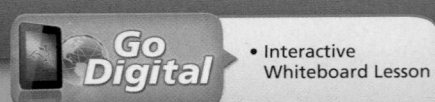
Go Digital • Interactive Whiteboard Lesson

JOURNEYS Phonics

Interactive Whiteboard Lesson:
Possessives with 's

Phonemic Awareness/Phonics

▶ SHARE OBJECTIVES
- Learn how to use an apostrophe.
- Blend and read possessives with 's.

▶ SKILLS TRACE

Possessives with 's	
Introduce	T148–T149
Differentiate	T188
Reteach	T196
Review	T160
Assess	Weekly Tests, Lesson 12

ELL **ENGLISH LANGUAGE LEARNERS**

Comprehensible Input

Beginning Write *Jim* and *Jim's* on the board. Circle *'s.* Point to and read each word. Have children repeat.

Low Intermediate Show **Sound/Spelling Card** *chick.* Write and read *the chick's pen.* Then have children read it with you.

High Intermediate Write and read with children the words *dog, cat, mom, Jim.* Then have children add an *'s* to each word and read the new words.

Proficient Have partners write their own names with *'s.* Then have them use the new word correctly in a sentence.

See ELL Lesson 12, p. E17, for scaffolded support.

Possessives with 's

PHONEMIC AWARENESS WARM-UP *Listen as I say a word:* sun. *If I change the first sound to /b/, I get* bun. *Let's say more words together. Listen to the word:* hip. *What word do I get if I change the first sound to /ch/?* chip **Repeat the process with these word pairs:** *cat, hat; Sam, jam; less, mess; pick, sick.*

1 Teach/Model

INTRODUCE POSSESSIVES WITH 'S Explain that sometimes nouns have letters added to the ends of them to tell us more about the word. When an *s* is added, it can make the word plural. When a special mark called an **apostrophe** is added before the *s*, it shows that the noun owns something.

- Write the words *cat, cats,* and *cat's* on the board. Point out that the second and third words have *s* added to the end of the word, but they mean different things. Circle the apostrophe in the third word. Tell children that this mark means the cat owns something. Read each word and have children repeat after you.

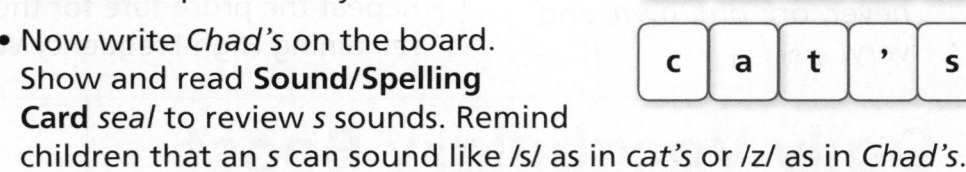

- Now write *Chad's* on the board. Show and read **Sound/Spelling Card** *seal* to review *s* sounds. Remind children that an *s* can sound like /s/ as in *cat's* or /z/ as in *Chad's.*

- Use the word *cat's* in a sentence: *My cat's dish is empty.* Have children repeat /k/ /ă/ /t/ /s/ with you.

- Repeat with *dog* and *dog's.*

COMMON CORE
RF.1.3a know the spelling-sound correspondences for common consonant digraphs; **RF.1.3b** decode regularly spelled one-syllable words; **RF.1.3f** read words with inflectional endings; **RF.1.3g** recognize and read irregularly spelled words; **L.1.2e** spell untaught words phonetically, drawing on phonemic awareness and spelling conventions

2 Guided Practice

CONTINUOUS BLENDING ROUTINE Display **Letter Cards** *b, u, g, s* to model blending *bug* and *bugs*. Blend the sounds, stretching out each word while pointing to the letters in a sweeping motion. *Listen: /b/ /ŭ/ /g/, bug; /b/ /ŭ/ /g/ /z/, bugs.*

Blend once more with children. Then have children blend the sounds and read the words on their own.

Write *bugs* on the board. Write an apostrophe between *g* and *s*. Remind children that the letter *s* with an apostrophe at the end of a word shows ownership. The word now means "something belongs to the bug."

REPEAT CONTINUOUS BLENDING ROUTINE with the words in Row 1 below. Use the **Corrective Feedback** steps if children need additional help.

DECODING Call on individuals to blend one or more words and to read the sample sentences. 🔵 RF.1.3a, RF.1.3b, RF.1.3f, RF.1.3g

---

1. Seth's   ant's   mom's   plant's   chick's
2. rug's   batch   limping   jumps   this

Beth's sis is <u>funny</u> <u>and</u> rich.

<u>My</u> <u>friend's</u> cat is black.

---

3 Apply

Use **Instructional Routine 6** and the sentences shown to teach connecting sounds to writing. Have children say each word aloud after you. Then have them identify the sounds and write the letters that stand for each sound. Print the words so children can check their work. 🔵 L.1.2e

---

- **Dad's**   Mitch is <u>Dad's</u> best friend.
- **pet's**   Put the scraps in the <u>pet's</u> dish.
- **Seth's**   <u>Seth's</u> snack is in the tent.

Corrective Feedback Work with the whole group to correct errors, following the model below.

Phonics Error:
A child reads *Seth's* as *Seth*.

Correct the error. Review the **Sound/Spelling Card.** Say the word and the sound. *The word is* Seth's. *The 's stands for the end sound /s/ in this word.*

Model by asking children what sound ends *Seth's.* Say the word, emphasizing the end sound /s/. *What is the word?* Seth's

Guide *Let's read the word together. The word is* Seth's.

Check *You read the word* Seth. *What is the correct word?* Seth's

Reinforce Go back three or four words and have children continue reading. Make note of errors and review those words during tomorrow's lesson.

SMALL GROUP Options   **Go to pp. T188 for additional Phonics support.**

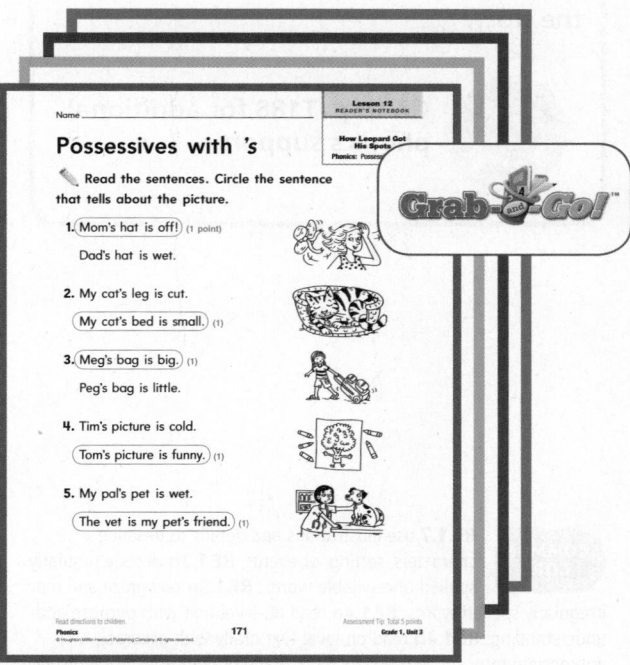

Reader's Notebook Vol. 1 p. 171
See Grab-and-Go™ Resources for additional leveled practice.

• Decodable Reader
• Cold Reads Online

Decodable Reader

▶ **SHARE OBJECTIVE**
• Read text with regularly spelled one-syllable words, digraphs, possessives with 's, and high-frequency words.

DAILY ASSESSMENT **RtI**

Corrective Feedback Work with the whole group to correct errors, following the model below.

Decoding Error:
A child reads *Fran's* as *Fran*.

Correct the error. Say the word. *That word is* Fran's. *The letter* s *at the end stands for the sound* /z/.

Guide Review the sound/spelling. *Remember that the* 's *at the end of a word makes a new word.* Have children blend and read the word. *What is the word?* Fran's

Check *Go back to the beginning of the sentence and read it again.*

Reinforce Record the error and review the word again before children reread the story.

Go to p. T188 for additional phonics support.

COMMON CORE **RL.1.7** use illustrations and details to describe characters, setting, or events; **RF.1.3b** decode regularly spelled one-syllable words; **RF.1.3g** recognize and read irregularly spelled words; **RF.1.4a** read on-level text with purpose and understanding; **RF.1.4b** read on-level text orally with accuracy, appropriate rate, and expression; **SL.1.5** add drawings or visual displays to descriptions to clarify ideas, thoughts, and feelings

Read *Champs*

Decodable Reader, Unit 3, pp. 39–44

REVIEW POSSESSIVE 's AND WORDS TO KNOW Tell children that this story has many words with 's. Review with them the following Words to Know, which they will also read in the story: *been, know,* and *own.*

PREVIEW Have children preview pages 39–41 and predict what they think the story is about. Ask volunteers to tell things they do with a pet. Then tell children they are going to read a story about two friends and how they play with their dogs.

MODEL FLUENCY AND RATE Have children follow along as you read page 39 aloud, very slowly. Tell children that when you read, you should read at a rate that is not too slow. If you read too slowly, it can be hard for listeners to understand what you are reading. Read the sentence again at a faster pace. Lead children in a choral reading, reading the page fluently and at an appropriate rate.

READ Remind children to track words from left to right. Have children read each page silently and then choral-read aloud. Coach them to read fluently and at an appropriate rate. Listen as children read to make sure they are correctly decoding the possessive words and accurately reading the Words to Know. ◼ **RF.1.3b, RF.1.3g**

RESPONDING Have children page through the story. Have children take turns pantomiming the things Bill and Fran do with their dogs. Encourage them to use the illustrations as a guide. ◼ **RL.1.7, SL.1.5**

Fluency

Rate

1 Teach/Model

Explain to children that good readers know how to adjust their reading rate, or speed. Display **Projectable 12.5**. Explain that sometimes it is necessary to read more slowly. Model reading the first four sentences of the paragraph quickly. Then stop and say: *There is a lot of information in this paragraph. I can't remember it all. I'm going to reread these sentences again, then read the rest more slowly.* Model rereading and reading the rest of the paragraph at a slower rate. Next, read question 1 and model how to reread to find the answer.

Go to p. T189 for additional fluency support.

Projectable 12.5

How Leopard Got His Spots Fluency Rate

Reading to Understand

Good readers read carefully. You should not be afraid to slow down and reread long sentences.

Listen to the paragraph.
Then write answers to each question.

Dutch is Bill's dog. Dutch and Bill play tug. Dutch is the tug champ. Bill sits on his bench to rest. Dutch has his own spot to rest. Dutch's spot is not a bench. Bill and Dutch do not get much rest. Bill's pal Fran is here.

1. Who is Dutch? Dutch is Bill's dog.
2. What do Bill and Dutch play? They play tug.
3. Where does Bill sit to rest? on his bench
4. Who is Bill's pal? Fran

2 Guided Practice

Read question 2. Reread the second sentence of the paragraph at a slow rate. Have children echo-read the answer. Repeat for questions 3 and 4, having children slowly echo-read each answer. ▬ RF.1.4a

3 Apply

Have pairs practice reading *How Leopard Got His Spots* to each other. Have volunteers read each page aloud. Guide children to read with accuracy, appropriate rate, and expression. Remind them that if they get to a part that is hard to understand, they should slow down so they can better understand what they are reading. ▬ RF.1.4a, RF.1.4b

Cold Reads: Support for fluent reading and comprehension

Independent Reading

▶ SHARE OBJECTIVES

- Read and comprehend literature.
- Ask and answer questions about key details in a story.
- Read independently from a "just right" book.
- Read fluently at an appropriate rate.

 **ENGLISH LANGUAGE LEARNERS**

Comprehensible Input

Beginning Ask children *yes/no* questions to review the important events in the story.

Low Intermediate Ask children some details about the story, such as *With whom was Fred Turtle playing catch?* and *Why did Len want spots too?*

High Intermediate Have children retell in their own words the trick Hal played on Fred and the trick Fred played on Hal.

Proficient Have partners create a chart describing the traits of each character in the story. Have them talk about how they feel about each character and tell why.

Reader's Guide

Revisit the Anchor Text

Lead children in a brief discussion about *How Leopard Got His Spots*. Have them recount the important events, and tell the lesson the story teaches. Remind children to follow rules for discussions, such as listening with care. As children speak, guide them to connect their ideas about the story to others' comments. 🔊 **RL.1.2, RL.1.3, SL.1.1a, SL.1.1b**

Have children read *How Leopard Got His Spots* on their own and think about key details about the story. Have them use the Reader's Guide pages in their **Reader's Notebook**, pp. 172–173. Explain that they should respond to the questions and support their responses with text evidence from the pictures and sentences in *How Leopard Got His Spots*. 🔊 **RL.1.1, RL.1.7, RL.1.10**

MODEL QUESTIONING Demonstrate asking a question about *How Leopard Got His Spots*. For example, write this question on the board: *Why did Fred Turtle paint Len?* Reread **Student Book** pp. 54, 58–59 with children, and work together to respond to the question.

GENERATE QUESTIONS Have children work independently or collaboratively to generate questions about *How Leopard Got His Spots* and share their questions with the class. Have them work together to use text evidence and their own experiences to answer the questions. 🔊 **RL.1.1**

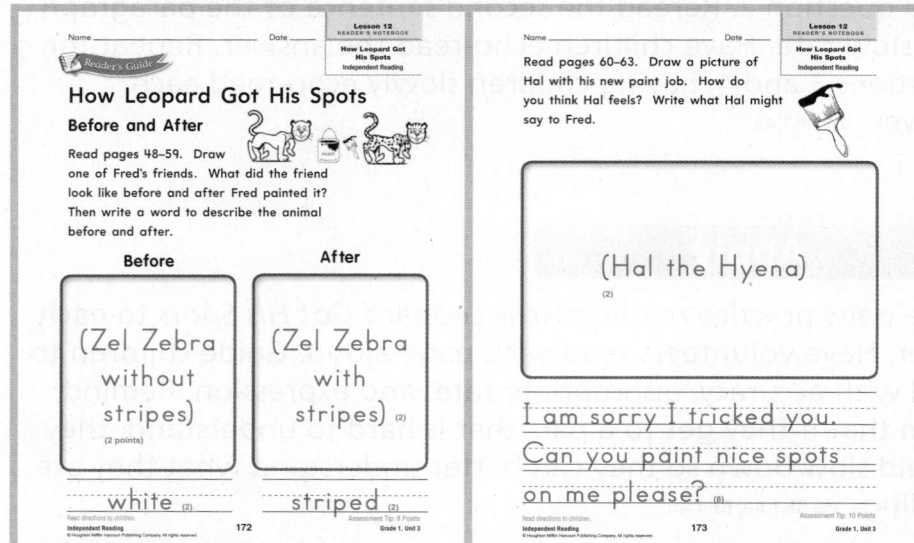

Reader's Notebook pp. 172–173

COMMON CORE
RL.1.1 ask and answer questions about key details; **RL.1.2** retell stories and demonstrate understanding of the message or lesson; **RL.1.3** describe characters, settings, and major events; **RL.1.7** use illustrations and details to describe characters, setting, or events; **RL.1.10** read prose and poetry; **RF.1.4b** read on-level text orally with accuracy, appropriate rate, and expression; **SL.1.1a** follow rules for discussions; **SL.1.1b** build on others' talk in conversations by responding to others' comments

Self-Selected Reading

Genres of Interest

Tell children that one way to choose a book is to think about a kind of book, or a genre, that they enjoy. Discuss these points with children.

- Ask yourself whether you want to read a book with information and facts about a topic or whether you want to read something make-believe.

- Think about whether you would like to read a picture book, a chapter book, a play, or a poem.

- Do you like realistic stories? Do you like fantasy stories?

- Flip through the book to find out what genre it is.

Tell children that once they have selected a book, they should open it and read one or two pages to be sure it is "just right." Guide children to choose appropriate books to read independently.

Self-Correction Strategies

Read for Fluency at an Appropriate Rate

Tell children that good readers read at different rates depending on what kind of text they are reading. When there is a lot of information in an informational text, for instance, they might read more slowly, so that they will be able to understand the information better.

Tell children that as they read their independent reading books, they will practice reading at an appropriate rate for the type of book they are reading. Model an example of appropriate rate for them. Let children know that reading at the correct rate takes practice.

Have partners read aloud to each other from their self-selected books. When one child has finished reading, his or her partner should provide feedback about rate. Each partner should read more than once to improve his or her fluency and rate. Guide children to practice reading at a rate that makes it easy for them to understand the text, slowing down as needed if comprehension breaks down. **RF.1.4b**

Apply Vocabulary Knowledge

▶ SHARE OBJECTIVES

- Use words and phrases acquired through conversations, reading and being read to, and responding to texts.
- Identify real-life connections between words and their use.
- Learn the different parts of a dictionary.

ELL ENGLISH LANGUAGE LEARNERS

Comprehensible Input

Beginning Discuss the words *change*, *redo*, and *transform*. Explain that these words mean about the same thing.

Low Intermediate Have children say other words that mean the same thing as *transform*.

High Intermediate Have children complete this sentence frame: _____ *can transform to* _____.

Proficient Have children tell about something that can *transform*. Have them use complete sentences.

See ELL Lesson 12, p. E16, for further vocabulary support.

✓ SELECTION VOCABULARY >> Review

Review with children the Selection Vocabulary words on p. T120. Call on children to explain how the words were used in *How Leopard Got His Spots*.

ENRICH VOCABULARY Write the following Related Words on the board. Read each word aloud, and have children repeat after you. Then read the student-friendly explanation for each word. Connect each word's meaning to the story *How Leopard Got His Spots* by writing the context sentences on the board and reading them aloud.

cruel: Something is cruel when it brings pain or makes you feel bad. *Hal Hyena played a cruel trick on Fred Turtle.*

transform: If you transform something, you totally change it. *Fred Turtle painted his friends to transform their looks.*

struggling: If you are struggling, you are making a great effort with your body or mind to do something. *Fred Turtle was struggling to get out of the plants.*

MAKE CONNECTIONS Discuss all of the words using the items below to help children make connections between vocabulary words and their use. **L.1.5b, L.1.5c**

- Which of these words names an animal with stripes: ***leopard***, *flag*, ***zebra***, *tie*?
- Tell about a time that you have ***danced***. Show what it was like.
- What are your favorite ***flowers***?
- Would it be ***cruel*** to invite someone to a party? Why or why not?
- Tell about something you would like to ***paint***.
- How would you look if you were ***struggling*** to remember something?
- What could you do to ***transform*** an old garden?
- Which of these words names an animal with spots: ***giraffe***, *map*, *Sun*, ***hyena***?

COMMON CORE **L.1.5b** define words by category and by key attributes; **L.1.5c** identify real-life connections between words and their use **L.1.6** use words and phrases acquired through conversations, reading and being read to, and responding to texts

T154 • Unit 3 Lesson 12

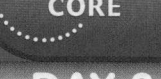
Dictionary Skills

DISCUSS USING A DICTIONARY Review with children that dictionary entries are in A, B, C order. Explain how this can help them find words.

The words in a dictionary or glossary are in alphabetical order. If I want to find the word zebra, *I must look at the beginning letter. Zebra begins with* z, *so I know I need to look near the end of the dictionary because* z *comes at the end of the alphabet.*

Guide children to look up the Lesson 12 Selection Vocabulary words *leopard* and *flowers* in a print dictionary or glossary. As a class, discuss how to look up the singular form of *flower* when you want to find the plural form. Then, show children how to look up the same words in an online dictionary.

Have partners work together to look up the new word *transform* in a print dictionary and an online dictionary. Discuss Internet safety rules before looking up any information online. Ask volunteers to read aloud the definitions. As a class talk about how the definitions are the same and how they are different.

Literacy and Language Guide
Additional Lesson 12 vocabulary lessons appear in the Literacy and Language Guide.

QUICKWRITE

Read aloud each question below. Pause a few minutes between each item to allow children to write a response. **L.1.6**

1. What subjects were you struggling with last year?

2. Would it be cruel to break your sister's toy on purpose? Why?

3. Name something you would like to transform. How would you change it?

- *my*WriteSmart
- eBook
- GrammarSnap Videos

Grammar Commands

▶ SHARE OBJECTIVES

- **Grammar** Identify and write simple commands using *that, these,* or *those.*
- **Spelling** Spell words with *ch* and *tch* using conventional spelling patterns.
- **Writing** Choose a topic and use a graphic organizer to plan instructions.

ELL ENGLISH LANGUAGE LEARNERS
Language Transfer

All Proficiencies Say, *Children, stand up.* Once all children are up, say, *Sit down, please.* Explain that *stand up* and *sit down* are commands. Tell children that we use commands to give orders or to tell people to do something. Encourage volunteers to give you more examples of commands.

1 Teach/Model

12.6 **COMMANDS** Display **Projectable 12.6**. Review that a *command* is a sentence that tells someone to do something.

- Tell children that a command can end in a period, or a command can end in an exclamation point to show strong feeling.

- Model reading the two examples to show how the exclamation point is used to show strong feeling.

Think Aloud *The command* Stop the car *tells the driver to stop, but does not suggest an emergency. The command* Stop the car! *tells the driver to stop at once.*

2 Guided Practice/Apply

- Work together to complete **Projectable 12.6**.
- Have children read the pairs of commands, showing strong feeling when an exclamation point is used.
- Provide sentence starters for children to use to produce commands. *(Hold that____; Collect these ____; Find those____.)*
- For additional practice, you may want to distribute **Reader's Notebook** Vol. 1 page 175. ⬤ **L.1.1j**

Spelling Words with *ch* and *tch*

SPELLING WORDS

BASIC	
chin	chop
much	chip
rich	chick
CHALLENGE	
match	pitch

Segment Sounds

- Model segmenting sounds. *Listen as I say* chin: /ch/ /ĭ/ /n/. *Repeat after me:* /ch/ /ĭ/ /n/.

- Tell children that saying the sounds in a word will help them spell it. Have children segment the sounds in *chop, much,* and *pitch.* ⬤ **RF.1.2d**

Build Words

- Use **Letter Cards** to model building *chin.* Have children read and write the word.

- Have partners use **Letter Cards** to build words with *ch* and *tch.* Have children read and spell one word they built.

- For additional practice, you may want to distribute **Reader's Notebook** Vol. 1 page 174. ⬤ **L.1.2d**

 COMMON CORE

RF.1.2d segment spoken single-syllable words into their complete sequence of individual sounds; **W.1.2** write informative/explanatory texts; **W.1.5** focus on a topic, respond to questions/suggestions from peers, and add details to strengthen writing; **L.1.1f** use frequently occurring adjectives **L.1.1h** use determiners; **L.1.1j** produce and expand simple and compound declarative, interrogative, imperative, and exclamatory

Informative Writing Prewriting

1 Teach/Model

PLANNING INSTRUCTIONS Explain to children that as they write a letter with instructions, they should use time-order words that make the order of steps clear.

- Display **Projectable 12.7.** Tell children that they can use a flow chart like this to plan their instructions. Read aloud the prompt. Then model filling in the graphic organizer.

Think Aloud
I want to write to my friend to tell her how to make a mouse puppet. I will use order words. In the first box, I will write the first step: First, cut a circle from gray paper.

- Have children help you think of three more steps to tell how to make a mouse puppet. Record these steps in the numbered boxes, using time-order words as possible.

- Save the completed flow chart for Day 4.

2 Independent Writing

- Display and read aloud the writing prompt. Ask children to share their ideas about possible topics. Help each child choose an animal that he or she might make a puppet for.

- Work with children to complete flow charts for their chosen topics like the one completed above. Remind them to use words such as *first, next,* and *last* to make the order of steps clear.
  ▬ W.1.2, W.1.5

Oral Language Conventions

Using Adjectives Remind children that they can use adjectives to make the steps in their instructions more specific and clear. To illustrate this point, identify one of the adjectives you used in your flow chart. Have children identify other adjectives on your chart and suggest additional ones that might be included to improve your instructions. ▬ L.1.1f

sentences; **L.1.2d** use conventional spelling for words with common spelling patterns and for frequently occurring irregular words

---

Daily Proofreading Practice

                          Dallas
There is a zoo in ~~dallas~~.
                  ^

     know   Texas
I ~~no~~ that is in ~~texas~~.
     ^   ^

Projectable 12.7

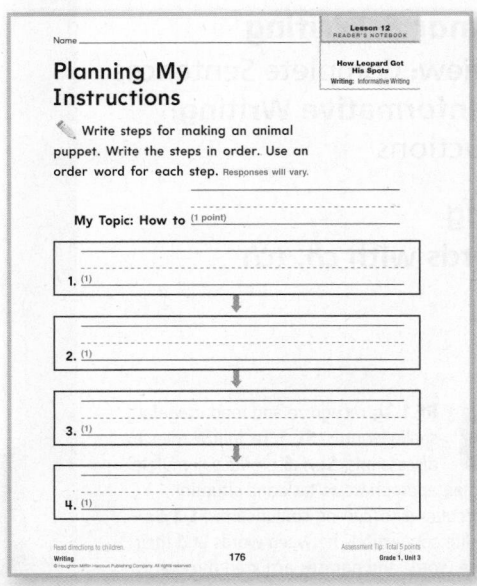

How Leopard Got His Spots Writing Informative Writing

Planning My Instructions

Write a letter to a friend. In your letter, write instructions that explain how to make an animal puppet.

Write steps for making an animal puppet. Write the steps in order. Use an order word for each step.

My Topic: How to Make a Mouse Puppet

1. First, cut a circle from gray paper.
2. Next, draw a mouse face on the paper.
3. Then, glue a stick to the bottom of the face.
4. Last, glue string whiskers on the face.

Writing   Grade 1, Unit 3

Lesson 12
READER'S NOTEBOOK

How Leopard Got His Spots
Writing: Informative Writing

Name _____

Planning My Instructions

✎ Write steps for making an animal puppet. Write the steps in order. Use an order word for each step. Responses will vary.

My Topic: How to _____ (1 point)

1. (1) _____
2. (1) _____
3. (1) _____
4. (1) _____

176   Grade 1, Unit 3

Reader's Notebook Vol. 1 p. 176

DAY 4

Today's Goals

Vocabulary & Oral Language
- **Vocabulary Strategies:** Homophones

Phonemic Awareness
- Substitute Initial Phonemes

Phonics & Fluency
- Words with *ch, tch*
- Possessives with *'s*
- Read Decodable Reader: *Kits, Chicks, and Pups*

☑ **WORDS TO KNOW**

been	off
brown	out
know	own
never	very

Text-Based Comprehension
Connect to the Topic
- **Read Informational Text:** *The Rain Forest*
- Compare Texts

Grammar & Writing
- **Review:** Complete Sentences
-  **Informative Writing:** Instructions

Spelling
- Words with *ch, tch*

COMMON CORE **RF.1.3g** recognize and read irregularly spelled words; **SL.1.1a** follow rules for discussions; **SL.1.6** produce complete sentences when appropriate to task and situation; **L.1.1g** use frequently occurring conjunctions; **L.1.5c** identify real-life connections between words and their use; **L.1.6** use words and phrases acquired through conversations, reading and being read to, and responding to texts

Opening Routines

Warm Up with Wordplay

The Never-Ending Story

Tell children that today they will help you write a story about animals, with all the events in order. Display and read aloud the following:

> **First, I saw a leopard in the grass. And then . . .**

Guide one child to continue the story by asking: *And then what happened?* When the child has continued the story, he or she says, "and then." The next child then adds the next event that happens. Encourage children to use time order words and complete sentences. Record the story as children speak and then read the whole story aloud. ◼ **SL.1.6, L.1.1g**

Daily Phonemic Awareness

Substitute Initial Phonemes

- *Today we're going to change the first sound in a word to make a new word. For example, change the /d/ in* den *to /t/. What do we get?* ten *Good! Now let's change the /t/ in* ten *to /m/. What word do we get?* men *Let's keep going.*

Change the . . .	Result
/h/ in *hop* to /ch/	chop
/w/ in *wild* to /ch/	child
/m/ in *miss* to /th/	this
/p/ in *pin* to /ch/	chin
/m/ in *mat* to /ch/	chat
/w/ in *wear* to /th/	there

Corrective Feedback

- If a child misses a word, say the correct word and model the task. *Listen to the word: mat, /m/, /ă/, /t/. Now change the /m/ to /ch/. What is the new word?* chat

- Have children do it once with you before doing it on their own. Then back up several words and continue the game.

Daily High-Frequency Words

Introduce

- Point to the **High-Frequency Word Card** *never.*

- *Say the word.* never *Spell the word.* n, e, v, e, r *Write the word. Check the word.*

- Repeat the procedure with the words *been, brown, know, off, out, own,* and *very.* 🔲 **RF.1.3g**

Explosion Game

- Have children take turns being the leader in a word-chanting game.

- The leader points to a High-Frequency Word and leads the class in chanting it three times: first as a whisper, then with normal volume, and then loudly. The effect is to create a verbal "explosion."

- Continue the procedure to have the class chant the remaining High-Frequency words for this week.

Corrective Feedback

- Say the correct word and have children repeat it. Own. *What is the word?* own

- Have children spell the word. *o, w, n How do we say this word?* own

- Have children reread all of the cards in random order.

Daily Vocabulary Boost

- Guide children to interact with the Oral Vocabulary words by asking the following questions. Remind them to speak clearly when participating in discussion.

  Think of a spy story you read or saw. What was the spy looking for?

  What can happen to a vase that tumbles off a shelf?

  What can you view through a telescope?

- Ask children to work together to explain *spy, tumbles,* and *view* in their own words. Make sure children follow appropriate rules for discussion, such as listening to speakers, taking turns, and staying on topic. 🔲 **SL.1.1a, L.1.5c, L.1.6**

 **Oral Vocabulary**

adventure
frisky
shiver
spy
tumbles
view

Whole Group

DAY 4

Go Digital
• Interactive Whiteboard Lesson
• Decodable Reader

JOURNEYS
Phonics

Interactive Whiteboard Lesson:
Words with Digraphs *ch*, *tch*, and Possessives with *'s*

Phonemic Awareness/Phonics

▶ SHARE OBJECTIVES
- Blend, build, and read possessives with *'s*.
- Review and sort words with consonant digraphs *ch*, *tch*.
- Read on-level text fluently and at an appropriate rate.

▶ SKILLS TRACE

Possessives with *'s*	
Introduce	T148–T149
Differentiate	T188
Reteach	T196
▶ **Review**	**T160**
Assess	Weekly Tests, Lesson 12

▶ SKILLS TRACE

Words with Digraphs *ch*, *tch*	
Introduce	T114–T115
Differentiate	T182
Reteach	T196
▶ **Review**	**T138, T160**
Assess	Weekly Tests, Lesson 12

COMMON CORE **RI.1.2** identify the main topic and retell key details; **RF.1.2c** isolate and pronounce sounds in spoken single-syllable words; **RF.1.3a** know the spelling-sound correspondences for common consonant digraphs; **RF.1.3b** decode regularly spelled one-syllable words; **RF.1.3g** recognize and read irregularly spelled words; **RF.1.4b** read on-level text orally with accuracy, appropriate rate, and expression; **L.1.2d** use conventional spelling for words with common spelling patterns and for frequently occurring irregular words

Review Possessives with *'s*; Digraphs *ch*, *tch*

PHONEMIC AWARENESS WARM-UP Tell children you will say a word and ask them to change the first sound to make a new word. *Listen: The word is* dad. *Change /d/ to /m/. What is the new word?* mad Continue with these words: *pat-hat, let-get, chin-pin.*

MAKE AND READ WORDS On the board, copy the letters and the phonogram -*atch* as shown below. Tell children they will help you make new words by saying which letter/s to add to complete the word. Explain that you will give clues to help them. As each word is suggested, write the missing letter/s. Model the first word. Read the following clues. Reread all the words to complete the activity.
▬ RF.1.3a, L.1.2d

1. You can play this with a ball.

2. This also means "fix."

3. This means to take quickly.

4. Baby chicks do this from eggs.

5. Do this when you have an itch.

6. You light a candle with this.

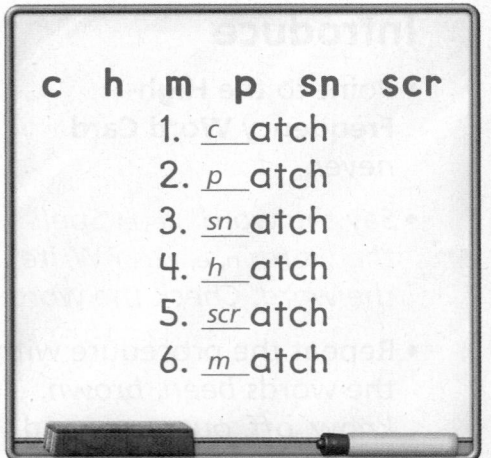

c h m p sn scr

1. _c_ atch
2. _p_ atch
3. _sn_ atch
4. _h_ atch
5. _scr_ atch
6. _m_ atch

GROUPING WORDS BY SOUND Display the **Sound/Spelling Card** *chick* on the board and review the digraphs *ch* and *tch*. Say the word *much*. Have children identify its end sound. Then ask if it belongs on the board with the card. Write the word. Continue sorting words: *that, rich, chip, thin, pitch, think, inch.*

Have children write the words. Then ask children to work with a partner to read each word.
▬ RF.1.2c

ch
_tch

Decodable Reader

  Go Digital

Read *Kits, Chicks, and Pups*

Decodable Reader,
Unit 3, pp. 45–50

Kits, Chicks, and Pups
by Lara Heisman

Cats, dogs, and ducks have moms and dads.
45

Dog moms have pups. This mom and her pups sit still. They make such a good picture.
46

Ducks do not have pups. Ducks have chicks. Ducks swim in a pond. Dad duck is with his chicks.
47

This mom duck has a nest. Eggs will hatch in it. Chicks will pop out! Mom will get off the nest.
48

This kit can run. Mom cat will run, too. The kit and her mom will run and then stop and nap.
49

This mom and dad know that chicks must eat. This mom's chicks will get fed. Mom and dad will do it. The chicks will get big.
50

REVIEW *'s* AND WORDS TO KNOW Remind children that *'s* at the end of a name or noun shows that something belongs to that person or thing. Have children tell what belongs to someone in their family. Explain that children will read possessives in the selection, as well as the following words they have learned: *know, off, out.*

PREVIEW Have children preview pages 45–47 and predict what the selection is about. Ask volunteers to tell what they think mother and father animals must do to take care of their babies.

MODEL FLUENCY AND RATE Read aloud page 49 as children follow along. Point out that you read the first part of the page quickly because the cats are running. Lead children in choral reading the page with fluency and an appropriate rate.

READ Remind children to track the words from left to right and to sweep their hand down from the end of one line to the beginning of the next and continue reading. Have children read each page silently and then choral-read aloud. Listen as children read to make sure they are correctly decoding the words with /ch/ and accurately reading the Words to Know. 🔲 RF.1.3a, RF.1.3b, RF.1.3g

RESPONDING Have partners share the information they have learned from the selection. As they share, monitor to see if they are speaking at an appropriate volume and speed to be clearly understood. 🔲 RI.1.2

DAILY ASSESSMENT 3 2 1 RtI

Corrective Feedback Work with the whole group to correct errors, following the model below.

Decoding Error:
A child reads *mom's* as *mom.*

Correct the error. Say the word. *That word is* mom's. *The letter* s *at the end stands for the sound /z/.*

Guide Have children repeat the word. *What is the word?* mom's

Check *Go back to the beginning of the sentence and read it again.*

Reinforce Record the error and review the word again before children reread the story.

Reread for Fluency/ Develop Automaticity

READ WITH A PARTNER Have partners reread *Kits, Chicks, and Pups* three or four times, taking turns reading aloud each page. Remind them to read words correctly and to read smoothly. Visit partners to listen to them read. Give feedback about reading accurately, at an appropriate rate, and with expression and provide guidance for improving fluency.

🔲 RF.1.4b

• eBook

Lesson 12

INFORMATIONAL TEXT

Read Together

☑ **GENRE**

Informational text gives facts about a topic. This is from a science textbook. What facts do the words give? What do the pictures show?

☑ **TEXT FOCUS**

A **map** is a drawing of a town, state, country, or the world. A map **key** tells more about what the map shows. What do you learn from the map on page 70?

RI.1.5 know and use text features to locate facts or information; **RI.1.10** read informational texts

Go Digital

68

The Rain Forest

A rain forest is a very wet and warm place. Rain forests have layers. Each layer has its own animals that live in it.

Canopy Layer The tops of trees poking out above the forest form this layer. The tree leaves and branches keep most sunlight off the layers below. Eagles, sloths, and monkeys live here.

Understory Layer This layer is above the ground. It is shady. Young trees and bushes grow here. Frogs, birds, and snakes live here.

sloth

eagle

monkey

toucan

jaguar

tapir

69

◆ **DOMAIN: Life Science**

LESSON TOPIC: Jungle Animals

Cross-Curricular Connection Tell children that jungle animals are wild and not like tame pets. Tell them that some jungle animals are predators, or animals that hunt other animals for food. Explain that a leopard is one of the top predators in the African jungle. Have children brainstorm questions they have about wild animals that live in the jungle or rain forest. Guide them to research in teams to answer the questions.

RL.1.3 describe characters, settings, and major events **RL.1.3** describe the connection between individuals, events, ideas or information in a text; **RI.1.5** know and use text features to locate facts or information; **RI.1.10** read informational texts; **W.1.3** write narratives

Connect to the Topic
Informational Text

Introduce Genre and Text Focus

• Read with children the genre and text focus information on p. 68. Review that informational texts give facts about a topic and have details in the words and pictures that support the topic.

🔊 **RI.1.5**

• Point out the headings, labels, map, map key, and caption. Have children tell how each text and graphic feature adds information to the selection and makes the information easier to find.

🔊 **RI.1.5**

• Then read the selection with children. After reading, help them use the map to identify where rain forests are located. Then discuss how each red heading tells what that section is about. Have children tell details about each layer and describe connections in the information, such as *How are anteaters and insects connected?* 🔊 **RI.1.3, RI.1.10**

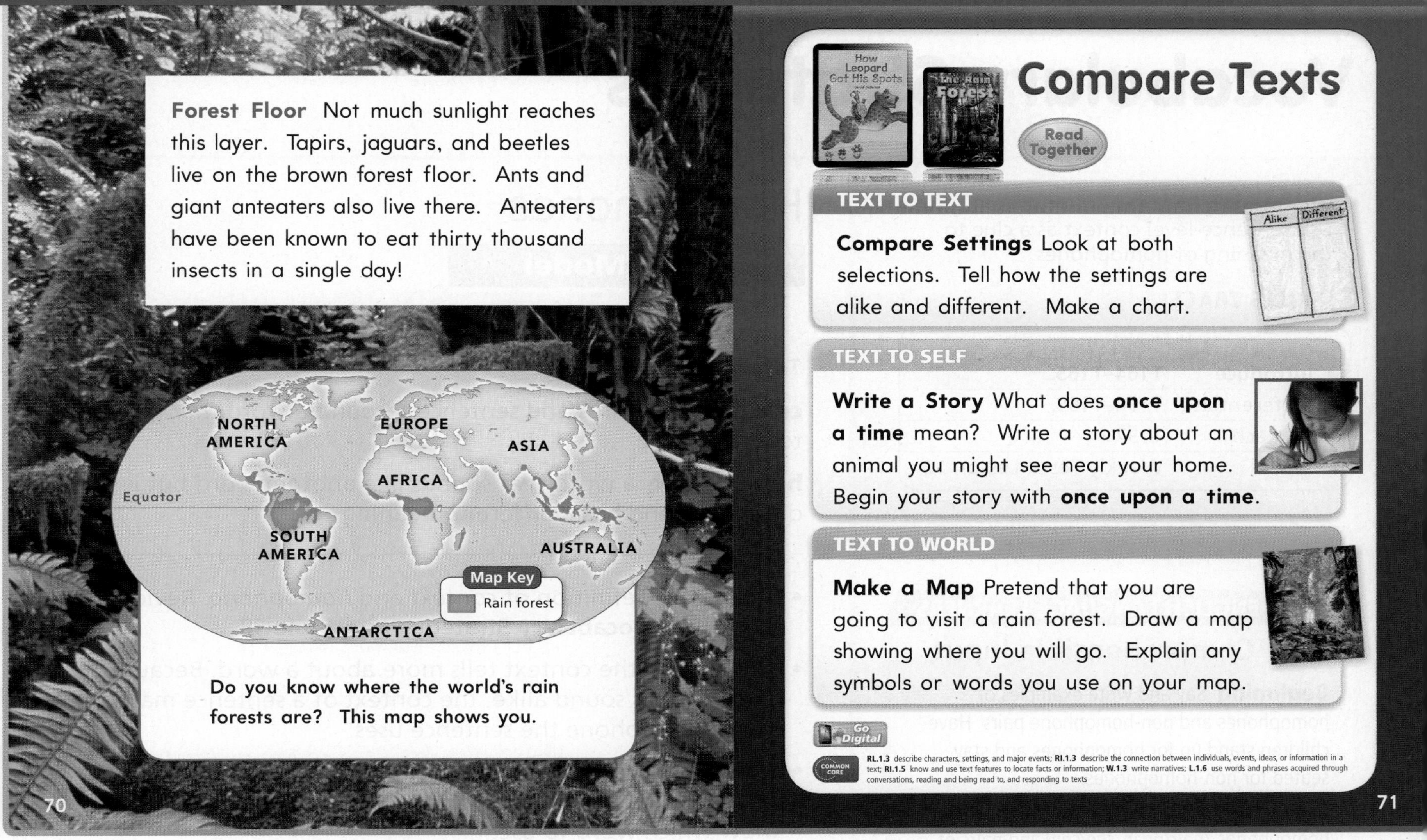

Forest Floor Not much sunlight reaches this layer. Tapirs, jaguars, and beetles live on the brown forest floor. Ants and giant anteaters also live there. Anteaters have been known to eat thirty thousand insects in a single day!

NORTH AMERICA
EUROPE
ASIA
AFRICA
Equator
SOUTH AMERICA
AUSTRALIA
ANTARCTICA

Map Key
Rain forest

Do you know where the world's rain forests are? This map shows you.

Compare Texts

Read Together

TEXT TO TEXT

Compare Settings Look at both selections. Tell how the settings are alike and different. Make a chart.

Alike | Different

TEXT TO SELF

Write a Story What does **once upon a time** mean? Write a story about an animal you might see near your home. Begin your story with **once upon a time**.

TEXT TO WORLD

Make a Map Pretend that you are going to visit a rain forest. Draw a map showing where you will go. Explain any symbols or words you use on your map.

Go Digital

COMMON CORE RL.1.3 describe characters, settings, and major events; RI.1.3 describe the connection between individuals, events, ideas, or information in a text; RI.1.5 know and use text features to locate facts or information; W.1.3 write narratives; L.1.6 use words and phrases acquired through conversations, reading and being read to, and responding to texts

70

71

Compare Texts

TEXT TO TEXT

Compare Settings Have children page through *How Leopard Got His Spots* and *The Rain Forest*. Have children tell how the places in the selections are alike and different. Have them make a chart and list text evidence from the words and pictures to show this information. ⬤ RL.1.3, RI.1.3

TEXT TO SELF

Write a Story Remind children that a story has characters, a setting, and events that happen. Explain that the phrase "once upon a time" can help introduce readers to the characters and setting at the beginning of a story. Before writing, have children discuss details about their characters, setting, and events with a partner. Then have children illustrate their finished stories and share them in small groups. ⬤ RL.1.3, W.1.3

TEXT TO WORLD

Make a Map Review the characteristics and purposes of maps. Children's finished maps should show a rain forest or the route to a rain forest. Have children explain the graphic features they used on their maps and the information the features give. Ask children to tell how the graphic features they included make information easier to find. ⬤ RI.1.5

Whole Group

DAY 4

Go Digital
• Interactive Whiteboard Lesson
• Literacy and Language Guide

JOURNEYS
Vocabulary Strategies

Interactive Whiteboard Lesson:
Homophones

Vocabulary Strategies

► SHARE OBJECTIVE

• Use sentence-level context as a clue to the meaning of homophones.

► SKILLS TRACE

Homophones	
Introduce	**T164–T165**
Differentiate	T194–T195
Reteach	T197
Assess	Weekly Tests, Lesson 12

ELL ENGLISH LANGUAGE LEARNERS
Comprehensible Input

Beginning Say and write examples of homophones and non-homophone pairs. Have children stand up for homophones and stay seated for non-homophones.

Low Intermediate Say and write pairs of homophones *(pair/pear, see/sea)* and pairs of non-homophones *(lose/loose, are/our, dog/cat)*. Children repeat and give the "thumbs up" for homophones, and repeat and give the "thumbs down" otherwise.

High Intermediate Have children copy *sea, sail, sight, sale, see,* and *site* to index cards and match the homophones.

Proficient Have children work in pairs to list pairs of homophones and use them in sentences.

See ELL Lesson 12, p. E17, for further support.

Homophones

1 Teach/Model

Terms About Language

context the words and sentences around a word that give clues to its meaning

homophone a word that sounds like another word but is spelled differently and has a different meaning

---

• Discuss the definition of *context* and *homophone*. Review step one on the **Vocabulary Strategy Projectable S8**.

• Explain that the context tells more about a word. Because homophones sound alike, the context of a sentence makes clear which homophone the sentence uses.

• We might read or hear words that sound alike when we read, write, and listen to stories. Knowing homophones helps readers know which word to use.

• Write *know* and *no* on the board. Read the following sentence from *How Leopard Got His Spots* aloud. Model using context to recognize the correct homophone, *know*.

> Do you know how Leopard got his spots?.

Think Aloud *To find out more about* know, *I listen to the words around it. I also think about the homophones* know *and* no. *The word* know *means understanding or learning something. The word* no *is the opposite of yes. The opposite of yes does not make sense in this sentence, because it is asking me* how. *This sentence uses the word* know.

Literacy and Language Guide
Additional Lesson 12 vocabulary lessons appear in the Literacy and Language Guide.

2 Guided Practice

- Display **Projectable 12.8** and read aloud the example sentence. Discuss the homophones and meanings in the first row of the chart.

- Read aloud the first sentence. Write *tail* and *tale* in the appropriate columns. Guide children to tell definitions for each word. Then have children use the words *rabbit* and *fluffy* to help them choose the correct word. Circle the word *tail* in the sentence.

- Explain to children that although they could be hearing a story or tale, this sentence is telling about a part of a rabbit's body.

Projectable 12.8

Projectable 12.8

How Leopard Got His Spots | Vocabulary Strategies | Homophones

Homophones

Example: [Meat / (Meet)] me at the park.

1. The rabbit has a fluffy [(tail) / tale].

2. I saw [wear / (where)] he ran.

3. Can you [sea / (see)] him there?

Homophone 1	Meaning	Homophone 2	Meaning
meat	a kind of food	meet	to join someone
tail	part of an animal's body	tale	a story
wear	to have on clothes	where	a place
sea	the ocean	see	to look at

Vocabulary Strategies
© Houghton Mifflin Harcourt Publishing Company. All rights reserved.

Grade 1, Unit 3

3 Apply

- Read aloud the second item on **Projectable 12.8** to children.

- Have children provide definitions for each homophone and then choose the correct word to complete the sentence, *where*.

- Ask them to point out the words in the sentence that helped them decide between the choices.

- Repeat the procedure with the last item. ◼ **L.1.4a**

Are children able to identify and use homophones correctly?

IF...	THEN...
children have difficulty identifying the correct homophone for a sentence,	▶ use Struggling Readers lesson, p. T194.
children can identify the correct homophone for a sentence,	▶ use On Level lesson, p. T194.
children can identify and use homophones correctly in sentences,	▶ use Advanced lesson, p. T195.

SMALL GROUP Options

Differentiate Vocabulary Strategies:
pp. T194–T195.
Group English Language Learners according to language proficiency.

- *my*WriteSmart
- eBook
- GrammarSnap Videos

Grammar Spiral Review: Complete Sentences

▶ SHARE OBJECTIVES

- **Grammar** Review that a complete sentence has a subject and a predicate.
- **Spelling** Spell words with *ch* and *tch* using conventional spelling patterns.
- **Handwriting** Print the spelling words.
- **Writing** Draft instructions.

ELL ENGLISH LANGUAGE LEARNERS

Language Transfer

All Proficiencies Display the sentence on **Student Book** p. 56 *I have big brown spots now.* Tell children that this is a complete sentence because it tells us about something. Have children read the completed sentence aloud and help them identify the subject and the predicate.

See ELL Lesson 12, p. E19, for scaffolded support.

1 Teach/Model

COMPLETE SENTENCES Write on the board: *The leopard runs fast.* *What is the naming part of the sentence?* The leopard *What is the action part of the sentence?* runs fast

- Review that every complete sentence has two parts. The naming part is called the *subject*. The action part is called the *predicate*.

- Use a chart to discuss subjects and predicates in sentences.

Subject	Predicate
The monkey	swings in a tree.
A lion	roars.
The giraffe	eats leaves.

2 Guided Practice/Apply

- Have volunteers add subjects and predicates to create additional complete sentences on the chart.

- Remind children to make sure they match the verbs to the nouns as they write subjects and predicates on the chart. ▬ **L.1.1c, L.1.1j**

Spelling Words with *ch* and *tch*

SPELLING WORDS

BASIC

chin	chop
much	chip
rich	chick

CHALLENGE

match	pitch

Connect to Writing

- Remind children that they have been learning about commands.

- Ask children to use the spelling words to write same commands. Remind them to proofread their sentences. Have children read their sentences aloud.

- Practice spelling the words as a class. Say each word and spell it aloud. ▬ **L.1.1j, L.1.2d**

Handwriting

Model how to form *chip, rich,* and *chick.* Have children use their best handwriting to print the spelling words. Handwriting and ball-and-stick models are available on the **Handwriting Models Blackline Masters.** ▬ **L.1.1a**

COMMON CORE

W.1.2 write informative/explanatory texts; **W.1.5** focus on a topic, respond to questions/suggestions from peers, and add details to strengthen writing; **L.1.1a** print upper- and lowercase letters; **L.1.1c** use singular and plural nouns with matching verbs in sentences; **L.1.1j** produce and expand simple and compound declarative, interrogative, imperative, and exclamatory sentences; **L.1.2d** use conventional spelling for words with

Informative Writing Drafting

1 Teach/Model

USING ORDER WORDS Remind children that they will use *order words* as they write their instruction letters. Then turn to p. 55 in *How Leopard Got His Spots* and review how order words help make the order of steps or events clear.

Connect to *How Leopard Got His Spots*

Fred mixed paints from many flowers.
Then he painted black stripes on Zel Zebra.

- *What is the order word on this page? How does it help make the author's meaning clear?* Then *helps make the author's meaning clear because it shows that Fred painted stripes on Zel Zebra after he mixed the paints.*

12.9
- Display **Projectable 12.7** from Day 3. Review your topic and the steps you wrote on the graphic organizer.
- Then display **Projectable 12.9**. Model drafting a letter with instructions based on your graphic organizer.

Think Aloud *I will write to my friend about making a mouse puppet. The first step I wrote about on my graphic organizer was about cutting the face. So I will copy that step into my letter:* First, cut a circle from gray paper.

- As you draft your letter, point out that it is important to write steps that explain exactly what the reader would do.

2 Independent Writing

Allow children to draft their instruction letters. Help them refer to their graphic organizer from Day 3 and the Focus Wall as they write. Remind them to be as specific as possible as they write their steps, so readers will understand their instructions. **W.1.2, W.1.5**

common spelling patterns and for frequently occurring irregular words

---

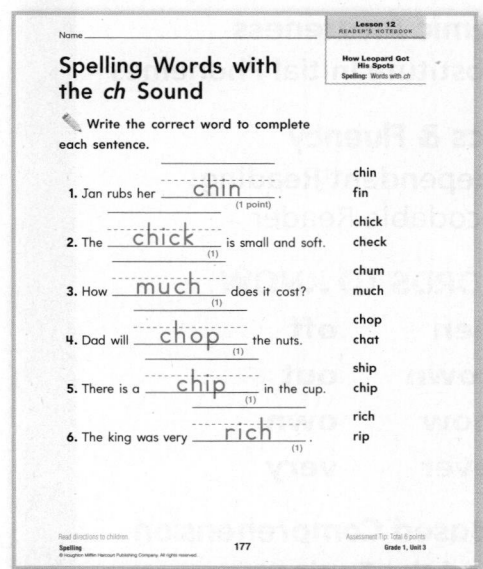

Reader's Notebook Vol. 1 p. 177

Reader's Notebook Vol. 1 p. 178

DAY 5

Today's Goals

Vocabulary & Oral Language
- Domain-Specific Vocabulary
- Speaking & Listening

Phonemic Awareness
- Substitute Initial Phonemes

Phonics & Fluency
- Independent Reading: Decodable Reader

☑ **WORDS TO KNOW**

been	off
brown	out
know	own
never	very

Text-Based Comprehension
Extend the Topic
- Speaking & Listening: Giving Clear Descriptions

Assess & Reteach
- Assess Skills
- Respond to Assessment

Grammar & Writing
- Commands
-  Informative Writing: Instructions

Spelling
- Words with *ch*, *tch*

COMMON CORE

RF.1.3g recognize and read irregularly spelled words; **SL.1.6** produce complete sentences when appropriate to task and situation; **L.1.2d** use conventional spelling for words with common spelling patterns and for frequently occurring irregular words; **L.1.6** use words and phrases acquired through conversations, reading and being read to, and responding to texts

Opening Routines

Warm Up with Wordplay

Homophone Match

Have children review this week's vocabulary strategy by playing a game with homophones. Write the following words, and read them aloud with children.

flour	bare
here	flower
bear	four
for	hear

Have children match each word in the left column with its homophone in the right column. Invite volunteers to draw a line on the board connecting each pair. Then work together to explain each word's meaning. Have children choose a homophone pair and say a complete sentence for each homophone.
SL.1.6

Daily Phonemic Awareness

Substitute Initial Phonemes

- *We're going to change sounds to make new words. What are the sounds in Sam? /s/ /ă/ /m/. Change the first sound in Sam to /j/. Now blend the sounds /j/ /ă/ /m/. What is the word?* jam *Let's try more.*

- Have children repeat with you before doing it on their own.

Change the . . .	Result
First sound in *hop* to /ch/	*chop*
First sound in *match* to /l/	*latch*
First sound in *get* to /m/	*met*
First sound in *fish* to /w/	*wish*
First sound in *bun* to /r/	*run*

Corrective Feedback

- If a child misses a word, say the correct word and model the task. *Listen to the sounds in* hop: /h/ /ŏ/ /p/. *What is the first sound?* /h/ *Now I'll change the* /h/ *to* /ch/: /ch/ /ŏ/ /p/. *What is the word?* chop

- Repeat the procedure with the word *match*. Have children do it with you before doing it on their own. *Change the first sound in* match *to* /l/. latch

- Back up several words and continue the game.

Daily High-Frequency Words

Introduce

- Point to the **High-Frequency Word Card** *very*.

- *Say the word.* very *Spell the word.* v, e, r, y *Write the word. Check the word.*

- Repeat the procedure with the words from this week and last week *(blue, cold, far, little, live, their, water, where)*. ⬤ RF.1.3g, L.1.2d

Find the Letter Game

- Choose a word from this week's or the previous week's High-Frequency Words. Write a dash on the board for each letter.

- Have children call out letters. If the letter is in the word, write it on the appropriate blank.

- Continue until children can guess the word.

- Ask the child who guesses the word correctly to come to the board to choose the next word.

Corrective Feedback

- Say the correct word and have children repeat it. Off. *What is the word?* off

- Have children spell the word. o, f, f *How do we say this word?* off

- Have children reread all of the cards in random order.

Daily Vocabulary Boost

- Reread "Turtle, Frog, and Rat" aloud to children. (See pp. T112–T113.)

- As you reach each Oral Vocabulary word in the selection, have a volunteer explain or describe its meaning.

- After reading, review the Oral Vocabulary words and their definitions. Challenge children to use the words in their everyday speech. ⬤ L.1.6

 ☑ Oral Vocabulary

adventure	spy
frisky	tumbles
shiver	view

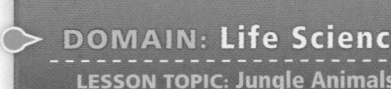
◇ **DOMAIN: Life Science**

LESSON TOPIC: Jungle Animals

Extend the Topic

▶ SHARE OBJECTIVES

- Acquire and use domain-specific vocabulary.
- Participate in conversations about a topic.
- Ask and answer questions about key details in a text.
- Describe characters, settings, and events in a story.

Words About the Topic: Jungle Animals

- **predator** an animal that hunts another animal for food
- **primate** a grouping of mammals that includes monkeys, apes, lemurs, and humans
- **jungle** a tropical forest with many plants and animals

◔ Domain-Specific Vocabulary

INTRODUCE WORDS ABOUT THE TOPIC Remind children that this week's topic is Jungle Animals. Display the words shown at the left. Tell children that these are words that can help them learn more about the topic. Read aloud the meaning of each word, and have children respond to the following prompts. ◼ **L.1.5c, L.1.6**

- *A lion attacks antelopes because the lion is a _____ and needs food.* predator
- *What group of animals includes monkeys and apes?* primates
- *A warm, wet tropical area where animals such as parrots and monkeys live is called a _____.* jungle

INTERACT WITH THE WORDS Have children work in small groups to create Four-Square Maps. For each of the domain-specific words, children should fold a blank sheet of paper into four equal sections. Work with them to follow the steps below for each word. As needed, display the meanings of the words on the board. Ask individual children to use the words in a sentence orally. Then write the sentence on the board for other children to refer to for ideas.

1 In the first corner, draw a picture for the word.

2 In the second corner, write the meaning of the word.

3 In the third corner, write a sentence using the word.

4 In the fourth corner, write the word.

When groups have finished, have them share their Four-Square Maps with the class. ◼ **L.1.5c, L.1.6**

Speaking and Listening
Giving Clear Descriptions

DISCUSS DESCRIPTIONS Tell the class they are going to describe things in *How Leopard Got His Spots.* Point out that one way to make sure they really understand a story is to clearly describe its characters, setting, and events. Display and discuss the Tips for Describing. Ask children to identify the characters in *How Leopard Got His Spots and make a list.* Fred Turtle, Hal Hyena, Len Leopard, Zel Zebra, Jill Giraffe

MODEL A CLEAR DESCRIPTION Model for children a clear description of Hal Hyena, such as the following:

Hal Hyena is a grayish-brown animal that looks like a dog. He has a ridge of hair standing up on his head and along his back. He has big, round ears. Hal is not very nice to Fred because he plays a trick on him. At the end of the story, Fred splashes paint on Hal so that Hal has messy brown spots on his back. Hal jumps in the air and looks shocked!

Have children find pictures of Hal in the **Student Book** and suggest details that could be added to make your description even clearer. Tell children that they will include clear details like the ones they heard about Hal when they tell their description to a group.

GIVE CLEAR DESCRIPTIONS Organize children into small groups. Have each child choose a character or event from *How Leopard Got His Spots* and give a talk to clearly describe that character or event. Have them show a picture from the story of the character or event to help make their description clearer as they speak. Remind children to include details such as adjectives, exact nouns, and action verbs to help make their descriptions clear for their listeners. Ask them to choose their words carefully to say exactly what they mean to say to express their ideas and feelings clearly. ▬ RL.1.3, SL.1.4

ASK AND ANSWER QUESTIONS After each child gives his or her talk, have group members ask the speaker questions to clear up any confusion about the topic or to gather additional information. Have the speaker answer the questions. For questions the speaker cannot answer, guide group members to work together to find the answers, returning to the story as needed to find text evidence. ▬ SL.1.1c, SL.1.2, SL.1.3

Tips for Describing

1. **Tell about characters, setting, and events.**

2. **Use details.**
   - **adjectives**
   - **exact nouns**
   - **action verbs**

3. **Use words that tell your ideas clearly.**

Name _____ Date _____

Listening Log

Title _____

What was your favorite part?

Write a question about what you heard.

Listening Log   13   Grade 1 Additional Resources

Listening Log

Grammar Weekly Review: Commands

▶ SHARE OBJECTIVES
- **Grammar** Review simple commands.
- **Spelling** Spell words with *ch* and *tch* using conventional spelling patterns.

ELL ENGLISH LANGUAGE LEARNERS

Language Transfer

Beginning Display the words *chick, much, clutch*. Read the words aloud and have children clap whenever they hear the /ch/ sound.

Low Intermediate Have children use **Letter Cards** to build and read *much, chop, pitch*.

High Intermediate Have children use **Letter Cards** to build and read *much*. Guide them in changing the cards to read *match, chop*.

Proficient Have children in groups use **Letter Cards** *t, c, h, a, i, e, t, s, w, r, p, m* to build and read as many words with the sound /ch/ as they can.

1 Review/Practice

- Read together the text at the top of **Student Book** p. 72. Discuss the commands in the box.

- Direct children's attention to the Try This! activity on **Student Book** p. 73. Have children write each command making sure that they begin each command with a capital letter and use the correct punctuation. Then, have children talk with partners about how they know which sentences are commands.

2 Connect to Writing

- Write the following commands on the board. Model using proofreading marks to correct the first sentence.

  come with me? leave that there now

- Ask a volunteer to correct the errors in the second sentence.

  C   L   !
  come with me? leave that there now.
    ^   ^ ^   ^

- Together read the directions for Grammar in Writing at the bottom of **Student Book** p. 73. Remind children to write commands correctly and to add words like *that, this,* or *those* to make their commands clear. ▭ **L.1.1h, L.1.1j, L.1.2b**

Spelling Words with *ch* and *tch*

SPELLING WORDS AND SENTENCES

BASIC

1. *chin* A fly was on his *chin*.
2. *chop* *Chop* the apples into small pieces.
3. *much* How *much* does that toy cost?
4. *chip* The cup has a *chip* in it.

5. *rich* He is *rich* and has many things.
6. *chick* The baby *chick* was yellow.

CHALLENGE

7. *match* Find the *match* for each card.
8. *pitch* *Pitch* the ball to me.

Assess

Say each spelling word. Then say it in a sentence and repeat the word. Have children write the word.
▭ **L.1.2d**

Corrective Feedback

Review any words that children misspell.

COMMON CORE **L.1.1h** use determiners; **L.1.1j** produce and expand simple and compound declarative, interrogative, imperative, and exclamatory sentences; **L.1.2b** use end punctuation for sentences; **L.1.2d** use conventional spelling for words with common spelling patterns and for frequently occurring irregular words

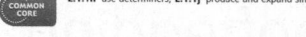

L.1.1h use determiners; L.1.1j produce and expand simple and compound declarative, interrogative, imperative, and exclamatory sentences

Grammar

Commands A sentence that tells someone to do something is a **command**. A command can end with a period. A command can end with an exclamation point when it is said with strong feeling.

Commands
Pick up that pencil.
Draw stripes on the zebra.
Help the turtle right now!
Save the rain forest!

Try This!

Read the sentences. Decide which ones are commands. Write each command on another sheet of paper. Then read the commands to a partner to check them.

1. Paint more spots on the giraffe.
2. Does the leopard like his spots?
3. Stand still while you paint.
4. Those paints are new.
5. Stay away from that wet paint!

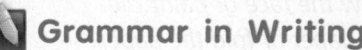 **Grammar in Writing**

When you proofread your writing, be sure you have written commands correctly.

72
73

Try This!

1. Paint more spots on the giraffe.
2. Stand still while you paint.
3. Stay away from that wet paint!

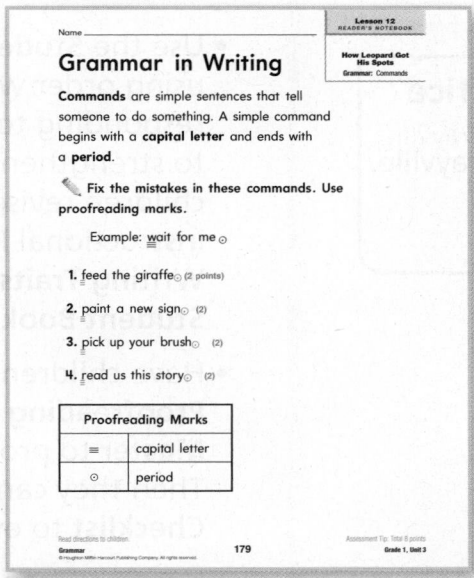

Name _____

Grammar in Writing

How Leopard Got His Spots
Grammar: Commands

Commands are simple sentences that tell someone to do something. A simple command begins with a **capital letter** and ends with a **period**.

✎ Fix the mistakes in these commands. Use proofreading marks.

Example: wait for me ⊙

1. feed the giraffe ⊙ (2 points)
2. paint a new sign ⊙ (2)
3. pick up your brush ⊙ (2)
4. read us this story ⊙ (2)

Proofreading Marks	
≡	capital letter
⊙	period

Read directions to children.

Grammar   179   Grade 1, Unit 3

Reader's Notebook Vol. 1 p. 179

DAY 5

Informative Writing Revising and Proofreading

► SHARE OBJECTIVE

• Revise and proofread letters with instructions.

ELL ENGLISH LANGUAGE LEARNERS
Comprehensible Input

Beginning Ask children yes/no questions to help them add order words to their instructions. For example: *Do you draw the face first? Do you cut the paper last?* Use hand gestures to support your meaning.

Low Intermediate Ask children simple questions to help them add details that will make their instructions more specific. For example: *Do you draw the face or paint the face? Do you cut the paper or fold the paper?*

High Intermediate Have children work with partners to brainstorm details they might add to make their instructions more specific.

Proficient Have children read their letters aloud to partners who can help them identify places for revision.

See ELL Lesson 12, p. E21, for scaffolded support.

Daily Proofreading Practice

Jan lives on ~~maple street~~ in ~~grayville~~.
        Maple Street   Grayville

I have never ~~ben~~ there.
         been

COMMON CORE **W.1.2** write informative/explanatory texts; **W.1.5** focus on a topic, respond to questions/suggestions from peers, and add details to strengthen writing

1 Teach/Model

• Display **Projectable 12.10**. Read aloud the text. Explain that a first grader named Akil wrote this letter about how to make a leopard puppet. Then review some of the reasons for revising a piece of writing.

• *Writers revise their work by changing it to make it better. Sometimes they add order words to make it clearer.*

• Use the **Talk About It** questions to help children analyze Akil's draft. Have children suggest revisions to the draft.

• Model revising the draft and then checking for spelling and correct capitalization and punctuation.

Projectable 12.10

How Leopard Got His Spots | Writing Informative Writing

Revising Akil's Draft

Read Akil's draft. Then think of ways to help Akil make his instructions better.

> Dear Pam,
>
> I made a leopard puppet. Here is how you can make one, too.
>   small paper
> 1. First, get a bag.
> 2. Next, fold the sides of the flap.
>   glue on
> 3. Then, ~~add~~ ears, eyes, a nose, and whiskers.
>   Last, c
> 4. Color brown spots.
>
> I hope you have fun making your puppet.
>   Your friend,
>   Akil

Talk About It
☐ Do the instructions have order words?
☐ Did Akil tell the steps in order?
☐ Did Akil include a greeting and a closing in his letter?

Writing   Grade 1, Unit 3

2 Independent Writing

• Use the **Student Book** pp. 74–75 to review the Writing Focus, using order words. Have children work with a partner, responding to questions and suggestions and adding details to strengthen writing. Then have children revise their own instructional letters, using the **Writing Traits Checklist** on **Student Book** p. 74.

• Have children use the **Proofreading Checklist Blackline Master** to proofread their drafts. Then they can use the **Writing Checklist** to evaluate their letters.

• Have children make clean copies of their revised work and then share it with the group.
💬 **W.1.2, W.1.5**

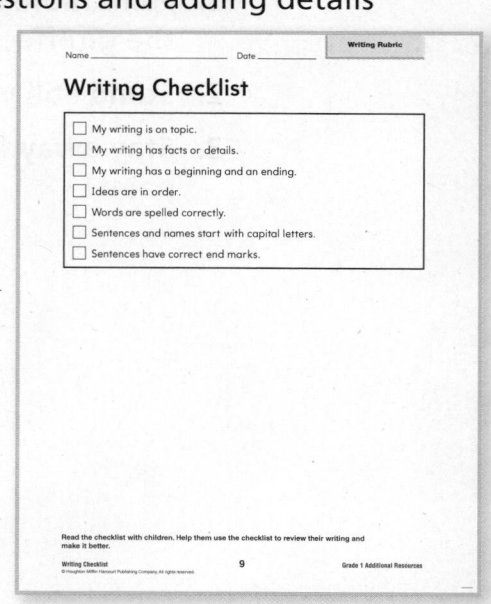

Name _____ Date _____ **Writing Rubric**

Writing Checklist
☐ My writing is on topic.
☐ My writing has facts or details.
☐ My writing has a beginning and an ending.
☐ Ideas are in order.
☐ Words are spelled correctly.
☐ Sentences and names start with capital letters.
☐ Sentences have correct end marks.

Read the checklist with children. Help them use the checklist to review their writing and make it better.

Writing Checklist   9   Grade 1 Additional Resources

Writing Checklist

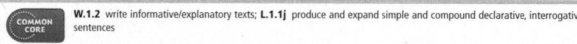 W.1.2 write informative/explanatory texts; L.1.1j produce and expand simple and compound declarative, interrogative, imperative, and exclamatory sentences

Informative Writing

☑ **Sentence Fluency** In good **instructions**, the sentences tell the steps in order. Order words help make the steps easy to follow.

Akil drafted his instructions in a letter to his friend Pam. Later, he added the order word **Last**.

Revised Draft

Last,
4. ~~C~~olor brown spots.

✏ Writing Traits Checklist

☑ **Sentence Fluency** Do my instructions have order words?

☑ Did I tell the steps in order?

☑ Did I include a greeting and a closing in my letter?

74

Revise your writing using the Checklist. You can follow the instructions in Akil's final copy to make a puppet!

Final Copy

Dear Pam,

I made a leopard puppet. Here is how you can make one, too.

1. First, get a small paper bag.
2. Next, fold the sides of the flap.
3. Then, glue on ears, eyes, a nose, and whiskers.
4. Last, color brown spots.

I hope you have fun making your puppet.

Your friend,
Akil

75

---

*See also the **Writing Rubric Blackline Master** on Teacher's Edition p. R11.*

WRITING TRAITS SCORING RUBRIC

	Focus/Support	Organization	Word Choice/Voice	Conventions/Sentence Fluency
6	Develops topic or events with relevant facts or details.	Introduces topic or situation clearly, organizes ideas to support purpose, has relevant conclusion.	Links ideas with words, phrases. Uses specific language. Connects with reader in unique way.	Demonstrates exemplary command of conventions of standard written English. Includes variety of complete sentences that flow smoothly, naturally.
5	Mostly develops topic or events with relevant facts or details.	Introduces topic or situation, mostly organizes ideas to support purpose, has mostly relevant conclusion.	Links most ideas with words, phrases. Uses specific language. Connects with reader.	Demonstrates good command of conventions of standard written English. Includes some variety of complete sentences that flow smoothly, naturally.
4	Adequately develops topic or events with relevant facts or details.	Introduces topic or situation, adequately organizes ideas to support purpose, has adequate conclusion.	Links some ideas with words, phrases. Uses some specific language. Connects with reader.	Demonstrates adequate command of conventions of standard written English. Includes some variety of complete sentences. Some flow smoothly, naturally.
3	Develops topic or events with some relevant facts or details.	Introduces topic or situation, organizes some ideas to support purpose, has somewhat relevant conclusion.	Links some ideas with words, phrases. May use some specific language. May connect with reader.	Demonstrates command of some conventions of standard written English. Includes little variety of complete sentences. Few flow smoothly, naturally.
2	Develops topic or events with few relevant facts or details.	May introduce topic or situation, organizes few ideas to support purpose, may have somewhat relevant conclusion.	Attempts to link ideas with words. Rarely uses specific language. May not connect with reader.	Demonstrates little command of conventions of standard written English. Includes little sentence variety. Incomplete sentences hinder meaning.
1	May not develop topic or events with relevant facts or details.	May attempt to introduce topic or situation, may not organize ideas to support purpose, may not have relevant conclusion.	May not link ideas with words. Does not use specific language or connect with reader.	Demonstrates little or no command of conventions of standard written English. Sentences do not vary. Incomplete sentences hinder meaning.

✓ Progress Monitoring

Assess

- **Weekly Tests**
- **Periodic Assessments**

Respond to Assessment

✓ Vocabulary

High-Frequency Words
Strategies: Homophones

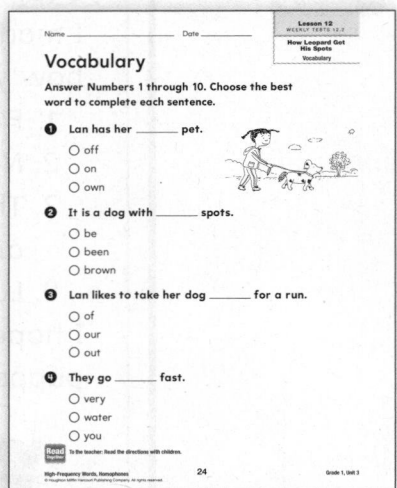

Weekly Tests 12.2–12.4

▇ **RF.1.3g** recognize and read irregularly spelled words; **L.1.4a** use sentence-level context as a clue to the meaning of a word or phrase

IF a Child Scores...	THEN...
7–10 of 10	▶ Continue Core Instructional Program
1–6 of 10	▶ **Reteaching Lesson,** p. T197

If a child scores below target on two or more tests, then consider using Diagnostic Assessment to pinpoint the child's instructional needs. The child may need systematic intervention.

✓ Phonics/Decoding

Words with Digraphs *ch, tch*
Possessives with *'s*
Phonogram: *-atch*

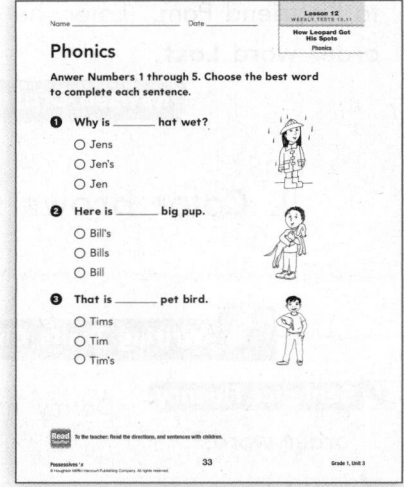

Weekly Tests 12.8–12.14
Phonemic Awareness
See Observation Checklist in Grab-and-Go™ Resources.

▇ **RF.1.3a** know the spelling-sound correspondences for common consonant digraphs; **RF.1.3b** decode regularly spelled one-syllable words

IF a Child Scores...	THEN...
7–10 of 10	▶ Continue Core Instructional Program
1–6 of 10	▶ **Reteaching Lesson,** p. T196

If a child scores below target on two or more tests, then consider using Diagnostic Assessment to pinpoint the child's instructional needs. The child may need systematic intervention.

COMMON CORE

Go Digital
- Grab-and-Go Weekly Tests
- Online Assessment System
- Cold Reads Online
- ExamView Banks

COMMON CORE

☑ Comprehension

Sequence of Events
Story Lesson

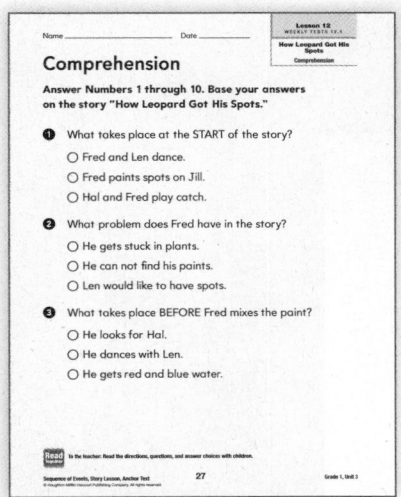

Weekly Tests 12.5–12.7

RL.1.1 ask and answer questions about key details; **RL.1.2** retell stories and demonstrate understanding of the message or lesson; **RL.1.3** describe characters, settings, and major events

---

IF a Child Scores...	THEN...
7–10 of 10	▶ Continue Core Instructional Program
1–6 of 10	▶ Reteaching Lesson, p. T97

If a child scores below target on two or more tests, then consider using Diagnostic Assessment to pinpoint the child's instructional needs. The child may need systematic intervention.

☑ Language Arts

Grammar: Commands

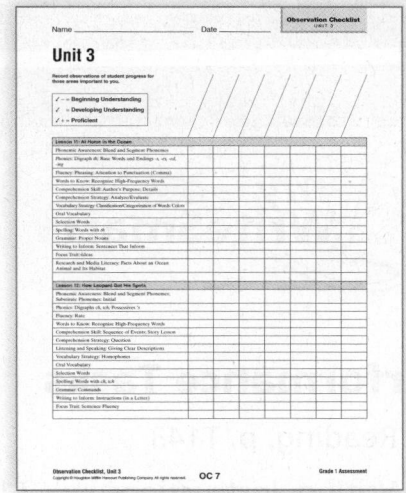

Observation Checklist,
Assessment, p. OC7

L.1.1h use determiners, **L.1.1j** produce and expand simple and compound declarative, interrogative, imperative, and exclamatory sentences

---

IF a Child Scores...	THEN...
Proficient	▶ Continue Core Instructional Program
Developing	▶ Review Instruction, p. T144, T156, T172–T173
Beginning	▶ Intervention Lesson 12, pp. S12–S21

If a child scores below target on two or more tests, then consider using Diagnostic Assessment to pinpoint the child's instructional needs. The child may need systematic intervention.

☑ FLUENCY

Fluency Plan Assess one group per week. Use the suggested plan below.

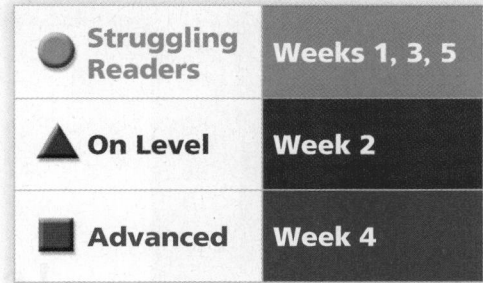

● **Struggling Readers**	Weeks 1, 3, 5
▲ **On Level**	Week 2
■ **Advanced**	Week 4

Fluency Scoring Rubrics
See *Grab-and-Go™ Resources Assessment* for help in measuring progress.

Oral Reading Practice
Use the **Student Book**, the **Leveled Readers**, or other reading materials in this unit to help children improve fluency.

☑ COLD READS

HOUGHTON MIFFLIN HARCOURT

JOURNEYS

Cold Reads

GRADE 1

Cold Reads *are leveled passages that can be used to practice and monitor fluency and comprehension.*

Performance Tasks

LESSON 12

Lesson Performance Tasks

- Write About Reading, p. T143
- Informative Writing: Instructions, pp. T174–T175
- Cumulative Performance Assessment: Task 2 of 5

Unit-Level Performance Tasks

- Research and Media Performance Task, pp. xxvi–xxvii
- Cumulative Performance Assessment
  Task 1: complete after Lesson 11
  Task 2: complete after Lesson 12
  Task 3: complete after Lesson 13
  Task 4: complete after Lesson 14
  Task 5: complete after Lesson 15

DAY 1

Differentiate
Phonics & Words to Know
- Digraphs *ch*, *tch*
- *been, brown, know, never, off, out, own, very*

Vocabulary Reader
- *Spots*

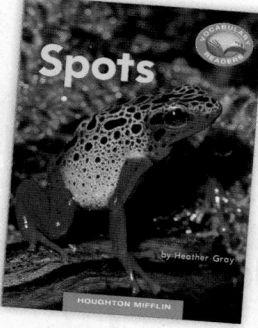

Vocabulary Reader

DAY 2

Differentiate Comprehension
- Sequence of Events
- Question

DAY 3

Differentiate
Phonics & Fluency
- Possessives with *'s*, Phonogram *-atch*
- Rate

Leveled Readers
- ● *Giraffe's Neck*
- ▲ *Bear's Tail*
- ■ *Peacock's Tail*
- ◆ *Bear's Long, Brown Tail*

Leveled Readers

DAY 4

Differentiate
Vocabulary Strategies
- Homophones

DAY 5

Options for Reteaching
- Phonics
- Vocabulary Strategies
- Comprehension

Literacy Centers

Independent Practice
- Word Study, T106
- Think and Write, T107
- Comprehension and Fluency, T106
- Digital Center, T107

Word Study

Think and Write

Comprehension and Fluency

Suggested Small Group Plan

Differentiated Instruction

Teacher-Led

	DAY 1	DAY 2	DAY 3
Struggling Readers	**Vocabulary Reader** *Spots,* Differentiated Instruction, p. T184 **Differentiate Phonics:** Digraphs *ch, tch,* p. T182	**Differentiate Comprehension:** Sequence of Events; Question Strategy, p. T186 **Reread** *Rich Gets a Dog,* p. T139	**Leveled Reader** *Giraffe's Neck,* p. T190 **Differentiate Phonics:** Possessives with *'s,* Phonogram *-atch,* p. T188 
On Level	**Vocabulary Reader** *Spots,* Differentiated Instruction, p. T184	**Differentiate Comprehension:** Sequence of Events; Question Strategy, p. T186 **Reread** *Rich Gets a Dog,* p. T139	**Leveled Reader** *Bear's Tail,* p. T191 **Differentiate Fluency:** Rate, p. T189 
Advanced	**Vocabulary Reader** *Spots,* Differentiated Instruction, p. T185	**Differentiate Comprehension:** Sequence of Events; Question Strategy, p. T187	**Leveled Reader** *Peacock's Tail,* p. T192 **Differentiate Fluency:** Rate, p. T189 
English Language Learners	**Vocabulary Reader** *Spots,* Differentiated Instruction, p. T185 **Differentiate Words to Know** Using Context Cards, p. T183	**Differentiate Comprehension:** Sequence of Events; Question Strategy, p. T187 **Reread** *Rich Gets a Dog,* p. T139	**Leveled Reader** *Bear's Long, Brown Tail,* p. T193 **Differentiate Fluency:** Rate, p. T189 

What are my other kids doing?

	DAY 1	DAY 2	DAY 3
Struggling Readers	**Word Building:** Build and read Spelling Words using Letter Cards **Complete** Leveled Practice, SR12.1–SR12.2	**Words to Know:** Partners practice reading Context Cards **Reread** *Scratch, Chomp* and *Rich Gets a Dog* **Complete** Leveled Practice, SR12.3	**Reread:** Partners read *Giraffe's Neck* **Complete** Leveled Practice, SR12.4
On Level	**Word Building:** Build and read Words to Know using Letter Cards	**Words to Know:** Practice reading Context Cards **Reread** *Scratch, Chomp* and *Rich Gets a Dog*	**Reread:** Partners read *Bear's Tail*
Advanced	**Context Cards** Assign Talk It Over activities **Complete** Leveled Practice, A12.1–A12.2	**Reread:** Partners read *How Leopard Got His Spots* **Complete** Leveled Practice, A12.3	**Reread** *Peacock's Tail* **Complete** Leveled Practice, A12.4
English Language Learners	**Listen** to Audio of *How Leopard Got His Spots* **Complete** Leveled Practice, ELL12.1–ELL12.2	**Listen:** Follow along with Audio of *How Leopard Got His Spots* **Retell:** Partners retell *How Leopard Got His Spots* using Retelling Cards **Complete** Leveled Practice, ELL12.3	**Reread:** Partners read *Bear's Long, Brown Tail* **Listen** to Audio of *The Rain Forest* **Complete** Leveled Practice, ELL12.4

For Strategic Intervention for this lesson, see pp. S12–S21.

DAY 4

Differentiate Vocabulary Strategies: Homophones, p. T194
Reread *Kits, Chicks, and Pups*, p. T161

Differentiate Vocabulary Strategies: Homophones, p. T194
Reread *Kits, Chicks, and Pups*, p. T161

Differentiate Vocabulary Strategies: Homophones, p. T195

Differentiate Vocabulary Strategies: Homophones, p. T195
Reread *Kits, Chicks, and Pups*, p. T161

Reread: Partners read *Kits, Chicks, and Pups*
Listen to Audio of *The Rain Forest*

Reread *Kits, Chicks, and Pups*

Reread: Partners read *The Rain Forest*

Listen to Audio of *The Rain Forest*
Reread: Partners read *Champs*

DAY 5

Options for Reteaching, pp. T196–T197
Reread one of this week's Decodable Reader selections.

Options for Reteaching, pp. T196–T197
Reread one of this week's Decodable Reader selections.

Options for Reteaching, pp. T196–T197
Reread one of this week's Decodable Reader selections.

Options for Reteaching, pp. T196–T197
Reread one of this week's Decodable Reader selections.

Reread: Choose among this week's stories
• Complete and share Literacy Center activities

Reread: Choose among this week's stories
• Complete and share Literacy Center activities

Reread: Choose among this week's stories
• Complete and share Literacy Center activities

Reread: Choose among this week's stories
• Complete and share Literacy Center activities

Weekly To-Do List

This Weekly To-Do List helps children see their own progress and move on to additional activities independently.

Differentiate Phonics and Words to Know

Struggling Readers

Phonemic Awareness/Phonics

Digraphs *ch, tch*

I DO IT

- Show **Picture Card** *chin*. Emphasize the */ch/* sound.
- Use **Instructional Routine 2** to model how to blend *chin*.

- Write and underline *ch*. *These letters stand for /ch/.*
- Repeat with *chick* and *patch*, pointing out the *ch* and *tch* spellings, respectively.
- Repeat with words with */ch/* in **Decodable Reader** selection *Scratch, Chomp*.

WE DO IT

- Review the *ch* and *tch* spellings on the **Sound/Spelling Card** *chick*.
- Ask children to say */ch/* each time they hear a word with the sound: *chin, punch, much, chat, champ, cheese, itch, stitch*.
- Help children blend the sounds to read the words below. Use the **Corrective Feedback** if children need additional help.

> chug   chin   chip   chant
> bunch   pinch   match   ditch

- Discuss the meanings of the words.

YOU DO IT

- Distribute **Letter Cards** to pairs of children so they can make */ch/* words.
- Have children make a list of their words and then read them with the group.

DAILY ASSESSMENT

Corrective Feedback Work with children to correct errors, following the model below.

Phonics Error:
A child reads *match* as *math*.

Correct the error. Say the word and emphasize the final sound. *The word is* match; *the letters* tch *stand for the sound /ch/.*

Model as you touch the letters. *I'll blend /m/ /ă/ /ch/. What is the word? match*

Guide *Let's blend together: /m/ /ă/ /ch/. What is the word? match*

Check *You blend. /m/ /ă/ /ch/ What is the word? match*

Reinforce Go back three or four words and have children continue reading. Make note of errors and review those words during tomorrow's lesson.

ELL English Language Learners

Words to Know

- Write this week's Words to Know on the board and read them aloud.
- Use the backs of the **Vocabulary in Context Cards** to review the explanations of the words.
- Tell children that they will see these words in this week's reading selections.
- Have children look for the words in the selection *How Leopard Got His Spots*.

☑ **WORDS TO KNOW**

been	off
brown	out
know	own
never	very

Vocabulary in Context Cards

Beginning
- Write the words on the board. Point to and read each word aloud. Repeat with the cards and have children say each word as you point to the pictures.

Low Intermediate
- Point to each word and picture on the context cards. Have children say the word. Have children repeat the activity with a partner.

High Intermediate
- Have children work with a partner to review the words. One partner will point to a picture and the other says the word. Have children switch roles and repeat.

Proficient
- Have children work in pairs. Each pair will choose a few of the cards and practice asking and answering questions using the word.

On Level

See Literacy Center Practice—Unit 3 Lesson 12 Word Study

If children have time after completing the purple activity, have them try moving on to the blue activity.

Advanced

See Literacy Center Practice—Unit 3 Lesson 12 Word Study

If children have time after completing the blue activity, have them reread the **Decodable Reader** selection *Scratch, Chomp*.

Vocabulary Reader

Spots

Summary

This book features the spots many animals have on their bodies.

☑ **WORDS TO KNOW**

been	off
brown	out
know	own
never	very

Struggling Readers

- Ask a volunteer to draw spots on the board. Then tell children that this selection is about spots found on animals.

- Preview the selection with a picture walk. Help children identify the animals on each page.

- Read the selection aloud. Point out that the first sentence on almost every page follows the pattern *The _____ has spots.* Then have children choral-read the selection with a partner. Guide them to use context clues when they come to an unfamiliar word (or phrase).

- Read the Words to Know and have children read them after you. Have them use each one in a sentence about spots. Have partners work together to complete the Responding page. Read aloud the directions on **Blackline Master 12.4** and guide children to complete it.

On Level

- Ask children to name animals they know about that have spots. Use the Words to Know in questions such as *Who has brown spots? What do you know about a leopard's spots? Do the spots wash off? Do you have your own spots?*

- Remind children that context clues can help them figure out unfamiliar words (or phrases) in a sentence.

- Read the selection aloud. Reread the selection, leaving the animal name blank and have children say the missing word. Have children read every other page with you. Then ask them to read the book to a partner. Remind them to use context clues when they come to an unfamiliar word (or phrase).

- Then assign the Responding page and **Blackline Master 12.4**. Review the directions with children and have them discuss their responses with a partner.

Advanced

- Have children preview the selection and make predictions about what they will read. Ask them to read aloud any words that repeat on each page.

- Before reading, remind children to use context clues to help them determine the meaning of unknown words (or phrases).

- Ask children to read the selection with a partner. Remind them to use context clues to find the meaning of any unfamiliar words (or phrases).

- Review the Words to Know and have children use them to discuss the selection. Then assign the Responding page and **Blackline Master 12.4**. For the Talk About It activity, remind children to include examples to support their ideas.

ELL English Language Learners

Beginning

Have children draw animals from the selection and help them label each one. Ask children to read the name of each animal they drew.

High Intermediate

Have children make word cards for each animal in the selection. Then have them name and sort the animals into animals that have fur, animals that have feathers, animals that have four feet, and so on.

Low Intermediate

Have children make and illustrate word cards for animals from the selection. Then write this sentence on the board: *The _____ has spots.* Display each word card. If the animal has spots, have children read the sentence and complete it with the animal name.

Proficient

Have children write a new book called *Animal Stripes.* Display pictures of animals with stripes and help children name and discuss them. Then have them write about the animals using this sentence frame: *The _____ has stripes on its body.*

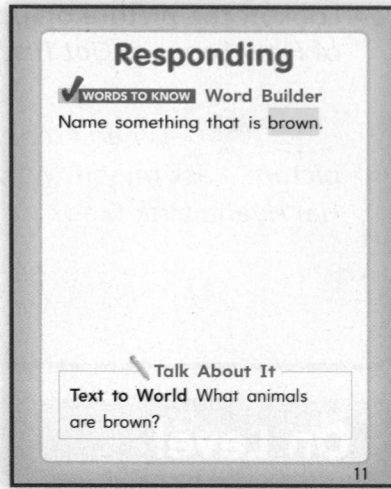

Spots, p. 11

Blackline Master 12.4

Differentiate Comprehension
Sequence of Events; Question

Struggling Readers

I DO IT
- Use **Projectable S5** to review the Question strategy.
- List the *W* and *H* question words on the board:

  who, what, when, where, why, how
- Look at the picture on pp. 48–49 of *How Leopard Got His Spots*.

  Think Aloud *When I see this picture, I ask myself: Why would Hal Hyena trick Fred?*

WE DO IT
- Have children page through *How Leopard Got His Spots*.
- Help children use the pictures to generate *W* and *H* questions about the story.
- Have children look at the illustration on p. 52. *How does Len help Fred? He chops the plants so Fred can be free.*
- Continue with the other pictures in the book.

YOU DO IT
- Have children fold a paper in half. Label the top half "Beginning" and bottom half "End."
- Have children draw one picture under each heading of an event that happened at the beginning and end of the story.

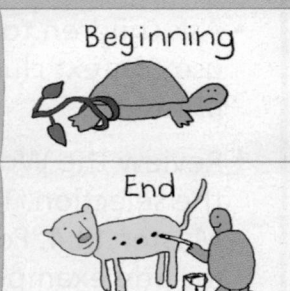

On Level

I DO IT
- Use **Projectable S5** to review the Question strategy.
- Review the *W* and *H* question words: *who, what, when, where, why, how*.
- Read aloud pp. 48–50 of *How Leopard Got His Spots*.

  Think Aloud *As I read these pages, I ask myself: Why does Hal trick Fred? How does Fred feel? What will Fred do?*

WE DO IT
- Remind children that illustrations can help answer questions they have while reading.
- Have them look at the picture on p. 53 and create questions about what they see.
- List children's questions with *W* and *H* question words on the board.
- Reread *How Leopard Got His Spots* with children and discuss their questions and answers.

YOU DO IT
- Have children write three sentences retelling three events that took place in the story.
- Have them start each sentence with *First, Next,* or *Last*.
- Children may illustrate their sentences.

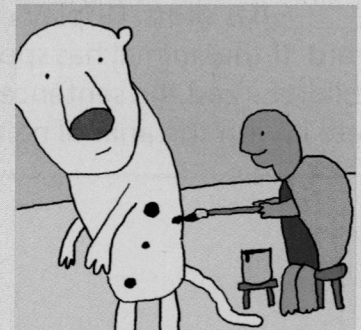

Advanced

I DO IT

- Explain that readers ask themselves questions before, during, and after reading a story.

- Write the following questions on the board: *What can I tell about this story before I read it? While I read it? After I have read it?*

- Answer the first question. *I know this story will tell me about the first leopard to get spots.*

WE DO IT

- Have children read *How Leopard Got His Spots*.

- Discuss their answers to the "During" and "After" questions as they read.

- Ask children how the illustrations helped them answer the "Before," "During," and "After" questions.

YOU DO IT

- Have children write their own version of *How Leopard Got His Spots*.

- Tell them to write four new sentences, paying attention to the sequence of events.

- Have children use the words *first, next, then,* and *last* to begin each sentence.

 **English Language Learners**

Review the **Question Strategy** and explain that good readers pause to ask themselves questions as they read. Then use the following activities with children according to their level of proficiency.

Beginning

Write the words *first, next,* and *last* on the board. Point to each word, say it, and have children repeat. Then describe three pictures in *How Leopard Got His Spots*. Use the words *first, next,* and *last* to show the sequence of events.

Low Intermediate

Reread the selection, having children pay attention to the sequence of events. Guide them to use the words *first, next,* and *last* to describe what happens.

High Intermediate

Explain that readers sometimes have to think about what the author does not tell or show in a story in order to understand the sequence of events. Give examples from the selection. Have children discuss what seems to have happened using the words *first, next,* and *last.*

Proficient

Prompt children to discuss the importance of understanding the sequence of events (stated and unstated) in a story. Guide them to retell *How Leopard Got His Spots* using the text and pictures for support.

Differentiate Comprehension • **T187**

Differentiate Phonics and Fluency

Struggling Readers

Phonics

Possessives with 's

I DO IT

- Write *Kim's* on the board. Read it aloud for children. Underline the word *Kim* and say it. Then point to and circle the *apostrophe s* and explain that it is added to a noun to show that something belongs to someone.

- Use **Instructional Routine 3** to model how to blend *Kim's*. Emphasize the last sound /z/ to differentiate *Kim's* from *Kim*.

- Use *Kim's* and *Kim* in oral sentences.

- Repeat with possessive words in the **Decodable Reader** story *Kits, Chicks, and Pups*.

WE DO IT

- Write *doll's* on the board.

- Have children use **Letter Cards** and hand-drawn cards with an apostrophe to build *doll's*.

- Ask children to identify the letters that spell each sound: /d/ d; /ŏ/ o; /l/ ll; /z/ s.

YOU DO IT

- Have children use **Letter Cards** and hand-drawn cards with an apostrophe to build *pet* and then *pet's*.

- Have partners explain the difference in the sounds and the spellings of the words. Then have the partners use the words in oral sentences.

- Offer **Corrective Feedback** as needed.

KIM'S BAG

Kim

DAILY ASSESSMENT

Corrective Feedback

If children consistently omit the sound of the possessive *s* at the end of nouns, practice with pairs of words: *Mom/Mom's, Gran/ Gran's, pup/pup's*. Use the pairs of words in sentences. Accentuate the final sound in each possessive form.

All Levels

Fluency

Rate

I DO IT

- Write *Chaz has never been out of his own town.*

- Model reading the sentence at an average pace.

- Use a Think Aloud as you run a finger under the sentence and reread it.

> **Think Aloud** *This is an easy sentence to understand. I don't have to slow down to read it. If the words were harder, I would have to slow down. If I were being tested, I would read it more slowly, too.*

WE DO IT

- Pick a page for children to turn to in the On-Level **Leveled Reader.**

- Have children move their fingers under the words as you read them aloud at a normal pace. Then challenge children to choral-read with you, keeping your pace.

- Tell children that if you were being tested on the page, you would read slower. Read the page slower, inviting children to choral-read. Provide **Corrective Feedback.**

YOU DO IT

- Have children pick a page from their **Leveled Reader.** Tell each child to read their page to him or herself.

- Have children pair up with a partner. The partner will be testing children on what they read. Have children reread the material, slower, with that in mind.

- Monitor and provide **Corrective Feedback** as needed.

DAILY ASSESSMENT

Corrective Feedback
If you notice children do not remember what they are reading, suggest they slow down. Remind them that good readers understand what they read; they don't read for speed.

Leveled Readers

☑ **TARGET SKILL**
Sequence of Events

☑ **TARGET STRATEGY**
Question

☑ **WORDS TO KNOW**

been	off
brown	out
know	own
never	very

Struggling Readers

 Giraffe's Neck

SUMMARY Giraffe is very hungry. She eats the leaves on the low and middle branches. She's still hungry, so she stretches her neck to reach the highest part of the tree.

GENRE: FOLKTALE

Introducing the Text

- Review and discuss this week's Words to Know.

- Take a picture walk through *Giraffe's Neck*. Have children talk about where the giraffe is getting the leaves and how her neck changes at the end.

- Review that events in a story happen in a certain order. Tell them a flow chart can help them keep the events in order.

Supporting the Reading

- **p. 3** *What is the first thing Giraffe does?* She eats some leaves on a low branch.

- **p. 9–10** *When does Giraffe eat the leaves on the high branch?* after she stretches her neck

Discussing and Revisiting the Text

CRITICAL THINKING Read aloud the top half of Responding p. 11 in *Giraffe's Neck*.

- Have children tell a partner what happens first, next, and last in *Giraffe's Neck*.

- Guide children to write what happens first, next, and last by using **Blackline Master 12.5.** Tell them to use the illustrations in *Giraffe's Neck* as a guide.

FLUENCY: RATE Model reading orally p. 10 to show children the appropriate rate to read the text. Then have them choral-read along with you at the same speed.

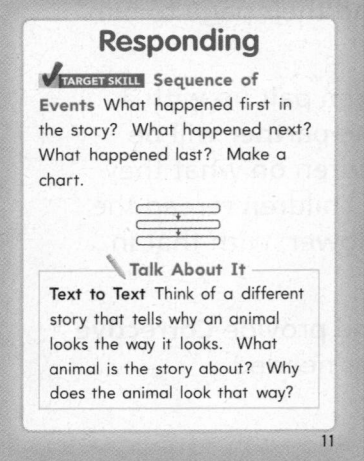

Responding

☑ **TARGET SKILL** Sequence of Events What happened first in the story? What happened next? What happened last? Make a chart.

Talk About It

Text to Text Think of a different story that tells why an animal looks the way it looks. What animal is the story about? Why does the animal look that way?

11

Giraffe's Neck, p. 11

Blackline Master 12.5

On Level

 Bear's Tail

SUMMARY Bear brags about his long tail so much that Fox plays a trick on him. Fox tells Bear to catch fish by putting his tail in a hole in the lake's ice. The water freezes around his tail and it finally snaps off. Bear learns not to brag so much.

GENRE: FOLKTALE

Introducing the Text

• Review and discuss this week's Words to Know.

• Discuss bragging with children. Ask children why bragging makes some people feel uncomfortable.

• Review with children how events happen first, next, and last in a story. Tell them that a flow chart can help them keep the events in order.

Supporting the Reading

• **p. 6** *What does Fox do after Bear asks about the fish Fox caught?* Fox tells Bear he caught the fish by putting his tail in the water.

• **p. 9** *What happened after Bear yanked his tail out of the ice?* The tail snapped right off. *What sentence gives the answer?* The last sentence on the page

Discussing and Revisiting the Text

CRITICAL THINKING Read aloud the top half of Responding p. 11 in *Bear's Tail*.

• Have partners tell what happens first, next, and last in *Bear's Tail*.

• Guide children to write what happens first, next, and last by using **Blackline Master 12.6**.

FLUENCY: RATE Have children echo-read p. 8 to practice reading at the appropriate rate.

Responding

✔ **TARGET SKILL** Sequence of Events What happened first in the story? What happened next? What happened last? Make a chart.

Write About It
Text to Text Think of a different story that tells why an animal looks the way it looks. Draw a picture of the animal. Write a sentence to tell about the animal.

11

Bear's Tail, p.11

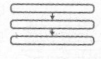

Flow Chart: Sequence of Events — Bear's Tail

Title: Bear's Tail

First
Bear brags a lot about his tail. Fox is tired of Bear bragging.

Next
Fox tricks Bear and tells him to get fish with his tail in the icy lake. Bear puts his tail in the water and sits for a long time.

Last
Bear's tail snaps off. He stops bragging.

Blackline Master 12.6

TARGET SKILL
Sequence of Events

TARGET STRATEGY
Question

WORDS TO KNOW

been	off
brown	out
know	own
never	very

Leveled Readers

Advanced

◼ *Peacock's Tail*

SUMMARY Peacock gets Crow to paint his feathers, and is so proud that he leaves Crow to show off his plumage to the world. Missing Crow, Peacock returns and they become friends again.

GENRE: FOLKTALE

Responding

✓ **TARGET SKILL** Sequence of Events What happened first in the story? What happened next? What happened last? Make a chart.

Write About It

Text to Text Think of a different story that tells why an animal looks the way it looks. Write two sentences about the animal and why it looks that way.

11

Peacock's Tail, p. 11

Introducing the Text

• Review and discuss this week's Words to Know.

• Explain that having too much pride can hurt friendships. Tell them this story is about what happens after one friend becomes too prideful.

• As children read, tell them to keep in mind what events happen first, next, and last.

Supporting the Reading

• **pp. 4–5** *What is the first thing that happens on these pages?* Crow paints Peacock's tail with colors and makes eyes on them.

• **pp. 6–7** *Why did Peacock pour paint on Crow's head?* Peacock didn't want to take the time to paint Crow. *What sentence explains this?* But Peacock didn't want to paint Crow.

Discussing and Revisiting the Text

CRITICAL THINKING Have children read the top half of Responding p. 11 in the **Leveled Reader.**

• Have children tell a partner what happens first, next, and last in *Peacock's Tail.*

• Have children write what happens in *Peacock's Tail* in order on **Blackline Master 12.7.**

FLUENCY: RATE Have children choose a page and read it aloud to practice reading at the appropriate rate.

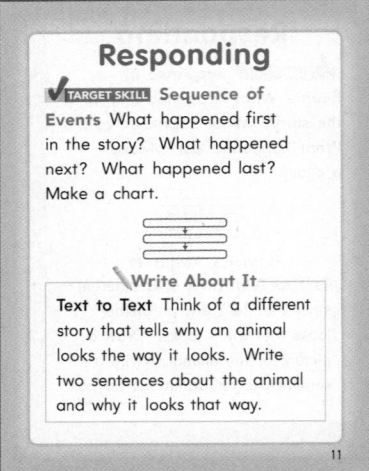

Name _____

Flow Chart: Sequence of Events

Title: Peacock's Tail

Possible responses shown.

First
Crow paints Peacock's feathers blue, green, and black. Peacock pours black paint on Crow.

Next
Peacock takes a trip around the world to show off his feathers while Crow stays in the forest.

Last
Peacock returns and says he is sorry. Crow is glad his friend is back.

Blackline Master 12.7

 ELL English Language Learners

◆ *Bear's Long, Brown Tail*

SUMMARY Fox doesn't like for Bear to brag about his long tail, so when he gets the chance he tells Bear that he can catch a fish in the frozen lake with his tail. Bear takes his advice, and in the end his tail snaps off when he pulls it out.

GENRE: FOLKTALE

Introducing the Text

- Review and discuss this week's Words to Know.

- Take a picture walk through *Bear's Long, Brown Tail* and have children tell what they think is happening in the story.

- Remind children that events happen in a certain order. As they read, have them think about what happens first, next, and last.

Supporting the Reading

- **p. 6** *What does Fox tell Bear to do to get a fish?* First, he tells Bear to make a hole in the ice. Then he puts his tail in the hole. Last, the tail catches the fish.

- **p. 5** *What sentences explain why Fox tricks bear?* Bear talks about his long tail all the time! I do not like that.

Discussing and Revisiting the Text

CRITICAL THINKING Help children read the top half of Responding p. 11 in *Bear's Long, Brown Tail*.

- Guide children to retell *Bear's Long, Brown Tail* and tell what happens first, next, and last.

- Have children write what happens first, next, and last by using **Blackline Master 12.8.**

FLUENCY: RATE Model reading orally p. 6 to show how to read dialogue and text at the appropriate rate. Then have children echo-read each sentence with you.

For more reading options, see ELL Lesson 12, pp. E12–E21.

Responding

✓ **TARGET SKILL** Sequence of Events What happened first in the story? What happened next? What happened last? Make a chart.

✎ **Write About It**
Text to Text Think of a different story that tells why an animal looks the way it looks. Draw a picture of the animal. Write a sentence to tell about the animal.

11

Bear's Long, Brown Tail, p. 11

Name _____

Flow Chart: Sequence of Events

Title: Bear's Long, Brown Tail
Possible responses shown.

First
Bear talks about his tail all the time. Fox tricks Bear and tells him to put his tail in the water to catch fish.

Next
Bear puts his tail in the cold water and sits for a long time.

Last
Bear's tail comes off.

Blackline Master 12.8

Differentiate Vocabulary Strategies
Homophones

Struggling Readers

I DO IT

- Explain that homophones are words that sound alike, but are spelled differently.

- Write the words *hair* and *hare* on the board and read them aloud. Explain what each word means.

- Ask volunteers to draw a head of hair and a rabbit on the board.

- Write these sentence frames: *I have _____ on my head. A _____ looks like a rabbit.* Draw lines to connect the sentences to the correct words.

WE DO IT

- Write the words *hear* and *here* on index cards. Show children the sentence strip: *I can _____ the band play.*

- Together, use the information in the sentence to decide whether the sentence uses *hear* or *here*.

- Place the card for *hear* in the sentence.

YOU DO IT

- Give children index cards with *see* and *sea* written on them. Show children the sentence strip, *Did you _____ that red car?*

- Have them place the correct index card in the sentence strip.

Did you _____ that red car?

see   sea

On Level

I DO IT

- Explain that homophones are words that sound alike, but are spelled differently.

- Write this sentence on the board: *The cake won first place at the _____.* Below the sentence, write the words *fare* and *fair*.

- Explain that the context of the sentence helps you know which word is correct.

> **Think Aloud** *When I read the words, they sound alike. But I know that* fare *is money. A* fair *is like a carnival with contests, so* fair *is the right word for the sentence.*

WE DO IT

- Write the following sentence on the board: *I can _____ the band play.* Below the sentence, write the words *hear* and *here*.

- Call on a child to read the sentence aloud and to point out the important words (and phrases) in the sentence that give clues about the missing word.

- Have children use the context to tell that *hear* is something that they could do near a band.

- Ask children to suggest a sentence that could include the word *here*, such as *I can sit here.*

YOU DO IT

- Have each child write sentences using the words *see* and *sea*. The sentence should contain context clues to show that the right homophone is in each of the sentences.

- Collect and read the sentences aloud.

- Based on the information, challenge children to tell which word, *see* or *sea*, is used in the sentences they hear.

Advanced

I DO IT

- Remind children that homophones are words that are spelled differently and have different meanings but sound alike.

- Write *fair* and *fare* on the board. Read the words aloud as you write them.

WE DO IT

- Ask children to explain how the words in the pair are alike. Then ask them to describe how the words are different.

- Write children's ideas on the board. Based on these ideas, ask children to create a sentence or a pair of sentences that makes the meaning of each homophone clear. Possible answer: *I paid bus fare to take me to the county fair.*

YOU DO IT

- Write the words *hear* and *here* on the board.

- Have the children write one sentence or a pair of sentences that makes the meaning of each word clear.

> I will stand here to hear the song.

ELL English Language Learners

Explain that homophones are words that sound alike but have different spellings and different meanings. Write *hair/hare* and *mail/male* on the board. Use the following activities with children according to their level of English proficiency.

Beginning

- Draw and label simple pictures for *hair/hare* and *mail/male* on the board.

- Read the words aloud as you point out the different spellings. Use the pictures to explain the different meanings.

- Give simple oral definitions for each word and ask children to point to the correct picture.

Low Intermediate

- Do the Beginning activity to the left with children.

- Ask children to give oral definitions for each word as they point to the correct picture.

- Have children draw their own pictures for *son/sun* and *rose/rows*. Then repeat the activity.

High Intermediate

- Discuss the meanings of the homophones listed on the board, using pictures as necessary.

- Write sentence frames such as the following on the board:
  My brother is a _____.
  I got a letter in the _____.

- Have children write the correct word to complete each sentence.

Proficient

- Do the High Intermediate activity to the left with children.

- Help children understand how the context of the sentence will help them figure out which homophone is correct.

Options for Reteaching

Reteach Phonics

Digraphs *ch* and *tch*

I DO IT

- Tell children that you will review some words that will help them read the **Decodable Reader** selection *Kits, Chicks, and Pups* on their own.

- Review **Instructional Routine 2.** Remind children that they have been reading *ch* and *tch* words this week.

- Review this week's Words to Know *been, brown, know, never, off, out, own,* and *very.*

- Have children open to p. 47 of *Kits, Chicks, and Pups.*

WE DO IT

- Write *chicks* on the board.

- Help children find the word *chicks* on the page.

- Model how to decode *chicks* step by step.

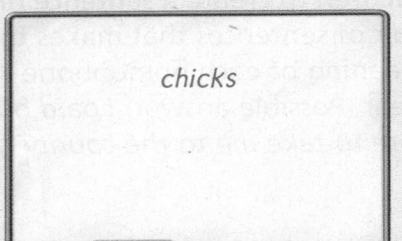

YOU DO IT

- Have partners work together to read *Kits, Chicks, and Pups.*

- Use the **Corrective Feedback** on p. T182 if children need additional help.

Ducks do not have pups. Ducks have chicks. Ducks swim in a pond. Dad duck is with his chicks.

47

Reteach Phonics

Possessives with *'s*, Phonogram *-atch*

I DO IT

- Tell children that you will review some words that will help them read the **Decodable Reader** selection *Kits, Chicks, and Pups* on their own.

- Review **Instructional Routine 2.** Remind children that they have been reading possessive words with *'s* this week.

- Review this week's Words to Know *been, brown, know, never, off, out, own,* and *very.*

- Have children open to p. 50 of *Kits, Chicks, and Pups.*

WE DO IT

- Write *mom's* on the board.

- Help children find the word *mom's* on the page.

- Model how to decode *mom's* step by step.

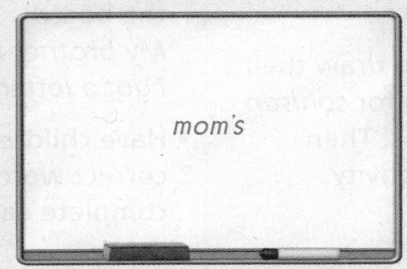

YOU DO IT

- Have partners work together to read *Kits, Chicks, and Pups.*

- Use the **Corrective Feedback** on p. T188 if children need additional help.

This mom and dad know that chicks must eat. This mom's chicks will get fed. Mom and dad will do it. The chicks will get big.

50

Reteach Vocabulary Strategies

Homophones

I DO IT

- Remind children that a homophone is a word that sounds like another word but is spelled differently and has a different meaning.

- Explain that looking around a word for context clues will help clarify which homophone a sentence uses.

WE DO IT

- Display **Projectable 12.8.**

- Help children figure out the meaning of the homophone used in each sentence.

- Read aloud sentence number one.

- Model how to figure out which homophone fits the sentence.

> **Think Aloud** *"The rabbit has a fluffy tail/tale." A tail, spelled T-A-I-L, is a part of an animal, and a tale, spelled T-A-L-E, is a story. So, in this sentence, tail, spelled T-A-I-L, is the correct homophone to use.*

- Have children fill in *tail, tale* and their meanings in the chart.

YOU DO IT

- Have partners work together to figure out the meanings of each homophone.

- Have them model applying the **Vocabulary Strategy** to know which homophone fits the sentence.

Reteach Comprehension Skill

Sequence of Events

I DO IT

- Remind children that events in a selection are usually told in the order they happen. *First, next, then,* and *finally* are signal words that show sequence.

WE DO IT

- Have children read aloud **Student Book** pp. 55–59.

- Model how to retell events in order.

> **Think Aloud** *Sometimes the author includes signal words, such as* then *and* next, *which help me know the sequence of events. I can read that Fred mixed paints.* **Then** *he painted black stripes on Zel Zebra. And he painted Jill Giraffe* **next**.

- Help volunteers continue retelling events in order.

YOU DO IT

- Distribute **Graphic Organizer 6: Flow Chart.**

- Have children fill in the boxes with events in order and use signal words. *First, Fred mixed paints. Then he painted black stripes on Zel. Fred painted Jill next. Len asked for spots. Len got spots of his own.*

- Have children work in pairs to complete the graphic organizer.

- Review the completed graphic organizers together.

Teacher Notes

LESSON **13**

See pages xvi-xvii in this Teacher's Edition for the full digital offering.

*my*SmartPlanner

Plan Across Disciplines, Schedule, Organize

Write, Collaborate, Respond

Online Assessment

Assess, Prescribe, Remediate, Report

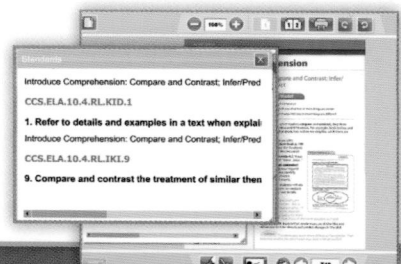

CHALLENGE

Survey Favorite Seasons

After reading the selection "Seasons," ask children to do a survey to find out everyone's favorite season.

- Tell children that a survey is a way to find out what people like. Explain that you can also find out reasons why people like one thing more than another.
- Ask children to work together to survey their classmates. Tell them to find out everyone's favorite season and why it is a favorite.
- Have children create charts or graphs to display their results. Ask them to share reasons that their classmates gave.

Informational Text

SCIENCE

Connection to Informational Text

SEASONAL CHORES "Seasons" tells about the fun things people can do during the different seasons. Point out to children that not everything about the seasons is necessarily fun. Ask children to think of a chore that people have to do in each season. Talk about how dead leaves have to be raked in the fall or how snow must be shoveled from streets and sidewalks in the winter. Ask children to name some summer and spring chores, such as mowing the lawn or pulling out weeds and planting flowers. Have each child choose a chore. Then have him or her draw an invention that helps with the chore. Ask children to show their inventions to the class. Children should say how the inventions work. **Common Core, *English Language Arts: SL.1.5** add drawings or visual displays to descriptions to clarify ideas, thoughts, and feelings

WHOLE GROUP

READING INFORMATIONAL TEXT

RI.1.1 ask and answer questions about key details

RI.1.3 describe the connection between individuals, events, ideas or information in a text

RI.1.4 ask and answer questions to determine or clarify the meaning of words and phrases

RI.1.5 know and use text features to locate facts or information

RI.1.9 identify similarities in and differences between texts on the same topic

FOUNDATIONAL SKILLS

RF.1.2b orally produce single-syllable words by blending sounds

RF.1.2d segment spoken single-syllable words into their complete sequence of individual sounds

RF.1.3a know the spelling-sound correspondences for common consonant digraphs

RF.1.4a read on-level text with purpose and understanding

RF.1.4b read on-level text orally with accuracy, appropriate rate, and expression

RF.1.4c use context to confirm or self-correct word recognition and understanding

WRITING

W.1.1 write opinion pieces

W.1.2 write informative/explanatory texts

W.1.8 recall information from experiences or gather information from sources to answer a question

SPEAKING AND LISTENING

SL.1.1a follow rules for discussions

SL.1.1b build on others' talk in conversations by responding to others' comments

SL.1.3 ask and answer questions about what a speaker says

SL.1.4 describe people, places, things, and events with details/express ideas and feelings clearly

SL.1.6 produce complete sentences when appropriate to task and situation

LANGUAGE

L.1.1j produce and expand simple and compound declarative, interrogative, imperative, and exclamatory sentences

L.1.1c use singular and plural nouns with matching verbs in sentences

L.1.4c identify frequently occurring root words and their inflectional forms

LESSON **13**  Our Focus Wall

ANCHOR TEXT

Seasons
Informational Text

Read Together

Four Seasons for Animals
Informational Text

ESSENTIAL QUESTION

What changes do the different seasons cause?

FOUNDATIONAL SKILLS

☑ Words to Know
HIGH-FREQUENCY WORDS

down	fall	goes
green	grow	new
open	yellow	

Phonics

Digraphs *sh, wh, ph*
Contractions with *'s, n't*

sh

Fluency

Accuracy: Word Recognition

READING LITERATURE & INFORMATIONAL TEXT

Comprehension Skills and Strategies

☑ **TARGET SKILL**
- Cause and Effect
- Sound Words

☑ **TARGET STRATEGY**
- Visualize

WRITING

Writing

Informative Writing: Sentences

Focus Trait: Ideas

LANGUAGE

Spelling

Digraphs *sh, wh, ph*

ship	when
shop	whip
which	fish

Grammar

Subjects and Verbs

Vocabulary Strategies

Words Ending in *-ed, -ing, -s*

Whole Group *At a Glance*

WHOLE GROUP

⌄ Reading

ANCHOR TEXT

⌐ DOMAIN: **Life Science**

LESSON TOPIC: Seasons

Seasons
Informational Text

Children will read *Seasons* to

• review that some events happen because of others.
• understand sound words and onomatopoeia.

Four Seasons for Animals
Informational Text

Children will read *Four Seasons for Animals* to

• learn about plants and animals throughout the seasons.
• use headings to know what each section will be about.

⌄ Language Arts

◯ Grammar

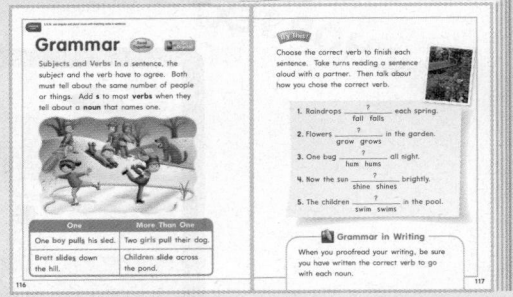

Children learn about sentence agreement through reading and choosing correct verb forms for sentences that relate to seasons.

◯ Writing

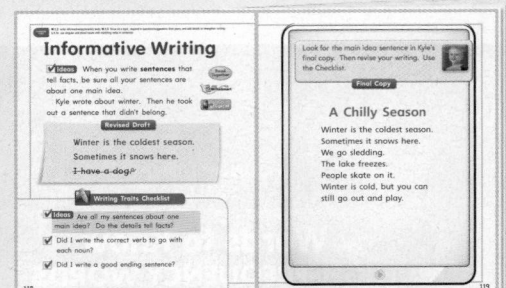

Children write sentences that inform using *Seasons* as a model for writing clear, factual information.

⚠ TEXT COMPLEXITY RUBRIC

Overall Text Complexity		Seasons INFORMATIONAL TEXT	Four Seasons for Animals INFORMATIONAL TEXT
		COMPLEX	COMPLEX
Quantitative Measures	Lexile	370	350
	Guided Reading Level	G	G
Qualitative Measures	Text Structure	Implicit compare/contrast text structure	Simple science concepts
	Language Conventionality and Clarity	Longer descriptions	Some unfamiliar language
	Knowledge Demands	Some specialized knowledge required	Some specialized knowledge required
	Purpose/Levels of Meaning	Single topic	Single topic

⌄ Additional Whole Group Resources

◉ Decodable Readers

- *Phil's New Bat,* pp. 51–56
- *In a Rush,* pp. 57–62
- *Ralph Goes to Camp,* pp. 63–68
- *Trish's Gift,* pp. 69–74

◉ Progress Monitoring

Assess and monitor children's progress to determine who is on track and who needs help. Clear prescriptions identify targeted instruction to address children's needs and get them back on track.

Respond to Assessment

- ☑ Vocabulary, p. T280
- ☑ Phonics, p. T280
- ☑ Comprehension, p. T281
- ☑ Language Arts, p. T281
- ☑ Fluency, p. T281

FOR STUDENTS

-  my WriteSmart
- eBook
- GrammarSnap Videos
- Destination Reading
- Context Cards

FOR TEACHERS

- Teacher One-Stop
- Interactive Whiteboard Lessons
- Literacy and Language Guide

- Lesson 13 Blackline Masters
- Additional Resources
- Assessment

Lesson resources organized by week.

◉ Lesson 13 Blackline Masters

- Home Letter 13.1
- Weekly To-Do List 13.2
- Vocabulary Word Cards 13.3
- Words to Know 13.4
- Leveled Reader Graphic Organizers 13.5–13.8
- Leveled Practice for Words to Know and Phonics SR13.1–SR13.4, A13.1–A13.4, ELL13.1–ELL13.4
- Weekly Tests 13.1–13.20

◉ Assessment

- Weekly Tests Answer Key
- Observation Checklists
- Fluency Tests
- Periodic Assessments

◉ Additional Resources

- Reading Log
- Vocabulary Log
- Listening Log
- Proofreading Checklist
- Writing Conference Form
- Writing Checklist
- Instructional Routines
- Graphic Organizer Blackline Masters
- Handwriting Models

SMALL GROUP

Weekly Leveled Readers

Struggling Readers

Guided Reading Level: B
Lexile: 20
DRA: 2

On Level

Guided Reading Level: I
Lexile: 460
DRA: 16

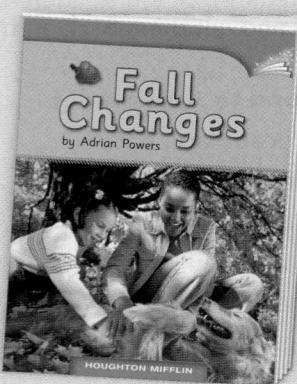

Advanced

Guided Reading Level: K
Lexile: 600
DRA: 20

English Language Learners

Guided Reading Level: H
Lexile: 300
DRA: 14

Leveled Reader Teacher's Guides

8-page lessons for each book support instruction in guided reading groups

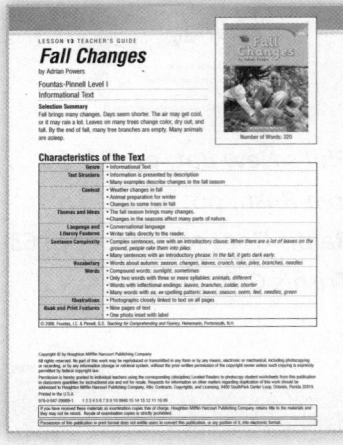

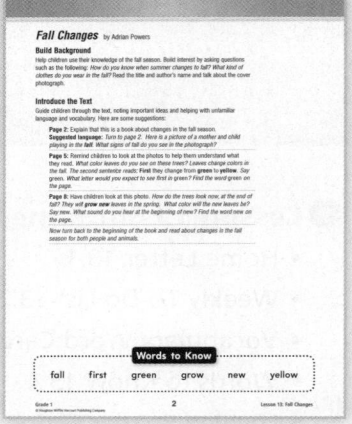

Vocabulary Reader

for all levels

Guided Reading Level: D
Lexile: 30
DRA: 6

What My Other Students Are Doing

Performance Task

- Write About Reading
- Informative writing
- Research and Media Literacy
- Unit Performance Assessment, Task 3 of 5

Literacy Centers

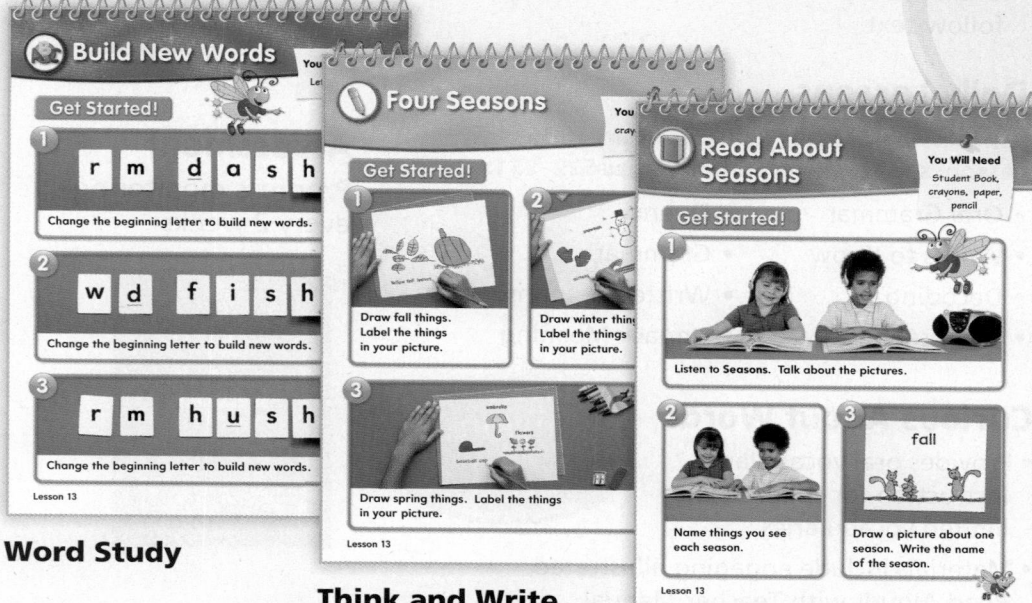

Build New Words

Get Started!

1 r m d a s h
Change the beginning letter to build new words.

2 w d f i s h
Change the beginning letter to build new words.

3 r m h u s h
Change the beginning letter to build new words.

Lesson 13

Word Study

Four Seasons

Get Started!

1 Draw fall things. Label the things in your picture.

2 Draw winter things. Label the things in your picture.

3 Draw spring things. Label the things in your picture.

Lesson 13

Think and Write

Read About Seasons

You Will Need
Student Book, crayons, paper, pencil

Get Started!

1 Listen to Seasons. Talk about the pictures.

2 Name things you see each season.

3 fall
Draw a picture about one season. Write the name of the season.

Lesson 13

Comprehension and Fluency

Reader's Notebook

Includes practice for:

- Text analysis and citing text evidence
- Words to Know
- Phonics
- Spelling
- Grammar
- Writing Traits

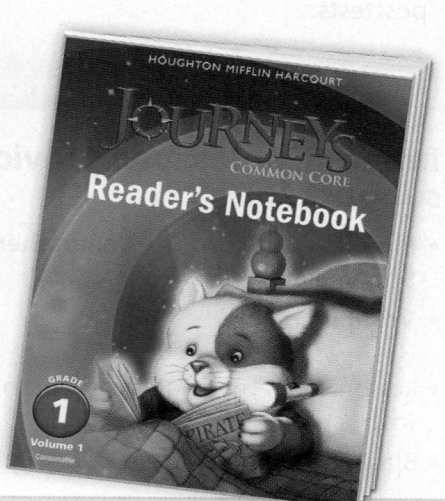

HOUGHTON MIFFLIN HARCOURT

JOURNEYS
COMMON CORE
Reader's Notebook

GRADE 1
Volume 1

Go Digital

FOR STUDENTS

- Leveled Readers Online
- Vocabulary Reader Online

FOR TEACHERS

- Teacher One-Stop
- Literacy and Language Guide
- Leveled Readers Database
- Leveled Reader Teacher's Guides

Grab-and-Go!

- Lesson 13 Blackline Masters
- Additional Resources
- Assessment

FOR STUDENTS

- Write-in Reader eBook
- Vocabulary Reader Online
- Struggling Readers Leveled Reader Online

FOR TEACHERS

- Leveled Reader Teacher's Guide

- Struggling Readers Blackline Masters

RtI INTERVENTION

∨ Strategic Intervention: TIER II

Use these materials to provide additional targeted instruction for children who need Tier II strategic intervention.

● Write-In Reader:
Max Has His Bath

- Engaging selection connects to main topic
- Interactive worktext reinforces this week's vocabulary and comprehension
- Opportunities for student interaction
- Builds the foundational skills for reading more complex texts
- Online version with dual-speed audio and follow-text

● Daily Lessons

For this week's daily Strategic Intervention Lesson, see Teacher's Edition pages S22–S31:

- Oral Grammar
- Words to Know
- Decoding
- Comprehension
- Fluency
- Grammar
- Written Response
- Unpack Meaning

Curious About Words

- Provides oral vocabulary instruction for children with limited vocabularies.
- Materials include engaging, illustrated Read Alouds with Teacher Manual.
- Teaches high-utility, research-based words, including academic vocabulary.
- Assessment includes weekly pretests and posttests.

● Assessment
Progress monitoring every 2 weeks.

∨ Intensive Intervention: TIER III

● Interactive lessons provide support for

- **Phonics and Word Study Skills**
- **Vocabulary**
- **Comprehension**
- **Fluency**

- Lesson cards for small-group or individual instruction
- Blackline masters for additional practice
- Leveled books for additional reading and skill application
- Lesson assessments evaluate the effectiveness of the intervention

ELL — ENGLISH LANGUAGE LEARNERS

⌄ Whole Group

Use these resources to help English Language Learners access the core content with the whole group.

Go Digital

FOR STUDENTS
- ELL Leveled Reader Online
- Vocabulary Reader Online
- Cross-Curricular Activity Bank
- Multimedia Grammar Glossary
- Picture Card Bank Online

● **Point-of-Use Scaffolded Support**
- Use Visuals
- Use Gestures
- Comprehensible Input
- Peer-Supported Learning
- Language Issues
- Idiomatic Language
- Use Sentence Frames
- Expand Language Production

● **Vocabulary in Context Cards**

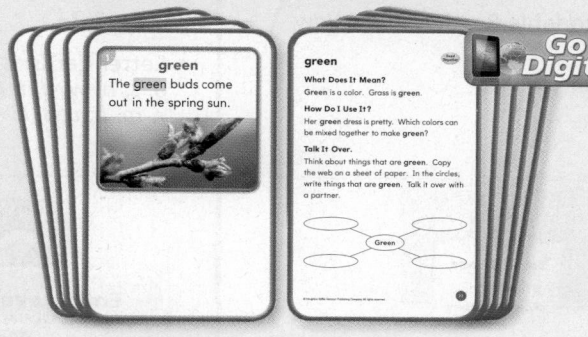

front   back

FOR TEACHERS
- ELD Station Online
- Leveled Readers Database
- Leveled Reader Teacher's Guide

⌄ Small Group

Use these resources to help English Language Learners access the core content with a smaller group.

● **ELL Leveled Reader**
- Contains the same content as the On-Level Reader but uses more accessible language
- ELL Leveled Reader Lesson Plan
- ELL Blackline Masters

Grab-and-Go!
- ELL Blackline Masters

⌄ ELL Extra Support

Use these additional resources to support English Language Learners as needed.

● **ELL Lesson 13 Resources**
- Daily Lessons to support the core
- Language Support Card 13
- ELL Blackline Masters
- ELL Teacher's Handbook
   Professional Development
   Peer Conferences Forms
   Cooperative Learning Guidelines

● **Building Background**
Video Clip for Lesson 13:
The Four Seasons

Literacy Centers

COMMON CORE Managing Independent Activities

Comprehension and Fluency

Materials
- Student Book: *Seasons*
- eBook
- Crayons
- Decodable Reader: *Phil's New Bat*
- Paper, pencil

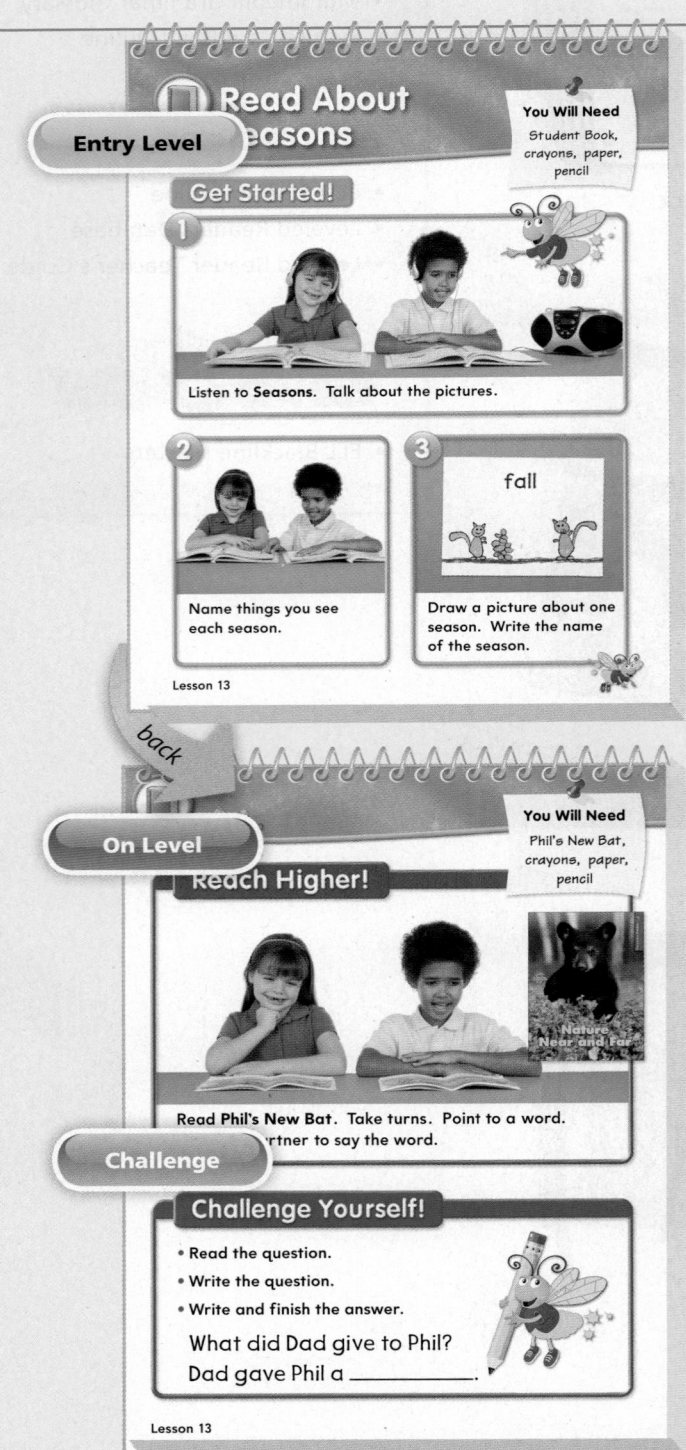

Entry Level

Read About Seasons

You Will Need
Student Book, crayons, paper, pencil

Get Started!

1. Listen to **Seasons**. Talk about the pictures.

2. Name things you see each season.

3. fall

Draw a picture about one season. Write the name of the season.

Lesson 13

On Level

Reach Higher!

You Will Need
Phil's New Bat, crayons, paper, pencil

Read **Phil's New Bat**. Take turns. Point to a word. ...rtner to say the word.

Challenge

Challenge Yourself!

- Read the question.
- Write the question.
- Write and finish the answer.

What did Dad give to Phil?
Dad gave Phil a _____.

Lesson 13

Word Study

Materials
- Letter Cards: *r, m, d, a, s, h; w, d, f, i, s, h; r, m, h, u, s, h*
- Crayons
- Word Cards: *bell, cut, feet, lip, mop*
- Paper, pencil

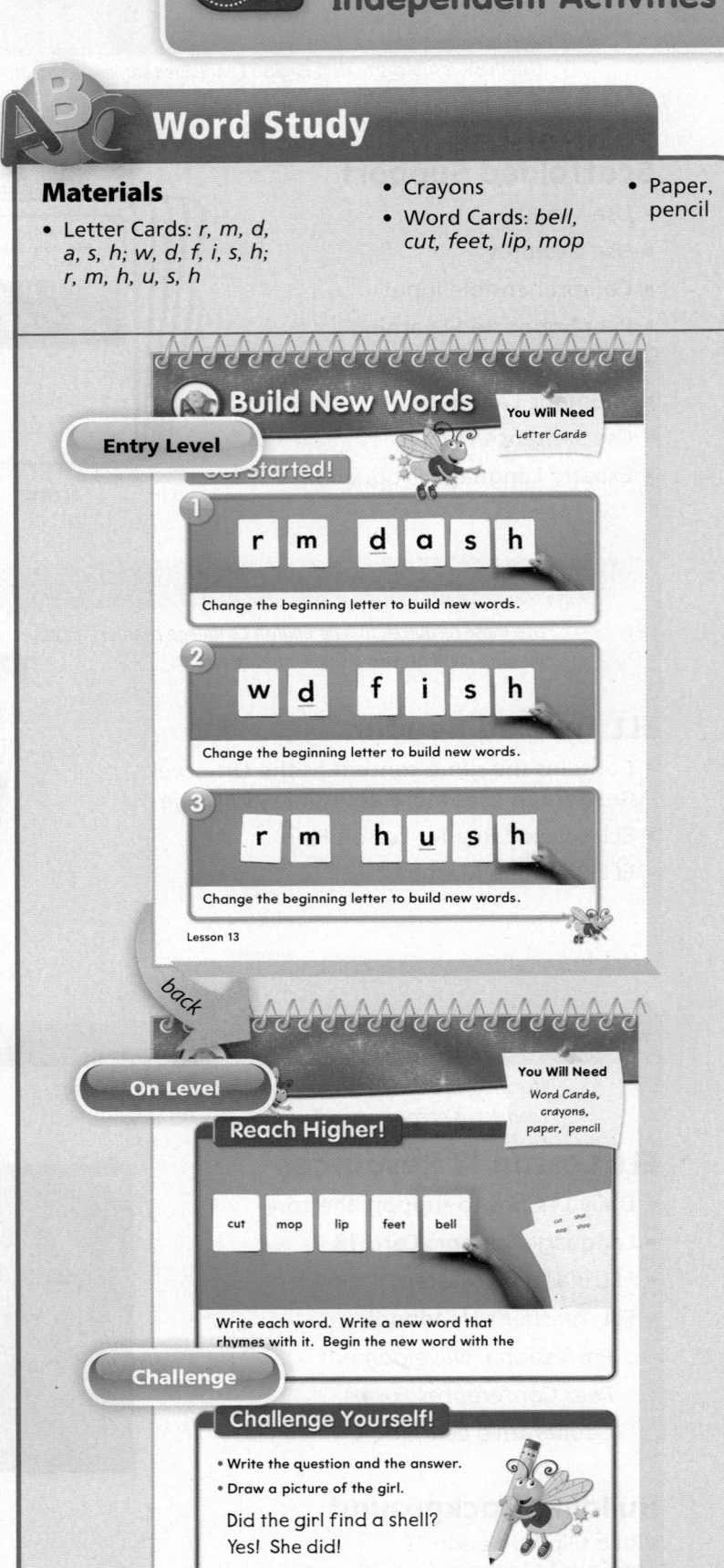

Entry Level

Build New Words

You Will Need
Letter Cards

Get Started!

1. r m **dash**

Change the beginning letter to build new words.

2. w **d** f i s h

Change the beginning letter to build new words.

3. r m h u s h

Change the beginning letter to build new words.

Lesson 13

On Level

Reach Higher!

You Will Need
Word Cards, crayons, paper, pencil

cut | mop | lip | feet | bell

Write each word. Write a new word that rhymes with it. Begin the new word with the ...

Challenge

Challenge Yourself!

- Write the question and the answer.
- Draw a picture of the girl.

Did the girl find a shell?
Yes! She did!

Lesson 13

Use Literacy Centers to support this week's Common Core focus. Each center contains three activities. Children who experience success with the entry-level activity move on to the on-level and challenge activities, as time permits.

Think and Write

Materials
- Crayons
- Paper
- Pencil

Four Seasons

Entry Level

You Will Need
crayons, paper, pencil

Get Started!

1. Draw fall things. Label the things in your picture.
2. Draw winter things. Label the things in your picture.
3. Draw spring things. Label the things in your picture.

Lesson 13

back

On Level

You Will Need
crayons, paper, pencil

Reach Higher!

This is a summer picnic.

Draw a summer picture. Show a picnic.
...ntence about a picnic.

Challenge

Challenge Yourself!
- What season is it now?
- Write the name of the season.
- Draw a picture about the season.

spring summer fall winter

Lesson 13

Go Digital

FOR STUDENTS

my WriteSmart

Children complete performance tasks related to the week's instruction.

eBook
Children read and listen to *Seasons* and *Four Seasons for Animals*, generate questions about the seasons, and reread the texts to deepen their knowledge.

Leveled Readers Online
Children read and listen to **Leveled Readers,** reinforcing lesson's Target Vocabulary, Target Skill, and Target Strategy.

Destination Reading
Children practice and apply key lesson skills through gamelike activities.

GrammarSnap Videos
Children practice and apply understanding of subjects and verbs.

Read

Independent Reading

Have children read daily from a self-selected trade book and record their progress in their Reading Log.

See p. T253 for support in guiding children to select an appropriate book.

LESSON 13 Weekly Planner

	DAY 1	**DAY 2**	**DAY 3**
Daily Language • Opening Routines • Oral Vocabulary • Listening Comprehension • Phonemic Awareness • Speaking and Listening	**Opening Routines,** T210–T211 • Phonemic Awareness • High-Frequency Words • Vocabulary Boost **Read Aloud,** "The Prickly Pride of Texas," T212–T213 **Introduce Oral Vocabulary Phonemic Awareness,** T214	**Opening Routines,** T236–T237 • Phonemic Awareness • High-Frequency Words • Vocabulary Boost **Phonemic Awareness,** T238	**Opening Routines,** T246–T247 • Phonemic Awareness • High-Frequency Words • Vocabulary Boost **Phonemic Awareness,** T248
Vocabulary **Text-Based Comprehension** • Skills and Strategies • Craft and Structure **Research and Media Literacy**	**Read**  ☑ **Introduce Words to Know** High-Frequently Words, T218–T219 ☑ **Read and Comprehend,** T220–T221 **FIRST READ Think Through the Text** Read the Anchor Text: *Seasons,* T222–T233	**Read**  ☑ **Dig Deeper: How to Analyze the Text,** T240–T241 • Cause and Effect • Sound Words **SECOND READ Analyze the Text** Reread the Anchor Text: *Seasons,* T222–T232 **Your Turn,** T242–T243	**Read**  **Independent Reading,** T252–T253 • Reader's Guide: *Seasons* • Self-Selected Reading **Apply Vocabulary Knowledge,** T254–T255
Foundational Skills • Phonics and Word Recognition • Fluency	☑ **Phonics** Words with Digraphs *sh, wh, ph,* T214–T216 **Read** *Phil's New Bat ,*T217 ☑ **Fluency** Model Accuracy, T212	☑ **Phonics** Words with Digraphs *sh, wh, ph,* T238 **Read** *In a Rush,* T239 ☑ **Fluency** Practice Accuracy, T239	☑ **Phonics** Contractions with *'s, n't,* T248–T249 **Read** *Ralph Goes to Camp,* T250 ☑ **Fluency** Accuracy: Word Recognition, T251
Spelling Grammar Writing	☑ **Spelling** Words with *sh, wh, ph,* T234 Pretest ☑ **Grammar** Introduce Subjects and Verbs, T234 Daily Proofreading Practice, T235 ☑ **Informative Writing: Sentences** Introduce the Model, T235	☑ **Spelling** Word Sort, T244 ☑ **Grammar** Subjects and Verbs, T244 Daily Proofreading Practice, T245 ☑ **Informative Writing: Sentences** Focus Trait: Ideas, T245	☑ **Spelling** Segment Sounds, T256 ☑ **Grammar** Subjects and Verbs, T256 Daily Proofreading Practice, T257 ☑ **Informative Writing: Sentences** Prewriting, T257

Whole Group

Whole Group Language Arts

Small Group

 Suggestions for Small Groups (See pp. T283–T301.)  **RtI** Suggestions for Intervention (See pp. S22–S31.)

COMMON CORE
State Standards

RI.1.1, RL.1.10, RF.1.2b, RF.1.2d, RF.1.3a, RF.1.3g, RF.1.4b, W.1.2, W.1.5, SL.1.1a, SL.1.2, L.1.1c, L.1.2d	RI.1.3, RI.1.4, RF.1.2b, RF.1.3a, RF.1.3g, RF.1.4b, W.1.2, SL.1.1b, SL.1.6, L.1.1a, L.1.1c, L.1.2d, L.1.4a, L.1.6	RI.1.2, RF.1.2b, RF.1.3b, RF.1.3g, RF.1.4a, RF.1.4b, RF.1.4c, W.1.2, W.1.5, SL.1.1b, L.1.1c, L.1.1j, L.1.2d, L.1.5a, L.1.5c

DAY 4

Opening Routines, T258–T259
- Phonemic Awareness
- High-Frequency Words
- Vocabulary Boost

Phonemic Awareness, T260

Connect to the Topic
- Read Informational Text: *Four Seasons for Animals*, T262–T266
- Think Through the Text, T262–T266
- ☑ **Compare Texts,** T267
- ☑ **Vocabulary Strategies**
Word Endings -*ed*, -*ing*, -*s*, T268–T269

☑ **Phonics**
- Words with Digraphs *sh, wh, ph*, T260
- Contractions with *'s, n't*, T260

Read *Trish's Gift*, T261

☑ **Fluency**
Accuracy: Word Recognition, T251

☑ **Spelling**
Connect to Writing, T270

☑ **Grammar**
Spiral Review: Statements, T270
Daily Proofreading Practice, T271

☑ **Informative Writing: Sentences**
Drafting, T257

 Suggestions for English Language Learners
(See pp. E22–E31.)

RI.1.2, RI.1.5, RI.1.10, RF.1.3b, RF.1.3f, RF.1.3g,
RF.1.4b, W.1.2, W.1.5, L.1.1j, L.1.2d, L.1.4c,
L.1.5c, L.1.6

DAY 5

Opening Routines, T272–T273
- Phonemic Awareness
- High-Frequency Words
- Vocabulary Boost

Phonemic Awareness, T273

Speaking and Listening, T275

Extend the Topic
- Domain-Specific Vocabulary, T274
- Speaking and Listening: Discuss Informational Text, T275
- Optional Second Read: *Four Seasons for Animals*, T262–T266

☑ **Phonics**
- Words with Digraphs *sh, wh, ph*, T280
- Contractions with *'s, n't*, T280

☑ **Fluency**
Accuracy: Word Recognition, T257

☑ **Spelling**
Assess, T276

☑ **Grammar**
Weekly Review: Subjects and Verbs,
T276–T277
Daily Proofreading Practice, T278

☑ **Informative Writing: Sentences**
Revising and Proofreading, T278–T279

RI.1.3, RI.1.9, RF.1.3g, W.1.2, W.1.5, SL.1.1b,
SL.1.1c, SL.1.6, L.1.1c, L.1.1j, L.1.2d, L.1.6

Go Digital

FOR STUDENTS

myWriteSmart

- eBook
- GrammarSnap Videos
- Destination Reading
- Context Cards

FOR TEACHERS

- Teacher One-Stop
- Interactive Whiteboard Lessons
- Literacy and Language Guide

Grab-and-Go!

- Lesson 13 Blackline Masters
- Additional Resources
- Assessment

DAY 1

Today's Goals

Vocabulary & Oral Language
- **Teacher Read Aloud:** "The Prickly Pride of Texas"
- **Oral Vocabulary**
- **Listening Comprehension**
- **Model Fluency**

Phonemic Awareness
- **Blend and Segment Phonemes**

Phonics & Fluency
- **Words with Digraphs** *sh, wh, ph*
- **Read Decodable Reader:** *Phil's New Bat*
- **Fluency:** Accuracy

☑ WORDS TO KNOW

down	grow
fall	new
goes	open
green	yellow

Text-Based Comprehension
- **Read and Comprehend**
- **Read the Anchor Text:** *Seasons*

Grammar & Writing
- **Subjects and Verbs**
- **Informative Writing:** Sentences

Spelling
- **Words with** *sh, wh, ph*

RF.1.2b orally produce single-syllable words by blending sounds; **RF.1.2d** segment spoken single-syllable words into their complete sequence of individual sounds; **RF.1.3g** recognize and read irregularly spelled words; **SL.1.1a** follow rules for discussions; **L.1.5c** identify real-life connections between words and their use

Opening Routines

Warm Up with Wordplay

How Do They Go Together?

Display and read the following:

snowy   rainy   sunny

Have children discuss how these words belong together. Have children compare their answers while following good discussion rules. Remind them to listen carefully to each other. Then tell them the correct answer: these words tell about different kinds of weather.

Encourage children to come up with more weather words. Write down the responses and say them aloud with children. Tell children that this week they will read selections about the seasons of the year and how nature changes. ◄► SL.1.1a

Daily Phonemic Awareness

Blend and Segment Phonemes

- *I'm going to say the sounds in a word and blend them. Then you say the word. Ready? Listen: /m/ /ŏ/ /p/. What is the word?* mop *Good. Now let's do some more.*

- Have children blend the following sounds with you and then by themselves.

/h/ /ŏ/ /t/ hot   /sh/ /ŏ/ /p/ shop   /w/ /ĕ/ /t/ wet

/p/ /ă/ /k/ pack   /w/ /ĭ/ /sh/ wish   /sh/ /ĭ/ /p/ ship

- Reverse the process. Say each word above and have children repeat it. *How many sounds are in the word* hot? *three Say the first sound. Say the middle sound. Say the last sound.* ◼ RF.1.2b, RF.1.2d

Corrective Feedback

- **Model the task.** *The word is* shop. *Listen: /sh/ /ŏ/ /p/. What is the word?* shop

- Have children do the blending with you before doing it on their own.

- Back up several words and continue the game.

Daily High-Frequency Words

Introduce

- **Point to the Words to Know on the Focus Wall.** *Our Words to Know for this week are* down, fall, goes, green, grow, new, open, *and* yellow. *You are going to see these words in your reading.*

- Use **Instructional Routine 10** and the **High-Frequency Word Card** to introduce the word *down*.

- Repeat the procedure with the words *fall, goes, green, grow, new, open,* and *yellow*. ◼ RF.1.3g

Corrective Feedback

- Say the correct word and have children repeat it. Down. *What is the word?* down

- Have children spell the word. *d-o-w-n How do we say this word?* down

- Have children reread all of the cards in random order.

Daily Vocabulary Boost

- Have children recall what they know about plants. Guide children to interact with the Oral Vocabulary words from previous weeks by asking the following questions about real-life experiences. Remind them to speak clearly when participating in discussion.

  - *What plants have you seen in* forests *or other places in nature?*

  - *Which plants do you you think are most* beautiful?

  - *What plants would be hard to* yank *out of the ground?*

  - *Do you think plants have* predators? *Explain.*

- Have children work together to explain *forests, beautiful, yank,* and *predators* in their own words. ◼ L.1.5c, L.1.6

☑ **Oral Vocabulary**

forests

beautiful

yank

predators

Teacher Read Aloud

▶ **SHARE OBJECTIVES**

- Listen to hear words read correctly.
- Ask and answer questions about a text read aloud.
- Participate in a class discussion.

Model Fluency

- Explain to children that good readers make sure that they read aloud accurately, or without mistakes. *As you read aloud, look carefully at the words. Listen to yourself as you read. If you skip a word, you can go back and read that part again.*

- Read the first sentence of "The Prickly Pride of Texas," but skip *heard*. Model how to recognize that you skipped a word, and then read the sentence correctly.

- Repeat for the second sentence, skipping *build*. Have children raise their hands when they notice a skipped word. *How did you know when I skipped a word?*

- Read the entire selection aloud. Ask children to listen carefully to the details about the prickly pear cactus.

COMMON CORE SL.1.1a follow rules for discussions; **SL.1.1c** ask questions to clear up confusion about topics and texts under discussion; **SL.1.2** ask and answer questions about details in a text read aloud, information presented orally, or through other media; **SL.1.3** ask and answer questions about what a speaker says; **SL.1.6** produce complete sentences when appropriate to task and situation

The Prickly Pride of Texas

Have you heard the legend of the prickly pear cactus? Long ago in Mexico, a group of people called the Aztecs wanted to build a great city. They searched for the right spot for hundreds of years. Finally, a signal told them where to build. It was an eagle, with a snake in its mouth, standing on a prickly pear cactus. The signal told the Aztecs that they had found the correct location. They built the city right there and called it Tenochtitlan (teh-noch-TIT-lan) or "The Place of the Prickly Pear Cactus." Today, that city is the capital of Mexico.

It is no wonder that the Aztecs wanted to live in a place where they could find the prickly pear cactus; people have used this plant for food, medicine, hair conditioner, and more for a very long time. It grows in warm places all over the world, including the United States. The prickly pear grows so much in Texas, for example, that it is the official Texas state plant!

You can easily spot a prickly pear cactus. This plant does not have **vines**, a woody trunk, or thin leaves like other familiar plants. Instead, it has flat, green paddles. They are shaped like tears.

A prickly pear cactus can be just a few inches high or up to 7 feet tall. You would need a **plow** to knock down a large prickly pear cactus!

Introduce Oral Vocabulary

Use **Instructional Routine 16** to define each highlighted oral vocabulary word.

- Discuss the meaning of each word as it is used in the story.

- For additional support and reinforcement, have children look up each word in a children's dictionary.

vines long, twisting stems • *This plant does not have vines, a woody trunk, or thin leaves like other familiar plants.*

plow a tool that pushes things over or to the side • *You would need a plow to knock down a large prickly pear cactus!*

Whether large or small, this plant usually produces beautiful flowers. Each flower is a bright **burst** of yellow that **glows** in the sun. Don't try to gather these flowers for a **bouquet**, though, because the prickly pear cactus is covered with sharp spines that look like needles. Sometimes the flowers **shrivel** and form fruits. These reddish-pink fruits are called prickly pears because they also have prickly spines. **3**

Many people like to eat the fruit and paddles of the prickly pear cactus. The fruits are red, sweet, and juicy inside and make delicious jams, candies, or sweet drinks. The seeds inside the fruits can even be used to make flour for bread. The paddles make tasty, healthy food too, but take a little more work. To eat them, people must first carefully pick the paddles and scrub or cut off the spines. After that, the paddles can be cooked like a vegetable or cut up and stirred like an omelet.

The prickly pear cactus has other uses besides serving as food. The red fruit can be made into dye for fabric. Other parts of the plant can be used as medicine. In some parts of the world, they are grown between houses as natural fences. **4**

The prickly pear cactus is a beautiful, useful, and important plant. So the next time you travel across the Texas countryside, try to spot one. Don't touch it, however— it's called "prickly" for a reason!

burst a short, intense action or event • *Each flower is a bright burst of yellow that glows in the sun.*

glows shows bright, warm, healthy color • *Each flower is a bright burst of yellow that glows in the sun.*

bouquet a group of picked or cut flowers • *Don't try to gather these flowers for a bouquet, though, because the prickly pear cactus is covered with sharp spines that look like needles.*

shrivel to shrink and become wrinkled • *Sometimes the flowers shrivel and form fruits.*

Listening Comprehension

Read aloud the selection. Pause at the numbered stopping points to ask children the questions below. Discuss the meanings of the highlighted words, as needed, to support the discussion.
🔊 **SL.1.2**

1 *How did the Aztecs know where to build their city?* Sample answer: When the Aztecs saw an eagle with a snake in its mouth on a prickly pear cactus, they knew that was the right place. **SUMMARIZE**

2 *What is this selection mostly about?* prickly pear cactuses **MAIN IDEA AND DETAILS**

3 *How did the writer show that the prickly pear cactus is a beautiful plant?* Sample answer: beautiful flowers, bright burst of yellow that glows, reddish pink fruits **PERSUASION**

4 *What can the prickly pear cactus be used for?* Sample answer: food, medicine, dye, and natural fences **DETAILS**

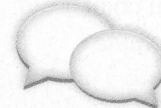

Classroom Collaboration

Guide children in a classroom discussion about the selection. Begin with a question: *Why do you think the Aztecs wanted to build their city where they found the eagle?* As children continue the discussion, have them ask and answer questions about the text and each others' comments. Remind children to speak in complete sentences and to follow good discussion rules, such as listening carefully and taking turns.

🔊 **SL.1.1a, SL.1.1c, SL.1.3, SL.1.6**

Whole Group

DAY 1

Go Digital • Interactive Whiteboard Lesson

JOURNEYS Phonics

Interactive Whiteboard Lesson:
Words with Digraphs *sh, wh, ph*

Phonemic Awareness/Phonics

▶ SHARE OBJECTIVES

- Learn the sound-spelling correspondences for digraphs *sh, wh, ph*.
- Blend and segment words with digraphs *sh, wh, ph*.
- Blend and decode regularly-spelled one-syllable words with digraphs *sh, wh, ph*.

▶ SKILLS TRACE

Words with Digraphs *sh, wh, ph*	
Introduce	T214–T215
Differentiate	T286
Reteach	T300
Review	T238, T260
Assess	Weekly Tests, Lesson 13

ELL ENGLISH LANGUAGE LEARNERS
Language Transfer

Beginning Review the consonant digraphs *sh*, *ph*, and *wh*. Say *shell*, *graph*, and *whip* and have children repeat the words.

Low Intermediate Write *sh*, *ph*, and *wh* on the board. Model each sound as you point to it. Have children repeat. Say *share*, *phone*, and *which*, and have children repeat.

High Intermediate Use letter cards to build *chip*, *hen*, *quiz*, *stop*. Have children change the first letter or letters to *sh* or *wh* and read the new words.

Proficient Have partners use letter cards to build and read *shop*, *ship*, and *whip*. Continue the word ladder, changing *whip* to *whiz* to *quiz*.

See ELL Lesson 13, p. E23, for scaffolded support.

COMMON CORE **RF.1.2b** orally produce single-syllable words by blending sounds; **RF.1.2d** segment spoken single-syllable words into their complete sequence of individual sounds; **RF.1.3a** know the spelling-sound correspondences for common consonant digraphs; **RF.1.3b** decode regularly spelled one-syllable words; **RF.1.3g** recognize and read irregularly spelled words; **SL.1.6** produce complete sentences when appropriate to task and situation

Words with Digraphs *sh, wh, ph*

PHONEMIC AWARENESS WARM-UP *Listen as I blend some sounds to say a word: /sh/ /ĭ/ /p/. The word is* ship. *Listen again. /sh/ /ĭ/ /p/,* ship. *Repeat with* whale *and* phone.

Now let's do it together. Listen. Blend the sounds: /f/ /ĭ/ /sh/. What is the word? fish *Now you blend the sounds, and tell me each word. /hw/ /ĭ/ /p/* whip, */d/ /ă/ /sh/* dash, */g/ /r/ /ă/ /f/* graph.

Reverse the process, segmenting instead of blending. Use the same words, but in random order. ▬ **RF.1.2b, RF.1.2d**

1 Teach/Model

SOUND/SPELLING CARDS Display the card for *sheep*. Name the picture and say the beginning sound. Have children repeat after you. *Listen: sheep, /sh/. Now you say it.*

- Say the sound and give the spelling. *Sheep begins with the sound /sh/. The letters* sh *can stand for the sound /sh/ at the beginning, middle, or end of a word.*

- Display the card for *whale*. Name the picture and say the beginning sound. Have children repeat after you. *Listen: whale, /hw/. Now you say it.*

- Say the sound and give the spelling. *Whale begins with the sound /hw/. The letters* wh *can stand for the sound /hw/ at the beginning or middle of a word.*

- Write and read *graph*. Point out the *ph* spelling at the end of *graph*. *Graph ends with the sound /f/.* Display the card for *fish*. *The letters* ph *can stand for the sound /f/ at the beginning, middle, or end of a word.*

- Repeat with the words *fish, elephant,* and *wheel*.

2 Guided Practice

CONTINUOUS BLENDING ROUTINE Use **Instructional Routine 3** to model blending *fish*. Write the word *fish* on the board.

RF.1.2b, RF.1.3a, RF.1.3b

• Remind children that knowing the sound/ spelling *sh* can help them read words.

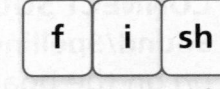

• Display **Letter Cards** *f, i,* and *sh.*

• Blend the sounds. *Listen: /f/ /ĭ/ /sh/.* Have children blend the sounds with you. *Now you blend the sounds. /f/ /ĭ/ /sh/, fish*

• Repeat the routine with letter cards for *whip,* and *graph.*

REPEAT CONTINUOUS BLENDING with the words in Row 1 below. Then write the words in Rows 1–3 and have children read them. Use the **Corrective Feedback** steps if children need additional help.

• Repeat until children are reading at a rate of three seconds per word.

DECODING Write the two sentences on the board. Call on individuals to blend one or more words and to read the sentences.

RF.1.3a, RF.1.3b, RF.1.3g

1. fish	when	whip	graph	shop
2. what	shell	which	ship	path
3. dish	whiz	check	crash	then

What can <u>a</u> math whiz <u>do</u>?

<u>Look</u> at <u>the</u> graphs in <u>the</u> shop.

3 Apply

Hands-on Practice

Have partners use letter cards to take turns building and reading words with digraphs *sh, wh,* and *ph.* After reading a word, each partner should use the word in a sentence.

RF.1.3a, RF.1.3b, SL.1.6

Corrective Feedback Work with the whole group to correct errors, following the model below.

Phonics Error:
A child reads *ship* as *sip.*

Correct the error. Review the **Sound/ Spelling Card.** Say the word and the sound. *The letters* sh *stand for the sound /sh/.*

Model as you touch the letters. *I'll blend: /sh/ /ĭ/ /p/. What is the word?* ship

Guide *Let's blend together: /sh/ /ĭ/ /p/. What is the word?* ship

Check *You blend: /sh/ /ĭ/ /p/. What is the word?* ship

Reinforce Go back three or four words and have children continue reading. Make note of errors and review those words during tomorrow's lesson.

SMALL GROUP Options Go to p. T286 for additional phonics support.

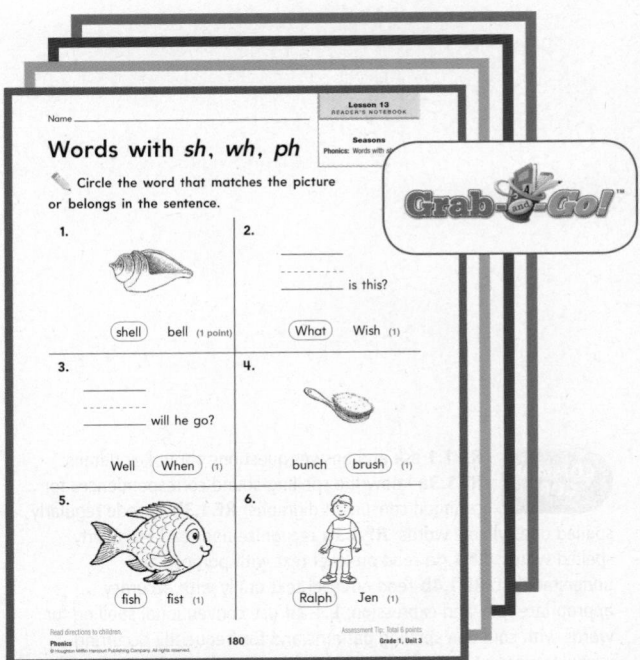

Reader's Notebook Vol. 1 p. 180
See Grab-and-Go™ Resources for additional leveled practice.

Go Digital
• Interactive Whiteboard Lesson
• Decodable Reader

Phonics/Spelling

▶ SHARE OBJECTIVES

- Write words with digraphs *sh*, *wh*, *ph*.
- Read decodable text with regularly spelled one-syllable words with digraphs and irregularly spelled high-frequency words.
- Practice reading on-level text fluently with accuracy and understanding.

▶ DICTATION SENTENCES

- **dish.** Mom broke a **dish**.
- **wash.** I help **wash** the car.
- **whiz.** Sally is a math **whiz**.
- **wham.** The door made a loud **wham**!
- **Phil.** This is my friend **Phil**.
- **shin.** Your **shin** is part of your leg.

Write Words with *sh*, *wh*, *ph*

1 Teach/Model

CONNECT SOUNDS TO SPELLING Review **Sound/Spelling Cards** *sheep* and *whale*. Write *ph* on the board and remind children that these letters can stand for the /f/ sound. Tell children that they will write words with the sounds /sh/, /hw/, or /f/.

Use **Instructional Routine 6** to dictate, using the first sentence at the left. *Listen as I say each word and use it in a sentence.*

- Model how to spell the word *dish*. Point to *sh* on the **Sound/Spelling Card**. *What is the ending sound? /sh/ I remember that these letters can stand for the /sh/ sound. I will write* sh *at the end of the word. Then I'll reread to check the whole word:* dish.

2 Guided Practice

CONNECT SOUNDS TO WRITING Continue the dictation, using the sentences at the left.

- Have children say each word aloud after you. Then have children identify the sounds they hear at the beginning, middle, and end, and write the letters that stand for each sound. ◖L.1.2e
- Remind children to write only the dictation word.

3 Apply

Read aloud the following sentence for children to write.

> Which dish is on the shelf?

Remind children that *the* is a Word to Know they learned in previous lessons.

Print the words and sentence for children to check their work.
◖L.1.2d

RL.1.1 ask and answer questions about key details; **RF.1.3a** know the spelling-sound correspondences for common consonant digraphs; **RF.1.3b** decode regularly spelled one-syllable words; **RF.1.3g** recognize and read irregularly spelled words; **RF.1.4a** read on-level text with purpose and understanding; **RF.1.4b** read on-level text orally with accuracy, appropriate rate, and expression; **L.1.2d** use conventional spelling for words with common spelling patterns and for frequently occurring irregular words; **L.1.2e** spell untaught words phonetically, drawing on phonemic awareness and spelling conventions

Decodable Reader

Read *Phil's New Bat*

Decodable Reader, Unit 3, pp. 51–56

REVIEW sh, wh, ph AND WORDS TO KNOW Tell children that many words in this story have *sh, wh,* or *ph*. Point out that children have learned the following words, which they will also read in the story: *down, fall, new.*

PREVIEW Have children preview pages 51–53 and predict what the story is about. Ask volunteers to tell about a time they have played or watched baseball.

MODEL FLUENCY AND ACCURACY Read aloud page 51 as children follow along. Point out that you do not misread, add, or skip words. Lead them in choral reading the page with fluency and accuracy.

READ Remind children to track the words from left to right. When they come to the end of a line, they should sweep their hand down to the beginning of the next line and continue reading. Have children read each page silently, and then choral-read aloud. Have them read to find out what Phil does with his bat. RF.1.3a, RF.1.3b, RF.1.3g, RF.1.4a

RESPONDING Have children ask themselves questions about the story, such as *How does Phil feel when he falls down on his leg? Why does Phil let his pal play with his bat?* Tell children to look back at the story to help them answer the questions. Have them write brief notes and then share their ideas with a partner. RL.1.1

Reread for Fluency/ Develop Automaticity

READ WITH A PARTNER Have partners reread *Phil's New Bat* three or four times, taking turns reading aloud each page. Remind them to read words correctly and to read smoothly. Visit partners to listen to them read. Give feedback about reading accurately, at an appropriate rate, and with expression and provide guidance for improving fluency. RF.1.4b

Whole Group

DAY 1

 **Go Digital**
• eBook
• Context Cards
• Vocabulary Reader

Introduce Words to Know

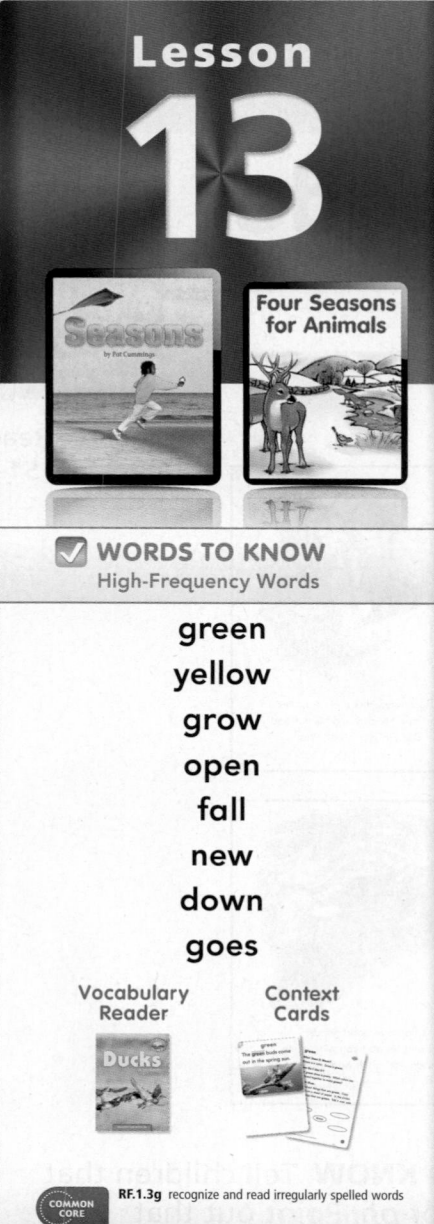

Lesson
13

Seasons

Four Seasons for Animals

✓ **WORDS TO KNOW**
High-Frequency Words

green
yellow
grow
open
fall
new
down
goes

Vocabulary Reader

Ducks

Context Cards

COMMON CORE RF.1.3g recognize and read irregularly spelled words

76  **Go Digital**

Words to Know

 **Read Together**

▶ Read each **Context Card.**

▶ Choose two blue words. Use them in sentences.

1 green
The green buds come out in the spring sun.

2 yellow
He put on yellow boots on a rainy day.

▷ **SHARE OBJECTIVE**
• Recognize and read irregularly spelled words.

Teach

Display and discuss the **Vocabulary in Context Cards,** using the routine below. See also **Instructional Routine 15.**

1 Read and pronounce the word. Read the word once alone and then together.

2 Explain the word. Read aloud the explanation under *What Does It Mean?*

3 Discuss vocabulary in context. Together, read aloud the sentence on the front of the card. Help children explain and use the word in new sentences.

4 Engage with the word. Ask and discuss *How Do I Use It?*

Give partners or small groups one or two **Vocabulary in Context Cards.** Help children complete the *Talk It Over* activities for each card. ⬤ **RF.1.3g**

ELL ENGLISH LANGUAGE LEARNERS

Language Transfer

Beginning Close the door and say *The door is closed.* Then open the door and say *The door is open.* Have children repeat *open* while a volunteer opens the door.

High Intermediate Have children complete this sentence frame: *We can open the door to ____.* Have them tell reasons why they might need to open a door.

Low Intermediate Close the door and ask *Is the door open?* Open the door and ask *Is the door open or closed?*

Proficient Have children use complete sentences to tell about why they might need to have a door open.

See ELL Lesson 13, p. E22, for vocabulary support.

3 grow
Many flowers grow in the summer.

4 open
The windows can be open on a hot day.

5 fall
The leaves change color in fall.

6 new
She has a brand new backpack for school.

7 down
Snow comes down on a cold day.

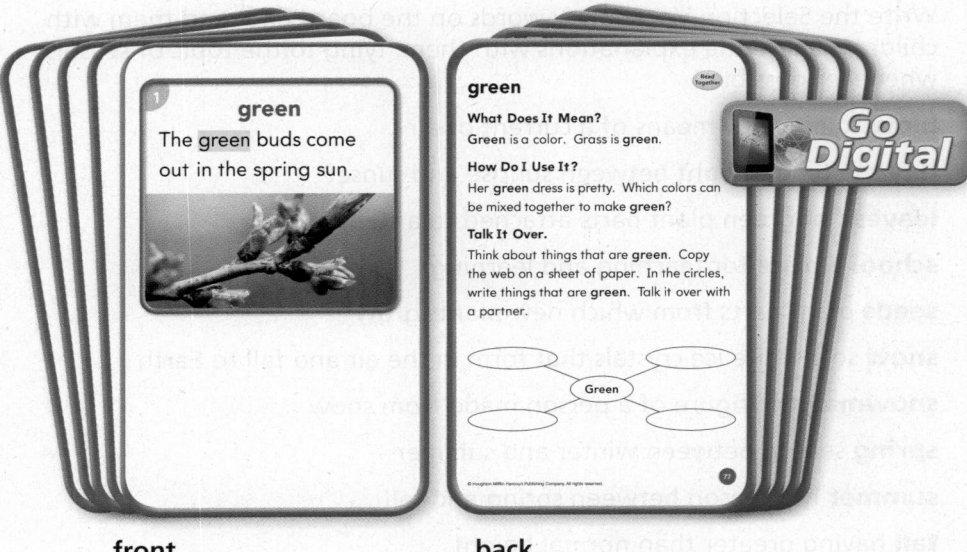

8 goes
She goes to the park to skate with her mom.

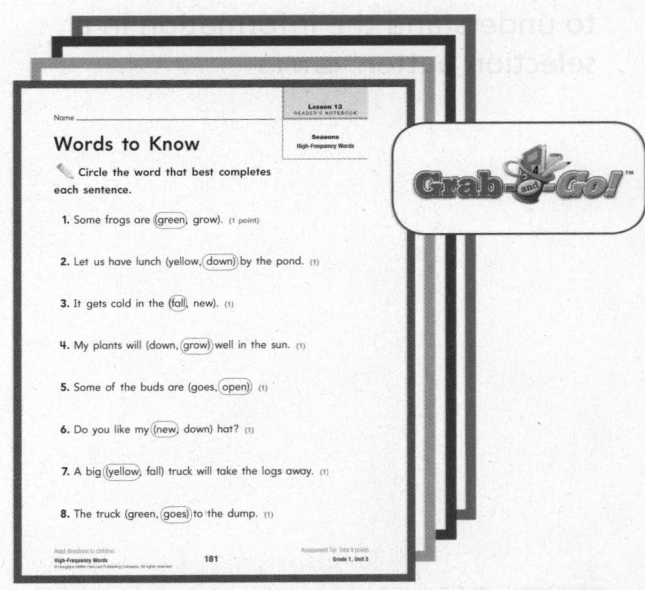

77

DAILY ASSESSMENT · RtI

Are children able to understand and use the Words to Know?

IF...	THEN...
children have difficulty understanding and using Words to Know,	▶ use **Vocabulary in Context Cards** and the Struggling Readers activity, p. T288. *See also Intervention Lesson 13, pp. S22–S31.*
children can understand and use most Words to Know,	▶ use **Vocabulary in Context Cards** and the On Level activity, p. T288.
children can understand and use all Words to Know,	▶ use the Advanced activity, p. T289.

SMALL GROUP Options

Vocabulary Reader pp. T288–T289
Provide support for English Language Learners according to language proficiency. See also Differentiate Words to Know, p. T287.

VOCABULARY IN CONTEXT CARDS 77–84

1 green
The green buds come out in the spring sun.

green

What Does It Mean?
Green is a color. Grass is green.

How Do I Use It?
Her green dress is pretty. Which colors can be mixed together to make green?

Talk It Over.
Think about things that are green. Copy the web on a sheet of paper. In the circles, write things that are green. Talk it over with a partner.

Green

Go Digital

Grab-and-Go!

front   back

Words to Know

✏ Circle the word that best completes each sentence.

Lesson 13 READER'S NOTEBOOK
Seasons
High-Frequency Words

1. Some frogs are (green), grow. (1 point)
2. Let us have lunch (yellow, down) by the pond. (1)
3. It gets cold in the (fall), new). (1)
4. My plants will (down, grow) well in the sun. (1)
5. Some of the buds are (goes, open) (1)
6. Do you like my (new), down) hat? (1)
7. A big (yellow), fall) truck will take the logs away. (1)
8. The truck (green, goes) to the dump. (1)

181

Reader's Notebook Vol. 1 p. 181
See Grab-and-Go™ Resources for additional leveled practice.

 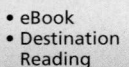
- eBook
- Destination Reading

Read and Comprehend

▶ **SHARE OBJECTIVES**
- Understand cause and effect.
- Visualize while reading a selection to aid comprehension.

☑ TARGET SKILL
Sequence of Events

- Read **Student Book** p. 78 with children.

- Explain to children that sometimes one event can cause another event to happen.

- Then tell them the **cause** happens first. The cause makes something else happen. The **effect** is what happens next.

- Draw children's attention to the graphic organizer on **Student Book** p. 78. Tell them that, as they read, they can use a graphic organizer like this one to show how events are connected, such as how one event causes another event to happen. Explain that this will help them to understand the information in a selection better. ⬛ **RI.1.3**

 **RI.1.3** describe the connection between individuals, events, ideas, or information in a text

---

Read and Comprehend

 Read Together / Go Digital

☑ TARGET SKILL

Cause and Effect Sometimes one event can **cause** another event to happen. The **cause** happens first. It makes something else happen. The **effect** is what happens next. As you read, think about what happens and why. You can use a chart like this to show how events are connected.

Cause		Effect
Event	→	Event

☑ TARGET STRATEGY

Visualize To understand a selection, picture events in your mind as you read.

COMMON CORE · **RI.1.3** describe the connection between individuals, events, ideas, or information in a text

78

SELECTION VOCABULARY

Tell children they may see words they do not recognize as they read *Seasons*. Write the Selection Vocabulary words on the board and read them with children. Share the explanations with them, tying to the topic of seasons whenever possible.

blow to move by means of a current of air

day the time of light between sunrise and sunset

leaves flat green plant parts attached to a stem

school a place for teaching and learning

seeds plant parts from which new plants grow

snow soft white ice crystals that form in the air and fall to Earth

snowman the figure of a person made from snow

spring season between winter and summer

summer hot season between spring and fall

tall having greater than normal height

winter cold season between fall and spring

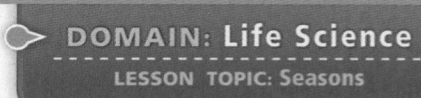

PREVIEW THE TOPIC
Seasons

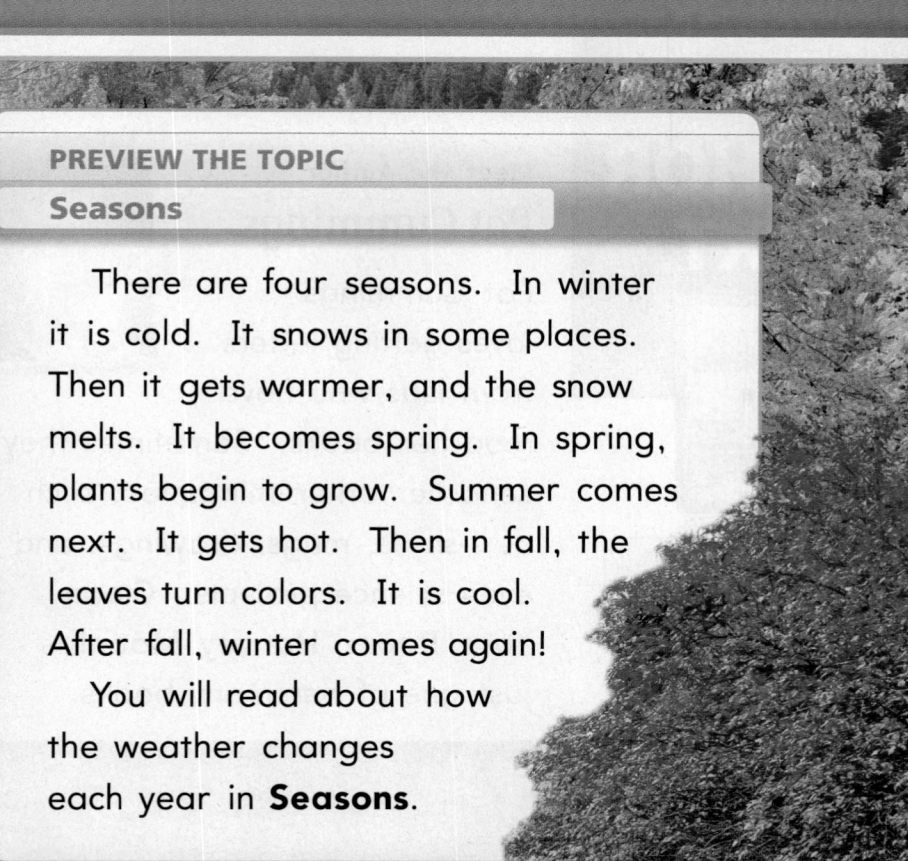

There are four seasons. In winter it is cold. It snows in some places. Then it gets warmer, and the snow melts. It becomes spring. In spring, plants begin to grow. Summer comes next. It gets hot. Then in fall, the leaves turn colors. It is cool. After fall, winter comes again!

You will read about how the weather changes each year in **Seasons**.

79

COMPREHENSION STRATEGIES

Use the following strategies flexibly as you read with children by modeling how they can be used to improve comprehension. See scaffolded support for the strategy shown in boldface during this week's reading.

- Monitor/Clarify
- Summarize
- Infer/Predict
- **Visualize**
- Analyze/Evaluate
- Question
- Phonics/Decoding

Use the Strategy Projectables, S1–S8, for additional support.

⬦ **DOMAIN: Life Science**
LESSON TOPIC: Seasons

☑ TARGET STRATEGY
Visualize

- Read the bottom of **Student Book** p. 78 with children.

- Tell children that good readers picture in their mind, or **visualize** things, as they read. Explain that children should make pictures in their mind of the places they read about and the events that are happening. This will help them understand the selection better.

- Then explain that you will show them how they should use this strategy when they read *Seasons* together.

Preview the Topic: Seasons

- Tell children that today they will begin reading *Seasons*.

- Read the information on **Student Book** p. 79 with children.

- Then write the word *seasons* on the board. Have children explain their understanding of what a season is using the information in the text and their own experiences. Have them name their favorite season and give reasons why they like it.

- To further explore seasons, work with children to investigate what happens to living things in your area during different seasons. Choose a nearby tree or other appropriate plant to have children visit throughout the seasons. Guide them to make careful observations, using their five senses. Have children keep a record of their observations, drawing pictures of the tree or plant during each season and writing notes about any changes they observe. During class discussions, have children compare their observations with their classmates'.

Read the Anchor Text

☑ TARGET SKILL
Cause and Effect

- Point out the graphic organizer on **Student Book** p. 80 to children.
- Tell children a graphic organizer can help them tell events that happen in the selection and why they happen.

☑ GENRE Informational Text

- Read the genre information on **Student Book** p. 80 with children.
- Preview the selection with children, and model identifying the characteristics of this informational text.

Think Aloud *Informational text gives facts and information about a topic. The title makes me think that the selection will describe the different seasons of the year. This selection also has rhyming words, like poetry.*

- *How do the photos help you know that the selection gives information about the seasons? The photos show real people, plants, and animals in each season.*

- As you preview, ask children to point out other features of informational text.

 **RI.1.10** read informational texts; **RF.1.4a** read on-level text with purpose and understanding

Lesson 13

ANCHOR TEXT

☑ TARGET SKILL

Cause and Effect
Tell what happens and why.

☑ GENRE

Informational text gives facts about a topic. As you read, look for:
▶ information and facts in the words
▶ photos that show the real world

COMMON CORE **RI.1.3** describe the connection between individuals, events, ideas, or information in a text; **RI.1.4** ask and answer questions to determine or clarify the meaning of words and phrases; **RI.1.10** read informational texts

80

Meet the Author

Pat Cummings

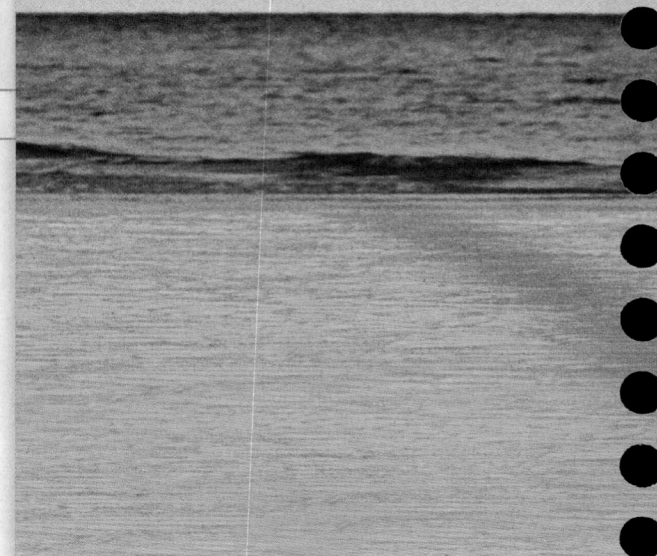

Pat Cummings loves getting letters from kids who have read her books. Sometimes they send her other things too, such as T-shirts, mugs, drawings, and even science projects. **Clean Your Room, Harvey Moon!** is just one of her many books.

🔲 RI.1.10

Scaffold Close Reading

Think Through the Text	Analyze the Text	Independent Reading
FIRST READ	**SECOND READ**	
Develop comprehension through	Support analyzing short sections of text:	• Children analyze the text independently, using the Reader's Guide on pp. 187–188 of the **Reader's Notebook**. (See p. T252 for instructional support.)
• Guided Questioning	• Cause and Effect	
• Target Strategy: Visualize	• Sound Words	
• Vocabulary in Context	Use directed note-taking by working with children to complete a graphic organizer during reading. Distribute copies of Graphic Organizer 2.	• Children read independently in a self-selected trade book.
IF children demonstrate understanding of what the selection is mostly about,		
THEN provide additional challenge using the questions labeled A Closer Look.		

Seasons

written by Pat Cummings

ESSENTIAL QUESTION

What changes do the different seasons cause?

81

Determine the level of additional support your children will need to read and comprehend *Seasons* successfully.

READERS

• **Motivate** Ask children to name the current season and describe what the weather is generally like and any major changes that usually happen during this season.

• **Access Knowledge and Experiences** Remind children of the Preview the Topic information on **Student Book** p. 79. Ask them to share with a partner what they recall, and if possible, share one other thing they know about the seasons.

TASKS

• **Increase Scaffolding** Stop periodically as you read to have children describe key ideas from the text and photographs.

• **Foster Independence** Have children read the selection in small groups. Tell them to pause throughout the selection to ask any questions they have about the information. Have them look together for text evidence in the words and photographs to help them answer the questions.

ESSENTIAL QUESTION

• Read aloud and discuss the Essential Question on **Student Book** p. 81: *What changes do the different seasons cause?* Tell children to think about this question as they read *Seasons*.

Predictive Writing

• Write the Essential Question on the board.

• Have partners work together to write what they expect *Seasons* to be about. Have them think about how the Essential Question relates to what they noticed while previewing the selection or what they already know about seasons from their own experiences.

• Guide children to think about the genre as they write. Discuss their predictions.

Set Purpose

• Tell children that good readers set a purpose for reading. *Think about the photos in the selection and what you know about informational text. What do you want to learn about the seasons?*

• Model setting a purpose for reading.

Think Aloud *I can think of lots of things I like to do in each season. Each season gives me different feelings, too. I will read to find out how the seasons are different and which one I like best.*

• Have children set their own purpose for reading. Ask volunteers to share their purpose for reading. Then have children read the selection.

🔲 **RI.1.10, RF.1.4.a**

Spring

In the spring,
fresh winds blow.
We plant new seeds,
and green buds grow.

82

83

ENGLISH LANGUAGE LEARNERS

Comprehensible Input

Beginning Have children act out a seed growing into a flower. As they "grow," guide them in understanding the content-area vocabulary, such as *seed* and *bud*.

Low Intermediate Have children look at the photos. Ask questions with imbedded answers, such as *Does it look cold or warm?*

High Intermediate *What happens after it rains? The grass gets wet.* Guide children to understand that this is an **effect**.

Proficient *Why does the grass make squishing noises? because it rained* Guide children to understand that this is a **cause**.

FIRST READ

Use Text Evidence

Think Through the Text

1 *Why do you think the author begins the selection with spring? Why didn't the author start with winter for example?* Spring is when things start to grow, so it is a good way to start a selection about the seasons.

2 *Look at the picture. What do you think the girl is holding in her hand?* seeds *Why do you think so?* The words tell about planting seeds. I see a watering can and a pot of soil. These are things you use when planting seeds. ▬ **RI.1.1, RI.1.3**

RI.1.1 ask and answer questions about key details; **RI.1.3** describe the connection between individuals, events, ideas, or information in a text; **RI.1.4** ask and answer questions to determine or clarify the meaning of words and phrases; **RF.1.3b** decode regularly spelled one-syllable words

KEY: ☑ **WORDS TO KNOW**
High-Frequency Words ▬
Decodable Words with ▬
Digraphs *sh, wh, ph*

COMMON CORE

DAY 1

Eggs hatch open.
Little chicks sing.
The sun is out.
It must be spring!

84

The grass gets wet.
Splish! Splash! Splish!
When we step,
we hear it squish. ③

85

☑ Phonics/Decoding STRATEGY

Use **Projectable S1** to help children apply the Phonics/Decoding strategy while reading p. 85. Write the word *splash* on the board. Model blending the sounds: /s/ /p/ /l/ /ă/ /sh/, *splash*. Have children repeat. Reread the page together to make sure *splash* makes sense.
▬ RF.1.3b

③ *Which words rhyme on pp. 84–85?* blow, grow; sing, spring; splash, squish *Why do you think the author wrote an informational text that rhymes?* The author wanted it to be fun to read and fun to learn the about the seasons. ▬ RI.1.1

SECOND READ | **DAY 2**

ANALYZE THE TEXT

Sound Words Reread p. 85 with children. Have them identify sound words in the first two lines. *Splish! Splash! Splish!* Guide children to use the sentences and photo to understand that these words describe the sounds of rain coming down and of feet walking through wet grass. Ask children to find another sound word, and have them use context to determine its meaning. *squish* As children read, have them find other sound words, such as *buzz, hum,* and *crunch*. Guide them to ask questions about the words and to use the context of the text and photos to determine their meanings. Discuss how the sound words help them visualize what is happening.
▬ RI.1.4

Summer

Then summer is here
and it gets hot.
We are not in school.
We play a lot. **4**

86

87

Use Visuals

Beginning Model cause and effect by cutting a piece of paper. Have children repeat the words *cause* and *effect* after you as you demonstrate.

Low Intermediate Model cause and effect using classroom objects. Use a chart to help children identify and record which is the cause and which is the effect.

High Intermediate Have partners use classroom objects to create and tell about an example of a cause and effect.

Proficient Have partners say sentences about causes and effects they see in daily life.

COMMON CORE **RI.1.1** ask and answer questions about key details; **RI.1.3** describe the connection between individuals, events, ideas, or information in a text; **RI.1.8** identify the reasons an author gives to support points; **RF.1.3b** decode regularly spelled one-syllable words; **RF.1.3g** recognize and read irregularly spelled words

FIRST READ

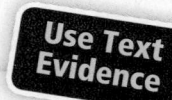
Use Text Evidence

Think Through the Text

4 *The selection says "We play a lot." Why can the children "play a lot"? It is summer. School is over and there is no homework, so there is more time to play.* ◯ **RI.1.1, RI.1.3**

☑ TARGET STRATEGY: Visualize

Reread **Student Book** pp. 86–87. Then model the strategy.

Think Aloud *The selection describes summer. I read this part and visualize what summer is like—no school and hot weather. I can close my eyes and picture myself blowing bubbles and playing and laughing with my friends.*

Guide children to use the Visualize strategy as they continue reading.

KEY: ✓ **WORDS TO KNOW**
High-Frequency Words
Decodable Words with
Digraphs *sh, wh, ph*

COMMON
CORE

DAY 1

Bugs buzz and hum.
The plants grow tall.
Next to them,
I look small.

Summer goes fast,
and when it ends,
we will go back to school
with all our friends. **5**

88

89

 A Closer Look

*What two things does the author compare on p. 88?
How does she compare them?* The author compares the boy
with the tall plants. The author says that the boy is smaller than
the plants. *What is the author trying to say about
summer by describing the plants?* The author is trying to
say that the seeds and buds in the spring have now grown into
large plants. ▬ **RI.1.1, RI.1.3, RI.1.8**

5 *What two events does the author use to talk
about the beginning of summer and the end of
summer?* The end of school is at the beginning of summer
and the first day of school is at the end of summer.
▬ **RI.1.1, RI.1.3**

Fall

In fall the leaves
are red, yellow, and brown.
In a gust of wind,
they will fall down. **6**   **7**

90

91

 ENGLISH LANGUAGE LEARNERS

Use Gestures

Beginning Have children act out being a leaf falling from a tree. Pantomime a "gust" of wind and have them respond.

Low Intermediate Have children look at the pictures. Ask: *Does it look hot or cold?* Have them act out the answer by shivering if it looks cold or fanning their face if it looks hot.

High Intermediate *What happens after the wind blows? The leaves fall down.* Have children act out the answer as they say it.

Proficient Have children tell what happens to the leaves after the wind blows. Have them say *The wind is the _____. cause The leaves falling down is the _____. effect*

COMMON CORE **RI.1.1** ask and answer questions about key details; **RI.1.3** describe the connection between individuals, events, ideas, or information in a text; **RI.1.4** ask and answer questions to determine or clarify the meaning of words and phrases; **RF.1.3g** recognize and read irregularly spelled words; **L.1.4a** use sentence-level context as a clue to the meaning of a word or phrase

FIRST READ

 **Use Text Evidence**

Think Through the Text

6 *What clues in the text around the word* gust *help you understand what* gust *means?* wind; they fall down; *These words help me understand that a gust is wind that blows hard enough to make leaves fall off trees.* ▬ **RI.1.4, L.1.4a**

7 *Look at p. 91. What happens to the leaves?* They fall down. *What causes this to happen?* The wind blows hard. ▬ **RI.1.1, RI.1.3**

KEY: ☑ **WORDS TO KNOW**
High-Frequency Words
Decodable Words with
Digraphs *sh, wh, ph* ▬

COMMON
CORE

DAY 1

The leaves crunch
as we jump and hop.
It is such fun,
we cannot stop!

8

92

Animals get nuts
and pack them away.
They will have lots to eat
on a cold day. 9

93

8 *Look at the picture on p. 92. Find something that happens and describe why.* The leaves crunch because the children jump and hop on them. ▬ RI.1.3

9 *When will the animals eat the nuts they collect and pack away?* They will eat them when it gets cold. *Why don't they just go get nuts when they are hungry?* They collect them in the fall because that's when they fall from trees and are easy to find. If they wait too long, it will be winter. There might be snow on the ground and animals might not be able to find nuts.
▬ RI.1.1, RI.1.3

ANALYZE THE TEXT

Cause and Effect Display **Projectable 13.2**, and distribute **Graphic Organizer 2**.

Recall with children from p. 91 that the leaves fall off the trees. Write this event under *Effect* on the T-Map. Ask children to use text evidence to tell what causes the leaves to fall down. *a gust of wind* Add this under *Cause*. Model describing the connection between these events: *A gust of wind blows hard and causes the leaves to fall.* Then have children identify other causes and effects from previous pages, tell how to fill in the T-Map, and describe the connection. Guide them to continue to find and describe causes and effects between individuals, events, ideas, and pieces of information. ▬ RI.1.3

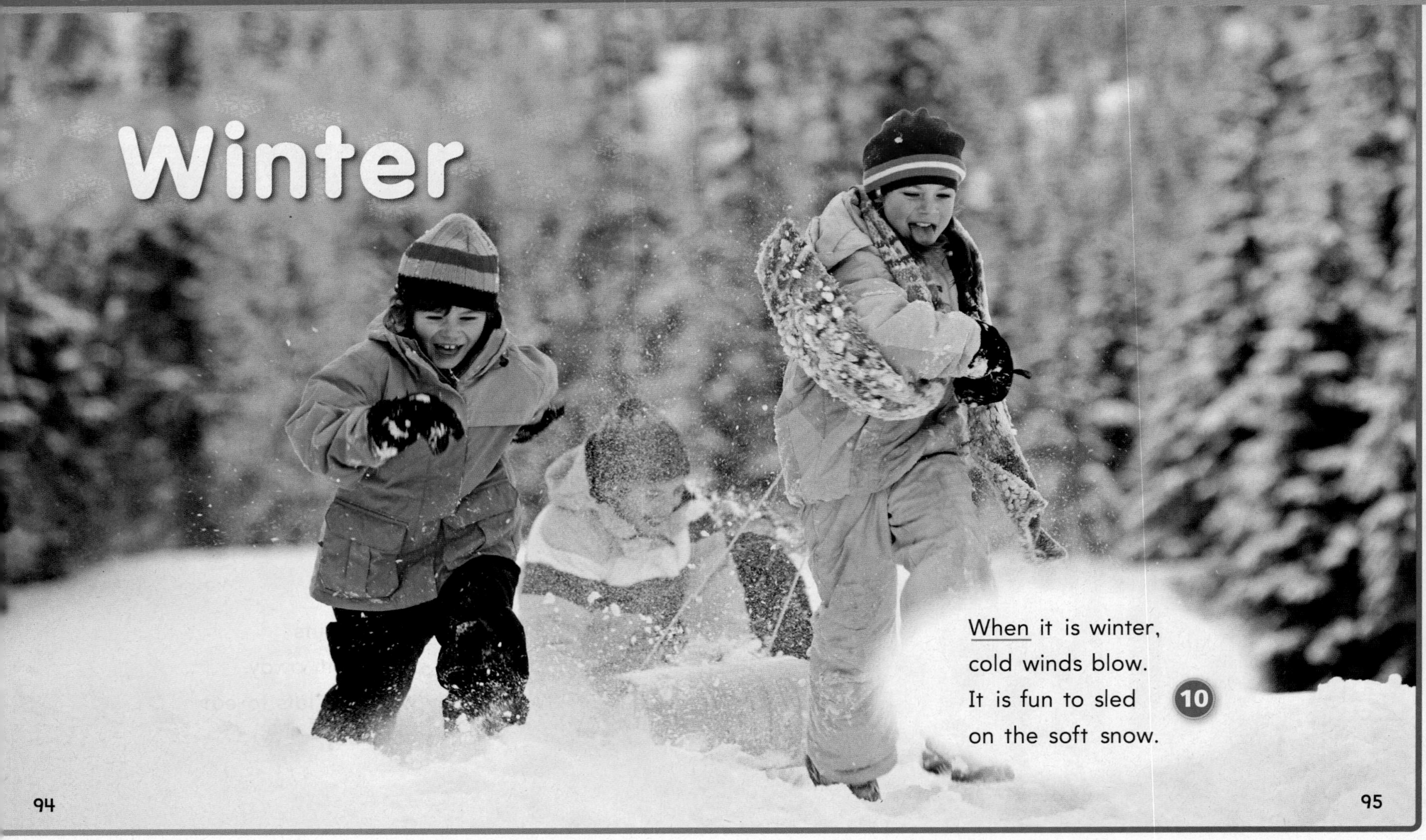
Winter
When it is winter,
cold winds blow.
It is fun to sled
on the soft snow.
10
94
95

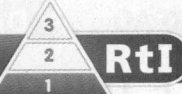

DAILY ASSESSMENT RtI

Visualize IF children have difficulty applying the Visualize strategy, **THEN** use this model:

Think Aloud *On pp. 94–95, I see a picture of a winter scene. When I look at the snow, I visualize what winter is like. I see little white snowflakes swirling around. I feel the cold on my cheeks and think of building a snowman.*

Have children share what they visualized about these pages.

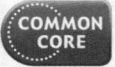

COMMON CORE **RI.1.1** ask and answer questions about key details; **RI.1.3** describe the connection between individuals, events, ideas or information in a text; **RI.1.7** use illustrations and details to describe key ideas; **RI.1.8** identify the reasons an author gives to support points; **RF.1.3b** decode regularly spelled one-syllable words

FIRST READ

Use Text Evidence

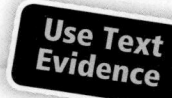

Think Through the Text

☑ TARGET STRATEGY: Visualize

Help children apply the Visualize Strategy after reading **Student Book** pp. 94–95. Tell children to spend a minute imagining winter and different winter activities. Ask them to tell a partner what they have visualized about different activities and images that make them think of winter and know what winter is like. Then ask volunteers to tell how they used the Visualize strategy to help them understand the information better.

10 *How do you think the author feels about winter?* *The author likes winter.* *What text evidence in the words and photo help you know?* *The author says it's fun to sled. The photo shows children smiling and having fun playing in the snow.*

RI.1.1, RI.1.7, RI.1.8

KEY: ☑ **WORDS TO KNOW**
High-Frequency Words
Decodable Words with
Digraphs *sh, wh, ph*

COMMON
CORE

DAY 1

When it is cold,
some animals rest.
This animal has
a nap in a nest.

96

A hat on a shelf
gives us a plan.
We will put the hat
on a big snowman! 11

97

▶ A Closer Look

Why do some animals rest in the winter? It is cold. There
isn't a lot of food to find so they can't use too much energy. ▬RI.1.1

11 *What made the children think of the idea of
making a snowman?* They saw a hat on a shelf and
realized they could put it on a snowman. ▬RI.1.3

Winter

Summer

Winter, Spring,
Summer, Fall.
Which is best?
We like them all!

Spring

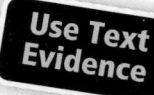

Fall

12   13

98

99

LESSON TOPIC: Seasons

Cross-Curricular Connection Remind children that there are four seasons in a year. Explain that in some places, all four seasons are experienced, but in others the weather might not be very different from one season to the next. Have children describe what the change of seasons is like where they live.

FIRST READ

Use Text Evidence

Think Through the Text

12 *What is the order of the seasons?* winter, spring, summer, fall *What season will come after fall?* winter *How are the seasons the same? How are they different?* There are fun activities to do each season. The weather can be very different in each season. ▬ **RI.1.1, RI.1.2, RI.1.3**

13 *What is the main idea of the whole selection?* Each of the four seasons is interesting and fun in its own way. ▬ **RI.1.3**

COMMON CORE
RI.1.1 ask and answer questions about key details;
RI.1.2 identify the main topic and retell key details;
RI.1.3 describe the connection between individuals, events, ideas, or information in a text; **RF.1.3b** decode regularly spelled one-syllable words; **RF.1.3g** recognize and read irregularly spelled words

Guided Summary

Oral Language Use the prompts on the **Retelling Cards** to guide children to identify the topic, the main idea, and retell key details as they summarize the selection. ◼ RI.1.2

front

New plants grow in spring.

Suggested Prompt:
Ask children to tell what else happens in spring.

back

front

It is fun to play outside in summer.

Suggested Prompt:
Have children share an outdoor activity that they enjoy in summer.

back

front

Squirrels find nuts in fall and save them for winter.

Suggested Prompt:
Ask children to tell other ways in which animals prepare for winter.

back

front

Winter weather is cold and snowy in many places.

Suggested Prompt:
Ask children which season comes after winter.

back

SUMMARIZING RUBRIC

4	**Highly Effective**	The child restates the main idea; identifies the important facts or details; retells the order of events by referring to the words and/or illustrations; requires little or no prompting.
3	**Generally Effective**	The child restates the main idea; identifies some important facts or details; retells the order of most events and may refer to the words and/or illustrations; may require some prompting.
2	**Somewhat Effective**	The child may restate the main idea; identifies some facts or details; retells the order of some events with some omissions or errors; requires some prompting.
1	**Ineffective**	The child is unable to restate the main idea; identifies some facts or details, possibly with errors; is unable to retell the order of events; is unable to summarize without prompting.

Go Digital
- *my*WriteSmart
- eBook
- GrammarSnap Videos
- Literacy and Language Guide

Grammar Introduce Subjects and Verbs

▶ SHARE OBJECTIVES

- **Grammar** Use subjects and matching verbs to produce complete sentences.
- **Spelling** Spell words with *sh, wh,* and *ph* drawing on phonemic awareness and spelling conventions.
- **Writing** Write together sentences that inform.

 **ENGLISH LANGUAGE LEARNERS**

Language Transfer

Beginning Display the words *fish, dish, photo, what, where.* Read the words aloud and have children clap whenever they hear the /sh/, /f/, or /hw/ sound.

Low Intermediate Have children use **Letter Cards** to build and read *fish, graph, when.*

High Intermediate Have children use **Letter Lards** to build and read *dish.* Guide them in changing the cards to read *dash, what, Phil.*

Proficient Have children in groups use **Letter Cards** *t, c, h, a, i, e, o, t, s, w, r, p, d, n* to build and read as many words with the /sh/, /f/, or /hw/ sound as they can.

1 Teach/Model

- Ask children to name their favorite seasons. Discuss the things they like to do during their favorite seasons.
- Record children's responses, such as *Orlando plays in the snow.*
- Point out the subject and verb in each sentence. Remind children that every complete sentence must have a *subject,* the naming part, and a *verb,* the action part. Explain that verbs in a sentence must match, or agree, with the subject nouns.

2 Guided Practice/Apply

- Model making a sentence about something to do in the summer, such as *The boy drinks lemonade; The boys drink lemonade.* Point out that in the first sentence the singular noun *boy* matches the verb *drinks.* In the second sentence the plural noun *boys* matches the verb *drink.*
- Have children brainstorm a list of subjects and verbs as a class. Then have children work in pairs to use those subjects and verbs to make up sentences about things to do in different seasons. Remind them to be sure to use matching subjects and verbs. **SL.1.6, L.1.1c, L.1.1j**

Spelling Words with *sh, wh,* and *ph*

SPELLING WORDS AND SENTENCES

BASIC

1. *ship*
The *ship* sails on the ocean.

2. *shop*
I like to *shop* for food.

3. *which*
Which hand is it in?

4. *when*
When will you go home?

5. *whip*
Whip the butter with a fork.

6. *fish*
The *fish* swim in the water.

CHALLENGE

7. *shell*
John found a *shell* on the beach.

8. *graph*
Please draw a picture *graph* on the board.

Administer the Pretest

Say the first word and read the sentence. Have children use what they know about letter-sounds to spell the word phonetically. Repeat the word as children write it. Write the word on the board and have children correct their spelling if needed. Repeat for words 2–8. Tell children that they can use their list to practice at home. **L.1.2e**

Teach the Principle

- Review **Sound/Spelling Cards** *sheep* and *whale.* Explain that the /sh/ sound can be spelled with the letters *sh.* Explain that the /hw/ sound can be spelled with the letters *wh.*
- Write *graph,* underlining *ph.* Explain that the letters *ph* stand for the /f/ sound.

 COMMON CORE **W.1.2** write informative/explanatory texts; **W.1.5** focus on a topic, respond to questions/suggestions from peers, and add details to strengthen writing; **SL.1.6** produce complete sentences when appropriate to task and situation; **L.1.1c** use singular and plural nouns with matching verbs

Informative Writing Introduce the Model

1 Teach/Model

- Remind children that sentences that inform tell facts about the world. Facts are things that are true, while opinions are beliefs.

- Display **Projectable 13.1**. Read aloud and discuss the model with children. Discuss the Talk About It questions.

- Sum up by reviewing the Writer's Checklist about sentences that inform.

Projectable 13.1

> Projectable 13.1
>
> Seasons Writing Informative Writing
>
> **Writing Model**
>
> **Sentences That Inform**
>
> The **topic sentence** tells what all the sentences are about.
>
> **Spring**
> → Many things change in the spring.
>
> **Detail sentences** tell facts about the topic. All the detail sentences are about one main idea.
> → Spring is the time of year when flowers bloom.
> In the spring, the days get longer.
> The weather gets warmer in the spring.
>
> **Talk About It**
> 1. What kind of writing is this? How do you know? writing to inform; it tells facts
> 2. What is the job of the topic sentence? to tell what all the sentences are about
> 3. What is the main idea of these sentences? Things change in the spring.
> 4. What are some facts in the detail sentences? flowers bloom in spring; the days get longer; the weather gets warmer
>
> Writing
> © Houghton Mifflin Harcourt Publishing Company. All rights reserved.
> Grade 1, Unit 3

2 Shared Writing

- Tell children that they will work together to write sentences that inform about summer. Ask volunteers to suggest things they might see on a summer day or activities they might do.

- Provide time for partners to brainstorm about summer. One child describes an activity or thing while the other records the information in pictures or words.

- Help the class write a topic sentence and detail sentences telling facts about summer. Remind them not to include opinions, such as "Summer is my favorite time of year." Make sure all the detail sentences tell facts about one main idea.

- As needed, prompt children with questions such as: *What do you know about summer? What is the weather like? What do you do in the summer?*

- Help the class come up with a closing sentence that retells the main idea of the sentences and ties the ideas together. ▄ **W.1.2, W.1.5**

Oral Language Conventions

Speak in Complete Sentences Remind children that a complete sentence has a subject and a verb. In order to share ideas that inform, children must speak in complete sentences. As they suggest sentences for the Shared Writing activity, coach children to speak in complete sentences. ▄ **SL.1.6**

in sentences; **L.1.1j** produce and expand simple and compound declarative, interrogative, imperative, and exclamatory sentences; **L.1.2e** spell untaught words phonetically, drawing on phonemic awareness and spelling conventions

Daily Proofreading Practice

down
The snow is falling doun.
                      ^

Kelly
My friend kelly has a sled.
          ^

Writer's Checklist

What Makes Great Sentences That Inform?

- The **topic sentence** tells what all the sentences are about.

- **Detail sentences** tell facts, not opinions.

- All the sentences are about one **main idea**.

Performance Task

 *my*WriteSmart Have children complete the writing assignment through *my*WriteSmart. Children will read the prompt and have access to multiple writing resources.

HOUGHTON MIFFLIN HARCOURT

Common Core Writing Handbook

Additional support for Informative Writing appears in the **Common Core Writing Handbook,** Lesson 13.

DAY 2

Today's Goals

Vocabulary & Oral Language
• Oral Vocabulary

Phonemic Awareness
• Blend and Segment Phonemes

Phonics & Fluency
• Words with Digraphs *sh, wh, ph*
• Read Decodable Reader: *In a Rush*
• Fluency: Accuracy

☑ **WORDS TO KNOW**

down	grow
fall	new
goes	open
green	yellow

Text-Based Comprehension
• **Dig Deeper:** How to Analyze the Text
• **Cause and Effect**
• **Sound Words**
• **Reread the Anchor Text:** *Seasons*

Grammar & Writing
• **Subjects and Verbs**
➡ **Informative Writing:** Sentences That Inform
Focus Trait: Ideas

Spelling
• **Words with** *sh, wh, ph*

RF.1.2b orally produce single-syllable words by blending sounds; **RF.1.2d** segment spoken single-syllable words into their complete sequence of individual sounds; **RF.1.3g** recognize and read irregularly spelled words; **L.1.6** use words and phrases acquired through conversations, reading and being read to, and responding to texts

Opening Routines

Warm Up with Wordplay

Share a Riddle

Display and read the following riddle:

> ### How does an elephant get down from a tree?

Have children discuss possible answers to this riddle. Guide them to listen to each other and build the conversation by responding to each others' comments. As children discuss, remind them they have been reading about seasons and that seasons may be part of the answer to the riddle. Have children offer their guesses about the answer before you read the correct one: They sit on a leaf and wait for fall!

Guide children to tell what makes this answer silly. They might remark on the size of an elephant compared to a leaf, or they might recognize the multiple meanings of the word *fall*. Invite children to explain any other responses they might have given to answer the riddle.

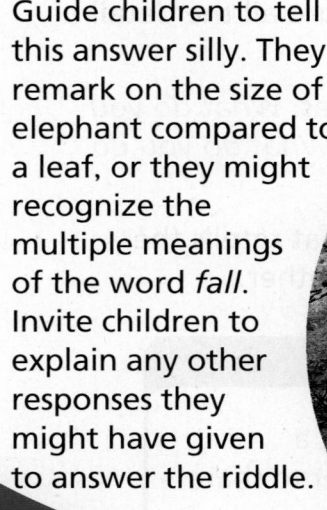

Daily Phonemic Awareness

Blend and Segment Phonemes

- *I'm going to say the sounds in a word and blend them. Then you say the word. Listen: /m/ /ŭ/ /d/. What is the word?* mud *Good.*

- Have children blend these sounds with you, then on their own.

/th/ /ĭ/ /s/ this	/r/ /ŏ/ /k/ rock	/m/ /ī/ /t/ might
/ch/ /ā/ /s/ chase	/d/ /ĭ/ /sh/ dish	/sh/ /ā/ /p/ shape
/d/ /ă/ /sh/ dash	/w/ /ĕ/ /l/ well	/k/ /ă/ /sh/ cash

- Reverse the process. Say each word below and have children repeat it. *How many sounds are in the word* this? *three Say the first sound. Say the middle sound. Say the last sound.*

  rock   might   chase   dish   shape   dash   well   cash

  🔊 RF.1.2b, RF.1.2d

Corrective Feedback

- Model the task. *The word is* dish. *Listen: /d/ /ĭ/ /sh/. What is the word?* dish

- Have children do the blending with you before doing it on their own.

- If a child misses a sound, repeat the word and model the task. *Listen to the sounds in* dish: */d/ /ĭ/ /sh/. What is the first sound? /d/ middle sound? /ĭ/ final sound? /sh/*

- Go back a few words and continue.

Daily High-Frequency Words

Introduce

- Point to the **High-Frequency Word Card** *fall*.

- *Say the word.* fall *Spell the word.* f, a, l, l *Write the word. Check the word.*

- Repeat the procedure with the words *down, goes, green, grow, new, open,* and *yellow.*

  🔊 RF.1.3.g

Word Box Game

- Write each High-Frequency Word on a piece of paper. Place the pieces of paper in a box.

- Have children take turns picking a word and reading it to the class.

- Have children repeat the word.

- Do the same for the remaining words.

Corrective Feedback

- Say the correct word and have children repeat it. Green. *What is the word?* green

- Have children spell the word. *g, r, e, e, n How do we say this word?* green

- Have children reread all of the cards in random order.

Daily Vocabulary Boost

- Review the Oral Vocabulary words and their definitions with children. (See pp. T212–T213.) Remind children that they heard these words in the Read Aloud "The Prickly Pride of Texas."

- Recall with children what they heard and then guide them to interact with each word's meaning.

  - *Each flower is a bright burst of yellow that glows in the sun. Which of the following can glow: a sunset, a football, a firefly?*

  - *Don't try to gather these flowers for a bouquet, though, because the prickly pear cactus is covered with sharp spines that look like needles. How would you feel if someone gave you a bouquet of flowers?*

- Continue in the same manner with *burst, plow, shrivel,* and *vines.* 🔊 L.1.6

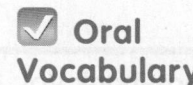
Oral Vocabulary

bouquet
burst
glows
plow
shrivel
vines

Whole Group

DAY 2

 **Go Digital**
- Interactive Whiteboard Lesson
- Decodable Reader

 **Journeys** Phonics

Interactive Whiteboard Lesson:
Words with Digraphs *sh, wh, ph*

Phonemic Awareness/Phonics

▶ SHARE OBJECTIVES
- Blend, build, and decode regularly spelled one-syllable words with digraphs *sh, wh,* and *ph*.
- Read on-level text with fluency and accuracy.

▶ SKILLS TRACE

Words with Digraphs *sh, wh, ph*	
Introduce	T214–T215
Differentiate	T286
Reteach	T300
▶ Review	**T238, T260**
Assess	Weekly Tests, Lesson 13

Reader's Notebook Vol. 1 p. 182
See Grab-and-Go™ Resources for additional leveled practice.

COMMON CORE **RF.1.2b** orally produce single-syllable words by blending sounds; **RF.1.3a** know the spelling-sound correspondences for common consonant digraphs; **RF.1.3b** decode regularly spelled one-syllable words; **RF.1.3g** recognize and read irregularly spelled words; **RF.1.4a** read on-level text with purpose and understanding; **RF.1.4b** read on-level text orally with accuracy, appropriate rate, and expression; **L.1.2e** spell untaught words phonetically, drawing on phonemic awareness and spelling conventions

Words with Digraphs *sh, wh, ph*

PHONEMIC AWARENESS WARM-UP *Let's play a game. I'll say each sound in a word. You blend the sounds to say the word. Listen: /hw/ /ĕ/ /n/ when.* **Repeat with these:** *rush, shell, which, graph.* ◼ **RF.1.2b**

1 Teach/Model

Review /sh/, /hw/, and /f/ with **Sound/Spelling Cards**.

CONTINUOUS BLENDING ROUTINE Use **Instructional Routine 3** to model blending *whiff*, displaying **Letter Cards** *wh, i,* and *ff*. Repeat the routine with the words in Row 1 below.

Write the words and sentence shown below. Call on individuals to blend and read one or more words and to read the sentence.

1. when   rush   shell   which   graph
2. scratch   miss   Seth   chin   whiff

Which shell did Seth rush to find?

2 Guided Practice

BUILD WORDS Model how to spell the word *rush. The letter r stands for the first sound. The next sound is /ŭ/. I know u stands for /ŭ/. The last sound is /sh/. I know that sh together stands for /sh/.*

- Guide children to identify sounds and spell the words *shop, shut, dish, crash, whiz, graph.* ◼ **L.1.2e**
- Call on individuals to spell the words with **Letter Cards** while other children check their work.

3 Apply

Hands-on Practice

Have partners use letter cards to take turns building and reading words with consonant digraphs *sh, wh,* and *ph*.
◼ **RF.1.3a, RF.1.3b**

Decodable Reader

Read *In a Rush*

**Decodable Reader,
Unit 3, pp. 57–62**

DAILY ASSESSMENT

 RtI

Corrective Feedback Work with the whole group to correct errors, following the model below.

Decoding Error:
A child reads *cash* as *cast*.

Correct the error. Say the word. *That word is cash. The end sound is /sh/. The letters sh stand for /sh/.*

Guide Have children repeat the word. *What is the word? cash*

Check *Go back to the beginning of the sentence and read it again.*

Reinforce Record the error and review the word again before children reread the story.

**Reread for Fluency/
Develop Automaticity**
READ WITH A PARTNER Have partners reread *In a Rush* three or four times, taking turns reading aloud each page. Remind them to read words correctly and to read smoothly. Visit partners to listen to them read. Give feedback about reading accurately, at an appropriate rate, and with expression and provide guidance for improving fluency. ▪RF.1.4b

REVIEW *sh, wh, ph* AND WORDS TO KNOW Tell children that many words in this story have *sh, wh,* or *ph.* Point out that they have learned the following words, which they will also read in the story: *down, goes, open, yellow.*

PREVIEW Have children preview pages 57–59 and predict what the story is about. Ask volunteers to tell how they dress when the weather is rainy or snowy and cold.

MODEL FLUENCY AND ACCURACY Read aloud page 57. As you read, substitute *rust* for *rush.* Ask if what you read made sense. Tell children that you will reread the sentence again. Lead children in choral reading the page with fluency and accuracy.

READ Remind children to track the words from left to right. When they come to the end of a line, they should sweep their hand down to the beginning of the next line and continue reading. Have children read each page silently and then choral-read aloud. Have them read to find out what Shan buys and why.

▪RF.1.3a, RF.1.3b, RF.1.3g, RF.1.4a

RESPONDING Have children talk with a partner about Shan's problem and how she solves it. Then ask them to draw and write about a problem they have had and how they solved it.

Whole Group

DAY 2

Go Digital
• eBook
• Interactive Whiteboard Lesson

JOURNEYS Text Analysis

Interactive Whiteboard Lesson:
Text Analysis: Informational Text

Dig Deeper: How to Analyze the Text

► SHARE OBJECTIVES
- Understand cause-and-effect relationships.
- Identify sound words and understand their use.

RI.1.3 describe the connection between individuals, events, ideas or information in a text; **RI.1.4** ask and answer questions to determine or clarify the meaning of words and phrases; **L.1.4a** use sentence-level context as a clue to the meaning of a word or phrase

Text-Based Comprehension

1 Teach/Model

Terms About Informational Text

cause the reason why something happens

effect the event that happens after the cause

onomatopoeia using words that sound like real noises

- Remind children that they have read *Seasons*, an informational text about seasons. Read and discuss **Student Book** p. 100 with children and help them understand the meaning of **cause** and **effect**.

- Explain to children that in informational texts, often two people, events, ideas, or pieces of information are connected, or joined in some way. In *Seasons*, many events are connected because one event causes another event to happen.

 Think Aloud *To understand a text, I think about how pieces of information are connected as I read. I can use a graphic organizer to show what happens and the reason why. We read about the winter. The cold causes things to happen. I will write* cold weather *under* Cause. *What is one thing that cold weather causes animals to do? They rest, or hibernate, in winter. I will write* animals rest *under* Effect. *I can describe the connection by saying:* Animals rest because the weather is too cold to go out. *What else does cold weather cause to happen?*

- Read and discuss **Student Book** p. 101 with children.

- Explain that the author used words that sound like real noises. This is called using **onomatopoeia**.

- Have children find words in the selection that are **sound words**. Guide them to ask questions about the meaning of the words and phrases. Help them use the other words in the sentence to figure out what the words are and what they mean. Talk about how the sound words help describe things in a clear way and make the selection fun and interesting to read.

COMPREHENSION

Dig Deeper

 Read Together

How to Analyze the Text
Use these pages to learn about Cause and Effect and Sound Words. Then read **Seasons** again.

Cause and Effect

In **Seasons**, many events cause other events to happen. The **cause** happens first. It is the reason why something else happens. The **effect** is what happens next. In **Seasons**, you read that it is cold in winter. What does the cold cause some animals to do? Use a chart to show what happens and why.

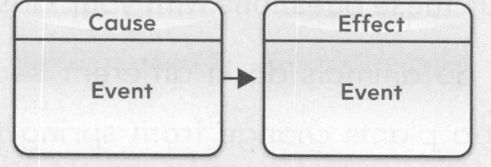

Cause		Effect
Event	→	Event

 **RI.1.3** describe the connection between individuals, events, ideas, or information in a text; **RI.1.4** ask and answer questions to determine or clarify the meaning of words and phrases

100

Go Digital

Sound Words

An author can use words that sound like real noises. In the part about spring, the author uses the words **Splish! Splash! Splish!** These words describe the sounds of rain and wet grass.

Find other words that tell about sounds in **Seasons**. Ask yourself what the words mean and what they describe. Use the other words and sentences to help you. Do sound words help you know what real things are like?

101

SECOND READ

2 Guided Practice/Apply

READ FOR TEXT EVIDENCE Begin a second read of *Seasons* with children. Use the instructional support to guide children to analyze the text:

• Cause and Effect, p. T229 ▬ RI.1.3

• Sound Words, p. T225 ▬ RI.1.4, L.1.4a

DIRECTED NOTE-TAKING The graphic organizer will be completed with children during the second read on p. T229.

DAILY ASSESSMENT  RtI

Are children able to understand cause-and-effect relationships?

IF...	THEN...
children have difficulty understanding cause and effect,	use **Differentiate Comprehension** for Struggling Readers, p. T290. See also Intervention Lesson 13, pp. S22–S23.
children can understand most cause-and-effect relationships,	use **Differentiate Comprehension** for On Level Readers, p. T290.
children can understand all cause-and-effect relationships,	use **Differentiate Comprehension** for Advanced Readers, p. T291.

 SMALL GROUP Options

Differentiate Comprehension, pp. T290–T291
Group English Language Learners according to language proficiency. See also ELL Lesson 13, p. E25, for scaffolded support.

Go Digital
- *my*WriteSmart
- eBook

SECOND READ

Your Turn

Use Text Evidence

▶ SHARE OBJECTIVES
- Respond to questions by talking with peers in complete sentences.
- Write a response to literature using complete sentences.

RETURN TO THE ESSENTIAL QUESTION

Have partners, discuss the Essential Question *What changes do the different seasons cause?* Have children provide text evidence from the words and photos in the selection to support their answers. Have children follow classroom discussion rules, such as listening carefully to the speaker, waiting their turn to talk, and staying on topic.
🔲 **RI.1.3, SL.1.1a**

 **Classroom Conversation** Have children continue their discussion of the changes the seasons cause, supporting their answers with text evidence and information from their own observations and experiences. Then ask children to explain and describe how the plants, trees, and animals are different or how the weather is different during different seasons where you live. Help children to build conversations by coaching them to have multiple exchanges with classmates, responding appropriately to others' comments and adding their own ideas. 🔲 **RI.1.1, RI.1.3, SL.1.1b**

 **COMMON CORE** **RI.1.1** ask and answer questions about key details; **RI.1.3** describe the connection between individuals, events, ideas or information in a text; **W.1.1** write opinion pieces; **SL.1.1a** follow rules for discussions; **SL.1.1b** build on others' talk in conversations by responding to others' comments

---

 **Read Together**

Your Turn

*my*WriteSmart

RETURN TO THE ESSENTIAL QUESTION

 Turn and Talk **What changes do the different seasons cause?** Talk with a partner about why changes happen in each season. Then look for text evidence to explain your answer. Take turns.

 **Classroom Conversation**

Talk about these questions with your class.

1. What do animals do in different seasons?
2. How do plants change from spring to summer to fall?
3. Tell what the seasons are like where you live.

102

ELL ENGLISH LANGUAGE LEARNERS

Use Visuals

Beginning Use **online Picture Cards** *swim* and *gloves*. Have children repeat the words after you and the name of the season that matches the pictures.

High Intermediate Use **online Picture Cards** *swim* and *gloves*. Have children identify which season matches the pictures, using a complete sentence.

Low Intermediate Use **online Picture Cards** *swim* and *gloves*. Have children say *spring*, *summer*, *fall*, or *winter* to identify the season that matches the pictures.

Proficient Use **online Picture Cards** *swim* and *gloves*. Have partners work together to name an activity and the season that matches the pictures. Have them use complete sentences.

See ELL Lesson 13, p. E24, for further comprehension support.

WRITE ABOUT READING

Response Write about your favorite season. First, tell what your topic is. Then give reasons why you like the season. Use text evidence from **Seasons** for ideas. Write an ending sentence.

Spring

Summer

Fall

Winter

Writing Tip

An ending sentence can tell your opinion again in different words.

 RI.1.1 ask and answer questions about key details; **RI.1.3** describe the connection between individuals, events, ideas, or information in a text; **W.1.1** write opinion pieces; **SL.1.1a** follow rules for discussions

103

WRITE ABOUT READING

 Performance Task

Tell children that they will write a response to the informational text *Seasons* to give their opinion about which season is their favorite.

- Read **Student Book** p. 103 with children.

- Explain that children will write about their favorite season.

- Make sure children understand they will give reasons why they like the season and use text evidence from the words and photos in *Seasons* for ideas.

- Guide children to write a topic sentence that names their favorite season and tells their opinion, followed by sentences that give reasons for their opinion, supported by examples. Help them to write an ending sentence. ▬ **W.1.1**

WRITING TIP Read the Writing Tip with children before they begin writing. Explain to them that an ending sentence tells their opinion again using different words. Model an example for them. ▬ **W.1.1**

Have children complete the Write About Reading activity through *my*WriteSmart. Children will read the prompt within *my*WriteSmart and have access to multiple writing resources, including the Student eBook, Writing Rubrics, and Graphic Organizers.

Grammar Subjects and Verbs

▶ **SHARE OBJECTIVES**

- **Grammar** Identify and use singular and plural nouns with matching verbs in sentences.

- **Spelling** Spell words with *sh*, *wh*, and *ph* using conventional spelling patterns.

- **Handwriting** Print the spelling words.

- **Writing** Print sentences that inform with a main idea and details.

ELL **ENGLISH LANGUAGE LEARNERS**

Language Transfer

All Proficiencies Using sentence strips, with red strips containing nouns/subjects, and blue strips containing verbs in each inflected present tense form (e.g. *make/makes, walk/walks*, etc.), guide the class in building complete sentences, matching each subject to the appropriately inflected verb.

---

1 Teach/Model

SUBJECTS AND VERBS Display **Projectable 13.3**.

- Review that the action word in a sentence is called a *verb*. It tells what the *subject*, or naming part, of the sentence is doing.

- Point out that verbs have to agree with the subjects. When a subject noun names one, you add *s* to most verbs. When it is plural, the verb usually has nothing added.

Think Aloud *In the first sentence, the word* children *is the subject.* Children *names more than one. It tells who is doing the action. The word* walk *is the verb. It names the action the subject does.* Walk *agrees with* children.

- Repeat with the second sentence.

2 Guided Practice/Apply

- Work together to complete **Projectable 13.3**. Support children as they select a verb from the box to tell what the subject of the sentence is doing.

- Have children practice saying sentences aloud whose subjects and verbs agree. Then have them write the sentences correctly.
  SL.1.6, L.1.1c, L.1.1j

Spelling Words with *sh, wh,* and *ph*

SPELLING WORDS

BASIC

ship	when
shop	whip
which	fish

CHALLENGE

shell	graph

Word Sort

- Review **Sound/Spelling Cards** *sheep* and *whale*. *What sound do you hear at the beginning of* sheep? *(/sh/) What sound do you hear at the beginning of* whale? *(/hw/)*

- Draw a two-column chart on the board. Write *sh* in the left column. Write *wh* in the right column. Ask children to sort the spelling words into the columns.

- For additional practice, use **Reader's Notebook** Vol. 1 page 183. **L.1.2d**

Handwriting

Model how to form *ship, shop,* and *which*. Have children use their best handwriting to write the spelling words, forming the letters correctly. Ball-and-stick and continuous stroke handwriting models are available on the **Handwriting Models Blackline Masters**.
L.1.1a

W.1.2 write informative/explanatory texts; **W.1.5** focus on a topic, respond to questions/suggestions from peers, and add details to strengthen writing; **W.1.8** recall information from experiences or gather information from sources to answer a question; **LACC.1.SL.2.6** produce complete sentences when appropriate to task and situation; **SL.1.6** produce complete sentences when appropriate to task and situation; **L.1.1a** print upper-

Informative Writing Focus Trait: Ideas

1 Teach/Model

MAIN IDEA Remind children that the main idea of a group of sentences is what these sentences are mostly about.

- Review that all the sentences in a group should be about the same main idea. Explain that sentences that are not about the main idea do not belong and should be deleted.

- Read aloud the following sentences, most of which are from *Seasons*. Ask children to find the sentence that does not belong and that did not appear in the selection.

Connect to *Seasons*
Which sentence does not belong?
Then summer is here and it gets hot. We are not in school. I like green more than yellow. We play a lot.

- *Which sentence does not belong? "I like green more than yellow."*

13.4

- Display **Projectable 13.4**. Point out that the beginnings of the sentences are already in place. Model how to use the frames to create facts about a season. Highlight the closing sentence, pointing out that it retells the main idea of all the sentences using different words. It gives the reader a sense of closure.

2 Guided Writing

- Ask children to choose a season that they would like to write about. Review the names of the seasons if necessary. Have children draw something about this season on a separate sheet of paper.

- Have children work with a partner asking and answering questions about their picture. As children describe their picture, have them include facts about the season. As needed, provide prompts such as: *How is spring different from fall?* or *What are some facts about winter?*

- Have children complete frames to write sentences that give facts about the season they chose. ■ **W.1.2, W.1.5, W.1.8**

and lowercase letters; **L.1.1c** use singular and plural nouns with matching verbs in sentences; **L.1.1j** produce and expand simple and compound declarative, interrogative, imperative, and exclamatory sentences; **L.1.2d** use conventional spelling for words with common spelling patterns and for frequently occurring irregular words

Daily Proofreading Practice

Flowers gro in the spring. *(grow)*

Tess plants yello flowers *(yellow)*

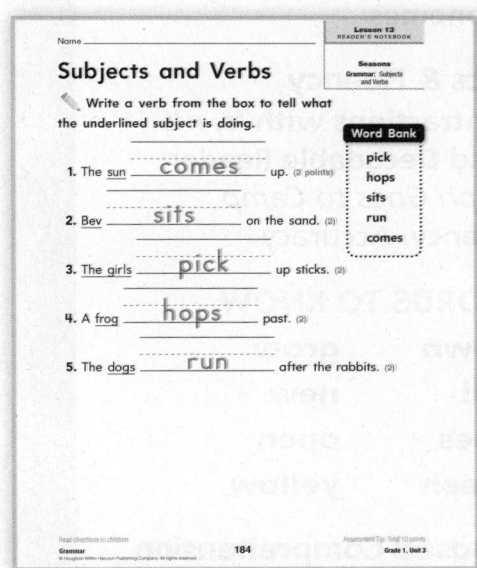

Reader's Notebook Vol. 1 p. 184

Reader's Notebook Vol. 1 p. 185

DAY 3

Today's Goals

Vocabulary & Oral Language
- Apply Vocabulary Knowledge

Phonemic Awareness
- Substitute Initial Phonemes
- Blend and Segment Phonemes

Phonics & Fluency
- Contractions with 's, n't
- Read Decodable Reader: *Ralph Goes to Camp*
- Fluency: Accuracy

 **WORDS TO KNOW**

down	grow
fall	new
goes	open
green	yellow

Text-Based Comprehension

Independent Reading
- Reader's Guide
- Self-Selected Reading

Grammar & Writing
- Subjects and Verbs
- ➡ Informative Writing: Sentences That Inform

Spelling
- Words with *sh, wh, ph*

 **COMMON CORE** **RF.1.3g** recognize and read irregularly spelled words; **SL.1.1a** follow rules for discussions; **L.1.5a** sort words into categories to gain a sense of concepts the categories represent; **L.1.5c** identify real-life connections between words and their use; **L.1.6** use words and phrases acquired through conversations, reading and being read to, and responding to texts

Opening Routines

Warm Up with Wordplay

Two Words

Remind children that they have been reading about seasons. Tell children to think of a season and say two words that have something to do with that season. Give examples such as *flowers* or *snow*.

hot	**sunny**
leaves	**chilly**
snowman	**cold**

Ask children to help you identify the longest word, the shortest word, and the most unusual word. Then have children work together to sort the words by season. Write headings on the board for each season and tell children to say which category each word belongs in. 🔲 L.1.5a

Daily Phonemic Awareness

Substitute Initial Phonemes

- *Today we're going to change the first sound in a word to make a new word. For example, change the /p/ in* pick *to /k/. What do you get?* kick *Good! Now let's change the /t/ in* top *to /ch/. What word do we get?* chop *Let's keep going.*

Change the . . .	Result
/l/ in *lid* to /d/	*did*
/b/ in *but* to /sh/	*shut*
/s/ in *sip* to /hw/	*whip*
/th/ in *thin* to /ch/	*chin*
/l/ in *lock* to /sh/	*shock*

Corrective Feedback

- If a child misses a word, say the correct word and model the task. *Listen:* lid, /l/ /ĭ/ /d/. *Now change the /l/ to /d/. What is the new word?* did

- Have children do it once with you before doing it on their own.

Daily High-Frequency Words

Introduce

- Point to the **High-Frequency Word Card** *goes*.

- *Say the word.* goes *Spell the word.* g, o, e, s *Write the word. Check the word.*

- Repeat the procedure with the words *down, fall, green, grow, new, open,* and *yellow.*
   RF.1.3g

Find the Letter Game

- Choose a word from this week's or the previous week's High-Frequency Words. Write a dash on the board to represent each letter in the word.

- Have children call out letters. If the letter is in the word, write it on the appropriate blank.

- Continue until children can guess the word.

- Ask the child who guesses the word correctly to come to the board to choose the next word.

Corrective Feedback

- If a child is unable to recognize the word *yellow,* say the correct word and have children repeat it. *Yellow. What is the word?* yellow

- Have children spell the word. *y, e, l, l, o, w How do we say this word?* yellow

- Have children reread all of the cards in random order.

Daily Vocabulary Boost

- Guide children to interact with the Oral Vocabulary words by asking the following questions. Remind them to speak clearly when participating in discussion.

  What is a bouquet *usually made of?*

  Where might you be if you hear a burst *of applause?*

  Have you seen something that glows *in the dark? What was it?*

- Ask children to work with a partner to explain *bouquet, burst,* and *glows* in their own words. Remind them that it is important to listen to what their partner says. Make sure children follow appropriate rules for discussion such as listening to speakers, taking turns, and staying on topic. ⬛ SL.1.1a, L.1.5c, L.1.6

☑ **Oral Vocabulary**

bouquet

burst

glows

plow

shrivel

vines

Whole Group

DAY 3

• Interactive Whiteboard Lesson

Interactive Whiteboard Lesson:
Contractions with *'s, n't*

Phonics

Phonemic Awareness/Phonics

▶ SHARE OBJECTIVES

• Learn about and use apostrophes in contractions.
• Blend and read contractions with *'s*, and *n't*.

▶ SKILLS TRACE

Contractions with *'s, n't*	
Introduce	**T248–T249**
Differentiate	T292
Reteach	T300
Review	T260
Assess	Weekly Tests, Lesson 13

ELL **ENGLISH LANGUAGE LEARNERS**

Language Transfer

Beginning Write *it's, she's, he's, there's,* and *that's* on the board. Read each word and have children repeat.

Low Intermediate Tell children to listen and raise their hands when you read a word that is a contraction: *is, not, wasn't, did, that, it's, there's, didn't.*

High Intermediate Write *it is, had not, she is,* and *was not.* Have children read the words, and write them as contractions.

Proficient Write *it, had, she, he, was, did,* and *there* on the board. Have children add *'s* or *n't* to make each word a contraction. Then have children read the contractions.

See ELL Lesson 13, p. E27, for scaffolded support.

COMMON CORE **RF.1.2b** orally produce single-syllable words by blending sounds; **RF.1.2d** segment spoken single-syllable words into their complete sequence of individual sounds; **RF.1.3b** decode regularly spelled one-syllable words; **RF.1.3g** recognize and read irregularly spelled words; **L.1.2e** spell untaught words phonetically, drawing on phonemic awareness and spelling conventions

Contractions with *'s, n't*

PHONEMIC AWARENESS WARM-UP *Listen as I blend some sounds to make a word. /hw/ /ĭ/ /ch/. Which. Now you try. Blend these sounds: /f/ /l/ /ă/ /sh/. What is the word?* flash **Repeat with** *dish, whale,* and *what.*

Now tell what sounds make up the word Phil. */f/ /ĭ/ /l/* **Repeat with** *shape, graph,* and *wash.* **RF.1.2b, RF.1.2d**

1 Teach/Model

INTRODUCE CONTRACTIONS Tell children that a **contraction** is a shorter, more informal way of saying two words together. The words *is* and *not* can sometimes be combined with other words. When this happens, an **apostrophe** takes the place of missing letters.

• Use **Letter Cards** to form the words *has not.* Read the words. Model forming the contraction *hasn't. This word is* hasn't. *It is a shorter way to say* has not. *To make this word, I replace the letter* o *in* not *with an apostrophe.* Have children read the word.

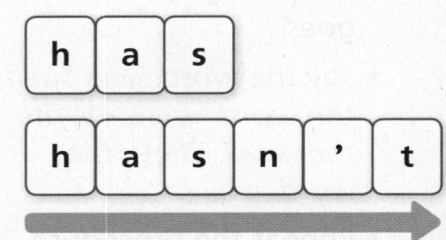

• Place the cards on the board and add an apostrophe between the *n* and the *t.* Use *hasn't* in a sentence: *She hasn't gone to the zoo.* Repeat with the words *was not* and *wasn't.* Use *wasn't* in a sentence: *He wasn't able to go.* Have children read the words.

• Use **Letter Cards** to form the words *it is.* Read the words. Model forming the contraction *it's. This word is* it's. *The word* it's *is a shorter way to say* it is. *To make this word, I replace the letter* i *in* is *with an apostrophe.* Have children read the word.

• Place the cards on the board and add an apostrophe between the *t* and the *s.* Read the word: *it's.* Use *it's* in a sentence: *It's not something that I want.* Repeat with the words *that is* and *that's.* Use *that's* in a sentence: *That's my favorite fruit.* Have children read the words.

2 Guided Practice

CONTINUOUS BLENDING ROUTINE Use **Instructional Routine 3** to model blending *it's*. ▬ RF.1.2b, RF.1.3b

- Display **Letter Cards** *i, t, s* on the board and add an apostrophe between *t* and *s*. Blend and say *it's*. *Listen: /ĭ/ /t/ /s/*, it's. Remind children that *it's* is a shorter way of saying *it is*.

- Now model how to blend *didn't*. Tell children that *didn't* is a shorter way of saying *did not*.

REPEAT CONTINUOUS BLENDING ROUTINE with the words in Row 1 below. Then write the words in Rows 1–3 and have children read them. Use the **Corrective Feedback** steps if children need help.

DECODING Write the two sentences on the board. Call on individuals to blend words, identify the contractions, and read the sentences. ▬ RF.1.3b, RF.1.3g

1. hadn't	wasn't	it's	that's	didn't
2. which	shed	graph	he's	splash
3. pitch	that	what's	then	missing

Chet didn't <u>fall</u> <u>down</u>.
That's <u>a</u> fish in <u>a</u> dish.

3 Apply

Use **Instructional Routine 6**. Have children repeat the words after you. Then have them identify the sounds and write the letters that spell each sound. Print the words so children can check their work. ▬ RF.1.3b, L.1.2e

1. It's	**It's** my new graph.
2. hadn't	Matt **hadn't** opened the latch.
3. didn't	**Didn't** the clock stop ticking?

Corrective Feedback Work with the whole group to correct errors, following the model below.

Phonics Error:
A child reads *he's* as *his*.

Correct the error. Say the word and the sound. *The word is he's.*

Model Model by reminding children that *he's* is a contraction. *He's is a shorter way of saying* he is. *What is the word?* he's

Guide *Let's read the word together. The word is he's.*

Check *You read the word. What is the correct word?* he's

Reinforce Go back three or four words and have children continue reading. Make note of errors and review those words during tomorrow's lesson.

SMALL GROUP Options

Go to p. T292 for additional phonics support.

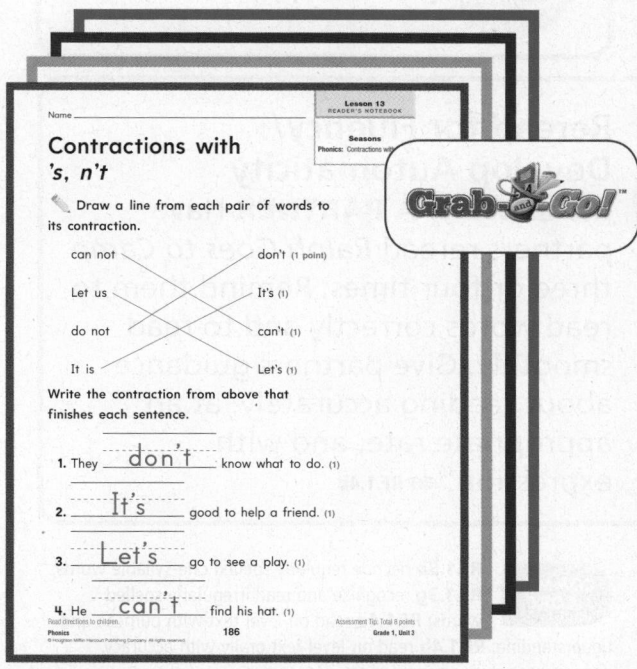

Reader's Notebook Vol. 1 p. 186
See Grab-and-Go™ Resources for additional leveled practice.

 • Decodable Reader
• Cold Reads Online

Decodable Reader

▶ **SHARE OBJECTIVE**
• Read text with digraphs, contractions, and high-frequency words.

Read *Ralph Goes to Camp*

Decodable Reader, Unit 3, pp. 63–68

DAILY ASSESSMENT | 3 2 1 | **RtI**

Corrective Feedback Work with the whole group to correct errors.

Decoding Error:
A child reads *it's* as *is*.

Correct the error. Say the word. *That word is* it's.

Guide Review the sound/spelling. *Remember that in a contraction, 's can be used in place of the word* is. Have children blend and read the word.

Check *Read the sentence again.*

Reinforce Review the word again before children reread the story.

 **Go to p. T292 for additional phonics support.**

Reread for Fluency/ Develop Automaticity

READ WITH A PARTNER Have partners reread *Ralph Goes to Camp* three or four times. Remind them to read words correctly and to read smoothly. Give partners guidance about reading accurately, at an appropriate rate, and with expression. ▬ RF.1.4b

COMMON CORE **RF.1.3b** decode regularly spelled one-syllable words; **RF.1.3g** recognize and read irregularly spelled words; **RF.1.4a** read on-level text with purpose and understanding; **RF.1.4b** read on-level text orally with accuracy, appropriate rate, and expression

REVIEW CONTRACTIONS WITH *'s, n't* AND WORDS TO KNOW
Tell children that this story has many contractions with *'s* and *n't*. Review with them the following Words to Know, which they will also read in the story: *goes* and *yellow*.

PREVIEW Have children preview pages 63–65 and predict what they think the story is about. Ask volunteers to tell about jobs they do at home. Tell children they are going to read about a boy who has jobs to do before he can go to camp.

MODEL FLUENCY AND ACCURACY Have children follow along as you read page 63 aloud, skipping the word *can*. Tell them you made a mistake by skipping the word *can*. Then read the sentence again accurately. Lead children in a choral reading, reading the page fluently and accurately.

READ Remind children to track words from left to right. Remind them that when they come to the end of a line, they should continue by reading at the beginning of the next line. Have children read each page silently and then choral-read aloud. Coach them to read fluently and accurately. Have children read to find out about the jobs Ralph does before he goes to camp.
▬ RF.1.3b, RF.1.3g, RF.1.4a

RESPONDING Have partners take turns retelling the story. Encourage them to use the illustrations as a guide.

Fluency

Accuracy: Word Recognition

1 Teach/Model

Remind children that good readers are able to recognize more and more words as soon as they see them. They learn new words the more they practice reading. Display **Projectable 13.5**. Tell children to watch and listen as you read a list of words. Cover all but the first word with a sheet of paper. Model reading the first word, then move down one word at a time reading each word smoothly, but at a slow rate. Explain that the next time you read the list of words you will be able to read them more quickly because you have practiced reading them once.

Projectable 13.5

Projectable 13.5

Seasons | Fluency Accuracy: Word Recognition

Getting to Know Words

Good readers know many words when they see them.
You will know many words if you practice.

Look at each word.
Read it as soon as you know it.

1. shop
2. splish
3. rush
4. crash
5. Ralph
6. shock
7. trash
8. splash
9. when
10. with

Fluency
© Houghton Mifflin Harcourt Publishing Company. All rights reserved.

Grade 1, Unit 3

2 Guided Practice

Cover the list again. This time read each word and have children echo-read the word before going on to the next. Repeat for all words on the list. Then uncover the words and have children choral-read the list several times.

3 Apply

Have pairs practice reading *Seasons* to each other. Encourage children to improve their accuracy by reading a sentence several times. Have volunteers read each page aloud with accuracy, appropriate rate, and expression. ▇ **RF.1.4b**

▶ SHARE OBJECTIVES

• Read on-level text fluently by recognizing words and reading with accuracy.

> SMALL GROUP Options
>
> **Go to p. T293 for additional fluency support.**

HOUGHTON MIFFLIN HARCOURT

JOURNEYS

Cold Reads

GRADE 1

Cold Reads: Support for fluent reading and comprehension

Independent Reading

▶ SHARE OBJECTIVES

- Read and comprehend informational text.
- Ask and answer questions about key details.
- Read independently from a "just right" book.

 **ENGLISH LANGUAGE LEARNERS**

Comprehensible Input

Beginning Ask children *yes/no* questions about key details in the selection.

Low Intermediate Ask children some details about the story, such as *What does rain do in the spring?* and *What do some animals do in the winter?* Have them use words or phrases to answer.

High Intermediate Have children use words and phrases to tell what happens in a single season.

Proficient Have partners summarize what happens in each season, using complete sentences.

Reader's Guide

Revisit the Anchor Text

Lead children in a brief discussion about *Seasons*. Have them recount the topic and important details they learned about seasons. Have them choose two seasons and tell how they are alike and how they are different. Remind children to follow the classroom rules for discussions and to speak one at a time. To build conversations, encourage them to connect their ideas about the text to others' comments.
🔲 **RI.1.2, RI.1.3, SL.1.1a, SL.1.1b**

Have children read *Seasons* on their own and think about important ideas in the text. Have children use the Reader's Guide pages in their **Reader's Notebook**, pp. 187–188. Explain that they should respond to the questions and support their responses with text evidence from the photos and sentences in *Seasons*. 🔲 **RI.1.1, RI.1.7, RI.1.10**

GENERATE QUESTIONS Have children work independently or collaboratively to generate questions about *Seasons*. Ask children to share their questions. List questions that children have in common or that are most significant to their understanding of the selection. Guide them to work together to find the answers. 🔲 **RI.1.1**

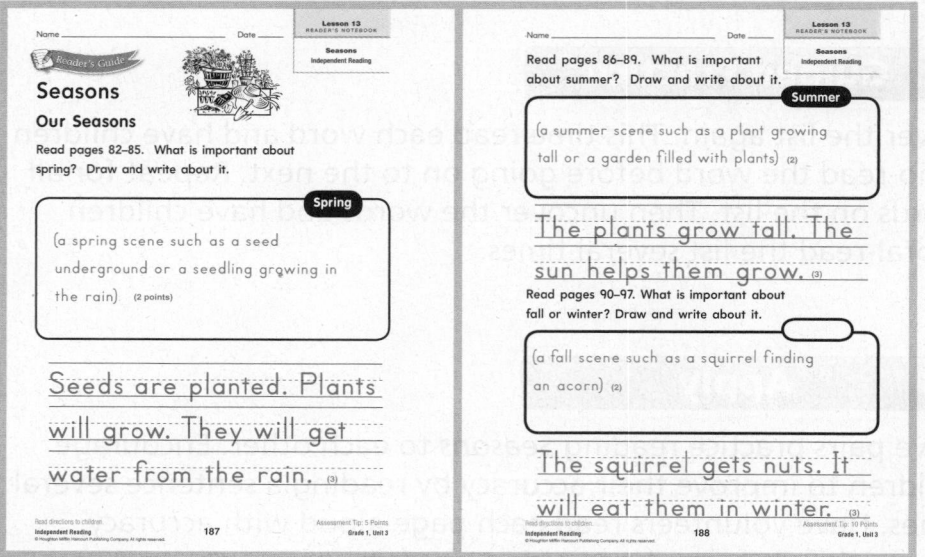

Reader's Notebook pp. 187–188

COMMON CORE **RI.1.1** ask and answer questions about key details; **RI.1.2** identify the main topic and retell key details; **RI.1.3** describe the connection between individuals, events, ideas, or information in a text; **RI.1.7** use illustrations and details to describe key; **RI.1.10** read informational texts; **RF.1.4b** read on-level text orally with accuracy, appropriate rate, and expression; **RF.1.4c** use context to confirm or self-correct word recognition and understanding; **SL.1.1a** follow rules for discussions; **SL.1.1b** build on others' talk in conversations by responding to others' comments

Self-Selected Reading

Topics of Interest

Help children choose a book that they will enjoy reading. Provide tips for self-selecting a nonfiction book based on interest.

• Ask yourself, *What would I like to learn more about*? Maybe there is something interesting that you have read recently or heard about, and you would like to know more.

• Make a list of the topics you like the most, such as seasons, animals, or trees.

• Look at books in the classroom or school library to find one about your topic of interest.

Tell children that once they have chosen a book, they should read one or two pages to be sure it is "just right" for their area of interest. Tell children that if they lose interest in the first few pages they should try another book. Guide them to find appropriate books to read independently.

Self-Correction Strategies

Self-Correct Word Recognition

Explain to children that if they do not recognize a word, it is a good idea to pause briefly to try to remember if it is a word they have read in another story. If not, they should use the sounds the letters stand for and word parts they know, such as -ed and -ing, to figure out the word.

Guide children to look at the first pages of their independent reading books to find high frequency words they know. Then ask them to identify which words are new. For each new word, have children look for known phonic elements, such as digraphs, and word parts to help them sound out the new word. Have them blend the sounds to read the word and then reread the sentence to check whether the word makes sense.

Have partners take turns reading aloud to each other from their self-selected books. When they come to a new word they practiced reading on their own, tell them to read the sentence smoothly and accurately to practice reading aloud the new word in context to aid fluency understanding. ◼ RF.1.4b, RF.1.4c

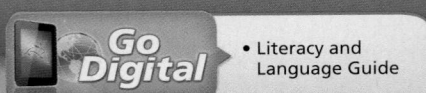

Apply Vocabulary Knowledge

▶ SHARE OBJECTIVES

- Use words and phrases acquired through conversations, reading and being read to, and responding to texts.
- Identify real-life connections between words and their use.
- Learn about the parts of a dictionary.

ELL ENGLISH LANGUAGE LEARNERS

Comprehensible Input

Beginning Have children act out feeling *elated*. Dicuss other words that mean almost the same thing as *elated*: *happy, joyful, excited*.

Low Intermediate Have children think of things that make them feel happy. Have them complete this sentence frame: *I feel elated when _____*.

High Intermediate Have partners work together to say sentences about things that make them fell *elated*.

Proficient Have children write a sentence about something that makes them feel *elated*.

See ELL Lesson 13, p. E26,
for further vocabulary support.

☑ SELECTION VOCABULARY >> Review

Review with children the Selection Vocabulary words on p. T220. Call on children to explain how the words were used in *Seasons*.

ENRICH VOCABULARY Write the following Related Words on the board. Read each word aloud, and have children repeat after you. Then read the student-friendly explanation for each word. Connect each word's meaning to the selection *Seasons* by writing the context sentences on the board and reading them aloud.

hibernate: If something hibernates, it spends the winter sleeping. *The little furry animal will hibernate while it is cold out.*

elated: If you are elated, you are very happy and excited about something. *The boys were elated to build their snowman.*

gradual: If something happens in a gradual way, it happens very slowly. *The change from summer to fall is gradual.*

MAKE CONNECTIONS Discuss all of the words using the items below to help children make connections between vocabulary words and their use. ▬ **L.1.5c, L.1.6**

- Name an animal that can **hibernate** in **winter**.
- When do you think is the best time to plant **seeds**?
- Describe a perfect **spring day**.
- Which event is the most **gradual**: a cake baking, a tree growing, building a **snowman**?
- Have you ever jumped in a pile of **leaves**? What was it like?
- What activities at **school** make you feel most **elated**?
- What kinds of things can you make from **snow**?
- What would the wind sound like if it were to **blow** through a **tall** tree?

COMMON CORE **RI.1.5** know and use text features to locate facts or information; **L.1.5c** identify real-life connections between words and their use; **L.1.6** use words and phrases acquired through conversations, reading and being read to, and responding to texts

Dictionary Skills

DISCUSS USING A DICTIONARY Hold up a beginning dictionary. Open to a page and point to the words at the top. Remind children that these are called *guide words*. Have a volunteer tell what the purpose of guide words is. *The guide words show what word starts the page and what word ends the page. You can use them to tell if the word you are looking for is on the page.*

Then point to an entry on the page. Point out the word in bold and its definition. Guide children to notice that dictionaries also give information about how to pronounce the word, the word's history, and how to use the word in a sentence.

Guide children to look up the Lesson 13 Selection Vocabulary words *snowman* and *summer* in a print dictionary. Then, have partners work together to look up the new words *hibernate* and *gradual*. Have volunteers identify each element of the dictionary entry for each word. Have one child read the definition, one child tell about the history of the word, and one child read the example sentence or sentences. RI.1.5

Literacy and Language Guide
Additional Lesson 13 vocabulary lessons appear in the Literacy and Language Guide.

QUICKWRITE

Read aloud each question below. Pause a few minutes between each item to allow children to write a response. L.1.5c

1. What do you think it would feel like to hibernate?

2. What do you do that makes you feel elated?

3. Is a caterpillar turning into a butterfly a gradual change? Why or why not?

Go Digital
• *my*WriteSmart
• eBook
• GrammarSnap Videos

Grammar Subjects and Verbs

▶ SHARE OBJECTIVES

- **Grammar** Identify and use singular and plural nouns with matching verbs in sentences.
- **Spelling** Spell words with *sh, wh,* and *ph* using conventional spelling patterns.
- **Writing** Choose a topic and use a graphic organizer to plan sentences that inform.

ELL ENGLISH LANGUAGE LEARNERS
Language Transfer

All Proficiencies Display the sentences from **Student Book** p. 88, *Bugs buzz and hum,* and *I look small.* Guide the class in finding the verbs. Explain that in the second sentence the verb ends in *s* because there is only one subject, while in the second sentence there is no *s* because the subject is plural. (Since many languages, such as Cantonese and Haitian Creole, do not inflect verbs for tense, extra modeling may be required.)

1 Teach/Model

13.6

VERBS WITH *s* Display **Projectable 13.6.** Review that a subject can name one or more than one. Point out that verbs have to agree with the subjects. When a noun subject names one, you add *s* to most verbs.

- Model identifying how verbs agree with the subjects.

> **Think Aloud**
> *The subject in the first sentence names one person,* Ken. *The verb* jumps *has an* s *at the end. The subject of the second sentence names more than one,* boys. *The verb* jump *does not have an* s *at the end.*

2 Guided Practice/Apply

- Work together to complete **Projectable 13.6.** Support children as they choose and write the correct verb to finish each sentence.
- Have children write two sentences on their own: one with a subject that names one and one with a subject that names more than one. Have partners work together to check that the correct verbs have been used.
- For additional practice, you may want to distribute **Reader's Notebook** Vol. 1 page 190. ◼ L.1.1c, L.1.1j

Spelling Words with *sh, wh,* and *ph*

SPELLING WORDS

BASIC	
ship	when
shop	whip
which	fish
CHALLENGE	
shell	graph

Segment Sounds

- Model segmenting sounds. *Listen as I say* ship: /sh/ /ĭ/ /p/. *Repeat after me:* /sh/ /ĭ/ /p/. *Now listen as I say* which: /hw/ /ĭ/ /ch/. *Repeat after me:* /hw/ /ĭ/ /ch/.
- Tell children that saying the sounds in a word will help them spell the words. Have children practice segmenting the sounds in *shop* and *when.* ◼ RF.1.2d

Build Words

- Use **Letter Cards** to model building the words *ship* and *which.* Have children read the word.
- Have partners use **Letter Cards** to build words with *sh, wh,* and *ph.* Have them read and write each word.
- For additional practice, you may want to distribute **Reader's Notebook** Vol.1 page 189. ◼ L.1.2d

COMMON CORE

RF.1.2d segment spoken single-syllable words into their complete sequence of individual sounds; **W.1.2** write informative/explanatory texts; **W.1.5** focus on a topic, respond to questions/suggestions from peers, and add details to strengthen writing; **W.1.8** recall information from experiences or gather information from sources to answer a question; **SL.1.6** produce complete sentences when appropriate to task and situation;

Informative Writing Prewriting

1 Teach/Model

MAIN IDEA Review with children that all sentences in a paragraph should be about the main idea introduced in the topic sentence.

- Display **Projectable 13.7.** Tell children that they can use a chart like this to prepare to write sentences that inform.

- Read the prompt aloud. Then model filling in the graphic organizer.

Think Aloud *I want to write about winter. I'll write facts about winter in my chart. "Winter is the coldest time of year" is a fact. I should not include opinions like "winter is fun" or facts that are not about winter.*

- Ask children to help you list facts about winter and write a closing sentence that retells the main idea.

- Save the completed chart for Day 4.

2 Independent Writing

- Write the prompt on the board and read it aloud with children.

- Help children decide which season to write about. Have them choose a different season than the one they used in the Day 2 activity. As needed, prompt them by asking questions about the season they know the most about.

- Have children fill in the graphic organizer. Remind them that they need to write the name of the season they chose at the top of the page. Remind them also that each statement they write must be a fact that tells about the main idea. Finally, their closing sentence should retell the main idea using different words.
W.1.2, W.1.5, W.1.8, L.1.1j

Oral Language Conventions

Speak in Complete Sentences Remind children that a complete sentence has a subject and a verb. As children discuss which season to write about, remind them to use complete sentences. Emphasize the subject and verb of each sentence. Orally correct any problems with subject-verb agreement. SL.1.6

L.1.1c use singular and plural nouns with matching verbs in sentences; **L.1.1j** produce and expand simple and compound declarative, interrogative, imperative, and exclamatory sentences; **L.1.2d** use conventional spelling for words with common spelling patterns and for frequently occurring irregular words

Daily Proofreading Practice

In summer the sun ~~shine~~. shines

The children play on the ~~grean~~ grass. green

Projectable 13.7

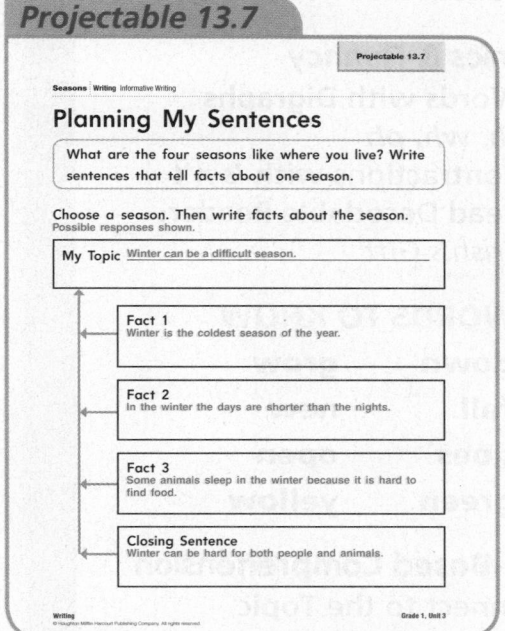

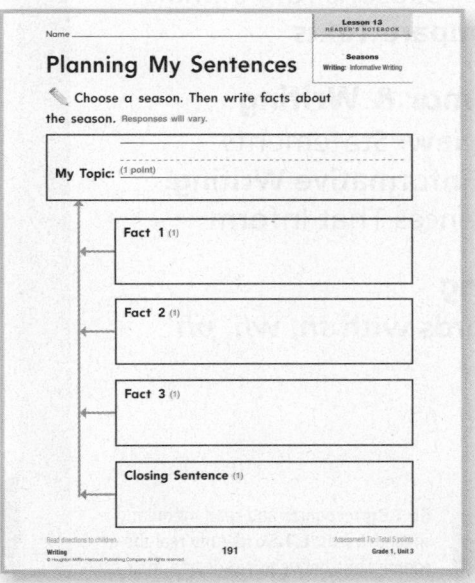

Reader's Notebook Vol. 1 p. 191

DAY 4

Today's Goals

Vocabulary & Oral Language
- Vocabulary Strategies: Word Endings *-ed, -ing, -s*

Phonemic Awareness
- Substitute Phonemes

Phonics & Fluency
- Words with Digraphs *sh, wh, ph*
- Contractions with *'s n't*
- Read Decodable Reader: *Trish's Gift*

☑ **WORDS TO KNOW**

down	grow
fall	new
goes	open
green	yellow

Text-Based Comprehension
Connect to the Topic
- Read Informational Text: *Four Seasons for Animals*
- Compare Texts

Grammar & Writing
- Review: Statements
- ➡ Informative Writing: Sentences That Inform

Spelling
- Words with *sh, wh, ph*

RF.1.3g recognize and read irregularly spelled words; **L.1.5c** identify real-life connections between words and their use; **L.1.6** use words and phrases acquired through conversations, reading and being read to, and responding to texts

Opening Routines

Warm Up with Wordplay

Make a Rhyme

Remind children that they have been learning about words that have the sound /sh/. Display and read the word *ash*.

Have children work with a partner to come up with as many other words in this word family (words that rhyme with *ash*) as they can. Call on children to share their words. Write down what children say. Then have children work together to use the rhyming words to make a short poem of two or four lines. Record the poem as children dictate, and then read it aloud with children.

cash	**dash**	**mash**
flash	**sash**	**crash**

Daily Phonemic Awareness

Substitute Initial Phonemes

- *Today we're going to change the first sound in a word to make a new word. For example, change the /s/ in sock to /r/. What do you get?* rock *Good! Now let's change the /r/ in rock to /d/. What word do we get?* dock *Let's keep going.*

Change the . . .	Result	Change the . . .	Result
/d/ in *dish* to /w/	wish	/th/ in *that* to /ch/	chat
/m/ in *mix* to /f/	fix	/b/ in *but* to /sh/	shut
/h/ in *hop* to /sh/	shop	/h/ in *hen* to /hw/	when

Corrective Feedback

- If a child misses a word, say the correct word and model the task. *Listen to the word: dish, /d/, /ĭ/, /sh/. Now change the /d/ to /w/. What is the new word?* wish

- Have children do it once with you before doing it on their own. Then back up several words and continue the game.

Daily High-Frequency Words

Introduce

- Point to the **High-Frequency Word Card** *green.*

- *Say the word.* green *Spell the word.* g, r, e, e, n *Write the word. Check the word.*

- Repeat the procedure with the words *down, fall, goes, grow, new, open,* and *yellow.*

  ◼ RF.1.3g

Cheerleader Call and Response Game

- Pick one child to be the Head Cheerleader and to stand in the front of the room.

- Have the Head Cheerleader call out each letter of a High-Frequency Word. The class responds. *Give me a G!* **G!** *Give me an R!* **R!** *Give me an O!* **O!** *Give me a W!* **W!** *What does that spell?* **GROW!**

- Choose different Head Cheerleaders for the remaining High-Frequency Words.

Corrective Feedback

- Say the correct word and have children repeat it. Open. *What is the word?* open

- Have children spell the word. *o, p, e, n How do we say this word?* open

- Have children reread all of the cards in random order.

Daily Vocabulary Boost

- Guide children to interact with the Oral Vocabulary words by asking the following questions. Have them relate the words to things they have seen or experienced when possible.

  How does a farmer plow *the fields?*

  What could make flowers shrivel*?*

  How do vines *cover a wall?*

- Have children work with a partner to explain *plow, shrivel,* and *vines* in their own words. Make sure children follow appropriate rules for discussion such as listening to speakers, taking turns, and staying on topic. ◼ L.1.5c, L.1.6

 **Oral Vocabulary**

bouquet

burst

glows

plow

shrivel

vines

Whole Group

DAY 4

• Interactive Whiteboard Lesson
• Decodable Reader

Phonics

Interactive Whiteboard Lesson:
Words with Digraphs *sh, wh, ph* and
Contractions with *'s, n't*

Phonemic Awareness/Phonics

▶ SHARE OBJECTIVES

- Blend, build, and decode contractions with *'s, n't*.
- Review and sort words with consonant digraphs.
- Read decodable text with contractions; consonant digraphs; and high-frequency words.

▶ SKILLS TRACE

Words with Digraphs *sh, wh, ph*	
Introduce	T214–T215
Differentiate	T286
Reteach	T300
▶ Review	**T238, T260**
Assess	Weekly Tests, Lesson 13

▶ SKILLS TRACE

Contractions with *'s, n't*	
Introduce	T248–T249
Differentiate	T292
Reteach	T300
▶ Review	**T260**
Assess	Weekly Tests, Lesson 13

Review Digraphs *sh, wh, ph* and Contractions with *'s, n't*

PHONEMIC AWARENESS WARM-UP Tell children that you will say a word and then ask them to change a sound to make a new word. *Listen: The word is* cape. *Change the /k/ to /sh/. What is the new word?* shape Continue the pattern using these words: *fit-fish, chair-where, grass-graph, pale-whale.*

MAKE AND READ WORDS Write the words and sentences below on the board. Have children identify the contraction that best completes each sentence. Then work with children to tell which two words make up each contraction.

> **Pam's He's There's It's What's**
> 1. _____ good at that. *Pam's*
> 2. _____ the best friend I have. *He's*
> 3. _____ a frog in the box. *There's*
> 4. _____ good that you are here. *It's*
> 5. _____ the best pet? *What's*

GROUPING WORDS BY SOUND Display the **Sound/Spelling Cards** *chick, sheep,* and *whale* to review digraphs *ch, tch, sh, wh.* Then make a three-column chart on the board, using the cards as headings. Say the word *catch.* Have children identify its end sound, /ch/. Then ask under which card you should write the word. Continue sorting these words: *check, fish, squish, chin, shack, pinch, when, whim, much, whiz.*

Have children copy the completed columns. Then ask children to work with a partner to read each word. 🔲 RF.1.2c, RF.1.3b

COMMON CORE

RF.1.2c isolate and pronounce sounds in spoken single-syllable words; **RF.1.3b** decode regularly spelled one-syllable words; **RF.1.3g** recognize and read irregularly spelled words; **RF.1.4a** read on-level text with purpose and understanding; **RF.1.4b** read on-level text orally with accuracy, appropriate rate, and expression

Decodable Reader

Read *Trish's Gift*

Decodable Reader,
Unit 3, pp. 69–74

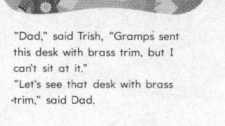

REVIEW CONTRACTIONS AND WORDS TO KNOW Tell children that this story has many words with *'s* and *n't*. Point out that children have learned the following words, which they will also read in the story: *green, grow, new, open.*

PREVIEW Have children preview pages 69–71 and predict what the story is about. Ask volunteers to tell about a gift they received.

MODEL FLUENCY AND ACCURACY Read aloud page 69, substituting *dust* for *desk.* Ask if what you read made sense. Tell children you will reread the sentence again. Then lead children in choral reading the page with fluency and accuracy.

READ Remind children to track the words from left to right. Remind them that when they come to the end of a line, they should sweep their hand down to the beginning of the next line and continue reading. Have children read each page silently and then choral-read aloud. Have them read to find out about Trish's gift and how Dad helps. 🔲 RF.1.3b, RF.1.3g, RF.1.4a

RESPONDING Write these sentences from the story on the board and have children read them aloud: *It was a new desk. Where is that bench? That's it!* Guide them to use the end marks to help them read each sentence with appropriate expression. Then have partners read the story aloud. Remind them to use end marks to help them.

Corrective Feedback Work with the whole group to correct errors, following the model below.

Decoding Error:
A child reads *let's* as *less.*

Correct the error. Say the word. *That word is* let's.

Guide Have children repeat the word. *What is the word?* let's

Check *Go back to the beginning of the sentence and read it again.*

Reinforce Record the error and review the word again before children reread the story.

Reread for Fluency/ Develop Automaticity

READ WITH A PARTNER Have partners reread *Trish's Gift* three or four times, taking turns reading aloud each page. Remind them to read words correctly and to read smoothly. Visit partners to listen to them read. Give feedback about reading accurately, at an appropriate rate, and with expression and provide guidance for improving fluency. 🔲 RF.1.4b

Lesson 13

INFORMATIONAL TEXT

Read Together

☑ **GENRE**

Informational text gives facts about a topic. Look for facts about what happens to plants and animals during the seasons.

☑ **TEXT FOCUS**

Headings are titles for different parts of an informational text. They tell you what each section will be about. What do the headings in this selection tell you?

 RI.1.5 know and use text features to locate facts or information; **RI.1.10** read informational texts

104

Four Seasons for Animals

written and illustrated
by Ashley Wolff

Spring

It is spring. Young animals run and play. Bird nests are full of eggs. Soon the eggs will hatch.

105

DOMAIN: Life Science

LESSON TOPIC: Seasons

Cross-Curricular Connection Ask children to name the four seasons in the year. Tell children to think about where they spend much of their time during each of the seasons. Tell them to think about the activities they do during each season. Then, with partners, have them discuss what they see, hear, feel, touch, and taste during each season.

 **RI.1.2** identify the main topic and retell key details; **RI.1.3** describe the connection between individuals, events, ideas or information in a text; **RI.1.5** know and use text features to locate facts or information; **RI.1.6** distinguish between information provided by pictures and words; **RI.1.7** use illustrations and details to describe key ideas; **RI.1.10** read informational texts

Connect to the Topic
Informational Text

Introduce Genre and Text Focus

• Read and discuss with the children the genre and text focus information on **Student Book** p. 104.

• Have children point to the heading *Spring* on p. 105 and read it aloud. Remind children that this is the name of a season. Recall with them that sometimes informational texts have **headings** to tell what a certain section of the selection will be about. Ask children what kind of information they think they will read in this section. Tell them to think about these ideas when they read to find out if the information is there. ▬ **RI.1.5**

• Tell children that they will read about the four seasons, as the title says. Before they begin, have children page through the selection to find the section about each season, using the headings to locate the information. Then read the selection with the children. ▬ **RI.1.5, RI.1.10**

Spring brings rain. Grass turns green and grows tall. Buds grow on trees and plants. Spring also brings rain puddles! Flower buds get wet. Rain helps the new plants grow. **1** **2**

3

106

107

Think Through the Text

1 *What is the main idea of this section?* Spring is the beginning of new life and growth. ▬RI.1.2

2 *What helps the new plants grow?* Rain falls on the new plants, which helps them grow. ▬RI.1.3

3 *How does the illustration connect to the information in the sentences?* The illustration shows rain falling, animals playing in puddles, and plants in the rain. The sentences tell about rain, puddles, and plants growing. *What more did you learn from the illustration that was not in the words?* I learned that animals like the rain just like plants do. I can see that flower buds are flowers that are not quite opened.
▬RI.1.3, RI.1.6, RI.1.7

Summer ④

It is summer. Buds open and flowers bloom in the bright sun. Insects buzz here and there. Now there are chicks in the bird nest! Their mother will teach them how to fly.

108

It can get very hot in the summer. Many animals live near the pond. ⑤ ⑥ Ducks swim in the pond. Fox pups cool off in the shade.

109

DOMAIN: Life Science

LESSON TOPIC: Seasons

Cross-Curricular Connection Have children raise questions about seasons, plants, animals, or other things in the natural world. Guide them to investigate the questions in teams, and to generate appropriate explanations. Help them use a variety of sources of information, such as direct observation using the five senses, books, the Internet, and other media to find answers.

COMMON CORE **RI.1.1** ask and answer questions about key details; **RI.1.2** identify the main topic and retell key details; **RI.1.3** describe the connection between individuals, events, ideas or information in a text; **RI.1.5** know and use text features to locate facts or information; **RI.1.6** distinguish between information provided by pictures and words; **RI.1.7** use illustrations and details to describe key ideas; **RI.1.9** identify similarities in and differences between texts on the same topic

Use Text Evidence

Think Through the Text

④ *What does the heading "Summer" tell you about this section?* It tells me that the section of this informational text will give me facts about summer. ◼ **RI.1.5**

⑤ *How is the weather in the spring different from the weather in the summer?* In the spring, it rains a lot. In the summer, it is hot and sunny. ◼ **RI.1.2, RI.1.3**

⑥ *What information about summer is the same as in* Seasons? plants grow; insects buzz; it is hot *What information in* Four Season for Animals *is different?* chicks hatched and will learn to fly; ducks, foxes, and other animals cool off in the water and shade *How are the pictures of summer different in the two selections?* Seasons *has photos that show children playing;* Four Seasons for Animals *has artwork that shows what different animals do in the summer.* ◼ **RI.1.3, RI.1.7, RI.1.9**

Fall

It is fall. Leaves fall down. Animals get ready for winter. Some animals eat as much as they can. They need to store fat because food is scarce in the winter. **7**

110

Squirrels and chipmunks gather nuts so they will have enough food for the winter.

8 **9**

111

7 *Why do animals need to store fat?* They need to store fat because there is not much food during the winter.
■ RI.1.1

8 *Look at the illustrations on pp. 106–107 and pp. 110–111. How are the illustrations different?* The spring illustration shows animals playing in the rain and puddles. The grass is green and plants are growing. The fall illustration shows brown grass, no rain, and fall leaves. The animals are not playing. They are busy eating.
■ RI.1.2, RI.1.7

9 *Look at the illustrations on pp. 110–111. What are the animals doing?* Different kinds of animals are eating different kinds of food. *What more do you learn from the sentences about why the animals are eating?* The animals are all busy eating food so they can store fat for winter. Food is hard to find during the winter. Squirrels and chipmunks gather nuts and save them to eat in winter. ■ RI.1.6, RI.1.7

Winter

It is winter. Winter can be very cold and wet. Bears hibernate in the winter. That means they sleep. **10**

Many other animals hibernate in the winter. They curl up in dens to keep safe from the cold and wet. **11**

ELL **ENGLISH LANGUAGE LEARNERS**
Comprehensible Input

All Proficiencies Support ELLs in understanding the concepts and vocabulary about the seasons by pointing out and discussing helpful pictures in *Four Seasons for Animals*. For example, point to the bear sleeping underground. Say the following, using gestures to clarify: *The bear is asleep because it is cold and snowy outside. It will sleep for a long, long time—all winter. This means that the bear is hibernating. What are the other animals doing?*

COMMON CORE **RI.1.2** identify the main topic and retell key details; **RI.1.3** describe the connection between individuals, events, ideas or information in a text; **RI.1.4** ask and answer questions to determine or clarify the meaning of words and phrases; **RI.1.7** use illustrations and details to describe key ideas; **RI.1.9** identify similarities in and differences between texts on the same topic; **SL.1.4** describe people, places, things, and events with details/express ideas and feelings clearly

Use Text Evidence

Think Through the Text

10 *What clues in the sentences and pictures help you know what* hibernate *means? The pictures show animals sleeping in dens they have made underground. The words "hibernate in winter" and "that means they sleep" tell me that* hibernate *means to sleep for a long time.* **RI.1.4**

11 *Look at the illustrations and read the sections about summer and winter. How are the animals different in the two seasons? In the summer, the animals are playing and eating in the pond. In the winter, they are trying to keep warm and are hibernating.* **RI.1.2, RI.1.3, RI.1.7**

12 *What season comes after winter? spring* **RI.1.2**

Like all the seasons, the winter will pass. The animals know that spring will come once again. **12**

114

Compare Texts

Read Together

TEXT TO TEXT

Make a Chart How are the selections alike and different? Make a chart to show evidence.

Pictures	Facts	Descriptions

TEXT TO SELF

Describe a Season Describe your favorite season. Tell why you like it. Use details to make your ideas and feelings clear.

TEXT TO WORLD

Tell About Seasons Find your state on a globe. Then locate a country. Tell how you think the seasons in both places might be the same or different.

Go Digital

COMMON CORE **RI.1.3** describe the connection between individuals, events, ideas, or information in a text; **RI.1.9** identify similarities in and differences between texts on the same topic; **SL.1.4** describe people, places, things, and events with details/express ideas and feelings clearly

115

Compare Texts

TEXT TO TEXT

Make a Chart Have children page through *Seasons* and *Four Seasons for Animals*. Have them tell how the selections are alike and different. Have them make a chart to show this information. Guide children to tell how the topic of both selections is the same: seasons. Help them compare examples of illustrations, descriptions and facts given about each season, and the way the information is presented.
RI.1.9

TEXT TO SELF

Describe a Season Remind children that when they tell about their favorite season, they need to provide details to give reasons why they like it. Explain that using details will make their ideas and feelings clear. Tell them to use adjectives and other details to describe things like colors, what the weather is like, and their feelings. Have children describe their seasons in small groups. SL.1.4

TEXT TO WORLD

Tell About Seasons Display a globe and guide children to understand its characteristics and purposes. Help them correctly locate their state and a country other than the United States on the globe. They tell a partner how the seasons in the two places are alike and different, using the locations on the globe to justify their reasoning. Have children include details as they describe places, things, and events to make their ideas clear.
SL.1.4

Whole Group

DAY 4

Go Digital
• Interactive Whiteboard Lesson
• Literacy and Language Guide

Interactive Whiteboard Lesson:
Words Endings *-ed, -ing,* or *-s*

Vocabulary Strategies

Vocabulary Strategies

SHARE OBJECTIVES
• Identify and read words with inflectional endings.
• Identify frequently occurring root words and their inflectional forms.

SKILLS TRACE

Word Endings *-ed, -ing,* or *-s*	
Introduce	**T268–T269**
Differentiate	T298–T299
Reteach	T301
Assess	Weekly Tests, Lesson 13

ELL ENGLISH LANGUAGE LEARNERS
Language Transfer

Beginning Write *cat* and *cats* on the board. Have children contrast the words. Repeat for words such as *eat/eating; walk/walked.*

Low Intermediate Children write -s, -ing and -ed on white index cards, and base words like *cat, eat,* and *walk* on yellow cards. Have them combine a base word and ending and read the new words.

High Intermediate Have children write *cats, dogs, birds.* Help them circle the base word in each. Repeat for words with -ed and -ing endings.

Proficient Have children copy words such as *cats, eating,* and *walked,* and circle the base words.

See ELL Lesson 13, p. E27,
for further support.

COMMON CORE **RF.1.3f** read words with inflectional endings; **L.1.4c** Identify frequently occurring root words and identify their inflectional forms

Word Endings *-ed, -ing,* or *-s*

1 Teach/Model

Terms About Language

base word a word to which beginning and ending word parts can be added; a base word is also known as a root word

---

• Discuss the definition of *base word*. Explain that a base word is also known as a root word. Review step two on the **Vocabulary Strategy Projectable S8.** Tell children to focus on the endings of words to learn more about them.

• Explain that the word ending *-ed* tells that something *happened already* and the word ending *-ing* tells that something is happening now. Explain that the word ending *-s* can make a singular noun plural. It can also be added to verbs to show present action.

• Write the word *look* on the board to model the use of inflectional forms. Below the word, write *looks, looked,* and *looking* and have children write each of the words. Then underline the base word, or root word, *look* in each word. Write a sentence for each of the words, and read each sentence aloud.

• Write the following sentence from *Seasons* on the board and read it aloud. Then model using word parts to figure out the meaning of a word.

> We play a lot.

Think Aloud Play *is a word I know. It is a base word or root word. If I add* -s, *it means one person or thing is doing the action. Now I can say "He plays a lot." If I want to change the meaning, I can add* -ed *and say "We played a lot." That means we played already. I can add* -ing *and say "We are playing a lot," which means we play right now. But I know a* play *is also a show on stage that people can watch. If I add* -s *to the noun* play, *I make* plays, *or more than one play.*

Literacy and Language Guide
Additional Lesson 13 vocabulary lessons appear in the Literacy and Language Guide.

2 Guided Practice

- Display **Projectable 13.8** and read aloud the example sentence. Explain how to complete the word by adding the correct ending for the sentence.

- Read aloud the first sentence. Have children use the clues *is* and *today* to help them choose the correct word ending. Write *-ing* on the line.

3 Apply

- Read aloud the second item on **Projectable 13.8** to children.

- Have children identify the base or root word in the sentence. Then have them choose the correct word ending for *shape*.

- Ask them to point out the words in the sentence that helped them decide which ending to use.

- Repeat the procedure with the remaining items. ▬ RF.1.3f, L.1.4c

Projectable 13.8

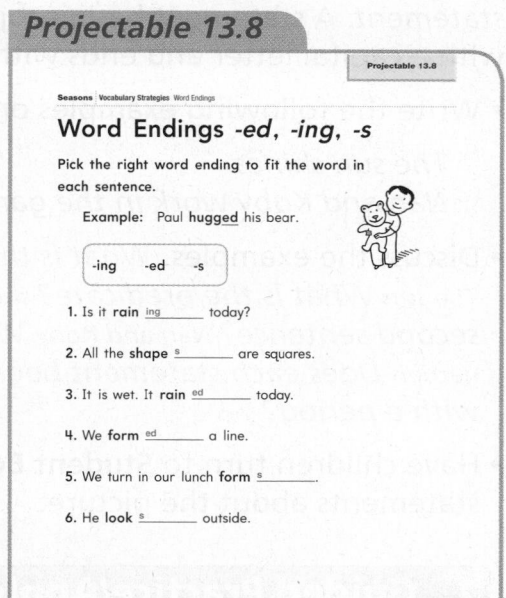

Projectable 13.8

Seasons | Vocabulary Strategies | Word Endings

Word Endings -ed, -ing, -s

Pick the right word ending to fit the word in each sentence.

Example: Paul **hugged** his bear.

| -ing | -ed | -s |

1. Is it **rain** _ing_____ today?

2. All the **shape** _s_____ are squares.

3. It is wet. It **rain** _ed_____ today.

4. We **form** _ed_____ a line.

5. We turn in our lunch **form** _s_____.

6. He **look** _s_____ outside.

Vocabulary Strategies
© Houghton Mifflin Harcourt Publishing Company. All rights reserved.
Grade 1, Unit 3

DAILY ASSESSMENT △ RtI

Can children use word endings to change the meaning of words?

IF...	THEN...
children have difficulty understanding how word endings change word meanings,	▶ use Struggling Readers lesson, p. T298.
children can add endings to familiar words and understand how word endings change word meanings,	▶ use On Level lesson, p. T298.
children can use word endings to change the meaning of most words correctly,	▶ use Advanced lesson, p. T299.

SMALL GROUP Options

Differentiate Vocabulary Strategies: pp. T298–T299.
Group English Language Learners according to language proficiency.

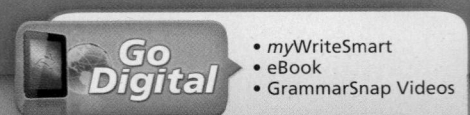

Grammar Spiral Review: Statements

▶ SHARE OBJECTIVES

- **Grammar** Review simple declarative statements.
- **Spelling** Spell words with *sh*, *wh*, and *ph* using conventional spelling patterns.
- **Handwriting** Print the spelling words.
- **Writing** Draft sentences that inform.

ELL ENGLISH LANGUAGE LEARNERS
Comprehensible Input

All Proficiencies Display a sentence frame with a verb most children are already familiar with, such as: _____ runs. Have children fill in the sentence frame with the name of a child in class. Have that child pantomime running.

See ELL Lesson 13, p. E29 for scaffolded support.

1 Teach/Model

STATEMENTS Review that a sentence that tells something is a *statement*. A statement has a subject and a predicate. It begins with a capital letter and ends with a period.

- Write the following examples on the board:

  The sun shines.
  Nan and Koby work in the garden.

- Discuss the examples. *What is the subject in the first statement? The sun What is the predicate? shines What is the subject in the second sentence? Nan and Koby What is the predicate? work in the garden Does each statement begin with a capital letter and end with a period? yes*

- Have children turn to **Student Book** p. 109. Model saying statements about the picture.

2 Guided Practice/Apply

- Have children complete the following statements about things that happen in the spring. Have them expand their statements using adjectives or other details. Remind them to use correct punctuation for their statements. ▬ **L.1.1j, L.1.2b**

  The flowers_____. _____*makes a nest.*

Spelling Words with *sh, wh,* and *ph*

SPELLING WORDS

BASIC

ship	when
shop	whip
which	fish

CHALLENGE

shell	graph

Connect to Writing

- Remind children that they have been learning how to use subjects and matching verbs.

- Have children use the spelling words to write sentences that include matching subjects and verbs. Have children read their sentences aloud.

- Practice spelling the words as a class. Say each word and spell it aloud. ▬ **L.1.1c, L.1.2d**

Handwriting

Model how to form *when, whip,* and *fish*. Have children use their best handwriting to print the spelling words. Ball-and-stick and continuous stroke handwriting models are on the **Handwriting Models Blackline Masters**. ▬ **L.1.1a**

COMMON CORE **W.1.2** write informative/explanatory texts; **W.1.5** focus on a topic, respond to questions/suggestions from peers, and add details to strengthen writing; **L.1.1j** produce and expand simple and compound declarative, interrogative, imperative, and exclamatory sentences; **L.1.2b** use end punctuation for sentences; **L.1.2d** use conventional spelling for words with common spelling patterns and for frequently occurring irregular words; **L.1.6** use words and phrases acquired through conversations, reading and being read to, and responding to texts

Informative Writing Drafting

1 Teach/Model

CAUSE AND EFFECT Tell children that their sentences can show cause and effect. For example, explain that some animals sleep in winter because the weather is cold and food is hard to find. Help children distinguish cause and effect in this sentence.

Connect to *Seasons*

In a gust of wind, leaves will fall down.

• *What is the cause?* the wind *What is the effect?* the leaves fall

• Display **Projectable 13.7** from Day 3. Review the facts you wrote about winter.

 **13.9**
• Then display **Projectable 13.9**. Model how to draft sentences that inform.

Think Aloud *I can use my graphic organizer to draft sentences about winter. First, I need a topic sentence. The topic sentence tells about the main idea, which is winter. I'll write the sentence:* Winter can be a difficult season.

• As you draft, ask children to help turn the list of facts into sentences.

2 Independent Writing

• Have children talk with a partner about how they can include cause and effect in one or more of their sentences. Guide them to use the word *because* to show the relationship in their writing.

• Allow time for children to draft their own facts about the season they chose. Help them refer to their graphic organizers from Day 3 and the Focus Wall as they write. Guide partners to incorporate each others' suggestions for strengthening writing and to include a closing sentence. **W.1.2, W.1.5, L.1.6**

Daily Proofreading Practice

In summer the pool is ~~opin~~. (open)

The children ~~swims~~ all day. (swim)

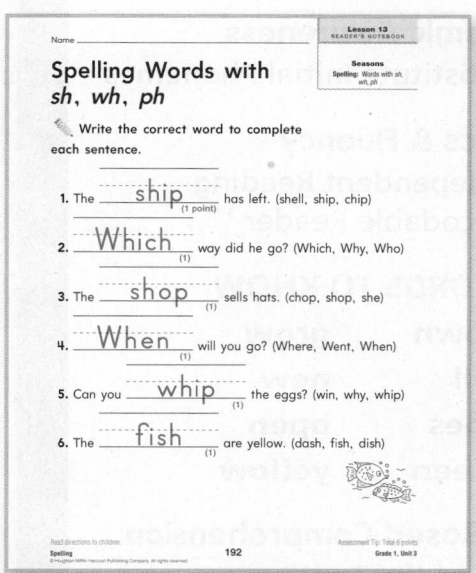

Reader's Notebook Vol. 1 p. 192

Reader's Notebook Vol. 1 p. 193

DAY 5

Today's Goals

Vocabulary & Oral Language
- Domain-Specific Vocabulary
- Speaking & Listening

Phonemic Awareness
- Substitute Initial Phonemes

Phonics & Fluency
- Independent Reading:
  Decodable Reader

☑ **WORDS TO KNOW**

down	grow
fall	new
goes	open
green	yellow

Text-Based Comprehension
Extend the Topic
- Speaking & Listening:
  Discuss Informational Text:
  Compare and Contrast

Assess & Reteach
- Assess Skills
- Respond to Assessment

Grammar & Writing
- Subjects and Verbs
- ✏ Informative Writing:
  Sentences That Inform

Spelling
- Words with *sh, wh, ph*

COMMON CORE **RF.1.3g** recognize and read irregularly spelled words; **SL.1.6** produce complete sentences when appropriate to task and situation; **L.1.6** use words and phrases acquired through conversations, reading and being read to, and responding to texts

Opening Routines

Warm Up with Wordplay

Ending with *-ing*

Remind children that they have been working with words that end with *-ing*. Tell children you are going to play an action game. Begin by asking a child *What are you doing?* He or she should think of action to pantomime such as walking or jumping. As he or she acts out the word, he or she should say *I am _____ing*. Then the child asks the next child *What are you doing?* Continue the game until everyone has pantomimed and said a complete sentence. ⬛ **SL.1.6**

Daily Phonemic Awareness

Substitute Initial Phonemes

- *We're going to change the sounds in words to make new words. For example, change the first sound in* sip *to /z/. /z/ /ĭ/ /p/. What is the word?* zip *Good! Let's try some more.*

- Have children repeat with you before doing it on their own. Have them continue with the words shown.

Change the . . .	Result
First sound in *hip* to /ch/	*chip*
First sound in *well* to /sh/	*shell*
First sound in *tone* to /ph/	*phone*

Corrective Feedback

- If a child misses a word, say the correct word and model the task. *Listen to the sounds in* hip: */h/ /ĭ/ /p/. What is the first sound? /h/ Now I'll change the /h/ to /ch/: /ch/ /ĭ/ /p/. What is the word?* chip

- Have children repeat the procedure with you before doing it on their own.

- Go back several words and continue the game.

Daily High-Frequency Words

Introduce

- Point to the **High-Frequency Word Card** *new.*
- *Say the word.* new *Spell the word.* n, e, w *Write the word. Check the word.*
- Repeat the procedure with the words from this week (*down, fall, goes, green, grow, open, yellow*) and last week (*been, brown, know, never, off, out, own, very*). ◼ RF.1.3g

Find the Letter Game

- Choose a word from this week's or the previous week's High-Frequency Words. Write a dash on the board for each letter.
- Have children call out letters. If the letter is in the word, write it on the appropriate blank.
- Continue until children can guess the word.
- Ask the child who guesses the word correctly to come to the board to choose the next word.

Corrective Feedback

- Say the correct word and have children repeat it. Fall. *What is the word?* fall
- Have children spell the word. *f, a, l, l How do we say this word?* fall
- Have children reread all of the cards in random order.

Daily Vocabulary Boost

- Reread "The Prickly Pride of Texas" aloud to children. (See pp. T212–T213.)
- As you reach each Oral Vocabulary word in the selection, have a volunteer explain or describe its meaning. Call on each child to make a sentence with a vocabulary word. Repeat the list until each child has used a vocabulary word.
- After reading, review the Oral Vocabulary words and their definitions. Challenge children to use the words in their everyday speech. ◼ L.1.6

☑ **Oral Vocabulary**

bouquet
burst
glows
plow
shrivel
vines

• eBook

Extend the Topic

▶ SHARE OBJECTIVES

- Acquire and use domain-specific vocabulary.
- Participate in conversations about a topic.
- Identify basic similarities in and differences between two texts on the same topic.
- Describe the connection between ideas in a text.

Words About the Topic: Seasons

- **weather** the temperature and what it is like outside (hot or cold, sunny or rainy, and so on)
- **cycle** a series of events that repeats over and over
- **sunlight** the light that comes from the Sun

▷ Domain-Specific Vocabulary

INTRODUCE WORDS ABOUT THE TOPIC Remind children that this week's topic is Seasons. Display the words shown at the left. Tell children that these are words that can help them learn more about the topic. Read aloud the meaning of each word, and have children respond to the following prompts. ◼ **L.1.5c, L.1.6**

- *If I want to find out if it's going to rain or be sunny today, what question might I ask? What will the weather be like today?*

- *If we watch the Moon during the year, there is a pattern to the way it seems to change shape. The changes in the way the moon looks happen in a _____.* cycle

- *During the day, we can see because of _____.* sunlight

INTERACT WITH THE WORDS Have children work in small groups to create Four-Square Maps. For each of the domain-specific words, children should fold a blank sheet of paper into four equal sections. Work with them to follow the steps below for each word. As needed, display the meanings of the words on the board. Ask individual children to use the words in a sentence orally. Then write the sentence on the board for other children to refer to for ideas.

1 In the first corner, draw a picture for the word.

2 In the second corner, write the meaning of the word.

3 In the third corner, write a sentence using the word.

4 In the fourth corner, write the word.

When groups have finished, have them share their Four-Square Maps with the class. ◼ **L.1.5c, L.1.6**

COMMON CORE **RI.1.3** describe the connection between individuals, events, ideas, or information in a text; **RI.1.9** identify similarities in and differences between two texts on the same topic; **SL.1.1b** build on others' talk in conversations by responding to others' comments; **SL.1.1c** ask questions to clear up confusion about topics and texts under discussion; **SL.1.3** ask and answer questions about what a speaker says; **L.1.5c** identify real-life connections between words and their use; **L.1.6** use words and phrases acquired through conversations, reading and being read to, and responding to texts

Speaking and Listening

Discuss Informational Text:
Compare and Contrast

COMPARING TWO TEXTS Display and review the Tips for Comparing and Contrasting. Point out that two texts can be the same in some ways and different in others. Tell the class that comparing and contrasting two selections is a good way to understand the topic better.

Have children look back at *Seasons* and *Four Seasons for Animals*. Ask how the topics are the same. *Both are about the seasons.* How are they different? *The second is about only animals.* 🔲 RI.1.3, RI.1.9

CLASS DISCUSSION Have children revisit *Seasons* and *Four Seasons for Animals* again, this time paying close attention to the illustrations. Ask questions to help children compare and contrast the illustrations in the two texts, such as: 🔲 RI.1.3, RI.1.9

- What things pictured in both selections are the same? *birds nests, fields, rain, flowers, sleeping animals, snow, and so on*

- What are the illustrations in both selections trying to show? *the seasons—spring, summer, fall, and winter*

- How are the illustrations different? *One has drawings and the other has photographs.*

GROUP DISCUSSION Organize children into small groups. Have each group compare and contrast the descriptions of spring, summer, fall, and winter in the two selections. How are the descriptions the same? How are they different?

Remind children to follow discussion rules, and to build the conversation by responding to what others in the group have said. Tell listeners to ask questions when they do not understand. The rest of the group works together to answer the questions in order to help clear up any confusion. Guide children to return to the selections to find text evidence to help them answer the questions, if needed. Then discuss children's findings about how the descriptions are alike and different with the whole class.

🔲 RI.1.3, RI.1.9, SL.1.1b, SL.1.1c, SL.1.3

Tips for Comparing and Contrasting

1. **Compare: Tell what is the same.**

   Words for comparing: *like, the same as, similar, equal, and, also.*

2. **Contrast: Tell what is different.**

   Words for contrasting: *different, unlike, more (less) than, on the other hand, but.*

Listening Log

Grammar Weekly Review: Subjects and Verbs

▶ SHARE OBJECTIVES

- **Grammar** Review and use singular and plural nouns with matching verbs in sentences.
- **Spelling** Spell words with *sh*, *wh*, and *ph* using conventional spelling patterns.

ELL ENGLISH LANGUAGE LEARNERS
Language Transfer

Beginning Display the words *wish, shirt, graph, what, where.* Read the words aloud and have children clap whenever they hear the /sh/, /f/, or /hw/ sound.

Low Intermediate Have children use letter cards to build and read *fish, shell, who.*

High Intermediate Have children use letter cards to build and read *wish.* Guide them in changing the cards to read *dish, shirt, photo, what.*

Proficient Have children in groups use **Letter Cards** *t, c, h, a, i, e, o, t, s, w, r, p, d, n* to build and read as many words with the /sh/, /f/, or /hw/ sound as they can.

1 Review/Practice

- Read together the text at the top of **Student Book p. 116.** Discuss the subjects and the verbs in the sentences.
- Direct children's attention to the **Try This!** activity on **Student Book p. 117.** Have children write the correct verb to finish each sentence. **L.1.1c**

2 Connect to Writing

- Write the following statements on the board. Ask children to identify the mistakes orally.

  Sam and Tom hikes in the woods. Sam see a deer.

- Model using proofreading marks to correct the first sentence.
- Ask a volunteer to correct the error in the second sentence.

  Sam and Tom h̶i̶k̶e̶s̶ ^hike^ in the woods. Sam s̶e̶e̶ ^sees^ a deer.

- Together read the directions for **Grammar in Writing** at the bottom of **Student Book** p. 117. Support children as they check for subject-verb agreement in their own writing. **L.1.1c, L.1.1j**

Spelling Words with *sh, wh,* and *ph*

SPELLING WORDS AND SENTENCES

BASIC

1. *ship* The *ship* sails on the ocean.
2. *shop* I like to *shop* for food.
3. *which* *Which* hand is it in?
4. *when* *When* will you go home?
5. *whip* *Whip* the butter with a fork,

6. *fish* The *fish* swim in the water.

CHALLENGE

7. *shell* John found a *shell* on the beach.
8. *graph* Please draw a picture *graph* on the board.

Assess

Say each spelling word. Then say it in a sentence and repeat the word. Have children write the word. **L.1.2d**

Corrective Feedback

Review any words that children misspell.

COMMON CORE **L.1.1c** use singular and plural nouns with matching verbs in sentences; **L.1.1j** produce and expand simple and compound declarative, interrogative, imperative, and exclamatory sentences; **L.1.2d** use conventional spelling for words with common spelling patterns and for frequently occurring irregular words

L.1.1c use singular and plural nouns with matching verbs in sentences

Grammar

Subjects and Verbs In a sentence, the subject and the verb have to agree. Both must tell about the same number of people or things. Add **s** to most **verbs** when they tell about a **noun** that names one.

One	More Than One
One boy **pulls** his sled.	Two girls **pull** their dog.
Brett **slides** down the hill.	Children **slide** across the pond.

116

Try This!

Choose the correct verb to finish each sentence. Take turns reading a sentence aloud with a partner. Then talk about how you chose the correct verb.

1. Raindrops _____?_____ each spring.
   fall   falls

2. Flowers _____?_____ in the garden.
   grow   grows

3. One bug _____?_____ all night.
   hum   hums

4. Now the sun _____?_____ brightly.
   shine   shines

5. The children _____?_____ in the pool.
   swim   swims

 Grammar in Writing

When you proofread your writing, be sure you have written the correct verb to go with each noun.

117

Try This!

1. fall
2. grow
3. hums
4. shines
5. swim

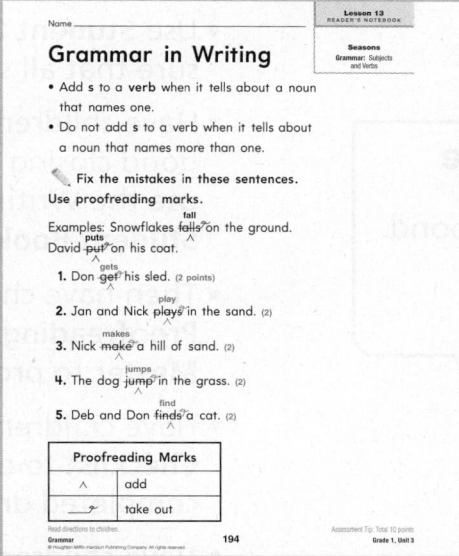

Reader's Notebook Vol. 1 p. 194

Go Digital
• eBook
• *my*WriteSmart

Informative Writing Revising and Proofreading

▶ **SHARE OBJECTIVE**
• Revise and proofread sentences that inform.

ELL ENGLISH LANGUAGE LEARNERS

Comprehensible Input

Beginning Have children draw pictures of activities they like to do during each season. Have them dictate to you simple sentences about their drawings.

Low Intermediate Have children draw pictures of activities they like to do during each season. Provide sentence frames for them to complete, such as *I ___ in spring.*

High Intermediate Have children write sentences about each season. Guide them to circle the subject and underline the verb.

Proficient Have children work with partners to read and revise one another's work.

See ELL Lesson 13, p. E31, for scaffolded support.

Daily Proofreading Practice

Karen and Bob skates on the pond.
skate
^

Bob fall down
falls
^   ^

COMMON CORE

W.1.2 write informative/explanatory texts; **W.1.5** focus on a topic, respond to questions/suggestions from peers, and add details to strengthen writing; **L.1.1c** use singular and plural nouns with matching verbs in sentences

---

1 Teach/Model

Display **Projectable 13.10**. Explain that a first grader named Kyle wrote these facts.

• Review what revision means.

• *Revising means making your writing better by changing and rewriting your sentences.*

• Use the **Talk About It** questions to help children analyze Kyle's draft.

• Have children suggest revisions. Help them identify that Kyle needs to add a closing sentence that retells the main idea using different words and offers a sense of closure.

• Model revising the draft and then checking for spelling and correct capitalization and punctuation.

Projectable 13.10

Seasons Writing Informative Writing

Revising Kyle's Draft

Read Kyle's draft. Then help Kyle think of ways to make his sentences better.

A Chilly Season

Winter is the coldest season.

Sometimes it snows here.

I have a dog.

We go sledding.

The lake freeze.
         s
         ^

People skate on it.

Winter is cold, but you can

still go out and play.

Talk About It
☐ Are all Kyle's sentences about one main idea?
☐ Does each detail sentence tell a fact?
☐ Did Kyle write the correct verb to go with each noun?

Writing   Grade 1, Unit 3

2 Independent Writing

• Use **Student Book pp. 118–119** to review the focus skill, making sure that all sentences are about the main idea.

• Have children revise their own papers, being sure to include a good closing sentence. Have them use the Writing Traits Checklist on **Student Book p. 118**.

• Then have children use the **Proofreading Checklist Blackline Master** to proofread their papers.

• Have children use the **Writing Checklist** to evaluate their completed drafts.

• Have children make clean copies of their revised work. Have them draw to illustrate their final draft. Provide time for children to share their sentences that inform.

🔲 **W.1.2, W.1.5, L.1.1c**

Name _____ Date _____   **Writing Rubric**

Writing Checklist

☐ My writing is on topic.
☐ My writing has facts or details.
☐ My writing has a beginning and an ending.
☐ Ideas are in order.
☐ Words are spelled correctly.
☐ Sentences and names start with capital letters.
☐ Sentences have correct end marks.

Read the checklist with children. Help them use the checklist to review their writing and make it better.

Writing Checklist   9   Grade 1 Additional Resources

Writing Checklist

W.1.2 write informative/explanatory texts; W.1.5 focus on a topic, respond to questions/suggestions from peers, and add details to strengthen writing; L.1.1c use singular and plural nouns with matching verbs in sentences

Informative Writing

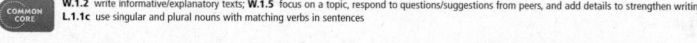

☑ **Ideas** When you write **sentences** that tell facts, be sure all your sentences are about one main idea.

Kyle wrote about winter. Then he took out a sentence that didn't belong.

Revised Draft

Winter is the coldest season.

Sometimes it snows here.

~~I have a dog.~~

Writing Traits Checklist

☑ **Ideas** Are all my sentences about one main idea? Do the details tell facts?

☑ Did I write the correct verb to go with each noun?

☑ Did I write a good ending sentence?

118

Look for the main idea sentence in Kyle's final copy. Then revise your writing. Use the Checklist.

Final Copy

A Chilly Season

Winter is the coldest season.
Sometimes it snows here.
We go sledding.
The lake freezes.
People skate on it.
Winter is cold, but you can
still go out and play.

119

WRITING TRAITS SCORING RUBRIC

See also the **Writing Rubric Blackline Master** on Teacher's Edition p. R11.

	Focus/Support	Organization	Word Choice/Voice	Conventions/Sentence Fluency
6	Develops topic or events with relevant facts or details.	Introduces topic or situation clearly, organizes ideas to support purpose, has relevant conclusion.	Links ideas with words, phrases. Uses specific language. Connects with reader in unique way.	Demonstrates exemplary command of conventions of standard written English. Includes variety of complete sentences that flow smoothly, naturally.
5	Mostly develops topic or events with relevant facts or details.	Introduces topic or situation, mostly organizes ideas to support purpose, has mostly relevant conclusion.	Links most ideas with words, phrases. Uses specific language. Connects with reader.	Demonstrates good command of conventions of standard written English. Includes some variety of complete sentences that flow smoothly, naturally.
4	Adequately develops topic or events with relevant facts or details.	Introduces topic or situation, adequately organizes ideas to support purpose, has adequate conclusion.	Links some ideas with words, phrases. Uses some specific language. Connects with reader.	Demonstrates adequate command of conventions of standard written English. Includes some variety of complete sentences. Some flow smoothly, naturally.
3	Develops topic or events with some relevant facts or details.	Introduces topic or situation, organizes some ideas to support purpose, has somewhat relevant conclusion.	Links some ideas with words, phrases. May use some specific language. May connect with reader.	Demonstrates command of some conventions of standard written English. Includes little variety of complete sentences. Few flow smoothly, naturally.
2	Develops topic or events with few relevant facts or details.	May introduce topic or situation, organizes few ideas to support purpose, may have somewhat relevant conclusion.	Attempts to link ideas with words. Rarely uses specific language. May not connect with reader.	Demonstrates little command of conventions of standard written English. Includes little sentence variety. Incomplete sentences hinder meaning.
1	May not develop topic or events with relevant facts or details.	May attempt to introduce topic or situation, may not organize ideas to support purpose, may not have relevant conclusion.	May not link ideas with words. Does not use specific language or connect with reader.	Demonstrates little or no command of conventions of standard written English. Sentences do not vary. Incomplete sentences hinder meaning.

✓ Progress Monitoring

Assess

- Weekly Tests
- Periodic Assessments

COMMON CORE

Respond to Assessment

✓ Vocabulary

High-Frequency Words
Strategies: Word Endings -ed, -ing, -s

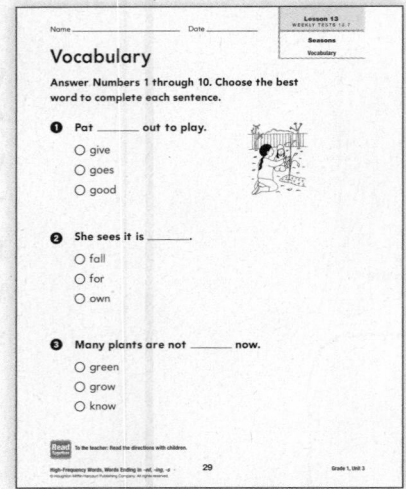

Weekly Tests 13.7–13.10

RF.1.3g recognize and read irregularly spelled words; **L.1.4c** identify frequently occurring root words and their inflectional forms

IF a Child Scores...	THEN...
7–10 of 10	▶ Continue Core Instructional Program
1–6 of 10	▶ Reteaching Lesson, p. T301

If a child scores below target on two or more tests, then consider using Diagnostic Assessment to pinpoint the child's instructional needs. The child may need systematic intervention.

✓ Phonics/Decoding

Words with Digraphs *sh, wh, ph*
Contractions with *'s, n't*

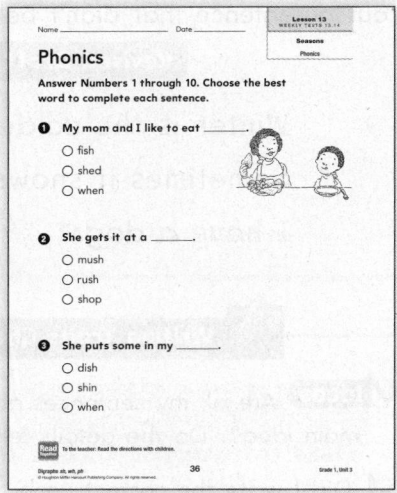

Weekly Tests 13.14–13.20
Phonemic Awareness
See Observation Checklist *in Grab-and-Go™ Resources.*

RF.1.3a know the spelling-sound correspondences for common consonant digraphs

IF a Child Scores...	THEN...
7–10 of 10	▶ Continue Core Instructional Program
1–6 of 10	▶ Reteaching Lesson, p. T300

If a child scores below target on two or more tests, then consider using Diagnostic Assessment to pinpoint the child's instructional needs. The child may need systematic intervention.

Go Digital

- Grab-and-Go Weekly Tests
- Online Assessment System
- Cold Reads Online
- ExamView Banks

COMMON CORE

✓ Comprehension

Cause and Effect
Sound Words

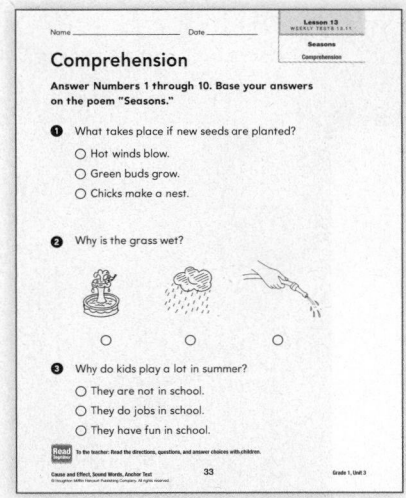

Weekly Tests 13.11–13.13

RI.1.3 describe the connection between individuals, events, ideas, or information in a text; **RI.1.4** ask and answer questions to determine or clarify the meaning of words and phrases

IF a Child Scores...	THEN...
7–10 of 10	▶ Continue Core Instructional Program
1–6 of 10	▶ Reteaching Lesson, p. T301

If a child scores below target on two or more tests, then consider using Diagnostic Assessment to pinpoint the child's instructional needs. The child may need systematic intervention.

✓ Language Arts

Grammar: Subjects and Verbs

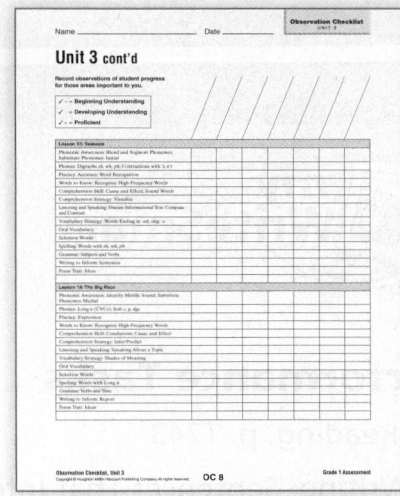

Observation Checklist,
Assessment, **p. OC8**

L.1.1c use singular and plural nouns with matching verbs in sentences

IF a Child Scores...	THEN...
Proficient	▶ Continue Core Instructional Program
Developing	▶ Review Instruction, pp. T234, T244, T256, T276–T277
Beginning	▶ Intervention Lesson 13, pp. S22–S31

If a child scores below target on two or more tests, then consider using Diagnostic Assessment to pinpoint the child's instructional needs. The child may need systematic intervention.

✓ FLUENCY

Fluency Plan Assess one group per week. Use the suggested plan below.

● **Struggling Readers**	**Weeks 1, 3, 5**
▲ **On Level**	**Week 2**
■ **Advanced**	**Week 4**

Fluency Scoring Rubrics
See *Grab-and-Go™ Resources Assessment* for help in measuring progress.

Oral Reading Practice
Use the **Student Book**, the **Leveled Readers**, or other reading materials in this unit to help children improve fluency.

✓ COLD READS

Cold Reads *are leveled passages that can be used to practice and monitor fluency and comprehension.*

LESSON 13

Performance Tasks

my WriteSmart

Lesson Performance Tasks

- Write About Reading, p. T243

- Informative Writing: Sentences That Inform, pp. T278–T279

- Cumulative Performance Assessment: Task 3 of 5

Unit-Level Performance Tasks

- Research and Media Performance Task, pp. xxvi–xxvii

- Cumulative Performance Assessment

  Task 1: complete after Lesson 11

  Task 2: complete after Lesson 12

  Task 3: complete after Lesson 13

  Task 4: complete after Lesson 14

  Task 5: complete after Lesson 15

SMALL GROUP

DAY 1

Differentiate
Phonics & Words to Know
- Digraphs *sh*, *wh*, *ph*
- *down, fall, goes, green, grow, new, open, yellow*

Vocabulary Reader
- *Ducks*

Vocabulary Reader

DAY 2

Differentiate Comprehension
- Cause and Effect
- Visualize

DAY 3

Differentiate
Phonics & Fluency
- Contractions with *'s*, *n't*
- Accuracy: Word Recognition

Leveled Readers
- ⬤ *Winter*
- ▲ *Fall Changes*
- ◼ *Seasons Around the World*
- ◆ *In the Fall*

Leveled Readers

DAY 4

Differentiate
Vocabulary Strategies
- Word Endings *-ed*, *-ing*, *-s*

DAY 5

Options for Reteaching
- Phonics
- Vocabulary Strategies
- Comprehension

Literacy Centers

Independent Practice
- Word Study, T206
- Think and Write, T207
- Comprehension and Fluency, T206
- Digital Center, T207

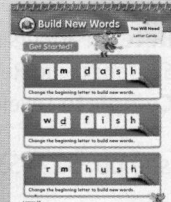
Word Study

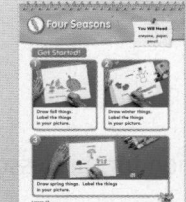
Think and Write

Comprehension and Fluency

Teacher-Led

	DAY 1	DAY 2	DAY 3
Struggling Readers	**Vocabulary Reader** *Ducks*, Differentiated Instruction, p. T288 **Differentiate Phonics:** Digraphs *sh, wh, ph*, p. T286	**Differentiate Comprehension:** Cause and Effect; Visualize Strategy, p. T290 **Reread** *In a Rush*, p. T239	**Leveled Reader** *Winter*, p. T294 **Differentiate Phonics:** Contractions with *'s, n't,* p. T292
On Level	**Vocabulary Reader** *Ducks*, Differentiated Instruction, p. T288	**Differentiate Comprehension:** Cause and Effect; Visualize Strategy, p. T290 **Reread** *In a Rush*, p. T239	**Leveled Reader** *Fall Changes*, p. T295 **Differentiate Fluency:** Accuracy: Word Recognition, p. T293
Advanced	**Vocabulary Reader** *Ducks*, Differentiated Instruction, p. T289	**Differentiate Comprehension:** Cause and Effect; Visualize Strategy, p. T291	**Leveled Reader** *Seasons Around the World*, p. T296 **Differentiate Fluency:** Accuracy: Word Recognition, p. T293
English Language Learners	**Vocabulary Reader** *Ducks*, Differentiated Instruction, p. T289 **Differentiate Words to Know** Using Context Cards, p. T287	**Differentiate Comprehension:** Cause and Effect; Visualize Strategy, p. T291 **Reread** *In a Rush*, p. T239	**Leveled Reader** *In the Fall*, p. T297 **Differentiate Fluency:** Accuracy: Word Recognition, p. T293

What are my other kids doing?

	DAY 1	DAY 2	DAY 3
Struggling Readers	**Word Building:** Build and read Spelling Words using Letter Cards **Complete** Leveled Practice, SR13.1–SR13.2	**Words to Know:** Partners practice reading Context Cards **Reread** *Phil's New Bat* and *In a Rush* **Complete** Leveled Practice, SR13.3	**Reread:** Partners read *Winter* **Complete** Leveled Practice, SR13.4
On Level	**Word Building:** Build and read Words to Know using Letter Cards	**Words to Know:** Practice reading Context Cards **Reread** *Phil's New Bat* and *In a Rush*	**Reread:** Partners read *Fall Changes*
Advanced	**Context Cards** Assign Talk It Over activities **Complete** Leveled Practice, A13.1–A13.2	**Reread:** Partners read *Seasons* **Complete** Leveled Practice, A13.3	**Reread** *Seasons Around the World* **Complete** Leveled Practice, A13.4
English Language Learners	**Listen** to Audio of *Seasons* **Complete** Leveled Practice, ELL13.1–ELL13.2	**Listen:** Follow along with Audio of *Seasons* **Retell:** Partners retell *Seasons* using Retelling Cards **Complete** Leveled Practice, ELL13.3	**Reread:** Partners read *In the Fall* **Listen** to Audio of *Four Seasons for Animals* **Complete** Leveled Practice, ELL13.4

For Strategic Intervention for this lesson, see pp. S22–S31.

DAY 4

Differentiate Vocabulary Strategies: Word Endings -ed, -ing, -s, p. T298
Reread Trish's Gift, p. T261

Differentiate Vocabulary Strategies: Word Endings -ed, -ing, -s, p. T298
Reread Trish's Gift, p. T261

Differentiate Vocabulary Strategies: Word Endings -ed, -ing, -s, p. T299

Differentiate Vocabulary Strategies: Word Endings -ed, -ing, -s, p. T299
Reread Trish's Gift, p. T261

Reread: Partners read Trish's Gift
Listen to Audio of Four Seasons for Animals

Reread Trish's Gift

Reread: Partners read Four Seasons for Animals

Listen to Audio of Four Seasons for Animals
Reread: Partners read Ralph Goes to Camp

DAY 5

Options for Reteaching, pp. T300–T301
Reread one of this week's Decodable Reader selections.

Options for Reteaching, pp. T300–T301
Reread one of this week's Decodable Reader selections.

Options for Reteaching, pp. T300–T301
Reread one of this week's Decodable Reader selections.

Options for Reteaching, pp. T300–T301
Reread one of this week's Decodable Reader selections.

Reread: Choose among this week's stories
• Complete and share Literacy Center activities

Reread: Choose among this week's stories
• Complete and share Literacy Center activities

Reread: Choose among this week's stories
• Complete and share Literacy Center activities

Reread: Choose among this week's stories
• Complete and share Literacy Center activities

Weekly To-Do List

This Weekly To-Do List helps children see their own progress and move on to additional activities independently.

Lesson 13
BLACKLINE MASTER 13.3

Name _____

Weekly To-Do List
Put an X in each box when you finish the activity.

Must Do	May Do
☐ Practice pages	☐ Reading Log
	☐ Vocabulary in Context Cards
☐ Comprehension and Fluency Literacy Center	☐ Spelling
☐ Word Study Literacy Center	☐ Writing
	☐ Other _____
☐ Think and Write Literacy Center	
☐ Read	
☐ Other _____	

I read . . .

☐ Monday	
☐ Tuesday	
☐ Wednesday	
☐ Thursday	
☐ Friday	

Weekly To-Do List
© Houghton Mifflin Harcourt Publishing Company. All rights reserved.
4
Grade 1, Unit 3

Differentiate Phonics and Words to Know

Struggling Readers

Phonemic Awareness/Phonics

Digraphs *sh, wh, ph*

I DO IT

- Show **Picture Card** *ship*. Emphasize the initial sound /sh/.

- Use **Instructional Routine 2** to model how to blend *ship*.

- Write and underline *sh*. *These letters stand for the sound /sh/ at the beginning of* ship.

- Show and name **Picture Card** *brush*, emphasizing final /sh/.

- Point to *sh*. *The letters* sh *stand for /sh/ at the end of this word.*

- Repeat with **Picture Cards** *wheel* and *photo*.

- Review /sh/, /hw/, and /f/ words in the **Decodable Reader** selection *Phil's New Bat*.

WE DO IT

- Use **Sound/Spelling Cards** *sheep*, *whale*, and *graph* to review the *sh* spelling for /sh/, the *wh* spelling for /hw/, and the *ph* spelling for /f/.

- Say the following words and have children say which sound they hear in each: shin, /sh/; why, /hw/; crush, /sh/; phone, /f/; rash, /sh/; photo, /f/; shine, /sh/; white, /hw/, phase, /f/.

- Help children blend the sounds to read the words below. Use the **Corrective Feedback** if children need additional help.

- Discuss the meanings of any unfamiliar words with children.

phone	when	phase	which
sh	rush	shop	shut
whiz	mesh	whip	photo

YOU DO IT

- Have partners copy the words from the previous activity onto individual index cards.

- Show children how to sort the words into three groups: *sh, wh,* and *ph*.

- Have children take turns reading the words in each group.

DAILY ASSESSMENT  **RtI**

Phonics Error:
A child reads *shop* as *chop*.

Correct the error. Say the word and its initial sound. *The word is* shop; *the letters* sh *stand for the sound /sh/.*

Model as you touch the letters. *I'll blend /sh/ /ŏ/ /p/. What is the word?* shop

Check *You blend. /sh/ /ŏ/ /p/. What is the word?* shop

Reinforce Go back three or four words and have children continue reading. Make note of errors and review those words during tomorrow's lesson.

 **English Language Learners**

Words to Know

- Write this week's Words to Know on the board and read them aloud.
- Use the backs of the **Vocabulary in Context Cards** to review the explanations of the words.
- Tell children that they will see these words in this week's reading selections.
- Have children look for the words in the selection *Seasons*.

☑ **WORDS TO KNOW**

down	grow
fall	new
goes	open
green	yellow

Vocabulary in Context Cards

Beginning

- Read each word aloud, and have children repeat after you. Use each word in a sentence, using visuals when possible. Have children raise their hands when they hear one of the Words to Know.

Low Intermediate

- Have children read each word aloud as you point to it. Have them work in pairs to practice matching the words to the pictures.

High Intermediate

- Ask questions about the selection, using the Words to Know. For example, *What color are the leaves in spring? green* Have children work with partners to find the answers.

Proficient

- Prompt children to use the Words to Know in sentences to retell parts of *Seasons*.

On Level

See Literacy Center Practice—Unit 3 Lesson 13 Word Study

If children have time after completing the purple activity, have them try moving on to the blue activity.

Advanced

See Literacy Center Practice—Unit 3 Lesson 13 Word Study

If children have time after completing the blue activity, have them reread the **Decodable Reader** selection *Phil's New Bat*.

Vocabulary Reader
Ducks

Summary

Ducks make a nest in the warm weather and swim with their ducklings. When the weather turns cold, the ducks migrate to a warmer place.

☑ WORDS TO KNOW

down	grow
fall	new
goes	open
green	yellow

Struggling Readers

- Explain to children that ducks live in and around bodies of water. Some ducks fly to warmer places in the winter, but some do not. Ask children to talk about ducks they have seen.

- Preview the selection and have children tell what they see on each page. Have them point to words they recognize.

- Read the selection aloud, tracking the print as you read. Then reread the selection and have children echo-read after you. Have children take turns reading a page aloud. Guide them to use context clues when they come to an unfamiliar word (or phrase).

- Read the Words to Know and have children read them after you. Have partners complete the Responding page. Read the directions on **Blackline Master 13.4** and guide children to complete it.

On Level

- Ask children to tell what they know about ducks. Record their responses in a word web. Call attention to any words in the web that are Words to Know.

- Remind children that context clues can help them figure out unfamiliar words (or phrases) in a sentence.

- Read the selection aloud as children follow along. Then ask children to read the book to a partner. Remind them to use context clues when they come to an unfamiliar word (or phrase).

- Then assign the Responding page and **Blackline Master 13.4**. Review the directions with children and have them discuss their responses with a partner.

Go Digital
• Vocabulary Reader Online
• Literacy and Language Guide
• Context Cards

COMMON CORE

DAY 1

Advanced

- Have children preview the selection and tell what they see happening on each page. Have them frame words they recognize.

- Before reading, remind children to use context clues to help them determine the meaning of unknown words (or phrases).

- Ask alternate children to read pages of the selection aloud. Have children stop and use context clues together when they see unfamiliar words (or phrases).

- Review the Words to Know and have children use them to discuss the selection. Then assign the Responding page and **Blackline Master 13.4**. For the Talk About It activity, remind children to include facts and details to support their ideas.

 ## English Language Learners

Beginning

Make word cards for the verbs in the book, such as *sit*, *fall*, *swim*, and so on. Then have children take turns choosing a card and pantomiming the action of the verb for the class.

High Intermediate

Make word cards for these words in the selection: *start*, *sun*, *ducks*, *swim*, *eggs*, *open*, *duck*, *sits*. Then have children sort the words into nouns and verbs. Encourage children to use one word in a sentence.

Low Intermediate

Create a flow chart that shows what ducks do, starting in the warm weather and going through the book. Have children dictate what happens first, next, and last. Then have them illustrate the flow chart.

Proficient

Have children practice subject and verb agreement with these words: *A duck sits. The ducks sit.* Make word cards for each word and have children rearrange them according to a singular or plural noun. Repeat with other verbs from the selection.

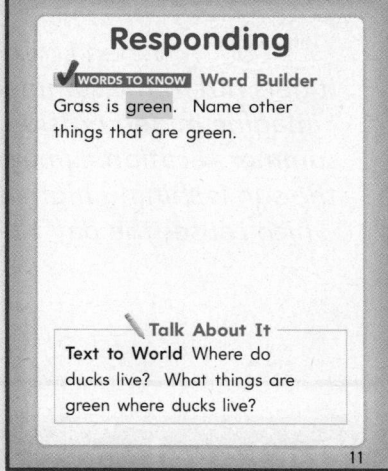

Responding

✓ WORDS TO KNOW Word Builder
Grass is green. Name other things that are green.

✏ **Talk About It**
Text to World Where do ducks live? What things are green where ducks live?

11

Ducks, p. 11

Blackline Master 13.4

Differentiate Comprehension
Cause and Effect; Visualize

Struggling Readers

I DO IT

- Review **Projectable S4** with children. Then display pages 86–87 of *Seasons*. Read the text aloud.

- Tell children that good readers picture story events in their minds as they read.

  Think Aloud *When I think of how it gets hot in the summer, I imagine myself outside during summer vacation. I imagine that the sun is shining high in the sky, which causes the day to be hot.*

WE DO IT

- Have children turn to page 91 of *Seasons*. Read the text aloud.

- Tell children to picture in their mind a tree in fall. Tell them to imagine what the leaves look like and how a big gust of wind causes the leaves to fall to the ground. Have volunteers share what they pictured.

- Repeat with other events described in the selection.

YOU DO IT

- Have children turn to page 85 and read the text as a group. Have children draw pictures of themselves stepping on spring grass and tell what happens after they step on the grass. *Sample response: The grass is wet in spring, so when I step on it it squishes under my feet.*

On Level

I DO IT

- Review **Projectable S4**.

- Display pages 86–87 of *Seasons* and read the text aloud.

- Tell children that good readers picture story events in their minds as they read. This helps them better understand why the events happen.

  Think Aloud *When I think of how it gets hot in the summer, I imagine myself outside during summer vacation. I imagine that the sun is shining high in the sky, which causes the day to be hot.*

WE DO IT

- Have children turn to page 91 of *Seasons*. Read the text aloud.

- Ask: *Why do the leaves fall from the tree?* Tell children to make a picture in their minds to help answer the question. *The leaves are dry and dead so when the wind blows, they fall right off the tree.*

- Repeat with other events described in the selection.

YOU DO IT

- Have children choose an event from the selection to visualize and illustrate. Have each child explain what is happening in the picture and what caused it to happen.

Advanced

I DO IT

- Tell children that good readers picture story events in their minds as they read. This helps them understand why the events happen. Then display page 87 of *Seasons* and read the text aloud.

Think Aloud *As I read this page, I wonder about why it gets hot in summer. I picture myself standing outside during summer vacation with the sun shining high in the sky. The day is very hot.*

WE DO IT

- Have children read the "Winter" section of *Seasons*, beginning on page 94.

- Have children describe some of their favorite winter experiences and explain why they enjoyed them.

YOU DO IT

- Have each child choose one of the seasons and draw a picture of himself or herself doing something in that season. Have children show a cause and effect in their pictures.

ELL English Language Learners

Review the **Visualize Strategy** and explain that good readers make pictures in their minds to understand what they read. Then use the following activities with children according to their level of English proficiency.

Beginning

Read aloud page 88 of *Seasons*. Have children draw pictures of what they see in their minds as you read. Ask them to share their pictures.

Low Intermediate

Read aloud page 88 of *Seasons*. Have children draw pictures of what they see in their minds as you read. Ask them to orally describe their pictures.

High Intermediate

Have each child choose a season and act out what he or she does during that season. Prompt classmates to guess which season is being shown.

Proficient

Have children play a guessing game with partners by providing clues to their favorite seasons. For example:
In my favorite season, you might _____.
In my favorite season, the weather is _____.

Differentiate Phonics and Fluency

Struggling Readers

Phonics

Contractions with *'s, n't*

I DO IT

- Write *it is* on the board and read it aloud.

- *I hear and see two words:* it *and* is. *I can put these words together to make* it's. *It's* is a shorter way to say it is. Remind children that this type of word is called a contraction.

- Write *it's* under *it is* on the board. Circle the *i* in *is* and the apostrophe in *it's*. *When I write* it's, *I take out the* i *in* is *and put an apostrophe in its place.*

- Repeat the procedure with *is not* and *isn't*.

- Tell children that knowing contractions and the words they stand for will help them read and understand better.

- Review contractions in the **Decodable Reader** story *Ralph Goes to Camp*.

WE DO IT

- Write *do not* on the board.

- Have children use **Letter Cards** to build the words. Have them make their own card for the apostrophe.

- Demonstrate and have children duplicate moving the words together and replacing the *o* in *not* with an apostrophe.

- Have children read the contraction and use it in a sentence.

YOU DO IT

- Have children use **Letter Cards** to build *it is, he is, she is, cannot, do not,* and *is not*.

- Have partners take turns replacing the correct letter or letters with an apostrophe and reading the new contraction.

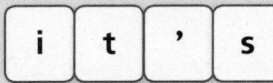

- Children can then take turns using the contractions in sentences.

DAILY ASSESSMENT   ### RtI
3 / 2 / 1

Corrective Feedback

Use **Letter Cards** to model correct answers. *My word pair is* he is. *I'll replace the* i *with an apostrophe. Now I have the smaller word* he's. Guide children. *What is the word?* he's *What are the two words that make* he's? he *and* is. Have children create the contraction on their own, and use it in tomorrow's lesson.

All Levels

Fluency

Accuracy: Word Recognition

I DO IT

- Write *Red, yellow, and green leaves fall down when summer ends.*

- Model underlining words you already know.

- Use a Think Aloud as you underline *red, and, green, fall, down,* and *ends.*

Think Aloud *I don't know all the words just by looking at them. I can sound them out. I will practice reading the sentence with the new words. Practicing the words helps me learn the words.*

WE DO IT

- Choose a sentence from each **Leveled Reader** and write it on the board.

- Ask three children to come up and underline the words he or she knows in the sentence from their reader.

- Choral-read each sentence twice with the entire class.

- Call the three children to the board again. Have them underline the words they recognize after practicing.

YOU DO IT

- Choose a spread from the On-Level **Leveled Reader**.

- Pair children at the same level. Have partners read a page aloud to each other, practicing until each knows all the words on his or her page by sight. Then have the children switch pages and repeat the exercise.

- Remind children to read along on the page as their partner reads aloud.

- Monitor and provide **Corrective Feedback** as needed.

DAILY ASSESSMENT

Corrective Feedback
Check children's understanding by asking them what steps they took to learn the new words. Guide children to see how practicing makes it easier to recognize words.

☑ **TARGET SKILL**
Cause and Effect

☑ **TARGET STRATEGY**
Visualize

☑ **WORDS TO KNOW**

down	grow
fall	new
goes	open
green	yellow

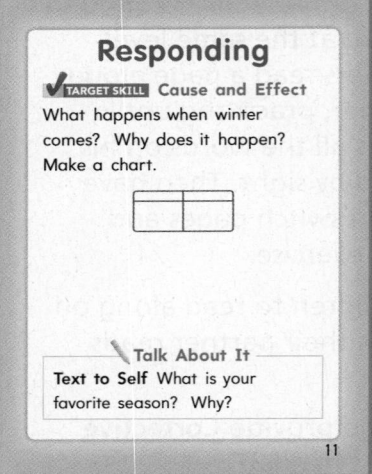

Winter, p. 11

Blackline Master 13.5

Leveled Readers

Struggling Readers

● *Winter*

SUMMARY Leaves are falling, people are raking, rabbits are eating, birds are flying, bears are sleeping, the wind is blowing, and the lake is freezing. Winter is coming!

GENRE: INFORMATIONAL TEXT

Introducing the Text

- Review and discuss this week's Words to Know.

- Take a picture walk through *Winter*. Explain that *Winter* shows how the weather changes and what animals and people do to prepare for the colder days.

- Review that for everything that happens, there is a cause. To find a cause, they need to ask, "Why did it happen?" Tell them to use a T-map to show causes and effects.

Supporting the Reading

- **p. 2** *What is happening to the leaves? They are falling. Why are they falling? They are falling because winter is coming.*

- **p. 6** *What do you think it is like inside the cave where the bears are sleeping? Sample answers: It's dry and warmer than outside. It's dark and cool.*

Discussing and Revisiting the Text

CRITICAL THINKING Read aloud the top half of Responding p. 11 in *Winter*.

- Have children talk about what happens when winter comes.

- Show children how to list what happens when winter comes in the left column of **Blackline Master 13.5**. Then help them write what causes each thing to happen in the right column.

FLUENCY: ACCURACY Model reading orally p. 6 to show children the correct words. Point out how the second sentence repeats on each page but p. 10. Then have them choral-read pp. 6–7 along with you.

On Level

Fall Changes

SUMMARY Fall brings many changes, like shorter days, colder temperatures, and changing colors of leaves.

GENRE: INFORMATIONAL TEXT

Introducing the Text

• Review and discuss this week's Words to Know.

• Have children discuss what they know about what changes in the fall season. Write their responses on chart paper.

• Review with children cause and effect relationships. Tell them that they can record what happens and why it happens in a T-map.

Supporting the Reading

• **p. 3** *Why do the days feel shorter in the fall? There is less sunlight each day.*

• **pp. 5–6** *Imagine you are outside on a fall day. What would the day be like? Possible answers: The day is cool, but the sun is shining. The leaves on the trees are bright red and yellow.*

Discussing and Revisiting the Text

CRITICAL THINKING Read aloud the top half of Responding p. 11 in *Fall Changes*.

• Have children gather in pairs and choose one action in the book and tell why it happens.

• Guide children to write two things that happen in *Fall Changes* on the left column on **Blackline Master 13.6.** Then have them record what makes each action happen in the right column.

FLUENCY: ACCURACY Model reading orally p. 6 to show children the correct words to read. Then record them as they read a page of their choice aloud. Have them listen to the recording and tell how accurate they were.

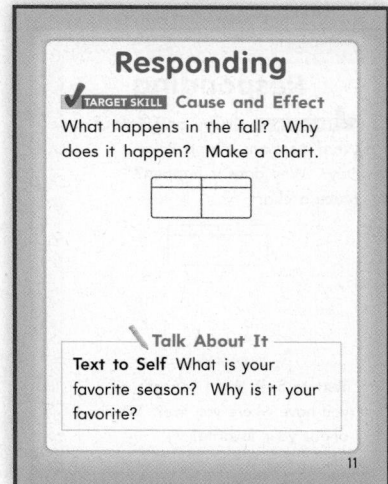

Fall Changes, p. 11

Blackline Master 13.6

Leveled Readers

TARGET SKILL
Cause and Effect

TARGET STRATEGY
Visualize

WORDS TO KNOW

down	grow
fall	new
goes	open
green	yellow

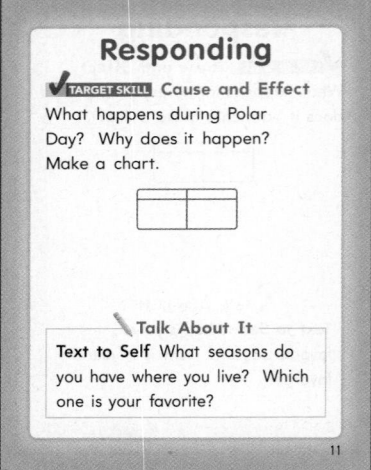

Responding

TARGET SKILL Cause and Effect
What happens during Polar Day? Why does it happen? Make a chart.

Talk About It
Text to Self What seasons do you have where you live? Which one is your favorite?

11

Seasons Around the World,
p. 11

T-Map: *Cause and Effect*

Title: *Seasons Around the World*
Possible responses shown.

What Happens?	Why?
You can see the sun at midnight.	The sun does not go down for many weeks.
It does not rain much.	It is the dry season.
A tornado forms.	The wind blows very fast and spins in a circle.

Graphic Organizer 2 | 9 | Grade 1, Unit 3

Blackline Master 13.7

Advanced

■ *Seasons Around the World*

SUMMARY All over the world, there are many more seasons than just fall, winter, spring, and summer. Some places have wet and dry seasons, polar days and polar nights, and hurricane and tornado seasons.

GENRE: INFORMATIONAL TEXT

Introducing the Text

- Review and discuss this week's Words to Know.

- Ask children what seasons they have where they live and have them describe each. As they read, have them look for other kinds of seasons.

- As children read, have them think about what causes things to happen in each season.

Supporting the Reading

- **p. 5** *Why do some places need both a wet and dry season?* The two seasons make it possible for plants to grow.

- **p. 7** *What do you think it would be like to experience a hurricane?* Possible answers: The wind would be blowing hard and rain would fall. The sky would be very dark, and it would be warm. It might be very scary to be in a place that has a hurricane season.

Discussing and Revisiting the Text

CRITICAL THINKING Have children read the top half of Responding p. 11 in *Seasons Around the World.*

- Have children tell why people call the time of year Polar Day when the sun does not set.

- Have children describe Polar Day and Polar Night in the left column of **Blackline Master 13.7.** Then have them write why they are called each name in the right column.

FLUENCY: ACCURACY Have children read aloud favorite parts of *Seasons Around the World* to practice reading words accurately. Before reading aloud, encourage them to make sure they recognize each word.

Differentiate Vocabulary Strategies

Word endings

ELL English Language Learners

◆ In the Fall

SUMMARY So much happens during the fall. Most leaves change color and animals look for places to sleep for the winter. Gradually, the weather gets cooler, and leaves fall on the ground.

GENRE: INFORMATIONAL TEXT

Introducing the Text

• Review and discuss this week's Words to Know.

• Take a picture walk through *In the Fall* and have children describe each picture. Have them point to pictures that show key words, like *leaves, animal, green,* and *yellow.*

• Remind children that when something happens, something causes it to happen. They can ask themselves, "What happened? Why did it happen?"

Supporting the Reading

• **p. 3** *Why does it get dark early in the fall?* The sun sets early in the day.

• **p. 7** *Imagine you are jumping in a pile of leaves. What is it like?* Sample answers: The leaves crunch under my feet. I laugh after I jump. The leaves scatter all around me.

Discussing and Revisiting the Text

CRITICAL THINKING Help children read the top half of Responding p. 11 in *In the Fall.*

• Have children tell why some trees don't have leaves in the winter. Ask them to find one other thing that happens in the fall and tell why.

• Guide children to write two things that happen in the fall in the left column of **Blackline Master 13.8.** Then have them tell why each thing happens in the right column.

FLUENCY: ACCURACY Look together at p. 9. Have children point to any words they do not know. Then have children echo-read each sentence with you so they know how to read the correct words.

For more reading options, see ELL Lesson 13, pp. E22–E31.

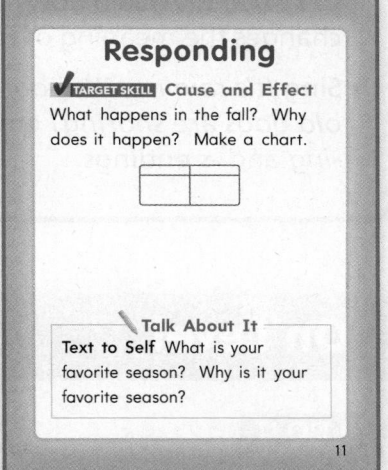

Responding

✓ **TARGET SKILL** Cause and Effect
What happens in the fall? Why does it happen? Make a chart.

✎ **Talk About It**
Text to Self What is your favorite season? Why is it your favorite season?

11

In the Fall, p. 11

Name _____

T-Map: Cause and Effect

Lesson 13
BLACKLINE MASTER 13.8

In the Fall
Graphic Organizer 2

Title: In the Fall
Possible responses shown.

What Happens?	Why?
It gets dark early.	The sun goes down early.
We rake the leaves.	So many leaves drop to the ground.
Some trees are green in the fall.	These trees have needles that do not drop to the ground.

Graphic Organizer 2   10   Grade 1, Unit 3

Blackline Master 13.8

Differentiate Vocabulary Strategies
Word Endings -ed, -ing, -s

Struggling Readers

I DO IT

- Explain that you can change the meaning of a word by adding a word ending.

- Write *rain, pour, snore, dog, head,* and *bump* on the board.

- Explain how word endings *-ed, -ing,* and *-s* change the meanings of words. Model how to add endings to *rain* and explain how each ending changes the meaning of *rain*.

- Sing *It's raining, it's pouring, the old dogs are snoring!* emphasizing *-ing* and *-s* endings.

WE DO IT

- As a class, sing the next line of the song. (*They bumped their heads and went to bed and didn't get up till the morning!*) Point to the words on the board again. Ask children which word ending you should add to each word to make the words in the song.

- Change *snore* to *snoring.* Call on individuals to come to the board to add *-ing* to *rain* and *pour*, *-s* to *dog* and *head*, and *-ed* to *bump*.

- Discuss how these word endings change the meanings of the words.

YOU DO IT

- Erase the endings from the words on the board. Sing the song again twice. Tell children to write every word they hear that ends with *-ed, -ing,* or *-s.*

- Have children exchange papers. Partners should circle the ending of each word.

- Call on individuals to tell what the different word endings mean.

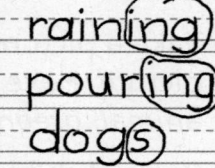

On Level

I DO IT

- Write *rain* on the board.

- Model how to add word endings to the base word (or root word) *rain.* Explain how each ending changes the meaning of *rain.* *When I add -ed, I make* rained. *The -ed ending tells me that rain fell in the past. When I add -ing, I make* raining. *The -ing ending tells me that rain is falling right now. When I add -s, I make* rains. *The -s ending also tells me that it is raining now.*

WE DO IT

- Work with children at the board to follow your model to add endings *-ing, -ed,* and *-s* to the verbs *plant* and *snow.*

- Have children list additional words they can make by adding *-ing, -s,* and *-ed* to *rain* and *storm.*

- Write the new words on the board. Discuss how the word endings have changed the base words (or root words).

YOU DO IT

- Have each child pick *rain* or *storm* and write three sentences with their verb and *-ing, -ed,* and *-s.*

- Ask children to read the sentences aloud. Others raise their hands when they hear a word ending.

It is storming.
I like the sound of storms.
I am glad it stormed.

Advanced

I DO IT

• Remind children that adding endings to words changes their meanings.

• Copy the chart below on the board. Then read the words and endings aloud. Discuss how each ending changes the meaning of the base word (or root word).

WE DO IT

• Add two new words to the chart: *form* and *show*. Ask volunteers to write the words and their endings in the chart.

• Ask children to explain how each ending changes the meaning of the base word (or root word).

• Have children add other base words (or root words) and their endings to the chart.

YOU DO IT

• Have each child choose a word from the chart and write a sentence for each of its endings.

• Have them trade with a partner and circle the word endings.

• Ask children to read their sentences aloud. Have others raise their hands when they hear a word ending.

Word	-ing	-s	-ed
snow	snowing	snows	snowed
hug	hugging	hugs	hugged

ELL English Language Learners

Write *rain, snow, storm, flow, turn, plant,* and *form* on the board. Provide extra practice with word endings using these base words (or root words). Use the following activities with children according to their level of English proficiency.

Beginning

• Add *-ing* to the end of each word. Point to each word as you read it. Have children repeat after you. Repeat with *-ed* and *-s* endings.

Low Intermediate

• Add the endings *-ing, -ed,* and *-s* to each word. Have children read the words aloud. Remind them that *-ing* means something is happening now and *-ed* means something has already happened.

High Intermediate

• Have children make up oral sentences using base words (or root words) with the endings *-ing, -ed,* and *-s.* Ask them to share their sentences with the class.

Proficient

• Have children work with partners to scan the text to find base words (or root words) that will work with the endings *-ing, -ed,* and *-s.* Prompt the partners to add the endings and use the words in sentences.

Options for Reteaching

Reteach Phonics

Digraphs *sh, wh, ph*

I DO IT

- Tell children that you will review words that will help them read the **Decodable Reader** story *Trish's Gift*.

- Review **Instructional Routine 3.** Remind children that they have been reading *sh*, *wh*, and *ph* words this week.

- Review this week's Words to Know *down, fall, goes, green, grow, new, open,* and *yellow.*

- Have children open to p. 72 of *Trish's Gift*.

WE DO IT

- Write *shed* on the board.

- Help children find the word *shed* on the page.

- Model how to decode *shed* step by step.

YOU DO IT

- Have partners work together to read *Trish's Gift*.

- Use the **Corrective Feedback** on p. T286 if children need additional help.

"Gramps put that bench in his shed," said Dad.
"Is that the shed Gramps had?" asked Trish.
"Yes, it's his shed," said Dad.
Dad and Trish ran fast.
72

Reteach Phonics

Contractions with *'s, n't*

I DO IT

- Tell children that you will review some words that will help them read the **Decodable Reader** story *Trish's Gift*.

- Review **Instructional Routine 3.** Remind children that they have been reading contractions with *'s* and *n't* this week.

- Review this week's Words to Know *down, fall, goes, green, grow, new, open,* and *yellow.*

- Have children open to p. 70 of *Trish's Gift*.

WE DO IT

- Write *let's* on the board.

- Help children find the word *let's* on the page.

- Model how to decode *let's* step by step.

YOU DO IT

- Have partners work together to read *Trish's Gift*.

- Use the **Corrective Feedback** on p. T292 if children need additional help.

"Dad," said Trish, "Gramps sent this desk with brass trim, but I can't sit at it."
"Let's see that desk with brass trim," said Dad.
70

Reteach Vocabulary Strategies

Word Endings -ed, -ing, -s

I DO IT

- Remind children that words can be made of a base word (or root word) plus an ending that changes the meaning of the word.

- Explain that -ed tells that something happened already, -ing tells that something is happening now, and -s can show that there is more than one.

WE DO IT

- Display **Projectable 13.8.**

- Help children choose the correct word ending to complete each sentence.

- Read aloud the first sentence.

- Model how to choose which word ending to add to the base word *rain*.

  Think Aloud *The word today is a clue word that the sentence is telling about something that's happening now. The ending -ing tells that something is happening now. So, the word rain should be changed to raining to complete this sentence.*

- Have children write *ing* after *rain*.

YOU DO IT

- Have partners work together to choose the correct word endings to complete the other sentences.

- Have them model applying the **Vocabulary Strategy** to show how an ending added to a base word (or root word) changes the meaning of the word.

Reteach Comprehension Skill

Cause and Effect

I DO IT

- Remind children that sometimes one story event makes, or causes, another event. The two events are linked.

WE DO IT

- Have children read aloud **Student Book** pp. 90–93.

- Model how to recognize events in fall that are causes and effects.

  Think Aloud *The author says that in a gust of wind leaves will fall down. The wind will cause the leaves to fall. The effect, or what happened, is the leaves will fall. The cause, or why it happened, is the gust of wind.*

- Help volunteers recognize other events that are linked as cause and effect.

YOU DO IT

- Distribute **Graphic Organizer 2: T-Map.**

- Have children write effects under *What happened?* and causes under *Why?* *leaves will fall* (effect), *a gust of wind* (cause); *leaves crunch* (effect), *we jump and hop* (cause); *they will have lots to eat* (effect), *animals pack nuts away* (cause)

- Have pairs complete the graphic organizer. Review the completed graphic organizers together.

Teacher Notes

See pages xvi-xvii in this Teacher's Edition for the full digital offering.

*my*SmartPlanner

Plan Across Disciplines, Schedule, Organize

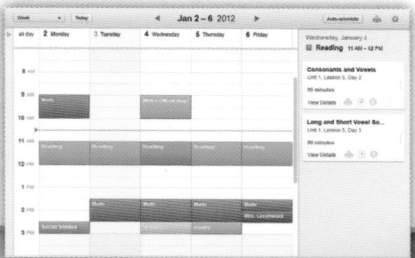

Write, Collaborate, Respond

Online Assessment

Assess, Prescribe, Remediate, Report

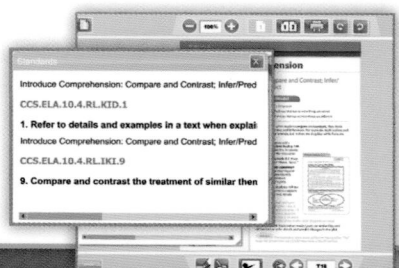

CHALLENGE

Research a Speedy Animal

After reading the selection "The Big Race," have children research speedy animals.

- Explain to children that some animals can move much faster than humans. For example, the fastest human can move at about twenty miles per hour. However, some dogs can move at forty miles per hour, and some big cats, like the cheetah, can move at eighty miles per hour.
- Give children access to books or an online resource. Have them research one speedy animal.
- Call on children to stand up and tell about the animal they researched.

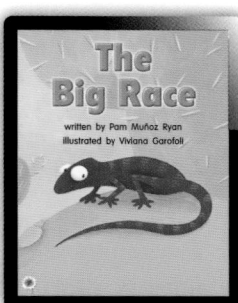

Fantasy

SCIENCE

Connection to Informational Text

RACES ALL AROUND "The Big Race" tells about five friends running in a race. Tell children that running races are held around the country every year. Running groups hold races. Other races are run for charities. Ask children to find out what kinds of races are run in your town, county, or state. Have them work in small groups to find two or three different races. They should record the name of each race, its distance, and how many people run. Invite groups to list the facts and figures they find in a chart. As a class, review each chart and discuss some of the facts. Ask: *Which race do you think would be the easiest to run? Why? Which one would be the hardest? Why?* Discuss children's answers. **Common Core, *English Language Arts*: W.1.8** recall information from experiences or gather information from sources to answer a question

READING LITERATURE

RL.1.1 ask and answer questions about key details

RL.1.5 explain major differences between story books and informational books

READING INFORMATIONAL TEXT

RI.1.5 know and use text features to locate facts or information

RI.1.9 identify similarities in and differences between texts on the same topic

FOUNDATIONAL SKILLS

RF.1.2a distinguish long from short vowel sounds in spoken single-syllable words

RF.1.2c isolate and pronounce sounds in spoken single-syllable words

RF.1.2d segment spoken single-syllable words into their complete sequence of individual sounds

RF.1.3c know final -e and vowel team conventions for representing long vowel sounds

RF.1.4a read on-level text with purpose and understanding

RF.1.4b read on-level text orally with accuracy, appropriate rate, and expression

WRITING

W.1.2 write informative/explanatory texts

W.1.7 participate in shared research and writing projects

W.1.8 recall information from experiences or gather information from sources to answer a question

SPEAKING AND LISTENING

SL.1.1a follow rules for discussions

SL.1.1b build on others' talk in conversations by responding to others' comments

SL.1.2 ask and answer questions about details in a text read aloud, information presented orally, or through other media

SL.1.3 ask and answer questions about what a speaker says

SL.1.4 describe people, places, things, and events with details/express ideas and feelings clearly

SL.1.6 produce complete sentences when appropriate to task and situation

LANGUAGE

L.1.1e use verbs to convey sense of past, present, and future

L.1.2d use conventional spelling for words with common spelling patterns and for frequently occurring irregular words

L.1.5d distinguish shades of meaning among verbs by defining or by acting out the meanings

L.1.6 use words and phrases acquired through conversations, reading and being read to, and responding to texts.

 **LESSON 14**

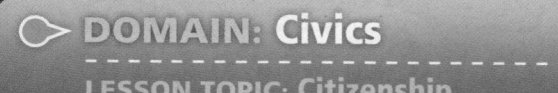 **Our Focus Wall**

ANCHOR TEXT

The Big Race
Fantasy

Read Together

Rules and Laws
Informational Text

ESSENTIAL QUESTION

Why is it important to have rules?

FOUNDATIONAL SKILLS

☑ Words to Know
HIGH-FREQUENCY WORDS

four	five	into
over	starts	three
two	watch	

Phonics

Long *a* (CVCe)

Soft *c, g, dge*

Phonograms
-ake, -ace

a
a_e
ai
_ay

Fluency

Expression

READING LITERATURE & INFORMATIONAL TEXT

Comprehension Skills and Strategies

☑ **TARGET SKILL**
- Conclusions
- Cause and Effect

☑ **TARGET STRATEGY**
- Infer/Predict

WRITING

Writing

Informative Writing: Report

Focus Trait: Ideas

LANGUAGE

Spelling

**Long *a* (CVCe)
Phonogram *-ake***

came	late
make	gave
brave	shape

Grammar

Verbs and Time

Vocabulary Strategies

Shades of Meaning

WHOLE GROUP

∨ Reading

DOMAIN: Civics
LESSON TOPIC: Citizenship

ANCHOR TEXT

The Big Race
Fantasy

Children will read *The Big Race* to

- draw conclusions using story clues and pictures.
- discover the relationship between cause and effect.

Rules and Laws
Informational Text

Children will read *Rules and Laws* to

- know why rules and laws are important.
- learn about and use labels.

∨ Language Arts

● Grammar

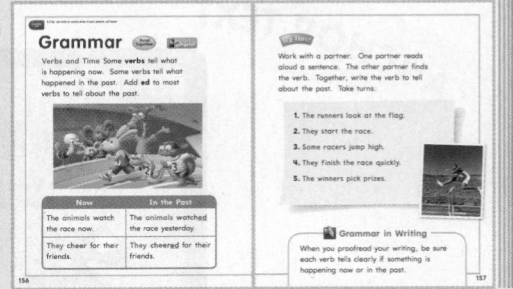

Children learn about verbs and time through reading and changing verbs to past tense in sentences that relate to running.

● Writing

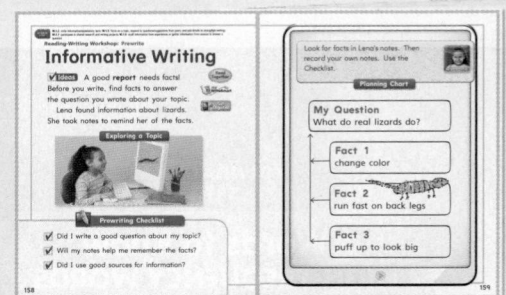

Children begin a report using *The Prickly Pride of Texas* as a model for writing factual information.

◢ TEXT COMPLEXITY RUBRIC

Overall Text Complexity		The Big Race FANTASY	Rules and Laws INFORMATIONAL TEXT
		ACCESSIBLE	MORE COMPLEX
Quantitative Measures	Lexile	330	320
	Guided Reading Level	G	J
Qualitative Measures	Text Structure	Simple, linear chronology	Somewhat complex civics concepts
	Language Conventionality and Clarity	Increased, clearly assigned dialogue	More complex sentence structure
	Knowledge Demands	Clearly fantastical situation	Specialized knowledge required
	Purpose/Levels of Meaning	Single level of simple meaning	Single topic

⌄ Additional Whole Group Resources

◉ Decodable Readers

- *Tate's Cakes*, pp. 75–80
- *Dave and the Whales*, pp. 81–86
- *A Safe Lodge*, pp. 87–92
- *The Race*, pp. 93–98

◉ Progress Monitoring

Assess and monitor children's progress to determine who is on track and who needs help. Clear prescriptions identify targeted instruction to address children's needs and get them back on track.

Respond to Assessment
- ☑ Vocabulary, p. T382
- ☑ Phonics, p. T382
- ☑ Comprehension, p. T383
- ☑ Language Arts, p. T383
- ☑ Fluency, p. T383

FOR STUDENTS
-  my WriteSmart
- eBook
- GrammarSnap Videos
- Destination Reading
- Context Cards

FOR TEACHERS
- Teacher One-Stop
- Interactive Whiteboard Lessons
- Literacy and Language Guide

- Lesson 14 Blackline Masters
- Additional Resources
- Assessment

Lesson resources organized by week.

◉ Lesson 14 Blackline Masters
- Home Letter 14.1
- Weekly To-Do List 14.2
- Vocabulary Word Cards 14.3
- Words to Know 14.4
- Leveled Reader Graphic Organizers 14.5–14.8
- Leveled Practice for Words to Know and Phonics SR14.1–SR14.4, A14.1–A14.4, ELL14.1–ELL14.4
- Weekly Tests 14.1–14.14

◉ Assessment
- Weekly Tests Answer Key
- Observation Checklists
- Fluency Tests
- Periodic Assessments

◉ Additional Resources
- Reading Log
- Vocabulary Log
- Listening Log
- Proofreading Checklist
- Writing Conference Form
- Writing Checklist
- Instructional Routines
- Graphic Organizer Blackline Masters
- Handwriting Models

SMALL GROUP

▽ Weekly Leveled Readers

● Struggling Readers
Guided Reading Level: D
Lexile: 290
DRA: 6

▲ On Level
Guided Reading Level: I
Lexile: 320
DRA: 16

■ Advanced
Guided Reading Level: K
Lexile: 440
DRA: 20

◆ English Language Learners
Guided Reading Level: I
Lexile: 300
DRA: 16

● Vocabulary Reader
for all levels
Guided Reading Level: E
Lexile: 330
DRA: 8

● Leveled Reader Teacher's Guides
8-page lessons for each book support instruction in guided reading groups

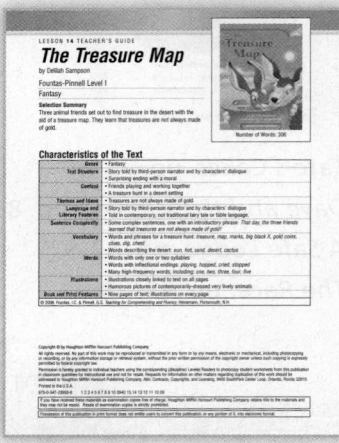
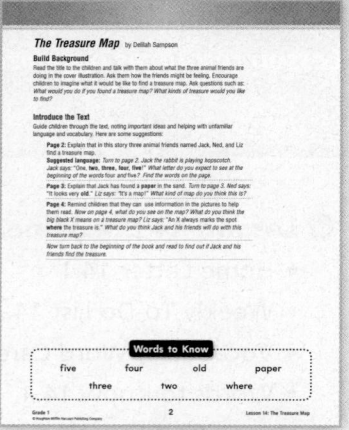

What My Other Students Are Doing

Performance Task

- Write About Reading
- Informative Writing
- Research and Media Literacy
- Unit Performance Assessment, Task 4 of 5

Literacy Centers

Number Fun

Get Started!

1 Read each card. Say the number words in order.

2 Write a number word. Draw a picture. Write the number.

3 Write numbers from 1 to 5. Write the words.

Lesson 14

Word Study

Sharing Time

Get Started!

1 Draw a pie. Show how two people can share it.

2 Show how four people share the pie.

3 Write about sharing with a friend. Tell what you shared.

Lesson 14

Think and Write

Read with a Partner

You Will Need
Tate's Cakes

Get Started!

1 Work with a partner. Read the story Tate's Cakes.

2 "Yes," said Tate, "let's ask Jade."

3 Take turns reading with your partner.

Point to a word. Ask your partner to read it.

Lesson 14

Comprehension and Fluency

Reader's Notebook

Includes practice for:

- Text analysis and citing text evidence
- Words to Know
- Phonics
- Spelling
- Grammar
- Writing Traits

HOUGHTON MIFFLIN HARCOURT

JOURNEYS
COMMON CORE

Reader's Notebook

GRADE 1 Volume 1

Go Digital

FOR STUDENTS

- Leveled Readers Online
- Vocabulary Reader Online

FOR TEACHERS

- Teacher One-Stop
- Literacy and Language Guide
- Leveled Readers Database
- Leveled Reader Teacher's Guides

Grab-and-Go!

- Lesson 14 Blackline Masters
- Additional Resources
- Assessment

Go Digital

FOR STUDENTS

- Write-in Reader eBook
- Vocabulary Reader Online
- Struggling Readers Leveled Reader Online

FOR TEACHERS

- Leveled Reader Teacher's Guide

Grab-and-Go!

- Struggling Readers Blackline Masters

RtI INTERVENTION

Strategic Intervention: TIER II

Use these materials to provide additional targeted instruction for children who need Tier II strategic intervention.

Write-In Reader:
Jake's Best Race

- Engaging selection connects to main topic
- Interactive worktext reinforces this week's vocabulary and comprehension
- Opportunities for student interaction
- Builds the foundational skills for reading more complex texts
- Online version with dual-speed audio and follow-text

Daily Lessons

For this week's daily Strategic Intervention Lesson, see Teacher's Edition pages S32–S41:

- Oral Grammar
- Words to Know
- Decoding
- Comprehension
- Fluency
- Grammar
- Written Response
- Unpack Meaning

Assessment
Progress monitoring every 2 weeks.

Curious About Words

- Provides oral vocabulary instruction for children with limited vocabularies.
- Materials include engaging, illustrated Read Alouds with Teacher Manual.
- Teaches high-utility, research-based words, including academic vocabulary.
- Assessment includes weekly pretests and posttests.

Intensive Intervention: TIER III

Interactive lessons provide support for

- Phonics and Word Study Skills
- Vocabulary
- Comprehension
- Fluency

- Lesson cards for small-group or individual instruction
- Blackline masters for additional practice

- Leveled books for additional reading and skill application
- Lesson assessments evaluate the effectiveness of the intervention

COMMON CORE

English Language Learners *At a Glance*

ENGLISH LANGUAGE LEARNERS

ELL

ENGLISH LANGUAGE LEARNERS

⌄ Whole Group

Use these resources to help English Language Learners access the core content with the whole group.

● Point-of-Use Scaffolded Support

- Use Visuals
- Use Gestures
- Comprehensible Input
- Peer-Supported Learning
- Language Issues
- Idiomatic Language
- Use Sentence Frames
- Expand Language Production

● Vocabulary in Context Cards

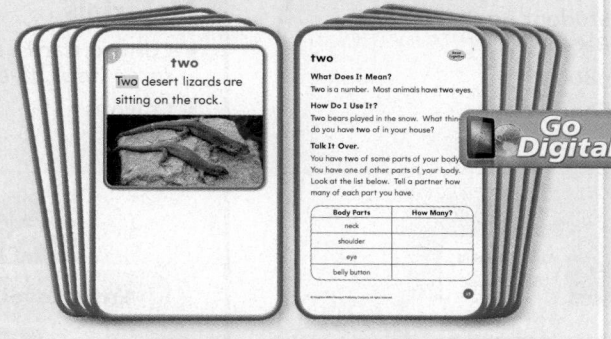

front   back

FOR STUDENTS

- ELL Leveled Reader Online
- Vocabulary Reader Online
- Cross-Curricular Activity Bank
- Multimedia Grammar Glossary
- Picture Card Bank Online

FOR TEACHERS

- ELD Station Online
- Leveled Readers Database
- Leveled Reader Teacher's Guide

Grab-and-Go!

- ELL Blackline Masters

⌄ Small Group

Use these resources to help English Language Learners access the core content with a smaller group.

● ELL Leveled Reader

- Contains the same content as the On-Level Reader but uses more accessible language
- ELL Leveled Reader Lesson Plan
- ELL Blackline Masters

⌄ ELL Extra Support

Use these additional resources to support English Language Learners as needed.

● ELL Lesson 14 Resources

- Daily Lessons to support the core
- Language Support Card 14
- ELL Blackline Masters
- ELL Teacher's Handbook
  Professional Development
  Peer Conferences Forms
  Cooperative Learning Guidelines

● Building Background

LESSON 14 Literacy Centers

 **COMMON CORE** Managing Independent Activities

Comprehension and Fluency

Materials
- Decodable Reader: *Tate's Cakes*
- Crayons
- Student Book: *The Big Race*
- eBook
- Pencil, paper

Read with a Partner

Entry Level

Get Started!

1. Work with a partner. Read the story **Tate's Cakes**.
2. "Yes," said Tate, "let's ask Jade." Take turns reading with your partner.
3. Point to a word. Ask your partner to read it.

You Will Need: *Tate's Cakes*

Lesson 14

On Level

Reach Higher!

You Will Need: Student Book, crayons, paper, pencil

Listen to **The Big Race**. Take turns. Act it out.

Challenge

Challenge Yourself!
- Read the sentence.
- Write the sentence.
- Draw a picture of the cake.

This cake is for the winner.

Lesson 14

Word Study

Materials
- Context Cards: *two, three, four, five*
- Crayons
- Paper, pencil
- High-Frequency Word Cards: *into, over, starts, watch*

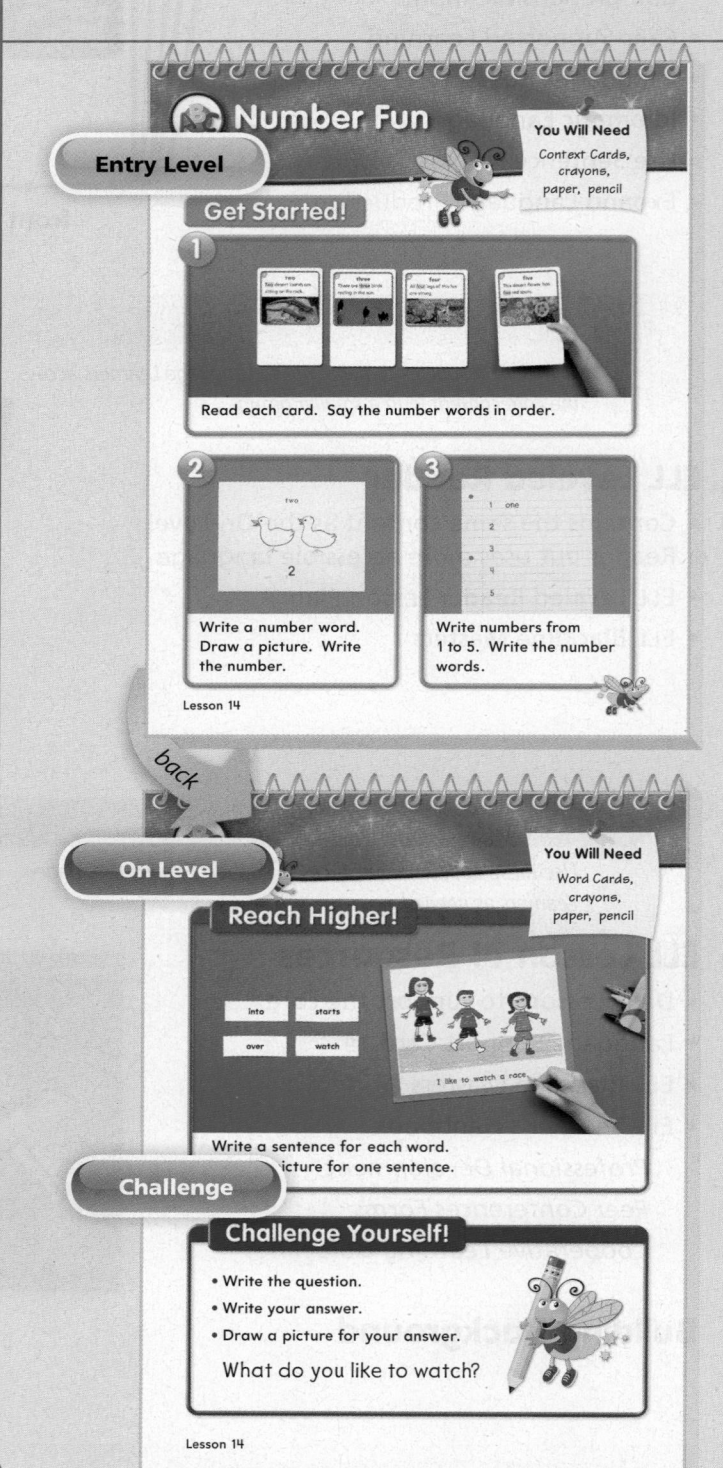

Number Fun

Entry Level

Get Started!

1. Read each card. Say the number words in order.
2. Write a number word. Draw a picture. Write the number.
3. Write numbers from 1 to 5. Write the number words.

You Will Need: Context Cards, crayons, paper, pencil

Lesson 14

On Level

Reach Higher!

You Will Need: Word Cards, crayons, paper, pencil

Write a sentence for each word. Draw a picture for one sentence.

Challenge

Challenge Yourself!
- Write the question.
- Write your answer.
- Draw a picture for your answer.

What do you like to watch?

Lesson 14

Use Literacy Centers to support this week's Common Core focus. Each center contains three activities. Children who experience success with the entry-level activity move on to the on-level and challenge activities, as time permits.

Think and Write

Materials

- Crayons
- Paper, pencil
- Books

- High-Frequency Word Cards: *five, four, into, over, starts, three, two, watch*

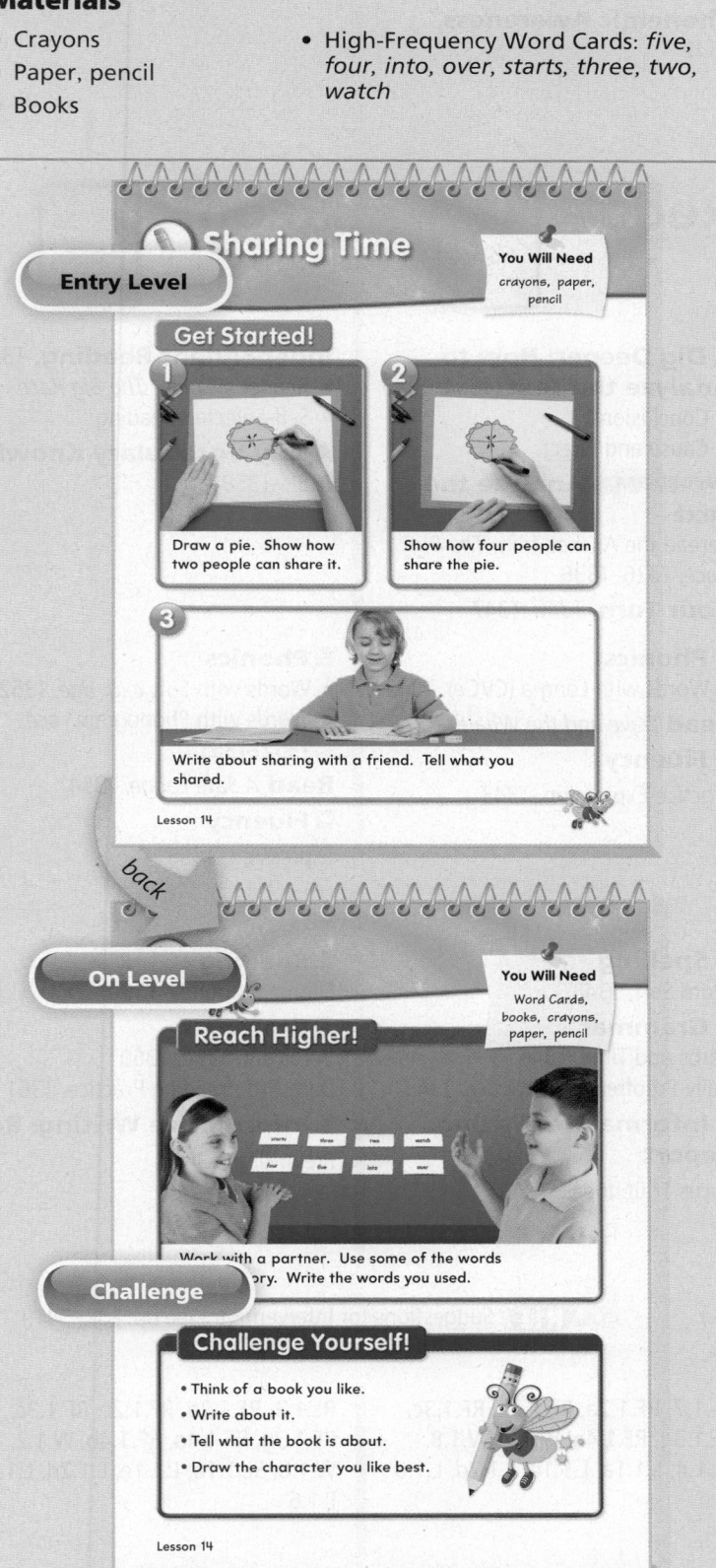

Sharing Time

Entry Level

You Will Need
crayons, paper, pencil

Get Started!

1. Draw a pie. Show how two people can share it.
2. Show how four people can share the pie.
3. Write about sharing with a friend. Tell what you shared.

Lesson 14

back

On Level

You Will Need
Word Cards, books, crayons, paper, pencil

Reach Higher!

Work with a partner. Use some of the words ... ory. Write the words you used.

Challenge

Challenge Yourself!

- Think of a book you like.
- Write about it.
- Tell what the book is about.
- Draw the character you like best.

Lesson 14

Go Digital

FOR STUDENTS

my WriteSmart

Children complete performance tasks related to the week's instruction.

eBook
Children read and listen to *The Big Race* and *Rules and Laws*, generate questions about citizenship, and reread the selections to deepen their knowledge.

Leveled Readers Online
Children read and listen to **Leveled Readers**, reinforcing lesson's Target Vocabulary, Target Skill, and Target Strategy.

Destination Reading
Children practice and apply key lesson skills through gamelike activities.

GrammarSnap Videos
Children practice and apply understanding of verbs and time.

Read

Independent Reading

Have children read daily from a self-selected trade book and record their progress in their Reading Log.

See p. T357 for support in guiding children to select an appropriate book.

LESSON 14 Weekly Planner

	DAY 1	**DAY 2**	**DAY 3**
Whole Group			
Daily Language • Opening Routines • Oral Vocabulary • Listening Comprehension • Phonemic Awareness • Speaking and Listening	**Opening Routines,** T314–T315 • Phonemic Awareness • High-Frequency Words • Vocabulary Boost **Read Aloud,** "The Tortoise and the Hare," T316–T317 **Introduce Oral Vocabulary Phonemic Awareness,** T318	**Opening Routines,** T340–T341 • Phonemic Awareness • High-Frequency Words • Vocabulary Boost **Phonemic Awareness,** T342	**Opening Routines,** T350–T351 • Phonemic Awareness • High-Frequency Words • Vocabulary Boost **Phonemic Awareness,** T352
Vocabulary **Text-Based Comprehension** • Skills and Strategies • Craft and Structure **Research and Media Literacy**	**Read**  ▢ **Introduce Words to Know** High-Frequency Words, T322–T323 ▢ **Read and Comprehend,** T324–T325 **FIRST READ** **Think Through the Text** Read the Anchor Text: *The Big Race*, T326–T337	**Read**  ▢ **Dig Deeper: How to Analyze the Text,** T344–T345 • Conclusions • Cause and Effect **SECOND READ** **Analyze the Text** Reread the Anchor Text: *The Big Race*, T326–T336 **Your Turn,** T346–T347	**Read** **Independent Reading,** T356–T357 • Reader's Guide: *The Big Race* • Self-Selected Reading **Apply Vocabulary Knowledge,** T358–T359
Foundational Skills • Phonics and Word Recognition • Fluency	▢ **Phonics** • Words with Long *a* (CVCe), T318–T320 • Words with Phonogram *-ake*, T318–T320 **Read** *Tate's Cakes*, T321 ▢ **Fluency** Model Expression, T316	▢ **Phonics** • Words with Long *a* (CVCe), T342 **Read** *Dave and the Whales*, T343 ▢ **Fluency** Practice Expression, T343	▢ **Phonics** • Words with Soft *c, g, dge*, T352–T353 • Words with Phonogram *-ace*, T352–T353 **Read** *A Safe Lodge*, T354 ▢ **Fluency** Expression, T355
Whole Group Language Arts			
Spelling **Grammar** **Writing**	▢ **Spelling** Words with Long *a*, T338 Pretest ▢ **Grammar** Introduce Verbs and Time, T338 Daily Proofreading Practice, T339 ▢ **Informative Writing: Report** Introduce the Model, T339	▢ **Spelling** Word Sort, T348 ▢ **Grammar** Verbs and Time, T348 Daily Proofreading Practice, T349 ▢ **Informative Writing: Report** Focus Trait: Ideas, T349	▢ **Spelling** Segment Sounds, T360 ▢ **Grammar** Verbs and Time, T360 Daily Proofreading Practice, T361 ▢ **Informative Writing: Report** Prewriting, T361
Small Group	Suggestions for Small Groups (See pp. T385–T403.)	 RtI Suggestions for Intervention (See pp. S32–S41.)	
COMMON CORE State Standards	RL.1.1, RL.1.10, RF.1.2a, RF.1.2c, RF.1.3c, RF.1.3g, W.1.2, SL.1.2, L.1.1e, L.1.2d, L.1.2e, L.1.4a	RL.1.7, RF.1.2a, RF.1.3b, RF.1.3c, RF.1.3g, RF.1.4a, W.1.2, W.1.8, SL.1.4, L.1.1a, L.1.1e, L.1.2d, L.1.6	RL.1.3, RF.1.2a, RF.1.2c, RF.1.3c, RF.1.3g, RF.1.4a, RF.1.4b, W.1.2, W.1.8, SL.1.1a, L.1.1e, L.1.2d, L.1.5c, L.1.6

DAY 4

Opening Routines, T362–T363
- Phonemic Awareness
- High-Frequency Words
- Vocabulary Boost

Phonemic Awareness, T364

Read

Connect to the Topic
- Read Informational Text: *Rules and Laws*, T366–T368
- Think Through the Text
- ☑ **Compare Texts,** T369
- ☑ **Vocabulary Strategies**
Shades of Meaning, T370–T371

☑ **Phonics**
- Words with Long *a* (CVC*e*), T364
- Words with Soft *c, g, dge,* T364
Read *The Race,* T365
☑ **Fluency**
Expression, T355

☑ **Spelling**
Connect to Writing, T372
☑ **Grammar**
Spiral Review: Singular and Plural Nouns, T372
Daily Proofreading Practice, T373
☑ **Informative Writing: Report**
Prewriting, T373

 Suggestions for English Language Learners
(See pp. E32–E41.)

RI.1.2, RI.1.5, RI.1.10, RF.1.3c, RF.1.3g,
RF.1.4b, W.1.2, W.1.6, W.1.8, SL.1.6, L.1.1c,
L.1.5d, L.1.6

DAY 5

Opening Routines, T374–T375
- Phonemic Awareness
- High-Frequency Words
- Vocabulary Boost

Phonemic Awareness, T375
Speaking and Listening, T377

Read

Extend the Topic
- Domain-Specific Vocabulary, T376
- Speaking and Listening: Speaking About a Topic, T377
- Optional Second Read: *Rules and Laws*, T366–T368

☑ **Phonics**
- Words with Long *a* (CVC*e*), T382
- Words with Soft *c, g, dge,* T382
- Phonograms *-ake, -ace,* T382
☑ **Fluency**
Expression, T355

☑ **Spelling**
Assess, T378
☑ **Grammar**
Verbs and Time, T378–T379
Daily Proofreading Practice, T380
☑ **Informative Writing: Report**
Prewriting, T380–T381

RI.1.2, RI.1.3, RF.1.2a, RF.1.3g, W.1.2, W.1.5,
W.1.8, SL.1.1a, SL.1.3, L.1.1e, L.1.2d, L.1.4c,
L.1.6

 Go Digital

FOR STUDENTS

 my WriteSmart

- eBook
- GrammarSnap Videos
- Destination Reading
- Context Cards

FOR TEACHERS

- Teacher One-Stop
- Interactive Whiteboard Lessons
- Literacy and Language Guide

 Grab-and-Go!

- Lesson 14 Blackline Masters
- Additional Resources
- Assessment

DAY 1

Today's Goals

Vocabulary & Oral Language
- **Teacher Read Aloud:** "The Tortoise and the Hare"
- **Oral Vocabulary**
- **Listening Comprehension**
- **Model Fluency**

Phonemic Awareness
- **Substitute Phonemes**
- **Identify Middle Sound**

Phonics & Fluency
- **Words with Long *a* (CVCe)**
- **Read Decodable Reader:** *Tate's Cakes*
- **Fluency:** Expression

☑ WORDS TO KNOW

four	starts
five	three
into	two
over	watch

Text-Based Comprehension
- **Read and Comprehend**
- **Read the Anchor Text:** *The Big Race*

Grammar & Writing
- **Verbs and Time**
-  **Informative Writing:** Report

Spelling
- **Words with Long *a***

COMMON CORE **RF.1.2a** distinguish long from short vowel sounds in spoken single-syllable words; **RF.1.2c** isolate and pronounce sounds in spoken single-syllable words; **RF.1.3g** recognize and read irregularly spelled words; **SL.1.1a** follow rules for discussions; **L.1.4a** use sentence-level context as a clue to the meaning of a word or phrase **L.1.6** use words and phrases acquired through conversations, reading and being read to, and responding to texts

Opening Routines

Warm Up with Wordplay

Share a Riddle

Display and read the following riddle:

> ## How is a rule like a mirror?

Have children discuss possible answers to the riddle with a partner. Remind them to follow good discussion rules and to take turns speaking. Then read the answer: both can be broken.

Point out that this riddle works because *broken* is used to mean two different things. Ask children to tell what it means to break something, such as mirror. Then have them tell what it means to break a rule. Guide children to recognize that they have to use the other words in a sentence or phrase to decide which meaning of *broken* is meant. Tell children that this week they will be reading some selections and stories about rules and good citizenship.

 **SL.1.1a, L.3.4a**

Daily Phonemic Awareness

Identify Middle Sounds and Substitute Phonemes

- *We're going to change the vowel sound in a word to make a new word. Start with* tack. *What is its vowel sound?* /ă/ *Change the short a to long a,* /ā/. *What is the new word?* take *Let's keep going.* ■ RF.1.2a, RF.1.2c

Change the . . .	Result
/ă/ in *lack* to /ā/	lake
/ă/ in *sack* to /ŏ/	sock
/ă/ in *pan* to /ĕ/	pen
/ŏ/ in *shop* to /ā/	shape
/ă/ in *hat* to /ĭ/	hit

- Have children repeat the "Result" words, then tell whether the vowel sound is long or short. Long: lake, shape; Short: sock, pen, hit

Corrective Feedback

- If a child misses a word, say the correct word and model the task. *Listen to the word: lack, /l/ /ă/ /k/. Now change /ă/ to /ā/: /l/ /ā/ /k/. What is the new word? lake*

- Have children complete the task with you before doing it on their own.

- Then have them continue with the remaining words.

Daily High-Frequency Words

Introduce

- Point to the Words to Know on the Focus Wall. *Our Words to Know for this week are* four, five, into, over, starts, three, two, *and* watch. *You are going to see these words in your reading.*

- Use **Instructional Routine 10** and the **High-Frequency Word Card** to introduce the word *four*.

- Repeat the procedure with the words *five, into, over, starts, three, two,* and *watch*. ■ RF.1.3g

Corrective Feedback

- If a child is unable to recognize the word *four*, say the correct word and have children repeat it. Four. *What is the word? four*

- Have children spell the word. f,o,u,r *How do we say this word? four*

- Have children reread all of the cards in random order.

Daily Vocabulary Boost

- Have children think about a time they were in a race. Guide them to apply the Oral Vocabulary words from previous weeks to their own experiences by asking the following questions. Remind them to speak clearly when participating in a discussion.

  Did you ever try *to win a race? Tell about it.*

  How did you practice *to get ready?*

  During the race, were you dashing *along?*

  After the race, did you glow *with happiness?*

- Have children work together to explain *try, practice, dashing,* and *glow* in their own words. Encourage them to use these words in their everyday speech. ■ L.1.6

 ☑ Oral Vocabulary

try
practiced
dashing
glow

Teacher Read Aloud

▶ **SHARE OBJECTIVES**
- Listen for natural expression during reading.
- Ask and answer questions about a text read aloud.
- Retell a story, and tell the lesson it teaches.

Model Fluency

- Explain to children that good readers read in a smooth and natural way, as if they were having a conversation. *As you read aloud, try to read in a natural way, as if you were just talking to a friend.*

- Read the first sentence of "The Tortoise and the Hare" aloud, once in a natural way and once in a stilted way.

- *Which reading sounded natural to you? Why? What did I do to make the reading sound natural?*

- Read the entire selection aloud. Ask children to listen carefully to find out who wins the race and what each animal learns at the end.

COMMON CORE **RL.1.2** retell stories and demonstrate understanding of the message or lesson; **SL.1.1c** ask questions to clear up confusion about topics and texts under discussion; **SL.1.2** ask and answer questions about details in a text read aloud, information presented orally, or through other media; **SL.1.3** ask and answer questions about what a speaker says

The Tortoise and the Hare

This story is about a desert tortoise and a hare. The hare is also known as a jack-rabbit because it is always running around really fast. This hare was extra fast and he knew it. "I am as fast as lightning," he said. "No animal in the desert **habitat** is as fast as I am."

The tortoise **mainly** took things more slowly. He moved at his own pace and was proud of it. One day, tired of the hare bragging about his speed, he said, "Hare, you are fast indeed, but I would like to race you anyway."

The hare laughed and laughed. "I will certainly beat you in a race," he said. "You could **search** your whole life and never find a faster opponent!"

The tortoise insisted, so the tortoise and the hare set up at the starting line. The other animals of the desert—the prairie dog, the coyote, the rattlesnake, the scorpion, and all the others—gathered to watch.

The rattlesnake called, "Get ready!" and the coyote gave a **howl** to start the race. The hare started off like a shot. He was so fast that he bent the **stems** on the plants nearby. The tortoise went off at his usual steady pace.

Introduce Oral Vocabulary

Use **Instructional Routine 16** to define each highlighted oral vocabulary word.

- Discuss the meaning of each word as it is used in the story.

- For additional support and reinforcement, have children look up each word in a children's dictionary.

habitat the place in nature where a plant or animal lives • *"No animal in the desert habitat is as fast as I am."*

mainly for the most part • *The tortoise mainly took things more slowly.*

After two minutes, the hare stopped and looked back. He was so far ahead that he could not even see the tortoise behind him. "That silly tortoise will never catch up with me," he thought. "I will just take a rest and finish the race later." ③

So the hare sat down by a **cactus** and soon fell asleep by dreaming about carrot ice cream. He slept so well that he didn't notice the tortoise slowly plodding by. When the hare woke up, he quickly finished the race, but was shocked to find the tortoise already across the finish line!

All of the animals in the desert cheered when the prairie dog handed the tortoise the trophy. The coyote reminded the hare that "there are times to set a fast pace, but slow and steady wins the race." ④

search to look for something • *"You could search your whole life and never find a faster opponent!"*

howl a loud cry • *The rattlesnake called, "Get ready!" and the coyote gave a howl to start the race.*

stems the long parts of plants where the leaves and flowers grow • *He was so fast that he bent the stems on the plants nearby.*

cactus a plant with sharp spikes that grows in hot, dry places • *So the hare sat down by a cactus and soon fell asleep by dreaming about carrot ice cream.*

Listening Comprehension

Read aloud the story. Pause at the numbered stopping points to ask children the questions below. Discuss the meanings of the highlighted words, as needed, to support the discussion.
SL.1.2

① *How are the tortoise and the hare different? Sample answer: The tortoise is slow and steady. The hare is fast and jumpy.* **COMPARE AND CONTRAST**

② *What details tell you that this story is made-up? Sample answer: The animals think, talk, and have feelings like humans.* **GENRE**

③ *What does the rabbit do two minutes into the race? Sample answer: He decides to rest and finish the race later.* **UNDERSTANDING CHARACTERS**

④ *What are some lessons you can learn from this story? Sample answers: Do things in your own way, and at your own pace, and you will succeed. There are times to set a fast pace, but slow and steady wins the race.* **THEME**

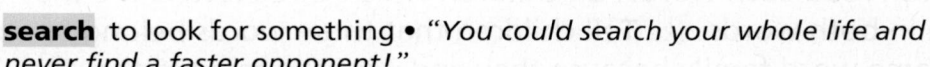

Classroom Collaboration

Begin a classroom discussion of the story by asking *What happened first? Then what happened? What happened last?* Then guide children to think about the lessons presented in the story. Have children ask and answer each other's questions about the lessons they learned from the story.
RL.1.2, SL.1.1c, SL.1.3

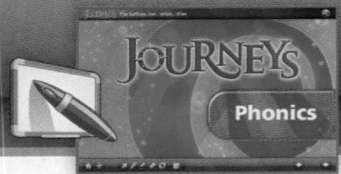
Phonemic Awareness/Phonics

▶ SHARE OBJECTIVES

- Isolate and pronounce medial sounds in words.
- Learn the sound-spelling correspondence for long *a* (CVCe).
- Blend and decode regularly spelled one-syllable words with *a_e*.

▶ SKILLS TRACE

Words with Long *a*	
▶ **Introduce**	**T318–T319**
Differentiate	T388
Reteach	T402
Review	T342, T364
Assess	Weekly Tests, Lesson 14

COMMON CORE **RF.1.2b** orally produce single-syllable words by blending sounds; **RF.1.2c** isolate and pronounce sounds in spoken single-syllable words; **RF.1.3b** decode regularly spelled one-syllable words; **RF.1.3c** know final -e and vowel team conventions for representing long vowel sounds; **RF.1.3g** recognize and read irregularly spelled words; **SL.1.6** produce complete sentences when appropriate to task and situation

Words with Long *a* (CVCe)

PHONEMIC AWARENESS WARM-UP Guide children to identify the middle sound in words. *I am going to say a word. Listen for the middle sound. The word is tack, /t/ /ă/ /k/. The middle sound is /ă/. Let's do another one: pace, /p/ /ā/ /s/. The middle sound is /ā/.*

Now you try. Listen: pick. What is the middle sound in pick? /ĭ/ Repeat with these words: *shop /ŏ/, bet /ĕ/, mate /ā/, lane /ā/.*
◼ **RF.1.2c**

1 Teach/Model

SOUND/SPELLING CARDS Display the card for *acorn*. Name the picture and say the sound. Have children repeat after you. *Listen: acorn, /ā/. Now you say it.*

- Point to the *a_e* spelling pattern. *When you see the letter a followed by a consonant and an e, the letter a will often stand for the long a sound, /ā/.*

- Write and read *made*. Cover the *e*. Read *mad*, pointing out the /ă/ sound. Uncover the *e* and point out the *a*-consonant-*e* pattern. Have children read *made*. Repeat with the words *pane* and *tape*.

PHONOGRAM -ake List *bake* and *take* on the board, and have children read each word. Ask children which three letters are the same in both words. *ake* Tell children that these words belong to the same word family because they end with the same letters and sounds. Guide children to list more -*ake* words such as *cake, fake, lake, make,* and *rake*. List them on the board and have children read them. ◼ **RF.1.3c**

2 Guided Practice

CONTINUOUS BLENDING ROUTINE Use **Instructional Routine 3** to model blending *cape*. Write the word *cape* on the board.
☐ **RF.1.2b, RF.1.3b, RF.1.3c**

• Point to **Sound/Spelling Card** *acorn* and remind children that knowing sound/spellings for /ā/ can help them when they read.

• Display **Letter Cards** *c, a, p,* and *e.*

• Blend the sounds. *Listen: /k/ /ā/ /p/.* Have children blend with you. *Now you blend the sounds. /k/ /ā/ /p/*

REPEAT CONTINUOUS BLENDING ROUTINE with the words in Row 1 below. Then write the words in Rows 1–3 and have children read them. Use the **Corrective Feedback** steps if children need additional help.

• Repeat until children are reading at a rate of three seconds per word.

DECODING Write the two sentences on the board. Call on individuals to blend one or more words and to read the sentences. ☐ **RF.1.3b, RF.1.3c, RF.1.3g**

1. take	plane	gave	made	lane
2. shake	crash	whale	shade	she's
3. gate	chase	it's	sat	whip

**Dave came and gave <u>me some</u> grapes.
<u>I</u> ate <u>the</u> cake that Jake made.**

3 Apply  Hands-on Practice

Have partners use letter cards to take turns building and reading words with long *a* and the *a_e* pattern. After reading a word, each partner should use the word in a sentence. ☐ **RF.1.3b, RF.1.3c, SL.2.6**

Corrective Feedback Work with the whole group to correct errors, following the model below.

Phonics Error:
A child reads *shake* as *shack*.

Correct the error. Review the **Sound/Spelling Card**. Say the word and the sound. *The word is shake. The a-consonant-e tells us that the letter a stands for the sound /ā/.*

Model as you touch the letters. *I'll blend: /sh/ /ā/ /k/. What is the word? shake*

Guide *Let's blend together: /sh/ /ā/ /k/. What is the word? shake*

Check *You blend: /sh/ /ā/ /k/. What is the word? shake*

Reinforce Go back three or four words and have children continue reading. Make note of errors and review those words during tomorrow's lesson.

SMALL GROUP Options Go to p. T388 for additional phonics support.

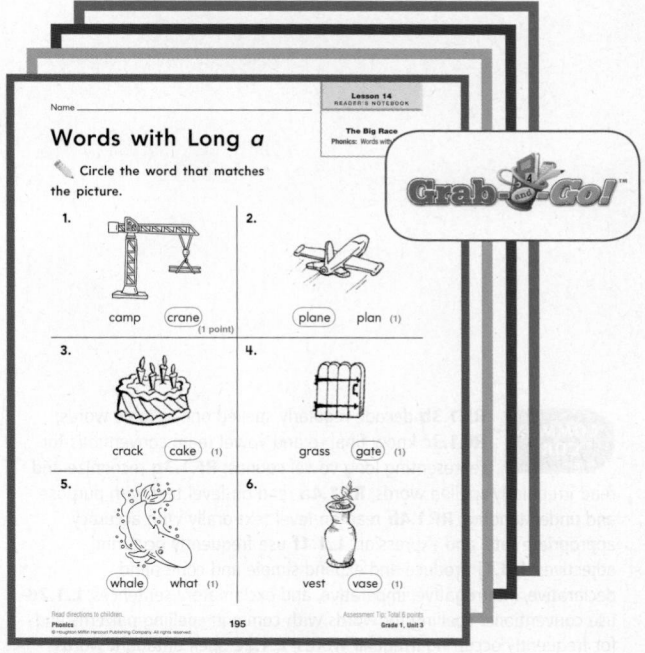

Reader's Notebook Vol. 1 p. 195
See Grab-and-Go™ Resources for additional leveled practice.

• Interactive Whiteboard Lesson
• Decodable Reader

Phonics/Spelling

▶ **SHARE OBJECTIVES**

• Write words with long *a* (CVCe).
• Decode text with regularly spelled one-syllable words with long *a* and high-frequency words.
• Practice reading on-level text accurately with fluency and expression.

▶ **DICTATION SENTENCES**

• **whale.** A **whale** is an animal.
• **name.** His **name** is Ron.
• **shake.** I can **shake** this can.
• **plate.** That is my **plate**.
• **save.** Will you **save** some grapes for me?
• **wake.** When did you **wake** up?

COMMON CORE

RF.1.3b decode regularly spelled one-syllable words; **RF.1.3c** know final -e and vowel team conventions for representing long vowel sounds; **RF.1.3g** recognize and read irregularly spelled words; **RF.1.4a** read on-level text with purpose and understanding; **RF.1.4b** read on-level text orally with accuracy, appropriate rate, and expression; **L.1.1f** use frequently occurring adjectives; **L.1.1j** produce and expand simple and compound declarative, interrogative, imperative, and exclamatory sentences; **L.1.2d** use conventional spelling for words with common spelling patterns and for frequently occurring irregular words; **L.1.2e** spell untaught words phonetically, drawing on phonemic awareness and spelling conventions

Write Words with Long *a* (CVCe)

1 Teach/Model

CONNECT SOUNDS TO SPELLING Review **Sound/Spelling Card** *acorn*. Tell children that they will now write words with /ā/.

Use **Instructional Routine 6** to dictate, using the first sentence at the left. *Listen as I say each word and use it in a sentence.*

• Model how to spell *whale*. Point to the *a_e* spelling on the **Sound/Spelling Card** *acorn*. *I know that the letter a followed by a consonant and e can stand for /ā/ in this word. I'll begin the word with the letters* wh. *I will write the letter a before the consonant* l *and e after it. Now I'll reread to check the whole word:* whale.

2 Guided Practice

CONNECT SOUNDS TO WRITING Continue the dictation, using the sentences at the left.

• Have children say each word aloud after you. Then have children identify the sounds they hear at the beginning, middle, and end, and write the letters that stand for each sound. **L.1.2e**

• Remind children to write only the dictation word.

3 Apply

• Read aloud the following sentence for children to write.

> Kate gave Nate <u>some</u> cake.

• Remind children that *some* is a Word to Know they learned in a previous lesson.

• Print the dictation words and the sentences for children to check their work. **L.1.2d**

Decodable Reader

 Go Digital

Read *Tate's Cakes*

Decodable Reader, Unit 3, pp. 75–80

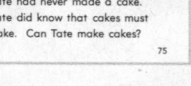

REVIEW /ā/ AND WORDS TO KNOW Tell children that many words in this story have the *a*-consonant-*e* pattern, which often stands for the long *a* sound. Point out that children have learned the following words, which they will also read in the story: *four, five, into, over.*

PREVIEW Have children preview pages 75–77 and predict what the story is about. Ask volunteers to tell about a time they helped to cook or bake something.

MODEL FLUENCY AND EXPRESSION Read aloud page 75 as children follow along. As you read have children note that you are reading the way you would speak, sounding like you are curious. Lead children in choral reading the page with fluency and expression.

READ Remind children to track the words from left to right and when they come to the end of a line, to sweep their hand down to the beginning of the next line and continue reading. Have children read each page silently and then choral read it. Have them read to find out if Tate bakes some cakes.
▪ RF.1.3b, RF.1.3c, RF.1.3g, RF.1.4a

RESPONDING Have children look at Jade's cakes. Ask them to draw a picture of the cake they would like to get. Then have them write sentences about the cake. Brainstorm some adjectives children can use to describe how the cake looks, smells, and tastes before they write their sentences. ▪ L.1.1f, L.1.1j

Corrective Feedback Work with the whole group to correct errors, following the model below.

Decoding Error:
A child reads *bake* as *back*.

Correct the error. Say the word. *That word is bake. The middle sound is /ā/. The letter a followed by a consonant and e often stands for the long a sound, /ā/.*

Guide Have children repeat the word. *What is the word? bake*

Check *Go back to the beginning of the sentence and read it again.*

Reinforce Record the error and review the word again before children reread the story.

 SMALL GROUP Options

Go to p. T388 for additional phonics support.

Reread for Fluency/ Develop Automaticity

READ WITH A PARTNER Have partners reread *Tate's Cakes* three or four times, taking turns reading aloud each page. Remind them to read words correctly and to read smoothly. Visit partners to listen to them read. Give feedback about reading accurately, at an appropriate rate, and with expression, and provide guidance for improving fluency. ▪ RF.1.4b

Go Digital
• eBook
• Context Cards
• Vocabulary Reader

Introduce Words to Know

▶ SHARE OBJECTIVE
• Recognize and read irregularly spelled words.

Teach

Display and discuss the **Vocabulary in Context Cards,** using the routine below. See also **Instructional Routine 15.**

1 **Read and pronounce the word.** Read the word once alone and then together.

2 **Explain the word.** Read aloud the explanation under *What Does It Mean?*

3 **Discuss vocabulary in context.** Together, read aloud the sentence on the front of the card. Help children explain and use the word in new sentences.

4 **Engage with the word.** Ask and discuss *How Do I Use It?*

Practice/Apply

Give partners or small groups one or two **Vocabulary in Context Cards.** Help children complete the *Talk It Over* activities for each card. **RF.1.3g**

COMMON CORE **RF.1.3g** recognize and read irregularly spelled words

---

Lesson 14

The Big Race
written by Pam Muñoz Ryan
Illustrated by Viviana Garofoli

Rules and Laws

✓ WORDS TO KNOW
High-Frequency Words

two
into
three
starts
over
four
five
watch

Vocabulary Reader

Desert Animals

Context Cards

COMMON CORE **RF.1.3g** recognize and read irregularly spelled words

120 Go Digital

Words to Know

Read Together

▶ Read each **Context Card.**

▶ Use a blue word to tell about something you did.

1 **two**
Two desert lizards are sitting on the rock.

2 **into**
The bird flew into the big cactus.

ELL ENGLISH LANGUAGE LEARNERS
Comprehensible Input

Beginning Hold up two fingers and say *How many fingers am I holding up? Two.* Then hold up three fingers and repeat the question. Continue with *four* and *five.* Have children repeat each number after you, holding up their own fingers.

High Intermediate Have children complete these sentence frames: *I have two _____. A tricycle has three _____. A car has four _____. I have five _____.*

Low Intermediate Hold up two fingers and ask *How many fingers am I holding up?* Continue with *three, four,* and *five.*

Proficient Have children write sentences using the numbers *two, three, four,* and *five.*

See ELL Lesson 14, p. E32, for vocabulary support.

3 three
There are three birds resting in the sun.

4 starts
The desert starts to cool down at sunset.

5 over
A hawk flew over the tall rocks.

6 four
All four legs of this fox are strong.

7 five
This desert flower has five red spots.

8 watch
The rabbits watch and listen for danger.

121

DAILY ASSESSMENT — RtI

Are children able to understand and use the Words to Know?

IF...	THEN...
children have difficulty understanding and using Words to Know,	▶ use **Vocabulary in Context Cards** and the Struggling Readers activity, p. T390. *See also Intervention Lesson 14, pp. S32–S41.*
children can understand and use most Words to Know,	▶ use **Vocabulary in Context Cards** and the On Level activity, p. T390.
children can understand and use all Words to Know,	▶ use the Advanced activity, p. T391.

SMALL GROUP Options

Vocabulary Reader pp. T390–T391
Provide support for English Language Learners according to language proficiency. See also Differentiate Words to Know, p. T389.

VOCABULARY IN CONTEXT CARDS 85–92

front

back

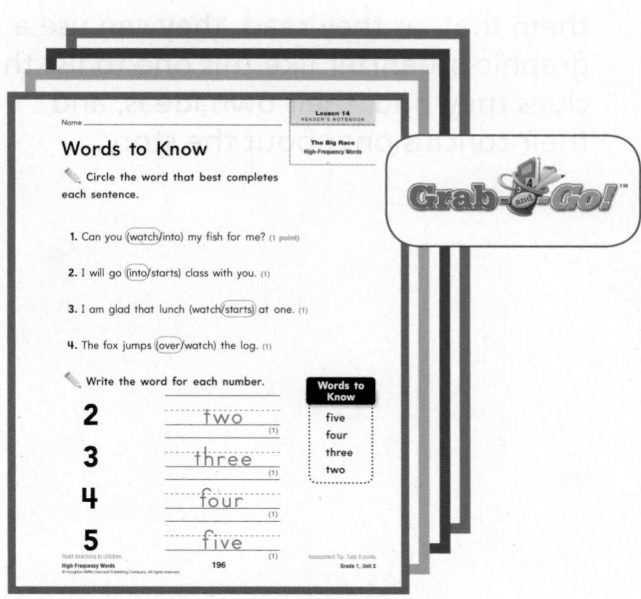

Reader's Notebook Vol. 1 p. 196
See Grab-and-Go™ Resources for additional leveled practice.

Introduce Words to Know (SB p. 121) • **T323**

Read and Comprehend

- Use text evidence and prior knowledge to draw conclusions about a story.
- Infer and predict while reading a story to aid comprehension.

☑ TARGET SKILL
Conclusions

- Read **Student Book** p. 122 with children.

- Tell children that sometimes authors do not give all the details in a story.

- Explain that readers must use clues in the words and pictures and think about what they already know to make a smart guess about what the author does not tell.

- Tell them the smart guess is called a **conclusion** and that often people say that when you are making a smart guess, you are **drawing a conclusion.**

- Draw children's attention to the graphic organizer on **Student Book** p. 122. Tell them that, as they read, they can use a graphic organizer like this one to list the clues they find, their own ideas, and their conclusions about the story.

Read and Comprehend

☑ TARGET SKILL

Conclusions Sometimes authors do not tell all the details in a story. Readers must use clues in the words and pictures and think about what they already know. This will help them make a smart guess about what the author does not tell. This smart guess is a **conclusion**. Use a chart to list the clues and your conclusions.

```
┌────────┐   ┌────────┐   ┌────────┐
│  Clue  │   │  Clue  │   │  Clue  │
└────────┘   └────────┘   └────────┘
     │            │            │
     └────────────┼────────────┘
                  ▼
       ┌────────────────────┐
       │     Conclusion     │
       └────────────────────┘
```

☑ TARGET STRATEGY

Infer/Predict Use text evidence to help you think of what might happen next.

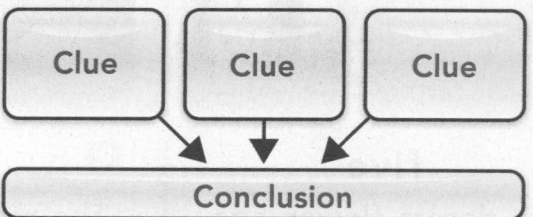

122 COMMON CORE · **RL.1.3** describe characters, settings, and major events; **RL.1.7** use illustrations and details to describe characters, setting, or events

---

SELECTION VOCABULARY

Tell children they may see words they do not recognize as they read *The Big Race*. Write the Selection Vocabulary words on the board and read them with children. Share the explanations with them.

cottontail a kind of rabbit

hay a dry grass that some animals eat

hooray a shout of joy or praise

lizard a reptile with scaly skin, a thin body, four legs, and a long tail

race a contest of speed

roadrunner a bird with a long feathered tail that can run quickly

Cross at the cross walk. This rule keeps you safe. **Wash your hands.** This rule keeps you healthy. Following rules makes you a good classmate. It makes you a good neighbor, too. What rules do you follow at school? What rules do you follow at home? What rules do you follow when you play?

When you read **The Big Race,** think about the rules and the different ways the animals race.

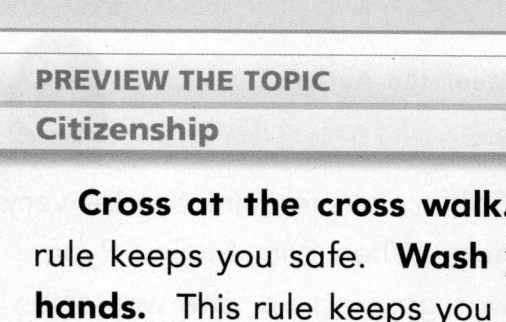

123

COMPREHENSION STRATEGIES

Use the following strategies flexibly as you read with children by modeling how they can be used to improve comprehension. See scaffolded support for the strategy shown in boldface during this week's reading.

- Monitor/Clarify
- Summarize
- **Infer/Predict**
- Visualize
- Analyze/Evaluate
- Question
- Phonics/Decoding

Use the Strategy Projectables, S1–S8, for additional support.

DOMAIN: **Civics**
- -
LESSON TOPIC: Citizenship

☑ TARGET STRATEGY
Infer/Predict

- Read the bottom of **Student Book** p. 122 with children.

- Tell children that they should look for clues, called **text evidence**, in the words and pictures of a story to help them figure out important ideas.

- Explain that good readers are like detectives—they think about these clues to figure out things the author does not say in the words.

- Tell children that good readers use what they have read and figured out in a story to make a good guess, or **predict**, what might happen next.

- Then explain that you will show them how they should use the Infer/Predict strategy when you read together.

Preview the Topic: Citizenship

- Tell children that today they will begin reading *The Big Race*.

- Read the information on **Student Book** p. 123 with children.

- Then write on the board the words *good citizen* and *citizenship*. Have children explain their understanding of what a good citizen and citizenship are using the information in the text and their own experiences.

- Have children describe what is happening in the photo on **Student Book** p. 123, using the words *rules, good citizen,* and *citizenship*. Expand the discussion to talk about why it is important to be good citizens in school and in the community. Have children describe ways they can be a responsible citizen at school and in their community.

Read the Anchor Text

☑ TARGET SKILL
Conclusions

- Point out the graphic organizer on **Student Book** p. 124 to children.

- Tell children that this kind of graphic organizer can help them list clues and draw conclusions about a story.

☑ GENRE **Fantasy**

- Read the genre information on **Student Book** p. 124 with children.

- Preview the story with children, and model identifying the characteristics of a fantasy.

Think Aloud *A fantasy tells about events that do not happen in real life. The Big Race seems to be a story about a group of animals that run in a race like people do. Animals do not wear numbers and run in races in real life, so I think this story is a fantasy.*

- *How do the illustrations help you know that* The Big Race *is a fantasy? The illustrations show animals wearing clothes, talking, and acting like people.*

- As you preview, ask children to point out other features of fantasies.

 **RL.1.10** read prose and poetry; **RF.1.4a** read on-level text with purpose and understanding

---

Lesson 14
ANCHOR TEXT

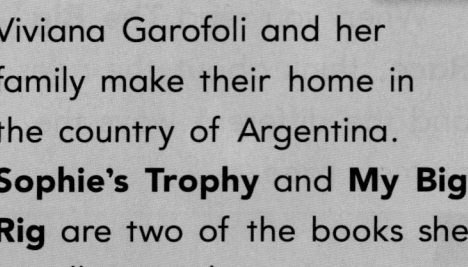
The Big Race
written by Pam Muñoz Ryan
Illustrated by Viviana Garofoli

☑ TARGET SKILL

Conclusions Use clues and what you know to figure out more about a story.

☑ GENRE

A **fantasy** could not happen in real life. As you read, look for:
▶ animals who talk and act like people
▶ events that could not really happen

 **RL.1.3** describe characters, settings, and major events; **RL.1.7** use illustrations and details to describe characters, setting, or events; **RL.1.10** read prose and poetry

124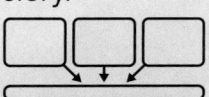

Meet the Author
Pam Muñoz Ryan

California summers can be very hot. When Pam Muñoz Ryan was growing up, she was often at the library on summer days. That's because the library was one of the few places nearby with air conditioning!

Meet the Illustrator
Viviana Garofoli

Viviana Garofoli and her family make their home in the country of Argentina. **Sophie's Trophy** and **My Big Rig** are two of the books she has illustrated.

🔲 RL.1.10

Scaffold Close Reading

Think Through the Text	Analyze the Text	Independent Reading
FIRST READ	**SECOND READ**	
Develop comprehension through	Support analyzing short sections of text:	• Children analyze the text independently, using the Reader's Guide on pp. 202–203 of the **Reader's Notebook**. (See p. T356 for instructional support.)
• Guided Questioning	• Conclusions	
• Target Strategy: Infer/Predict	• Cause and Effect	
• Vocabulary in Context	Use directed note-taking by working with children to complete a graphic organizer during reading. Distribute copies of Graphic Organizer 7.	• Children read independently in a self-selected trade book.
IF children demonstrate understanding of what the story is mostly about,		
THEN provide additional challenge using the questions labeled A Closer Look.		

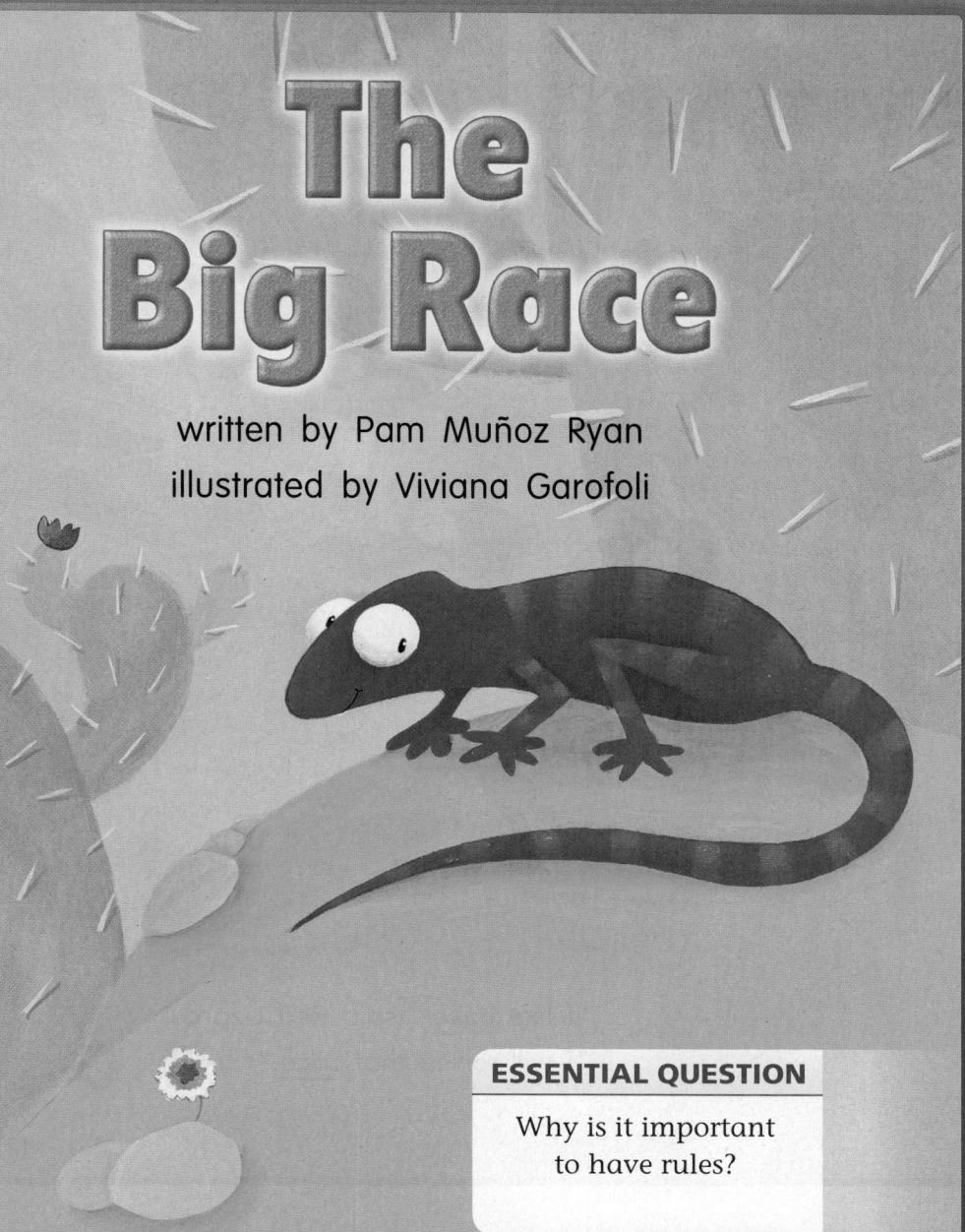

The Big Race

written by Pam Muñoz Ryan

illustrated by Viviana Garofoli

ESSENTIAL QUESTION

Why is it important to have rules?

125

Anchor Text (SB p. 125) • **T327**

ESSENTIAL QUESTION

- Read aloud and discuss the Essential Question on **Student Book** p. 125: *Why is it important to have rules?* Tell children to think about this question as they read *The Big Race*.

Predictive Writing

- Write the Essential Question on the board.

- Explain that children will work with a partner to write about what they expect *The Big Race* to be about. Tell them to think about how the Essential Question relates to what they noticed while previewing the story or what they already know about the Essential Question from their own experiences with races.

- Guide children to think about the genre as they write. Then discuss children's predictions.

Set Purpose

- Tell children that good readers set a purpose for reading. *Look at the pictures in the story. Think about what you know about a fantasy. What do you hope to enjoy about* The Big Race?

- Model setting a reading purpose.

Think Aloud *The title tells me the story is about a race. The illustration shows a lizard in the desert. I wonder who will be in the race and who will win. I will read to find out.*

- Have children set their own purpose for reading. Ask volunteers to share their purpose for reading. Then have children read the story. ◼ RL.1.10, RF.1.4a

READER AND TASK CONSIDERATIONS

Determine the level of additional support your children will need to read and comprehend *The Big Race* successfully.

READERS

- **Motivate** Ask children to tell about rules at school or in the community that they think are good to have. Have them tell why.

- **Access Knowledge and Experiences** Remind children of the Preview the Topic information on **Student Book** p. 123. Ask them to share with a partner what they recall, and if possible, share one other thing they know about following the rules and being a good citizen.

TASKS

- **Increase Scaffolding** Stop periodically as you read to have children retell events that happen and tell what causes them to happen.

- **Foster Independence** Have children read the story in small groups. Tell them to pause throughout the story to ask any questions they have about the characters, setting, or events. Have them look together for text evidence in the words and pictures to help them answer the questions.

Today is the big <u>race</u>. **1**

126

"I like <u>cake</u>!" said Red Lizard.
"I will run in that <u>race</u>." **2** **3**

127

 **DOMAIN: Civics**

LESSON TOPIC: Citizenship

Cross-Curricular Connection Remind children that there are rules they have to follow when they are at school. Explain that when they follow rules at school, they are being good citizens. Have children identify several rules of the school or classroom. Then have them explain why we have rules at school and in the community. Discuss with children their rights and responsibilities in the school community. Then have children explain them in their own words.

COMMON CORE **RL.1.1** ask and answer questions about key details; **RL.1.3** describe characters, settings, and major events; **RL.1.7** use illustrations and details to describe characters, setting, or events; **RF.1.3b** decode regularly spelled one-syllable words; **RF.1.3g** recognize and read irregularly spelled words

---

FIRST READ

Think Through the Text

1 *What can we tell about the race from p. 126?* There is a race today. The prize for the winner is a big cake. ◼ RL.1.7

2 *Why does Red Lizard want to run in the race?* Red Lizard wants to win the cake. ◼ RL.1.1, RL.1.3

3 *Why does the author let us know that Red Lizard likes cake?* The author wants to give a reason why Red Lizard wants to race. ◼ RL.1.1

KEY: ☑ **WORDS TO KNOW**
High-Frequency Words
Decodable Words with
Long a: a_e

COMMON CORE

DAY 1

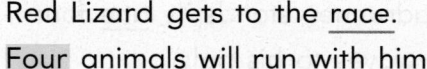

Red Lizard gets to the race.
Four animals will run with him.

128

Cottontail is not late.
She will run in lane one.

129

☑ TARGET STRATEGY: Infer/Predict

Reread **Student Book** pp. 128–129 with children, and
model the Infer/Predict strategy. Then guide them to
use the strategy as they continue reading.

Think Aloud   *There are many clues in the illustrations
and text on pages 128–129. I read that Red Lizard is at
the race and four animals will run with him. The author
didn't say it, but I figured out that five animals will be
in the race. I read that Cottontail was not late and she
is wearing number one. Red Lizard will wear number
five. I can infer that Cottontail got to the race first and
Red Lizard got to the race last. I predict that Cottontail
will run faster than Red Lizard because she is bigger
and she got to the race on time.*

Rat naps in the shade.
She will run in lane two.

Snake takes his spot in lane three.
Roadrunner stands in lane four.
He waves to his pals.

130

131

COMMON CORE
RL.1.1 ask and answer questions about key details;
RL.1.3 describe characters, settings, and major events;
RL.1.7 use illustrations and details to describe characters, setting, or events; **RF.1.3b** decode regularly spelled one-syllable words;
RF.1.3g recognize and read irregularly spelled words

FIRST READ

Use Text Evidence

Think Through the Text

4 *What is rat doing? She is taking a nap in the shade.* ◼ RL.1.1

▶ A Closer Look

Describe Rat based on what you've read and seen in pictures so far. She is a small, pink rat with a red bow on her head. She might be tired, because she is taking a nap. She might be lazy. How does Rat act differently from the other animals before the race? Rat rests before the race. The other animals are in their lanes, getting ready. ◼ RL.1.3, RL.1.7

KEY: ☑ **WORDS TO KNOW**
High-Frequency Words ▬
Decodable Words with ▬
Long *a*: *a_e*

COMMON CORE

DAY 1

Get set.

Go!

Red Lizard is in <u>lane</u> <u>five</u>.
The animals bend and hop.

132

The flag is down, and the <u>race</u> starts! **5**
Many animals watch and clap. **6**

133

5 *What happens when Tortoise puts the flag down?*
The race begins. **Describe what you think the animals
do when the flag goes down.** *They start running as
fast as they can.* ▬ **RL.1.1, RL.1.3**

6 *What do the animals in the crowd do when the
race starts?* *They watch and clap.* **How do the animals
in the crowd feel about the race?** *They are excited.*
▬ **RL.1.3**

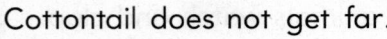

Cottontail does not get far.

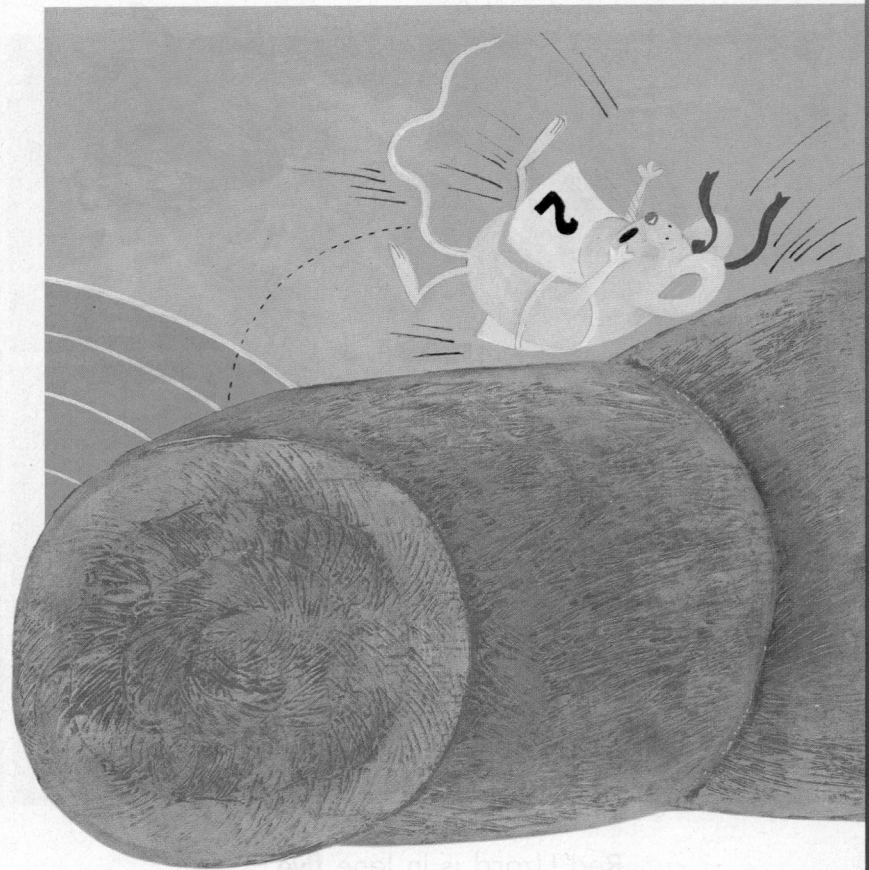

Rat falls into the hay.

134

135

Question IF children have difficulty applying the Infer/Predict strategy, **THEN** use this model:

Think Aloud *I predicted Cottontail would run faster than Red Lizard, but that was wrong. I will use other story clues to make a new prediction. Roadrunner has the longest legs and is still in the race. I predict he will win.*

Have children share what they infer/predict after reading pp. 136–137.

RL.1.1 ask and answer questions about key details;
RL.1.3 describe characters, settings, and major events;
RL.1.7 use illustrations and details to describe characters, setting, or events

FIRST READ

Use Text Evidence

Think Through the Text

7 *On page pp. 134–135, why does Cottontail stop running in the race?* Cottontail sees a butterfly and follows it. *Why does Rat stop running in the race?* Rat falls into some hay. *How many animals are left in the race?* three **RL.1.1, RL.1.3**

▸ A Closer Look

Why does Red Lizard have a better chance of winning now? Red Lizard has a better chance of winning because there are fewer animals in the race that he will need to beat.
RL.1.1

KEY: ☑ **WORDS TO KNOW**
High-Frequency Words
Decodable Words with
Long a: a_e

COMMON
CORE

DAY 1

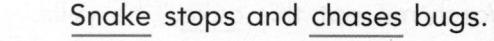
Snake stops and chases bugs. **8**

136

Roadrunner trips over a rake.
Who will win?

137

8 *Describe how Snake and Cottontail are alike.* They both stop racing when they see some bugs.
  🔲 RL.1.1, RL.1.3, RL.1.7

☑ TARGET STRATEGY: Infer/Predict

Help children apply the Infer/Predict Strategy after reading **Student Book** pp. 136–137. Ask several children to tell what they inferred and predicted and identify the text evidence from the words and illustrations that helped them. Guide children to predict how the race will end and then read on to confirm their prediction.

SECOND READ DAY 2

ANALYZE THE TEXT

Cause and Effect Remind children that one event in a story can cause another event to happen. Have children use text evidence to describe why Cottontail leaves the race. *Cottontail runs off to chase a pretty butterfly. This causes her to leave the race.* Point out that the **cause** is *Cottontail chases the butterfly* and the **effect** is *Cottontail leaves the race.* As children continue reading, guide them to identify similar cause-and-effect relationships to explain why Rat, Snake, and Roadrunner leave the race. Lead them to realize that the causes are different for each animal, but the effect is the same: The animal leaves the race and doesn't win. 🔲 RL.1.3, RL.1.7

Hip, Hip, Hooray!

5

It's Red Lizard who wins! **9**

138

"Watch me eat this <u>cake</u>," he yells.
Red Lizard looks at his big <u>cake</u>. **10**

139

ELL **ENGLISH LANGUAGE LEARNERS**
Comprehensible Input

Beginning Have children echo-read pages 138–141. Use intonation and expression to emphasize the emotions of the passages and the suspense of what Red Lizard will do.

Low Intermediate Have children describe the pictures in simple sentences.

High Intermediate Ask children: *What words help you guess what Red Lizard will do?*

Proficient Have children describe details that help them guess what Red Lizard will do.

RL.1.1 ask and answer questions about key details; **RL.1.3** describe characters, settings, and major events; **RL.1.7** use illustrations and details to describe characters, setting, or events; **RF.1.3b** decode regularly spelled one-syllable words; **RF.1.3c** know final -*e* and vowel team conventions for representing long vowel sounds; **RF.1.3g** recognize and read irregularly spelled words

---

FIRST READ

Use Text Evidence

Think Through the Text

☑ Phonics/Decoding Strategy

Use **Projectable S1** to help children apply the Phonics/Decoding strategy while reading p. 139. Write *cake*. Model blending the sounds: /k/ /ā/ /k/, *cake*. Have children repeat. Review with them that the *e* is silent. Then reread the page together to make sure *cake* makes sense. 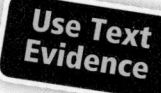 **RF.1.3b, RF.1.3c**

9 *Who wins the race?* Red Lizard *What does Red Lizard say when he wins?* Hip, Hip Hooray! *How does Red Lizard feel about winning the race?* He is excited, happy, and proud.
 RL.1.1, RL.1.3, RL.3.7

Red Lizard looks at his pals.

140

His pals like <u>cake</u>, too.
What will Red Lizard do now? **11**

141

10 *Why does Red Lizard get the cake?* He won the race. ▭ **RL.1.1**

11 *How do you think Red Lizard's pals feel? What text evidence helps you know?* They feel sad because they wish they had the cake. The picture shows their sad faces. The words say that they like cake. *What do you think Red Lizard will do next?* Red Lizard might decide to share the cake with his pals. ▭ **RL.1.3, RL.1.7**

SECOND READ **DAY 2**

ANALYZE THE TEXT

🗂 **14.2**

Conclusions Display **Projectable 14.2,** and distribute **Graphic Organizer 7.** Explain that the author does not tell exactly what kind of character Red Lizard is, but instead lets us make smart guesses, or draw **conclusions,** based on the things Red Lizard does. Ask children to describe what each character does during and after the race, and add these events as Clues to the Inference Map. Guide children to draw conclusions with questions like the following, and add the clues and their conclusions to the Inference Map: *What kind of racer is Red Lizard? What kind of friend is he? What story clues help you draw these conclusions?* ▭ **RL.1.3, RL.3.7**

Red Lizard gets five <u>plates</u>.
He gets <u>cake</u> for his pals, too. **12**
Hip, Hip, Hooray for Red Lizard!

142

143

Think Through the Text

12 *What does Red Lizard do with his cake?* He shares it with his pals. *Is this what you predicted would happen? Why or why not?* Yes, because the cake is big, so Red Lizard has enough to share. Also, the animals are his friends. 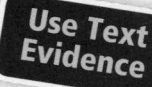 **RL.1.3**

▶ A Closer Look

What does Red Lizard do to show that he is a good pal? Red Lizard shares the cake. *How do you think his pals feel now? What text evidence helps you know?* happy; The story says they like cake. They each have a piece of cake and look happy. They say, "Hip, Hip, Hooray."  **RL.1.3, RL.3.7**

 **COMMON CORE** **RL.1.2** retell stories and demonstrate understanding of the message or lesson; **RL.1.3** describe characters, settings, and major events, **RL.3.7** use illustrations and details to describe characters, setting, or events

Guided Retelling

Oral Language Use the prompts on the **Retelling Cards** to guide children to retell the story, describing characters, settings, and the important events. Have them explain what the main message of the story is. 🔲 **RL.1.2, RL.1.3**

front

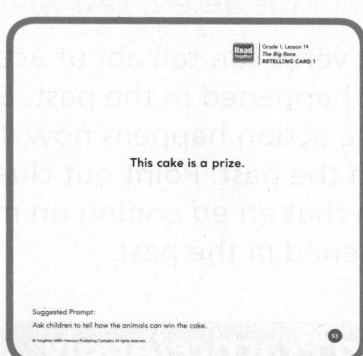

back

This cake is a prize.

front

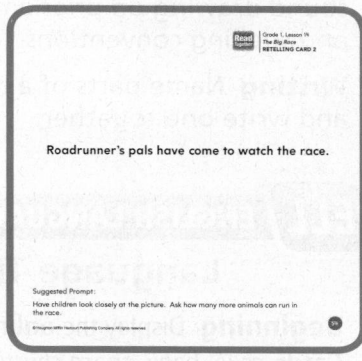

back

Roadrunner's pals have come to watch the race.

front

back

Red Lizard wins the race!

front

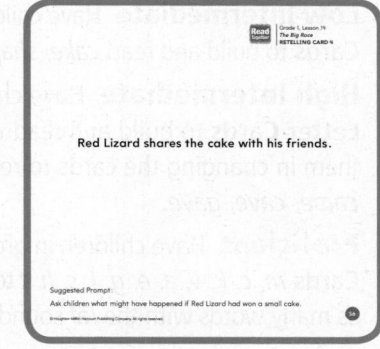

back

Red Lizard shares the cake with his friends.

RETELLING RUBRIC	
4 Highly Effective	The child describes the plot (problem and solution); retells the beginning, middle, and end, with attention to the sequence of events; describes the characters and the reasons for their actions and feelings; requires little or no prompting.
3 Generally Effective	The child describes most of the plot; retells most of the beginning, middle, and end, with some attention to the sequence of events; describes the characters and may provide some reasons for their actions and feelings; may require some prompting.
2 Somewhat Effective	The child describes some plot details; retells some of the beginning, middle, and end, with some omissions or errors; describes some of the characters; requires some prompting.
1 Ineffective	The child retells few, if any, details about the story elements, possibly with errors; is unable to retell the story without prompting.

Go Digital
- *my*WriteSmart
- eBook
- GrammarSnap Videos
- Literacy and Language Guide
- Interactive Whiteboard Lesson

Grammar Introduce Verbs and Time

▶ SHARE OBJECTIVES

- **Grammar** Learn about present and past tense verbs.
- **Spelling** Spell words with the long *a* sound drawing on phonemic awareness and spelling conventions.
- **Writing** Name parts of a research report and write one together.

ELL ENGLISH LANGUAGE LEARNERS
Language Transfer

Beginning Display the **online Picture Cards** *cake, baby, space shuttle*. Read the words aloud and have children clap whenever they hear the /ā/ sound.

Low Intermediate Have children use **Letter Cards** to build and read *cake, shape, make*.

High Intermediate Have children use **Letter Cards** to build and read *cake*. Guide them in changing the cards to read *make, came, cave, gave*.

Proficient Have children in groups use **Letter Cards** *m, c, k, v, a, e, g, l, s, h, t* to build and read as many words with the /ā/ sound as they can.

1 Teach/Model

- Model using verbs that tell about present and past time. *Today we* learn *about the desert. Last week we* learned *about seasons.*

- Explain that verbs can tell about actions that happen now, and actions that happened in the past. Explain that in the first sentence, the action happens now. In the second, the action happened in the past. Point out clue words *today* and *last week*. Also explain that an *ed* ending on many verbs shows that the action happened in the past.

2 Guided Practice/Apply

- Use the verbs in the chart to model sentences with actions that happen now and that happened in the past. Then have children work with partners to complete these sentences: *Today I _____. Yesterday I _____.*

Present Time	Past Time
walk	walked
play	played
talk	talked

- Have children create additional past and present tense sentences of their own. Write examples on the board and have children point to the base word and *-ed* endings. 🔲 SL.1.6, L.1.1e, L.1.4c

Spelling Words with Long *a*

SPELLING WORDS AND SENTENCES

BASIC

1. *came*
   Sam *came* to my party.

2. *make*
   Will you *make* me a cake?

3. *brave*
   He was *brave* and did not cry.

4. *late*
   Don't be *late* for school.

5. *gave*
   I *gave* Maria a ride on my bike.

6. *shape*
   The cake was in a round *shape*.

CHALLENGE

7. *waves*
   Big *waves* crashed on the beach.

8. *chases*
   My cat always *chases* his tail.

Administer the Pretest

Say the first word and read the sentence. Have children try to spell the untaught words phonetically, drawing on phonemic awareness and spelling conventions. Repeat the word as children write it. Write the word on the board and have children correct their spelling if needed. Repeat for words 2–8. 🔲 L.1.2e

Teach the Principle

Review **Sound/Spelling Card** *acorn*. List *came, late*, and *gave*, underlining the *a* and *e* in each word. Say the words aloud. Explain that the *a*-consonant-*e* pattern can stand for the long *a* sound.

COMMON CORE

W.1.2 write informative/explanatory texts; **W.1.5** focus on a topic, respond to questions/suggestions from peers, and add details to strengthen writing; **SL.1.6** produce complete sentences when appropriate to task and situation; **L.1.1e** use verbs to convey sense of past, present, and future; **L.1.1j** produce and expand simple and compound declarative, interrogative, imperative, and exclamatory sentences; **L.1.2e** spell untaught words

Informative Writing Introduce the Model

1 Teach/Model

- Explain that a report tells facts about a topic. Tell children that when they write reports, they can find the facts they need in books.

- Display **Projectable 14.1**. Read and discuss the model. Use the Talk About It questions.

- Sum up by reviewing the Writer's Checklist for research reports. Point out the purpose of the topic sentence and the closing sentence.

2 Shared Writing

- Work with children to research and write facts about the prickly pear cactus. Reread the Read Aloud *The Prickly Pride of Texas* from Lesson 13 to children. Have children tell what they remember about the article. Then remind children that this article gives facts about the prickly pear cactus.

- Ask partners to tell each other what they learned from this article. Prompt them with questions like these: *What do you remember about the prickly pear? Why is this plant famous?*

- Record a topic sentence and facts about the prickly pear as children suggest ideas. Help them compose an ending sentence that restates the main idea of their sentences about the prickly pair cactus. Review that all of the sentences must connect to what children learned from the Read Aloud.
🔲 W.1.2, W.1.5, L.1.1j

Projectable 14.1

> **Projectable 14.1**
>
> The Big Race Writing Informative Writing
>
> **Writing Model**
>
> **Report**
>
> The **topic sentence** tells what the report is about.
>
> **Coyotes**
>
> Coyotes are animals that can live in the desert. Coyotes hunt at night when it is cooler. They eat many kinds of desert plants and animals. They often live in holes they dig in the ground. Coyotes are well-suited to life in the desert.
>
> **Detail sentences** tell facts about the topic.
>
> The **closing sentence** retells the main idea in different words.
>
> **Talk About It**
>
> 1. What kind of writing is this? How do you know?
> report; it tells facts about a topic
> 2. What is the job of the topic sentence?
> to tell what the report is about
> 3. What is the job of the detail sentences?
> to tell facts about the topic
> 4. Do the detail sentences tell facts or opinions?
> facts
> 5. What is the job of the closing sentence?
> to retell the main idea in different words
>
> Writing
> © Houghton Mifflin Harcourt Publishing Company. All rights reserved.
> Grade 1, Unit 3

Daily Proofreading Practice

goes
The runner gos very fast.
          ^

jumps
He jump over the finish line.
   ^

Writer's Checklist

What Makes a Great Report?

- The **topic sentence** tells what the report is about.

- **Detail sentences** give facts about the topic.

- The **closing sentence** retells the main idea in different words.

Performance Task

my WriteSmart Have children complete the writing assignment through *my*WriteSmart. Children will read the prompt and have access to multiple writing resources.

HOUGHTON MIFFLIN HARCOURT
Common Core Writing Handbook

GRADE 1

Additional support for Informative Writing appears in the **Common Core Writing Handbook,** Lesson 14.

Oral Language Conventions

Using Verbs Remind children that a verb is an action word, or a word that tells what someone or something did or does. Have children name verbs they know.

phonetically, drawing on phonemic awareness and spelling conventions

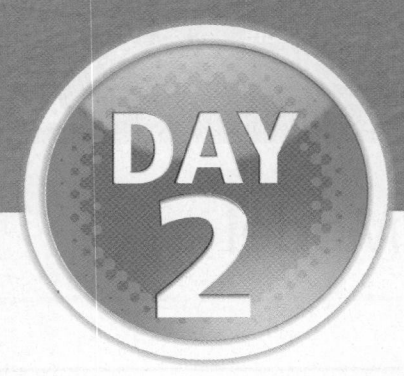

DAY 2

Today's Goals

Vocabulary & Oral Language
- Oral Vocabulary

Phonemic Awareness
- Substitute Phonemes
- Identify Middle Sound

Phonics & Fluency
- Words with Long *a* (CVC*e*)
- Phonogram *-ake*
- Read Decodable Reader: *Dave and the Whales*
- Fluency: Expression

☑ **WORDS TO KNOW**

four	starts
five	three
into	two
over	watch

Text-Based Comprehension
- **Dig Deeper:** How to Analyze the Text
- Conclusions
- Cause and Effect
- Reread the Anchor Text: *The Big Race*

Grammar & Writing
- Verbs and Time
- Informative Writing: Report
  Focus Trait: Ideas

Spelling
- Words with Long *a*

COMMON CORE

RF.1.2a distinguish long from short vowel sounds in spoken single-syllable words; **RF.1.3g** recognize and read irregularly spelled words; **L.1.6** use words and phrases acquired through conversations, reading and being read to, and responding to texts

Opening Routines

Warm Up with Wordplay

Make a Rhyme

Remind children that they have been learning about words that have the sound /ā/ spelled *a_e*. Display and read *Kate*.

Have children turn and talk to a partner to come up with as many other words in this word family (*-ate*) as they can. Call on children to share the words they came up with. Write down what children say and read the words aloud with children. Then have the class work together to make a short two- or four-line poem using the words from the list. Read the poem aloud with children.

grate	plate	Nate
rate	late	fate

Daily Phonemic Awareness

Identify Middle Sounds and Substitute Phonemes

- *Today we're going to change the vowel sound in a word to make a new word. Let's start with the word* tap. *What is its vowel sound?* /ă/, short a *Change the short a to long a. What is the word?* tape *Let's do some more.*

Change the . . .	Result
/ă/ in *pack* to /ĭ/	pick
/ă/ in *tack* to /ā/	take
/ĭ/ in *since* to /ĕ/	sense
/ă/ in *can* to /ā/	cane
/ā/ in *glade* to /ă/	glad
/ă/ in *quack* to /ā/	quake

- Have children repeat the "Result" words, then tell whether the vowel sound is long or short. Long: *take, cane, quake*; Short: *sense, glad, pick* ⬤ **RF.1.2a**

Corrective Feedback

- If a child misses a word, say the correct word and model the task. *Listen to the word* pack, /p/ /ă/ /k/. *Now change* /ă/ *to* /ĭ/: /p/ /ĭ/ /k/. *What is the new word?* pick

- Have children complete the task with you before doing it on their own.

- Then have them continue with the remaining words.

Daily High-Frequency Words

Introduce

- Point to the **High-Frequency Word Card** *five*.

- *Say the word.* five *Spell the word.* f, i, v, e *Write the word. Check the word.*

- Repeat the procedure with the words *four, into, over, starts, three, two,* and *watch*. ⬤ **RF.1.3g**

Hopscotch Game

- Make a hopscotch board on the floor with tape or on the playground with chalk.

- Choose a High-Frequency Word. Write one letter in each box and the word at the top.

- Have children hop, say each letter to spell the word, and say the word at the end.

- Repeat for the remaining words.

Corrective Feedback

- If a child is unable to recognize the word *five*, say the correct word and have children repeat it. *Five. What is the word?* five

- Have children spell the word. *f,i,v,e How do we say this word?* five

- Have children reread all of the cards in random order.

Daily Vocabulary Boost

- Review the Oral Vocabulary words and their definitions with children. (See pp. T316–T317.) Remind children that they heard these words in the Read Aloud "The Tortoise and the Hare."

- Recall with children the story events and then guide them to interact with each word's meaning.

  "No animal in the desert habitat is as fast as I am." What is a desert habitat *like?*

  "So the hare sat down by a cactus and soon fell asleep by dreaming about carrot ice cream." Would you like to touch a cactus? Why or why not?

- Continue in the same manner with *mainly, search, stems,* and *howl*. ⬤ **L.1.6**

 **Oral Vocabulary**

cactus
habitat
mainly
search
stems
howl

Interactive Whiteboard Lesson:
Words with Long *a* (CVCe)

Go Digital
• Interactive Whiteboard Lesson
• Decodable Reader

JOURNEYS
Phonics

Phonemic Awareness/Phonics

SHARE OBJECTIVES

• Blend, read, and decode regularly spelled one-syllable words with long *a* (CVCe).

• Read on-level text with words with long *a* and high-frequency words.

SKILLS TRACE

Words with Long *a*	
Introduce	T318–T319
Differentiate	T388
Reteach	T402
Review	**T342, T364**
Assess	Weekly Tests, Lesson 14

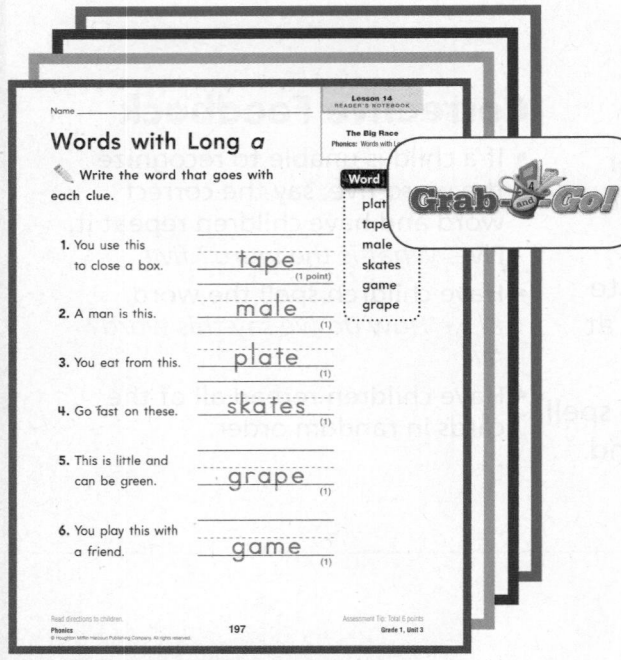

Reader's Notebook Vol. 1 p. 197
See Grab-and-Go™ Resources for additional leveled practice.

COMMON CORE
RF.1.2c isolate and pronounce sounds in spoken single-syllable words; **RF.1.3b** decode regularly spelled one-syllable words; **RF.1.3c** know final -e and vowel team conventions for representing long vowel sounds; **RF.1.3g** recognize and read irregularly spelled words; **RF.1.4a** read on-level text with purpose and understanding; **RF.1.4b** read on-level text orally with accuracy, appropriate rate, and expression; **L.1.2e** spell untaught words phonetically, drawing on phonemic awareness and spelling conventions

Words with Long *a* (CVCe)

PHONEMIC AWARENESS WARM-UP *Let's play a game. I'll say a word. You tell what the middle sound is. Listen: /r/ /ā/ /k/. /ā/* Repeat with these words: *miss, pack, mop, rush, cane.* RF.1.2c

1 Teach/Model

Review the **Sound/Spelling Card** *acorn, /ā/*.

CONTINUOUS BLENDING ROUTINE Use **Instructional Routine 3** to model blending *shake*. Display **Letter Cards** *sh, a, k*, and *e*. Repeat with Row 1 below.

Write the words and sentence shown below. Call on individuals to blend and read one or more words and to read the sentence.

1. bake   same   grade   plane   flake
2. whale   shade   sale   cash   shake

I ate <u>some</u> cake <u>and</u> gave <u>some</u> <u>to</u> Pat.

2 Guided Practice

BUILD WORDS Model how to spell the word *chase. The letters* ch *stand for the first sound. The next sound is /ā/. I know that* a *followed by a consonant and* e *can stand for /ā/. The last sound is /s/. The letter* s *can stand for the /s/ sound.*

• Guide children to identify the sounds in and spell the words *make, late, gave, cake,* and *wave.* L.1.2e

• Call on individuals to spell the words with **Letter Cards** while other children check their work.

3 Apply

Hands-on Practice

Have partners use Letter Cards to take turns building and reading words with long *a*. RF.1.3b, RF.1.3c

Decodable Reader

 Go Digital

Read *Dave and the Whales*

Decodable Reader,
Unit 3, pp. 81–86

REVIEW /ā/ AND WORDS TO KNOW Tell children that many words in this story have the pattern *a*-consonant-*e*, which often stands for the long *a* sound. Point out that children have learned the following words, which they will also read in the story: *five, four, three, two, watch.*

PREVIEW Have children preview pages 81–83 and predict what the story is about. Ask volunteers to tell about a skill or talent they have.

MODEL FLUENCY AND EXPRESSION Read aloud page 81 as children follow along. As you read, have children note that you make your voice sound excited because that's how Dave feels. Lead children in choral reading the page with fluency and expression.

READ Remind children to track the words from left to right and, when they come to the end of a line, to sweep their hand down to the beginning of the next line and continue reading. Have children read each page silently and then choral read it. Tell them to read to find out what Dave and the whales do.
📖 RF.1.3b, RF.1.3c, RF.1.3g, RF.1.4a

RESPONDING Have partners take turns reading the story aloud to each other. Guide them as needed to read different characters' words with appropriate expression. 📖 RF.1.4b

---

DAILY ASSESSMENT △ RtI

Corrective Feedback Work with the whole group to correct errors, following the model below.

Decoding Error:
A child reads *made* as *mad*.

Correct the error. Say the word. *That word is* made. *The middle sound is the long a sound. The letter a followed by a consonant and e often stands for the long a sound.*

Guide Have children repeat the word. *What is the word? made*

Check *Go back to the beginning of the sentence and read it again.*

Reinforce Record the error and review the word again before children reread the story.

Reread for Fluency/ Develop Automaticity

READ WITH A PARTNER Have partners reread *Dave and the Whales* three or four times, taking turns reading aloud each page. Remind them to read words correctly and to read smoothly. Visit partners to listen to them read. Give feedback about reading accurately, at an appropriate rate, and with expression and provide guidance for improving fluency.
📖 RF.1.4b

Whole Group

DAY 2

• eBook
• Interactive
  Whiteboard Lesson

Interactive Whiteboard Lesson:
Text Analysis: Fantasy

Dig Deeper: How to Analyze the Text

▶ SHARE OBJECTIVES

• Use text evidence and prior knowledge to draw conclusions about a story.
• Identify cause-and-effect relationships.

ELL ENGLISH LANGUAGE LEARNERS
Comprehensible Input

Have a volunteer act out something he or she might do on the playground.

Beginning Model how to draw a conclusion. *I see Anna jumping and spinning her arms. I draw the conclusion that she is jumping rope.*

Low Intermediate Have children repeat your thinking about how to identify clues and draw a conclusion.

High Intermediate Have children complete each of these sentence frames. *I see ____. I draw the conclusion that ____.*

Proficient Have children use complete sentences to draw a conclusion about what the volunteer is doing. Have them explain their thinking.

Text-Based Comprehension

1 Teach/Model

Terms About Literature

conclusion a smart guess about something the author does not say

cause why something happens in a story

effect the result of something that happens in a story

___

• Remind children that they have read *The Big Race*, a fantasy about animals in a race. Read and discuss **Student Book** p. 144 with them.

• Tell children that authors do not always tell every detail in a story. Explain that readers must make smart guesses, or draw **conclusions**, about things the author does not say using story clues and what they already know. Model how to use an inference map to draw a conclusion.

> **Think Aloud** *You can list story clues on a chart like the one on p. 144 to help you draw conclusions. I will write story clues in the boxes at the top. The author gives clues to help me figure out who won the race. The first clue is that Cottontail chases a butterfly and leaves the race. I will write that in the Clue box. A conclusion I can draw from this clue and what I know about races is that Cottontail does not win the race. She wouldn't be able to catch up to the others, even if she stopped chasing the butterfly. What do the other characters do? What conclusions can we draw?*

• Next, read and discuss **Student Book** p. 145 with children.

• Explain that sometimes one event in a story can cause another event to happen. The **cause** happens first. The **effect** is what happens next.

• Discuss the photos on p. 145 with children. Tell them that the boy blowing into the balloon **causes** something to happen. Ask: *What is the effect of the boy blowing into the balloon?* the balloon gets big and round; it inflates

• As children reread *The Big Race*, guide them to identify cause-and-effect relationships to help them understand the story better.

COMMON CORE **RL.1.3** describe characters, settings, and major events; **RL.1.7** use illustrations and details to describe characters, setting, or events

COMPREHENSION

Dig Deeper

Read Together

How to Analyze the Text

Use these pages to learn about
Conclusions and Cause and Effect.
Then read **The Big Race** again.

Conclusions

You can use clues in **The Big Race** to
think about things the author does not say.
The author does not tell you why Cottontail
does not win. What do the pictures and
words show that help you make a smart
guess about why? What do you know
about races that helps you understand?
Use a chart to list clues and conclusions.

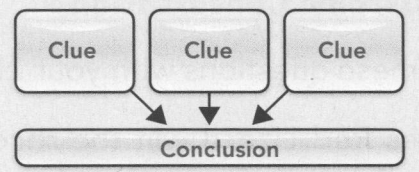

  **RL.1.3** describe characters, settings, and major events; **RL.1.7** use illustrations and details to describe characters, setting, or events

144

Go Digital

Cause and Effect

Sometimes one event in a story causes
another event to happen. As you read,
ask yourself what happens and why.

In **The Big Race**, why doesn't Snake
win? He does not win because he stops to
chase bugs. Snake stopping is the **cause**.
What happens after that? Snake loses
the race. That is the **effect**.

145

SECOND READ

2 Guided Practice/Apply

READ FOR TEXT EVIDENCE Begin a second read of *The
Big Race* with children. Use the instructional support to
guide children to analyze the text:

- Conclusions, p. T335 ▬ **RL.1.3, RL.1.7**
- Cause and Effect, p. T333 ▬ **RL.1.3, RL.1.7**

DIRECTED NOTE-TAKING The graphic organizer will
be completed with children during the second read on
p. T335.

DAILY ASSESSMENT ⟁ RtI

*Are children able to draw
conclusions?*

IF...	THEN...
children have difficulty drawing conclusions,	use **Differentiate Comprehension** for Struggling Readers, p. T392. *See also Intervention Lesson 14, pp. S36–S37.*
children can draw most conclusions,	use **Differentiate Comprehension** for On Level Readers, p. T392.
children can draw all conclusions,	use **Differentiate Comprehension** for Advanced Readers, p. T393.

**Differentiate Comprehension:
pp. T392–T393**
*Group English Language Learners according to
language proficiency. See also ELL Lesson 14,
p. E35, for scaffolded support.*

Your Turn

 **Use Text Evidence**

▶ SHARE OBJECTIVES

- Respond to questions by talking with peers in complete sentences, using text evidence.
- Write an opinion piece about a favorite story character.

RETURN TO THE ESSENTIAL QUESTION

Have partners discuss the Essential Question as it relates to rules in general and then as it applies to *The Big Race*. Have them describe what happens to the animals during the race when they don't follow the rules, such as leaving the race to chase bugs. Have children return to the story to find text evidence to support their responses. Tell them to be sure to describe the characters and events with details from the story to make their ideas and feelings clear. Tell children to speak in complete sentences, and guide them to do so, modeling as needed. 💬 **RL.1.7, SL.1.4, SL.1.6**

 ## Classroom Conversation Have

children continue their discussion of the story using questions 1–3. Tell them to include details and examples to make their ideas and feelings clear when they describe the characters and events. Remind children to listen respectfully to their classmates. Help them to build conversations by coaching them to have multiple exchanges with classmates, responding appropriately to others' comments and adding their own ideas. 💬 **RL.1.7, SL.1.1b, SL.1.4**

COMMON CORE **RL.1.7** use illustrations and details to describe characters, setting, or events; **W.1.1** write opinion pieces; **SL.1.1b** build on others' talk in conversations by responding to others' comments; **SL.1.4** describe people, places, things, and events with details/express ideas and feelings clearly; **SL.1.6** produce complete sentences when appropriate to task and situation; **L.1.6** use words and phrases acquired through conversations, reading and being read to, and responding to texts

---

Your Turn

RETURN TO THE ESSENTIAL QUESTION

Turn and Talk **Why is it important to have rules?** Describe what happens to the animals in the story when they do not follow the rules. Use text evidence to help you answer. Speak in complete sentences.

 ### Classroom Conversation

Talk about these questions with your class.

1. Why does Red Lizard win the race?
2. How does Red Lizard feel when he wins?
3. Red Lizard shares the cake. Is this the right thing to do? Why or why not?

146

ELL ENGLISH LANGUAGE LEARNERS

Comprehensible Input

Beginning Use simple *yes/no* questions to help children draw conclusions about who will win in *The Big Race*. *Is it a good idea to stop during a race? Can you win a race if you trip?*

High Intermediate Have children complete this sentence: *To win a race, it is important to ____.*

Low Intermediate Use simple questions to help children draw a conclusion based on *The Big Race*. *Do you have to be fast or slow to win a race? Is it better to trip or keep running?*

Proficient Have children tell whether they think the race would have the same results if the animals raced again. Ask them to write about what might happen.

See ELL Lesson 14, p. E34, for further comprehension support.

WRITE ABOUT READING

Response Choose a favorite character from **The Big Race**. Write sentences to give reasons why you like him or her. Use details from the story to explain your opinion.

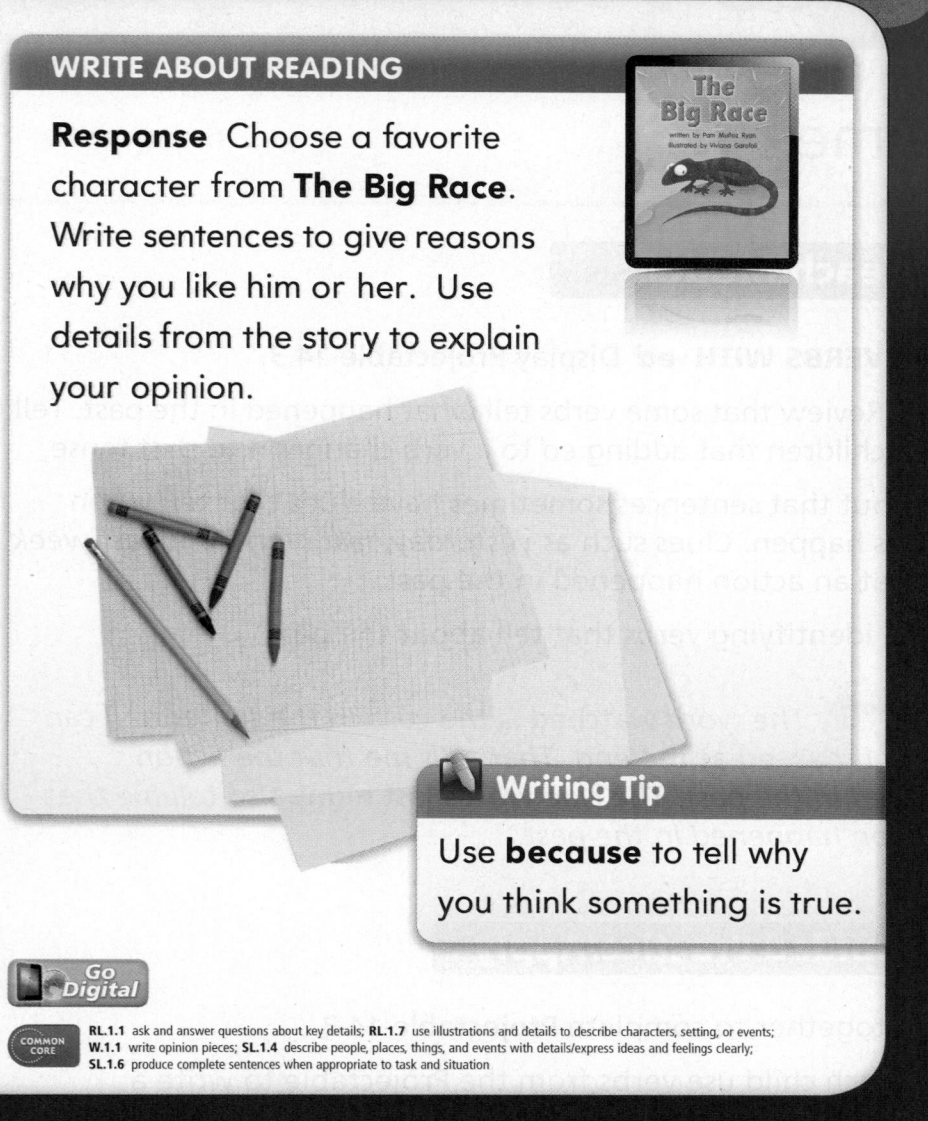

Writing Tip

Use **because** to tell why you think something is true.

Go Digital

COMMON CORE
RL.1.1 ask and answer questions about key details; **RL.1.7** use illustrations and details to describe characters, setting, or events; **W.1.1** write opinion pieces; **SL.1.4** describe people, places, things, and events with details/express ideas and feelings clearly; **SL.1.6** produce complete sentences when appropriate to task and situation

147

WRITE ABOUT READING   Performance Task

Tell children that they will write sentences that tell their opinion about a character from *The Big Race*.

- Read **Student Book** p. 145 with children.

- Explain that they will write about their favorite character from *The Big Race*.

- Make sure children understand they must give reasons why they like the character and use details from *The Big Race* to help explain why they feel as they do.

- Guide children to begin with a topic sentence that identifies the character and tells their opinion, followed by sentences that give reasons for their opinion backed up with examples.

- Help them to write an ending sentence to give their writing a sense of closure. ◀ **W.1.1**

WRITING TIP Read the Writing Tip with children before they begin writing. Explain to them that they can use the word *because* to give a reason when writing. Tell children that *because* is a word that signals that a reason will come next in a sentence. Model with an example on the board, such as *Red Lizard is nice because _____.* Have volunteers say various reasons that complete the sentence, based on the story and their own opinions.
◀ **W.1.1, L.1.6**

Have children complete the Write About Reading activity through *my*WriteSmart. Children will read the prompt within *my*WriteSmart and have access to multiple writing resources, including the Student eBook, Writing Rubrics, and Graphic Organizers.

Grammar Verbs and Time

▶ SHARE OBJECTIVES

- **Grammar** Use verbs that tell about actions that happened in the past.
- **Spelling** Spell words with the long *a* sound using conventional spelling patterns.
- **Handwriting** Print the spelling words.
- **Writing** Take notes for a report.

ELL ENGLISH LANGUAGE LEARNERS

Language Transfer

All Proficiencies Using sentence strips, with red strips containing nouns/subjects, and blue strips containing verbs inflected for present tense and past tense, ending in *-ed* (e.g. *jump/jumped, walk/walked,* etc.), guide the class in building sentences in the present tense, then changing so that they happen in the past.

1 Teach/Model

VERBS WITH -ed Display **Projectable 14.3**.

Review that some verbs tell what happened in the past. Tell children that adding *ed* to a verb changes it to past tense.

- Point out that sentences sometimes have clues that tell when actions happen. Clues such as *yesterday, last night*, and *last week* tell that an action happened in the past.
- Model identifying verbs that tell about the past.

> **Think Aloud** *The word* watched *is the verb in the sentence. I can see that it has* -ed *at the end. That tells me that the action happened in the past. The clue words* last night *also tell me that the action happened in the past.*

2 Guided Practice/Apply

- Work together to complete **Projectable 14.3**.
- Have each child use verbs from the Projectable to write a sentence about right now and a sentence about the past. ▬ **L.1.1e, L.1.1j**

Spelling Words with Long *a*

SPELLING WORDS

BASIC	
came	make
brave	late
gave	shape
CHALLENGE	
waves	chases

Word Sort

- Review **Sound/Spelling Card** *acorn*. *What sound do you hear at the beginning of* acorn? /ā/ *This is the long a sound. The letter a stands for the long a sound.*

- Write the spelling words on the board as well as the following short *a* words: *cat, ran*, and *add*. Ask volunteers to come up to the board and circle the words that have the long *a* sound.

- For additional practice, you may want to distribute **Reader's Notebook** Vol. 1 page 198. ▬ **L.1.2d**

Handwriting

Model how to form the basic words *came, make*, and *brave*. Have children use their best handwriting to write the spelling words, forming letters correctly. Ball-and-stick and continuous stroke handwriting models are available on the **Handwriting Models Blackline Masters**. ▬ **L.1.1a**

COMMON CORE

W.1.2 write informative/explanatory texts; **W.1.8** recall information from experiences or gather information from sources to answer a question; **L.1.1a** print upper- and lowercase letters; **L.1.1e** use verbs to convey sense of past, present, and future; **L.1.1j** produce and expand simple and compound declarative, interrogative, imperative, and exclamatory sentences; **L.1.2d** use conventional spelling for words with common spelling patterns and for frequently occurring irregular words

T348 • Unit 3 Lesson 14

Informative Writing Focus Trait: Ideas

1 Teach/Model

TAKING NOTES Remind children that writers need to do research if they are going to write a report. Explain that writers often take notes to help remind them what they learned and to help them come up with ideas for their reports.

- Tell children that notes can be words or phrases that answer a question. Add that notes can also be drawings with labels.

- Have children listen to this excerpt from "The Prickly Pride of Texas" to answer the question: *What does a prickly pear cactus look like?* Then use the board to model how to take notes.

Connect to "The Prickly Pride of Texas"

You can easily spot a prickly pear cactus. This plant does not have vines, a woody trunk, *or* thin leaves like other familiar plants. Instead, it has flat, green paddles. They are shaped like tears.

- *I will make notes about facts we learn that answer the question: What does a prickly pear cactus look like? I'll sketch a picture of a flat paddle that is shaped like a tear. I will write the words* green paddle *underneath. I will also write* no vines, leaves, woody trunk.

- Display **Projectable 14.4**. Read aloud the facts at the top.

2 Guided Writing

- Have each child tell a partner what they recall about roadrunners from **Projectable 14.4**. Explain that children will be taking notes to help them remember this information.

- Remind children that they can use words and phrases or pictures with labels to take their notes.

- Have children take notes about roadrunners. Have them use their notes to answer the question: *What do roadrunners eat?* Then have volunteers suggest entries that will help you complete **Projectable 14.4**.

- For additional practice, you may want to distribute **Reader's Notebook** Vol. 1, page 200. Have children use their notes to answer the following question: *Why can camels live in the desert?* ■ **W.1.2, W.1.8**

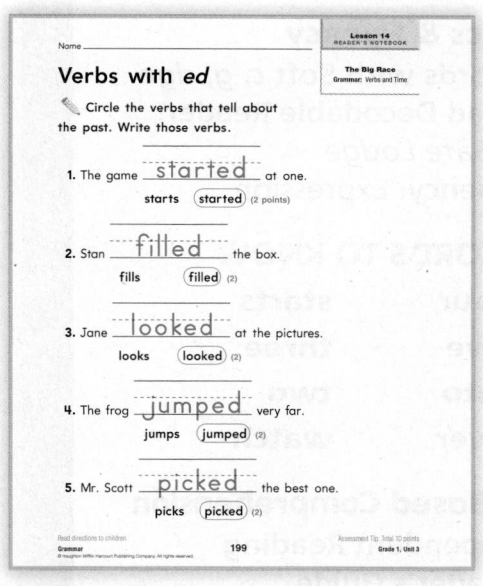

Reader's Notebook Vol. 1 p. 199

Reader's Notebook Vol. 1 p. 200

DAY 3

Today's Goals

Vocabulary & Oral Language
• Apply Vocabulary Knowledge

Phonemic Awareness
• Substitute Phonemes
• Identify Middle Sound

Phonics & Fluency
• **Words with Soft *c, g, dge***
• **Read Decodable Reader:** *A Safe Lodge*
• **Fluency:** Expression

☑ **WORDS TO KNOW**

four	starts
five	three
into	two
over	watch

Text-Based Comprehension
Independent Reading
• **Reader's Guide**
• **Self-Selected Reading**

Grammar & Writing
• **Verbs and Time**
 **Informative Writing:** Report

Spelling
• **Words with Long *a***

COMMON CORE **RF.1.2a** distinguish long from short vowel sounds in spoken single-syllable words; **RF.1.3g** recognize and read irregularly spelled words; **SL.1.1a** follow rules for discussions; **SL.1.1b** build on others' talk in conversations by responding to others' comments; **L.1.5c** identify real-life connections between words and their use; **L.1.6** use words and phrases acquired through conversations, reading and being read to, and responding to texts

Opening Routines

Warm Up with Wordplay

The Never-Ending Story

Have children recall the story they read about animal friends racing. Tell children that today they will help you write a story about friends playing a game. Display and read aloud the following:

> ## Some friends and I started to play a game. And then . . .

Have one child continue the story by asking him or her: *And then what happened?* When the child has told about one thing that happens, he or she says, "and then." The next child then adds something else that happens. Write down what the children say. After each child has taken a turn, read the whole story with children.

Daily Phonemic Awareness

Substitute Medial Phonemes

- *We're going to change one sound in the middle of a word to make a new word. For example, change the /ă/ in cap to /ā/. What do you get?* cape *Now change the /ā/ to /ŭ/. What is the new word?* cup *Let's keep going.*

Change the . . .	Result
/ă/ in *can* to /ā/	cane
/ā/ in *made* to /ă/	mad
/ŭ/ in *run* to /ă/	ran
/ī/ in *line* to /ā/	lane
/ă/ in *rack* to /ā/	rake
/ā/ in *tape* to /ă/	tap

- Say the words listed under "Result." Have children repeat the word and identify its vowel sound. Short *a: mad, ran, tap;* Long *a: cane, lane, rake* **RF.1.2a**

Corrective Feedback

- If a child misses a word, say the correct word and model the task. *Listen to the word can, /k/ /ă/ /n/. Now change /ă/ to /ā/: /k/ /ā/ /n/. What is the new word?* cane

- Have children complete the task with you before doing it on their own.

- Then have them continue with remaining words.

Daily High-Frequency Words

Introduce

- Point to the **High-Frequency Word Card** *into*.

- *Say the word.* into *Spell the word.* i, n, t, o *Write the word. Check the word.*

- Repeat the procedure with the words *four, five, over, starts, three, two,* and *watch.* **RF.1.3g**

Stomp and Clap Game

- Have a volunteer name the vowels. Remind them that the other letters are called consonants.

- Choose a High-Frequency Word and point to each letter as you spell it aloud.

- Have children repeat each letter. As they say each letter, have them stomp for vowels and clap for consonants.

- Repeat for the remaining words.

Corrective Feedback

- If a child is unable to recognize the word *into*, say the correct word and have children repeat it. Into. *What is the word?* into

- Have children spell the word. *i,n,t,o How do we say this word? into*

- Have children reread all of the cards in random order.

Daily Vocabulary Boost

- Guide children to interact with the Oral Vocabulary words by asking the following questions. Remind them to speak clearly when participating in a discussion.

  How is a cactus different from other kinds of plants?

  Why might you like to visit a desert habitat?

  What kind of programs do you mainly watch on TV?

- Ask children to work with a partner to explain *cactus, habitat, and mainly* in their own words. Have each child respond to what his or her partner says so that they build a conversation. Make sure children follow appropriate rules for discussion, such as listening to speakers, taking turns, and staying on topic. **SL.1.1a, SL.1.1b, L.1.5c, L.1.6**

 Oral Vocabulary

cactus
habitat
mainly
search
stems
howl

Interactive Whiteboard Lesson:
Words with Soft *c, g, dge*

Phonemic Awareness/Phonics

▶ **SHARE OBJECTIVES**
- Recognize medial sounds.
- Blend, read, and decode regularly spelled one-syllable words with soft *c, g,* and *dge*.
- Blend read, and decode regularly spelled words with phonogram *-ace*.

▶ **SKILLS TRACE**

Words with Soft *c, g, dge*	
Introduce	T352–T353
Differentiate	T394
Reteach	T402
Review	T364
Assess	Weekly Tests, Lesson 14

ELL ENGLISH LANGUAGE LEARNERS

Language Transfer

Beginning Say *page* and *badge*, emphasizing the /j/ sound. Have children repeat. Repeat with *rice* and *piece*.

Low Intermediate Write *age*. Read the word together. Have children identify the final sound. Point to *g* and repeat the sound. Repeat with *race, mice,* and *fudge*.

High Intermediate Use **Letter Cards** to build and read *page* and *cage*. Have children say more words that end in the phonogram *-age*. Repeat for *-ace*.

Proficient Have partners use letter cards to build and read as many words as they can with the phonograms *-age* and *-ace*.

See ELL Lesson 14, p. E37, for scaffolded support.

COMMON CORE **RF.1.2b** orally produce single-syllable words by blending sounds; **RF.1.2c** isolate and pronounce sounds in spoken single-syllable words; **RF.1.3b** decode regularly spelled one-syllable words; **RF.1.3c** know final -e and vowel team conventions for representing long vowel sounds; **RF.1.3g** recognize and read irregularly spelled words; **L.1.2e** spell untaught words phonetically, drawing on phonemic awareness and spelling conventions

Words with Soft *c, g, dge*

PHONEMIC AWARENESS WARM-UP Guide children to listen for and say the vowel sound they hear in the middle of each word. *I'll say a word and you say the vowel sound you hear. Listen:* bake. *Do you hear the vowel sound? The vowel sound is /ā/.*

Let's do some together. Listen: stack. *The vowel sound is /ă/. Listen:* stage. *The vowel sound is /ā/.*

Now let's do more: mat /ă/, date /ā/, badge /ă/, page /ā/. ▬ **RF.1.2c**

1 Teach/Model

INTRODUCE WORDS WITH SOFT *c, g, dge*
Display the **Picture Card** *mice*. Name the picture and say the end sound /s/.

- Repeat *mice* and give the spelling. *The word* mice *ends with /s/. Say the word with me and listen for the sound at the end of* mice. *The letter* c *stands for /s/ at the end of* mice.

- Write the word *race*. Say the word and have children repeat it after you. *The letter* c *stands for the /s/ sound at the end of* race. *Read the word with me:* race.

- Display **Sound/Spelling Card** *jump*. Point to each spelling and say /j/. Explain that *g* and *dge* can stand for the sound /j/ in some words. Write *badge*. Say the word and have children repeat it. *The letters* dge *stand for the /j/ sound in* badge.

- Display the **Picture Card** *cage*. Name the picture and say the end sound. Have children repeat after you. *Listen:* cage, /j/. *Write and read* cage. *The letter* g *stands for the /j/ sound in* cage.

PHONOGRAM *-ace* Write *lace* and *trace* on the board, and have children read each word. Ask children which three letters are the same in both words. Tell children that these words belong to the same word family because they end with the same letters and sounds. Guide children to think of more words with *-ace*, such as *face* and *place*. Write them on the board and have children read them. ▬ **RF.1.3c**

2 Guided Practice

CONTINUOUS BLENDING ROUTINE Display **Letter Cards** *c, a, g, e*. Blend the sounds, stretching out the word while pointing to each letter in a sweeping motion. *Listen:* /k/ /ā/ /j/, cage.

Together with children, blend the sounds. *Blend the word with me:* /k/ /ā/ /j/, cage. Then have children blend the sounds. *Now you read it.*
🔹 RF.1.2b, RF.1.3b, RF.1.3c

REPEAT CONTINUOUS BLENDING ROUTINE with Row 1 below. Use the **Corrective Feedback** steps if children need additional help.

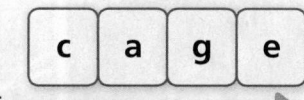

• Repeat until children are reading at a rate of three seconds per word.

DECODING Write the sentence on the board. Call on individuals to blend one or more words and to read the sentence.
🔹 RF.1.3b, RF.1.3c, RF.1.3g

1. lace   cage   badge   space   place
2. page   fudge   wish   gem   cell

Kate came <u>to</u> judge <u>who</u> wins <u>the</u> race.

3 Apply

Use **Instructional Routine 6** and the sentences below to connect sounds to writing. Have children say each word aloud. Then have them identify the sounds and write the letters that stand for each sound. Print the words so that children can check their work. 🔹 RF.1.3b, RF.1.3c, L.1.2e

• **fudge**   Jack likes to eat **fudge**.
• **trace**   Kim will **trace** her hand.
• **gem**   The **gem** is blue.

Corrective Feedback Work with the whole group to correct errors, following the model below.

Phonics Error:
A child reads *page* as *pig*.

Correct the error. Review the **Sound/Spelling Cards**. Say the word and the sound. *The word is* page. *The letter g stands for the sound /j/ in this word.*

Model by asking children what the end sound in *page* is. Say the word, emphasizing the end sound /j/. *What is the word?* page

Guide *Let's read the word together. The word is* page.

Check *You read the word* pig. *What is the correct word?* page

Reinforce Go back three or four words and have children continue reading. Make note of errors and review those words during tomorrow's lesson.

Go to p. T394 for additional phonics support.

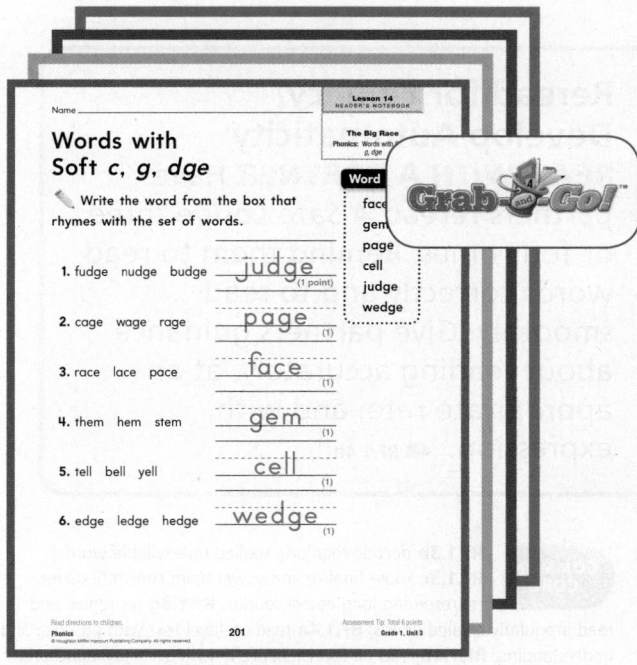

Reader's Notebook Vol. 1 p. 201
See Grab-and-Go™ Resources for additional leveled practice.

Phonemic Awareness/Phonics • **T353**

Decodable Reader

▶ SHARE OBJECTIVE

• Read text with regularly spelled words with soft *c, g,* and *dge* and high-frequency words.

DAILY ASSESSMENT · RtI

Corrective Feedback Work with the whole group to correct errors.

Decoding Error:
A child reads *lodge* as *log.*

Correct the error. *That word is* lodge. *Look closely at the last three letters.*

Guide *Remember that the letters* dge *stand for the /j/ sound.* Have children blend and read the word.

Check *Read the sentence again.*

Reinforce Review the word again before children reread the story.

SMALL GROUP Options Go to p. T394 for additional phonics support.

Reread for Fluency/Develop Automaticity

READ WITH A PARTNER Have partners reread *A Safe Lodge* three or four times. Remind them to read words correctly and to read smoothly. Give partners guidance about reading accurately, at an appropriate rate, and with expression. ◼ RF.1.4b

COMMON CORE **RF.1.3b** decode regularly spelled one-syllable words; **RF.1.3c** know final -e and vowel team conventions for representing long vowel sounds; **RF.1.3g** recognize and read irregularly spelled words; **RF.1.4a** read on-level text with purpose and understanding; **RF.1.4b** read on-level text orally with accuracy, appropriate rate, and expression

Read *A Safe Lodge*

**Decodable Reader,
Unit 3, pp. 87–92**

REVIEW SOFT *c, g, dge*; PHONOGRAM *-ace*; AND WORDS TO KNOW Tell children that this selection has many words with soft *c, g, dge,* and phonogram *-ace.* Review with them the following Words to Know, which they will read in the selection: *over, starts, watch.*

PREVIEW Tell children to preview pages 87–89 and predict what they think the selection is about. Ask volunteers to tell what they know about beavers. Tell children they are going to read lots of interesting facts about how beavers build their homes.

MODEL FLUENCY AND EXPRESSION Have children follow along as you read page 90 aloud, using expression to show how interesting the facts are. Remind children that they can change their voices to go up or down to express different feelings about what they are reading. Lead children in a choral reading, reading the page fluently and with appropriate expression.

READ Remind children to track words from left to right and when they come to the end of a line, to continue reading at the beginning of the next line. Have children read each page silently and then choral-read aloud. Coach them to read fluently, using appropriate expression. Have children read to find out what a beaver's lodge is like. ◼ RF.1.3b, RF.1.3c, RF.1.3g, RF.1.4a

RESPONDING Have children work with a partner to write a list of things they learned about beavers' lodges, or homes.

Fluency

Expression

1 Teach/Model

Remind children that good readers make their reading sound like they are speaking. They help listeners understand the meaning by using their voices to show feelings. Display **Projectable 14.5**. Tell children you will read the first sentence with and without expression. Read the sentence without pausing or expression. Then reread it with a pause at the slash mark and expression in your voice. Ask children which way sounded more natural, like you were speaking rather than reading. Repeat with sentence 2.

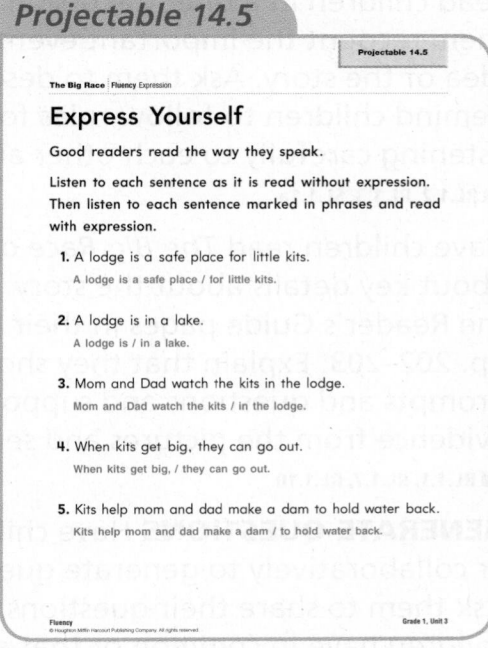

Projectable 14.5

Projectable 14.5

The Big Race | Fluency Expression

Express Yourself

Good readers read the way they speak.

Listen to each sentence as it is read without expression. Then listen to each sentence marked in phrases and read with expression.

1. A lodge is a safe place for little kits.
   A lodge is a safe place / for little kits.

2. A lodge is in a lake.
   A lodge is / in a lake.

3. Mom and Dad watch the kits in the lodge.
   Mom and Dad watch the kits / in the lodge.

4. When kits get big, they can go out.
   When kits get big, / they can go out.

5. Kits help mom and dad make a dam to hold water back.
   Kits help mom and dad make a dam / to hold water back.

Fluency
© Houghton Mifflin Harcourt Publishing Company. All rights reserved.

Grade 1, Unit 3

2 Guided Practice

Read sentence 3 with expression and a pause after the slash mark. Have children echo-read the sentence. Repeat with sentences 4 and 5. Have children choral-read sentences 1 through 5 using proper expression.

3 Apply

Have pairs practice reading *The Big Race*. Remind them to track the print from left to right as they read. Coach children to connect words to read them smoothly and accurately. Have volunteers read each page aloud with accuracy, appropriate rate, and expression. ▰ RF.1.4b

▶ SHARE OBJECTIVE

• Read on-level text fluently with accuracy and proper expression.

SMALL GROUP Options

Go to p. T395 for additional fluency support.

HOUGHTON MIFFLIN HARCOURT

JOURNEYS

Cold Reads

GRADE 1

Cold Reads: Support for fluent reading and comprehension

Independent Reading

- Read and comprehend literature.
- Ask and answer questions about key details in a story.
- Read independently from a "just right" book.
- Read aloud with appropriate expression.

ELL ENGLISH LANGUAGE LEARNERS
Comprehensible Input

Beginning Ask children *yes/no* questions about *The Big Race*.

Low Intermediate Ask children about some key details about the story, such as *What does Red Lizard do with his cake?* and *Why does Red Lizard run in the race?*

High Intermediate Have children explain what happens to one of the racers who is not Red Lizard.

Proficient Have partners summarize what happens to each racer in the story.

Reader's Guide

Revisit the Anchor Text

Lead children in a brief discussion about *The Big Race*. Have them recount the important events, and summarize the main idea of the story. Ask them to describe Red Lizard in detail. Remind children to follow rules for discussions, such as listening carefully to each other and taking turns speaking.
▬ **RL.1.2, RL.1.3, SL.1.1a**

Have children read *The Big Race* on their own and to think about key details about the story. Have children use the Reader's Guide pages in their **Reader's Notebook**, pp. 202–203. Explain that they should respond to the prompts and questions and support their responses with text evidence from the pictures and sentences in *The Big Race*.
▬ **RL.1.1, RL.1.7, RL.1.10**

GENERATE QUESTIONS Have children work independently or collaboratively to generate questions about *The Big Race*. Ask them to share their questions. Discuss questions that children have in common or that are most significant to their understanding of the story, and work with them to answer the questions. ▬ **RL.1.1**

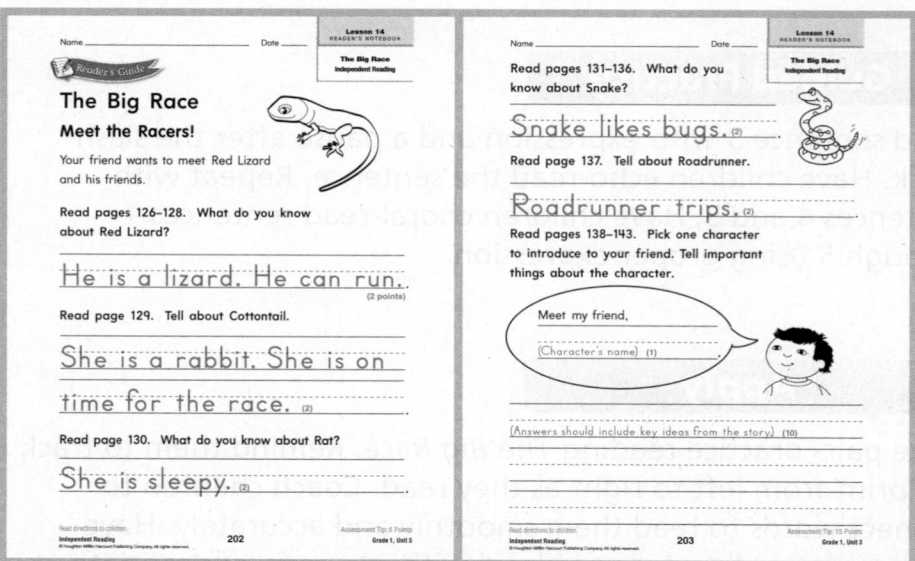

Reader's Notebook pp. 202–203

COMMON CORE **RL.1.1** ask and answer questions about key details; **RL.1.2** retell stories and demonstrate understanding of the message or lesson; **RL.1.3** describe characters, settings, and major events; **RL.1.7** use illustrations and details to describe characters, setting, or events; **RL.1.10** read prose and poetry; **RF.1.4c** use context to confirm or self-correct word recognition and understanding; **SL.1.1a** follow rules for discussions

Self-Selected Reading

Five Finger Rule

Help children use the Five Finger Rule for choosing a "just right" book.

• Choose a book that you like, and read the first page or two.

• Put up one finger for every word you don't know.

• If five of your fingers go up while reading, choose another book.

• If only two or three fingers go up, you've found a "just right" book.

Review with children why it is important to choose a book that is neither too easy nor too difficult. Guide them to choose appropriate books to read independently.

Self-Correction Strategies

Read for Fluency and Expression

Tell children that understanding what they read takes more than being able to read every word. They must also understand how the words work together to make sense.

Tell children that as they read their independent reading books, they will pay attention to reading smoothly and with a natural expression that is like their own speaking voice. Explain that this will help what they are reading sound like it makes sense, and they will understand it better. Model reading with expression a few pages from *The Big Race*. Have children join in echo reading the pages and then choral reading them. Point out how end marks in sentences, such as question marks and exclamation points, can help children know what expression to use when reading. As a class, discuss how using expression helps us understand and enjoy what we read.

Have partners practice reading aloud to each other from their self-selected books. Have them practice reading smoothly with appropriate expression. When one child has finished reading, his or her partner should provide feedback about expression. Each partner can read more than once to improve his or her fluency and expression. ▬ RF.1.4b

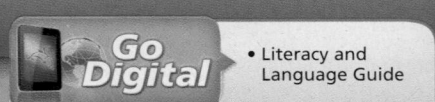
Apply Vocabulary Knowledge

▶ SHARE OBJECTIVES

- Use words and phrases acquired through conversations, reading and being read to, and responding to texts.
- Identify real-life connections between words and their use.
- Use a dictionary to find word meanings.

☑ SELECTION VOCABULARY ›› Review

Review with children the Selection Vocabulary words on p. T324. Call on children to explain how the words were used in *The Big Race*.

ENRICH VOCABULARY Write the following Related Words on the board. Read each word aloud, and have children repeat after you. Then read the student-friendly explanation for each word. Connect each word's meaning to the story *The Big Race* by writing the context sentences on the board and reading them aloud.

pace: Your pace is how fast you are going. *Red Lizard ran at a quick pace.*

anticipate: When you anticipate something, you look forward to it. *The animals anticipate running in the race and winning the big cake.*

clumsy: If you are clumsy, you do things in a messy way or without skill. *Roadrunner was clumsy to trip over the rake.*

continue: If you continue to do something, you keep doing it. *Red Lizard will win the race because he will continue running when the other animals stop.*

MAKE CONNECTIONS Discuss all of the words using the items below to help children make connections between vocabulary words and their use. ● L.1.5c

- Show how a **cottontail** moves.
- Have you ever been in a **race**? Tell about it.
- How is a **lizard** different from a bird?
- Tell about something you **anticipate** doing this year.
- Are ballerinas **clumsy**? Explain.
- Does a **roadrunner** move at a quick or slow **pace**?
- If you try to do something that is hard, would you **continue** doing it? Why or why not?
- Name some animals you know that eat **hay**.
- What kinds of things make you say "**Hooray**"?

COMMON CORE **RI.1.5** know and use text features to locate facts or information; **L.1.5c** identify real-life connections between words and their use; **L.1.6** use words and phrases acquired through conversations, reading and being read to, and responding to texts

Dictionary Skills

DISCUSS USING A DICTIONARY Remind children that the entries in a dictionary are in A, B, C order. Have a volunteer explain how this feature helps to find words.

Guide children to look up the Lesson 14 Selection Vocabulary words *hay* and *race* in a print dictionary. Have them explain how they found the words. Then have partners work together to look up *pace*, *cottontail*, and *lizard*. Ask volunteers to read aloud the definitions. ▬ RI.1.5

QUICKWRITE

Read aloud each question below. Pause a few minutes between each item to allow children to write a response. ▬ L.1.6

1. Would you anticipate taking a test? Why or why not?

2. When is it a good idea to go at a slow pace?

3. Tell about a time you or someone you know was clumsy.

4. What is something you continue to do, even if you do not like it?

Literacy and Language Guide
Additional Lesson 14 vocabulary lessons appear in the Literacy and Language Guide.

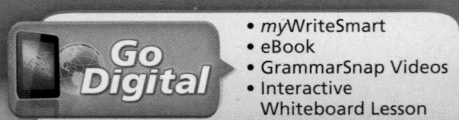

• *my*WriteSmart
• eBook
• GrammarSnap Videos
• Interactive Whiteboard Lesson

Grammar Verbs and Time

▶ SHARE OBJECTIVES

• **Grammar** Identify and use verbs that tell about present and past time.

• **Spelling** Spell words with the long *a* sound using conventional spelling patterns.

• **Writing** Choose a topic and explore ideas for a research report.

ELL ENGLISH LANGUAGE LEARNERS
Comprehensible Input

All Proficiencies Use sentence strips, with red strips containing nouns/subjects, and blue strips containing verbs inflected for present tense and past tense ending in -*ed* (e.g., *jump/jumped, walk/walked*, etc.). Guide the class in building sentences in the present tense, then changing so that they happen in the past.

1 Teach/Model

 **14.6**

PRESENT AND PAST TIME Display **Projectable 14.6**. Review that some verbs tell what is happening *now*, and some verbs tell what happened in the *past*.

• Remind children that they can add -*ed* to most verbs to tell about the past. Clue words such as *today, now, yesterday*, and *last night* can help tell when an action happens or happened.

• Model identifying present and past time verbs.

> **Think Aloud** *In the first sentence, the verb* starts *and the clue word* now *tell me that the action happens in the present time. In the second sentence, the verb* started *has -ed at the end. That tells me that the action happened in the past. The clue word* yesterday *also tells me that the action happened in the past.*

2 Guided Practice/Apply

• Work together to complete **Projectable 14.6**.

• Have each child choose verbs from the Projectable to write a sentence about now and a sentence about the past. Then have children circle the base word in their verbs and underline the -*ed* endings. ▬ **L.1.1e, L.1.1j, L.1.4c**

Spelling Words with Long *a*

SPELLING WORDS

BASIC	
came	make
brave	late
gave	shape
CHALLENGE	
waves	chases

Segment Sounds

• Model segmenting sounds. *Listen as I say the sounds in* came: /k/ /ā/ /m/. *Repeat after me:* /k/ /ā/ /m/.

• Repeat with the remaining words. Have children say the sounds in a word one at a time and write the letter or letters that stand for each sound to help them spell words correctly. ▬ **RF.1.2d, L.1.2d**

Build Words

• Use **Letter Cards** to model building the word *came*. Have children read and write the word.

c	a	m	e

• Have partners use **Letter Cards** to build words with the long *a* sound and add each word to their lists.

• For additional practice, you may want to distribute **Reader's Notebook** Vol. 1 page 204.

 **COMMON CORE**

RF.1.2d segment spoken single-syllable words into their complete sequence of individual sounds; **W.1.2** write informative/explanatory texts; **W.1.8** recall information from experiences or gather information from sources to answer a question; **L.1.1e** use verbs to convey sense of past, present, and future; **L.1.1j** produce and expand simple and compound declarative, interrogative, imperative, and exclamatory sentences;

Informative Writing Prewriting

1 Teach/Model

CHOOSING A TOPIC Tell children that they will begin writing their own research reports.

- Write the following prompt on the board and read it aloud for children: *Write a report about an animal.* Leave the prompt on the board throughout the workshop.

- Use questions like these to help children think of topic ideas: *What animals do you like? What animals did you learn about in the books we just read? What animals do you wonder about?*

- List animals as children suggest them. Make reference sources available for as many of the animals on the list as possible.

EXPLORING A TOPIC Explain that once children choose an animal for their report, they can write questions about their animals.

- Model writing questions about an animal you choose.

> **Think Aloud**
> *I plan to write about tigers. I have questions about tigers. For instance, I wonder what things they can do. I'll write that as a question: What can tigers do?*

2 Independent Writing

- Reread the writing prompt with children. Help each child choose an animal to write about. Tell them that they may use the list on the board, or choose an animal that is not on the list. Check that there are classroom resources for each of their choices.

- Then have children work in pairs. Have partners help each other ask and write questions about their animals. 🔊 **W.1.2, W.1.8**

Oral Language Conventions

Using Verbs Remind children that verbs can tell about things that happened in the past. Have children suggest verbs to tell about what their chosen animals might do; then ask them to tell how these verbs might change if used to describe something that already happened. 🔊 **L.1.1e**

L.1.2d use conventional spelling for words with common spelling patterns and for frequently occurring irregular words;
L.1.4c identify frequently occurring root words and their inflectional forms

Daily Proofreading Practice

Four   picked
~~Fore~~ winners ~~pick~~ a prize last night.
     ^   ^

                       ate
Then we ~~ait~~ some cake.
              ^

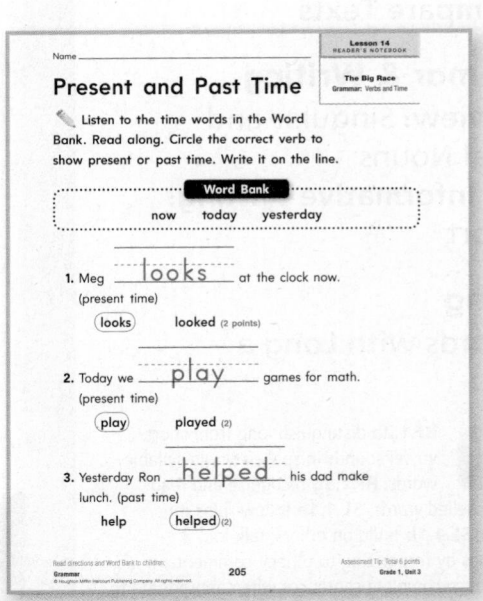

Reader's Notebook Vol. 1 p. 205

DAY 4

Today's Goals

Vocabulary & Oral Language
- **Vocabulary Strategies:**
  Shades of Meaning

Phonemic Awareness
- **Substitute Phonemes**

Phonics & Fluency
- **Words with Long a (CVCe)**
- **Words with Soft c, g, dge**
- **Read Decodable Reader:**
  The Race

☑ **WORDS TO KNOW**

four	starts
five	three
into	two
over	watch

Text-Based Comprehension
  Connect to the Topic
- **Read Informational Text:**
  Rules and Laws
- **Compare Texts**

Grammar & Writing
- **Review:** Singular and
  Plural Nouns
-  **Informative Writing:**
  Report

Spelling
- **Words with Long a**

COMMON CORE **RF.1.2a** distinguish long from short vowel sounds in spoken single-syllable words; **RF.1.3g** recognize and read irregularly spelled words; **SL.1.1a** follow rules for discussions; **SL.1.1b** build on others' talk in conversations by responding to others' comments; **SL.1.6** produce complete sentences when appropriate to task and situation; **L.1.6** use words and phrases acquired through conversations, reading and being read to, and responding to texts

T362 • Unit 3 Lesson 14

Opening Routines

Warm Up with Wordplay

Make a Sentence

Remind children that they have learned some new words this week. Display and read the following:

anticipate	**clumsy**	**hooray**
lizard	**pace**	**roadrunner**

Have children explain the meaning of each word in their own words. Then call on a child to make a sentence with the first word from the list. Call on another child to make a sentence with the next word. Repeat the list until each child has made up a sentence. ▭ **SL.1.6, L.1.6**

Daily Phonemic Awareness

Substitute Medial Phonemes

- *We're going to change the middle sound in a word to make a new word. For example, let's change short a to long a. Change the short a in mad to a long a: /m/ /ā/ /d/. made Good! Let's keep going.*

Change the . . .	Result
/ă/ in *plan* to /ā/	plane
/ā/ in *tame* to /ĭ/	Tim
/ī/ in *line* to /ā/	lane
/ā/ in *hate* to /ă/	hat
/ă/ in *back* to /ā/	bake

- Have children repeat the "Result" words and tell whether the vowel sound in each one is long or short. Long: *plane, lane, bake;* Short: *Tim, hat* ▬ **RF.1.2a**

Corrective Feedback

- If a child misses a word, say the correct word and model the task. *Listen to the word plan, /p/ /l/ /ă/ /n/. Now change /ă/ to /ā/: /p/ /l/ /ā/ /n/. What is the new word? plane*

- Have children complete the task with you before doing it on their own.

- Then have them continue with the remaining words.

Daily High-Frequency Words

Introduce

- Point to the **High-Frequency Word Card** *over*.

- *Say the word. over Spell the word. o, v, e, r Write the word. Check the word.*

- Repeat the procedure with the words *four, five, into, starts, three, two,* and *watch.* ▬ **RF.1.3g**

Word Jar Game

- Write each High-Frequency Word on a piece of paper.

- Place the papers in a big jar.

- Have children take turns picking out a word and reading it to the class.

- Have children repeat each word.

Corrective Feedback

- If a child is unable to recognize the word *watch*, say the correct word and have children repeat it. *Watch. What is the word? watch*

- Have children spell the word. *w,a,t,c,h How do we say this word? watch*

- Have children reread all of the cards in random order.

Daily Vocabulary Boost

- Guide children to interact with the Oral Vocabulary words by asking the following questions. Remind them to speak clearly when participating in a discussion.

  Why would you search for something?

  Where are the stems on flowers?

  Why would a dog howl?

- Ask children to work with a partner to explain *search, stems,* and *howl* in their own words. Have each child respond to what their partner says so that they build a conversation. Make sure children follow appropriate rules for discussion such as listening to speakers, taking turns, and staying on topic. ▬ **SL.1.1a, SL.1.1b, L.1.6**

 **Oral Vocabulary**

- cactus
- habitat
- mainly
- search
- stems
- howl

Whole Group

DAY 4

Go Digital
• Interactive Whiteboard Lesson
• Decodable Reader

JOURNEYS
Phonics

Interactive Whiteboard Lesson: Words with Long *a* (CVCe) and Words with Soft *c, g, dge*

Phonemic Awareness/Phonics

SHARE OBJECTIVES

• Blend, read, and decode regularly spelled one-syllable words with long *a* and soft *c*, *g*, and *dge*.

• Review and sort words with long *a*, *sh*, and *wh*.

• Read on-level decodable text with soft *c*, *g*, *dge* and high-frequency words.

SKILLS TRACE

Words with Long *a*	
Introduce	T318–T319
Differentiate	T388
Reteach	T402
▶ **Review**	**T342, T364**
Assess	Weekly Tests, Lesson 14

SKILLS TRACE

Words with Soft *c, g, dge*	
Introduce	T352–T353
Differentiate	T394
Reteach	T402
▶ **Review**	**T364**
Assess	Weekly Tests, Lesson 14

COMMON CORE **RL.1.2** retell stories and demonstrate understanding of the message or lesson; **RF.1.2c** isolate and pronounce sounds in spoken single-syllable words; **RF.1.3b** decode regularly spelled one-syllable words; **RF.1.3c** know final -e and vowel team conventions for representing long vowel sounds; **RF.1.3g** recognize and read irregularly spelled words; **RF.1.4a** read on-level text with purpose and understanding; **RF.1.4b** read on-level text orally with accuracy, appropriate rate, and expression; **L.1.2d** use conventional spelling for words with common spelling patterns and for frequently occurring irregular words

Review Long *a* (CVCe) and Soft *c, g, dge*

PHONEMIC AWARENESS WARM-UP Tell children that you will say a word and then ask them to change the middle sound to make a new word. *Listen: The word is* tack. *Change the* /ă/ *to* /ĭ/. *What is the new word?* tick Continue the pattern using these words: *lot-late, pin-pan, wig-wag, stack-stake.*

MAKE AND READ WORDS On the board, copy the letters and incomplete words below. Tell children they will help you make new words by adding the missing letters to complete a word. Explain that you will give clues to help them. As each word is suggested, write the missing letters. Model with the first word. Read the following clues. Reread all the words to complete the activity. ▭ RF.1.3b, L.1.2d

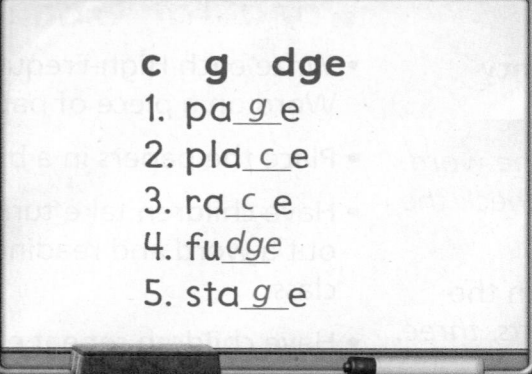

c g dge
1. pa_g_e
2. pla_c_e
3. ra_c_e
4. fu_dge_
5. sta_g_e

1. This is a part of a book.
2. This is somewhere to go.
3. People run in this.
4. This is a chocolate treat.
5. This is a place to perform.

GROUPING WORDS BY SOUND Display **Sound/Spelling Card** *acorn* and review the *a_e* spelling. Say *shape.* Have children identify the vowel sound. Then make a two-column chart on the board, using **Letter Cards** for *sh* and *wh* as headings. Have children identify the beginning sound in *shape* and tell you under which letters to write the word. Continue sorting: *whale, shade, whip, shop, shut, which, shame, when.*

Have children copy the completed chart. Then have them work with partners to read the words and underline those that do not have the long *a* sound. Review their work. ▭ RF.1.2c, RF.1.3b

a
a_e
ai
_ay

Decodable Reader

Read *The Race*

Decodable Reader,
Unit 3, pp. 93–98

REVIEW SOFT *c, g, dge* AND WORDS TO KNOW Tell children that many words in this story have soft *c, g,* or *dge.* Point out that children have learned the following words, which they will also read in the story: *four, into, over, starts, two, watch.*

PREVIEW Have children preview pages 93–95 and predict what the story is about. Ask volunteers to tell about a race they either saw or took part in.

MODEL FLUENCY AND EXPRESSION Read aloud page 95 as children follow along. As you read, have children note how excited you sound when you read the last sentence. Lead children in choral reading the page with fluency and expression.

READ Remind children to track the words from left to right, and when they come to the end of a line, to sweep their hand down to the beginning of the next line and continue reading. Have children read each page silently and then choral read it. Have them read to find out what happens during the race.
🔲 RF.1.3b, RF.1.3c, RF.1.3g, RF.1.4a

RESPONDING Have partners retell the story to each other. Ask them to identify their favorite part of the story and tell why they like it. 🔲 RL.1.2

Corrective Feedback Work with the whole group to correct errors, following the model below.

Decoding Error:
A child reads *pace* as *pack.*

Correct the error. Say the word. *That word is* pace. *The middle sound is long* a. *The a-consonant-e pattern often stands for the long a sound.*

Guide Have children repeat the word. *What is the word?* pace

Check *Go back to the beginning of the sentence and read it again.*

Reinforce Record the error and review the word again before children reread the story.

Reread for Fluency/ Develop Automaticity

READ WITH A PARTNER Have partners reread *The Race* three or four times, taking turns reading aloud each page. Remind them to read words correctly and to read smoothly. Visit partners to listen to them read. Give feedback about reading accurately, at an appropriate rate, and with expression and provide guidance for improving fluency. 🔲 RF.1.4b

Lesson 14

INFORMATIONAL TEXT

Read Together

☑ **GENRE**

Informational text gives facts on a topic. It can be from a textbook, article, or website. Look for facts about rules and laws as you read.

☑ **TEXT FOCUS**

Labels are words that tell more about a picture or photo. They can name parts of or the whole picture. What information do the labels in this selection give?

  RI.1.5 know and use text features to locate facts or information; **RI.1.10** read informational texts

148

Rules and Laws

by J. C. Cunningham

Health Rule

Rules

Who needs rules? We all do! Some rules keep us safe and healthy. Some rules help us learn. There are even rules to help us have fun!

Safety Rule

Can you find the child following this rule? **Raise your hand to speak.** What other rules are the children following? What could happen if they did not follow the rules?

School Rule

Game Rule

 1

149

DOMAIN: Civics

LESSON TOPIC: Citizenship

Cross-Curricular Connection Remind children that there are rules for everyone at school and in a community. Discuss classroom rules and rules for citizens in a neighborhood community, such as stopping at stop signs and not littering. Have groups or partners discuss the purpose of having rules at school and in their community and why it is important to follow the rules.

 **RI.1.2** identify the main topic and retell key details; **RI.1.3** describe the connection between individuals, events, ideas, or information in a text; **RI.1.5** know and use text features to locate facts or information; **RI.1.7** use illustrations and details to describe key ideas; **RI.1.8** identify the reasons an author gives to support points; **RI.1.10** read informational texts

Connect to the Topic
Informational Text

Introduce Genre and Text Focus

- Read with children the genre and text focus information on **Student Book** p. 148. Review that informational texts give facts about a topic.

- Point out a few labels and read them with children. Remind them that labels are words that tell more about a picture or photo. Have children point to labels, tell what information they give, and explain how the labels make the information easier to find. 🔊 **RI.1.5**

- Read the selection with children. 🔊 **RI.1.10**

- After reading, discuss the information with children. Direct them to use the labels to find key facts and information about the different rules and laws. Have children retell key details they learned from the photos and the text about rules and laws. 🔊 **RI.1.2, RI.1.5, RI.1.7**

② Traffic Law

Laws

Our government has rules, too. The rules are called laws. Laws keep us safe and healthy. Laws make sure we treat each other fairly.

150

EMPLOYEES MUST WASH HANDS

Can you find the person who obeyed this law? Employees must wash hands. What other laws do you think the pictures show?

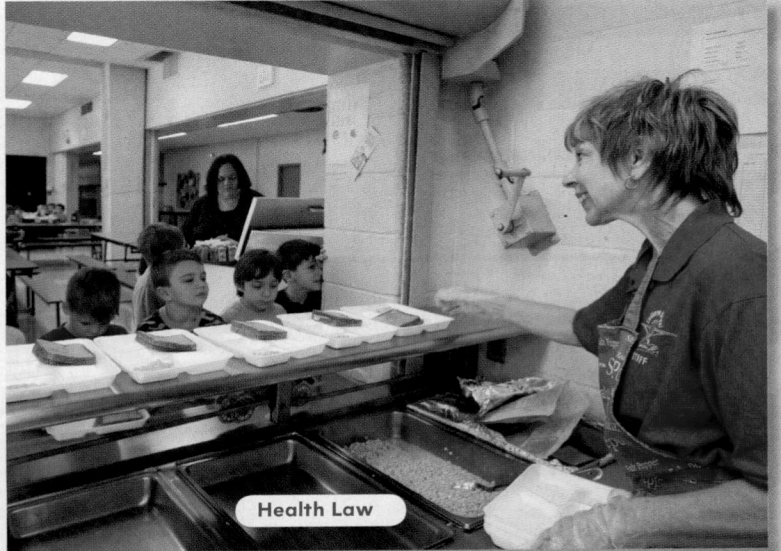

Health Law

151

FIRST READ

Use Text Evidence

Think Through the Text

① *The author gives several reasons why we need rules. What are some of the reasons?* Rules keep us safe and healthy, help us learn, and even help us have fun.
RI.1.2, RI.1.8

② *Look at the label on p. 150. What information does the label help you find?* It points out a car stopped at a stoplight. It is obeying a traffic law. *How does the label "Traffic Law" relate to the text that says "Laws keep us safe and healthy"?* When people follow traffic laws, we are safe because we don't get into accidents. **RI.1.3, RI.1.5**

• eBook

Laws help us to be good neighbors and good citizens. **3**

STOP **4**

What laws do you think these people are following? How do the laws help?

5

152

153

ELL **ENGLISH LANGUAGE LEARNERS**

Comprehensible Input

All Proficiencies Support ELLs in understanding the concepts and vocabulary about rules and laws by discussing helpful photographs and details in *Rules* and *Laws*. For example, point to the stop sign. Say the following, using gestures to clarify: *When drivers or bike riders come to a stop sign, they must stop. It is a law. This law keeps people safe. After they stop, they look both ways. If no car or truck is coming, they can go.*

COMMON CORE **RI.1.2** identify the main topic and retell key details; **RI.1.3** describe the connection between individuals, events, ideas, or information in a text; **RI.1.7** use illustrations and details to describe key ideas; **W.1.2** write informative/explanatory texts; **SL.1.1a** follow rules for discussions; **SL.1.1b** build on others' talk in conversations by responding to others' comments

Think Through the Text

Use Text Evidence

3 *How do laws help us be good neighbors?* When we follow the laws, we make our neighborhood cleaner and safer. ▪ **RI.1.2**

4 *Look at the photographs on pp. 152–153. How are they alike?* They both have stop signs. They show signs that help keep us safe. *How are they different?* One stop sign is on the bus and one is on a pole on the side of a road. ▪ **RI.1.3, RI.1.7**

5 *Look at each photograph on pp. 152–153. What rules and laws do you think the people are following?* Discuss each photo with children and guide them to understand the rules and laws. ▪ **RI.1.2, RI.1.3, RI.1.7**

Who needs
rules and laws?
We all do!

154

Compare Texts

Read Together

TEXT TO TEXT

Compare Stories Think about the
selections. Which is real and which is
make-believe? Tell how you know. Take
turns sharing evidence with a partner.

TEXT TO SELF

Write a List Write a list of rules the
runners should follow in **The Big Race**.
Tell why the rules make sense.

TEXT TO WORLD

Map a Race Course Pretend you will
run a race through your neighborhood.
Where does the race begin? Where is
the finish line? Draw a map.

Go Digital

RL.1.5 explain major differences between story books and informational books; W.1.2 write informative/explanatory texts; SL.1.1a follow rules for discussions; SL.1.1b build on others' talk in conversations by responding to others' comments

155

Compare Texts

TEXT TO TEXT

Compare Stories Have
children page through *The Big
Race* and *Rules and Laws* and
tell a partner which selection is
make-believe and which gives
real information. Have them
give details about how they
know which is which. As
partners discuss, have them
follow discussion rules, such as
listening carefully to each other
and taking turns speaking. Tell
them to build the conversation
by adding their ideas to what
their partner says.
RL.1.5, SL.1.1a, SL.1.1b

TEXT TO SELF

Write a List Have children
recall the beginning, middle,
and end of the race in the story
and think of rules that are
needed to make sure the race is
fair. Then children write a list
of the rules. Tell them that
when they write the list, they
can use a number to begin
each item. Have children
explain to a partner or group
why they think the rules they
wrote are good rules for
a race. W.1.2

TEXT TO WORLD

Map a Race Course Guide
children to understand map
symbols and cardinal directions
and use them when they make
their maps. Have them check
that their maps include a
starting point and finish line.
Then ask children to share their
maps in small groups. Have
them point out the route and
describe what the race would
be like.

Whole Group

DAY 4

- Interactive Whiteboard Lesson
- Literacy and Language Guide

Interactive Whiteboard Lesson:
Shades of Meaning

Vocabulary Strategies

▶ SHARE OBJECTIVES

- Distinguish shades of meaning among verbs and adjectives.

▶ SKILLS TRACE

Shades of Meaning	
Introduce	Unit 1 T64–T65
Differentiate	T400–T401
Reteach	T403
Review	T370–T371
Assess	Weekly Tests, Lesson 14

ELL ENGLISH LANGUAGE LEARNERS
Comprehensible Input

Beginning Ask children, *When do we usually sleep?* Help them answer, *at night. When do we usually nap?* Help them answer, *during the day. Are sleeping and napping the same thing?* Help them express the differences.

Low Intermediate Help children see the difference between *sleeping* and *napping* by comparing usual habits of either adults and children, people and animals, or different kinds of pets.

High Intermediate Help children compare *sleeping* with *napping* by asking questions such as *When do you nap/sleep? For how long do you nap/sleep? What do you wear to nap/to sleep?*

Proficient Have children work in pairs to name synonyms of *sleeping* and explain their differences.

See ELL Lesson 14, p. E37 for further support.

 **COMMON CORE** **L.1.5d** distinguish shades of meaning among verbs by defining or by acting out the meanings

Shades of Meaning

1 Teach/Model

Terms About Language

classify to place similar things in a group

categorize to name a group of similar things

context words and sentences around a word; a word's context gives clues to its meaning.

- Review the definitions of *classify, categorize,* and *context.* Explain that words in the same category may have similar meanings. Good readers use nearby words and sentences as clues to a word's meaning.

- Point out that acting out words that mean almost the same thing can help show how the words are slightly different. Write *stare* and *glance* on the board. Tell children that these words both mean *to look,* but each means looking in a different way. Model staring at the door. Then model glancing at the door. Discuss how your actions show that glancing is shorter than staring.

- Model using context to figure out the meanings of similar words. Write the following sentences on the board and read them aloud.

> The dog <u>slept</u> all night. The cat <u>napped</u> a few minutes. The <u>chilly</u> breeze moved through the tree. The <u>cold</u> wind blew the door open.

Think Aloud *Slept and* napped *are verbs. They both mean to close your eyes to rest. But I can tell from the other words in the sentences that they mean this in different ways.* All night *tells me that* slept *means for a longer time.* A few minutes *shows that* napped *is for a short time.* Chilly *and* cold *mean almost the same thing, too. They describe how something feels.* Breeze moved *and* wind blew *are clues. I think* cold *is a stronger feeling than* chilly.

Model acting out *slept, napped, chilly,* and *cold* to show the difference in meaning for each word.

Literacy and Language Guide
Additional Lesson 14 vocabulary lessons appear in the Literacy and Language Guide.

2 Guided Practice

- Display the word bank at the top of **Projectable 14.7**. Read the words aloud.

- Display the rest of **Projectable 14.7**. Point out the chart headings and read them aloud. Explain that you will work together to sort the words into the correct categories.

- Point to the first category title and ask children to say a verb from the box (*sweep*). Record it in the chart.

- Then have a volunteer act out the word and tell what it means. Write the definition in the chart. Repeat with an adjective.

Projectable 14.7

The Big Race | Vocabulary Strategies | Shades of Meaning

Shades of Meaning

| sweep | huge | scrub | small |
| big | dust | gigantic | mop |

Action Words	
sweep	to clean with a broom
scrub	to clean by rubbing
dust	to clean the dust off
mop	to clean with a mop

Descriptive Words	
huge	very large
small	little
big	large
gigantic	extremely large

Vocabulary Strategies
© Houghton Mifflin Harcourt Publishing Company. All rights reserved.

Grade 1, Unit 3

3 Apply

- Have partners work together to complete the charts. Remind them to choose the verbs or adjectives that belong in each category, act them out quietly to help them understand each word's meaning, and then give a definition for the word.

- After all the words have been sorted, have children discuss the definitions. Tell them to compare and contrast words in the same category. How are they similar? How are they different?

L.1.5d

Are children able to distinguish shades of meaning among words?

IF...	THEN...
children have difficulty distinguishing shades of meaning among words,	▶ **Differentiate Vocabulary Strategies** for Struggling Readers, p. T400
children can distinguish shades of meaning among most words,	▶ **Differentiate Vocabulary Strategies** for On-Level Readers, p. T400
children can easily distinguish shades of meaning among words,	▶ **Differentiate Vocabulary Strategies** for Advanced Readers, p. T401

SMALL GROUP Options

Differentiate Vocabulary Strategies: pp. T400–T401.
Group English Language Learners according to academic ability and language proficiency.

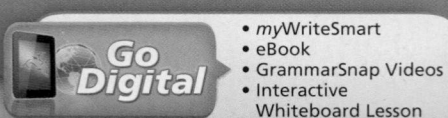
* *my*WriteSmart
* eBook
* GrammarSnap Videos
* Interactive Whiteboard Lesson

Grammar Spiral Review: Singular and Plural Nouns

▶ SHARE OBJECTIVES

* **Grammar** Review singular and plural nouns with matching verbs in a sentence.
* **Spelling** Spell words with the long *a* sound using conventional spelling patterns.
* **Handwriting** Print the spelling words.
* **Writing** Use a graphic organizer to begin planning a report.

 **ENGLISH LANGUAGE LEARNERS**

Language Transfer

All Proficiencies Display pairs of words representing both singular and plural (e.g., *girl/girls, man/men, lunch/lunches, child/children,* etc.). Guide children in telling which one is singular (only one), and which one is plural (more than one).

See ELL Lesson 14, p. E39, for scaffolded support.

1 Teach/Model

SINGULAR AND PLURAL NOUNS Write these sentences on the board: *Two children watch a race. The rabbits run in the park. Which words name one?* race, park *Which words name more than one?* children, rabbits

* Review that some nouns name one, and some nouns name more than one. An *s* ending means more than one. Point out that some special nouns change their spelling to name more than one.

man	men
child	children
woman	women
girl	girls

* Use a chart like the one pictured to model writing nouns that name one and more than one.
* Review that singular and plural nouns need matching verbs to make a complete sentence.

2 Guided Practice/Apply

* Have volunteers suggest nouns that name one and more than one to add to the chart. Then have children write sentences using singular and plural nouns from the chart with matching verbs. **L.1.1b, L.1.1c, L.1.1j**

Spelling Words with Long *a*

SPELLING WORDS

BASIC

came	make
brave	late
gave	shape

CHALLENGE

waves	chases

Connect to Writing

* Remind children that they have been learning to use verbs with *-ed* endings.
* Ask children to use the spelling words to write sentences that contain verbs with *-ed* endings. Remind them to proofread their sentences. Then invite volunteers to read their sentences aloud.
* Finally, tell children that the class will practice spelling the words together. Say each word and spell it aloud with children. **L.1.2d**

Handwriting

Model how to form the basic words *late* and *shape* using handwriting models available on **Handwriting Models Blackline Masters**. Have children print the spelling words using their best handwriting. **L.1.1a**

COMMON CORE **W.1.2** write informative/explanatory texts; **W.1.5** focus on a topic, respond to questions/suggestions from peers, and add details to strengthen writing; **W.1.6** use digital tools to produce and publish writing; **W.1.8** recall information from experiences or gather information from sources to answer a question; **L.1.1a** print upper- and lowercase letters; **L.1.1b** use common, proper, and possessive nouns; **L.1.1c** use singular and plural nouns with matching verbs in sentences; **L.1.1j** produce and expand simple and compound declarative, interrogative, imperative, and exclamatory sentences; **L.1.2d** use conventional spelling for words with common spelling patterns and for frequently occurring irregular words

T372 • Unit 3 Lesson 14

Informative Writing Prewriting

1 Teach/Model

PLANNING A RESEARCH REPORT Tell children that they can find information about animals in books or magazines or on the computer. Use the Study Skills lessons on pp. R2–R3 to help children find relevant books in the library and distinguish nonfiction from fiction. Show children how they can use sticky notes to mark places with important information.

- Read aloud the first paragraph of "The Prickly Pride of Texas" on page T212. Have children say what it tells them about the prickly pear cactus. *The Aztecs built their city where they saw the cactus.* Put a sticky note next to the sentence, *The signal told the Aztecs that they had found the correct location. This can help remind me that I learned something important about the prickly pear cactus.*

- Display **Projectable 14.8**. Read the prompt.
- Review that your topic is tigers. Then model filling in the graphic organizer.

Think Aloud *My question was about what tigers can do. I'll write that as a question in the first box. Now, I'll use books and other sources to find some answers to my question.*

- Model looking up this information online or in books or magazines.
- Save the completed chart for use on Day 1 next week.

2 Independent Writing

- Have children copy and begin completing a graphic organizer such as the one shown on **Projectable 14.8**. Remind them to focus on their topic. You may also want to distribute **Reader's Notebook** Vol. 1 page 208.
- Remind children that their questions should be broad enough to be answered in several ways.
- Review that questions and answers should be interesting to people who read the finished report. Have children ask and answer questions with a partner and add details to their graphic organizers as needed.
- Guide children to use digital tools such as a word processing program to help them edit and publish their work.

W.1.2, W.1.5, W.1.6, W.1.8

Reader's Notebook Vol. 1 p. 207

Reader's Notebook Vol. 1 p. 206

DAY 5

Today's Goals

Vocabulary & Oral Language
- Domain-Specific Vocabulary and Speaking & Listening

Phonemic Awareness
- Identify Middle Sounds and Substitute Phonemes

Phonics & Fluency
- Independent Reading: Decodable Reader

☑ **WORDS TO KNOW**

four	starts
five	three
into	two
over	watch

Text-Based Comprehension
  Extend the Topic
- Speaking & Listening: Speaking About a Topic

Assess & Reteach
- Assess Skills
- Respond to Assessment

Grammar & Writing
- Verbs and Time
- ➡ Informative Writing: Report

Spelling
- Words with Long *a*

RF.1.2a distinguish long from short vowel sounds in spoken single-syllable words; **RF.1.3g** recognize and read irregularly spelled words; **L.1.6** use words and phrases acquired through conversations, reading and being read to, and responding to texts

Opening Routines

Warm Up with Wordplay

How Do They Go Together?

Display and read aloud the following:

laws   rules   police

Have children discuss with a partner to figure out how these words belong together. Have children listen and take turns as they compare their answers. Then tell them the correct answer: these words are all things that help keep us safe.

Have children come up with other words about rules and safety. Write down the responses and say them aloud with children. Have them brainstorm people that keep us safe or certain rules in games or public places.

Daily Phonemic Awareness

Identify Middle Sounds and Substitute Phonemes

- *Today we're going to change the vowel sound in a word to make a new word. Let's start with the word cut. What is its vowel sound? short u Change the short u to short a. What is the word? cat Good!*

Change the . . .	Result
/ă/ in *black* to /ŏ/	block
/ă/ in *fast* to /ĭ/	fist
/ă/ in *rack* to /ā/	rake
/ă/ in *mast* to /ŭ/	must
/ŭ/ in *run* to /ā/	rain

- Have children repeat the "Result" words and tell whether its vowel sound is long or short. *Long: rake, rain; Short: block, fist, must* **RF.1.2a**

Corrective Feedback

- If a child misses a word, say the correct word and model the task. *Listen to the word: black, /b/ /l/ /ă/ /k/. Now change /ă/ to /ŏ/: /b/ /l/ /ŏ/ /k/. What is the new word? block*
- Have children complete the task with you before doing it on their own.
- Then have them continue with the remaining words.

Daily High-Frequency Words

Introduce

- Point to the **High-Frequency Word Card** *starts*.
- *Say the word. starts Spell the word. s, t, a, r, t, s Write the word. Check the word.*
- Repeat the procedure with the words from this week (*four, five, into, over, three, two, watch*) and last week (*down, fall, goes, green, grow, new, open, yellow*). **RF.1.3g**

Find the Letter Game

- Choose a word from this week's or the previous week's High-Frequency Words. Write a dash on the board to represent each letter in the word.
- Have children call out letters. If the letter is in the word, write it on the appropriate blank.
- Continue until children can guess the word. Ask the child who guesses the word correctly to come to the board to choose the next word.

Corrective Feedback

- If a child is unable to recognize the word *three*, say the correct word and have children repeat it. *Three. What is the word? three*
- Have children spell the word. *t,h,r,e,e How do we say this word? three*
- Have children reread all of the cards in random order.

Daily Vocabulary Boost

- Reread "The Tortoise and the Hare" aloud to children. (See pp. T316–T317.)
- As you read each Oral Vocabulary word in the selection, have a volunteer explain or describe its meaning. Have each child think of a sentence for each Oral Vocabulary word. Repeat the list until each child has come up with a sentence.
- After reading, review the Oral Vocabulary words and their definitions. Challenge children to use the words in their everyday speech. **L.1.6**

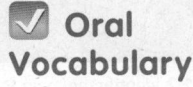 **Oral Vocabulary**

cactus

habitat

mainly

search

stems

howl

 DOMAIN: Civics

LESSON TOPIC: Citizenship

Extend the Topic

▶ SHARE OBJECTIVES

- Acquire and use domain-specific vocabulary.
- Participate in conversations about a topic.
- Follow agreed-upon rules for discussions.
- Ask and answer questions about key details in information presented orally.

Words About the Topic: Citizenship

- **legal** allowed by the law
- **rule** a guide for how to stay safe or to behave
- **duty** a job you should do

◗ Domain-Specific Vocabulary

INTRODUCE WORDS ABOUT THE TOPIC Remind children that this week's topic is Citizenship. Display the words shown at the left. Tell children that these are words that can help them learn more about the topic. Read aloud the meaning of each word, and have children respond to the following prompts. ▬ **L.1.5c, L.3.6**

- *If you have a driver's license, it is _____ for you to drive a car.* legal

- **Without using the term** *rule*, **name a rule that you have established for your classroom. For example,** *Before you speak in our class, you must raise your hand and wait to be called on. What do we call that?* _____. *a rule*

- *Can you name one example of a duty that members of our classroom have?* Accept reasonable responses.

INTERACT WITH THE WORDS Have children work in small groups to create Four-Square Maps. For each of the domain-specific words, children should fold a blank sheet of paper into four equal sections. Work with them to follow the steps below for each word. As needed, display the meanings of the words on the board. Ask individual children to use the words in a sentence orally. Then write the sentence on the board for other children to refer to for ideas.

1 In the first corner, draw a picture for the word.

2 In the second corner, write the meaning of the word.

3 In the third corner, write a sentence using the word.

4 In the fourth corner, write the word.

When groups have finished, have them share their Four-Square Maps with the class. ▬ **L.1.5c, L.3.6**

COMMON CORE **RI.1.2** identify the main topic and retell key details; **RI.1.3** describe the connection between individuals, events, ideas, or information in a text; **SL.1.1a** follow rules for discussions; **SL.1.1c** ask questions to clear up confusion about topics and texts under discussion; **SL.1.2** ask and answer questions about details in a text read aloud, information presented orally, or through other media; **SL.1.3** ask and answer questions about what a speaker says; **L.1.5c** identify real-life connections between words and their use; **L.1.6** use words and phrases acquired through conversations, reading and being read to, and responding to texts

Speaking and Listening
Speaking About a Topic

REVIEW RULES AND LAWS Have the class look back at *Rules and Laws*. Ask children to give an example from the selection of a rule or law and then explain what is good about it. What problem does it prevent? 🔲 RI.1.2, RI.1.3

Brainstorm with the class other rules or laws from school, home, social groups, or the neighborhood. Tell children that they are going to give a speech about why a particular rule or law is good. Display and review the Tips for Giving a Speech.

GIVING GROUP SPEECHES Organize children into groups. Have each group prepare a speech about why a rule or law is good. First groups should discuss and take notes. Then they plan the speech by deciding on the main idea and important details. The speech should include reasons why the rule or law is good, using the word *because*.

Remind children to follow the discussion rules as they plan their speeches, and guide them to build the conversation with each other through multiple exchanges by responding to the comments of others and adding their own ideas. 🔲 SL.1.1a, SL.1.1b

Have each group choose one member to give the speech, practice it together, and then present it to the class. After the speech is over, have listeners ask questions about key details in the information presented to gather more information or to clarify something they don't understand. Have group members answer the questions, or work with children to find the answers together. 🔲 SL.1.1c, SL.1.2, SL.1.3

PRACTICE GIVING A SPEECH Have children imagine that they are the President and are able to make up a new law. Tell them to think through the new law. What would it tell people to do, or not to do? Why is the law good and what problem would it help solve?

Have children write notes about their main idea and reasons why the law would be good. Have partners practice their speeches with each other, and then ask children to present their speeches in small groups. Tell them to use the word *because* when they give reasons in their speech. Have groups ask and answer questions about the new laws. 🔲 SL.1.1c, SL.1.2, SL.1.3, SL.1.6

Tips for Giving a Speech

1. **Plan your speech.**

2. **Write notes to remember important ideas.**

3. **Say your main idea at the beginning. Give reasons.**

4. **Speak clearly and loudly enough to be heard.**

Name _____ Date _____ | Listening Log

Listening Log
Title _____

| What was your favorite part? |

| Write a question about what you heard. |

Listening Log | 13 | Grade 1 Additional Resources

Listening Log

• eBook
• GrammarSnap Videos

Grammar Weekly Review: Verbs and Time

▶ SHARE OBJECTIVES

- **Grammar** Write present and past tense verbs correctly.
- **Spelling** Spell words with the long *a* sound using conventional spelling patterns.

ELL ENGLISH LANGUAGE LEARNERS
Language Transfer

Beginning Display the words *make, place, name, cape.* Read the words aloud and have children clap whenever they hear the /ā/ sound.

Low Intermediate Have children use letter cards to build and read *place, name, cape.*

High Intermediate Have children use letter cards to build and read *place.* Guide them in changing the cards to read *case, cake, make, name.*

Proficient Have children in groups use letter cards *m, c, k, v, a, e, g, l, s, h, t, m, n* to build and read as many words with the /ā/ sound as they can.

1 Review/Practice

- Together read the text at the top of **Student Book** p. 156. Discuss the verbs that tell about actions that happen now and that happened in the past.

- Direct children's attention to the Try This! activity on **Student Book** p. 157. Have children write the verb so it tells about the past.

2 Connect to Writing

CONVENTIONS: PROOFREADING Write the following statements on the board:

The running race starts yesterday.

The swimming race started now.

- Ask children to identify the mistakes orally.
- Model using proofreading marks to correct the first sentence.
- Have children identify and correct the errors in the second sentence. Have them identify the base word in each verb and the ending that helps tell time. **L.1.4c**
- Remind children to use verbs to tell about action that happens now and action that happened in the past to make their own writing clear. **L.1.1e, L.1.1j**

Spelling Words with Long *a*

SPELLING WORDS AND SENTENCES

BASIC

1. **came** Sam *came* to my party.
2. **make** Will you *make* me a cake?
3. **brave** He was *brave* and did not cry.
4. **late** Don't be *late* for school.
5. **gave** I *gave* Maria a ride on my bike.
6. **shape** The cake was in a round *shape*.

CHALLENGE

7. **waves** Big *waves* crashed on the beach.
8. **chases** My cat always *chases* his tail.

Assess

Say each spelling word, read the sentence, and then repeat the word. Have children write the word. **L.1.2d**

Corrective Feedback

Review any words that children misspell.

L.1.1e use verbs to convey sense of past, present, and future; **L.1.1j** produce and expand simple and compound declarative, interrogative, imperative, and exclamatory sentences; **L.1.2d** use conventional spelling for words with common spelling patterns and for frequently occurring irregular words; **L.1.4.c** identify frequently occurring root words and their inflectional forms

COMMON CORE L.1.1e use verbs to convey sense of past, present, and future

Grammar Read Together  Go Digital

Verbs and Time Some **verbs** tell what is happening now. Some verbs tell what happened in the past. Add **ed** to most verbs to tell about the past.

Now	In the Past
The animals **watch** the race now.	The animals **watch<u>ed</u>** the race yesterday.
They **cheer** for their friends.	They **cheer<u>ed</u>** for their friends.

156

 **Try This!**

Work with a partner. One partner reads aloud a sentence. The other partner finds the verb. Together, write the verb to tell about the past. Take turns.

1. The runners look at the flag.
2. They start the race.
3. Some racers jump high.
4. They finish the race quickly.
5. The winners pick prizes.

 Grammar in Writing

When you proofread your writing, be sure each verb tells clearly if something is happening now or in the past.

157

 **Try This!**

1. looked
2. started
3. jumped
4. finished
5. picked

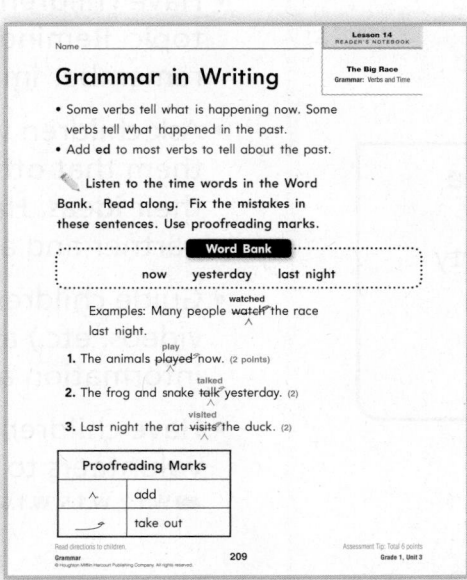

Reader's Notebook Vol. 1 p. 209

Informative Writing Prewriting

▶ SHARE OBJECTIVE

- **Writing** Use a graphic organizer to finish planning an animal report.

 **ENGLISH LANGUAGE LEARNERS**

Use Visuals

Beginning Tell children to include pictures in their charts to illustrate facts that they are not sure how to describe in words. Work with them to label the pictures.

Low Intermediate Have children draw pictures in their charts to illustrate facts that they are not sure how to describe in words.

High Intermediate Work with each child to brainstorm additional facts that he or she can add to the chart based on research.

Proficient Have children work with partners to revise and complete their graphic organizers.

*See ELL Lesson 14, p. E41,
for scaffolded support.*

Daily Proofreading Practice

The turtle and snake ~~gafe~~ gave a party last night.

All the animals ~~enjoy~~ enjoyed the party.

1 Teach/Model

PLANNING A REPORT Tell children that they will see how a first grader named Lena planned her report.

- Read together **Student Book** pp. 158–159 and discuss them with children.

- Point out that Lena used phrases to take notes for all three of the answers to her question. She also drew a picture. Explain that Lena could have drawn an arrow to the back legs of the lizard in the picture to help her remember that her note told about lizards' back legs.

- Discuss the question on **Student Book** p. 159. Use prompts like these to focus discussion: *Are these facts or opinions? How do you know? How do you think Lena found these facts? Do the facts answer her question? Why or why not?*

2 Independent Writing

- Ask children to complete their graphic organizers from Day 4. Have them refer to the Prewriting Checklist on **Student Book** p. 158.

- Have children check that they asked a good question about their topic. Remind them to make sure their notes help them remember important facts and details.

- Ask children who the audience for their reports will be. Remind them that other people need to be able to read and understand their ideas. Have children ask and answer questions with a partner and add details to their graphic organizers as needed.

- Guide children to use digital tools on the computer (Internet, videos, etc.) along with books and magazines to find more information about their topics.

- Have children make clean, final copies of their charts. Invite volunteers to display their work for classmates and read it aloud.
  🔲 W.1.2, W.1.5, W.1.6, W.1.8

COMMON CORE **W.1.2** write informative/explanatory texts; **W.1.5** focus on a topic, respond to questions/suggestions from peers, and add details to strengthen writing; **W.1.6** use digital tools to produce and publish writing; **W.1.8** recall information from experiences or gather information from sources to answer a question

W.1.2 write informative/explanatory texts; W.1.5 focus on a topic, respond to questions/suggestions from peers, and add details to strengthen writing; W.1.7 participate in shared research and writing projects; W.1.8 recall information from experiences or gather information from sources to answer a question

Reading-Writing Workshop: Prewrite

Informative Writing

✓ **Ideas** A good **report** needs facts! Before you write, find facts to answer the question you wrote about your topic. Lena found information about lizards. She took notes to remind her of the facts.

 Read Together

 my WriteSmart

Go Digital

Exploring a Topic

Prewriting Checklist

- ☑ Did I write a good question about my topic?
- ☑ Will my notes help me remember the facts?
- ☑ Did I use good sources for information?

158

Look for facts in Lena's notes. Then record your own notes. Use the Checklist.

Planning Chart

My Question
What do real lizards do?

Fact 1
change color

Fact 2
run fast on back legs

Fact 3
puff up to look big

159

See also the **Writing Rubric Blackline Master** on Teacher's Edition p. R11.

WRITING TRAITS SCORING RUBRIC

	Focus/Support	Organization	Word Choice/Voice	Conventions/Sentence Fluency
6	Develops topic or events with relevant facts or details.	Introduces topic or situation clearly, organizes ideas to support purpose, has relevant conclusion.	Links ideas with words, phrases. Uses specific language. Connects with reader in unique way.	Demonstrates exemplary command of conventions of standard written English. Includes variety of complete sentences that flow smoothly, naturally.
5	Mostly develops topic or events with relevant facts or details.	Introduces topic or situation, mostly organizes ideas to support purpose, has mostly relevant conclusion.	Links most ideas with words, phrases. Uses specific language. Connects with reader.	Demonstrates good command of conventions of standard written English. Includes some variety of complete sentences that flow smoothly, naturally.
4	Adequately develops topic or events with relevant facts or details.	Introduces topic or situation, adequately organizes ideas to support purpose, has adequate conclusion.	Links some ideas with words, phrases. Uses some specific language. Connects with reader.	Demonstrates adequate command of conventions of standard written English. Includes some variety of complete sentences. Some flow smoothly, naturally.
3	Develops topic or events with some relevant facts or details.	Introduces topic or situation, organizes some ideas to support purpose, has somewhat relevant conclusion.	Links some ideas with words, phrases. May use some specific language. May connect with reader.	Demonstrates command of some conventions of standard written English. Includes little variety of complete sentences. Few flow smoothly, naturally.
2	Develops topic or events with few relevant facts or details.	May introduce topic or situation, organizes few ideas to support purpose, may have somewhat relevant conclusion.	Attempts to link ideas with words. Rarely uses specific language. May not connect with reader.	Demonstrates little command of conventions of standard written English. Includes little sentence variety. Incomplete sentences hinder meaning.
1	May not develop topic or events with relevant facts or details.	May attempt to introduce topic or situation, may not organize ideas to support purpose, may not have relevant conclusion.	May not link ideas with words. Does not use specific language or connect with reader.	Demonstrates little or no command of conventions of standard written English. Sentences do not vary. Incomplete sentences hinder meaning.

☑ Progress Monitoring

Assess

Grab-&-Go!

- Weekly Tests
- Periodic Assessments

COMMON CORE

Respond to Assessment

☑ Vocabulary

High-Frequency Words
Strategies: Shades of Meaning

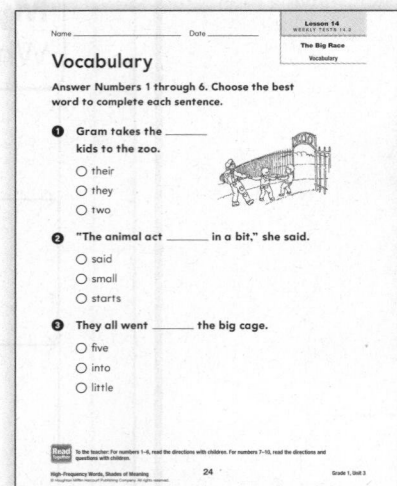

Weekly Tests 14.2–14.4

RF.3.3g recognize and read irregularly spelled words; **L.1.5d** distinguish shades of meaning among verbs and adjectives

IF a Child Scores...	THEN...
7–10 of 10	▶ Continue Core Instructional Program
1–6 of 10	▶ Reteaching Lesson, p. T403

If a child scores below target on two or more tests, then consider using Diagnostic Assessment to pinpoint the child's instructional needs. The child may need systematic intervention.

☑ Phonics/Decoding

Words with Long *a* (CVCe)
Words with Soft *c, g, dge*
Phonograms: -ake, -ace

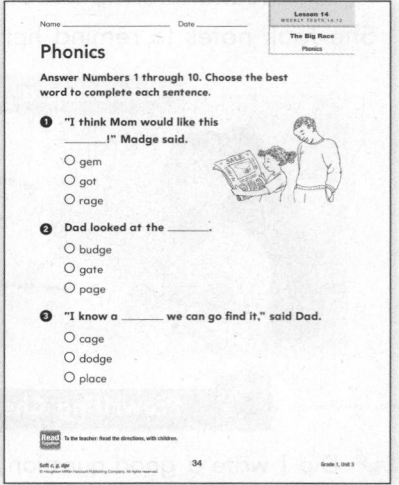

Weekly Tests 14.8–14.14
Phonemic Awareness
See Observation Checklist *in Grab-and-Go™ Resources.*

RF.1.3c know final -e and vowel team conventions for representing long vowel sounds

IF a Child Scores...	THEN...
7–10 of 10	▶ Continue Core Instructional Program
1–6 of 10	▶ Reteaching Lesson, p. T402

If a child scores below target on two or more tests, then consider using Diagnostic Assessment to pinpoint the child's instructional needs. The child may need systematic intervention.

 **Go Digital**
- Grab-and-Go Weekly Tests
- Online Assessment System
- Cold Reads Online
- ExamView Banks

 COMMON CORE

✓ Comprehension

Conclusions
Cause and Effect

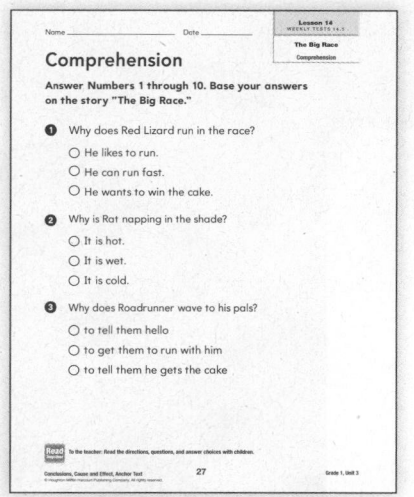

Weekly Tests 14.5–14.7

RL.1.3 describe characters, settings, and major events; **RL.1.7** use illustrations and details to describe characters, setting, or events

---

IF a Child Scores...	THEN...
7–10 of 10	▶ Continue Core Instructional Program
1–6 of 10	▶ Reteaching Lesson, p. T403

If a child scores below target on two or more tests, then consider using Diagnostic Assessment to pinpoint the child's instructional needs. The child may need systematic intervention.

✓ Language Arts

Grammar: Verbs and Time

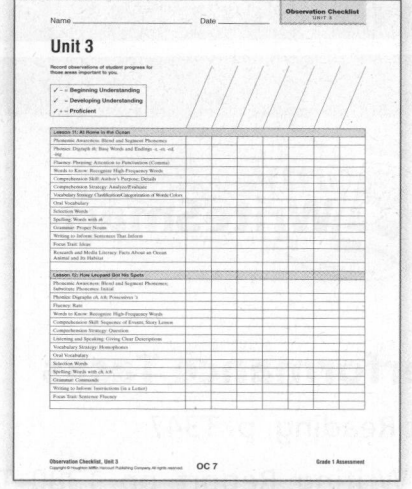

Observation Checklist, Assessment, p. OC7

L.1.1e use verbs to convey sense of past, present, and future

---

IF a Child Scores...	THEN...
Proficient	▶ Continue Core Instructional Program
Developing	▶ Review Instruction, pp. T338, T348, T360, T378–T379
Beginning	▶ Intervention Lesson 14, pp. S32–S41

If a child scores below target on two or more tests, then consider using Diagnostic Assessment to pinpoint the child's instructional needs. The child may need systematic intervention.

✓ FLUENCY

Fluency Plan Assess one group per week. Use the suggested plan below.

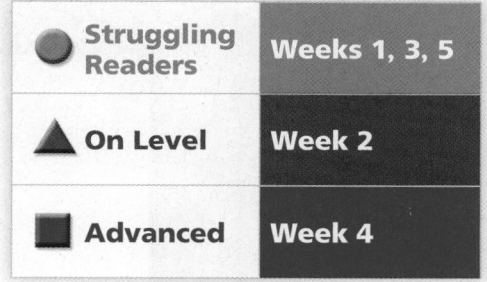

●	Struggling Readers	Weeks 1, 3, 5
▲	On Level	Week 2
■	Advanced	Week 4

Fluency Scoring Rubrics
See *Grab-and-Go™ Resources Assessment* for help in measuring progress.

Oral Reading Practice
Use the **Student Book**, the **Leveled Readers**, or other reading materials in this unit to help children improve fluency.

✓ COLD READS

Cold Reads *are leveled passages that can be used to practice and monitor fluency and comprehension.*

LESSON 14

Performance Tasks

Lesson Performance Tasks

- Write About Reading, p. T347
- Informative Writing: Report, pp. T380–T381
- Cumulative Performance Assessment, Task 4 of 5

Unit-Level Performance Tasks

- Research and Media Performance Task, pp. xxvi–xxvii
- Cumulative Performance Assessment

  Task 1: complete after Lesson 11

  Task 2: complete after Lesson 12

  Task 3: complete after Lesson 13

  Task 4: complete after Lesson 14

  Task 5: complete after Lesson 15

 **Weekly**
Small Group Instruction  **Go Digital**

 **DAY 1**

Differentiate
Phonics & Words to Know
- Words with Long *a* (CVCe)
- *four, five, into, over, starts, three, two, watch*

Vocabulary Reader
- *Desert Animals*

Vocabulary Reader

 **DAY 2**

Differentiate Comprehension
- Conclusions
- Infer/Predict

 **DAY 3**

Differentiate
Phonics & Fluency
- Soft *c, g, dge*
- Expression

Leveled Readers
- 🔴 *Izzy's Move*
- 🔺 *The Treasure Map*
- ⬛ *Cam the Camel*
- ◆ *The Map and the Treasure*

Leveled Readers

 **DAY 4**

Differentiate
Vocabulary Strategies
- Shades of Meaning

 **DAY 5**

Options for Reteaching
- Phonics
- Vocabulary Strategies
- Comprehension

Literacy Centers

Independent Practice
- Word Study, T310
- Think and Write, T311
- Comprehension and Fluency, T310
- Digital Center, T311

Word Study　　**Think and Write**　　**Comprehension and Fluency**

Suggested Small Group Plan

Differentiated Instruction

Teacher-Led		DAY 1	DAY 2	DAY 3
	Struggling Readers	**Vocabulary Reader** *Desert Animals*, Differentiated Instruction, p. T390 **Differentiate Phonics:** Long *a* (CVC*e*), p. T388	**Differentiate Comprehension:** Conclusions; Infer/Predict Strategy, p. T392 **Reread** *Dave and the Whales*, p. T343	**Leveled Reader** *Izzy's Move*, p. T396 **Differentiate Phonics:** Soft *c*, *g*, *dge*, T394 
	On Level	**Vocabulary Reader** *Desert Animals*, Differentiated Instruction, p. T390	**Differentiate Comprehension:** Conclusions; Infer/Predict Strategy, p. T392 **Reread** *Dave and the Whales*, p. T343	**Leveled Reader** *The Treasure Map*, p. T397 **Differentiate Fluency:** Expression, p. T395 
	Advanced	**Vocabulary Reader** *Desert Animals*, Differentiated Instruction, p. T391	**Differentiate Comprehension:** Conclusions; Infer/Predict Strategy, p. T393	**Leveled Reader** *Cam the Camel*, p. T398 **Differentiate Fluency:** Expression, p. T395 
	English Language Learners	**Vocabulary Reader** *Desert Animals*, Differentiated Instruction, p. T391 **Differentiate Words to Know** Using Context Cards, p. T389	**Differentiate Comprehension:** Conclusions; Infer/Predict Strategy, p. T393 **Reread** *Dave and the Whales*, p. T343	**Leveled Reader** *The Map and the Treasure*, p. T399 **Differentiate Fluency:** Expression, p. T395 

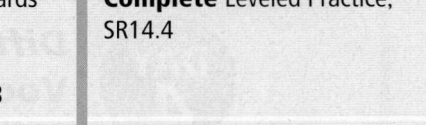

What are my other kids doing?				
	Struggling Readers	**Word Building:** Build and read Spelling Words using Letter Cards **Complete** Leveled Practice, SR14.1–SR14.2	**Words to Know:** Partners practice reading Context Cards **Reread** *Tate's Cakes* and *Dave and the Whales* **Complete** Leveled Practice, SR14.3	**Reread:** Partners read *Izzy's Move* **Complete** Leveled Practice, SR14.4
	On Level	**Word Building:** Build and read Words to Know using Letter Cards	**Words to Know:** Practice reading Context Cards **Reread** *Tate's Cakes* and *Dave and the Whales*	**Reread:** Partners read *The Treasure Map*
	Advanced	**Context Cards:** Assign Talk It Over activities **Complete** Leveled Practice, A14.1–A14.2	**Reread:** Partners read *The Big Race* **Complete** Leveled Practice, A14.3	**Reread** *Cam the Camel* **Complete** Leveled Practice, A14.4
	English Language Learners	**Listen** to Audio of *The Big Race* **Complete** Leveled Practice, ELL14.1–ELL14.2	**Listen:** Follow along with Audio of *The Big Race* **Retell:** Partners retell *The Big Race* using Retelling Cards **Complete** Leveled Practice, ELL14.3	**Reread:** Partners read *The Map and the Treasure* **Listen** to Audio of *Rules and Laws* **Complete** Leveled Practice, ELL14.4

For Strategic Intervention for this lesson, see pp. S32–S41.

DAY 4

Differentiate Vocabulary Strategies: Classify and Categorize Number Words, p. T400
Reread *The Race*, p. T365

Differentiate Vocabulary Strategies: Classify and Categorize Number Words p. T400
Reread *The Race*, p. T365

Differentiate Vocabulary Strategies: Classify and Categorize Number Words, p. T401

Differentiate Vocabulary Strategies: Classify and Categorize Number Words, p. T401
Reread *The Race*, p. T365

Reread: Partners read *The Race*
Listen to Audio of *Rules and Laws*

Reread *The Race*

Reread: Partners read *Rules and Laws*

Listen to Audio of *Rules and Laws*
Reread: Partners read *A Safe Lodge*

DAY 5

Options for Reteaching, pp. T402–T403
Reread one of this week's Decodable Reader selections.

Options for Reteaching, pp. T402–T403
Reread one of this week's Decodable Reader selections.

Options for Reteaching, pp. T402–T403
Reread one of this week's Decodable Reader selections.

Options for Reteaching, pp. T402–T403
Reread one of this week's Decodable Reader selections.

Reread: Choose among this week's stories
• Complete and share Literacy Center activities

Reread: Choose among this week's stories
• Complete and share Literacy Center activities

Reread: Choose among this week's stories
• Complete and share Literacy Center activities

Reread: Choose among this week's stories
• Complete and share Literacy Center activities

Weekly To-Do List

This Weekly To-Do List helps children see their own progress and move on to additional activities independently.

Name _____

Lesson 14
BLACKLINE MASTER 14.2

Weekly To-Do List

Put an X in each box when you finish the activity.

Must Do
☐ Practice pages
☐ Comprehension and Fluency Literacy Center
☐ Word Study Literacy Center
☐ Think and Write Literacy Center
☐ Read
☐ Other _____

May Do
☐ Reading Log
☐ Vocabulary in Context Cards
☐ Spelling
☐ Writing
☐ Other _____

I read . . .

☐ Monday	
☐ Tuesday	
☐ Wednesday	
☐ Thursday	
☐ Friday	

Read directions to students.
Weekly To-Do List
© Houghton Mifflin Harcourt Publishing Company. All rights reserved.
4
Grade 1, Unit 3

Differentiate Phonics and Words to Know

Struggling Readers

Phonemic Awareness/Phonics

Long *a* (CVC*e*)

I DO IT

- Show **Picture Card** *game*. Name the picture, emphasizing the long *a* sound, /ā/.

Use **Instructional Routine 2** to model how to blend *game*.

- Write *a_e*. *This pattern lets you know that the letter a stands for the long a sound, /ā/.*

- Review long *a* words in the **Decodable Reader** selection *Tate's Cakes*.

WE DO IT

- Use **Sound/Spelling Card** *acorn* to review the *a_e* pattern for /ā/.

- Ask children to identify the /ā/ word in each of the following pairs: *bat, bake; take, tack; page, pack*.

- Help children blend the sounds to read the words in the box below. Use the **Corrective Feedback** if children need additional help.

plane	late	make	grape
lake	trade	same	shake

- Discuss the meaning of any unfamiliar words with children.

YOU DO IT

- Have partners take turns using **Letter Cards** to create the following short *a* words: *cap, can, mad, plan,* and *tap.* Then have partners add the letter card *e* to the end of each word to create the following long *a* words: *cape, cane, made, plane,* and *tape.*

- Have children record the words in two separate lists and read the lists to the group.

DAILY ASSESSMENT

Corrective Feedback Work with children to correct errors, following the model below.

Phonics Error:
A child reads *lake* as *lack*.

Correct the error. Say the word and its vowel sound. *The word is* lake; *the letters* a_e *stand for the sound* /ā/.

Model as you touch the letters. *I'll blend /l/ /ā/ /k/. What is the word?* lake

Check *You blend. /l/ /ā/ /k/ What is the word?* lake

Reinforce Go back three or four words and have children continue reading. Make note of errors and review those words during tomorrow's lesson.

ELL English Language Learners

Words to Know

- Write this week's Words to Know on the board and read them aloud.
- Use the backs of the **Vocabulary in Context Cards** to review the explanations of the words.
- Tell children that they will see these words in this week's reading selections.
- Have children look for the words in the selection *The Big Race*.

☑ **WORDS TO KNOW**

four	starts
five	three
into	two
over	watch

Vocabulary in Context Cards

Beginning

- Read each word as you point to it on a **Vocabulary in Context Card**. Encourage children to repeat after you as they point to each word.

Low Intermediate

- Use each word in a simple sentence. Then write it on the board. Have children echo-read the sentences. Have volunteers underline the Words to Know in each sentence.

High Intermediate

- Have children use Words to Know to complete sentence frames. Have them read their sentences aloud to a partner.

Proficient

- Have children work in pairs to scan *The Big Race* to find sentences with the Words to Know. Then have children read the sentences aloud.

On Level

See Literacy Center Practice—Unit 3 Lesson 14 Word Study

If children have time after completing the purple activity, have them try moving on to the blue activity.

Advanced

See Literacy Center Practice—Unit 3 Lesson 14 Word Study

If children have time after completing the blue activity, have them reread the **Decodable Reader** selection *Tate's Cakes*.

Vocabulary Reader
Desert Animals

by Kaitlyn Robinson

HOUGHTON MIFFLIN

Summary

The desert is a hot and dry place, but some animals live comfortably there and find food to eat.

☑ **WORDS TO KNOW**

five	starts
four	three
into	two
over	watch

Struggling Readers

- Explain to children that some animals live in the desert. Display a photograph of the desert and tell them that a desert gets little rain and is sometimes very hot.

- Preview the selection and ask *yes* or *no* questions about what is on the page. For example, for p. 5, ask: *Is the sun hot? Is this the desert? Does a fox live here?*

- Read the selection aloud to children. Then reread it and ask children to join in with you. Have volunteers read a page aloud. Guide them to use context clues when they come to an unfamiliar word (or phrase).

- Read the Words to Know and have children repeat. Have partners work together to complete the Responding page. Read the directions on **Blackline Master 14.4** and guide children to complete it.

On Level

- Ask children to tell what they know about the desert and animals that live there. Record their responses on the board. Preview the book and have children match the animals in the pictures to the animal names in the text.

- Remind children that context clues can help them figure out unfamiliar words (or phrases) in a sentence.

- Read the selection aloud as children follow along. Then ask children to read the selection to a partner. Remind them to use context clues when they come to an unfamiliar word (or phrase).

- Then assign the Responding page and **Blackline Master 14.4**. Review the directions with children and have them discuss their responses with a partner.

Go Digital
• Vocabulary Reader Online
• Literacy and Language Guide
• Context Cards

COMMON CORE

DAY 1

Advanced

- Read the title and invite children to preview the selection. Have them identify the animal on each page and describe what it is doing.

- Before reading, remind children to use context clues to help them determine the meaning of unknown words (or phrases).

- Have children alternate reading pages of the selection aloud. Tell them to use context clues when they see unfamiliar words (or phrases).

- Review the Words to Know and have them use each word in a sentence that tells what they learned about animals in the desert. Then assign the Responding page and **Blackline Master 14.4**. For the Talk About It activity, remind children to include facts and details to support their ideas.

ELL English Language Learners

Beginning

Have children choose one animal that lives in the desert. Have them draw the animal. Then have them copy and complete this sentence frame: *This desert animal is a _____*. Ask children to share their work with the class.

Low Intermediate

For each page in the selection, ask questions such as: *What is the sun like*? *When does a snake hunt*? Have children read the sentence that gives the answer.

High Intermediate

Make a content web for *Desert Animals* and have children tell what they learned about animals in the desert. Record their answers in the web and then have volunteers use the web to summarize the story.

Proficient

Point out that *hot* and *cool* are opposites. Ask them what is cool and what is hot. Then have them list antonyms for other words in the selection, such as *hard*, *dark*, and *dry*. Have partners illustrate and label one pair of antonyms.

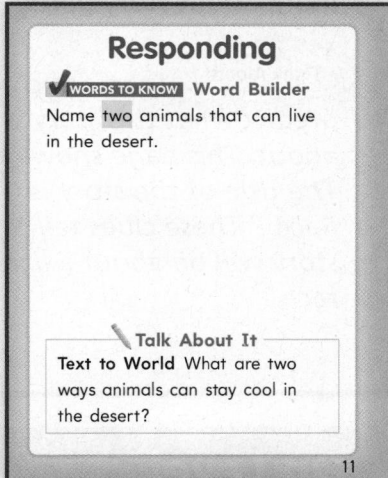

Desert Animals, p. 11

Blackline Master 14.4

Differentiate Comprehension
Conclusions; Infer/Predict

Struggling Readers

I DO IT

- Review **Projectable S2** with children. Then display p. 125 of *The Big Race* and read the title aloud. Tell children that good readers infer and predict as they read, or use clues to figure out more about story parts.

  Think Aloud *I can use clues to predict what this story will be about. This page shows a lizard. The title of the story is "The Big Race." These clues tell me that the story will be about a lizard and a race.*

WE DO IT

- Have children turn to pp. 126–127 of *The Big Race*. Read the text aloud. *What clues on this page tell you that this story will be about a lizard that runs a race?*

- Have children list clues they find on these pages that support the previous prediction.

YOU DO IT

- *When you read these pages, do you think Red Lizard will win the race? What clues tell you so?* Have children work together to make a prediction based on clues from pp. 134–137.

On Level

I DO IT

- Review **Projectable S2**. Then display pp. 124–127 of *The Big Race* and read the text aloud. Tell children that good readers infer and predict, or use clues to figure out more about story parts.

  Think Aloud *I can use clues to predict what this story will be about. The title of the story is "The Big Race." Then the words on the next page say, "Today is the big race." The picture shows a lizard looking at a big cake. I think the story will be about a lizard who runs a race for a cake.*

WE DO IT

- *Do you think Red Lizard will win the race? What clues tell you so?*

- Have children work together to make a prediction based on clues from pp. 126–127. Remind them to use clues from the text and pictures.

YOU DO IT

- Read pp. 128–137 of *The Big Race* with children, and have them identify additional clues that support their earlier prediction.

- Have children record the clues they found with words and pictures. If they cannot find additional clues to support their earlier prediction, have them revise their prediction based on information from the story.

Advanced

I DO IT

- Tell children that good readers infer and predict as they read, or use clues to figure out story parts. Explain that they must sometimes draw conclusions about things the author has not said directly.

- Display pp. 126–127 of *The Big Race* and read the text aloud. Tell children that you will use clues from the story to draw a conclusion about Red Lizard and predict what the story will be about.

WE DO IT

- Have children read up to p. 130 of *The Big Race*. *Who do you think wants to win the race more, Red Lizard or Rat? What makes you think so?* Help children identify clues from the story so far that can help them draw a conclusion.

YOU DO IT

- Have children finish reading the story and ask them to predict what the animals will do now.

- Have them explain what conclusions they can draw about Red Lizard based on the story and how this helps them predict what will happen next.

ELL English Language Learners

Review the **Infer/Predict Strategy** and explain that good readers use story clues to figure out story parts as they read. Then use the following activities with children according to their level of English proficiency.

Beginning

Display p. 125 of *The Big Race*. *Will this story be about a cat? Will this story be about a lizard?* Have children point to the part of the picture that helps them know what the story will be about.

Low Intermediate

Display p. 125 of *The Big Race*. *What animal do you think this story will be about?* Have children give their answers orally and point to the part of the picture that provides a clue.

High Intermediate

Display p. 125 of *The Big Race*. *How do the picture and words help you know that the story will be about a lizard?* Have children explain their answers, using the picture and title for support.

Proficient

Display p. 125 of *The Big Race*. Have each child write a sentence to explain how they know from the picture or words on this page that the story will be about a lizard.

Differentiate Phonics and Fluency

Struggling Readers

Phonics

Soft *c, g, dge*

I DO IT

- Use **Letter Cards** to form the word *wag*.
- Read the word and note the /ă/ sound in the middle and the /g/ sound at the end.
- Hold up the **Letter Card** *e*. *This letter does two jobs.* Add *e* to the end of *wag*.

| w | a | g | e |

- *Listen as I say the new word:* wage. *Adding the e to the end changed the /ă/ to /ā/.*
- *Listen for the end sound as I say the words again:* wag, wage. *Adding the e changes the sound for g from /g/ to /j/.*
- Explain the words to children as necessary.
- Repeat with soft *c, g,* and *dge* words in the **Decodable Reader** selection *A Safe Lodge*.

WE DO IT

- Write *jug* on the board.
- Have children use **Letter Cards** to build *jug*.
- Demonstrate and have children replace the final *g* with *dge*.
- Have children read *jug* and *judge*, noting that replacing the *g* with *dge* changes the /g/ sound to /j/.
- Repeat with *rack* and *race*. Provide **Corrective Feedback**.

YOU DO IT

- Have partners use **Letter Cards** to build the words *bag, leg, stag, rack, lack,* and *pack*.
- Have partners take turns replacing the final sound with /j/ (*ge, dge*) or /s/ (*ce*) and reading the new words.
- Help children check their spellings and list their new words by end sound.

DAILY ASSESSMENT ▲ 3 2 1 **RtI**

Corrective Feedback
Use **Letter Cards** to model correct answers. *My word is* stag. *I replace the* g *with* ge. *Now I have the word* stage. Guide children. *What is the word?* stage *What is the end sound?* /j/ Have children build the word on their own, and use it again in tomorrow's lesson.

All Levels

Fluency

Expression

I DO IT

- Write this sentence on the board: *My dog won the contest at the fair!*

- Model reading the sentence with no expression or feeling, without any phrasing breaks.

- Use a Think Aloud to model figuring out why the sentence didn't sound right. Then reread the sentence with expression and feeling, using slashes to break it into meaningful chunks.

> **Think Aloud** *Something didn't seem right. The exclamation point at the end of the sentence shows excitement. I didn't sound excited. I didn't break the sentence into phrases either.*

WE DO IT

- Pick a page for children to turn to in the On Level **Leveled Reader**. Look for a page with sentences that are easier to break into chunks.

- Copy the page onto the board. Call on a child to read it aloud. Encourage him or her to read with feeling.

- Have another child come to the board and insert slashes between phrases, based on how the first child reads. Provide **Corrective Feedback**.

YOU DO IT

- Have children pick a page from their **Leveled Reader**. Tell children to read their pages to themselves, concentrating on reading with expression. Then have children read the page aloud to the class.

- Monitor and provide **Corrective Feedback** as needed.

DAILY ASSESSMENT

Corrective Feedback
Help children read with expression by showing them an exaggerated example.

TARGET SKILL
Conclusions

TARGET STRATEGY
Infer/Predict

WORDS TO KNOW

four	starts
five	three
into	two
over	watch

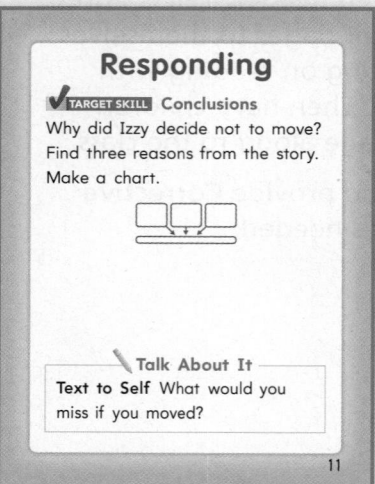

Responding

☑TARGET SKILL **Conclusions**

Why did Izzy decide not to move? Find three reasons from the story. Make a chart.

Talk About It

Text to Self What would you miss if you moved?

Izzy's Move, p. 11

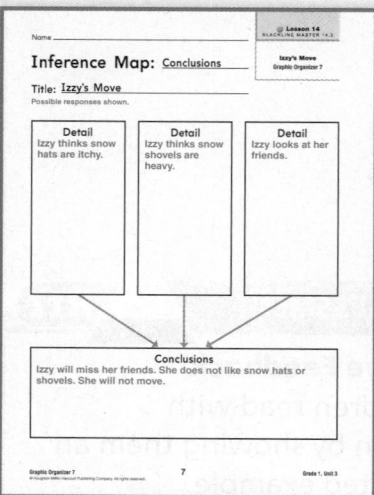

Name _____

Inference Map: **Conclusions**

Title: Izzy's Move

Possible responses shown.

Detail	Detail	Detail
Izzy thinks snow hats are itchy.	Izzy thinks snow shovels are heavy.	Izzy looks at her friends.

Conclusions
Izzy will miss her friends. She does not like snow hats or shovels. She will not move.

Blackline Master 14.5

Leveled Readers

Struggling Readers

 Izzy's Move

SUMMARY Izzy decides to move. When she realizes what changes she will have to make, she decides she belongs at home with her friends.

GENRE: FANTASY

Introducing the Text

• Review and discuss this week's Words to Know.

• Display the first picture of *Izzy's Move*. Explain that a desert is a hot and dry place. Desert plants don't need much water to live. Some desert animals are snakes, lizards, and jackrabbits. *Have you been to a desert? What did you see?*

• Review with children that using an inference map can help them put together clues in a story to figure out ideas the author suggests but does not state.

Supporting the Reading

• **pp. 6–7** *Do you think Izzy knew she would need a snow hat? How do you know? Sample answer: No, she says she doesn't like snow hats because they are itchy.*

• **p. 9** *What do you think Izzy will do now that she knows what she needs to take to a cold place? Sample answer: She won't move. How do you know that? Sample answer: She doesn't look as happy as she did; she doesn't like snow hats or snow shovels.*

Discussing and Revisiting the Text

CRITICAL THINKING Read aloud the top half of Responding, p. 11 in the **Leveled Reader**.

• Have children describe what Izzy did in the story. Then have them think about why Izzy acted the way she did.

• Have children write three details about Izzy on **Blackline Master 14.5** and then write what they figured out about Izzy in the bottom box.

FLUENCY: EXPRESSION Read aloud pp. 4–5 to model reading with expression. Then have children echo-read the next two pages with you to practice reading with expression.

On Level

▲ *The Treasure Map*

SUMMARY Jack, Ned, and Liz follow a treasure map through the desert and dig up a buried chest. They expect to see gold coins. Instead they find something for Jack to eat, Ned to drink, and Liz to keep warm. They realize that not all treasure is gold.

GENRE: FANTASY

Introducing the Text

• Review and discuss this week's Words to Know.

• Explain that in stories the location of a treasure is usually shown with a big *X* to mark the spot where it's buried. *Have you read a story about buried treasure? What kind of treasure was it?*

• Remind children that authors don't always tell everything in a story. Readers can use clues and details to figure out an author's idea. Explain that an inference map can help them gather clues to draw a conclusion.

Supporting the Reading

• **p. 6** *What does Liz do to help the friends hunt for the treasure?* Sample answer: She gets up on rocks to look for clues. *How would this help them find the treasure?* Sample answer: Liz can climb high and see far to find things shown on the map.

• **p. 10** *What do you think the author means when she states that not all treasure is made of gold?* Sample answer: Treasure is valuable and having something to eat, drink, and keep warm with in the desert is more valuable than gold.

Discussing and Revisiting the Text

CRITICAL THINKING Help children read the top half of Responding, p. 11 in the **Leveled Reader**.

• Have children work in pairs to look for clues and details that help them figure out ideas that the author doesn't state in the story.

• Have children use **Blackline Master 14.6** to record why the friends think the objects are treasures.

FLUENCY: EXPRESSION Use pp. 2–3 to model reading dialogue and narration with expression. Then have children choral-read pp. 4–5.

Responding

✔ **TARGET SKILL** **Conclusions**
The things the animals find in the box are treasures. What three details tell you why? Make a chart.

✎ **Write About It**
Text to Self Draw three pictures of things that are treasures to you. Write a sentence about your favorite.

11

The Treasure Map, p. 11

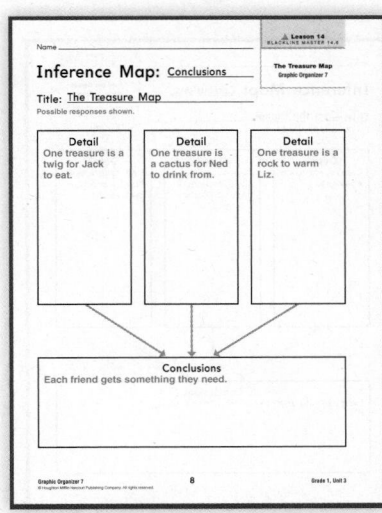

Blackline Master 14.6

✓ TARGET SKILL
Conclusions

✓ TARGET STRATEGY
Infer/Predict

✓ WORDS TO KNOW

four	starts
five	three
into	two
over	watch

Leveled Readers

Advanced

■ *Cam the Camel*

SUMMARY Cam finds out that she can't do any of the Camel School lessons as well as the other camels. She worries that she can't do anything right until the teacher falls in the water and Cam saves him!

GENRE: FANTASY

Introducing the Text

- Review and discuss this week's Words to Know.

- Explain that young animals learn from adult animals just as children learn in school. *What do you have a hard time doing? What do you do well?*

- Have children think about how they form ideas as they read. Point out that using what they read and what they know to figure out something the author doesn't say is called drawing a conclusion.

Supporting the Reading

- **pp. 2–3** *Do you think that Cam is doing her best? How do you know? Yes, she runs as fast as she can and she wants to be a good camel and do well in school.*

- **p. 10** *How do you think Mr. Camel's opinion of Cam changed? He may have thought she wasn't very good at being a camel, but now he thinks she's brave and smart. What do you think school will be like for Cam now? It will be easier; she will do better.*

Discussing and Revisiting the Text

CRITICAL THINKING Have children read the top half of Responding, p. 11 in the **Leveled Reader**.

- Have children work in pairs to review the story and think about what clues they used to draw conclusions about the characters and events.

- Have children list on **Blackline Master 14.7** the clues and details they used to draw their conclusions.

FLUENCY: EXPRESSION Have groups take turns playing the parts of Cam, Mr. Camel, and the narrator to read the story with expression.

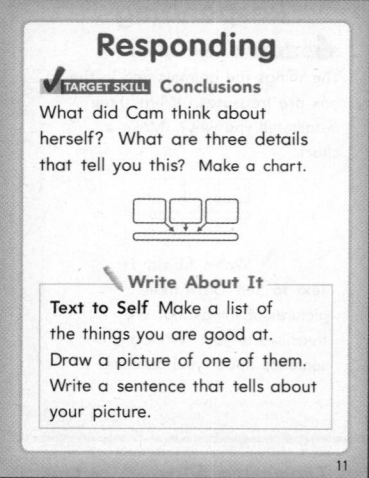

Cam the Camel, p. 11

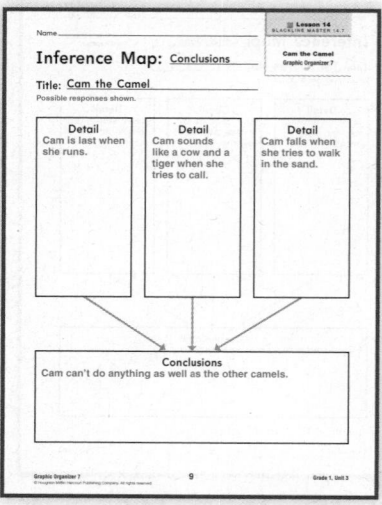

Blackline Master 14.7

 **ELL** **English Language Learners**

 ## The Map and the Treasure

SUMMARY Three friends find an old map and decide to follow it in the hopes of finding a treasure. What they find isn't gold, but it is a treasure to each of them.

GENRE: FANTASY

Introducing the Text

- Review and discuss this week's Words to Know.

- Take a picture walk through *The Map and the Treasure* and read the labels. Ask children what they think a treasure buried in a box would be.

- Remind children that when they read they can figure out ideas about a story that the author doesn't actually say. They can use clues they read along with things they already know to draw conclusions.

Supporting the Reading

- **p. 6** *Why do you think Liz wanted to find the treasure?* Sample answer: She thinks the treasure is gold, and gold is very valuable.

- **pp. 9–10** *What does Liz mean when she says she understands?* Sample answer: She knows why the things they found are a treasure. *Why are these things a treasure?* Sample answer: If you are hungry, thirsty, or cold, you would think that something to eat, drink, and to keep warm with would be valuable.

Discussing and Revisiting the Text

CRITICAL THINKING Help children read the top half of Responding, p. 11 in the **Leveled Reader**.

- Have children work in pairs to look for clues that help them figure out ideas about the treasure the friends find.

- Have children record their ideas on **Blackline Master 14.8**.

FLUENCY: EXPRESSION Have children choral-read pp. 9–10 of *The Map and the Treasure* with expression. Point out that quotation marks show the words a character says and should be read like a person is speaking.

For more reading options, see ELL Lesson 14, pp. E32–E41.

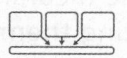

Responding

✓ **TARGET SKILL** Conclusions

The things the animals find in the box are treasures. What three details tell you why? Make a chart.

✏️ **Write About It**

Text to Self Draw three pictures of things that you think are treasures. Write a sentence about your favorite treasure.

11

The Map and the Treasure, p. 11

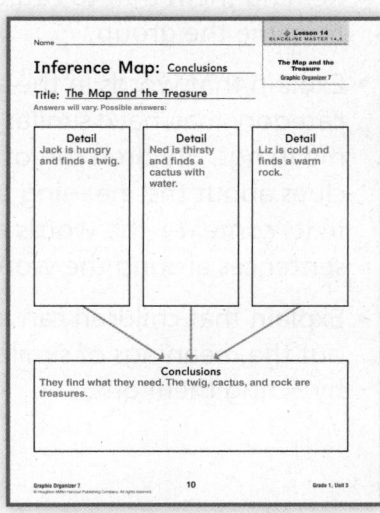

Blackline Master 14.8

Differentiate Vocabulary Strategies
Shades of Meaning

Struggling Readers

I DO IT

- Remind children that a *category* is a group of similar objects or things. Explain that to *classify* is to put similar things in such a group. And to *categorize* is to name the group.

- Words in the same category may have similar meanings, and clues about the meaning of a word may be found in its *context*—the words and sentences around the word.

- Explain that children can also figure out the meanings of similar words by acting them out.

WE DO IT

- Write the following sentences on the board: *Larry swept his room. Lisa scrubbed her desk.*

- Have a volunteer pretend to sweep part of the classroom. Have another pretend to scrub a desk.

- Have children discuss the words and the actions they saw. Say, *Sweep and scrub are action words about cleaning. But we can see how they're different. When you sweep, you use a broom. When you scrub, you use a brush to rub.*

YOU DO IT

- Write the following sentences on the board: *Melanie drew a big square. Hank drew a huge square.* Underline the adjectives.

- Have children work with partners to distinguish the meanings of *big* and *huge*. Have them draw examples of big and huge squares.

- Have children use their drawings to write meanings of *big* and *huge*.

On Level

I DO IT

- Remind children that to *classify* is to put similar things in a group. Remind them that to *categorize* is to name the group.

- Explain that words in the same category may have similar meanings. Children can often find clues about the meaning of a word in its *context*—the words and sentences around the word.

- Explain that children can also figure out the meanings of similar words by acting them out.

WE DO IT

- Write the following sentences on the board: *Judy was so happy that she skipped all the way to school. Fred was late so he ran to school.* Underline the verbs.

- Say, *Skipped and ran are action words. When a person skips or walks, he uses his legs and feet. He moves faster than a walk. But the words have different meanings.*

- Have children look for clues about the words' meanings in their contexts. Then have volunteers act out the words.

YOU DO IT

- Write the following sentences on the board: *Mr. Thompson grew a large pumpkin. His wife grew a gigantic pumpkin.* Underline the adjectives.

- Have children work with partners to distinguish the meanings of *large* and *gigantic*. Have them draw examples of large and gigantic pumpkins.

- Have children use their drawings to write meanings of *large* and *gigantic*.

Advanced

I DO IT

- Remind children that to *classify* is to put similar things in a group. Remind them that to *categorize* is to name the group.

- Explain that words in the same category may have similar meanings. Children can often find clues about the meaning of a word in its *context*—the words and sentences around the word.

WE DO IT

- Write the following sentences on the board: *The duck dives under the water. A dog swims across the pond.* Underline the verbs.

- Say, Dives *and* swims *are action words, or verbs. And both the duck and the dog are in water. Let's look at the words around the verbs for clues about their meanings.*

- Have children discuss how *dive* and *swim* are similar, and how they are different. Then have volunteers offer definitions of *dive* and *swim*.

YOU DO IT

- Write the following sentences on the board: *Ms. Gregg told a funny joke, and everyone laughed. Steve made a silly face when he saw the test.* Underline the adjectives.

- Have children work with partners to distinguish the meanings of *funny* and *silly*. What do the words' contexts tell them about the words' meanings?

- Have children tell a funny joke and draw a silly face.

ELL English Language Learners

Group English Language Learners according to language proficiency.

Beginning

- Tell children that words with the same or very similar meanings are called *synonyms*. Explain that synonyms usually belong to the same category of words but they may have a different shade of meaning.

- Write *sweep* and *scrub* on the board. Explain that both words mean *to clean*.

- Have children act out sweeping and scrubbing.

Low Intermediate

- Write *cat* and *kitten* on the board.

- Have children use each word in a sentence.

- Have the class discuss the similarities and the differences between a cat and a kitten.

High Intermediate

- Write *skip* and *run* on the board.

- Have the class describe things that make them skip, and things that make them run.

- Have the class think about the differences between the two actions.

Proficient

- Have children make a list of things that are big and a list of things that are gigantic.

- Have partners explain the difference to each other.

Options for Reteaching

Reteach Phonics

Long *a* (CVC*e*)

I DO IT

- Tell children that you will review some words that will help them read the **Decodable Reader** story *The Race*.
- Review **Instructional Routine 3.** Remind children that they have been reading words with long *a* this week.
- Review this week's Words to Know *four*, *five*, *into*, *over*, *starts*, *three*, *two*, and *watch*.
- Have children open to p. 95 of *The Race*.

WE DO IT

- Write *lane* on the board.
- Help children find the word *lane* on the page.
- Model how to decode *lane* step by step.

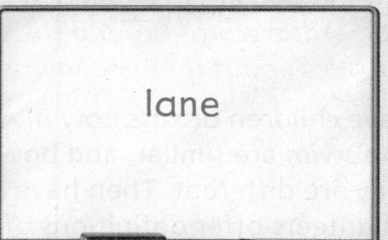

lane

YOU DO IT

- Have partners work together to read *The Race*.
- Use the **Corrective Feedback** on **p. T388** if children need additional help.

Dave has a lane. It is his space. Ace has a lane. It is his space. They must run and jump in that lane. They can't trade lanes.

95

Reteach Phonics

Soft *c*, *g*, *dge*

I DO IT

- Tell children that you will review some words that will help them read the **Decodable Reader** story *The Race*.
- Review **Instructional Routine 3.** Remind children that they have been reading soft *c*, *g*, and *dge* words this week.
- Review this week's Words to Know *four*, *five*, *into*, *over*, *starts*, *three*, *two*, and *watch*.
- Have children open to p. 96 of *The Race*.

WE DO IT

- Write *Madge* on the board.
- Help children find the word *Madge* on the page.
- Model how to decode *Madge* step by step.

Madge

YOU DO IT

- Have partners work together to read *The Race*.
- Use the **Corrective Feedback** on **p. T394** if children need additional help.

Madge and Grace got in this race. They will skate fast. Go, Madge! Go, Grace! Skate as fast as you can. Race, race, race.

96

Reteach Vocabulary Strategies

Shades of Meaning

I DO IT

- Remind children that to *classify* is to put similar things in a group, or category. Remind them that to *categorize* is to name the group.

- Remind children that words in the same category can have similar meanings. Children can often find clues about the meaning of a word in its *context*—the words and sentences around the word. They can also figure out the meanings of words by acting them out.

WE DO IT

- Display **Projectable 14.7**. Read the words aloud with children.

- Point to *big* and *gigantic*.

> **Think Aloud** *These are words I can use to describe things.* I made a big pizza. The family ordered a gigantic pizza. *So I can put both of these words in the second group,* Descriptive Words. *But I wonder what the difference is between* big *and* gigantic.

- Have a volunteer draw a big pizza on the board. Have another volunteer draw a gigantic pizza on the board. Have children discuss the difference between the pizzas and the difference between the adjectives.

YOU DO IT

- Have children work with their partners to classify the words in **Projectable 14.7**.

- Have children write a short definition of each word, showing how it is different from the other words in its category.

Reteach Comprehension Skill

Conclusions

I DO IT

- Remind children that a conclusion is a smart guess about something the author does not say. They can draw a conclusion by adding their own ideas to details in the text.

WE DO IT

- Have children read aloud **Student Book** pp. 126–142.

- Model how to draw a conclusion from details about the race.

> **Think Aloud** *I think the race is an exciting event for the animals. Several details suggest that this race is exciting. It is called a big race. Lots of animals want to join.*

- Help volunteers find other details that suggest the race is an exciting event.

YOU DO IT

- Distribute **Graphic Organizer 7: Inference Map**.

- Have children write the conclusion in the bottom box and details in the three boxes above. *Conclusion: The race is an exciting event. Details: called a big race; lots of animals join; a cake is the prize; animals watch and clap; they cheer "Hip, hip, hooray!"*

- Have children work in pairs to complete the graphic organizer.

- Review the completed graphic organizers together.

Teacher Notes

Go Digital

See pages xvi-xvii in this Teacher's Edition for the full digital offering.

*my*SmartPlanner
Plan Across Disciplines, Schedule, Organize

my WriteSmart

Write, Collaborate, Respond

Online Assessment
Assess, Prescribe, Remediate, Report

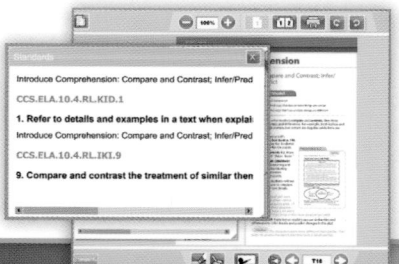

CHALLENGE

Research Animals and Their Babies

After reading the selection "Animal Groups," ask children to research animals and their babies.

• Have children choose animal groups they read about. Tell them they will research the animals and their babies.

• Encourage children to use books or an online resource to find information. Ask: *What are the babies called? How are the babies like the adults? How are they different? How do the babies grow and change?*

• Have children create posters about the animals and their babies and use pictures and captions to tell what they learned.

Animal Groups
by James Bruchac

Informational Text

SCIENCE

Connection to Informational Text

OFFICIAL ANIMALS "Animal Groups" is a selection about different types of animals. Tell children that states around the country have a number of official state animals. Ask: *Can you name the official animals of our state?* Help children use print or online resources to learn more about the state animals. Ask them to find the state bird, reptile, and fish. Also have them find out which state animals are mammals. Ask: *Where in the state are these animals found? What do they need for healthy growth?* Have children work in small groups to design posters. The posters should show pictures of and facts about the state animals.
Common Core, *English Language Arts:* W.1.7 participate in shared research and writing projects

READING INFORMATIONAL TEXT

RI.1.1 ask and answer questions about key details

RI.1.3 describe the connection between individuals, events, ideas or information in a text

RI.1.4 ask and answer questions to determine or clarify the meaning of words and phrases

RI.1.5 know and use text features to locate facts or information

RI.1.7 use illustrations and details to describe key ideas

RI.1.9 identify similarities in and differences between texts on the same topic

FOUNDATIONAL SKILLS

RF.1.2b orally produce single-syllable words by blending sounds

RF.1.2c isolate and pronounce sounds in spoken single-syllable words

RF.1.3a know the spelling-sound correspondences for common consonant digraphs

RF.1.3c know final -e and vowel team conventions for representing long vowel sounds

RF.1.4a read on-level text with purpose and understanding

RF.1.4c use context to confirm or self-correct word recognition and understanding

WRITING

W.1.2 write informative/explanatory texts

W.1.5 focus on a topic, respond to questions/suggestions from peers, and add details to strengthen writing

W.1.6 use digital tools to produce and publish writing

SPEAKING AND LISTENING

SL.1.1a follow rules for discussions

SL.1.1b build on others' talk in conversations by responding to others' comments

SL.1.1c ask question to clear up confusion about topics and texts under discussion

SL.1.2 ask and answer questions about details in a text read aloud, information presented orally, or through other media

SL.1.6 produce complete sentences when appropriate to task and situation

LANGUAGE

L.1.1h use determiners

L.1.1c use singular and plural nouns with matching verbs in sentences

L.1.1e use verbs to convey sense of past, present, and future

L.1.4b use frequently occurring affixes as a clue to the meaning of a word

LESSON 15

Our Focus Wall

ANCHOR TEXT

Animal Groups
Informational Text

Read Together

Animal Picnic
Play

ESSENTIAL QUESTION

What makes birds different from mammals?

FOUNDATIONAL SKILLS

☑ Words to Know
HIGH-FREQUENCY WORDS

bird	both	eyes
fly	long	or
those	walk	

Phonics

Long *i* (CVCe)
Digraphs *kn*, *wr*, *gn*, *mb*
Phonograms *-ine*, *-ite*

i
i_e
ie
igh
–y

Fluency

Intonation

READING LITERATURE & INFORMATIONAL TEXT

Comprehension Skills and Strategies

☑ **TARGET SKILL**
• Compare and Contrast
• Text and Graphic Features

☑ **TARGET STRATEGY**
• Monitor/Clarify

WRITING

Writing

Informative Writing: Report
Focus Trait: Word Choice

LANGUAGE

Spelling

Long *i* (CVCe)

time	bike
like	white
kite	drive

Grammar

The Verb *be*

Vocabulary Strategies

Suffixes *-er*, *-est*

WHOLE GROUP

⌄ Reading

ANCHOR TEXT

⌐ **DOMAIN: Life Science**
- -
LESSON TOPIC: Animals

Animal Groups
Informational Text

Children will read *Animal Groups* to

- compare and contrast animals in groups.
- review text and graphic features, such as labels.

Animal Picnic
Play/Readers' Theater

Children will read *Animal Picnic* to

- participate in Readers' Theater.
- learn about stage directions.

⌄ Language Arts

○ Grammar

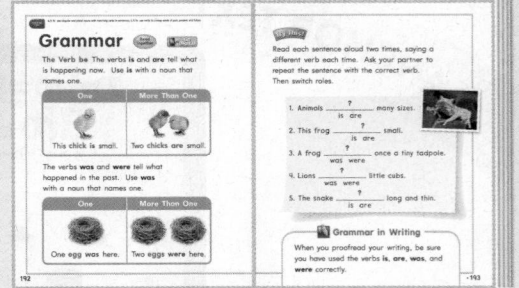

Children learn about the verb *be* through using the correct form of *be* in sentences that relate to animals.

○ Writing

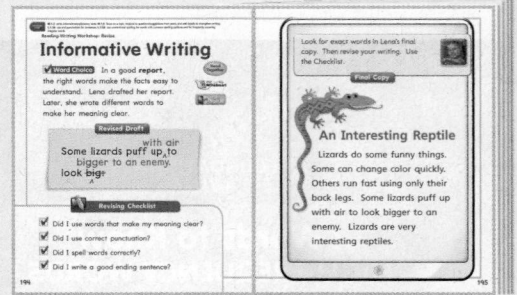

Children continue their work on the report from the previous lesson using *Animal Groups* as a model for including factual details.

△ TEXT COMPLEXITY RUBRIC

Overall Text Complexity		Animal Groups INFORMATIONAL TEXT	Animal Picnic PLAY
		MORE COMPLEX	ACCESSIBLE
Quantitative Measures	Lexile	360	NP
	Guided Reading Level	H	F
Qualitative Measures	Text Structure	More unconventional compare/contrast text structure	Less familiar story structure
	Language Conventionality and Clarity	Increased unfamiliar language	Some natural dialogue
	Knowledge Demands	Some specialized knowledge required	Situation includes unfamiliar aspects
	Purpose/Levels of Meaning	Implied, but easy to identify from context	Single level of simple meaning

⌄ Additional Whole Group Resources

● Decodable Readers

Mike's Bike

- *Mike's Bike,* pp. 99–104
- *The Nest,* pp. 105–110
- *The Nice Vet,* pp. 111–116
- *Kite Time,* pp. 117–122

● Progress Monitoring

Assess and monitor children's progress to determine who is on track and who needs help. Clear prescriptions identify targeted instruction to address children's needs and get them back on track.

Respond to Assessment
- ☑ Vocabulary, p. T482
- ☑ Phonics, p. T482
- ☑ Comprehension, p. T483
- ☑ Language Arts, p. T483
- ☑ Fluency, p. T483

FOR STUDENTS

- my WriteSmart
- eBook
- GrammarSnap Videos
- Destination Reading
- Context Cards

FOR TEACHERS
- Teacher One-Stop
- Interactive Whiteboard Lessons
- Literacy and Language Guide

- Lesson 15 Blackline Masters
- Additional Resources
- Assessment

Lesson resources organized by week.

○ Lesson 15 Blackline Masters
- Home Letter 15.1
- Weekly To-Do List 15.2
- Vocabulary Word Cards 15.3
- Words to Know 15.4
- Leveled Reader Graphic Organizers 15.5–15.8
- Test Power 15.9
- Leveled Practice for Words to Know and Phonics SR15.1–SR15.4, A15.1–A15.4, ELL15.1–ELL15.4
- Weekly Tests 15.1–15.14

○ Assessment
- Weekly Tests Answer Key
- Observation Checklists
- Fluency Tests
- Periodic Assessments

○ Additional Resources
- Reading Log
- Vocabulary Log
- Listening Log
- Proofreading Checklist
- Writing Conference Form
- Writing Checklist
- Instructional Routines
- Graphic Organizer Blackline Masters
- Handwriting Models

 **SMALL GROUP**

⌄ Weekly Leveled Readers

Struggling Readers

Guided Reading Level: D
Lexile: 220
DRA: 6

Making a Home
by Cecilia Méndez

HOUGHTON MIFFLIN

▲ On Level

Guided Reading Level: J
Lexile: 520
DRA: 18

All About Bats
by Mary Dell Hartman

HOUGHTON MIFFLIN

■ Advanced

Guided Reading Level: L
Lexile: 640
DRA: 24

Bald Eagles
by Philip Mayer

HOUGHTON MIFFLIN

◆ English Language Learners

Guided Reading Level: J
Lexile: 530
DRA: 18

Many Kinds of Bats
by Mary Dell Hartman

HOUGHTON MIFFLIN

● Vocabulary Reader
for all levels

Guided Reading Level: E
Lexile: 190
DRA: 8

Animals
by James Metzger

HOUGHTON MIFFLIN

● Leveled Reader Teacher's Guides

8-page lessons for each book support instruction in guided reading groups

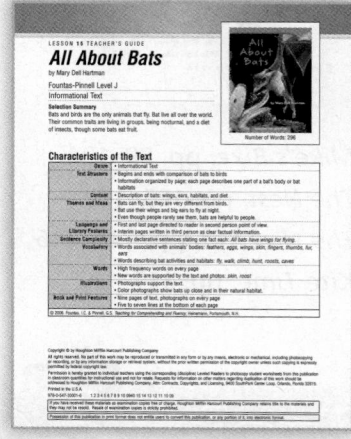

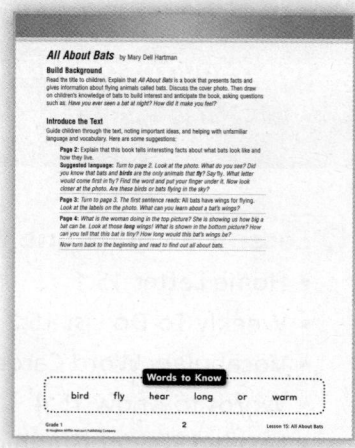

What My Other Students Are Doing

Performance Task

- Write About Reading
- Informative Writing
- Research and Media Literacy
- Unit Performance Assessment, Task 5 of 5

Literacy Centers

Make It Long

Get Started!

1.
| can | kit | mat | pin | sit | v |

Read each word. Write each word.

2.
| kit | pin | sit | e |

Add the letter e to each word. Write the new wor

3.
| can | mat | van | e |

Add the letter e to each word. Write the new wor

Lesson 15

Word Study

Animal Groups

Get Started!

Name each picture.
Find the birds.
Find the mammals.

Put the birds in a
Put the mammals
group.

Draw a group of reptiles.

Lesson 15

Think and Write

Read About Animals

You Will Need
Student Book, crayons, paper, pencil

Get Started!

1. Listen to **Animal Groups**. Talk about the pictures.

2. Talk about the different groups. Name the animals in each group.

3. Write an animal group name. Draw some animals for that group.

Lesson 15

Comprehension and Fluency

Reader's Notebook

Includes practice for:

- Text analysis and citing text evidence
- Words to Know
- Phonics
- Spelling
- Grammar
- Writing Traits

HOUGHTON MIFFLIN HARCOURT

JOURNEYS
COMMON CORE

Reader's Notebook

GRADE 1 Volume 1

Go Digital

FOR STUDENTS
- Leveled Readers Online
- Vocabulary Reader Online

FOR TEACHERS
- Teacher One-Stop
- Literacy and Language Guide
- Leveled Readers Database
- Leveled Reader Teacher's Guides

Grab-and-Go!

- Lesson 15 Blackline Masters
- Additional Resources
- Assessment

FOR STUDENTS

- Write-in Reader eBook
- Vocabulary Reader Online
- Struggling Readers Leveled Reader Online

FOR TEACHERS

- Leveled Reader Teacher's Guide

- Struggling Readers Blackline Masters

RtI INTERVENTION

∨ Strategic Intervention: TIER II

Use these materials to provide additional targeted instruction for children who need Tier II strategic intervention.

⬤ Write-In Reader:
Cats

- Engaging selection connects to main topic
- Interactive worktext reinforces this week's vocabulary and comprehension
- Opportunities for student interaction
- Builds the foundational skills for reading more complex texts
- Online version with dual-speed audio and follow-text

⬤ Daily Lessons

For this week's daily Strategic Intervention Lesson, see Teacher's Edition pages S42–S51:

- Oral Grammar
- Words to Know
- Decoding
- Comprehension
- Fluency
- Grammar
- Written Response
- Unpack Meaning

⬤ Assessment

Progress monitoring every 2 weeks.

Curious About Words

- Provides oral vocabulary instruction for children with limited vocabularies.
- Materials include engaging, illustrated Read Alouds with Teacher Manual.
- Teaches high-utility, research-based words, including academic vocabulary.
- Assessment includes weekly pretests and posttests.

∨ Intensive Intervention: TIER III

⬤ Interactive lessons provide support for

- **Phonics and Word Study Skills**
- **Vocabulary**
- **Comprehension**
- **Fluency**

- Lesson cards for small-group or individual instruction
- Blackline masters for additional practice

- Leveled books for additional reading and skill application
- Lesson assessments evaluate the effectiveness of the intervention

English Language Learners *At a Glance*

 **ENGLISH LANGUAGE LEARNERS**

∨ Whole Group

Use these resources to help English Language Learners access the core content with the whole group.

● Point-of-Use Scaffolded Support

- Use Visuals
- Use Gestures
- Comprehensible Input
- Peer-Supported Learning
- Language Issues
- Idiomatic Language
- Use Sentence Frames
- Expand Language Production

● Vocabulary in Context Cards

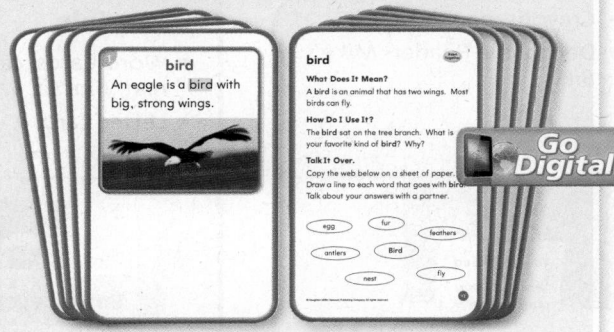

front   back

Go Digital

∨ Small Group

Use these resources to help English Language Learners access the core content with a smaller group.

◉ ELL Leveled Reader

- Contains the same content as the On-Level Reader but uses more accessible language
- ELL Leveled Reader Lesson Plan
- ELL Blackline Masters

∨ ELL Extra Support

Use these additional resources to support English Language Learners as needed.

◉ ELL Lesson 15 Resources

- Daily Lessons to support the core
- Language Support Card 15
- ELL Blackline Masters
- ELL Teacher's Handbook
    Professional Development
    Peer Conferences Forms
    Cooperative Learning Guidelines

◉ Building Background

Video Clip for Lesson 15:
Colorful Birds

Go Digital

FOR STUDENTS

- ELL Leveled Reader Online
- Vocabulary Reader Online
- Cross-Curricular Activity Bank
- Multimedia Grammar Glossary
- Picture Card Bank Online

FOR TEACHERS

- ELD Station Online
- Leveled Readers Database
- Leveled Reader Teacher's Guide

Grab-and-Go!™

- ELL Blackline Masters

Literacy Centers

 **COMMON CORE** — Managing Independent Activities

Comprehension and Fluency

Materials
- Student Book: *Animal Groups*
- eBook
- Crayons, paper, pencil
- Decodable Reader: *Mike's Bike*

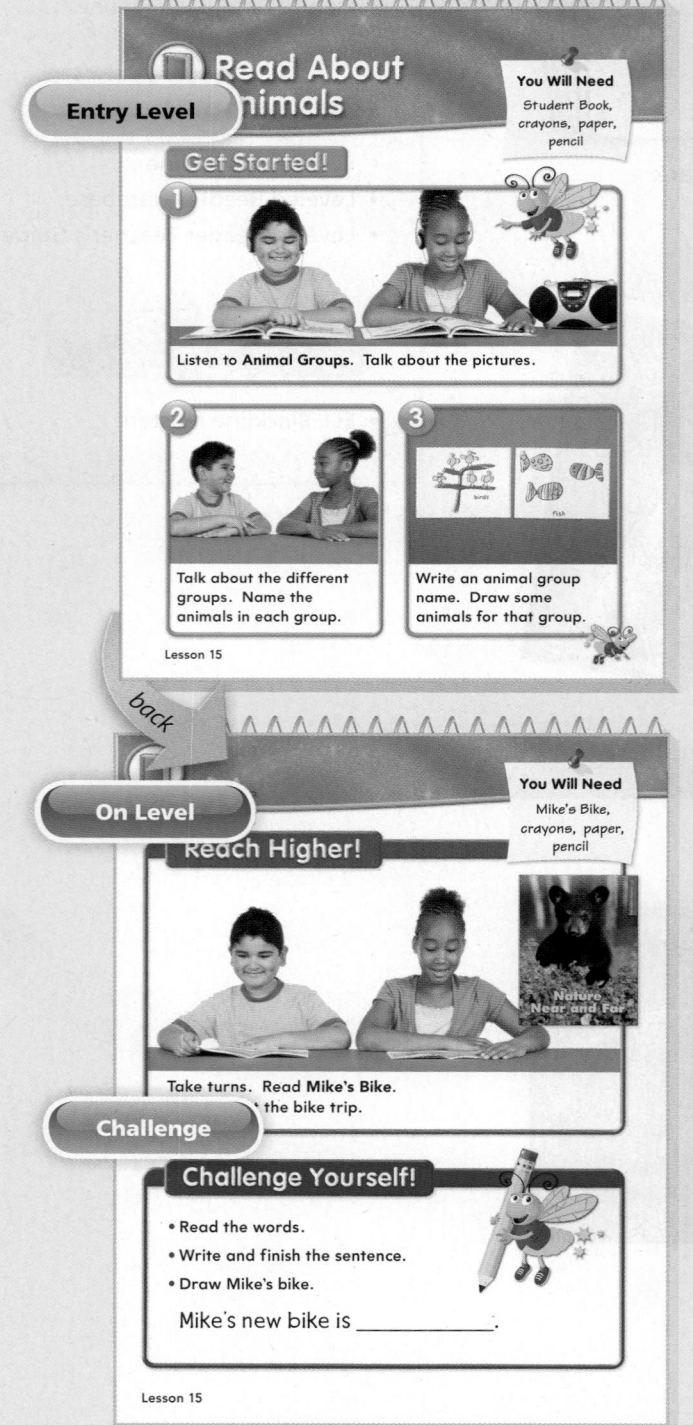

Read About Animals

Entry Level

Get Started!

You Will Need
Student Book, crayons, paper, pencil

1. Listen to **Animal Groups**. Talk about the pictures.

2. Talk about the different groups. Name the animals in each group.

3. Write an animal group name. Draw some animals for that group.

Lesson 15

back

On Level

Reach Higher!

You Will Need
Mike's Bike, crayons, paper, pencil

Take turns. Read Mike's Bike.
___ the bike trip.

Challenge

Challenge Yourself!
- Read the words.
- Write and finish the sentence.
- Draw Mike's bike.

Mike's new bike is _____.

Lesson 15

Word Study

Materials
- Word Cards: *can, kit, mat, pin, sit, van*
- Letter Card: *e*
- Picture Cards: *bike, dime, five, game, rake, skate, slide, vase*
- Crayons, pencil, paper

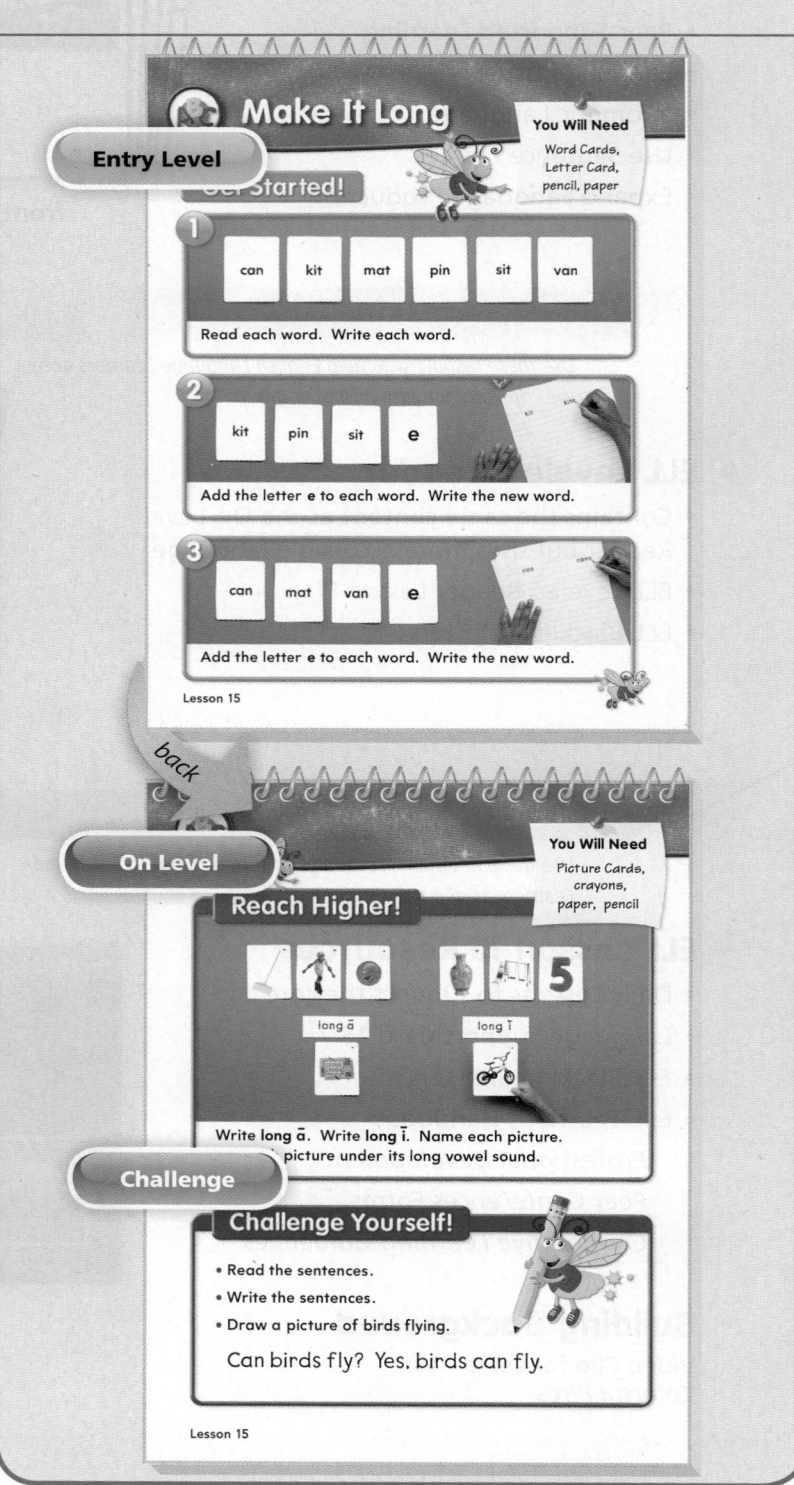

Make It Long

Entry Level

Get Started!

You Will Need
Word Cards, Letter Card, pencil, paper

1. can kit mat pin sit van

Read each word. Write each word.

2. kit pin sit e

Add the letter e to each word. Write the new word.

3. can mat van e

Add the letter e to each word. Write the new word.

Lesson 15

back

On Level

Reach Higher!

You Will Need
Picture Cards, crayons, paper, pencil

long ā   long ī

Write **long ā**. Write **long ī**. Name each picture.
___ picture under its long vowel sound.

Challenge

Challenge Yourself!
- Read the sentences.
- Write the sentences.
- Draw a picture of birds flying.

Can birds fly? Yes, birds can fly.

Lesson 15

Use Literacy Centers to support this week's Common Core focus. Each center contains three activities. Children who experience success with the entry-level activity move on to the on-level and challenge activities, as time permits.

Think and Write

Materials
- Picture Cards: *cat, chick, crow, dog, duck, fox, goat, hawk, horse, lion, mice, sheep, whale*
- Crayons
- Paper, pencil
- Paper bag

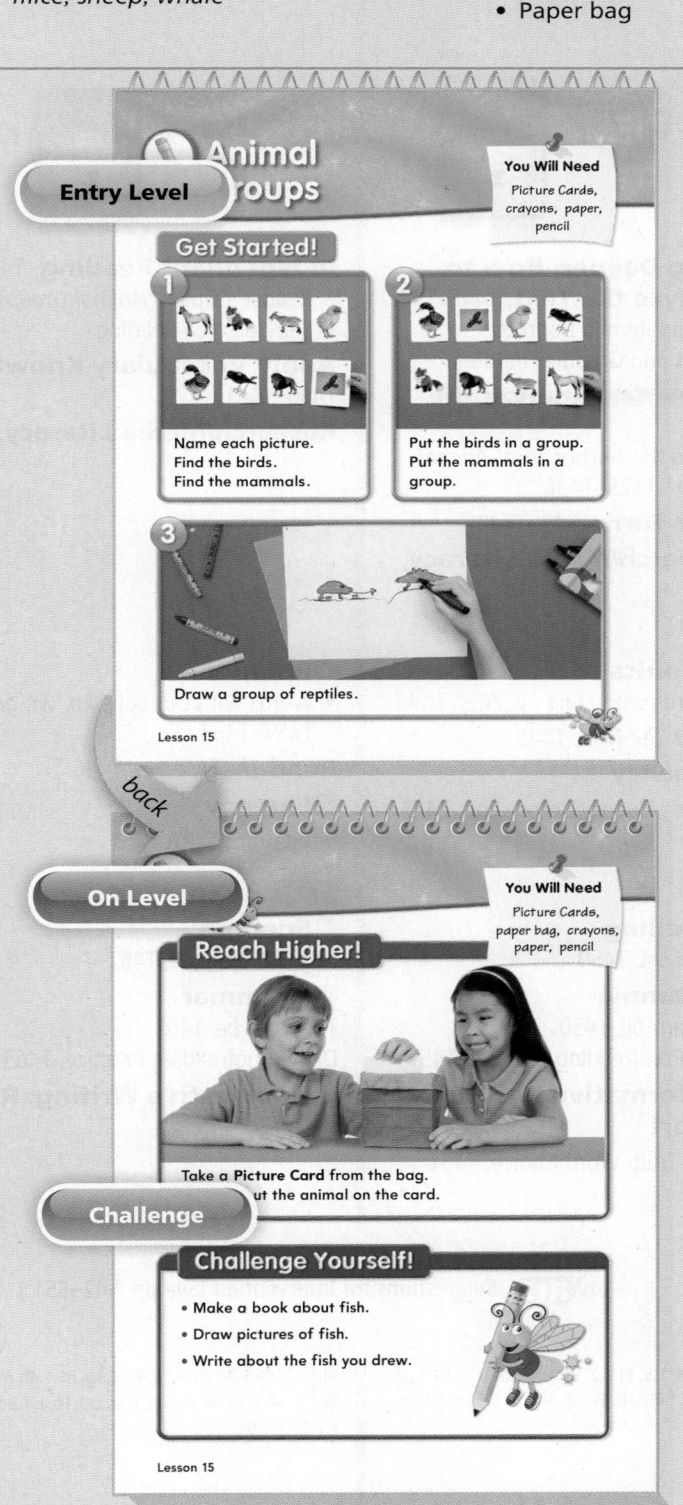

Entry Level

Animal Groups

You Will Need
Picture Cards, crayons, paper, pencil

Get Started!

1. Name each picture. Find the birds. Find the mammals.
2. Put the birds in a group. Put the mammals in a group.
3. Draw a group of reptiles.

Lesson 15

On Level

Reach Higher!

Take a Picture Card from the bag.
...ut the animal on the card.

You Will Need
Picture Cards, paper bag, crayons, paper, pencil

Challenge

Challenge Yourself!
- Make a book about fish.
- Draw pictures of fish.
- Write about the fish you drew.

Lesson 15

Go Digital

FOR STUDENTS

my WriteSmart

Children complete performance tasks related to the week's instruction.

eBook
Children read and listen to *Animal Groups* and *Animal Picnic*, generate questions about animals, and reread the selections to deepen their knowledge.

Leveled Readers Online
Children read and listen to **Leveled Readers,** reinforcing lesson's Target Vocabulary, Target Skill, and Target Strategy.

Destination Reading
Children practice and apply key lesson skills through gamelike activities.

GrammarSnap Videos
Children practice and apply understanding of the verb *be.*

Read

Independent Reading

Have children read daily from a self-selected trade book and record their progress in their Reading Log.

See p. T459 for support in guiding children to select an appropriate book.

LESSON 15 Weekly Planner

	DAY 1	**DAY 2**	**DAY 3**
Daily Language • Opening Routines • Oral Vocabulary • Listening Comprehension • Phonemic Awareness • Speaking and Listening	**Opening Routines,** T416–T417 • Phonemic Awareness • High-Frequency Words • Vocabulary Boost **Read Aloud,** "The Dancing Wolves," T418–T419 **Introduce Oral Vocabulary Phonemic Awareness,** T420	**Opening Routines,** T442–T443 • Phonemic Awareness • High-Frequency Words • Vocabulary Boost **Phonemic Awareness,** T444	**Opening Routines,** T452–T453 • Phonemic Awareness • High-Frequency Words • Vocabulary Boost **Phonemic Awareness,** T454

Whole Group

| **Vocabulary**

Text-Based Comprehension
• Skills and Strategies
• Craft and Structure
Research and Media Literacy | 
☑ **Introduce Words to Know**
High-Frequency Words, T424–T425
☑ **Read and Comprehend,** T426–T427
FIRST READ **Think Through the Text**
Read the Anchor Text: *Animal Groups*, T428–T439
Research/Media Literacy, T477 | 
☑ **Dig Deeper: How to Analyze the Text,** T446–T447
• Compare and Contrast
• Text and Graphic Features
SECOND READ **Analyze the Text**
Reread the Anchor Text: *Animal Groups*, T428–T438
Your Turn, T448–T449
Research/Media Literacy, T477 | 
Independent Reading, T458–T459
• Reader's Guide: *Animal Groups*
• Self-Selected Reading
Apply Vocabulary Knowledge, T460–T461
Research/Media Literacy, T477 |
| **Foundational Skills**
• Phonics and Word Recognition
• Fluency | ☑ **Phonics**
• Words with Long *i* (CVC*e*), T420–T422
Read *Mike's Bike*, T423
☑ **Fluency**
Model Fluency: Intonation, T418 | ☑ **Phonics**
• Words with Long *i* (CVC*e*), T444
Read *The Nest*, T445
☑ **Fluency**
Practice Fluency: Intonation, T445 | ☑ **Phonics**
• Words with Digraphs *kn, wr, gn, mb*, T454–T455
Read *The Nice Vet*, T456
☑ **Fluency**
Intonation, T457 |

Whole Group Language Arts

| **Spelling Grammar Writing** | ☑ **Spelling**
Words with Long *i*, T440
Pretest
☑ **Grammar**
Introduce the Verb *be*, T440
Daily Proofreading Practice, T441
☑ **Informative Writing: Report**
Drafting, T441 | ☑ **Spelling**
Word Sort, T450
☑ **Grammar**
The Verb *be*, T450
Daily Proofreading Practice, T451
☑ **Informative Writing: Report**
Focus Trait: Word Choice, T451 | ☑ **Spelling**
Segment Sounds, T462
☑ **Grammar**
The Verb *be*, T462
Daily Proofreading Practice, T463
☑ **Informative Writing: Report**
Drafting, T463 |

Small Group

 Suggestions for Small Groups (See pp. T489–T507.)    Suggestions for Intervention (See pp. S42–S51.)

COMMON CORE

State Standards

| RI.1.1, RI.1.3, RI.1.4, RI.1.10, RF.1.2c, RF.1.3c, RF.1.3g, RF.1.4a, W.1.2, W.1.5, W.1.6, W.1.8, SL.1.2, L.1.1c, L.1.1e, L.1.2e, L.1.6 | RI.1.3, RI.1.5, RI.1.7, RF.1.2c, RF.1.3c, RF.1.3g RF.1.4a, RF.1.4b, W.1.2, W.1.6, L.1.1c, L.1.1e, L.1.2d | RI.1.10, RF.1.2c, RF.1.3a, RF.1.3g, RF.1.4b, W.1.2, W.1.8, SL.1.1a, SL.1.1b, L.1.1c, L.1.1e, L.1.2d, L.1.5a, L.1.5c, L.1.6 |

DAY 4

Opening Routines, T464–T465
- Phonemic Awareness
- High-Frequency Words
- Vocabulary Boost

Phonemic Awareness, T466

Read

Connect to the Topic
- Read Play: *Animal Picnic*, T468
- Think Through the Text, T468
- ☑ **Compare Texts,** T469
- ☑ **Vocabulary Strategies,** Suffixes -er, -est, T470–T471

Research/Media Literacy, T477

☑ **Phonics**
- Words with Long *i* (CVC*e*), T466
- Words with Digraphs *kn, wr, gn, mb,* T466
- Phonograms -*ine,* -*ite,* T466

Read *Kite Time,* T467

☑ **Fluency**

Intonation, T457

☑ **Spelling**

Connect to Writing, T472

☑ **Grammar**

Spiral Review: Articles and Demonstrates, T472

Daily Proofreading Practice, T473

☑ **Informative Writing: Report**

Drafting and Revising, T473

 Suggestions for English Language Learners (See pp. E42–E51.)

RL.1.10, RI.1.9, RF.1.2c, RF.1.3c, RF.1.3g, RF.1.4b, W.1.2, W.1.5, W.3.8, SL.1.1a, SL.1.1b, L.1.1h, L.1.2d, L.1.4b, L.3.6

DAY 5

Opening Routines, T474–T475
- Phonemic Awareness
- High-Frequency Words
- Vocabulary Boost

Phonemic Awareness, T475

Read

Extend the Topic
- Domain-Specific Vocabulary, T476
- Research/Media Literacy: Ask and Answer Questions, T477
- Optional Second Read: *Animal Picnic,* T468

☑ **Phonics**
- Words with Long *i* (CVC*e*), T482
- Words with Digraphs *kn, wr, gn, mb,* T482
- Phonograms -*ine,* -*ite,* T482

☑ **Fluency**

Intonation, T457

☑ **Spelling**

Assess, T478

☑ **Grammar**

Weekly Review: The Verb *be,* T478–T479

Daily Proofreading Practice, T480

☑ **Informative Writing: Report**

Revising and Proofreading, T480–T481

RI.1.1, RF.1.2c, RF.1.3g, W.1.2, W.1.6, SL.1.1c, SL.1.2, SL.1.3, L.1.1c, L.1.1e, L.1.1j, L.1.2d, L.1.6

FOR STUDENTS

- eBook
- GrammarSnap Videos
- Destination Reading
- Context Cards

FOR TEACHERS

- Teacher One-Stop
- Interactive Whiteboard Lessons
- Literacy and Language Guide

- Lesson 15 Blackline Masters
- Additional Resources
- Assessment

DAY 1

Today's Goals

Vocabulary & Oral Language
- **Teacher Read Aloud:** "The Dancing Wolves"
- **Oral Vocabulary**
- **Listening Comprehension**
- **Model Fluency**

Phonemic Awareness
- **Substitute Phonemes**
- **Identify Middle Sound**

Phonics & Fluency
- **Words with Long *i* (CVCe)**
- **Read Decodable Reader:** *Mike's Bike*
- **Fluency:** Intonation

☑ **WORDS TO KNOW**

bird	long
both	or
eyes	those
fly	walk

Text-Based Comprehension
- **Read and Comprehend**
- **Read the Anchor Text:** *Animal Groups*

Grammar & Writing
- **The Verb *be***
- ✏ **Informative Writing:** Report

Spelling
- **Words with Long *i***

 **COMMON CORE** **RF.1.2c** isolate and pronounce sounds in spoken single-syllable words; **RF.1.3g** recognize and read irregularly spelled words; **SL.1.1a** follow rules for discussions; **L.1.6** use words and phrases acquired through conversations, reading and being read to, and responding to texts

Opening Routines

Warm Up with Wordplay

Share a Rhyme

Display and read the following rhyme with children:

> **Eeny meeny miny mo.**
> **Catch a tiger by the toe.**
> **If he hollers, let him go.**
> **Eeny meeny miny mo.**

Guide children to notice the nonsense words and to discuss why the rhyme uses nonsense words. Ask: *Is this a silly rhyme or a serious rhyme? How do you know?* Then have children point out the rhyming words, and have volunteers underline each one on the board. Challenge children to come up with more rhyming words. Then have children tell which word in the rhyme names an animal. Tell children they will be reading more selections about animals this week.

Daily Phonemic Awareness

Identify and Substitute Medial Phonemes

- *We're going to change the vowel sound in a word to make a new word. Listen to* mad, /m/ /ă/ /d/. *What is its vowel sound?* /ă/, short a *Change the short* a, /ă/, *to long* a, /ā/. *What is the new word?* made

- Have children repeat with you, then by themselves. Have them continue with the words shown to say the word, name the vowel sound, change the vowel sound, and say the new word. 🔊 **RF.1.2c**

Word	Change the . . .	Result
rid	/ĭ/ to /ī/	*ride*
hat	/ă/ to /ĭ/	*hit*
lake	/ā/ to /ī/	*like*
kit	/ĭ/ to /ī/	*kite*
Kate	/ā/ to /ă/	*cat*

Corrective Feedback

- If a child misses a word, say the correct word and model the task. *Listen to the word,* rid, /r/ /ĭ/ /d/. *Now change* /ĭ/ *to* /ī/: /r/ /ī/ /d/. *What is the new word?* ride

Daily High-Frequency Words

Introduce

- Point to the Words to Know on the Focus Wall. *Our Words to Know for this week are* bird, both, eyes, fly, long, or, those, *and* walk. *You are going to see these words in your reading.*

- Use **Instructional Routine 10** and the **High-Frequency Word Card** to introduce the word *bird.*

- Repeat the procedure with the words *both, eyes, fly, long, or, those,* and *walk.* 🔊 **RF.1.3g**

Corrective Feedback

- If a child is unable to recognize the word *both,* say the correct word and have children repeat it. *Both. What is the word?* both

- Have children spell the word. *b-o-t-h How do we say this word?* both

- Have children reread all of the cards in random order.

Daily Vocabulary Boost

- Demonstrate fluent reading by reading aloud the Big Book *Vulture View.* Tell children to listen carefully for rhyming words. Then reread the story and ask children to join in. Stop occasionally and ask a volunteer to read the rhyming words on the page. Then have children generate a series of words that rhyme with the rhyming pair.

- Review words that may be unfamiliar to children. Guide them to use the pictures to help them determine what the words mean.

- Have children discuss vultures using previously learned vocabulary, such as *search, habitat, view,* and *predators.* Challenge them to use these words in their everyday speech. Remind children to stay on topic and follow classroom rules. 🔊 **SL.1.1a, L.1.6**

Teacher Read Aloud

▶ SHARE OBJECTIVES

• Listen to hear how a reader's voice goes up and down.
• Answer questions about a text read aloud.
• Participate in a classroom discussion.

Model Fluency

• Explain to children that good readers use correct intonation, or pitch, as they read aloud. *As you read aloud, make your voice deeper at the end of a statement and higher at the end of a question.*

• Read aloud the second paragraph of "The Dancing Wolves." Ask children to give a "thumbs up" when they hear your voice go up at the end of a question and a "thumbs down" when your voice goes down at the end of a statement.

• *When did my voice go up as I read? When did my voice go down? How did this change help you understand what I was reading?*

• Read the entire selection aloud. Ask children to listen carefully to find out how the rabbit tricks the wolves.

SL.1.1a follow rules for discussions; SL.1.1b build on others' talk in conversations by responding to others' comments; SL.1.1c ask questions to clear up confusion about topics and texts under discussion; SL.1.2 ask and answer questions about details in a text read aloud, information presented orally, or through other media

The Dancing Wolves

A rabbit walked through the woods on his way to visit his friend the woodchuck. The woodchuck lived in a deep, warm hole under an old tree stump. Excited to share the woodchuck's cookies and milk, the rabbit was not as **sensitive** to the dangers in the forest as usual. He did not notice, until it was too late, that a pack of hungry wolves surrounded him and **threatened** to eat him.

The rabbit was frightened, but stayed **alert**. He said to the wolves, "I am too small for all of you to eat. I am just a little bite for big wolves like you. One of you will get me, but which one will it be?"

The wolves looked at the rabbit and sized him up. They imagined him on a **scale** and saw that he was too small for them to share. So, of course, the wolves began to argue. **①**

The rabbit cried, "Stop! I have an idea to solve your problem. I will teach you a new dance and the best dancer will win me as the prize."

The wolves, who loved to dance, agreed to this solution. The rabbit gave **directions**. "Line up. I will stand by this tree and sing. You dance away from me until I call 'Turn!' and then you dance back to me in a line." **②**

The wolves did as they were told. After hearing the cry "Turn!" they danced back to the rabbit. **③**

Introduce Oral Vocabulary

Use **Instructional Routine 16** to define each highlighted oral vocabulary word.

• Discuss the meaning of each word as it is used in the story.

• For additional support and reinforcement, have children look up each word in a children's dictionary.

sensitive aware of changes or details • *Excited to share the woodchuck's cookies and milk, the rabbit was not as sensitive to the dangers in the forest as usual.*

threatened said you were going to do harm • *He did not notice, until it was too late, that a pack of hungry wolves surrounded him and threatened to eat him.*

"Great!" said the rabbit. "You are marvelous dancers. Now for the next part, you will dance as before. But on every seventh step, you must **swivel** in place. I will sing and call to you from that tall tree *over there.*"

The wolves did as they were told, having even more fun. When they came back, the rabbit said, "Terrific! You did even better than the first time. For the next part, you will dance away from me again but this time you will hop on every fourth step and clap your paws on every fifth step. I will sing from that tree *way over there.*"

And so it went. The dances got harder and harder so that the wolves had to think more and more about what they were doing. The rabbit moved farther and farther away to trees that were closer and closer to the woodchuck's hole.

Finally, the rabbit yelled, "This is the last dance! It is a race. You must run away as fast as you can, do a flip every seventh step, and jump every tenth step. The first wolf that returns after I yell 'Turn!' will get to eat me."

The wolves took off. The rabbit waited until they were far away. Then he called "Turn" and darted into the woodchuck's hole. The wolves ran back, extra-hungry from all of the dancing, and expecting to eat rabbit for lunch. When they returned, though, the rabbit had disappeared. **4**

The wolves plopped down on the ground, moaning with hunger and disappointment. Each wolf thought he could hear the distant sound of a rabbit eating cookies, but none would admit it.

alert aware of what is happening and ready for action • *The rabbit was frightened, but stayed alert.*

scale a tool that measures weight • *They imagined him on a scale and saw that he was too small for them to share.*

directions instructions about how to do something • *The rabbit gave directions.*

swivel turn or spin on one spot • *But on every seventh step, you must swivel in place.*

Listening Comprehension

Read aloud the story. Pause at the numbered stopping points to ask children the questions below. Discuss the meanings of the highlighted words, as needed, to support the discussion.
SL.1.2

1 *Why don't the wolves eat the rabbit at first? Sample answer: They saw that the rabbit was too small to share, and they began to argue.* **CHARACTER MOTIVES**

2 *What details tell you that this story is made-up? Sample answer: The animals, think, talk, and have feelings like humans.* **GENRE**

3 *Why do the wolves do what the rabbit says? Sample answer: They enjoy dancing and they believe they might get a tasty rabbit to eat as a reward.* **UNDERSTANDING CHARACTERS**

4 *How did the rabbit get away? Sample answers: He dove into the woodchuck's hole.* **IDENTIFY STORY STRUCTURE**

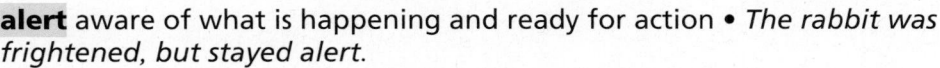

Classroom Collaboration

Begin the discussion by inviting students to ask questions to clear up any confusion about the story. Then, expand the discussion to include children's thoughts and personal responses to the story. Encourage children to respond to each other, rather than looking to you to step in on every question. Remind them to follow classroom rules for discussions, such as staying on topic, speaking one by one, and listening attentively when someone is speaking.
SL.1.1a, SL.1.1b, SL.1.1c

Whole Group

DAY 1

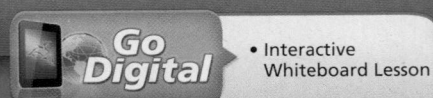

• Interactive Whiteboard Lesson

Phonics

Interactive Whiteboard Lesson:
Words with Long i (CVCe)

Phonemic Awareness/Phonics

▶ SHARE OBJECTIVES

- Identify medial sounds in words.
- Learn the sound-spelling correspondence for long *i* (CVCe).
- Blend and decode regularly spelled one-syllable words with *i_e*.

▶ SKILLS TRACE

Words with Long *i* (CVCe)	
Introduce	T420–T421
Differentiate	T492
Reteach	T506
Review	T444, T466
Assess	Weekly Tests, Lesson 15

ELL ENGLISH LANGUAGE LEARNERS
Use Visuals

Beginning Show **Picture Cards** *kite, slide, dime*. Point to each picture and say the words, emphasizing the long *i* sound. Have children repeat.

Low Intermediate Use **Letter Cards** to build and read the word *pine*. Have children repeat. Point out the long *i* sound and the silent *e*. Repeat with *nine* and *fine*.

High Intermediate Write and read *vine, hide, shine*. Point out the sound-spelling for long *i* in these words. Have children copy the words and read them with a partner.

Proficient Show **Letter Cards** for *kit*. Have children tell how to change it to *kite*. Read the new word. Repeat with *pin/pine, bit/bite, hid/hide*.

See ELL Lesson 15, p. E43, for scaffolded support.

COMMON CORE **RF.1.2b** orally produce single-syllable words by blending sounds; **RF.1.2c** isolate and pronounce sounds in spoken single-syllable words; **RF.1.3c** know final -e and vowel team conventions for representing long vowel sounds; **RF.1.3b** decode regularly spelled one-syllable words; **RF.1.3g** recognize and read irregularly spelled words; **SL.1.6** produce complete sentences when appropriate to task and situation

Words with Long *i* (CVCe)

PHONEMIC AWARENESS WARM-UP Guide children to listen for the middle sound in words. *I will say some words. Listen: kit. /k/ /ĭ/ /t/. The middle sound is /ĭ/. Let's do some more. Listen: kite. /k/ /ī/ /t/. The middle sound is /ī/.*

Now you do it. Listen: like. What is the middle sound? /ī/
Repeat with time /ī/, pack /ă/, mine /ī/, fit /ĭ/, map /ă/, bike /ī/.
▬ RF.1.2c

1 Teach/Model

SOUND/SPELLING CARDS Display the card for *ice cream*. Name the picture and say the sound. Have children repeat after you. *Listen: ice cream, /ī/. Now you say it.*

- Point to the *i_e* spelling. *When you see the letter* i *followed by a consonant and an* e*, the letter* i *will often stand for the long* i *sound, /ī/.*

- Write and read *hide*. Cover the *e*. Read *hid*, pointing out the short *i* sound, /ĭ/. Uncover the *e* and point out the *i*-consonant-*e* pattern. *The letter* i *stands for the /ī/ sound in* hide. *Read with me:* hide. Repeat with the words *slid/slide* and *rid/ride*.

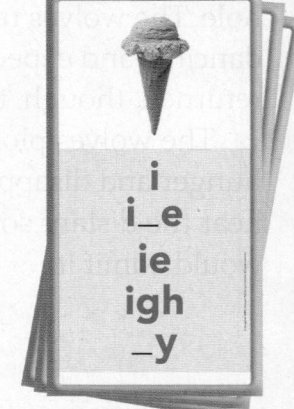

2 Guided Practice

CONTINUOUS BLENDING ROUTINE Use **Instructional Routine 3** to model blending *time*. Write *time* on the board. ■ RF.1.2b, RF.1.3b, RF.1.3c

- Point to **Sound/Spelling Card** *ice cream* and remind children that knowing that *i*-consonant-*e* can stand for the long *i* sound can help them when they read.

- Display **Letter Cards** *t, i, m,* and *e*.

- Point out the *i*-consonant-*e* pattern. Blend the sounds. *Listen: /t/ /ī/ /m/.* Have children blend with you. *Now you blend the sounds.* /t/ /ī/ /m/, *time*

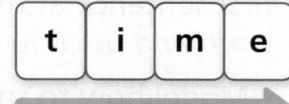

REPEAT CONTINUOUS BLENDING with the words in Row 1 below. Then write the words in Rows 1–3 and have children read them. Use the **Corrective Feedback** steps if children need additional help.

- Repeat until children are reading at a rate of three seconds per word.

DECODING Write the two sentences on the board. Call on individuals to blend one or more words and to read the sentences. ■ RF.1.3b, RF.1.3c, RF.1.3g

> **1.** time bite kite slide dime
> **2.** shake press whale shade he's
> **3.** chime chase that's sat white
>
> Mike <u>and</u> <u>I</u> had time <u>for</u> <u>a</u> walk.
> Miles can <u>fly</u> a kite <u>over</u> <u>the</u> pine tree.

3 Apply

Hands-on Practice

Have partners use letter cards to take turns building and reading words with long *i*. After reading a word, each partner should use the word in a sentence. ■ RF.1.3c, SL.1.6

DAILY ASSESSMENT

Corrective Feedback Work with the whole group to correct errors, following the model below.

Phonics Error:
A child reads *pine* as *pin*.

Correct the error. Review the **Sound/Spelling Card**. Say the word and the sound. *The word is* pine. *The pattern i-consonant-e tells me that the letter* i *stands for the /ī/ sound.*

Model as you touch the letters. *I'll blend: /p/ /ī/ /n/. What is the word?* pine

Guide *Let's blend together: /p/ /ī/ /n/. What is the word?* pine

Check *You blend: /p/ /ī/ /n/ What is the word?* pine

Reinforce Go back three or four words and have children continue reading. Make note of errors and review those words during tomorrow's lesson.

SMALL GROUP Options

Go to p. T492 for additional phonics support.

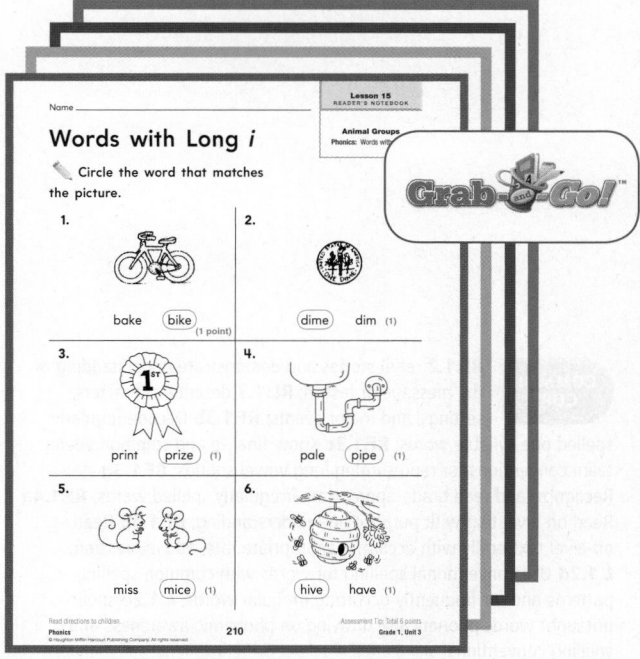

Reader's Notebook Vol. 1 p. 210
See Grab-and-Go™ Resources for additional leveled practice.

Phonemic Awareness/Phonics • **T421**

Phonics/Spelling

▶ SHARE OBJECTIVES

- Write words with long *i* (CVCe).
- Read text with regularly spelled one-syllable words with long *i* and high-frequency words.
- Practice reading on-level text while using proper intonation.

▶ DICTATION SENTENCES

- **lime.** A **lime** is a sour fruit.
- **wide.** I am **wide** awake.
- **ice.** May I have **ice** in my glass?
- **side.** This **side** is red.
- **while.** We will go in a little **while**.
- **rise.** She will watch the dough **rise**.

Write Words with Long *i* (CVCe)

1 | Teach/Model

CONNECT SOUNDS TO SPELLING Review **Sound/Spelling Card** *ice cream*. Tell children that they will now write words with /ī/.

Use **Instructional Routine 6** to dictate, using the first sentence at the left. *Listen as I say each word and use it in a sentence.*

- Model how to spell the word *lime*. Point to the *i_e* spelling on the **Sound/Spelling Card** *ice cream*. *What is the sound? /ī/ I know that the letters* i_e *stand for /ī/ in this word. I'll begin with the letter* l. *Now I will write* im. *I end with an* e. *Now I'll reread to check the whole word:* lime.

2 | Guided Practice

CONNECT SOUNDS TO WRITING Continue the dictation, using the sentences at the left. Remind children to only write the dictation word.

- Have children say each word aloud after you. Then have them identify the sounds they hear, and write the letters that stand for each sound. ◾ **L.1.2e**

3 | Apply

Read aloud the following sentence for children to write.

> Mike rides <u>a</u> bike <u>for</u> nine miles.

Remind children that *a* and *for* are Words to Know that they learned in previous lessons.

Print the words and sentence for children to check their work. ◾ **L.1.2d**

COMMON CORE **RL.1.2** retell stories and demonstrate understanding of the message or lesson; **RL.1.3** describe characters, settings, and major events; **RF.1.3b** Decode regularly spelled one-syllable words; **RF.1.3c** Know final -e and common vowel team conventions for representing long vowel sounds; **RF.1.3g** Recognize and read grade-appropriate irregularly spelled words; **RF.1.4a** Read on-level text with purpose and understanding; **RF.1.4b** Read on-level text orally with accuracy, appropriate rate, and expression; **L.1.2d** Use conventional spelling for words with common spelling patterns and for frequently occurring irregular words; **L.1.2e** spell untaught words phonetically, drawing on phonemic awareness and spelling conventions

Decodable Reader

Go Digital

Read *Mike's Bike*

Decodable Reader, Unit 3, pp. 99–104

Corrective Feedback Work with the whole group to correct errors, following the model below.

Decoding Error:
A child reads *like* as *lick*.

Correct the error. Say the word. *That word is* like. *The i-consonant-e pattern means the letter i stands for the sound /ī/.*

Guide Have children repeat the word. *What is the word?* like

Check *Go back to the beginning of the sentence and read it again.*

Reinforce Record the error and review the word again before children reread the story.

Go to p. T492 for additional phonics support.

REVIEW /ī/ AND WORDS TO KNOW Tell children that many words in this story have the letters *i_e*, which can stand for the long *i* sound. Point out that children have learned the following words which they will also read in the story: *both, long, or.*

PREVIEW Have children preview pages 99–101 and predict what the story is about. Ask volunteers to tell about a bike ride they took or would like to take.

MODEL FLUENCY AND INTONATION Read aloud page 101 as children follow along. Have children note the words that you say a little louder as you read what Nell says. Lead children in choral reading the page with fluency and appropriate intonation.

READ Remind children to track the words from left to right. Remind them that when they come to the end of a line, they should sweep their hand down to the beginning of the next line and continue reading. Have children read each page silently and then choral-read aloud. Have them read to find out what happens on Mike's bike ride. ⬤ RF.1.3b, RF.1.3c, RF.1.3g, RF.1.4a

RESPONDING Have children work with partners to retell the story. Remind them to retell the events in the order in which they happened. ⬤ RL.1.2, RL.1.3

Reread for Fluency/ Develop Automaticity

READ WITH A PARTNER Have partners reread *Mike's Bike* three or four times, taking turns reading aloud each page. Remind them to read words correctly and to read smoothly. Visit partners to listen to them read. Give feedback about reading accurately, at an appropriate rate, and with expression, and provide guidance for improving fluency. ⬤ RF.1.4b

- eBook
- Context Cards
- Vocabulary Reader

Introduce Words to Know

Teach

Display and discuss the **Vocabulary in Context Cards,** using the routine below. See also **Instructional Routine 15.**

1 **Read and pronounce the word.** Read the word once alone and then together.

2 **Explain the word.** Read aloud the explanation under *What Does It Mean?*

3 **Discuss vocabulary in context.** Together, read aloud the sentence on the front of the card. Help children explain and use the word in new sentences.

4 **Engage with the word.** Ask and discuss *How Do I Use It?*

Practice/Apply

Give partners or small groups one or two **Vocabulary in Context Cards.** Help children complete the *Talk It Over* activities for each card. ⬤ **RF.1.3g**

COMMON CORE **RF.1.3g** recognize and read irregularly spelled words

---

Lesson 15

✓ **WORDS TO KNOW**
High-Frequency Words

bird
fly
both
long
eyes
or
those
walk

Vocabulary Reader

Context Cards

 COMMON CORE **RF.1.3g** recognize and read irregularly spelled words

160  Go Digital

---

Words to Know

 Read Together

▶ Read each **Context Card.**

▶ Ask a question that uses one of the blue words.

1 **bird**
An eagle is a bird with big, strong wings.

2 **fly**
Bats are mammals that are able to fly.

 **ENGLISH LANGUAGE LEARNERS**

Use Gestures

Beginning Pantomime looking at something far away. *I see with my eyes.* Have children point to their eyes and repeat the sentence. *Do you see with your eyes?* yes

High Intermediate Have children point to their eyes and pronounce *see*. Point to your eyes. *What do we use to see? eyes* Have children name something they see using the sentence frame *I can see _____ with my eyes.*

Low Intermediate Point to your eyes and say, *These are my eyes. What are these?* Help children answer *your eyes.*

Proficient Have children take turns saying things they can see with their eyes. Have them imagine they are in different environments.

See ELL Lesson 15, p. E42 for vocabulary support.

3 both
The lizard has both stripes and spots.

4 long
This kangaroo has a long tail.

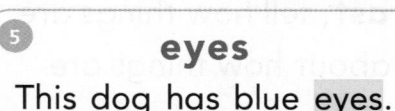

5 eyes
This dog has blue eyes.

6 or
Ducks can either swim or fly.

7 those
Those fish are not the same colors.

8 walk
The elephants walk together in a group.

161

DAILY ASSESSMENT RtI

Are children able to understand and use the Words to Know?

IF...	THEN...
children have difficulty understanding and using Words to Know,	▶ use **Vocabulary in Context Cards** and the Struggling Readers activity, p. T494. *See also Intervention Lesson 15, pp. S42–S51.*
children can understand and use most Words to Know,	▶ use **Vocabulary in Context Cards** and the On Level activity, p. T494.
children can understand and use all Words to Know,	▶ use the Advanced activity, p. T495.

SMALL GROUP Options

Vocabulary Readers pp. T494–T495
Provide support for English Language Learners according to language proficiency. See also Differentiate Words to Know, p. T493.

VOCABULARY IN CONTEXT CARDS 93–100

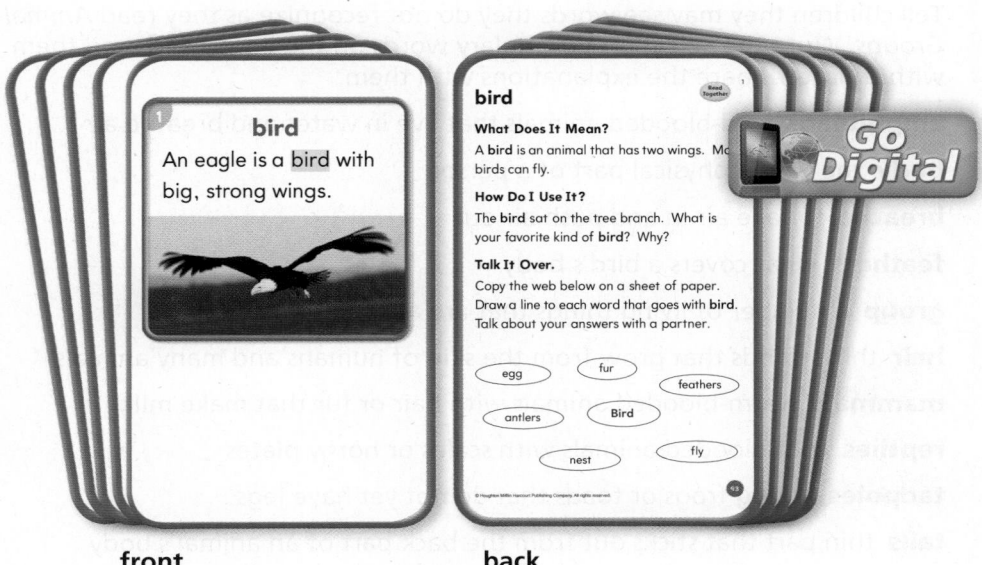

front

back

Go Digital

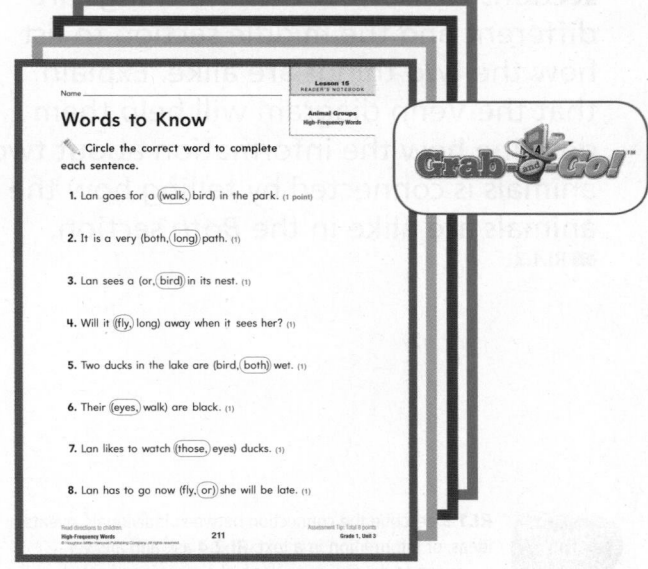

Grab and Go™

Reader's Notebook Vol. 1 p. 211
See Grab-and-Go™ Resources for additional leveled practice.

Introduce Words to Know (SB p. 161) • **T425**

Read and Comprehend

▶ SHARE OBJECTIVES
- Compare and contrast to understand a selection bettter.
- Monitor and clarify while reading a selection to aid comprehension.

☑ TARGET SKILL
Compare and Contrast

- Read **Student Book** p.162 with children.

- Explain to children that when you **compare** two things, you tell how they are alike. Then tell them when you **contrast** two things, you tell how they are different.

- Tell children that good readers think about how things are alike and different to understand what they are reading better.

- Draw children's attention to the graphic organizer on **Student Book** p. 162. Tell them that a Venn diagram will help them compare and contrast two things. Explain that they will use the outer sections to list how the two things are different and the middle section to list how the two things are alike. Explain that the Venn diagram will help them describe how the information about two animals is connected by telling how the animals are alike in the *Both* section.
  🔲 **RI.1.3**

 **RI.1.3** describe the connection between individuals, ideas, or information in a text; **RI.2.4** ask and answer questions to determine or clarify the meaning of words and phrases

---

Read and Comprehend

☑ TARGET SKILL

Compare and Contrast When you **compare**, tell how things are alike. When you **contrast**, tell how things are different. Think about how things are alike and different to understand a selection better. You can use a diagram to **compare** and **contrast** two things.

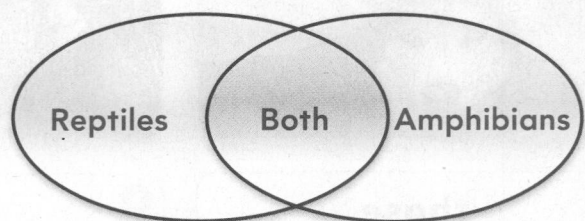

☑ TARGET STRATEGY

Monitor/Clarify If a word or a part does not make sense, you can ask questions, reread, or use the pictures for help.

162 **COMMON CORE** **RI.1.3** describe the connection between individuals, events, ideas, or information in a text; **RI.1.4** ask and answer questions to determine or clarify the meaning of words and phrases

---

SELECTION VOCABULARY

Tell children they may see words they do not recognize as they read *Animal Groups*. Write the Selection Vocabulary words on the board and read them with children. Share the explanations with them.

amphibians cold-blooded animals that live in water and breathe air

body the whole physical part of a person

breathe to take air in and push air out

feathers what covers a bird's body

group a number of living things that are alike in some way

hair thin strands that grow from the skin of humans and many animals

mammals warm-blooded animals with hair or fur that make milk

reptiles cold-blooded animals with scales or horny plates

tadpoles young frogs or toads that do not yet have legs

tails thin part that sticks out from the back part of an animal's body

wings parts of birds that let them fly

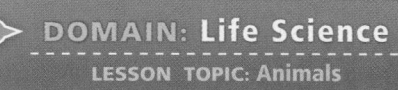
PREVIEW THE TOPIC

Animals

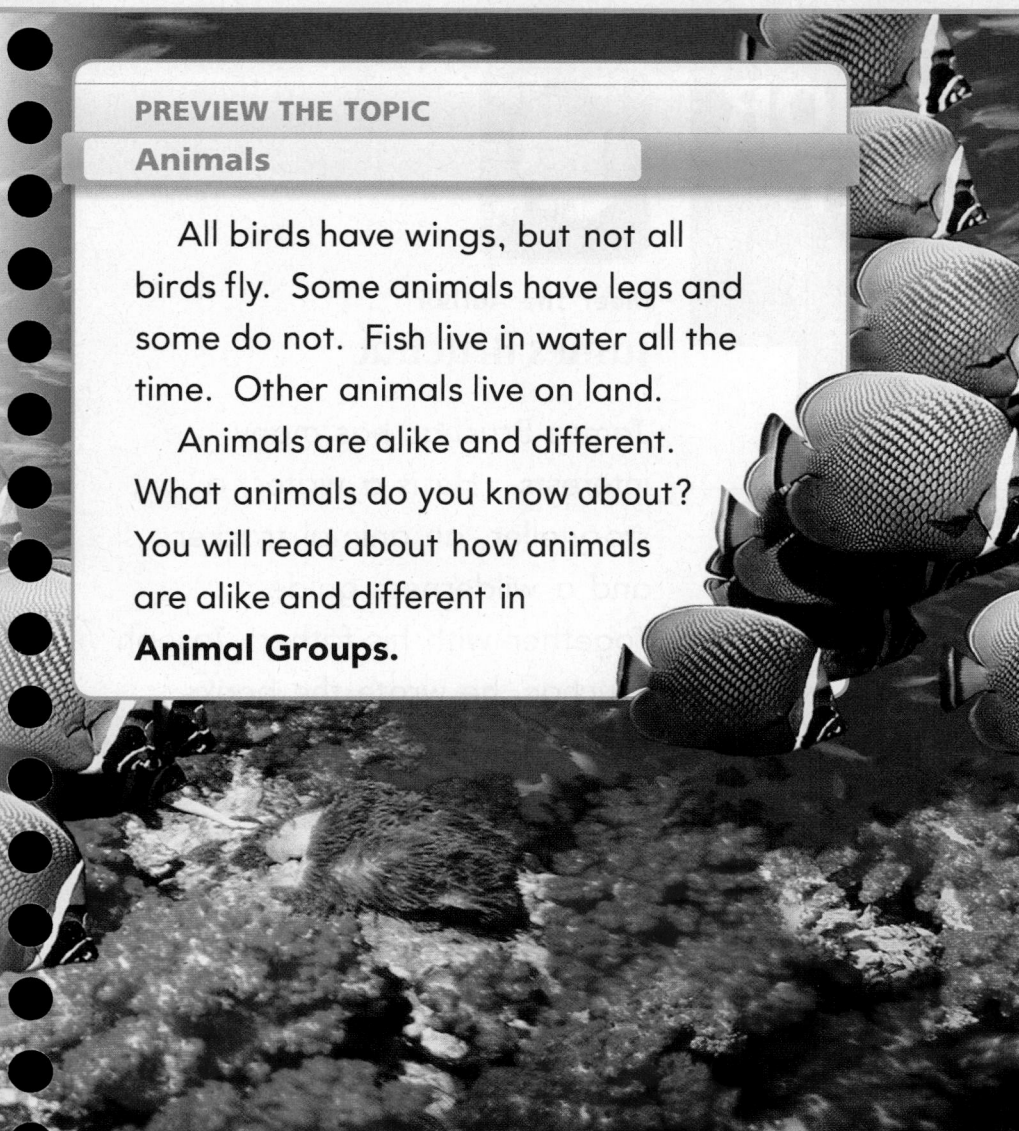

All birds have wings, but not all birds fly. Some animals have legs and some do not. Fish live in water all the time. Other animals live on land.

Animals are alike and different. What animals do you know about? You will read about how animals are alike and different in **Animal Groups.**

163

COMPREHENSION STRATEGIES

Use the following strategies flexibly as you read with children by modeling how they can be used to improve comprehension. See scaffolded support for the strategy shown in boldface during this week's reading.

- **Monitor/Clarify**
- **Summarize**
- **Infer/Predict**
- **Visualize**
- **Analyze/Evaluate**
- **Question**
- **Phonics/Decoding**

Use the Strategy Projectables, S1–S8, for additional support.

○ **DOMAIN: Life Science**

LESSON TOPIC: Animals

☑ TARGET STRATEGY
Monitor/Clarify

- Read the bottom of **Student Book** p. 162 with children.

- Tell children that if a part of a selection or words or phrases in a selection do not make sense, they can ask themselves questions about what the words or phrases mean. Then they can reread that part to find clues to help them understand the meaning of the words and phrases. They can also use the pictures for help.

- Explain that you will show them how they should use this strategy when they read *Animal Groups*. ⬛ RI.1.4

Preview the Topic: Animals

- Tell children that today they will begin reading *Animal Groups*.

- Read the information on **Student Book** p. 163 with them.

- Have children explain characteristics of animals, using the information in the text and their own experiences.

- Have them describe the photo on p. 163, using the word *animals*.

- To further explore the topic, brainstorm with children a list of animals that live in your area and help them choose ones to research. Guide them to use appropriate media and resources, and if possible, to use their five senses to observe the animals in nature. As children research, have them keep a record of what they find out, including drawings and facts about the animals. Have children publish their work as posters or reports and share them in small groups.

Read the Anchor Text

☑ **TARGET SKILL**
Compare and Contrast

- Point out the graphic organizer on **Student Book** p. 164 to children.
- Tell children a Venn diagram can help them describe how things are alike and how they are different.

☑ **GENRE** Informational Text

- Read the genre information on **Student Book** p. 164 with children.
- Preview the selection with children, and model identifying the characteristics of an informational text.

Think Aloud *An informational text gives information about a topic. It has details to explain important ideas. The title* Animal Groups *makes me think the selection will give information about kinds of animals. I think it's an informational text.*

- *How can the pictures in* Animal Groups *help you figure out that the selection is an informational text? It has photos of real animals. They give information, too.*

- As you preview, ask children to point out other features of informational texts, such as headings and labels.

- To help children distinguish genres, have them identify the general characteristics of informational texts they have read. Some examples are: sentences tell facts; photographs give information; it has labels and headings. Then have children explain the major differences between story books and informational books. ▭ **RL.1.5**

COMMON CORE **RI.1.10** read informational texts; **RF.1.4a** read on-level text with purpose and understanding

---

Lesson 15

ANCHOR TEXT

Animal Groups
by James Bruchac

Meet the Author

James Bruchac

James Bruchac has many interests. He is a writer, a storyteller, an animal tracker, and a wilderness guide. Together with his father, Joseph Bruchac, he wrote the books **How Chipmunk Got His Stripes** and **Turtle's Race with Beaver**.

☑ **TARGET SKILL**

Compare and Contrast
Tell how two things are alike and different.

☑ **GENRE**

Informational text gives facts about a topic. As you read, look for:
▸ information and facts in the words
▸ photos that show the real world

COMMON CORE **RI.1.3** describe the connection between individuals, events, ideas, or information in a text; **RI.1.7** use illustrations and details to describe key ideas; **RI.1.10** read informational texts

164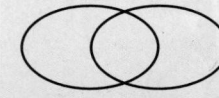

▭ **RI.1.10**

Scaffold Close Reading

Think Through the Text **FIRST READ**	Analyze the Text **SECOND READ**	Independent Reading
Develop comprehension through • Guided Questioning • Target Strategy: Monitor/ Clarify • Vocabulary in Context **IF** children demonstrate understanding of what the selection is mostly about, **THEN** provide additional challenge using the questions labeled A Closer Look.	Support analyzing short sections of text: • Compare and Contrast • Text and Graphic Features Use directed note-taking by working with children to complete a graphic organizer during reading. Distribute copies of Graphic Organizer 8.	• Children analyze the text independently, using the Reader's Guide on pp. 217–218 of the **Reader's Notebook**. (See p. T458 for instructional support.) • Children read independently in a self-selected trade book.

Animal Groups

written by James Bruchac

ESSENTIAL QUESTION

What makes birds
different from
mammals?

165

⚠ READER AND TASK CONSIDERATIONS

Determine the level of additional support your children will need to
read and comprehend *Animal Groups* successfully.

READERS

- **Motivate** Ask children to name
  different kinds of fish and birds they
  know about.
- **Access Knowledge and
  Experiences** Remind children of
  the Preview the Topic information on
  Student Book p. 163. Ask them to
  share with a partner what they recall,
  and if possible, share one other thing
  they know about how animals are
  alike or how they are different.

TASKS

- **Increase Scaffolding** Stop
  periodically as you read to have
  children retell key details from the
  text and the photographs.
- **Foster Independence** Have
  children read the selection in small
  groups. Tell them to pause throughout
  the selection to ask any questions they
  have about the information. Have
  them look together for text evidence in
  the sentences, labels, and photographs
  to help them answer the questions.

ESSENTIAL QUESTION

- Read aloud and discuss the Essential
  Question on **Student Book** p. 165:
  *What makes birds different from
  mammals?* Tell children to think
  about this question as they read.

Predictive Writing

- Write the Essential Question on the
  board.
- Explain that partners will work
  together to write what they expect
  Animal Groups to be about. Have
  them think about how the Essential
  Question relates to what they noticed
  while previewing the selection or
  what they already know from their
  own experiences or past readings.
- Guide children to think about the
  genre as they write their ideas. Then
  discuss their predictions.

Set Purpose

- Tell children that good readers set a
  purpose for reading. *Look at the
  photos. Think about what you know
  about an informational text. What do
  you hope to learn from Animal Groups?*
- Model setting a reading purpose.

> **Think Aloud** *I know about many
> different kinds of animals, but I do not
> know which animals are in a group
> together. I wonder what makes animals
> belong in a group together. I will read
> to find out.*

- Have children set their own purpose
  for reading. Ask several volunteers to
  share their purpose for reading. Then
  have children read the selection.

▄ RI.1.10, RF.1.4a

Fish

Reptile

Amphibian

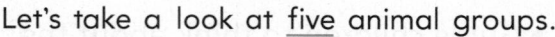

①

Let's take a look at <u>five</u> animal groups.

166

Bird

Mammal

How are animals in a group the same?

167

Comprehensible Input

Beginning Have children complete the sentence frame: *Each animal belongs to an animal group. I see _____ animal groups.* five

Low Intermediate *What are five animal groups?* fish, amphibian, reptile, bird, mammal *Which group has wings?*

High Intermediate *How are animals in a group the same?* look the same, move the same, live in the same places

Proficient *What does it mean when we compare animals?* tell how they are the same *What does it mean when we contrast animals?* tell how they are different

COMMON CORE **RI.1.1** ask and answer questions about key details; **RI.1.2** identify the main topic and retell key details; **RI.1.3** describe the connection between individuals, events, ideas or information in a text; **RI.1.4** ask and answer questions to determine or clarify the meaning of words and phrases; **RI.1.7** use illustrations and details to describe key ideas; **RF.1.3b** decode regularly spelled one-syllable words; **RF.1.3g** recognize and read irregularly spelled words

FIRST READ

Use Text Evidence

Think Through the Text

① *What is one difference you see between the fish and the reptile on p.166?* The fish has fins and the reptile has legs.
🔊 **RI.1.1**

☑ **TARGET STRATEGY: Monitor/Clarify**

Read **Student Book** pp. 166–167 with children. Model the strategy.

Think Aloud *The text says "animal groups," but I only see five single animals. I ask myself, What does animal groups mean? I think a group needs to have more than one. I will read the next few pages. Maybe I will find out about more than one kind of fish in the Fish group.*

Guide children to practice using the Monitor/Clarify strategy as they continue reading. 🔊 **RI.1.4**

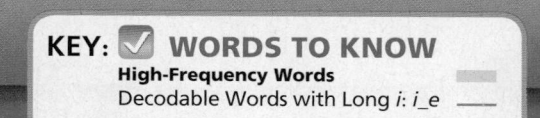 
Fish

fin

eye

mouth

tail

gill

fin

Fish must live in water. Fish have gills that help them breathe in water.

Fish have fins and tails. Those help them swim. **2**

168

169

▶ A Closer Look

How are all fish alike? They live in water and have gills, fins, and tails to help them breathe and swim in water. Make a smart guess, or draw a conclusion, about how one fish might be different from other fish. One fish might be different from other fish in color and size. Fish might also swim in different kinds of water such as salt water and fresh water. ◼ **RI.1.3, RI.1.7**

2 *What is the most important idea on pp. 168–169? Fish live in water. What details help explain that idea? Fish have gills, fins, and tails to help them live in water.*
◼ **RI.1.1, RI.1.2, RI.1.7**

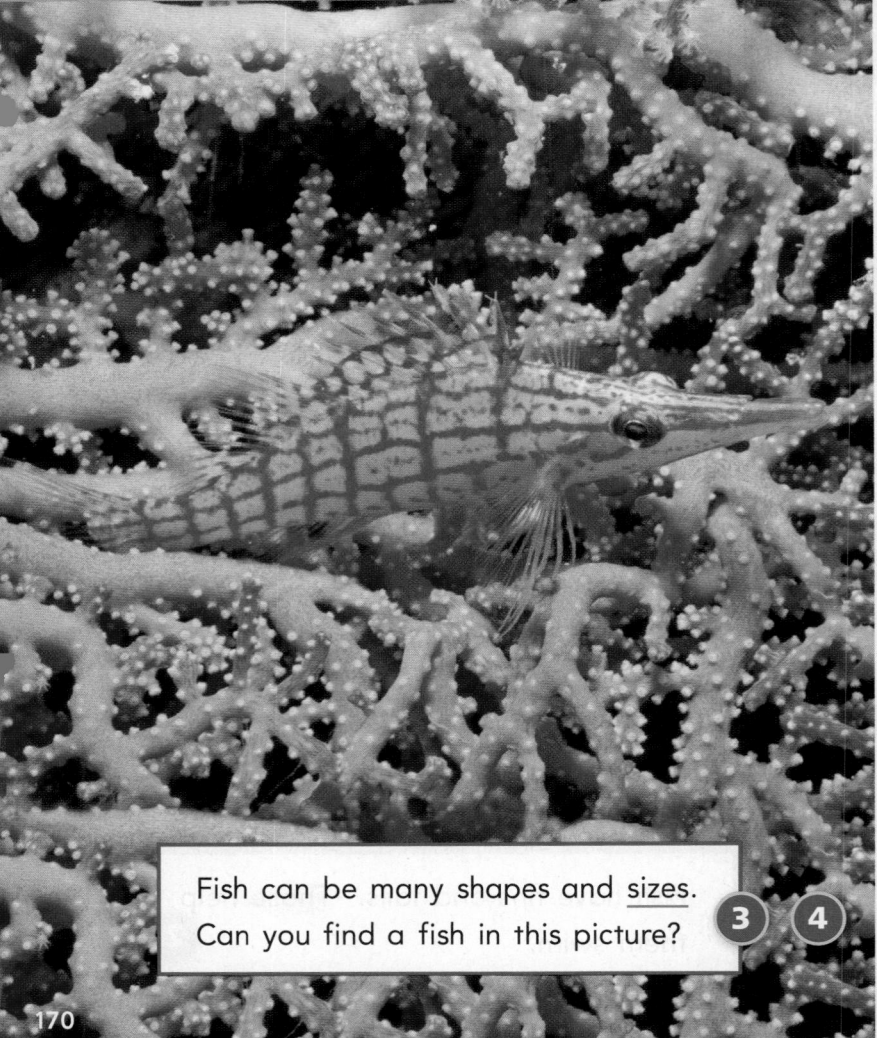

Fish can be many shapes and <u>sizes</u>. Can you find a fish in this picture?  ④

170

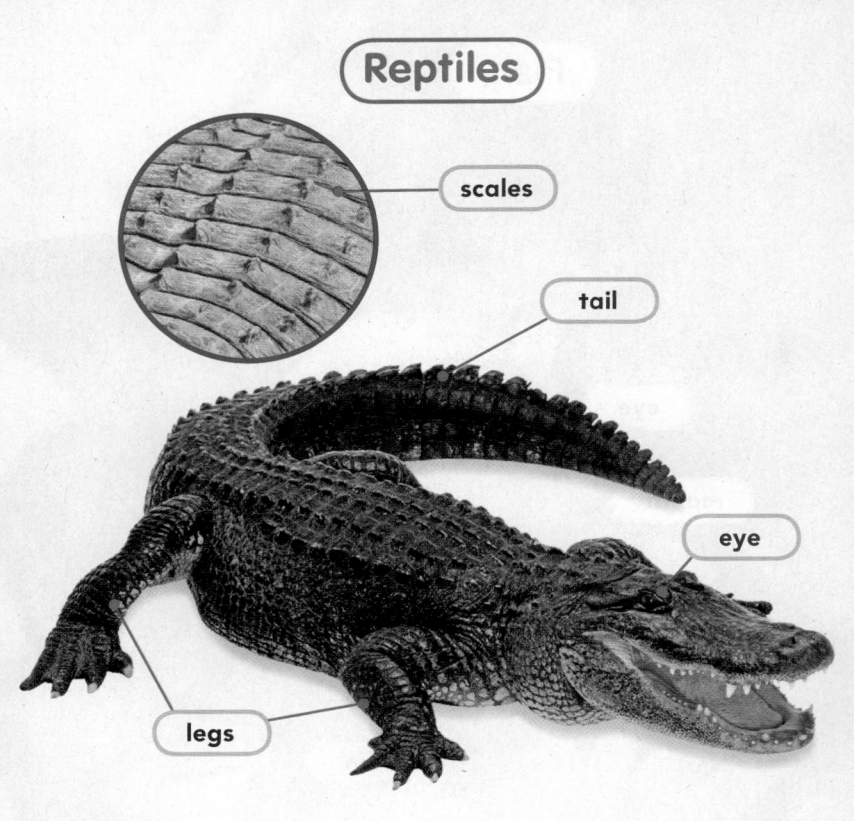

Reptiles

scales

tail

eye

legs

Reptiles can live on land. Some <u>like</u> to be in water. Reptiles have scales on their skin. ⑤

171

 **DOMAIN: Life Science**

LESSON TOPIC: Animals

Cross-Curricular Connection Tell children that animals, like humans, need things to survive. Remind them that humans cannot survive without air, water, food, and enough room to live and grow. Discuss each group of animals. Guide children to understand that the animals in each group need air, water, food, and space and how they get these basic necessities.

COMMON CORE **RI.1.1** ask and answer questions about key details; **RI.1.3** describe the connection between individuals, events, ideas, or information in a text; **RI.1.5** know and use text features to locate facts or information; **RI.1.7** use illustrations and details to describe key ideas; **RF.1.3b** decode regularly spelled one-syllable words; **RF.1.3g** recognize and read irregularly spelled words

FIRST READ

Use Text Evidence

Think Through the Text

③ *What are some ways one fish can be different from another?* They can have different shapes and sizes. ▬ RI.1.1

④ *What does the picture on p. 170 tell you about the fish?* It looks like the things around it, so it is hard to see. ▬ RI.1.7

⑤ *Where do reptiles have scales?* on their skin *What information do you find by the label "scales"?* You find out a photo that shows what scales are and what they look like close up. *If you touched a reptile's skin, how would the scales make it feel?* rough or bumpy ▬ RI.1.1, RI.1.5, RI.1.7

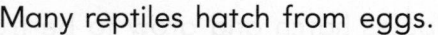

Many reptiles hatch from eggs.

172

Snakes cannot walk. They do not have legs. This snake slides its long body on the grass.

173

6 *What do the pictures on p. 172 show?* a turtle swimming and a baby turtle hatching from an egg *How is the turtle hatching connected to the turtle swimming?* They are both turtles; the baby hatching will grow up to be like the turtle that is swimming.
🔖 **RI.1.3, RI.1.7**

7 *Describe what is different about how turtles and snakes move.* Turtles swim or walk. Snakes slide on the ground. *What do turtles have that snakes do not?* Turtles have legs, so they can swim and walk. They also have shells. 🔖 **RI.1.1, RI.1.3, RI.1.7**

SECOND READ DAY 2

ANALYZE THE TEXT

15.2

Compare and Contrast
Display **Projectable 15.2** and distribute **Graphic Organizer 8**. Ask children to tell how fish and reptiles are alike. *have eyes, a mouth, and a tail; Fish live in water. Some reptiles live in water.* Add this information under *Both* on the Venn diagram. Model describing the connection between pieces of information: *Fish and reptiles are alike in some ways. Both groups have eyes, a mouth, and a tail. Fish live in water, and so do some reptiles.* Then have children identify ways that fish and reptiles are different and record their responses. Continue working with children to find and describe connections between individual animals, animal groups, events, ideas, and pieces of information as they read. 🔖 **RL.1.3**

Amphibians

eye

wet skin

legs

Amphibians spend <u>time</u> both on land and in water. They do not have scales. Their skin is wet.

174

8

tadpoles

Amphibians hatch from eggs. Tadpoles hatch and grow to be frogs.

175

Comprehensible Input

Beginning Have children draw a place where an amphibian might live.

Low Intermediate *Do amphibians live only on land, only in water, or both on land and in water? both on land and in water*

High Intermediate Have children look at the page and complete the sentence frame: *An amphibian's skin stays _____.* wet

Proficient Have children take turns telling a detail that amphibians have in common.

COMMON CORE **RI.1.1** ask and answer questions about key details; **RI.1.3** describe the connection between individuals, events, ideas, or information in a text; **RI.1.4** ask and answer questions to determine or clarify the meaning of words and phrases; **RI.1.5** know and use text features to locate facts or information; **RI.1.7** use illustrations and details to describe key ideas; **RF.1.3b** decode regularly spelled one-syllable words; **RF.1.3g** recognize and read irregularly spelled words

FIRST READ

Use Text Evidence

Think Through the Text

 A Closer Look

How are amphibians like reptiles? They hatch from eggs. *How are amphibians different from reptiles?* Amphibians do not have scales and their skin is wet. **RL.1.1, RI.1.3, RI.1.7**

8 *What text evidence in the words and photos helps you know what the word* tadpoles *means?* The label "tadpoles" helps me find the photo that shows them. I see that they look like little fish. The sentences say that tadpoles hatch from eggs and grow up to be frogs. Now I know that tadpoles are baby frogs. **RI.1.4, RI.1.5, RI.1.7**

KEY: ☑ **WORDS TO KNOW**
High-Frequency Words
Decodable Words with Long *i*: *i_e* ___

COMMON
CORE

DAY 1

Birds

eye

bill

wing

9

feathers

A bird has feathers and wings. This bird's eyes are on the sides of its face!

176

Many birds can fly. Some can run or swim fast.

10

177

---

9 *How are birds the same as amphibians?* They both have eyes, mouths, and legs. They are both kinds of animals. *How are birds different from amphibians?* Birds have two legs and two wings, not four legs. Birds have feathers and amphibians do not. ▬ **RI.1.1, RI.1.3, RI.1.7**

10 *Why can most birds fly?* They have wings.
▬ **RI.1.1, RI.1.3**

ANALYZE THE TEXT

Text and Graphic Features Remind children an author can use special features, such as headings and labels to point out information. Have children identify the heading and labels on p. 176. *What is this section about?* birds *What do the labels tell us? The labels tell us the names of a bird's body parts. What does the photo show? It shows what these body parts look like and where they are on the bird.* As children continue reading, guide them to use the headings to find out what the section will be about and use labels and photos to learn important details about the animals. Have children tell how these special features help them locate and learn information.
▬ **RI.1.5, RI.1.7**

Birds hatch from eggs. This hen made a nest for its eggs.

178

Mammals ⑪

eye

hair

tail

legs

Mammals can be many shapes and <u>sizes</u>. They have hair on their skin. ⑫

179

3
2
1
DAILY ASSESSMENT  **RtI**

Monitor/Clarify IF children have difficulty applying the Monitor/Clarify strategy, **THEN** use this model:

> **Think Aloud** *The sentence on p. 179 says mammals have hair. I ask myself what their hair looks like. I find out from the photo what a lion's hair looks like. I'll read on to find out about other mammals' hair.*

COMMON CORE **RI.1.1** ask and answer questions about key details; **RI.1.3** describe the connection between individuals, events, ideas, or information in a text; **RI.1.4** ask and answer questions to determine or clarify the meaning of words and phrases; **RI.1.5** know and use text features to locate facts or information; **RI.1.7** use illustrations and details to describe key ideas; **RF.1.3c** know final -e and vowel team conventions for representing long vowel sounds

---

FIRST READ

Use Text Evidence

Think Through the Text

☑ TARGET STRATEGY: Monitor/Clarify

Help children apply the Monitor/Clarify strategy after reading **Student Book** pp. 178–181. Have children ask themselves what the word *mammal* means. Then have them find evidence in the words and pictures to clarify the meaning of the word. As children read, continue guiding them to ask and answer questions to help determine or clarify the meaning of words and phrases. ◖RI.1.4

⑪ *What do you think we will read about in the section called "Mammals"?* "Mammals" is the name of an animal group. A lion is probably a mammal. We will learn how mammals are alike. ◖RI.1.5

⑫ *Birds and mammals have different things covering their skin. How are they different?* Birds have feathers and mammals have hair. ◖RI.1.1, RI.1.3, RI.1.7

A mammal mom can
make milk for its baby.

180

Lots of mammals live on land,
but some live in water.

181

☑ Phonics/Decoding Strategy

Use **Projectable S1** to help children apply the Phonics/
Decoding strategy while reading. Ask children to look
at the first sentence on **Student Book** p. 179 and point
to the last word. *How can you predict the vowel sound
in this word? by using the spelling pattern What is the
spelling pattern? consonant-vowel-consonant-e plus the –s
ending. What vowel sound does the i probably stand
for? long i What sound does the e stand for? It is silent.*
Lead children to blend the sounds and read the word:
/s//ī//z//əz/, *sizes*. Then read the sentence together to
confirm that *sizes* makes sense. ⬛ **RF.1.3c**

Did you know that you are a mammal, too?

13 14

182   183

FIRST READ

Use Text Evidence

Think Through the Text

13 *What important details have you learned about mammals in this section?* Mammals can be many shapes and sizes. They have hair on their bodies. Mammal mothers make milk for their babies. Mammals can live in water or on land. People are mammals, too.
RI.1.1, RI.1.2, RI.1.7

14 *Why do you think the author James Bruchac wrote this selection?* to give information; to tell about how groups of animals are alike and different

RI.1.1 ask and answer questions about key details; **RI.1.2** identify the main topic and retell key details; **RI.1.7** use illustrations and details to describe key ideas;

Guided Summary

Oral Language Use the prompts on the **Retelling Cards** to guide children to identify the main topic, retell key details, and summarize the selection. ▬ **RI.1.2, RI.1.7**

front

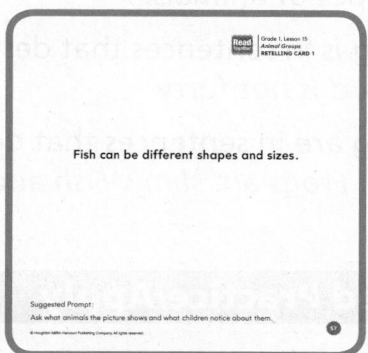

Fish can be different shapes and sizes.

Suggested Prompt:
Ask what animals the picture shows and what children notice about them.

back

front

Snakes are reptiles. They have scales on their skin.

Suggested Prompt:
Ask children to tell other ways in which reptiles are alike.

back

front

Amphibians have wet skin.

Suggested Prompt:
Ask children to guess how wet skin might help an amphibian spend time on land.

back

front

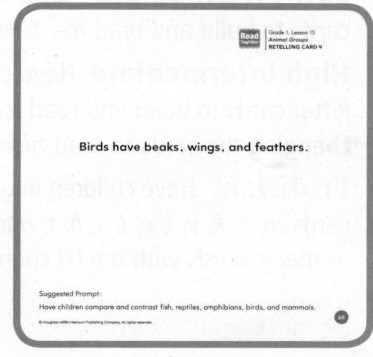

Birds have beaks, wings, and feathers.

Suggested Prompt:
Have children compare and contrast fish, reptiles, amphibians, birds, and mammals.

back

SUMMARIZING RUBRIC	
4 Highly Effective	The child restates the main idea; identifies the important facts or details; retells the order of events by referring to the words and/or illustrations; requires little or no prompting.
3 Generally Effective	The child restates the main idea; identifies some important facts or details; retells the order of most events and may refer to the words and/or illustrations; may require some prompting.
2 Somewhat Effective	The child may restate the main idea; identifies some facts or details; retells the order of some events with some omissions or errors; requires some prompting.
1 Ineffective	The child is unable to restate the main idea; identifies some facts or details, possibly with errors; is unable to retell the order of events; is unable to summarize without prompting.

Go Digital
• *my*WriteSmart
• eBook
• GrammarSnap Videos
• Literacy and Language Guide
• Interactive Whiteboard Lesson

Grammar Introduce the Verb *be*

▶ SHARE OBJECTIVES

- **Grammar** Learn about using *is* and *are* in sentences.
- **Spelling** Spell words with the long *i* sound drawing on phonemic awareness and spelling conventions.
- **Writing** Begin drafting a report.

ELL ENGLISH LANGUAGE LEARNERS
Language Transfer

Beginning Display the words *ice, time, like*. Read the words aloud and have children clap whenever they hear the /ī/ sound.

Low Intermediate Have children use letter cards to build and read *ice, time, like*.

High Intermediate Have children use letter cards to build and read *ice*. Guide them in changing the cards to read *nice, line, like*.

Proficient Have children in groups use letter cards *m, c, k, v, i, e, l, s, h, t, n* to build and read as many words with the /ī/ sound as they can.

1 Teach/Model

- Have children recall some of the facts they have learned about different types of animals.

- Model using *is* in sentences that describe one animal. Say: *A cat is furry. A lizard is not furry.*

- Model using *are* in sentences that describe more than one animal. Say: *Frogs are slimy. Fish and birds are colorful.*

2 Guided Practice/Apply

- Write these sentence frames on the board and read them with children. Have partners work together to complete them orally with information about animals. Point out that these sentences tell about now.

  A _____ is _____.

  Two _____ are _____.

- Then have children write their sentences with their partner.

- Have partners share their sentences with the class. Choose a few examples and discuss with the class why the sentences are correct. ◼ **SL.1.6, L.1.1c, L.1.1e, L.1.1j**

Spelling Words with Long *i*

SPELLING WORDS AND SENTENCES

BASIC

1. *time*
   What *time* is it?
2. *like*
   I *like* to eat oranges.
3. *kite*
   The *kite* was high in the sky.
4. *bike*
   My *bike* is blue.

5. *white*
   Snow is *white*.
6. *drive*
   Can you *drive* me to school?

CHALLENGE

7. *stripe*
   A skunk has a white *stripe*.
8. *mice*
   The *mice* ran under a bush.

Administer the Pretest

Say the first word and read the sentence. Repeat the word as children write it. Guide children to try to spell new words phonetically, drawing on phonemic awareness and spelling conventions. Write the word on the board and have children correct their spelling if needed. Repeat for words 2–8. ◼ **L.1.2e**

Teach the Principle

Review **Sound/Spelling Card**: *ice cream*. Say the name of the card. Point out *i_e*. Write *time*, underlining *i* and *e*. Read the word aloud. Explain that the /ī/ sound can be spelled with the letters *i_e*.

COMMON CORE
W.1.2 write informative/explanatory texts; **W.1.5** focus on a topic, respond to questions/suggestions from peers, and add details to strengthen writing; **W.1.6** use digital tools to produce and publish writing; **W.1.8** recall information from experiences or gather information from sources to answer a question; **SL.1.6** produce complete sentences when appropriate to task and situation; **L.1.1c** use singular and plural nouns with matching verbs in sentences;

Informative Writing Drafting

1 Teach/Model

- Review with children that a report has a topic sentence that tells what the report is about, detail sentences that give facts, and a closing sentence that retells the main idea.

- Display **Projectable 14.10** from Lesson 14. Review the question and answers you wrote on the graphic organizer.

- Then display **Projectable 15.1**. Model drafting a report. Ask the class to help you.

Think Aloud *I'll start with a topic sentence that tells the reader my report will be on tigers. Detail sentences will tell more about my topic.*

Projectable 15.1

Animal Groups Writing Informative Writing

Projectable 15.1

Drafting My Report

What animal would you like to know more about? Find facts about the animal and write a report.

Title: _Tigers_

Topic sentence tells what the report is about.	Sample report: → Tigers can do many things. They are good → at hunting for their food. Tigers can also jump high in the air. Not many animals can run as fast as a tiger.
Detail sentences tell facts about the topic.	
Closing sentence retells the main idea in different words.	→ Tigers are good at hunting, jumping, and running.

Writing
© Houghton Mifflin Harcourt Publishing Company. All rights reserved.

Grade 1, Unit 3

2 Shared Writing

- Write these two details on the board: cold nose; smell everything.

- Tell children to imagine they are writing a report about dogs. Ask children to help you turn the two details into sentences by adding information about the details.

APPLY Children can begin drafting their own reports by including a topic sentence, detail sentence, and a closing sentence. Remind children they can use information that they recall from their own experiences. Have them use their graphic organizers and the Focus Wall.

- Have children work with a partner to ask and respond to questions. They may use digital tools such as word processing applications to draft their writing. **W.1.2, W.1.5, W.1.6, W.1.8**

Oral Language Conventions

Using Verbs Remind children that a complete sentence includes a verb, a word that tells what someone or something does. Have them orally identify the verbs they used in their sentences to tell about their animals. **L.1.1e**

L.1.1e use verbs to convey sense of past, present, and future; **L.1.1j** produce and expand simple and compound declarative, interrogative, imperative, and exclamatory sentences; **L.1.2e** spell untaught words phonetically, drawing on phonemic awareness and spelling conventions

Daily Proofreading Practice

Two   jump

~~Twoo~~ monkeys ~~jumped~~ up now.
  ^   ^

                watch
Lisa and Ted ~~watc~~.
                   ^

Performance Task

my WriteSmart   Have children complete the writing assignment through *my*WriteSmart. Children will read the prompt and have access to multiple writing resources.

Common Core Writing Handbook

Additional support for Informative Writing appears in the **Common Core Writing Handbook,** Lesson 15.

DAY 2

Today's Goals

Vocabulary & Oral Language
- Oral Vocabulary

Phonemic Awareness
- Substitute Phonemes
- Identify Middle Sound

Phonics & Fluency
- Words with Long *i* (CVC*e*)
- Read Decodable Reader: *The Nest*
- Fluency: Intonation

 **WORDS TO KNOW**

bird	long
both	or
eyes	those
fly	walk

Text-Based Comprehension
- **Dig Deeper:** How to Analyze the Text
- **Compare and Contrast**
- **Text and Graphic Features**
- **Reread the Anchor Text:** *Animal Groups*

Grammar & Writing
- The Verb *be*
- ➡ **Informative Writing:** Report
  Focus Trait: Word Choice

Spelling
- Words with Long *i*

 **COMMON CORE**

RF.1.2c isolate and pronounce sounds in spoken single-syllable words; **RF.1.3c** know final -e and vowel team conventions for representing long vowel sounds; **RF.1.3g** recognize and read irregularly spelled words; **L.1.5c** identify real-life connections between words and their use; **L.1.6** use words and phrases acquired through conversations reading and being read to, and responding to texts

Opening Routines

Warm Up with Wordplay

Make a Rhyme

Remind children that they have been learning about words that have the sound /ī/ spelled *i*-consonant-e. Display and read the word *vine*.

Have children work with a partner to come up with as many other words in this word family (-*ine*) as they can. Call on children to share their words. Write down what children say. Then have the class work together to make a short two- or four-line poem using the rhyming words. 🔲 **RF.1.3c**

mine	line	dine
fine	nine	pine

Daily Phonemic Awareness

Identify and Substitute Medial Phonemes

- *Listen to the word tap, /t/ /ă/ /p/. What is its vowel sound? /ă/, short a Change the short a, /ă/, to long a, /ā/. What is the new word? tape*

- Have children repeat with you, then by themselves. Have them continue with the words shown to say the word, name the vowel sound, change the vowel sound, and say the new word. **RF.1.2c**

Word	Change the . . .	Result
sit	/ĭ/ to /ī/	sight
sight	/ī/ to /ă/	sat
sat	/ă/ to /ĕ/	set
duck	/ŭ/ to /ŏ/	dock
dock	/ŏ/ to /ĕ/	deck

Corrective Feedback

- If a child misses a word, say the correct word and model the task. *Listen to the word, sit, /s/ /ĭ/ /t/. Now change /ĭ/ to /ī/: /s/ /ī/ /t/. What is the new word? sight*

Daily High-Frequency Words

Introduce

- Point to the **High-Frequency Word Card** *both*.

- *Say the word. both Spell the word. b, o, t, h Write the word. Check the word.*

- Repeat the procedure with the words *bird, eyes, fly, long, or, those,* and *walk*. **RF.1.3g**

Cheerleader Game

- Choose a child as Head Cheerleader to stand in front of the room.

- Have the Head Cheerleader call out each letter of a High-Frequency Word. The whole class responds. *Give me an F! F! Give me an L! L! Give me a Y! Y!* What's that spell? **FLY!**

- Choose different Head Cheerleaders for the other words.

Corrective Feedback

- If a child is unable to recognize the word *fly*, say the correct word and have children repeat it. *Fly. What is the word? fly*

- Have children spell the word. *f,l,y How do we say this word? fly*

- Have children reread all of the cards in random order.

Daily Vocabulary Boost

- Review the Oral Vocabulary words and their definitions with children. (See pp. T418–T419.) Remind children that they heard these words in the Read Aloud "The Dancing Wolves."

- Recall with children the story events, and then guide them to interact with each word's meaning.

  - *The rabbit gave directions. What kind of* directions *might you find in a cake recipe?*

  - *But on every seventh step, you must swivel in place. Can you* swivel *in the chair you are sitting on? Why or why not?*

- Continue in the same manner with *alert, scale, sensitive,* and *threatened*. **L.1.5c, L.1.6**

☑ **Oral Vocabulary**

alert
directions
scale
sensitive
swivel
threatened

Interactive Whiteboard Lesson:
Words with Long *i* (CVCe)

Go Digital
• Interactive Whiteboard Lesson
• Decodable Reader

JOURNEYS
Phonics

RF.1.2c

Phonemic Awareness/Phonics

► SHARE OBJECTIVES

• Blend, read, and decode regularly spelled one-syllable words with long *i* (CVCe).

• Read on-level text with words with long *i* and high-frequency words with correct intonation.

► SKILLS TRACE

Reader's Notebook Vol. 1 p. 212
See Grab-and-Go™ Resources for additional leveled practice.

COMMON CORE
RI.1.7 use illustrations and details to describe key ideas; **RF.1.2c** isolate and pronounce sounds in spoken single-syllable words; **RF.1.3b** decode regularly spelled one-syllable words; **RF.1.3c** know final -e and vowel team conventions for representing long vowel sounds; **RF.1.3g** recognize and read irregularly spelled words; **RF.1.4a** read on-level text with purpose and understanding; **RF.1.4b** read on-level text orally with accuracy, appropriate rate, and expression; **L.1.2d** use conventional spelling for words with common spelling patterns and for frequently occurring irregular words

Words with Long *i* (CVCe)

PHONEMIC AWARENESS WARM-UP *Let's play a game. I'll say some words. You say what the middle sound is. Listen: rice, /r/ /ī/ /s/. /ī/* Repeat with these: *bag, pick, same, nice, bake.* **RF.1.2c**

1 Teach/Model

Review **Sound/Spelling Card** *ice cream, /ī/.*

CONTINUOUS BLENDING ROUTINE Use **Instructional Routine 3** to model blending *drive*. Display **Letter Cards** *d, r, i, v,* and *e*. Repeat the routine with the words in Row 1 below.

Write the words and sentence shown below. Call on individuals to blend and read words and to read the sentence.

> 1. drive   rice   ride   Mike   nine
> 2. mile   shame   dish   cash   take
>
> **Ike rides <u>a</u> bike <u>to</u> the sale.**

2 Guided Practice

BUILD WORDS Model how to spell the word *drive. The letter* d *stands for the first sound /d/. The letter* r *stands for the second sound /r/. The next sound is /ī/. I know that long* i *words can end with a silent* e. *The next sound is /v/. The letter* v *stands for /v/. Last I write a silent* e: /d/ /r/ /ī/ /v/, *drive.*

• Guide children to identify sounds and spell *time, like, kite.* **L.1.2d**

• Call on individuals to spell the words with **Letter Cards** while other children check their work.

3 Apply

Hands-on Practice

Have partners use letter cards to take turns building and reading words with long *i*. **RF.1.3b, RF.1.3c**

Decodable Reader

Go Digital

Read *The Nest*

Decodable Reader,
Unit 3, pp. 105–110

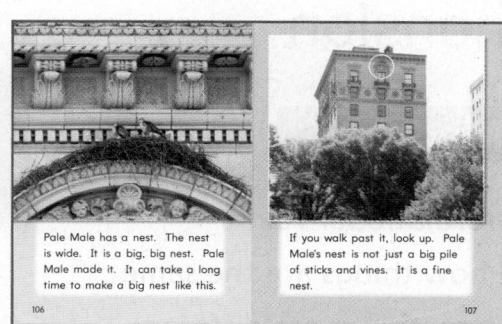

REVIEW /ī/ AND WORDS TO KNOW Tell children that many words in this selection have the *i_e* pattern, which can stand for the long *i* sound. Point out that children have learned the following words, which they will also read in the selection: *bird, both, fly, long, those, walk.*

PREVIEW Have children preview pages 105–107 and predict what the selection is about. Ask volunteers to tell what they know about birds, including what birds look like, do, and eat.

MODEL FLUENCY AND INTONATION Read aloud page 110 as children follow along. As you read have children note how the tone in your voice changes when you read the word *Fly!* Lead children in choral reading the page with fluency and intonation.

READ Remind children to track the words from left to right. When they come to the end of a line, they should sweep their hand down to the beginning of the next line and continue reading. Have children read each page silently and then choral-read aloud. Have them read to find out what is in the nest.
📖 RF.1.3b, RF.1.3c, RF.1.3g, RF.1.4a

RESPONDING Have partners work together to summarize the selection. Tell them they can page through the selection to remind themselves of events to include as they work. 📖 RI.1.7

DAILY ASSESSMENT 3 2 1 RtI

Corrective Feedback Work with the whole group to correct errors, following the model below.

Decoding Error:
A child reads *quite* as *quit.*

Correct the error. Say the word. *That word is* quite. *The i-consonant-e pattern means the letter* i *stands for the sound /ī/.*

Guide Have children repeat the word. *What is the word? quite*

Check *Go back to the beginning of the sentence and read it again.*

Reinforce Record the error and review the word again before children reread the story.

Reread for Fluency/ Develop Automaticity

READ WITH A PARTNER Have partners reread *The Nest* three or four times, taking turns reading aloud each page. Remind them to read words correctly and to read smoothly. Visit partners to listen to them read. Give feedback about reading accurately, at an appropriate rate, and with expression and provide guidance for improving fluency. 📖 RF.1.4b

Dig Deeper: How to Analyze the Text

Animal Groups
by James Bruchac

SHARE OBJECTIVES
- Compare and contrast to understand a selection better.
- Use text and graphic features to find and understand information.

 **ELL** **ENGLISH LANGUAGE LEARNERS**

Use Visuals

Beginning Show pictures of two animals. Have children say *alike* if the animals are the same and *different* if they are different. Repeat with other pairs of pictures.

Low Intermediate Show children two pictures of animals. Have children complete the sentence frame: *The two animals are _____.* using the words *alike* or *different*.

High Intermediate Show children pictures of two animals. Have them use complete sentences to say if the animals are alike or different. Then have them say how.

Proficient Have children draw two animals that are the same. Have them write a sentence about how they are the same. Then tell children to draw two animals that are different. Have them write a sentence about how they are different.

Text-Based Comprehension

 **1** **Teach/Model**

Terms About Informational Text

compare tell how things are the same

contrast tell how things are different

text and graphic features labels, headings, pictures, and other special features that point out information

---

- Remind children that they have read *Animal Groups*, an informational text about animal groups. Read and discuss **Student Book** p. 184 with children and help them understand the meaning of **compare** and **contrast**.

- Explain that in informational texts, often two individuals, events, ideas, or pieces of information are connected, or joined in some way. In *Animal Groups*, many of the animals are connected because they are alike in one or more ways.

Think Aloud *To understand a text, I think about how pieces of information are connected as I read. I can use a Venn diagram to show how animals are alike and how they are different. We read about reptiles and amphibians. One way I read that these two groups are alike is they both hatch from eggs. I will write* hatch from eggs *under Both. I can describe the connection by saying:* Both reptiles and amphibians hatch from eggs. *How else are these two groups alike? How are the two groups different?*

- Next, read and discuss **Student Book** p. 185 with children.

- Explain how authors use special features, such as photographs, headings, and labels, to point out information so that it is clearer and easier to find.

- Explain that headings are often at the top of the page and tell what you will read about. Labels are words that give more information about pictures. Have children turn to pp. 168–169. Guide them to use the heading and labels and to look carefully at the photo. Have children describe the information these special features helped them find and understand.

 **COMMON CORE** **RI.1.3** describe the connection between individuals, events, ideas, or information in a text; **RI.1.5** know and use text features to locate facts or information; **RI.1.7** use illustrations and details to describe key ideas

COMPREHENSION

Dig Deeper

 Read Together

How to Analyze the Text

Use these pages to learn about Compare and Contrast and Text and Graphic Features. Then read **Animal Groups** again.

Compare and Contrast

In **Animal Groups,** you learned what makes animals in a group the same and different. Think about reptiles and amphibians. **Compare** the groups to tell how they are alike. **Contrast** the groups to tell how they are different. Use a diagram to compare and contrast groups.

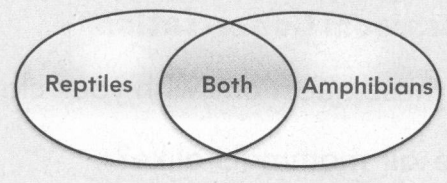

Reptiles   Both   Amphibians

 RI.1.3 describe the connection between individuals, events, ideas, or information in a text; **RI.1.5** know and use text features to locate facts or information; **RI.1.7** use illustrations and details to describe key ideas

184    Go Digital

Text and Graphic Features

Authors use special features to point out information. **Headings** are often at the top of a page and tell what part you are reading. **Labels** are words that give more information about details in pictures.

The heading on page 168 is **Fish**. What is this part about? There are also labels that give information. What do you learn about a fish's body?

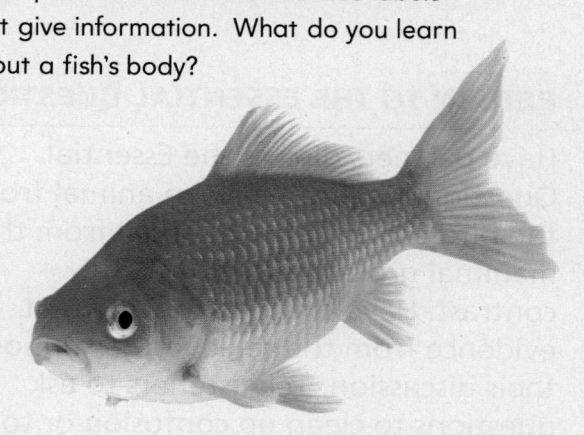

185

SECOND READ

2 Guided Practice/Apply

READ FOR TEXT EVIDENCE Begin a second read of *Animal Groups* with children. Use the instructional support to guide children to analyze the text:

• Compare and Contrast, p. T433 ▬ **RI.1.3**

• Text and Graphic Features, p. T435 ▬ **RI.1.5, RI.1.7**

DIRECTED NOTE-TAKING The graphic organizer will be completed with children during the second read on p. T433.

DAILY ASSESSMENT  RtI

Are children able to compare and contrast?

IF...	THEN...
children have difficulty comparing and contrasting,	use **Differentiate Comprehension** for Struggling Readers, p. T496. *See also Intervention Lesson 15, p. S51.*
children can mostly compare and contrast,	use **Differentiate Comprehension** for On Level Readers, p. T496.
children can always compare and contrast,	use **Differentiate Comprehension** for Advanced Readers, p. T497.

 SMALL GROUP Options

Differentiate Comprehension, pp. T496–T497
Group English Language Learners according to language proficiency. See also ELL Lesson 15, p. E45, for scaffolded support.

Go Digital
• *my*WriteSmart
• eBook

DAY 2

Your Turn  Use Text Evidence

▶ SHARE OBJECTIVES

- Respond to questions by talking with peers and asking and answering questions.
- Write a riddle in response to literature, using facts from the selection.

RETURN TO THE ESSENTIAL QUESTION

Have partners discuss the Essential Question. Children pick an animal from the bird group and an animal from the mammal group to compare and contrast. Have children provide text evidence from the selection to support their discussion. Tell listeners to ask questions to clean up confusion or to gather more information. Have speakers answer the questions.
▬ RI.1.3, RI.1.7, SL.1.1c, SL.1.3

 **Classroom Conversation** Have children continue their discussion of how the animals are alike and different. Help them summarize by telling how all the animal groups are alike. Ask children to use text evidence to support their answers and to add their own ideas. Help them to build conversations by coaching them to have multiple exchanges with classmates, responding appropriately to other's comments and adding their own ideas.
▬ RI.1.3, RI.1.7, SL.1.1b

 **COMMON CORE** **RI.1.3** describe the connection between individuals, events, ideas or information in a text; **RI.1.7** use illustrations and details to describe key ideas; **W.1.8** recall information from experiences or gather information from sources to answer a question; **SL.1.1b** build on others' talk in conversations by responding to others' comments; **SL.1.1c** ask questions to clear up confusion about topics and texts under discussion; **SL.1.3** ask and answer questions about what a speaker says; **L.1.2b** use end punctuation for sentence

---

Read Together

Your Turn  *my* WriteSmart

RETURN TO THE ESSENTIAL QUESTION

 **Turn and Talk** **What makes birds different from mammals?** Choose an animal from each group. Use words and pictures from the selection to tell how the animals are alike and different. Ask questions if you do not understand your partner's ideas.

 Classroom Conversation

Talk about these questions with your class.

1 How are all mammals alike?

2 How are fish different from mammals?

3 What are the five animal groups? What new things did you learn?

186

 **ENGLISH LANGUAGE LEARNERS**

Use Visuals

Beginning Show **online Picture Cards** *cat* and *dog*. Name characteristics and have children say *alike* or *different*. For example: *Number of legs: alike*

Low Intermediate Show **online Picture Cards** *cat* and *dog*. Have children name one similarity and one difference.

High Intermediate Have children choose two **online Picture Cards** depicting animals and tell one way they are alike and one way they are different.

Proficient Have children choose two **online Picture Cards** depicting animals and tell multiple ways they are alike and different.

See ELL Lesson 15, p. E44, for further comprehension support.

WRITE ABOUT READING

Response Use facts you learned from the selection to write a riddle about an animal. Write clues. Do not give its name. Read your riddle to a partner. Have your partner use the evidence in the clues to guess the answer.

I have gills and live in water.

Writing Tip

Use a question mark (**?**) at the end of a question.

Go Digital

COMMON CORE **RI.1.3** describe the connection between individuals, events, ideas, or information in a text; **RI.1.7** use illustrations and details to describe key ideas; **W.1.8** recall information from experiences or gather information from sources to answer a question; **SL.1.1c** ask questions to clear up confusion about topics and texts under discussion; **SL.1.3** ask and answer questions about what a speaker says

187

WRITE ABOUT READING

Performance Task

Tell children that they will write a response to the informational text *Animal Groups*.

• Read **Student Book** p. 187 with children.

• Tell them that they will write a riddle about an animal from *Animal Groups*. Explain that a riddle has sentences that give clues and ends with a question.

• Make sure children understand the clues are facts about the animal they learned from the words and photos in *Animal Groups*. The clues do not tell the name of the animal.

• Tell children to use complete sentence as they write.

• Have them share their riddles in small groups.

• Then have children draw and label a picture to answer the riddle and help them publish the riddles in a class book.

 **WRITING TIP** Read the Writing Tip with children before they begin writing. Explain to them that they should use a question mark at the end of the question. Model an example on the board.
🔲 **W.1.8, L.1.2b**

Go Digital   myWriteSmart

Have children complete the Write About Reading activity through *my*WriteSmart. Children will read the prompt within *my*WriteSmart and have access to multiple writing resources, including the Student eBook, Writing Rubrics, and Graphic Organizers.

- *my*WriteSmart
- eBook
- GrammarSnap Videos
- Interactive Whiteboard Lesson

Grammar The Verb *be*

▶ SHARE OBJECTIVES

- **Grammar** Use *is* and *are* as main verbs in sentences.
- **Spelling** Sort words with the long *i* sound using conventional spelling patterns.
- **Handwriting** Print the spelling words.
- **Writing** Draft report sentences using exact words.

ELL ENGLISH LANGUAGE LEARNERS

Language Transfer

All Proficiencies Using sentence strips, with red strips containing nouns/subjects, green strips containing adjectives, and blue strips containing the verb *be* inflected for different numbers in the present tense (e.g., *am/is/are*), guide the class in building sentences describing the different nouns using the appropriate conjugation of *be*. (Speakers of some languages, such as Spanish and Portuguese, may use multiple words for the same uses as the English verb *be* and may require extra modeling.)

1 Teach/Model

USING *IS* AND *ARE* Display **Projectable 15.3**. Review when to use *is* and *are*.

- Remind children that sentences with *is* and *are* tell about what is happening now or what something is like now. Review that they should use *is* in a sentence with a noun that names one and *are* with a noun that names more than one.

- Model using *is* and *are* to agree with the noun.

Think Aloud *The noun in the first sentence is* cat. *It names one. The verb is* goes *with a noun that names one. The noun in the second sentence is* cats. *This noun names more than one. The verb* are *goes with a noun that names more than one*

2 Guided Practice/Apply

- Work together to complete **Projectable 15.3**.

- Have children use nouns from the **Projectable** to write a sentence using *is* and a sentence using *are*. Have them share them with the class. Discuss correct examples and guide children to identify why they are correct. **L.1.1c, L.1.1e, L.1.1j**

Spelling Words with Long *i*

SPELLING WORDS

BASIC

time	like
kite	bike
white	drive

CHALLENGE

stripe	mice

Word Sort

- Review **Sound/Spelling Card**: *ice cream*. *What sound do you hear at the beginning of* ice? the long i sound /ī/

- Set up a five-column chart with headings *-ime*, *-ike*, *-ite*, *-ice*, and *-ive*. Model adding a spelling word to the chart. Place *bike* under the *-ike* column. Have children put each spelling word in the correct column. **L.1.2d**

Handwriting

Model how to form *time*, *like*, and *kite*. Have children use their best handwriting to print the spelling words. Ball-and-stick and continuous stroke handwriting models are available on the **Handwriting Models Blackline Masters**. **L.1.1a**

COMMON CORE **W.1.2** write informative/explanatory texts; **W.1.5** focus on a topic, respond to questions/suggestions from peers, and add details to strengthen writing; **W.1.6** use digital tools to produce and publish writing; **W.1.8** recall information from experiences or gather information from sources to answer a question; **L.1.1a** print upper- and lowercase letters; **L.1.1c** use singular and plural nouns with matching verbs in sentences; **L.1.1e** use verbs to convey sense of past, present, and future; **L.1.1f** use frequently occurring adjectives; **L.1.1j** produce and expand simple and compound declarative,

T450 • Unit 3 Lesson 15

Informative Writing Focus Trait: Word Choice

1 Teach/Model

USING CLEAR WORDS Explain that good writers try to choose words that are as clear as possible to let the reader know exactly what is happening.

- Tell children that it is easy for readers to make pictures in their minds if writers use clear words. Add that clear words also make writing more interesting. Explain that clear words often include adjectives, or describing words, such as *long, furry*, and *sharp*.

- Discuss how the author of *Animal Groups* uses clear words that help the reader understand what is happening.

Connect to *Animal Group*

Instead of this...	...the author wrote this.
Fish **can** breathe in water.	Fish **have gills that help them** breathe in water.
This snake **moves** on the grass.	This snake **slides its long body** on the grass.

- *Why are the author's sentences better? Clear words make the writing more interesting and help you picture the animals.*

- Display **Projectable 15.4**. Read each sentence aloud. Model how to fill the first sentence frame with clear words that will make the sentence clearer.

2 Guided Writing

- Have partners work together to complete the **Projectable**. Guide them to use the pictures to help them fill in the frames with exact words.

APPLY Have children continue drafting their research reports. Remind them to use exact words. Guide children to work with partners to use digital tools, such as a word processing program, to draft their writing. For additional practice, have them use **Reader's Notebook** Vol. 1 page 215.

■ W.1.2, W.1.5, W.1.6, W.1.8, L.1.1f, L.1.1j

interrogative, imperative, and exclamatory sentences; **L.1.2d** use conventional spelling patterns for words with common spelling patterns for frequently occurring irregular words

Daily Proofreading Practice

The ~~burds is~~ in the nest.
(birds are)

The nest ~~are~~ in a tree.
(is)

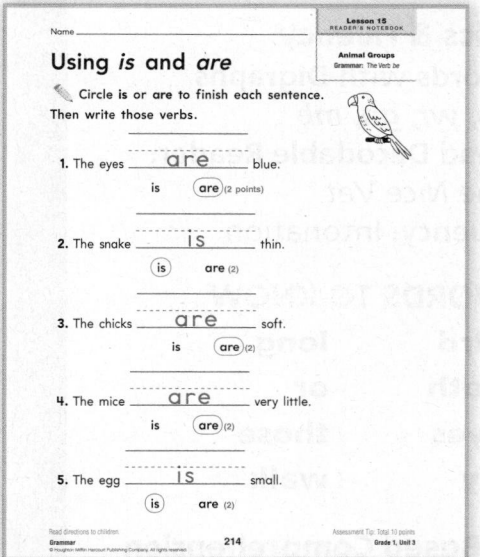

Reader's Notebook Vol. 1 p. 214

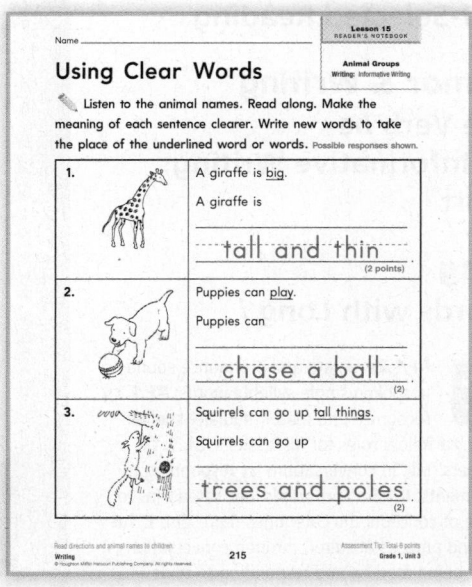

Reader's Notebook Vol. 1 p. 215

DAY 3

Today's Goals

Vocabulary & Oral Language
- Apply Vocabulary Knowledge

Phonemic Awareness
- Identify Middle Sound
- Substitute Phonemes

Phonics & Fluency
- Words with Digraphs *kn, wr, gn, mb*
- Read Decodable Reader: *The Nice Vet*
- Fluency: Intonation

☑ **WORDS TO KNOW**

bird	long
both	or
eyes	those
fly	walk

Text-Based Comprehension

Independent Reading
- Reader's Guide
- Self-Selected Reading

Grammar & Writing
- The Verb *be*
-  Informative Writing: Report

Spelling
- Words with Long *i*

COMMON CORE **RF.1.2c** isolate and pronounce sounds in spoken single-syllable words; **RF.1.3g** recognize and read irregularly spelled words; **SL.1.1a** follow rules for discussions; **SL.1.1b** build on others' talk in conversations by responding to others' comments; **L.1.5a** sort words into categories to gain a sense of concepts the categories represent; **L.1.6** use words and phrases acquired through conversations, reading and being read to, and responding to texts

Opening Routines

Warm Up with Wordplay

How Do They Go Together?

Display and read the following:

> **penguin   parrot   eagle**

Have children work with a partner to figure out how these words belong together. Have children compare their answers, and then tell them the correct answer: they are all birds.

Challenge children to add more types of birds to list. Then have them come up with examples from other animal groups. Write down the responses and say them aloud with children. ▬ **L.1.5a**

Daily Phonemic Awareness

Identify and Substitute Medial Phonemes

- *Listen to rack, /r/ /ă/ /k/. What is the middle sound?* /ă/, short a
  Change the short a, /ă/, to long a, /ā/. What is the new word? rake

- Have children repeat with you, then by themselves. Have them continue with the words shown to say the word, name the middle sound, change the middle sound, and say the new word.

RF.1.2c

Word	Change the . . .	Result
fit	/ĭ/ to /ī/	*fight*
fight	/ī/ to /ā/	*fate*
bat	/ă/ to /ī/	*bite*
kite	/ī/ to /ŭ/	*cut*
lit	/ĭ/ to /ī/	*light*

Corrective Feedback

- If a child misses a word, say the correct word and model the task. *Listen to the word fit, /f/ /ĭ/ /t/. Now change /ĭ/ to /ī/: /f/ /ī/ /t/. What is the new word?* fight

Daily High-Frequency Words

Introduce

- Point to the **High-Frequency Word Card** *eyes.*

- *Say the word.* eyes *Spell the word.* e, y, e, s *Write the word. Check the word.*

- Repeat the procedure with the words *bird, both, fly, long, or, those,* and *walk.*

  RF.1.3g

Tic-Tac-Toe Game

- Create a Tic-Tac-Toe board with a High-Frequency Word in each box. Choose a word from a previous week to fill in the remaining box.

- Divide children into teams, one for **X**s and one for **O**s.

- Have volunteers take turns reading a word. If the child reads the word correctly, he or she may put an **X** or an **O** in that box.

Corrective Feedback

- If a child is unable to recognize the word *long*, say the correct word and have children repeat it. *Long. What is the word?* long

- Have children spell the word. *l,o,n,g How do we say this word?* long

- Have children reread all of the cards in random order.

Daily Vocabulary Boost

- Guide children to interact with the Oral Vocabulary words by asking them the following questions. Remind them to speak clearly when participating in discussion.

  What alerts an animal that there is danger?

  Why would you give someone directions?

  What can you measure on a scale?

- Ask children to work with a partner to explain *alert, directions,* and *scale* in their own words. Have each child respond to what their partner says so that they build a conversation. Make sure children follow appropriate rules for discussion such as listening to speakers, taking turns, and staying on topic. SL.1.1a, SL.1.1b, L.1.6

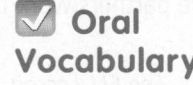 **Oral Vocabulary**

alert
directions
scale
sensitive
swivel
threatened

Whole Group

DAY 3

Go Digital • Interactive Whiteboard Lesson

JOURNEYS Phonics

Interactive Whiteboard Lesson:
Words with Digraphs *kn, wr, gn, mb*

Phonemic Awareness/Phonics

▶ SHARE OBJECTIVES

- Substitute medial sounds in words.
- Blend and decode regularly-spelled one-syllable words with digraphs *kn, wr, gn, mb*.

▶ SKILLS TRACE

Words with Digraphs *kn, wr, gn, mb*	
Introduce	**T454–T455**
Differentiate	T498
Reteach	T506
Review	T466
Assess	Weekly Tests, Lesson 15

ELL ENGLISH LANGUAGE LEARNERS
Comprehensible Input

Beginning Say *knot, knife, know.* Emphasize the /n/ sound. Have children repeat. Write the words on the board and circle *kn.* Have children repeat /n/.

Low Intermediate Write *knot, wren, gnat.* Circle *kn, wr, gn* and read the words together. Then have children read each word and repeat the beginning sounds.

High Intermediate Use **Letter Cards** to build and read together *knot, wren, gnat.* Then remove the *kn, wr, gn* cards from each word, mix the cards, and have children put the cards back where they belong.

Proficient Use **Letter Cards** to build/read together *know, wren, gnat.* Then mix the cards and have partners work together to rebuild the words.

See ELL Lesson 15, p. E47, for scaffolded support.

COMMON CORE **RF.1.2b** orally produce single-syllable words by blending sounds; **RF.1.3a** know the spelling-sound correspondences for common consonant digraphs; **RF.1.3b** decode regularly spelled one-syllable words; **RF.1.3g** recognize and read irregularly spelled words; **L.1.2d** use conventional spelling for words with common spelling patterns and for frequently occurring irregular words; **L.1.2e** spell untaught words phonetically, drawing on phonemic awareness and spelling conventions

Words with Digraphs
kn, wr, gn, mb

PHONEMIC AWARENESS WARM-UP *I'm going say a word and then change its middle sound to make a new word. Listen:* bake. *What word do I get if I change /ā/ to /ī/?* bike.

Now you try. Listen: sick. *What word do I get if I change /ĭ/ to /ŏ/?* sock. **Continue with these words:** *rash-rush, tick-tack, like-lock.*

1 Teach/Model

INTRODUCE WORDS WITH DIGRAPHS *kn, wr, gn, mb*

- Display **Sound/Spelling Card** *noodles* to review /n/. Read *noodles,* and say the beginning sound /n/. Then point to the *kn* and *gn* spellings on the card. Explain that these letter combinations can stand for the /n/ sound. Write *knock* and *gnat* on the board and read each word. Circle *kn* and *gn* and say /n/. Reread the words and have children repeat.

- Display **Sound/Spelling Card** *rooster* to review /r/. Read *rooster,* and say the beginning sound /r/. Then point to the *wr* spelling on the card. Explain that this letter combination can stand for the /r/ sound. Write *wren* on the board and read it. Circle *wr* and say /r/. Reread the word and have children repeat.

- Display **Sound/Spelling Card** *mouse* to review /m/. Read *mouse,* and say the beginning sound /m/. Then point to the *mb* spelling on the card. Explain that this letter combination can stand for the /m/ sound. Write *numb* on the board and read it. Circle *mb* and say /m/. Reread the word and have children repeat.

2 Guided Practice

CONTINUOUS BLENDING ROUTINE Use **Instructional Routine 3** to model blending *knot*. Write the word *knot* on the board.
■ RF.1.2b, RF.1.3a, RF.1.3b

- Point to **Sound/Spelling Card** *noodles,* and remind children that knowing the sound/spelling *kn* can help them read words.

- Display **Letter Cards** *kn, o, t*. Blend the sounds, stretching out the sounds. *Listen: /n/ /ŏ/ /t/,* knot. Then have children blend the sounds. *Now you read it.*

- Repeat the routine with *gnat, wrist,* and *lamb*.

REPEAT CONTINUOUS BLENDING ROUTINE with Row 1 below. Use the **Corrective Feedback** steps if children need additional help.

DECODING Write the words from Rows 1–2 and the sentences on the board. Call on individuals to blend one or more words and to read the sentences. ■ RF.1.3a, RF.1.3b, RF.1.3g

1. knock	gnash	wrist	thumb	knot
2. cage	judge	isn't	gem	will
3. lamb	place	wren	when	gnat

A gnat lands on <u>my</u> wrist <u>as</u> <u>I</u> <u>walk</u>.
The wren didn't <u>fly</u> <u>over</u> the <u>blue</u> <u>water</u>.

3 Apply

Use **Instructional Routine 6** and the sentences below. Have children say each word after you. Then have them identify the sounds and write the letters that stand for each sound. Print the words so children can check their work. ■ RF.1.3a, RF.1.3b, L.1.2d, L.1.2e

- **lamb**   I like to see the **lamb**.
- **knot**   Mom put a **knot** in the lace.
- **gnat**   We saw a **gnat** fly by.

DAILY ASSESSMENT   ▲3 2 1   **RtI**

Corrective Feedback Work with the whole group to correct errors, following the model below.

Phonics Error:
A child reads *wren* as *when*.

Correct the error. Review the **Sound/Spelling Card.** Say the word and the sound. *The word is* wren. *The letters* wr *stand for the sound /r/ in this word.*

Model as you touch the letters. *I'll blend: /r/ /ĕ/ /n/. wren*

Guide *Let's read the word together. The word is* wren.

Check *You read the word* when. *What is the correct word?* wren

Reinforce Go back three or four words and have children continue reading. Make note of errors and review those words during tomorrow's lesson.

Go to p. T498 for additional phonics support.

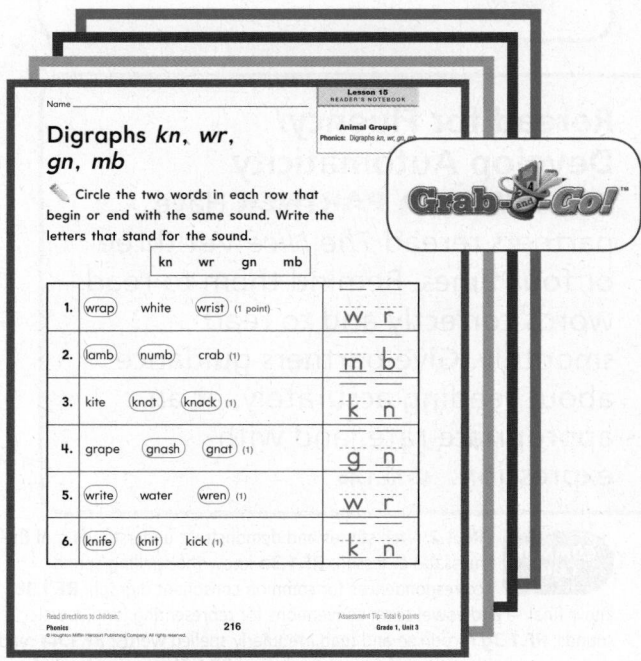

Reader's Notebook Vol. 1 p. 216
See Grab-and-Go™ Resources for additional leveled practice.

Decodable Reader

▶ SHARE OBJECTIVE

• Read text with long *i* words; words with digraphs *wr*, *mb*; and high-frequency words.

DAILY ASSESSMENT — RtI

Corrective Feedback Work with the whole group to correct errors.

Decoding Error:
A child reads *numb* as *nub*.

Correct the error. Say the word. *That word is* numb.

Guide *Remember that the digraph* mb *stands for the /m/ sound.* Have children blend and read the word.

Check *Read the sentence again.*

Reinforce Review the word again before children reread the story.

 Go to p. T498 for additional phonics support.

Reread for Fluency/ Develop Automaticity

READ WITH A PARTNER Have partners reread *The Nice Vet* three or four times. Remind them to read words correctly and to read smoothly. Give partners guidance about reading accurately, at an appropriate rate, and with expression. ◼ RF.1.4b

 **RL.1.2** retell stories and demonstrate understanding of the message or lesson; **RF.1.3a** know the spelling-sound correspondences for common consonant digraph; **RF.1.3c** know final -e and vowel team conventions for representing long vowel sounds; **RF.1.3g** recognize and read irregularly spelled words; **RF.1.4a** read on-level text with purpose and understanding; **RF.1.4b** read on-level text orally with accuracy, appropriate rate, and expression

Read *The Nice Vet*

Decodable Reader, Unit 3, pp. 111–116

REVIEW DIGRAPHS *wr*, *mb* AND WORDS TO KNOW Tell children that many words in this story begin with *wr* or end with *mb*. Review with them the following Words to Know, which they will also read in the story: *eyes, long, walk.*

PREVIEW Tell children to preview pages 111–113 and predict what they think the story is about. Ask children why people and pets go to a doctor. Tell children they are going to read about a dog that has to go to the vet. Explain that a vet is an animal doctor.

MODEL FLUENCY AND INTONATION Have children follow along as you read aloud page 116, misreading questions as statements. Tell children you made a mistake by not changing your voice when you read a sentence that ended in a question mark. Read the page again, changing your voice to ask the questions. Lead children in a choral reading, reading fluently and with appropriate intonation.

READ Remind children to track words from left to right. When they come to the end of a line, they should continue by reading at the beginning of the next line. Have children read each page silently and then choral-read aloud. Coach them to read fluently, using appropriate intonation. Have children read to find out who the nice vet is. ◼ RF.1.3a, RF.1.3c, RF.1.3g, RF.1.4a

RESPONDING Have children work with partners to retell the story. Remind them to retell the events in the order in which they happened. ◼ RL.1.2

Fluency

Intonation

1 Teach/Model

Remind children that good readers change the sound of their voices as they read so that they sound like they do in conversations. Tell children that the pitch of your voice changes when you are asking a question or when you are excited. Display **Projectable 15.5.** Tell children that you will use the end marks to decide which tone to use when you read. Model changing pitch as you read each question, statement, and exclamation in set 1. Guide children to see that the words in each sentence were the same, but the changes in your intonation changed the meaning of each sentence. Repeat for set 2.

Projectable 15.5

Projectable 15.5

Animal Groups | Fluency Intonation

Meaning What You Read

Good readers change the sound of their voices as they read aloud.

Practice reading the sets of sentences while you change your intonation.

1. Is Spike's vet nice?   (pitch low in beginning, higher at end, question)
   Spike's vet is nice.   (pitch high in beginning, lower at end, statement)
   Spike's vet is nice!   (pitch high all through, shows exclamation; stress "nice")

2. The vet can help Spike.   (pitch high in beginning, lower at end, statement)
   Can the vet help Spike?   (pitch low in beginning, higher at end, question)
   The vet can help Spike!   (pitch high all through, shows exclamation; stress "can")

3. Kate's dad is Spike's nice vet!   (pitch high all through, shows exclamation; stress "dad")
   Kate's dad is Spike's nice vet.   (pitch high in beginning, lower at end, statement)
   Is Kate's dad Spike's nice vet?   (pitch low in beginning, higher at end, question)

Fluency

Grade 1, Unit 3

2 Guided Practice

Read the sentences in set 3 and have children echo-read. Then have children choral-read all three sets of sentences using proper intonation.

3 Apply

Have pairs practice reading *Animal Groups*. Remind them to track the print from left to right as they read. Coach children to connect words to read them smoothly and accurately. Have volunteers read each page aloud with correct intonation and at an appropriate rate. **RF.1.4b**

▶ SHARE OBJECTIVE

- Read on-level text fluently with correct intonation.

SMALL GROUP Options

Go to p. T499 for additional fluency support.

HOUGHTON MIFFLIN HARCOURT

JOURNEYS

Cold Reads

GRADE 1

Cold Reads: Support for fluent reading and comprehension

Independent Reading

▶ SHARE OBJECTIVES

- Read and comprehend informational text.
- Ask and answer questions about key details in a selection.
- Read independently from a "just right" book.

ELL ENGLISH LANGUAGE LEARNERS
Comprehensible Input

Beginning Ask children *yes/no* questions about the animals in *Animal Groups.*

Low Intermediate Ask children some details about the selection, such as *What kind of animal is a lion?* and *How are amphibians born?*

High Intermediate Have children use a page from *Animal Groups* and tell the characteristics of one animal.

Proficient Have partners compare and contrast two animals from *Animal Groups.*

Reader's Guide

Revisit the Anchor Text

Lead children in a brief discussion about *Animal Groups.* Have them recount the topic, main idea, and important details to summarize the selection. Remind children to follow the classroom rules for group discussions and to listen with care. As children speak, guide them to connect their ideas about the text to others' comments. ◼ **RI.1.2, SL.1.1a, SL.1.1b**

Have children read *Animal Groups* on their own and to think about important ideas in the text. Have children use the Reader's Guide pages in their **Reader's Notebook,** pp. 217–218. Explain that they should respond to the prompts and questions and support their responses with text evidence from the sentences and photos in *Animal Groups.* ◼ **RI.1.1, RI.1.7, RI.1.10**

GENERATE QUESTIONS Have children work independently or collaboratively to generate questions about *Animal Groups.* Ask children to share their questions. List questions that children have in common or that are most significant to their understanding of the selection. Guide them to work together to find the answers. ◼ **RI.1.1**

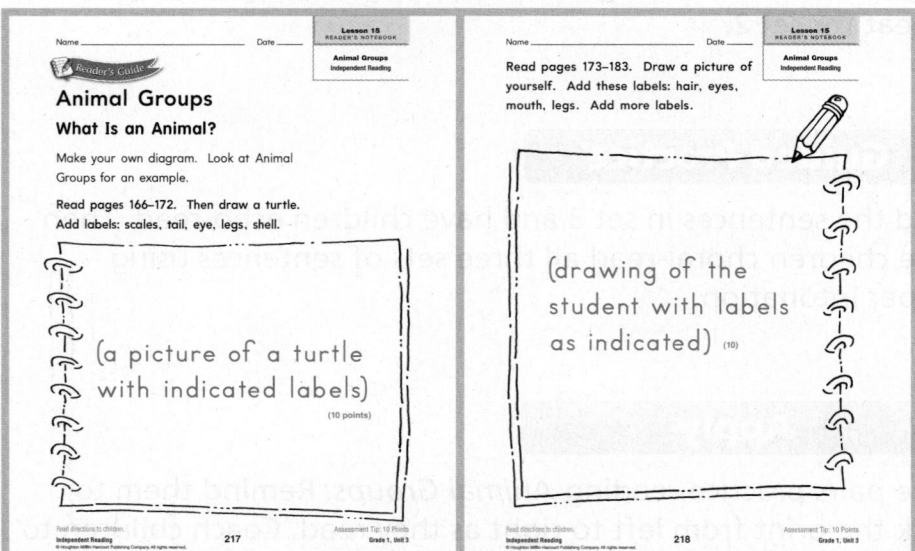

Reader's Notebook pp. 217–218

COMMON CORE

RI.1.1 ask and answer questions about key details; **RI.1.2** identify the main topic and retell key details; **RI.1.7** use illustrations and details to describe key ideas; **RI.1.10** read informational texts; **RF.1.4b** read on-level text orally with accuracy, appropriate rate, and expression; **RF.1.4c** use context to confirm or self-correct word recognition and understanding; **SL.1.1a** follow rules for discussions; **SL.1.1b** build on others' talk in conversations by responding to others' comments; **L.1.4a** use sentence-level context as a clue to the meaning of a word

Self-Selected Reading

Read the Summary

Tell children that when they choose books for reading, they should learn something about the books first. Guide children in selecting a book based on reading summaries.

- Think of a topic or a kind of story that you like, and find a few books that look interesting.

- Look at the pictures on the covers of the books, and read the titles and the authors' names.

- Look for summaries of the books on the back covers, or inside the book jackets, and read about the books. Choose the book that sounds the most interesting.

Tell children that once they have selected a book, they should open it and read one or two pages to be sure it is "just right." Guide them to choose appropriate books to read independently.

Self-Correction Strategies

Read for Fluency and Understanding

Tell children that it is important to read the words correctly and make sure they understand what they are reading. If they come to a word they cannot read or do not understand, they should pause and reread the other words in the sentence and the sentences nearby to look for clues. Then, they should use the clues to confirm what the word is and what it means. Then they can reread the sentence to check whether the word makes sense.

Have partners practice reading aloud to each other from their self-selected books. Have them reread parts of the text they do not understand and use context clues to help them make sense of confusing or unfamiliar words and phrases.

When one child has finished reading, his or her partner should provide feedback about accuracy. Then have partners switch roles. Have each partner read one more time, working to improve his or her accuracy and fluency. ◼ RF.1.4b, RF.1.4c, L.1.4a

Apply Vocabulary Knowledge

- Use words and phrases acquired through conversations, reading and being read to, and responding to texts.
- Identify real-life connections between words and their use.
- Use a dictionary to find definitions.

ELL ENGLISH LANGUAGE LEARNERS
Comprehensible Input

Beginning Discuss the words *same*, *alike*, and *similar*. Explain that these words mean about the same thing.

Low Intermediate Have children say other words that mean the same thing as *similar*.

High Intermediate Have children complete this sentence frame with one thing they do every day: *On a typical day I _____.*

Proficient Have children tell one thing they do on a typical day. Have them use complete sentences.

See ELL Lesson 15, p. E46, for further vocabulary support.

☑ SELECTION VOCABULARY >> Review

Review with children the Selection Vocabulary words on p. T426. Call on children to explain how the words were used in *Animal Groups*.

ENRICH VOCABULARY Write the following Related Words on the board. Read each word aloud, and have children repeat after you. Then read the student-friendly explanation for each word. Connect each word's meaning to the selection *Animal Groups* by writing the context sentences on the board and reading them aloud.

typical: If something is typical, it often is or happens a certain way all the time. *It is typical for reptiles to hatch from eggs.*

camouflage: When an animal can change the way it looks to blend into its surroundings, it is using camouflage. *The pink fish uses camouflage to hide in the pink coral.*

similar: If two things are similar, they are alike in some ways. *Frogs and toads are similar.*

MAKE CONNECTIONS Discuss all of the words using the items below to help children make connections between vocabulary words and their use. ◼ **L.1.5a, L.1.5c, L.1.6**

- Think about what you know about **tadpoles**. What happens to their **tails** as they grow up?
- Show how you **breathe**. Now tell how fish breathe.
- Is it **typical** for birds to have **hair**? Is it typical for birds to have **feathers**?
- How is a snake's **body similar** to a lizard's body?
- What animals or insects do you know that use **camouflage**?
- Do **amphibians** have wings? Name some animals that have wings.
- Which of the following animals would belong in a **group** called **mammals**: tiger, shark, bear, frog, pig?
- Which of the following animals would belong in a group called **reptiles**: cat, snake, turtle, panda, alligator?

COMMON CORE **RI.1.5** know and use text features to locate facts or information; **L.1.5a** sort words into categories to gain a sense of concepts the categories represent; **L.1.5c** identify real-life connections between words and their use; **L.1.6** use words and phrases acquired through conversations, reading and being read to, and responding to texts

Dictionary Skills

DISCUSS USING A DICTIONARY Display a beginning dictionary and review with children how to use it to find words that are unfamiliar. Remind children that words in a dictionary are in alphabetical order. Explain that this makes it easier to find the word you are looking for on the page. Open to a page and point to the guide words at the top. Ask children to tell how guide words can help them. *Guide words show what word is at the beginning of the page and what word is at the end of the page. If the word we are looking for is between those two words, we are on the right page.*

Guide children to look up the Lesson 15 Selection Vocabulary words *body, feathers,* and *hair* in a print dictionary. Remind children to look up the singular form of a noun if it is plural. Have volunteers read the definitions they find. Then have partners work together to look up the new vocabulary word *similar*. Have children tell whether they found the word toward the beginning or end of the dictionary and what guide words are at the top of the page. ◾ RI.1.5

Literacy and Language Guide
Additional Lesson 15 vocabulary lessons appear in the Literacy and Language Guide.

QUICKWRITE

Read aloud each question below. Pause a few minutes between each item to allow children to write a response. ◾ L.1.5c

1. What could you use in your backyard to camouflage yourself?

2. What do you do to get ready on a typical morning?

3. Do you think you and your best friend are similar? Why or why not?

Go Digital
• *my*WriteSmart
• eBook
• GrammarSnap Videos
• Interactive Whiteboard Lesson

Grammar The Verb *be*

▶ SHARE OBJECTIVES

- **Grammar** Use *was* and *were* as main verbs in sentences.
- **Spelling** Spell words with the long *i* sound using conventional spelling patterns.
- **Writing** Continue drafting a research report.

ELL ENGLISH LANGUAGE LEARNERS

Language Transfer

All Proficiencies Using sentence strips, with red strips containing nouns/subjects, green strips containing adjectives, and blue strips containing the verb *be* inflected for both past tense and present tense (e.g., *am/is/are, was/were,* etc.), guide the class in building sentences in the present tense, then changing so that they happen in the past.

1 Teach/Model

15.6 **USING *WAS* AND *WERE*** Display **Projectable 15.6**. Discuss when to use *was* and *were* to tell about the past.

- Tell children that they should use *was* in a sentence with a noun that names one and *were* with a noun that names more than one.

- Model using *was* and *were* to agree with the noun to tell about the past.

Think Aloud *The noun in the first sentence is* chick. *It names one. The verb* was *goes with a noun that names one. The noun in the second sentence is* chicks. *This noun names more than one. The verb* were *goes with a noun that names more than one.*

2 Guided Practice/Apply

- Work together to complete **Projectable 15.6**. Then have children say or write their own past tense sentences using *was* and *were*. Remind them to use the correct verbs with singular and plural subject nouns. ◼ **SL.1.6, L.1.1c, L.1.1e, L.1.1j**

Spelling Words with Long *i*

SPELLING WORDS

BASIC	
time	like
kite	bike
white	drive
CHALLENGE	
stripe	mice

Segment Sounds

- Model segmenting sounds. *Listen as I say* time: /t/ /ī/ /m/. *Repeat after me:* /t/ /ī/ /m/.

- Repeat with *like* and *kite*. Have children say the sounds in a word one at a time and write the letter or letters that stand for that sound to help them spell words correctly. ◼ **RF.1.2d, L.1.2d**

Build Words

- Use **Letter Cards** to model building the word *time*. Have children read and write the word.

- Have partners use **Letter Cards** to build words with the long *i* sound and add each word to their lists. Have partners read and spell one word they built.

- For additional practice, you may want to use **Reader's Notebook** Vol. 1 page 219.

COMMON CORE **RF.1.2d** segment spoken single-syllable words into their complete sequence of individual sounds; **W.1.2** write informative/explanatory texts; **W.1.5** focus on a topic, respond to questions/suggestions from peers, and add details to strengthen writing; **W.1.6** use digital tools to produce and publish writing; **W.1.8** recall information from experiences or gather information from sources to answer a question; **SL.1.6** produce complete sentences when appropriate

Informative Writing Drafting

1 Teach/Model

VOICE Explain that writers get their facts from other sources when writing a research report, but that they use their own words to write their reports. Emphasize that children will need to use their own words as they put their reports together.

- Model how to use your own words to write down some facts from *Animal Groups*.

Connect to *Animal Groups*

Many birds can fly. Some can run or swim fast.

- *I can write this information in my own words. I'll write*: Birds fly, run, or swim fast.

2 Independent Writing

- Have children continue drafting their research reports, referring to their graphic organizers.

- Remind children that they need to use their own words to write the facts they gather from various sources. Have pairs check each other's work to make sure they are not copying information from the sources word for word.

- As an option, guide children to work with partners to use digital tools to draft their writing on a computer. They may work together to use word processing programs, online reference materials, or appropriate tablet apps. ▬ **W.1.2, W.1.5, W.1.6, W.1.8**

to task and situation; **L.1.1c** use singular and plural nouns with matching verbs in sentences; **L.1.1e** use verbs to convey sense of past, present, and future; **L.1.1j** produce and expand simple and compound declarative, interrogative, imperative, and exclamatory sentences; **L.1.2d** use conventional spelling for words with common spelling patterns and for frequently occurring irregular words

---

Daily Proofreading Practice

This   was
~~Dis~~ fox ~~were~~ once a little pup.
  ^   ^

                     tail
It has a bushy ~~taile~~.
                     ^

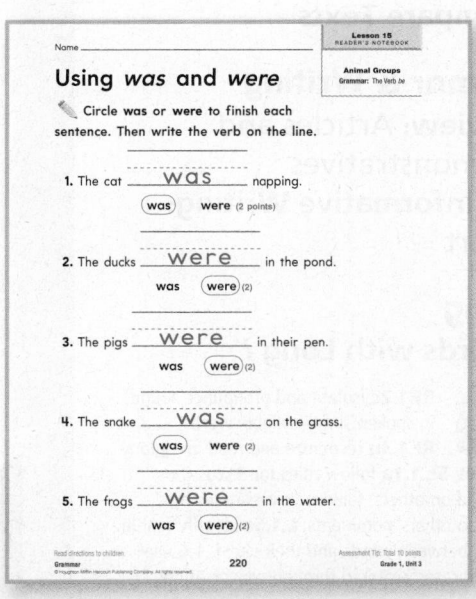

Reader's Notebook Vol. 1 p. 220

DAY 4

Today's Goals

Vocabulary & Oral Language
- **Vocabulary Strategies:** Suffixes *-er, -est*

Phonemic Awareness
- **Identify Middle Sound**
- **Substitute Phonemes**

Phonics & Fluency
- **Words with Long *i* (CVCe)**
- **Words with Digraphs *kn, wr, gn, mb***
- **Read Decodable Reader:** *Kite Time*

✅ **WORDS TO KNOW**

bird	long
both	or
eyes	those
fly	walk

Text-Based Comprehension
Connect to the Topic
- **Read Play:** *Animal Picnic*
- **Compare Texts**

Grammar & Writing
- **Review:** Articles and Demonstratives
- ➡ **Informative Writing:** Report

Spelling
- **Words with Long *i***

 **COMMON CORE** **RF.1.2c** isolate and pronounce sounds in spoken single-syllable words; **RF.1.3g** recognize and read irregularly spelled words; **SL.1.1a** follow rules for discussions; **SL.1.1b** build on others' talk in conversations by responding to others' comments; **L.1.5c** identify real-life connections between words and their use; **L.1.6** use words and phrases acquired through conversations, reading and being read to, and responding to texts

Opening Routines

Warm Up with Wordplay

Two Words

Remind children that they have been learning about animal groups. Tell children to think about the animal group fish. Have them each say two words that tell about fish. Write the words on the board and read them aloud with children.

gills	**fins**
swim	**scales**
water	**tail**

Repeat with other animal groups, such as mammals or amphibians.

Daily Phonemic Awareness

Identify and Substitute Medial Phonemes

- *Listen to the word* dim, /d/ /ĭ/ /m/. *What is its middle sound?* ĭ, *short* i
  Change the short i, /ĭ/, *to long* i, /ī/. *What is the new word?* dime

- Have children repeat with you, then by themselves. Have them continue with the words shown to say the word, name the middle sound, change the middle sound, and say the new word. 🔊 **RF.1.2c**

Word	Change the . . .	Result
fin	/ĭ/ to /ī/	*fine*
right	/ī/ to /ā/	*rate*
clam	/ă/ to /ī/	*climb*
climb	/ī/ to /ā/	*claim*

Corrective Feedback

- If a child misses a word, say the correct word and model the task. *Listen to the word,* fin, /f/ /ĭ/ /n/. *Now change* /ĭ/ *to* /ī/: /f/ /ī/ /n/. *What is the new word?* fine

Daily High-Frequency Words

- Point to the **High-Frequency Word Card** *those*.

- *Say the word.* those *Spell the word.* t, h, o, s, e *Write the word. Check the word.*

- Repeat the procedure with the words *bird, both, eyes, fly, long, or,* and *walk.* 🔊 **RF.1.3g**

Find the Letter Game

- Choose a High-Frequency Word. Write a dash on the board to represent each letter in the word.

- Have children call out letters. If the letter is in the word, write it on the appropriate blank. Continue until children guess the word.

- Ask the child who guesses the word correctly to come to the board to choose the next word.

Corrective Feedback

- If a child is unable to recognize the word *those*, say the correct word and have children repeat it. *Those. What is the word?* those

- Have children spell the word. t,h,o,s,e *How do we say this word?* those

- Have children reread all of the cards in random order.

Daily Vocabulary Boost

- Guide children to interact with the Oral Vocabulary words by asking them the following questions. Remind them to speak clearly when participating in discussion.

  Do you think a dog's ears are more sensitive *than ours? Why or why not?*

  What can you swivel *in?*

  What animals run when they are threatened?

- Ask children to work with a partner to explain *sensitive, swivel,* and *threatened* in their own words. Have each child respond to what his or her partner says so that they build a conversation. Challenge children to use these words in their everyday language. Make sure children follow appropriate rules for discussion such as listening to speakers, taking turns, and staying on topic. 🔊 **SL.1.1a, SL.1.1b, L.1.5c, L.1.6**

☑ **Oral Vocabulary**

alert
directions
scale
sensitive
swivel
threatened

Whole Group

DAY 4

Interactive Whiteboard Lesson: Words with Long *i* (CVCe) and Words with Digraphs *kn, wr, gn, mb*

Go Digital
• Interactive Whiteboard Lesson
• Decodable Reader

Phonics

Phonemic Awareness/Phonics

▶ SHARE OBJECTIVES

- Blend, read, and decode regularly spelled one-syllable words with long *i* and digraphs *kn, wr, gn, mb.*
- Review and sort words with long *i* and long *a.*
- Read on-level text fluently with appropriate intonation.

▶ SKILLS TRACE

Words with Long *i* (CVCe)	
Introduce	T420–T421
Differentiate	T492
Reteach	T506
▶ **Review**	**T444, T466**
Assess	Weekly Tests, Lesson 15

▶ SKILLS TRACE

Words with Digraphs *kn, wr, gn, mb*	
Introduce	T454–T455
Differentiate	T498
Reteach	T506
▶ **Review**	**T466**
Assess	Weekly Tests, Lesson 15

RI.1.7 use illustrations and details to describe key ideas; **RF.1.2c** isolate and pronounce sounds in spoken single-syllable words; **RF.1.3b** decode regularly spelled one-syllable words; **RF.1.3c** know final -e and vowel team conventions for representing long vowel sounds; **RF.1.3g** recognize and read irregularly spelled words **RF.1.4a** read on-level text with purpose and understanding; **RF.1.4b** read on-level text orally with accuracy, appropriate rate, and expression

Review Long *i*; Digraphs *kn, wr, gn, mb*

PHONEMIC AWARENESS WARM-UP Tell children that you will say a word and ask them to change the middle sound to make a new word. *Listen: The word is* twin. *Change the /ĭ/ to /ī/. What is the new word?* twine Continue with these words: *mat-moat, line-lane, pick-pack, rip-ripe.*

PHONOGRAMS *-ine, -ite* List *fine* and *mine* on the board. Point out that the last three letters are the same in each word. Explain that these words belong to the same word family because they end with the same letters and sounds. Guide children to add and read additional words, such as *dine, line, nine.* Repeat with *-ite,* using words like *bite, kite,* and *write.* 🔊 **RF.1.3b, RF.1.3c**

FILL IN THE BLANK Write the words and sentences below on the board. Have children read each word with you. Then guide them to choose a word that correctly completes each sentence. Model with the first sentence. Read the completed sentences with children.

1. A <u>gnat</u> is a little bug.

2. Dad cuts with a <u>knife</u>.

3. Mom will <u>knit</u> a cap.

4. A baby sheep is a <u>lamb</u>.

5. A <u>wren</u> is a little bird.

knit	lamb
wrist	gnat
thumb	knife
gnash	wren

GROUPING WORDS BY SOUND Display **Sound/Spelling Cards** *acorn* and *ice cream* and review long vowel *a_e* and *i_e* spellings. Make a two-column chart on the board, using the cards as headings. Then have children say *file,* identify its vowel sound, and tell you under which card to write the word. Continue with *state, mile, tame, face, smile, pile, blaze, mine.*

Have children copy the completed columns. Then ask children to work with partners to underline the long vowel spelling in each word. Review their work. 🔊 **RF.1.2c, RF.1.3c**

Decodable Reader

Read *Kite Time*

Decodable Reader, Unit 3, pp. 117–122

REVIEW DIGRAPHS *kn, wr* AND WORDS TO KNOW Tell children that some words in this selection have *kn* or *wr*. Point out that children have learned the following words, which they will also read in the selection: *bird, fly, or.*

PREVIEW Have children preview pages 117–119 and predict what the selection is about. Ask volunteers to tell what they know about flying a kite.

MODEL FLUENCY AND INTONATION Read aloud page 121 as children follow along. As you read, have children note how the tone in your voice changes each time you tell what the kite is doing. Lead children in choral reading the page with fluency and appropriate intonation.

READ Remind children to track the words from left to right. When they come to the end of a line, they should sweep their hand down to the beginning of the next line and continue reading. Have children read each page silently and then choral-read aloud. Have them read to find out about flying a kite.

RF.1.3b, RF.1.3c, RF.1.3g, RF.1.4a

RESPONDING Have partners read *Kite Time* again. Ask them to look for important information about how to fly a kite, both in the text and in the illustrations. Then have them make a list of the important details they learned about how to fly a kite. RI.1.7

DAILY ASSESSMENT 3 2 1 **RtI**

Corrective Feedback Work with the whole group to correct errors, following the model below.

Decoding Error:
A child reads *wrap* as *whap*.

Correct the error. Say the word. *That word is* wrap. *It begins with the letters* wr. *The letters* wr *stand for /r/.*

Guide Have children repeat the word. *What is the word?* wrap

Check *Go back to the beginning of the sentence and read it again.*

Reinforce Record the error and review the word again before children reread the story.

Reread for Fluency/ Develop Automaticity

READ WITH A PARTNER Have partners reread *Kite Time* three or four times, taking turns reading aloud each page. Remind them to read words correctly and to read smoothly. Visit partners to listen to them read. Give feedback about reading accurately, at an appropriate rate, and with expression and provide guidance for improving fluency. RF.1.4b

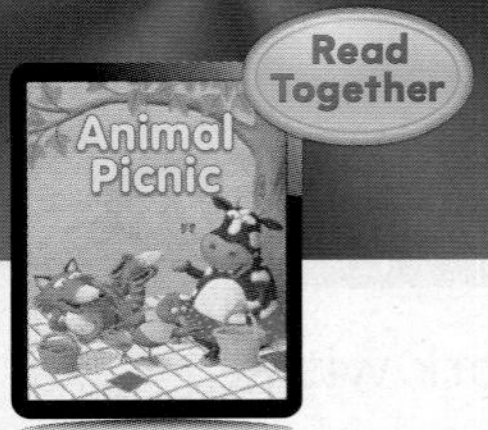

Read Together

Animal Picnic

A **play** is a story that people act out. Most of the words in a play are the words the characters say.

Stage directions are extra words in a play that tell about the characters and setting. They also tell what actions characters do. What are the stage directions in this play? How do you know?

COMMON CORE — RL.1.10 read prose and poetry

Go Digital

188

Animal Picnic

by Debbie O'Brien

Cast of Characters

Fox

Cow

Bird

Fox: Hi, Cow and Bird. How was your trip?

Cow: I had to walk to get here.

Bird: I had to fly.

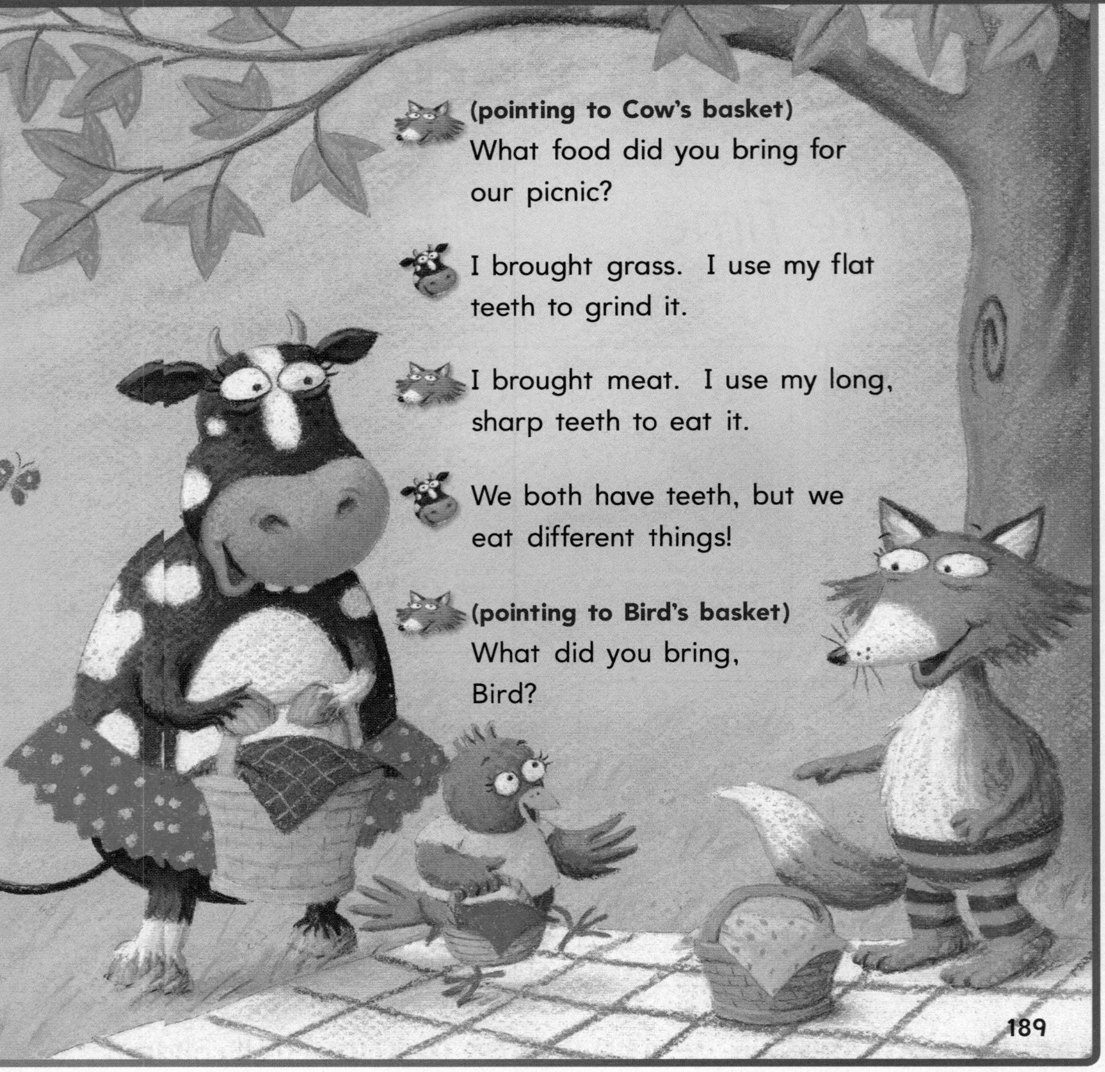

Fox: (pointing to Cow's basket) What food did you bring for our picnic?

Cow: I brought grass. I use my flat teeth to grind it.

Fox: I brought meat. I use my long, sharp teeth to eat it.

Cow: We both have teeth, but we eat different things!

Fox: (pointing to Bird's basket) What did you bring, Bird?

189

> **DOMAIN: Life Science**

LESSON TOPIC: Animals

Cross-Curricular Connection Have children identify some of the different environments that animals live in, such as the desert, a rain forest, a lake, or the ocean. Have children identify body parts that help animals survive in these environments. Guide them to explain or to find out how animals get the things they need to live and grow: air, water, food, and space.

Connect to the Topic
Play

Introduce Genre and Text Focus

- Read with children the genre and text focus information on **Student Book** p. 188. Explain that a **play** is a story that people act out, and that the story is told through characters' words and actions.

- Point out the cast of characters and the stage directions in the play. Explain that these stage directions tell actions that readers should do while performing.

- Read the play with children. After reading through the play once, discuss how the different animals' body parts help them survive. ▬ RL.1.10

- Have small groups choose parts, practice the play several times, and then read and perform it together as a Readers' Theater activity for the class. Have children practice reading smoothly and with expression. ▬ RL.1.10, RF.1.4b

I did not bring grass or meat. I brought seeds. Birds don't have any teeth!

How will you eat those seeds without teeth?

Watch this!
(Bird eats some seeds.)
Yum, yum, yum!

190

Compare Texts

Animal Groups

Animal Picnic

Read Together

TEXT TO TEXT

Compare Information Think about both selections. How are they alike and different? What information do you learn in each selection?

Alike	Different

TEXT TO SELF

Talk About Animals Which animal group is your favorite? Talk about it with a partner. Use complete sentences.

TEXT TO WORLD

Write a Question Write a question you have about an animal in the selections. Use this book or other books to find the answer.

Go Digital

COMMON CORE **RI.1.1** ask and answer questions about key details; **RI.1.9** identify similarities and differences between texts on the same topic; **W.1.8** recall information from experiences or gather information from sources to answer a question; **SL.1.6** produce complete sentences when appropriate to task and situation

191

Compare Texts

TEXT TO TEXT

Compare Information Have children make a chart like the one shown to compare and contrast what they learned about animals in both selections. Through discussion and by revisiting the selections to find text evidence, guide children to identify ways the two selections are alike and different—topic, illustrations (photos versus artwork), information and descriptions, and the way the information is presented (facts with labeled photos versus a play format). **RI.1.1, RI.1.9**

TEXT TO SELF

Talk About Animals Tell children to use complete sentences when they speak. Remind them to listen carefully when others speak and wait for their turn to talk. Have partners ask each other questions when they talk about their favorite animal groups, to clear up confusion or to find out more information. Tell children to respond to what others say during the discussion and to add their own ideas. **SL.1.1a, SL.1.1b, SL.1.1c, SL.1.6**

TEXT TO WORLD

Write a Question After children think of the animals they would like to know more about and write their questions, brainstorm with them where they could learn more about the animals and find the answers to their questions. Guide them to use *Animal Groups*, other books, or online resources to learn more about their animal. Have children share their findings in small groups. **RI.1.1, W.1.8**

Whole Group

DAY 4

• Interactive Whiteboard Lesson
• Literacy and Language Guide

Interactive Whiteboard Lesson:
Suffixes *-er, -est*

Vocabulary Strategies

▶ **SHARE OBJECTIVE**

• Use knowledge of the suffixes *-er* and *-est* to figure out the meanings of words.

▶ **SKILLS TRACE**

Suffixes *-er, -est*	
Introduce	T470–T471
Differentiate	T504–T505
Reteach	T507
Assess	Weekly Tests, Lesson 15

ELL **ENGLISH LANGUAGE LEARNERS**
Comprehensible Input

Beginning Write on the board *horse, frog, dog.* Have children dictate the name of the animals by size, starting with the frog. Use the sequence to clarify meaning while introducing comparatives with suffixes *-er* and *-est.*

Low Intermediate Write on the board *horse, frog, dog.* Ask *Which one is smaller, the horse or the frog? the frog* Continue with other similar questions.

High Intermediate Have volunteers show two classroom objects. Ask, *Which one is smaller/bigger, the _____ or the ____?* Have children answer using the sentence frame *The _____ is smaller/bigger than the ____.*

Proficient Have children work in pairs to choose two classroom objects and say a sentence about them comparing their size.

See ELL Lesson 15, p. 47 for scaffolded support.

COMMON CORE **L.1.4b** Use frequently occurring affixes as a clue to the meaning of a word

Suffixes *-er, -est*

1 Teach/Model

Terms About Language

suffix one or more letters that are added to the end of a root word to make a new, related word

---

• Discuss the definition of a *suffix*. Review step two on the **Vocabulary Strategy Projectable S8**. Tell children that recognizing a word part they know, such as a suffix, can help them understand the meaning of a new word.

• Tell children that the suffix *-er* is used to compare two people or things, and that *-est* is used to compare more than two people or things. Explain that children can use what they know about *-er* and *-est* to figure out the meanings of new words that have one of the suffixes.

• Remind children that they learned in *Animal Groups* that animals can be different sizes. Display p. 177 of the selection and have children look at the photos. Then write the following sentence on the board and read it aloud. Model using your knowledge of how the suffix *-er* is used to figure out the meaning of *smaller*.

> A penguin is <u>smaller</u> than an ostrich.

Think Aloud *If I didn't know the meaning of the word* smaller, *I would look to see if it has any word parts I know. I notice that it ends with the suffix* -er. *I know that* -er *is used to compare two things. If I cover* -er, *I see a word I know:* small. *So the sentence is comparing the size of the penguin to the size of the ostrich. The ostrich is not as small as the penguin.*

• Follow the same procedure to model using your knowledge of the suffix *-est* to figure out the meaning of *smallest*. Write a sentence about the photos on p. 177 using *smallest*.

Literacy and Language Guide
Additional Lesson 15 vocabulary lessons appear in the Literacy and Language Guide.

2 Guided Practice

- Display the top of **Projectable 15.7**. Read the first sentence aloud. Point to the boldfaced word (*shortest*) and re-read it.

- Display the rest of **Projectable 15.7**. Write *shortest* in the chart.

- Ask a volunteer to name the root word (*short*) and suffix (*-est*). Write them in the chart. Ask the volunteer what is being compared (more than two ways home). Write what is being compared in the chart. Review that the suffix *-est* means that *more than two* ways home are being compared.

- Have children use what they know about the suffix *-est* to discuss the meaning of *shortest*.

3 Apply

- Read the rest of the sentences aloud with children and have them complete the chart with you.

- Have children use what they know about the suffixes to discuss each word's meaning.

- When children have completed the chart, have them choose two of the boldfaced words from the top of the **Projectable** to make their own sentences. Write a few of the new sentences below the chart and discuss how the words were used. ◗ **L.1.4b**

Are children able to use their knowledge of the suffixes -er and -est to figure out the meanings of words?

IF...	THEN...
children have difficulty using their knowledge of the suffixes *-er* and *-est* to figure out the meanings of words,	▶ **Differentiate Vocabulary Strategies** for Struggling Readers, p. T504
children can use their knowledge of the suffixes *-er* and *-est* to figure out the meanings of most words,	▶ **Differentiate Vocabulary Strategies** for On-Level Readers, p. T504
children can easily use their knowledge of the suffixes *-er* and *-est* to figure out the meanings of words,	▶ **Differentiate Vocabulary Strategies** for Advanced Readers, p. T505

Differentiate Vocabulary Strategies:
pp. T504–T505.
Group English Language Learners according to academic ability and language proficiency.

Go Digital
- *my*WriteSmart
- eBook
- GrammarSnap Videos
- Interactive Whiteboard Lesson

Grammar Spiral Review: Articles and Demonstratives

▶ SHARE OBJECTIVES

- **Grammar** Review using the determiners *a*, *an*, and *the* and demonstratives.
- **Spelling** Spell words with the long *i* sound using conventional spelling patterns.
- **Handwriting** Print the spelling words.
- **Writing** Finish drafting a research report and have a writing conference.

ELL ENGLISH LANGUAGE LEARNERS
Language Transfer

Beginning Display the **online Picture Cards** *arm*, *shirt*. Write *an arm*, *a shirt*. Have children read it aloud. Explain that the articles *a/an* tell us that there is only one arm or one shirt.

Low Intermediate Display the cards above. Guide children in adding the article *a* or *an* so that we know it is only one arm and one shirt.

High Intermediate Display the sentence frame *I bought _____ shirt.* Have children complete the frame with the correct article.

Proficient Display a series of **online Picture Cards** and have children write each word, adding the article *a* or *an* to show there is only one of each.

1 Teach/Model

ARTICLES AND DEMONSTRATIVES Review that *a*, *an*, and *the* are special adjectives called *articles*. Remind children they have also learned the words *this*, *that*, *these*, and *those* are special adjectives that show a specific noun.

- Write these examples on the board: *a pear, an apple, the bear, this orange, that grape, these ducks, those trees*.

- Point out that *a* is used before a noun that names one item and begins with a consonant sound. *An* is used before a noun that names one item and begins with a vowel sound. *The* is used before a noun that names one or more than one. *This* and *that* are used with singular nouns. *These* and *those* are used with plural nouns.

2 Guided Practice/Apply

- Have children add examples to the list on the board. Then have them tell why each article or demonstrative is used and what noun it refers to.

- Have children work with partners to create oral sentences using some of the examples on the board. Have them write their sentences and share them with the class. **SL.1.6, L.1.1h**

Spelling Words with Long *i*

SPELLING WORDS

BASIC

time	like
kite	bike
white	drive

CHALLENGE

shell	mice

Connect to Writing

- Remind children that they have been learning how to use the verb *be*.

- Ask children to use the spelling words to write sentences using the verb *be*. Remind them to proofread their sentences. Then invite volunteers to read their sentences aloud.

- Finally, tell children that the class will practice spelling the words together. Say each word and spell it aloud with children. **L.1.2d**

Handwriting

Model how to form *bike, white,* and *drive*. Then have children use their best handwriting to print the spelling words. Ball-and-stick and continuous stroke handwriting models are available on the **Handwriting Models Blackline Masters**.

COMMON CORE

W.1.2 write informative/explanatory texts; **W.1.5** focus on a topic, respond to questions/suggestions from peers, and add details to strengthen writing; **W.1.6** use digital tools to produce and publish writing; **W.1.8** recall information from experiences or gather information from sources to answer a question; **L.1.1h** use determiners; **L.1.2d** use conventional spelling for words with common spelling patterns and for frequently occurring irregular words

Informative Writing Drafting and Revising

1 Teach/Model

USING THE VERB *be* Remind children that the words *is* and *are* are related. Use *is* in a sentence with a noun that names one, and *are* in a sentence with a noun that names more than one. Use *is* and *are* to tell about something that is happening now, not in the past.

• Point out examples of these words in *Animal Groups*.

Connect to *Animal Groups*

Their skin **is** wet.

This bird's eyes **are** on the sides of its face!

• *Why does the first sentence use* is? *There is only one skin.* *Why does the second sentence use* are? *There are two eyes.*

• Write the following sentences on the board:

   The girl _____ at the movies.

   Tom and Josie _____ at the zoo.

• *Which sentence should have the word* are *in the blank? the last Why? The subject names more than one. Which sentence should have the word* is *in the blank? the first Why? The subject names only one.*

2 Independent Writing

• Have children finish drafting their research reports. Then ask them to read their completed papers silently.

WRITING CONFERENCE Remind the class that in a writing conference, partners help one another improve their writing.

• Distribute the **Writing Conference Form**. Have children hold writing conferences, using the page as a guide. Have them respond to questions and suggestions from their partners to strengthen their own writing. ● W.1.5

• Then have children begin revising their research reports.
● W.1.2, W.1.8

Daily Proofreading Practice

Frogs are
Froggs is small animals.
^

They have big eyes.
            ^ eyes

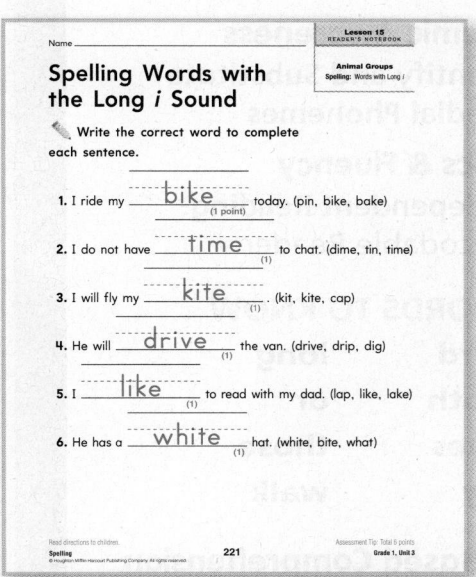

Reader's Notebook Vol. 1 p. 221

Reader's Notebook Vol. 1 p. 222

DAY 5

Today's Goals

Vocabulary & Oral Language
- Domain-Specific Vocabulary
- Speaking & Listening

Phonemic Awareness
- Identify and Substitute Medial Phonemes

Phonics & Fluency
- Independent Reading: Decodable Reader

☑ **WORDS TO KNOW**

bird	long
both	or
eyes	those
fly	walk

Text-Based Comprehension
Extend the Topic
- Research & Media Literacy: Ask and Answer Questions Using Information from Media

Assess & Reteach
- Assess Skills
- Respond to Assessment

Grammar & Writing
- The Verb *be*
- Informative Writing: Report

Spelling
- Words with Long *i*

RF.1.2c isolate and pronounce sounds in spoken single-syllable words; **RF.1.3g** recognize and read irregularly spelled words; **L.1.6** use words and phrases acquired through conversations, reading and being read to, and responding to texts

Opening Routines

Warm Up with Wordplay

Ending with *-er* or *-est*

Remind children that they have been working with words that end with *-er* and *-est*. Display and read the following words:

small	**slow**	**soft**

Have children add *-er* or *-est* to say new words. Then have children use the new words in sentences about animals. Challenge children to come up with more words that end with *-er* or *-est*. Write the words on the board and read them aloud with children.

Daily Phonemic Awareness

Identify and Substitute Medial Phonemes

- *Listen to the word* time, /t/ /ī/ /m/. *What is its middle sound?* /ī/, long i *Change the long* i, /ī/, *to long a*, /ā/. *What is the new word?* tame

- Have children repeat with you, then by themselves. Have them continue with the words shown to say the word, name the middle sound, change the middle sound, and say the new word. **◀ RF.1.2c**

Word	Change the . . .	Result
bike	/ī/ to /ā/	*bake*
bake	/ā/ to /ă/	*back*
gave	/ā/ to /ĭ/	*give*
when	/ĕ/ to /ī/	*whine*
ride	/ī/ to /ā/	*raid*

Corrective Feedback

- If a child misses a word, say the correct word and model the task. *Listen to the word,* bike, /b/ /ī/ /k/. *Now change* /ī/ *to* /ā/: /b/ /ā/ /k/. *What is the new word?* bake

Daily High-Frequency Words

Introduce

- Point to the **High-Frequency Word Card** *fly.*

- *Say the word.* fly *Spell the word.* f, l, y *Write the word. Check the word.*

- Repeat the procedure with the words from this week and last week (*five, four, into, over, starts, three, two, watch*). **◀ RF.1.3g**

Hopscotch Game

- Make a hopscotch board on the classroom floor with tape or on the playground with chalk.

- Choose a High-Frequency Word. Write one letter in each box and the whole word at the top.

- Have children hop and say each letter to spell the word and then say the word at the end.

- Do the same for additional words.

Corrective Feedback

- If a child is unable to recognize the word *walk*, say the correct word and have children repeat it. *Walk. What is the word?* walk

- Have children spell the word. *w,a,l,k How do we say this word?* walk

- Have children reread all of the cards in random order.

Daily Vocabulary Boost

- Reread "The Dancing Wolves" aloud to children. (See pp. T418–T419.)

- As you reach each Oral Vocabulary word in the selection, have a volunteer explain or describe its meaning. Have children make a sentence with each Oral Vocabulary word. Repeat the list until each child has come up with a sentence.

- After reading, review the Oral Vocabulary words and their definitions. Challenge children to use the words in their everyday speech. **◀ L.1.6**

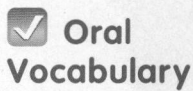
☑ Oral Vocabulary

alert
directions
scale
sensitive
swivel
threatened

• *my*WriteSmart
• eBook

> **DOMAIN: Life Science**
> **LESSON TOPIC:** Animals

Extend the Topic

▶ SHARE OBJECTIVES

- Acquire and use domain-specific vocabulary.
- Participate in conversations about a topic.
- Ask questions to clear up confusion or to gain information about the topics under discussion.
- Ask and answer questions about key details in information presented orally or through other media.

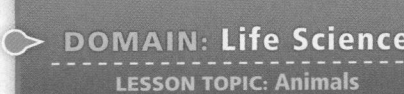

Words About the Topic: Animals

- **trait** a specific characteristic or behavior of an animal
- **adapt** to change or get used to a new situation
- **survive** to go on living

Domain-Specific Vocabulary

INTRODUCE WORDS ABOUT THE TOPIC Remind children that this week's topic is Animals. Display the words shown at the left. Tell children that these are words that can help them learn more about the topic. Read aloud the meaning of each word, and have children respond to the following prompts. 🔲 **L.1.5c, L.1.6**

- *What is one trait of dogs?* Accept reasonable responses, such as dogs bark or dogs wag their tails.

- *Do you remember when the school year first started? How did you get used to school and to our class?* Accept reasonable responses. *What word do we use to describe getting used to something?* adapt

- *What do animals need to survive?* Accept reasonable responses.

INTERACT WITH THE WORDS Have children work in small groups to create Four-Square Maps. For each of the domain-specific words, children should fold a blank sheet of paper into four equal sections. Work with them to follow the steps below for each word. As needed, display the meanings of the words on the board. Ask individual children to use the words in a sentence orally. Then write the sentence on the board for other children to refer to for ideas.

1 In the first corner, draw a picture of the word.

2 In the second corner, write the meaning of the word.

3 In the third corner, write a sentence using the word.

4 In the fourth corner, write the word.

When groups have finished, have them share their Four-Square Maps with the class. 🔲 **L.1.5c, L.1.6**

> **COMMON CORE** **RI.1.1** ask and answer questions about key details; **SL.1.1c** ask question to clear up confusion about topics and texts under discussion; **SL.1.2** ask and answer questions about details in a text read aloud, information presented orally, or through other media; **SL.1.3** ask and answer questions about what a speaker says; **L.1.5c** identify real-life connections between words and their use; **L.1.6** use words and phrases acquired through conversations, reading and being read to, and responding to texts

Research and Media Literacy

Ask and Answer Questions:
Using Information from Media

REVIEW THE TOPIC Ask the class to tell about the selection, *Animal Groups*. What were the five animal groups described in the book? What are some of the common traits in each group?

A RESEARCH QUESTION Explain that every animal has different traits—characteristics—that are notable about it. These traits help the animal to survive. For example, a shark has sharp teeth that help it attack and eat its prey.

Tell the class that they are each going to pick an animal, identify one of its traits, and then ask this important question: *How does _____ help the animal to survive?* This will be their research question.

FIND THE ANSWER Tell the class that they can find the answer to their research question using various media, including books, magazines, and websites. Give children time to research. Guide them to find appropriate resources and to use websites. Remind children to take notes about important facts they find that help answer their question. ▬ RI.1.1

PREPARE A PRESENTATION Have children organize their notes into a short report that they will present orally. Remind them to include a title, to present the main idea at the beginning, and to tell facts and details that explain the main idea. Have children draw a picture of the animal to include.

PRESENT AND ANSWER In groups, have each child give his or her presentation and share the picture of the animal. The other group members should ask questions about important details and facts to clear up confusion or to find out more information. The speaker should answer the questions. If there are any questions the speaker cannot answer, guide the group to work together to find answers, using print and nonprint media sources.
▬ SL.1.1c, SL.1.2, SL.1.3

DAY 1 Review the topic.

DAY 2 Ask a research question.

DAY 3 Find the answer.

DAY 4 Prepare a presentation.

DAY 5 Present and answer.

Performance Task

 **Have children complete the Research and Media Literacy task through *my*WriteSmart. Children will read a prompt within *my*WriteSmart and have access to multiple writing resources, including the Student eBook, a Writing Checklist, and Graphic Organizers.**

Go Digital
• eBook
• GrammarSnap Videos

Grammar Weekly Review: The Verb *be*

▶ SHARE OBJECTIVES

- **Grammar** Identify and use *is, are, was*, and *were* as main verbs in sentences.
- **Spelling** Spell words with the long *i* sound using conventional spelling patterns.

ELL ENGLISH LANGUAGE LEARNERS
Language Transfer

Beginning Display the words *kite, bike, white, stripe*. Read the words aloud and have children clap whenever they hear the /ī/ sound.

Low Intermediate Have children use letter cards to build and read *bike, white, stripe*.

High Intermediate Have children use letter cards to build and read *kite*. Guide them in changing the cards to read *bike, white, like*.

Proficient Have children in groups use letter cards *m, c, k, v, i, e, l, s, h, t, n* to build and read as many words with the /ī/ sound as they can.

1 Review/Practice

Together read the text at the top of **Student Book** p. 192. Discuss the example sentences and their use of *is, are, was,* and *were*.

- Direct children's attention to the Try This! activity on **Student Book** p. 193. Have children finish each sentence with the correct form of *be*.

2 Connect to Writing

CONVENTIONS: PROOFREADING Write the following statements on the board. Ask children to identify the mistakes orally.

> *The cat were once a kitten.*
> *Cats is soft and furry*

- Model using proofreading marks to correct the first sentence.
- Have children correct the errors in the second sentence.

> *was*
> *The cat were once a kitten.*

> *are*
> *Cats is soft and furry.*

- Remind children to use correct subject-verb agreement in their own writing and to use the right verbs to tell about the present or past. 🎧 **SL.1.6, L.1.1c, L.1.1e, L.1.1j**

Spelling Words with Long *i*

SPELLING WORDS AND SENTENCES

BASIC
1. **time** What *time* is it?
2. **like** I *like* to eat oranges.
3. **kite** The *kite* was high in the sky.
4. **bike** My *bike* is blue.
5. **white** Snow is *white*.

6. **drive** Can you *drive* me to school?

CHALLENGE
7. **stripe** A skunk has a white *stripe*.
8. **mice** The *mice* ran under a bush.

Assess
Say each spelling word, read the sentence, and then repeat the word. Have children write the word.
🎧 **L.1.2d**

Corrective Feedback
Review any words that children misspell.

COMMON CORE **SL.1.6** produce complete sentences when appropriate to task and situation; **L.1.1c** use singular and plural nouns with matching verbs in sentences; **L.1.1e** use verbs to convey sense of past, present, and future; **L.1.1j** produce and expand simple and compound declarative, interrogative, imperative, and exclamatory sentences; **L.1.2d** use conventional spelling for words with common spelling patterns and for frequently occurring irregular words

L.1.1c use singular and plural nouns with matching verbs in sentences; L.1.1e use verbs to convey sense of past, present, and future

Grammar

The Verb be The verbs **is** and **are** tell what is happening now. Use **is** with a noun that names one.

One	More Than One
This **chick is** small.	Two **chicks are** small.

The verbs **was** and **were** tell what happened in the past. Use **was** with a noun that names one.

One	More Than One
One **egg was** here.	Two **eggs were** here.

192

Try This!

Read each sentence aloud two times, saying a different verb each time. Ask your partner to repeat the sentence with the correct verb. Then switch roles.

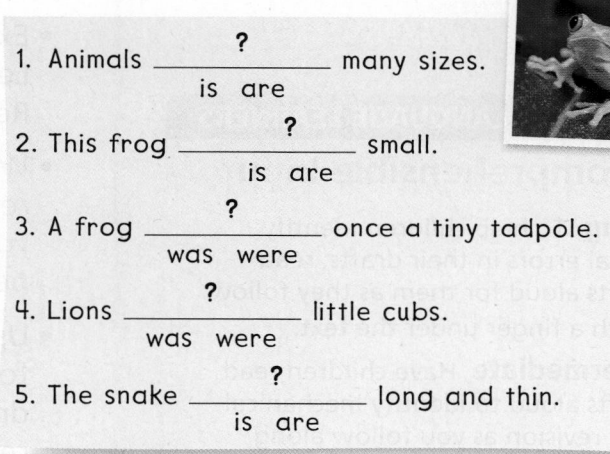

1. Animals _____ many sizes.
   is are
2. This frog _____ small.
   is are
3. A frog _____ once a tiny tadpole.
   was were
4. Lions _____ little cubs.
   was were
5. The snake _____ long and thin.
   is are

Grammar in Writing

When you proofread your writing, be sure you have used the verbs **is**, **are**, **was**, and **were** correctly.

193

Try This!

1. are
2. is
3. was
4. were
5. is

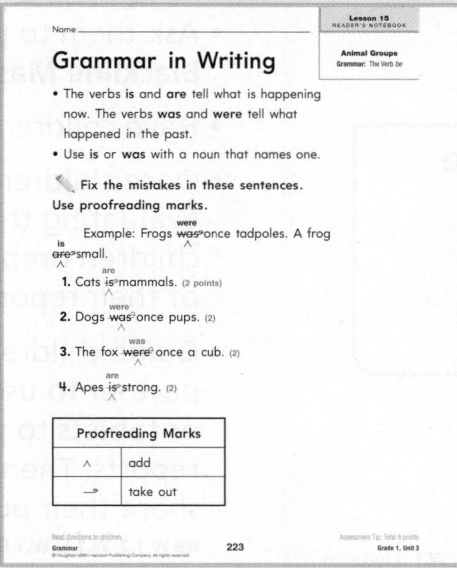

Reader's Notebook Vol. 1 p. 223

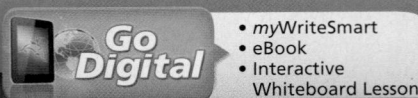
DAY 5

Informative Writing Revising and Proofreading

▶ **SHARE OBJECTIVE**
- Revise and proofread a research report.
- Publish a research report.

ELL ENGLISH LANGUAGE LEARNERS
Comprehensible Input

Beginning To help children identify mechanical errors in their drafts, read their drafts aloud for them as they follow along with a finger under the text.

Low Intermediate Have children read their drafts aloud to identify mechanical errors for revision as you follow along with your finger under the text.

High Intermediate Have children read their drafts aloud to partners to identify mechanical errors for revision.

Proficient Have children work with partners to identify places they can add more exact details to their writing.

See ELL Lesson 15, p. E51, for scaffolded support.

Daily Proofreading Practice

The birds ~~flie~~ fly in the sky.
^

Their feathers ~~is wite~~ are white.
^

COMMON CORE **W.1.2** write informative/explanatory texts; **W.1.5** focus on a topic, respond to questions/suggestions from peers, and add details to strengthen writing; **W.1.6** use digital tools to produce and publish writing; **W.1.8** recall information from experiences or gather information from sources to answer a question; **L.1.2b** use end punctuation for sentences; **L.1.2d** use conventional spelling for words with common spelling patterns and for frequently occurring irregular words

1 Teach/Model

- Display **Projectable 15.8**.

- Explain that a first grader named Lena wrote this research report. Review what *revision* is.

- *What parts of Lena's report are really good? Why? What parts do you think she can make even better?*

- Use the Talk About it questions to help children analyze the draft. Have children suggest revisions.

- Model revising the draft.

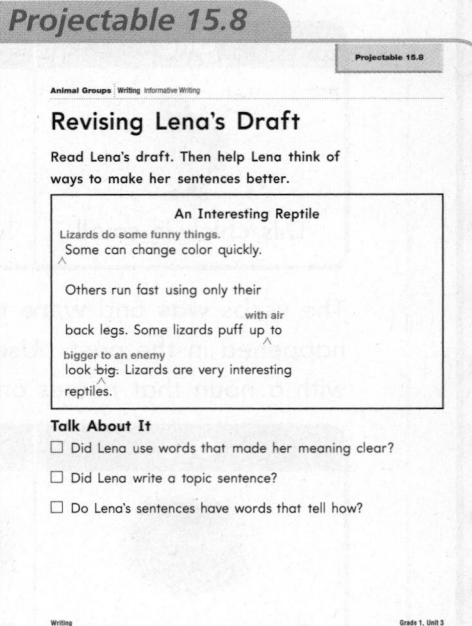

Projectable 15.8

2 Independent Writing

- Use **Student Book** pp. 194–195 to review the focus skill, using exact words. Then have children revise their own papers, using the Revising Checklist on **Student Book** p. 194.

- Ask them to proofread, referring to the **Proofreading Checklist Blackline Master**.

- Have children use the **Writing Checklist** to evaluate their drafts.

- Once children have finished evaluating their reports, have children prepare a clean final copy of their report.

- Guide children to work with a partner to use classroom computers or tablets to print or illustrate their reports. Then invite volunteers to share their published writing.

▬ W.1.2, W.1.5, W.1.6, W.1.8, L.1.2b, L.1.2d

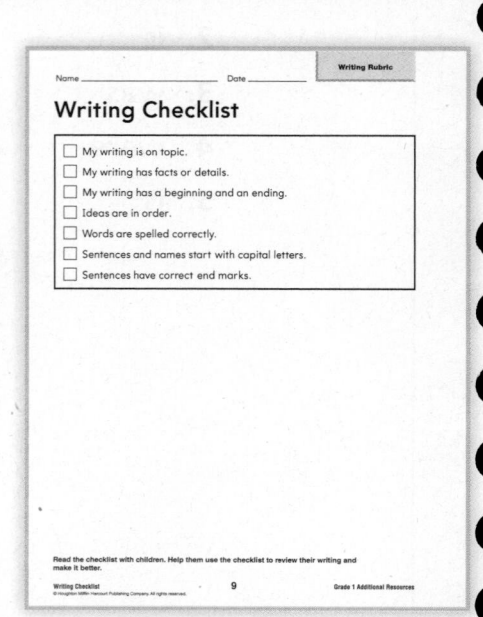

Writing Checklist

W.1.2 write informative/explanatory texts; W.1.5 focus on a topic, respond to questions/suggestions from peers, and add details to strengthen writing; L.1.2b use end punctuation for sentences; L.1.2d use conventional spelling for words with common spelling patterns and for frequently occurring irregular words

Reading-Writing Workshop: Revise

Informative Writing

✓ **Word Choice** In a good **report**, the right words make the facts easy to understand. Lena drafted her report. Later, she wrote different words to make her meaning clear.

 Read Together

 my WriteSmart

 Go Digital

Revised Draft

Some lizards puff up ˄to
~~bigger to an enemy.~~
look ~~big~~.

with air

Revising Checklist

☑ Did I use words that make my meaning clear?

☑ Did I use correct punctuation?

☑ Did I spell words correctly?

☑ Did I write a good ending sentence?

194

Look for exact words in Lena's final copy. Then revise your writing. Use the Checklist.

Final Copy

An Interesting Reptile

Lizards do some funny things. Some can change color quickly. Others run fast using only their back legs. Some lizards puff up with air to look bigger to an enemy. Lizards are very interesting reptiles.

195

See also the **Writing Rubric Blackline Master** on Teacher's Edition p. R11.

WRITING TRAITS SCORING RUBRIC

	Focus/Support	Organization	Word Choice/Voice	Conventions/Sentence Fluency
6	Develops topic or events with relevant facts or details.	Introduces topic or situation clearly, organizes ideas to support purpose, has relevant conclusion.	Links ideas with words, phrases. Uses specific language. Connects with reader in unique way.	Demonstrates exemplary command of conventions of standard written English. Includes variety of complete sentences that flow smoothly, naturally.
5	Mostly develops topic or events with relevant facts or details.	Introduces topic or situation, mostly organizes ideas to support purpose, has mostly relevant conclusion.	Links most ideas with words, phrases. Uses specific language. Connects with reader.	Demonstrates good command of conventions of standard written English. Includes some variety of complete sentences that flow smoothly, naturally.
4	Adequately develops topic or events with relevant facts or details.	Introduces topic or situation, adequately organizes ideas to support purpose, has adequate conclusion.	Links some ideas with words, phrases. Uses some specific language. Connects with reader.	Demonstrates adequate command of conventions of standard written English. Includes some variety of complete sentences. Some flow smoothly, naturally.
3	Develops topic or events with some relevant facts or details.	Introduces topic or situation, organizes some ideas to support purpose, has somewhat relevant conclusion.	Links some ideas with words, phrases. May use some specific language. May connect with reader.	Demonstrates command of some conventions of standard written English. Includes little variety of complete sentences. Few flow smoothly, naturally.
2	Develops topic or events with few relevant facts or details.	May introduce topic or situation, organizes few ideas to support purpose, may have somewhat relevant conclusion.	Attempts to link ideas with words. Rarely uses specific language. May not connect with reader.	Demonstrates little command of conventions of standard written English. Includes little sentence variety. Incomplete sentences hinder meaning.
1	May not develop topic or events with relevant facts or details.	May attempt to introduce topic or situation, may not organize ideas to support purpose, may not have relevant conclusion.	May not link ideas with words. Does not use specific language or connect with reader.	Demonstrates little or no command of conventions of standard written English. Sentences do not vary. Incomplete sentences hinder meaning.

✓ Progress Monitoring

Assess

- **Weekly Tests**
- **Periodic Assessments**

COMMON CORE

Respond to Assessment

✓ Vocabulary

High-Frequency Words
Strategies: Suffixes *-er, -est*

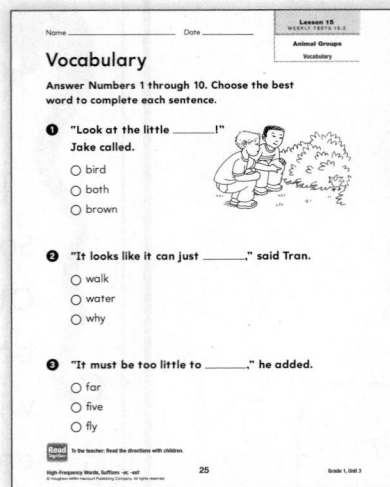

Weekly Tests 15.2–15.5

RF.1.3g recognize and read irregularly spelled words; **L.1.4b** use frequently occurring affixes as a clue to the meaning of a word

IF a Child Scores...	THEN...
7–10 of 10	▶ Continue Core Instructional Program
1–6 of 10	▶ Reteaching Lesson, p. T507

If a child scores below target on two or more tests, then consider using Diagnostic Assessment to pinpoint the child's instructional needs. The child may need systematic intervention.

✓ Phonics/Decoding

Words with Long *i* (CVCe);
Words with Digraphs *kn, wr, gn, mb*
Phonograms: *-ine, -ite*

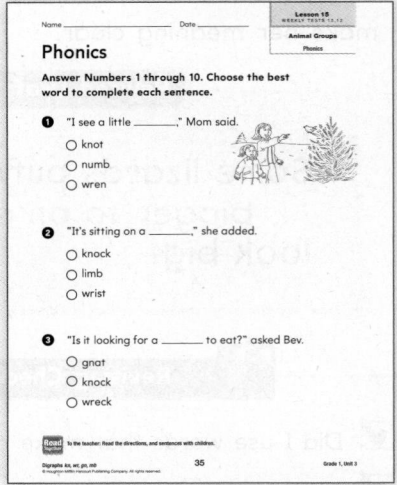

Weekly Tests 15.9–15.14

Phonemic Awareness
See Observation Checklist in Grab-and-Go™ Resources.

RF.1.3a know the spelling-sound correspondences for common consonant digraphs; **RF.1.3c** know final -e and vowel team conventions for representing long vowel sounds

IF a Child Scores...	THEN...
7–10 of 10	▶ Continue Core Instructional Program
1–6 of 10	▶ Reteaching Lesson, p. T506

If a child scores below target on two or more tests, then consider using Diagnostic Assessment to pinpoint the child's instructional needs. The child may need systematic intervention.

 **Go Digital**
- Grab-and-Go Weekly Tests
- Online Assessment System
- Cold Reads Online
- ExamView Banks

 COMMON CORE

☑ Comprehension

Compare and Contrast
Text and Graphic Features

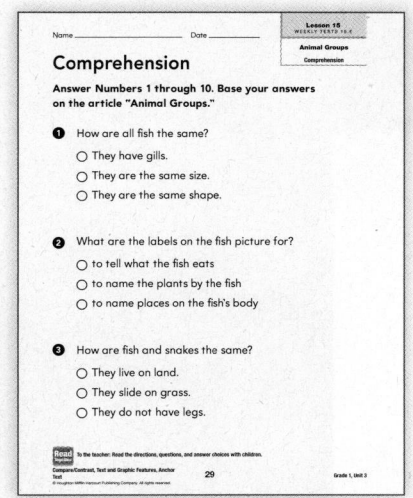

Weekly Tests 15.6–15.8

RI.1.3 describe the connection between individuals, events, ideas, or information in a text; **RI.2.5** know and use text features to locate facts or information; **RI.1.7** use illustrations and details to describe key ideas

---

IF a Child Scores...	THEN...
7–10 of 10	▶ Continue Core Instructional Program
1–6 of 10	▶ **Reteaching Lesson,** p. T507

If a child scores below target on two or more tests, then consider using Diagnostic Assessment to pinpoint the child's instructional needs. The child may need systematic intervention.

☑ Language Arts

Grammar: The Verb *be*

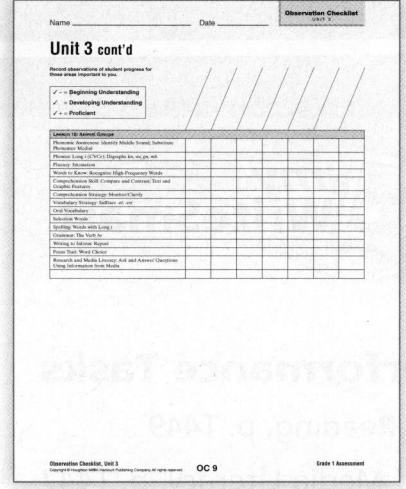

Observation Checklist, *Assessment,* **p. OC9**

L.1.1c use singular and plural nouns with matching verbs in sentences; **L.1.1e** use verbs to convey sense of past, present, and future

---

IF a Child Scores...	THEN...
Proficient	▶ Continue Core Instructional Program
Developing	▶ **Review Instruction,** pp. T440, T450, T462, T478–T479
Beginning	▶ **Intervention** Lesson 15, pp. S42–S51

If a child scores below target on two or more tests, then consider using Diagnostic Assessment to pinpoint the child's instructional needs. The child may need systematic intervention.

☑ FLUENCY

Fluency Plan Assess one group per week. Use the suggested plan below.

● **Struggling Readers**	**Weeks 1, 3, 5**
▲ **On Level**	**Week 2**
■ **Advanced**	**Week 4**

Fluency Scoring Rubrics
See *Grab-and-Go™ Resources Assessment* for help in measuring progress.

Oral Reading Practice
Use the **Student Book,** the **Leveled Readers,** or other reading materials in this unit to help children improve fluency.

☑ COLD READS

Cold Reads *are leveled passages that can be used to practice and monitor fluency and comprehension.*

LESSON 15

Performance Tasks

my WriteSmart

Lesson Performance Tasks

• Write About Reading, p. T449

• Research and Media Literacy, p. T447

• Informative Writing: Report, pp. T480–T481

• Cumulative Performance Assessment: Task 5 of 5

Unit-Level Performance Tasks

• Research and Media Performance Tasks, pp. xxvi–xxvii

• Cumulative Performance Assessment

Task 1: complete after Lesson 11

Task 2: complete after Lesson 12

Task 3: complete after Lesson 13

Task 4: complete after Lesson 14

Task 5: complete after Lesson 15

Discuss Taking a Test

TEST-TAKING STRATEGIES Remind children that using strategies when they take a test can help them better understand what they read. Display and discuss with children the following strategies:

• Read the title and preview the text.

• Look at any photographs or illustrations. Read the captions.

• Make notes in your test booklet or underline things that seem to be important.

• Ask yourself questions as you read: *Can I use what I have read and what I already know to figure out things the author has not said in the text? Can I make a prediction about what might happen?*

KINDS OF TEXTS Discuss kinds of texts that are found on tests, focusing on informational texts. Point out that the material children will need to understand on tests can be very challenging. Remind children to:

• Reread any sections that are not clear.

• Look at the other words in the sentence to help you understand the meaning of a different word or phrase.

• Look for the main idea and how it is supported with facts and important details.

• Think about how events, individuals, ideas, and information are connected.

• Think about the purpose of a text.

QUESTIONS Then discuss the questions children will encounter on tests. Remind children:

• For questions that ask you to write a response, include important examples and details from the text to support your answer.

• Look back at the text if the answer to the question is not clear.

• Remember to look for text evidence in the words and pictures to find important details and ideas to help you with your answer.

▶ SHARE OBJECTIVES

• Learn and apply test-taking strategies.
• Practice reading and understanding complex text.
• Practice using text-based evidence to respond to questions about text.

▶ SKILL TRACE

Test Power Focus
Unit 1 Read Literature
Unit 2 Read Literature
Unit 3 Read Informational Texts
Unit 4 Compare Texts
Unit 5 Read Literature and Informational Texts
Unit 6 Compare Texts

Think Through the Text

Tell children that a test may ask them to read informational texts and answer questions about them.

- Distribute **Blackline Master 15.9**.

- Have children read the first part of the article beginning on **Student Book** p. 196 and the first question. Tell them to stop after they read the first question. **RI.1.10**

- Read the first question aloud.

1 *Where do frogs and toads live when they are small? Frogs and toads both live in the water when they are small.*  **RI.1.1, RI.1.3**

- Call on volunteers to suggest answers. Remind children to provide evidence from the article to support their answers.

- Have children continue reading the article, stopping at each question and answering it. After children have answered each question, discuss the question and possible answers. Explore the text-based evidence for each answer.

COMMON CORE **RI.1.1** ask and answer questions about key details; **RI.1.3** describe the connection between individuals, events, ideas, or information in a text; **RI.1.4** ask and answer questions to determine or clarify the meaning of words and phrases; **RI.1.8** identify the reasons an author gives to support points; **RI.1.10** read informational text; **L.1.4a** use sentence-level context as a clue to the meaning of a word or phrase.

 Read Together

Read each article. As you read, stop and answer each question. Use text evidence.

Frogs and Toads

Frogs and toads are alike in some ways. They both lay eggs in water. They both live in water when they are small. They both eat lots of bugs.

1 Where do frogs and toads live when they are small?

Frogs and toads are different in some ways, too. Frogs have smooth, wet skin. Frogs live in or near water. They have long back legs, too. This helps them hop and swim.

196 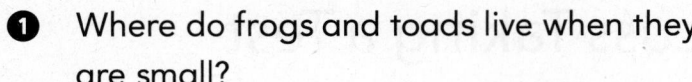 **COMMON CORE** **RI.1.1** ask and answer questions about key details; **RI.1.3** describe the connection between individuals, events, ideas, or information in a text; **RI.1.4** ask and answer questions to determine or clarify the meaning of words and phrases; **RI.1.8** identify the reasons an author gives to support points; **RI.1.10** read informational texts; **L.1.4a** use sentence-level context as a clue to the meaning of a word or phrase

---

ELL **ENGLISH LANGUAGE LEARNERS**

Expand Language Production

Beginning For each question, accept one-word responses and expand them. For example, if a child's response to question 1 is "water," expand it by saying, "Yes, frogs and toads live in the water when they are small."

High Intermediate Have children respond to the questions in complete sentences. Provide corrective feedback as needed.

Low Intermediate Provide part of a response for each question and have children complete it. Then have children repeat the complete response and confirm their understanding.

Proficient Have children tell how they know the answer to each question based on details from the selection.

Toads have dry, bumpy skin. Toads spend much of their time on land. They have small back legs. This helps them walk.

> **❷** How are frogs different from toads?

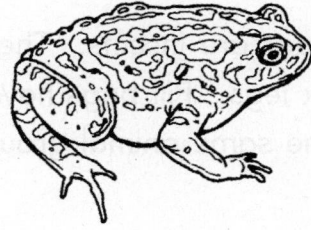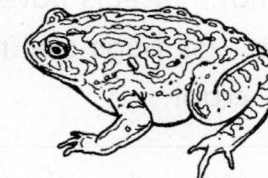

197

> A Closer Look

❷ *How are frogs different from toads?*
Frogs have smooth, wet skin. Toads have dry, bumpy skin. Frogs live in or near water. Toads live on land. Frogs have long back legs. Toads have small back legs.

◼ RI.1.1, RI.1.3

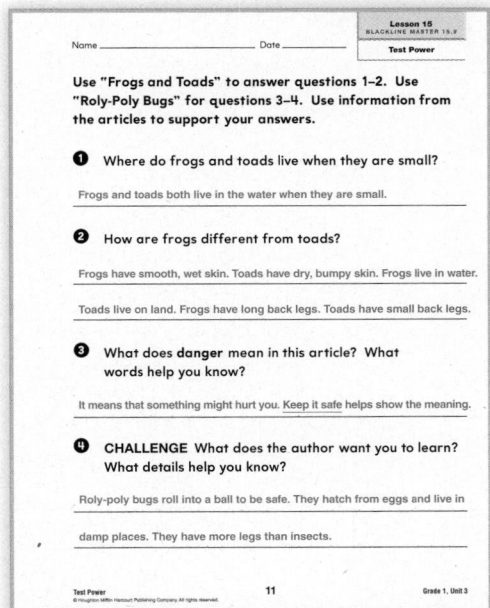

Blackline Master 15.9

Test Power (SB p. 197) • **T487**

3 *What does danger mean in this article? What words help you know?* "Danger" means that something might hurt you. "Keep it safe" helps show the meaning. ▰ RI.1.4, L.1.4a

4 **CHALLENGE** *What does the author want you to learn? What details help you know?* The author wants me to learn about roly-poly bugs. Roly-poly bugs roll into a ball to be safe. They hatch from eggs and live in damp places. The have more legs than insects. ▰ RI.1.1, RI.1.8

If time permits after children have read the articles and answered the questions, have them go back and check their answers. Tell children they should:

• Answer questions that they were unable to answer the first time.

• Make sure that their answers to the questions are correct.

• Review their answers and improve them, making sure they provide enough text evidence to support their answers.

Roly-Poly Bugs

A pill bug is a very small animal. It is also called a roly-poly. It can roll into a little ball that looks like a pill. This helps keep it safe from danger.

> **3** What does **danger** mean in this article? What words help you know?

Pill bugs hatch from eggs. They live in damp places. They live under leaves, rocks, or logs.

Some people think pill bugs are insects. They are not. Insects have six legs. Pill bugs have more. Pill bugs are in the same animal group as a crab!

> **4** What does the author want you to learn? What details help you know?

198

DAY 1

Differentiate
Phonics & Words to Know
- Long *i* (CVCe)
- *bird, both, eyes, fly, long, or, those, walk*

Vocabulary Reader
- *Animals*

Vocabulary Reader

DAY 2

Differentiate Comprehension
- Compare and Contrast
- Monitor/Clarify

DAY 3

Differentiate
Phonics & Fluency
- Digraphs *kn, wr, gn, mb*
- Intonation

Leveled Readers
- ⬤ *Making a Home*
- ▲ *All About Bats*
- ◼ *Bald Eagles*
- ◆ *Many Kinds of Bats*

Leveled Readers

DAY 4

Differentiate
Vocabulary Strategies
- Suffixes *-er, -est*

DAY 5

Options for Reteaching
- Phonics
- Vocabulary Strategies
- Comprehension

Literacy Centers

Independent Practice
- Word Study, T412
- Think and Write, T413
- Comprehension and Fluency, T412
- Digital Center, T413

Word Study

Think and Write

Comprehension and Fluency

Suggested Small Group Plan

Differentiated Instruction

Teacher-Led

	DAY 1 	DAY 2 	DAY 3
Struggling Readers	**Vocabulary Reader** *Animals*, Differentiated Instruction, p. T494 **Differentiate Phonics:** Long *i* (CVC*e*) p. T492	**Differentiate Comprehension:** Compare and Contrast; Monitor/Clarify Strategy, p. T496 **Reread** *The Nest*, p. T445	**Leveled Reader** *Making a Home*, p. T500 **Differentiate Phonics:** Digraphs *kn*, *wr*, *gn*, *mb*, p. T498 
On Level	**Vocabulary Reader** *Animals*, Differentiated Instruction, p. T494	**Differentiate Comprehension:** Compare and Contrast; Monitor/Clarify Strategy, p. T496 **Reread** *The Nest*, p. T445	**Leveled Reader** *All About Bats*, p. T501 **Differentiate Fluency:** Intonation, p. T499 
Advanced	**Vocabulary Reader** *Animals*, Differentiated Instruction, p. T495	**Differentiate Comprehension:** Compare and Contrast; Monitor/Clarify Strategy, p. T497	**Leveled Reader** *Bald Eagles*, p. T502 **Differentiate Fluency:** Intonation, p. T499 
English Language Learners	**Vocabulary Reader** *Animals*, Differentiated Instruction, p. T495 **Differentiate Words to Know** Using Context Cards, p. T493	**Differentiate Comprehension:** Compare and Contrast; Monitor/Clarify Strategy, p. T497 **Reread** *The Nest*, p. T445	**Leveled Reader** *Many Kinds of Bats*, p. T503 **Differentiate Fluency:** Intonation, p. T499 

What are my other kids doing?

	DAY 1	DAY 2	DAY 3
Struggling Readers	**Word Building:** Build and read Spelling Words using Letter Cards **Complete** Leveled Practice, SR15.1–SR15.2	**Words to Know:** Partners practice reading Context Cards **Reread** *Mike's Bike* and *The Nest* **Complete** Leveled Practice, SR15.3	**Reread:** Partners read *Making a Home* **Complete** Leveled Practice, SR15.4
On Level	**Word Building:** Build and read Words to Know using Letter Cards	**Words to Know:** Practice reading Context Cards **Reread** *Mike's Bike* and *The Nest* 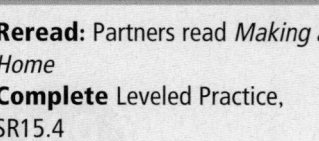	**Reread:** Partners read *All About Bats*
Advanced	**Context Cards:** Assign Talk It Over activities **Complete** Leveled Practice, A15.1–A15.2 	**Reread:** Partners read *Animal Groups* **Complete** Leveled Practice, A15.3 	**Reread** *Bald Eagles* **Complete** Leveled Practice, A15.4
English Language Learners	**Listen** to Audio of *Animal Groups* **Complete** Leveled Practice, ELL15.1–ELL15.2	**Listen:** Follow along with Audio of *Animal Groups* **Retell:** Partners retell *Animal Groups* using Retelling Cards **Complete** Leveled Practice, ELL15.3	**Reread:** Partners read *Many Kinds of Bats* **Listen** to Audio of *Animal Picnic* **Complete** Leveled Practice, ELL15.4

For Strategic Intervention for this lesson, see pp. S42–S51.

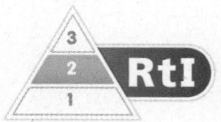

DAY 4

Differentiate Vocabulary
Strategies: Suffixes *-er*, *-est*, p. T504
Reread *Kite Time*, p. T467

Differentiate Vocabulary
Strategies: Suffixes *-er*, *-est*, p. T504
Reread *Kite Time*, p. T467

Differentiate Vocabulary
Strategies: Suffixes *-er*, *-est*, p. T505

Differentiate Vocabulary
Strategies: Suffixes *-er*, *-est*, p. T505
Reread *Kite Time*, p. T467

Reread: Partners read *Kite Time*
Listen to Audio of *Animal Picnic*

Reread *Kite Time*

Reread: Partners read
Animal Picnic

Listen to Audio of *Animal Picnic*
Reread: Partners read *The Nice Vet*

DAY 5

Options for Reteaching,
pp. T506–T507
Reread one of this week's Decodable
Reader selections.

Options for Reteaching,
pp. T506–T507
Reread one of this week's Decodable
Reader selections.

Options for Reteaching,
pp. T506–T507
Reread one of this week's Decodable
Reader selections.

Options for Reteaching,
pp. T506–T507
Reread one of this week's Decodable
Reader selections.

Reread: Choose among this week's
stories
• Complete and share Literacy Center
activities

Reread: Choose among this week's
stories
• Complete and share Literacy Center
activities

Reread: Choose among this week's
stories
• Complete and share Literacy Center
activities

Reread: Choose among this week's
stories
• Complete and share Literacy Center
activities

Weekly To-Do List

This Weekly To-Do List helps children
see their own progress and move on
to additional activities independently.

Differentiate Phonics and Words to Know

Struggling Readers

Phonemic Awareness/Phonics

Long *i* (CVC*e*)

I DO IT

- Show **Picture Card** *kite*. Emphasize the long *i* sound, /ī/.

  Use **Instructional Routine 2** to model how to blend *kite*.

- Write and underline *i_e*. *This pattern lets you know that the letter* i *stands for the long* i *sound, /ī/.*

- Review long *i* words with the **Decodable Reader** selection *Mike's Bike*.

WE DO IT

- Use **Instructional Routine 2** and the *ice cream* card to review the *i_e* spelling for /ī/.

- Ask children to name the /ī/ word in each of the following pairs: *bit, bite, bite; dime, dim, dime; pine, pin, pine.*

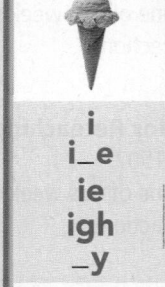

i
i_e
ie
igh
_y

- Help children blend the sounds to read the words below. Use the **Corrective Feedback** if children need additional help.

- Discuss the meanings of any unfamiliar words with children.

dive	nice	side	fine
mine	stripe	pride	tribe

YOU DO IT

- Have partners take turns using **Letter Cards** to create the following short *i* words: *bit, dim, fin, kit,* and *pin.* Then have partners add the letter card *e* to the end of each word to create these words: *bite, dime, fine, kite,* and *pine.*

- Have children record the words in two separate lists and read the lists to the group.

DAILY ASSESSMENT  **RtI** 3 2 1

Corrective Feedback Work with children to correct errors, following the model below.

Phonics Error:
A child reads *fine* as *fin.*

Correct the error. Say the word and its vowel sound. *The word is* fine; *the* i-consonant-e *pattern means that the letter* i *stands for the sound /ī/.*

Model as you touch the letters. *I'll blend /f/ /ī/ /n/. What is the word?* fine

Check *You blend. /f/ /ī/ /n/ What is the word?* fine

Reinforce Go back three or four words and have children continue reading. Make note of errors and review those words during tomorrow's lesson.

Words to Know

- Write this week's Words to Know on the board and read them aloud.
- Use the backs of the **Vocabulary in Context Cards** to review the explanations of the words.
- Tell children that they will see these words in this week's reading selections.
- Have children look for the words in the selection *Animal Groups*.

☑ **WORDS TO KNOW**

bird	long
both	or
eyes	those
fly	walk

Vocabulary in Context Cards

Beginning

- Read each word as you point to it on the **Vocabulary in Context Cards**, and have children repeat after you. Then point to the pictures and have children say the words.

Low Intermediate

- Have children say each word as you point to it and its picture. Have them work in pairs to repeat the activity.

High Intermediate

- Have children work with a partner. The first partner points to a picture and the other says the word. Then they switch roles and repeat the activity.

Proficient

- Have partners pick a few **Vocabulary in Context Cards**. Ask partners to take turns asking and answering questions about the pictures.

On Level

Have partners show each other the **Vocabulary in Context Cards** for this week's words and use each word in an oral sentence.

Advanced

Have partners use the **Vocabulary in Context Cards** for this week's words to give clues about each word for the other to guess. Ask them to write each word they guess correctly.

Vocabulary Reader
Animals

Struggling Readers

- Explain that different animals live in different places. Display pictures of an elephant, bear, and whale. Ask children yes and no questions such as *Does a whale have a tail?*

- Preview the selection and have children take a picture walk. Have them frame the words *whale*, *elephant*, and *bird*.

- Read the selection aloud and have children echo-read after you. Then have children take turns reading a page aloud. Guide them to use context clues when they come to an unfamiliar word (or phrase).

- Read the Words to Know and have children repeat. Have partners find *bird* and *long* in the selection. Then ask children to work together to complete the Responding page. Read aloud the directions on **Blackline Master 15.4** and guide children to complete it.

On Level

- Ask children to tell what they know about animals that live in the forest and in the water. Call attention to any words they use that are Words to Know. Then preview the pictures in the selection and have children identify the animals they see.

- Remind children that context clues can help them figure out unfamiliar words (or phrases) in a sentence.

- Read the selection aloud as children follow along. Then ask children to read two pages to a partner. Remind them to use context clues when they come to an unfamiliar word (or phrase).

- Then assign the Responding page and **Blackline Master 15.4**. Review the directions with children and have them discuss their responses with a partner.

Summary
This book explores a whale, an elephant, a parrot, and a child and shows where they live and what they look like.

☑ **WORDS TO KNOW**

bird	long
both	or
eyes	those
fly	walk

Go Digital
• Vocabulary Reader Online
• Literacy and Language Guide
• Context Cards

COMMON CORE

DAY 1

Advanced

- Have children preview the selection and tell what they see happening on each page. Have them frame words they recognize.

- Before reading, remind children to use context clues to help them determine the meaning of unknown words (or phrases).

- Ask alternate children to read pages of the selection aloud. Have children stop and use context clues together when they see unfamiliar words (or phrases).

- Review the Words to Know and have children use them to discuss the selection. Then assign the Responding page and **Blackline Master 15.4**. For the Talk About It activity, remind children to include facts and details to support their ideas.

ELL English Language Learners

Beginning

Ask children questions about each animal and have them look at the photographs to find the answers. For example, *Are elephants big? Do they have four legs? Do they have a trunk?* Have children use complete sentences to answer the questions.

Low Intermediate

Create a forest on butcher paper and have children draw animals that live there. Then have them label the animals and read the labels aloud.

High Intermediate

Have children compare and contrast two of the animals in the book. Have them use a Venn diagram to make their comparisons.

Proficient

Have children draw a bear, a whale, and a bird. Then have them label different parts of each animal, such as nose, mouth, claws, fur, wing, and so on. Ask them to share their pictures with others.

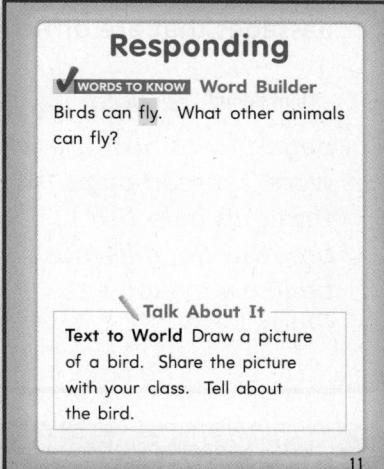

Animals, p. 11

Blackline Master 15.4

Differentiate Comprehension

Compare and Contrast; Monitor/Clarify

Struggling Readers

I DO IT

- Use **Projectable S3** to review the Monitor/Clarify strategy.
- Display pages 168–169 of *Animal Groups*.
- Tell children that you always think about the words, sentences, or passages that are difficult.

> **Think Aloud** *When I read these pages, I was not sure what gills were. I reread page 168. I read that gills help fish breathe. So, gills must be like a person's lungs.*

WE DO IT

- Have children page through *Animal Groups*.
- Have them identify things they do not understand.
- Have children assist each other with concepts that need to be clarified for better comprehension.
- Have children continue to monitor and clarify their understanding while identifying what is the same and different between two animal groups.

YOU DO IT

- Write the following words on the board: *scales, fin, eye, tail, leg, gill, mouth*.
- Have children draw a picture of a fish and a reptile.
- Have them use one of the words from the board to label something on each animal.
- Have them tell how the animals are alike and different.

On Level

I DO IT

- Use **Projectable S3** to review the Monitor/Clarify strategy.
- Tell children to remember to always think about the words, sentences, or passages that are difficult.
- Read aloud pp. 171–173 of *Animal Groups*.

> **Think Aloud** *When I was reading page 171, I was not sure what scales meant. Then I read that reptiles have "scales" on their skin. So, now I know that scales are the small circles found on reptile skin.*

WE DO IT

- Remind children to use strategies to help them clarify parts of the selection they do not understand.
- On the board, write the following:

> - I do not know this word.
> - I need help with this sentence.
> - I don't understand the part where . . .
> - I can't figure out . . .

- Have children page through *Animal Groups*. Use the diagram to find features only reptiles have and features only amphibians have.

YOU DO IT

- Have children use a Venn diagram to compare and contrast "Fish" and another animal group of their choice.
- Have them write a sentence about how the animal groups are the same and a sentence about how they are different under the Venn diagram.

Advanced

I DO IT

- Explain that readers can better understand what they read if they use strategies to figure out what does not make sense.

- Display pp. 168–169. Read the pages aloud. *When I saw the words* gills, fins, *and* tails, *I had to look at the picture to figure out what these things were. I read that the fish use gills to breathe, but I wanted to see what gills look like. Then I wanted to find the fins and the tails on the fish.*

WE DO IT

- Have children read *Animal Groups*.

- Have them identify any struggles they had while reading.

- Ask children to tell what struggles they had and how they helped themselves answer their questions.

- Discuss how amphibians and mammals are alike and different. Ask children what other topics they would like to compare and contrast from the text.

YOU DO IT

- Have children tell how they are like an animal group of their choice (fish, amphibian, reptile, or bird).

- Ask them to create another Venn diagram to compare and contrast themselves with an animal group.

- Have children write one sentence about how they are the same and several sentences about how they are different under the Venn diagram.

ELL English Language Learners

Review the **Monitor/Clarify Strategy** and explain to children that good readers stop to make sure they understand everything as they read. Then use the following activities with children according to their level of English proficiency.

Beginning

- Use visuals to show how to compare and contrast pairs of objects. Remind children that comparing tells how things are alike, and contrasting tells how things are different. Display each pair and have children say whether they are the same or different.

Low Intermediate

- Display **Picture Cards** of pairs of animals. Have children compare and contrast the animals. Ask them to say one way the animals are alike and one way they are different.

High Intermediate

- Help children compare and contrast animal groups. Have them name the animal groups, suggest characteristics of each, and then say what is the same about the groups and what is different.

Proficient

- Have children work in pairs. Each partner will choose an animal to draw and describe. The partners should discuss how their animals are alike and different.

Differentiate Phonics and Fluency

Struggling Readers

Phonics

Digraphs *kn, wr, gn, mb*

I DO IT

- Write *knife* on the board, and read it aloud, knife.
- Use **Instructional Routine 2** to model blending *knife*.

- Underline the letters *kn*. *The letters* kn *stand for the sound* /n/ *at the beginning of* knife.
- Write *gnat* on the board, underlining the *gn*. *The letters* gn *can also stand for* /n/. *In* gnat, /n/ *is spelled* gn.
- Repeat for /r/ in *wrist* and /m/ in *thumb*.
- Preview words with digraphs *kn, wr, gn,* and *mb* in the **Decodable Reader** selection *Kite Time*.

WE DO IT

- Display **Picture Cards** *knife* and *thumb*. Have children match them to the words on the board.
- *What letters stand for the* /n/ *sound at the beginning of* knife? *kn What letters stand for the* /m/ *sound at the end of* thumb? *mb*
- Write the words *gnaw* and *write* on the board next to *wrist* and *thumb*. Have children match the words that begin with the same sound.
- *What letters stand for the* /r/ *sound at the beginning of* wrist *and* write? *wr What letters stand for the* /n/ *sound at the beginning of* gnat *and* gnaw? *gn*

YOU DO IT

- Have partners use **Letter Cards** for *kn, gn, wr,* and *mb* to finish these incomplete words:

  __ot   __ife   __at   __aw
  __ist   __ite   li__   cru__

- Have partners take turns using the letter cards to complete the words.
- Use the **Corrective Feedback** if children need additional help.

DAILY ASSESSMENT  RtI

Corrective Feedback
Use **Letter Cards** to model correct answers. *My word is* crumb. *I added* mb *to* cru___ *to make the* /m/ *sound in* crumb. **Guide children.** *What is the word?* crumb. *What letters stand for the* /m/ *sound at the end of* crumb? mb **Have children build the word again on their own and use it again in tomorrow's lesson.**

All Levels

Fluency

Intonation

I DO IT

- Write *Do you know how far some birds can fly? They can go from Canada to Florida. That is a long trip!*

- Model reading the sentences in a monotone voice. Then ask children to explain what was wrong with your reading.

- Use a Think Aloud based on children's answers.

> **Think Aloud** *I didn't read the way I speak. How do I know when to change my voice? I know punctuation marks offer clues. I see a question mark, a period, and an exclamation point. Each sentence should be read differently, because it has different punctuation.*

- Model reading the sentences correctly after thinking aloud.

WE DO IT

- Choose three sentences from a **Leveled Reader** and write them on the board. Each sentence should be an example of a different type of punctuation.

- Read the first sentence without intonation.

- Choose a child to read it correctly. Have the child explain how he or she knew how to read the sentence correctly.

- Repeat with the remaining two sentences.

YOU DO IT

- Present small groups of children with a page from a **Leveled Reader.**

- Have each child take turns reading the page.

- Remind children to practice intonation, or changing their voices to read the same way they speak.

- Monitor and provide **Corrective Feedback** as needed.

DAILY ASSESSMENT

Corrective Feedback
Use contrast to reinforce the idea of punctuation dictating intonation. Allow children to choose sentences in the **Leveled Reader.** Have them read the sentence aloud in a monotone voice, and then read it with exaggerated intonation.

Leveled Readers

☑ **TARGET SKILL**
Compare and Contrast

☑ **TARGET STRATEGY**
Monitor/Clarify

☑ **WORDS TO KNOW**

bird	long
both	or
eyes	those
fly	walk

Struggling Readers

 Making a Home

SUMMARY All animals have homes. The animals have homes that are suited for them—whether it's by the water, in the water, in a tree, or in a cave.

GENRE: INFORMATIONAL TEXT

Introducing the Text

- Review and discuss this week's Words to Know.

- Take a picture walk through *Making a Home*. Explain that this book shows how different homes are good places for animals to live.

- Review that two things can be the same or different in many ways. Children can use a Venn diagram to show these likenesses and differences.

Supporting the Reading

- **pp. 8–9** *How are crabs' and frogs' homes alike? How are they different?* *Sample answer: They are both near the water. Crabs' homes are near the sea and frogs' homes are by a pond.*

- **p. 10** *You want to know how all animals' homes are alike. What sentence would you read again to find out?* *Sample answer: The homes are good places to live!*

Discussing and Revisiting the Text

CRITICAL THINKING Read the top half of Responding, p. 11 in *Making a Home*.

- Have children discuss together how the bird and beaver homes are alike and different.

- Show children how to list the ways the bird and beaver homes are the same in the overlapping part of **Blackline Master 15.5**. Then have them list how the homes are different on the outside parts.

FLUENCY: INTONATION Model reading orally p. 10 to show children the correct way to intonate. Then have them choral-read along with you.

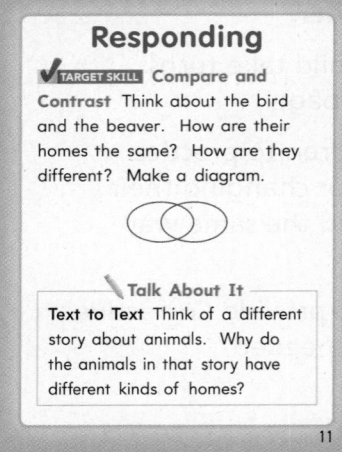

Making a Home, p. 11

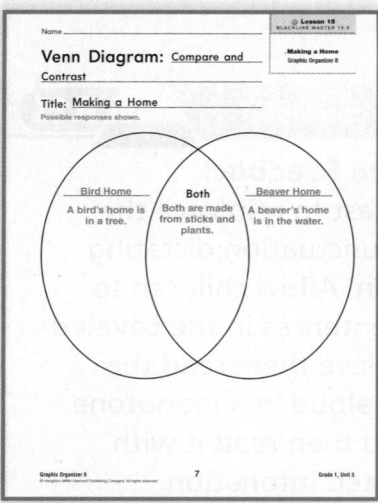

Blackline Master 15.5

On Level

 All About Bats

SUMMARY Bats fly like birds, but they don't have feathers or lay eggs. This book explores what bats eat, how they move, what they look like, how they fly, and where they live.

GENRE: INFORMATIONAL TEXT

Introducing the Text

• Review and discuss this week's Words to Know.

• Display a picture of a bat and ask children to tell what they know about the animal. Write their responses on the board.

• Review with children how they can compare and contrast two things. Tell them that a Venn diagram can help show how things are similar and different.

Supporting the Reading

• **p. 2** *How are bats and birds alike and different?* They both can fly, but birds have feathers and bats don't; birds lay eggs and bats don't.

• **p. 3** *How would you describe a bat?* They have wings with thin skin. They have long fingers and thumbs. *Look again at page 3. Did you leave anything out in your description?* Answers will vary.

Discussing and Revisiting the Text

CRITICAL THINKING Read the top half of Responding, p. 11 in *All About Bats*.

• Have partners tell how bats and birds are alike and different.

• Guide children to record the similarities in the overlapping part of **Blackline Master 15.6**. Have them record differences in the outside parts. Ask them to find more differences than the ones stated on page 2. Encourage them to use prior knowledge in their answers.

FLUENCY: INTONATION Model reading orally p. 4 to show children the proper way to intonate. Then have them echo-read to practice reading with correct intonation.

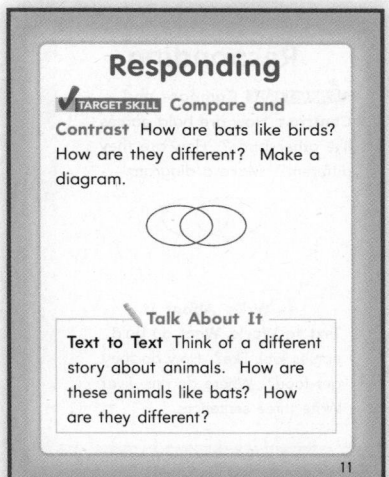

All About Bats, p. 11

Blackline Master 15.6

☑ TARGET SKILL
Compare and Contrast

☑ TARGET STRATEGY
Monitor/Clarify

☑ WORDS TO KNOW

bird	long
both	or
eyes	those
fly	walk

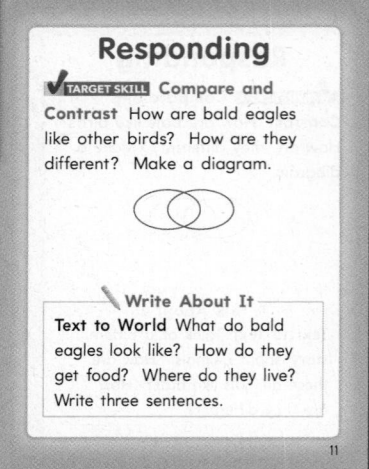

Responding

✓ TARGET SKILL Compare and Contrast How are bald eagles like other birds? How are they different? Make a diagram.

⬭⬭

Write About It
Text to World What do bald eagles look like? How do they get food? Where do they live? Write three sentences.

11

Bald Eagles, p. 11

Venn Diagram: Compare and Contrast

Title: Bald Eagles
Answers will vary. Possible answers:

Bald Eagles — have long wings, are heavy, hunt together, nests are big, are America's national bird

Both — have hollow bones, make nests, lay eggs and raise babies in a nest

Other Birds — are small, are light, nests are small

Blackline Master 15.7

Leveled Readers

Advanced

■ *Bald Eagles*

SUMMARY Bald eagles are strong hunters that live in all but one state of the United States. Their strength and freedom is symbolic of our country, so that is why it is our national bird.

GENRE: INFORMATIONAL TEXT

Introducing the Text

• Review and discuss this week's Words to Know.

• Explain that the bald eagle is our national bird. As they read, have them think about why our country would honor the bird in this way.

• As children read, have them compare and contrast the bald eagle to other birds they know.

Supporting the Reading

• **p. 3** *How is the bald eagle the same as and different from other birds?* Bald eagles have hollow bones like other birds, but they are much larger.

• **p. 4** *How does an eagle hunt for food?* They fly down and grab their prey. They also walk in water to catch fish. *Look at page 4. How well did you explain the text?* Answers will vary.

Discussing and Revisiting the Text

CRITICAL THINKING Have children read the top half of Responding, p. 11 in *Bald Eagles*.

• Have children compare a bald eagle to other birds they know about.

• Have children write the similarities and differences of bald eagles and other birds on **Blackline Master 15.7**.

FLUENCY: INTONATION Have children read aloud their favorite part of *Bald Eagles* to practice reading with intonation.

English Language Learners

Many Kinds of Bats

SUMMARY Bats come in many different colors and sizes, but they all have fur and fly like birds. This book explores what bats eat, where they live, and how they look.

GENRE: INFORMATIONAL TEXT

Introducing the Text

• Review and discuss this week's Words to Know.

• Take a picture walk through *Many Kinds of Bats* and have children describe each picture they see. Call out words in the text that are illustrated such as *bats, ears,* and *wing*.

• Remind children that they can compare two or more things to see how they are alike. They can contrast two or more things to see how they are different.

Supporting the Reading

• **p. 4** *How are all bats alike and different?* They all have soft fur, but they are different colors. They are different sizes, too.

• **pp. 8–9** *What do bats eat? Where can you find this information?* Bats eat insects or fruit. This information is on pages 8 and 9.

Discussing and Revisiting the Text

CRITICAL THINKING Help children read the top half of Responding, p. 11 in *Many Kinds of Bats*.

• Have children recall one way that bats and birds are alike. Then have them tell as many ways as they can how they are different.

• Guide children to write how birds and bats are alike and different by using **Blackline Master 15.8.**

FLUENCY: INTONATION Model reading orally p. 8 to show how to read with proper intonation. Then have children echo-read each sentence with you.

For more reading options, see ELL Lesson 15, pp. E42–E51.

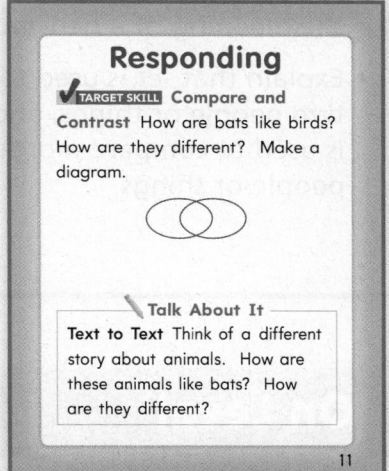

Responding

✓ **TARGET SKILL** **Compare and Contrast** How are bats like birds? How are they different? Make a diagram.

Talk About It
Text to Text Think of a different story about animals. How are these animals like bats? How are they different?

11

Many Kinds of Bats, p. 11

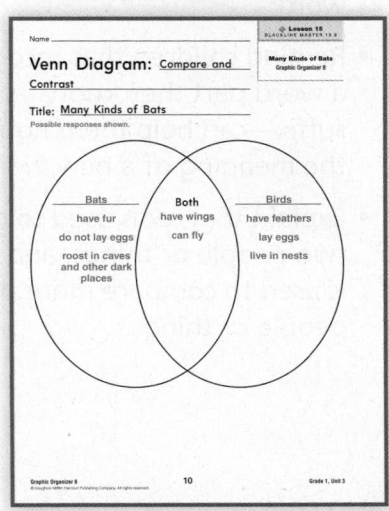

Blackline Master 15.8

Differentiate Vocabulary Strategies

Suffixes -er, -est

Struggling Readers

I DO IT

- Explain that a *suffix* is one or more letters that are added to the end of a word to make a new, related word.

- Tell children that recognizing a word part they know—such as a suffix—can help them understand the meaning of a new word.

- Explain that *-er* is used to compare two people or things, and that *-est* is used to compare more than two people or things.

WE DO IT

- Draw two lines on the board, one longer than the other. Write the following on the board: *This line is longer than that one.*

- Say, *Here's a word I don't know. To figure out its meaning, I can look for word parts I know.*

- Have children identify the suffix (-er). Cover the suffix and have children name the root word (long). Point out that the sentence is comparing the length of two lines. One of them is longer.

YOU DO IT

- Write the following sentences on the board: *Bill is taller than Jose. Erin is the fastest person on the team.* Underline *taller* and *fastest*.

- Have children work with partners to figure out the meanings of *taller* and *fastest*. Have them write the suffixes and tell how many things are being compared. Have them identify the root words.

- Challenge children to use the words in their own sentences.

On Level

I DO IT

- Explain that a *suffix* is one or more letters that are added to the end of a word to make a new, related word.

- Remind children that recognizing a word part they know—such as a suffix—can help them figure out the meaning of a new word.

- Explain that *-er* is used to compare two people or things, and that *-est* is used to compare more than two people or things.

WE DO IT

- Write the following sentence on the board: *Our dog is the smartest animal I know.* Underline *smartest*.

- Say, *Let's figure out the meaning of this word. We can look for word parts we know.*

- Have children identify the suffix (-est). Cover the suffix and have children name the root word (smart). Ask children how many dogs the sentence is comparing (more than two).

- Have students use the word *smartest* in their own sentences.

YOU DO IT

- Write the following sentences on the board: *Which is the shorter straw? This is the cleanest plate.* Underline *shorter* and *cleanest*.

- Have children analyze the meanings of *shorter* and *cleanest*. Have them write the suffixes and tell how many things are being compared. Have them identify the root words.

- Have children write their own sentences with *shorter* and *cleanest*.

Advanced

I DO IT

- Remind children that a *suffix* is one or more letters added to the end of a word to make a new, related word.

- Explain that *-er* is used to compare two people or things, and that *-est* is used to compare more than two people or things.

- The word endings *-er* and *-est* are not always suffixes. Some words simply end with the letters *-er* or *-est*. Write the following on the board: *test, chapter*.

WE DO IT

- Write the following sentences on the board: *A <u>rooster</u> woke me up. It was the <u>loudest</u> bird on the farm.*

- Point out that the word *rooster* ends with *-er*. Say, *But this -er isn't a suffix. It's part of the word* rooster. Have volunteers tell the meaning of *rooster*.

- Have children identify the suffix of *loudest*, name the root word, and tell how many are being compared.

- Have students use the word *loudest* in their own sentences.

YOU DO IT

- Write the following sentences on the board: *This room is quieter. My mom is the greatest cook I know.*

- Have children analyze the meanings of *quieter* and *greatest*. Have them write the suffixes and tell how many things are being compared, and identify the root words.

- Challenge children to write their own sentences with *quieter* and *greatest*.

ELL English Language Learners

Group English Language Learners according to language proficiency.

Beginning

- Remind children that a *suffix* is one or more letters added to the end of a word to make a new, related word.

- Explain that *-er* is used to compare two people or things, and that *-est* is used to compare more than two people or things.

- Explain that the endings *-er* and *-est* are not always suffixes. Some words, such as *test* and *chapter*, simply end with the letters *-er* or *-est*.

Low Intermediate

- Explain that the ending *-er* is used to compare two people or things, and that *-est* is used to compare more than two people or things.

- Explain that the endings *-er* and *-est* are not always suffixes.

- Write *bigger*, *chapter*, *faster*, *whitest*, and *test* on the board. Have children name the words in which *-er* and *-est* are suffixes.

High Intermediate

- Write *bigger* and *softer* on the board.

- Have the class form sentences using those words.

- Repeat with *biggest* and *softest*.

Proficient

- Have partners compare their favorite story characters. Have them tell why they are their favorite ones.

- Help them use the comparative and superlative suffixes in their conversation.

Options for Reteaching

Reteach Phonics

Long *i* (CVC*e*)

I DO IT

- Tell children that you will review some words that will help them read the **Decodable Reader** selection *Kite Time*.

  Review **Instructional Routine 3**. Remind children that they have been reading long *i* words this week.

- Review this week's Words to Know *bird*, *both*, *eyes*, *fly*, *long*, *or*, *those*, and *walk*.

- Have children open to p. 117 of *Kite Time*.

WE DO IT

- Write *time* on the board.

- Help children find the word *time* on the page.

- Model how to decode *time* step by step.

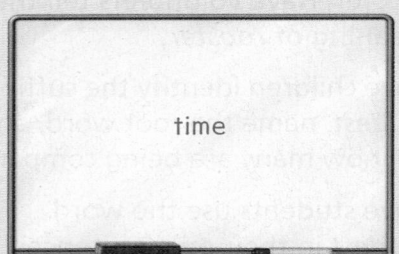

YOU DO IT

- Have partners work together to read *Kite Time*.

- Use the **Corrective Feedback** on p. T492 if children need additional help.

Kite Time
by Zach Mathews
illustrated by Chi Chung

The wind is up. It's time to fly a kite. It's kite time! It's fun time!

117

Reteach Phonics

Digraphs *kn, wr, gn, mb*

I DO IT

- Tell children that you will review some words that will help them read the **Decodable Reader** story *Kite Time*.

  Review **Instructional Routine 3**. Remind children that they have been reading *kn*, *wr*, *gn*, and *mb* words this week.

- Review this week's Words to Know *bird*, *both*, *eyes*, *fly*, *long*, *or*, *those*, and *walk*.

- Have children open to p. 118 of *Kite Time*.

WE DO IT

- Write *knock* on the board.

- Help children find the word *knock* on the page.

- Model how to decode *knock* step by step.

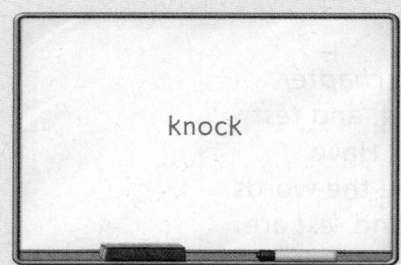

YOU DO IT

- Have partners work together to read *Kite Time*.

- Use the **Corrective Feedback** on p. T498 if children need additional help.

A kite can ride on the wind. It can glide up on the wind. Wind takes a kite up and up. Wind can knock it down, too.

118

Reteach Vocabulary Strategies

Suffixes -er, -est

I DO IT

- Remind children that the suffix -er is used to compare two people or things, and that the suffix -est is used to compare more than two people or things.

- Remind children that recognizing a word part they know—such as a suffix—can help them figure out the meaning of a new word.

WE DO IT

- Display **Projectable 15.7**. Read the second sentence aloud.

- Point to *cleaner*.

> **Think Aloud** *I don't recognize this word. If I can find some word parts I know, I might be able to figure out what it means. It looks like it has a suffix.*

- Have a volunteer identify the suffix. Write -er in the chart. Have another volunteer name the root word. Write *clean* in the chart. Have children discuss what is being compared. Make sure everyone understands that only two rooms are being compared. Complete the row for *cleaner* by writing what is being compared.

YOU DO IT

- Have children work with their partners to analyze the other boldface words in **Projectable 15.7**. They should write each word's suffix and root word and tell how many things are being compared.

- Challenge children to write their own sentences using the boldface words.

Reteach Comprehension Skill

Compare and Contrast

I DO IT

- Remind children that to compare things is to find ways they are the same. To contrast things is to find ways they are different.

WE DO IT

- Have children read aloud **Student Book** pp. 176–182.

- Model how to compare and contrast birds and mammals.

> **Think Aloud** *The author writes that birds have feathers, wings, and eyes on the side of their faces. Many can fly. They hatch from eggs. He writes that mammals have hair and come in many shapes and sizes. They make milk for their babies. Both have eyes and both have babies.*

- Help volunteers identify other similarities and differences between mammals and birds.

YOU DO IT

- Distribute **Graphic Organizer 8: Venn Diagram**.

- Have children list similarities about birds and mammals in the center and differences on either side. *Birds: feathers, wings, fly, eyes on side of face, hatch from eggs. Both: animals, some live on land, some run, some swim. Mammals: hair, make milk for babies*

- Have children work in pairs to complete the graphic organizer.

- Review the completed graphic organizers together.

Teacher Notes

Lesson 11

Pup's Bath

(Write-In Reader pages 105–110)

Words to Know: far, little, water, where

Blend and Segment Phonemes

Digraph *th*; Endings *-s*, *-es*, *-ed*, *-ing*; Phonogram *-ath*

Author's Purpose

Lesson 12

Al and Lop

(Write-In Reader pages 115–120)

Words to Know: never, off, own, very

Blend and Segment Phonemes; Substitute Initial Phonemes

Digraphs *ch*, *tch*; Possessive *'s*; Phonogram *-atch*

Sequence of Events

Lesson 13

Max Has His Bath

(Write-In Reader pages 125–130)

Words to Know: down, goes, open, yellow

Substitute Initial Phonemes; Blend and Segment Phonemes

Digraphs *sh*, *wh*, *ph*; Contractions with *'s*, *n't*; Phonogram *-ash*

Cause and Effect

Lesson 14

Jake's Best Race

(Write-In Reader pages 135–140)

Words to Know: over, three, two, watch

Identify Medial Phonemes; Substitute Medial Phonemes

Long *a* (CVCe); Soft *c*, *g*, *dge*; Phonograms *-ake*, *-ace*

Conclusions

Lesson 15

Cats

(Write-In Reader pages 145–150)

Words to Know: eyes, long, or, walk

Substitute Medial Phonemes; Identify Medial Phonemes

Long *i* (CVCe); Digraphs *kn*, *wr*, *gn*, *mb*; Phonograms *-ine*, *-ite*

Compare and Contrast

INTRODUCE THE WRITE-IN READER

"Be a Reading Detective!"

Write-In Reader pages ii-iii

- Have children open their **Write-In Readers** to pages ii-iii.

- Point out that a police detective looks for clues to solve a crime. A reading detective looks for clues to understand a story or a nonfiction selection.

- Explain that looking for clues can make reading easier and more fun.

- Read page ii with children. Say, *What questions will you think about when you read?* (Who? Where? When? What? Why?) *Remember to look for clues to answer the questions.*

TRY IT!

- Read the first part of page iii with children. Say, *What clues are you going to look for as you read?* (clues that answer the questions *Who? Where?* and *When?*)

- Then read the passage as children listen for clues.

- Discuss the answers to the questions. If children have difficulty, reread the passage, and have volunteers point to the places where clues can be found.

💬 Classroom Collaboration

- Use the question at the bottom of page iii to discuss the clues children found and how they helped them answer the questions.

- Explain that children will be reading detectives as they read each selection in the **Write-In Reader**.

RETURN TO THE ANCHOR TEXT

At the end of each lesson, children will return to the Anchor Text and look for clues to deepen their understanding. (See the "A" and "B" pages at the end of each lesson in the **Write-In Reader**.)

SHARE OBJECTIVES

- Blend and segment words.
- Read words with digraph *th*.
- Read High-Frequency Words in context.

MATERIALS

Sound/Spelling Card: *thumb*

Write-In Reader Vol. 1 pages 102–103

Context Cards: *far, little, water, where*

Phonemic Awareness

Blend and Segment

- Say, *First, I'll say the sounds in a word, then I will blend the sounds and say the word. Then I will say the sounds again:* /th/ /ĭ/ /k/, thick, /th/ /ĭ/ /k/.

- Have children say /th/ /ĭ/ /k/, *thick*, /th/ /ĭ/ /k/ with you.

- Have children say /th/ /ĭ/ /k/, *thick*, /th/ /ĭ/ /k/ on their own.

- Continue, using the following words:

/m/ /ŭ/ /ch/	much	/m/ /ŭ/ /ch/
/m/ /ā/ /th/	math	/m/ /ā/ /th/
/th/ /ĭ/ /n/	thin	/th/ /ĭ/ /n/

- Correct errors by repeating the process. ◼ **RF.1.2b, RF.1.2d**

RETEACH

Phonics: Digraph *th*

Sound/Spelling Card

- Display the **Sound/Spelling Card** for *thumb*. Say the word, and ask, *What sound do you hear at the beginning of thumb?* (/th/) Point to *th* and teach that *th* stands for /th/. Have children say /th/ several times.

- Write the following words on the board or on a pad:

thin	thick	bath	Beth	math	with

- Point under the *th*. Have children say the sounds, and then blend the sounds to read the word.

- Correct errors by modeling how to sound out the word.
  ◼ **RF.1.3a**

COMMON CORE **RF.1.2b** orally produce single-syllable words by blending sounds; **RF.1.2d** segment spoken single-syllable words into their complete sequence of individual sounds; **RF.1.3a** know the spelling-sound correspondences for common consonant digraphs; **RF.1.3g** recognize and read irregularly spelled words; **SL.1.1a** follow rules for discussions

Talk About It

- Ask children to think about creatures that live under the sea. Ask, *What do you know about sea animals?*

- Then ask, *What would you do if you wanted to learn more?* Have children suggest sources of information. Record their ideas on the board or on a pad. Ask questions such as:

    Where could you read about sharks?
    Have you ever seen a TV show about the ocean? **SL.1.1a**

RETEACH

Words to Know

Write-In Reader Vol. 1 pages 102–103

- Introduce *Sea Animals.* Ask children to look at the photographs and guess what these pages are about.

- Discuss each photograph, asking questions such as *What do you see in this picture? Where was this picture taken? What are all these pictures about?*

- Read each sentence aloud with children as they point to each word. Ask what the highlighted word in each sentence means. See suggested definitions in the right-hand column. Then have children write the target word.

- Have children take turns rereading each sentence. Then have them choral read the words in the Words to Know box with you. **RF.1.3g**

[**Quick Check** **Words to Know**]

Have children use one of the Words to Know in a sentence.

✓ WORDS TO KNOW

Far means a long distance between two places.

Little means a small amount of something, or to be small in size.

Water is what is in oceans, lakes, and rivers. It comes out of the faucet in a sink.

Where means the spot that someone or something is in.

DAILY FLUENCY

Build automaticity by using **Context Cards** or word lists on display. Point to the words in any order and have children read them aloud. Continue until children can read all words fluently.

DAY 2

Warm Up

Words to Know

far, little, water, where

Distribute the **Context Cards** to children. Include *far, little, water,* and *where.* Have partners practice reading the words. Then ask each child to use one word in a sentence. For a challenge, ask if anyone can use two words in just one sentence. ⬤ RF.1.3g

---

REVIEW

Phonics: Digraph *th*

Write-In Reader Vol. 1 page 104

- Introduce the **Write-In Reader.** Have children choral read the words in the word box. Have them identify the last two letters in each word. Ask, *What sound do these letters stand for?* (/th/) Then direct their attention to the images in the first row.

- Say, *Look at the pictures in the first row. Point to each one as I name it.* (moth, path) Then have children say the name of each object together.

- Follow the same procedure in the second row. (bath, math)

- Assign children to work on their own, writing the correct word below each object.

- Check children's work. If any children have written the incorrect word, determine whether the misunderstanding results from being unable to name the pictured objects or from being unable to read the words. ⬤ RF.1.3a

Teacher Read Aloud

Leveled Reader: *The Amazing Octopus*

Leveled Reader

- Use the **Think Aloud** to introduce author's purpose. Tell children that you are going to read aloud a story called *The Amazing Octopus*.

Think Aloud *As I read to you, think about the story. What kind of story is this? What reasons did the author have for writing it?*

- Read the story aloud. Ask questions such as:

After page 2: *What does an octopus use its arms for?* (to crawl on the ocean floor) *What does* crawl *mean?* (to move slowly or to creep)

After page 3: *What was this section mostly about?* (different ways an octopus moves around) *What is this story about?* (what an octopus is like)

After page 4: *What is an octopus's arm like?* (It is long and has little cups that can stick to things.) *I just read, "The little cups on their arms can grip the food that they find." What does* grip *mean?* (to hold onto)

After page 7: *Why does an octopus change color?* (to hide, or to show how it feels)

After page 8: *An octopus has no shell. Why is this helpful?* (It can squeeze into small places to hide.) *What does* squeeze *mean?* (to squish down and make yourself little)

After page 10: *Why did the author write this story?* (to teach us about the octopus) *What did you learn from this story?* (Answers will vary.) ▬ **SL.1.1c, SL.1.2**

Quick Check | **Comprehension**

Ask, *Do you think the author is more likely to be a teacher or a farmer? Tell why.*

ORAL VOCABULARY

- crawl
- grip
- squeeze

DAILY FLUENCY

Build automaticity by using **Context Cards** or word lists on display. Point to the words in any order and have children read them aloud. Continue until children can read all words fluently.

SHARE OBJECTIVES

- Blend and segment words.
- Read words with inflected endings.
- Read to apply comprehension skills.

MATERIALS

Write-In Reader Vol. 1 pages 105–110

TERMS ABOUT READING/ LANGUAGE ARTS

base word

Warm Up

Phonemic Awareness

Blend and Segment

- Say, *First, I'll say the sounds in a word, then I'll say the word. Then I will say the sounds again: /s/ /m/ /ī/ /l/, smile, /s/ /m/ /ī/ /l/.*

- Have children say /s/ /m/ /ī/ /l/, smile, /s/ /m/ /ī/ /l/ with you.

- Have children say /s/ /m/ /ī/ /l/, smile, /s/ /m/ /ī/ /l/ on their own.

- Continue, using the following words:

/ch/ /ē/ /p/	cheep	/ch/ /ē/ /p/
/t/ /ē/ /th/	teeth	/t/ /ē/ /th/
/d/ /r/ /ō/ /v/	drove	/d/ /r/ /ō/ /v/

- Correct errors by repeating the process. ▬ **RF.1.2b, RF.1.2d**

RETEACH

Phonics: Inflected Endings

- Write *-s, -es, -ed,* and *-ing* on the board or on a pad. Teach that when a word ends in *-s, -es, -ed,* or *-ing*, we find the base word first, then read the word with the ending.

- Write the following words on the board or on a pad:

| runs | dresses | dressed | jumped | jumping |

- Point under *run*. Say *run*, then say *runs*. Have children say *run* and *runs* with you as you point under them. Finally, have children read *run* and *runs* on their own.

- Follow the same procedure with the remaining words and endings.

- Correct errors by repeating the process. ▬ **RF.1.3f**

COMMON CORE **RL.1.1** ask and answer questions about key details; **RL.1.10** read prose and poetry; **RF.1.2b** orally produce single-syllable words by blending sounds; **RF.1.2d** segment spoken single-syllable words into their complete sequence of individual sounds; **RF.1.3f** read words with inflectional endings

READ

Pup's Bath

Write-In Reader Vol. 1 pages 105–110

Preview *Pup's Bath* using the **Think Aloud** to reteach author's purpose.

Think Aloud *Authors write for many different reasons. Sometimes they write to make us laugh. Sometimes they write to teach us something. As you read, think about why the author wrote this story. What was her purpose for writing it?*

READ

Have children choral read the story for accuracy. If they mispronounce or hesitate over a word, stop the reading and tell the class the correct word. Have all children repeat the word, and then continue reading from the beginning of the sentence.

REREAD

Reread the story with children. Use the following questions to determine children's understanding of the selection.

After page 105: *Where is Pup? What is he doing?* (He is in the bath-tub. He is taking a bath.)

After page 106: *Where is Pup now?* (underwater) *What does he see?* (He sees fish and a little boat.)

After page 107: *What is Pup looking at?* (a turtle) *Does it seem like he likes the turtle?* (No, he looks scared.) *Think about the art on these pages. Does the story seem real or made-up?* (made-up) If students have difficulty answering this, ask *Does the art look more like cartoons or like photographs?*

After page 109: *Reread the first line on this page.* (Then Pup sat up.) *Where was Pup this whole time?* (in his bathtub) *Why do you think that the author wrote this story?* (for fun) If students have trouble answering this, ask, *Do you think this story was written to teach you something? Or was it written so that you would have fun reading it?* **RL.1.1, RL.1.10**

Quick Check | Comprehension

Ask, *Do you think Pup's trip was real or not real? Tell why.*

DAILY FLUENCY

Build automaticity by using **Context Cards** or word lists on display. Point to the words in any order and have children read them aloud. Continue until children can read all words fluently.

SHARE OBJECTIVES

- Read and use High-Frequency Words.
- Build a word family using the phonogram -ath.
- Review decodable story to build fluency and comprehension.

MATERIALS

Context Cards: blue, cold, far, little, live, their, water, where

Letter Cards

Write-In Reader Vol. 1 pages 105–111

TERMS ABOUT READING/ LANGUAGE ARTS

comma   punctuation

☑ WORDS TO KNOW

Blue is a color. The sky is **blue**.

Cold means to have a low temperature.

Live means to breathe, eat, and grow. It also means to have a home.

Their is a word that shows that something belongs to a group.

COMMON CORE   **RL.1.1** ask and answer questions about key details; **RF.1.3b** decode regularly spelled one-syllable words; **RF.1.3g** recognize and read irregularly spelled words; **RF.1.4a** read on-level text with purpose and understanding

Warm Up

Words to Know

blue, cold, far, little, live, their, water, where

- Distribute the **Context Cards** to children. Include *blue, cold, far, little, live, their, water,* and *where.*
- Have children practice reading the words. Then challenge children to use as many of these words as possible in one sentence. 🔊 **RF.1.3g**

Quick Check | Words to Know

Ask each child to use one of the week's words in a sentence.

RETEACH

Phonics: Phonogram -ath

Letter Cards

- Create the phonogram -ath with the **Letter Cards**.
- Model using additional **Letter Cards** to add one or two letters in front of -ath to create words.
- Challenge children to create as many words as they can by adding one or two letters in front of the phonogram -ath. Record words on the board or on a pad. If children create nonsense words, say, *That's not a real word, but we can read it anyway.*
- Have children read the list of words. 🔊 **RF.1.3b**

a   t   h

Possible Words

bath	path	math

RETEACH

Fluency: Commas

Write-In Reader Vol. 1 page 108

- Explain that you are going to read a page in two different ways. Children will listen and give you some tips after each reading. First, read page 108 quickly, ignoring the commas. Ask, *What do you think about my first reading?* Encourage feedback.

- Point out the commas on this page. Say, *Commas are one kind of punctuation, or marks, that we see in writing. Commas can help readers break sentences into chunks. This makes stories easier to follow and understand.*

- Model how to use commas to guide pacing. Have children reread page 108, paying attention to the commas. **RF.1.4a**

Look Back and Respond

Write-In Reader Vol. 1 pages 105–111

Read aloud each question and the answer choices with children. Help children find answers using the suggestions below. Model how to look back at the story to find the answer.

1. What is this text for? (to tell a story) *What did you enjoy about this story?* (Answers will vary.) *Were the characters real or made-up?* (They were made-up. It was a story about a puppy who talks.)

2. What is the story about? (Pup's bath time) *Think about the story. Did you learn anything about how to keep clean?* (no)

3. What scares Pup? (a big turtle) *On what page does Pup get scared?* (page 107) *What is he looking at?* (the smiling turtle)

Turn and Talk 4. Have children talk about what they read. Ask questions such as *What kinds of animals did Pup see? What other things were there?* Ask for volunteers and write several responses on the board. Then have the children draw or write their responses. **RL.1.1**

DAILY FLUENCY

Build automaticity by using **Context Cards** or word lists on display. Point to the words in any order and have children read them aloud. Continue until children can read all words fluently.

SHARE OBJECTIVES

- Blend and segment words.
- Read words with *ch* and *tch*.
- Apply the author's purpose skill to real life and reading.

MATERIALS

Sound/Spelling Card: *chick*

Word Cards: *chick, chin, patch*

Picture Cards: *chick, chin, patch*

Write-In Reader Vol. 1 pages 105–110

TERMS ABOUT READING/ LANGUAGE ARTS

| author | purpose |
| entertain | persuade |

COMMON CORE **RF.1.2b** orally produce single-syllable words by blending sounds; **RF.1.2d** segment spoken single-syllable words into their complete sequence of individual sounds; **RF.1.3a** know the spelling-sound correspondences for common consonant digraphs

Warm Up

Phonemic Awareness

Blend and Segment

- Say, *First, I'll say the sounds in a word, then I will say the word. Then I will say the sounds again:* /s/ /p/ /l/ /ĭ/ /t/, *split*, /s/ /p/ /l/ /ĭ/ /t/.

- Have children say /s/ /p/ /l/ /ĭ/ /t/, *split*, /s/ /p/ /l/ /ĭ/ /t/ with you.

- Have children say /s/ /p/ /l/ /ĭ/ /t/, *split*, /s/ /p/ /l/ /ĭ/ /t/ on their own.

- Continue, using the following words:

/m/ /ŭ/ /ch/	much	/m/ /ŭ/ /ch/
/k/ /ā/ /k/	cake	/k/ /ā/ /k/
/ch/ /ŏ/ /p/	chop	/ch/ /ŏ/ /p/

- Correct errors by repeating the process. ⬤ **RF.1.2b, RF.1.2d**

PRETEACH

Phonics: Digraphs *ch, tch*

Sound/Spelling Card, Word Cards, Picture Cards

- Display the **Sound/Spelling Card** for *chick*. Say the word, and ask, *What sound do you hear at the beginning of* chick? (/ch/) Teach that *ch* and *tch* stand for /ch/. Have children say /ch/ several times.

- Show the **Word Card** for *chick*. Point under the *ch* and say /ch/. Then say the word. Have children say the sound as you point under *ch* and then say the word. Have children say the sound and word on their own. Show the **Picture Card** for *chick*.

- Follow the same procedure using the **Word** and **Picture Cards** for *chin* and *patch*. Remind children that *tch* also stands for /ch/.

- Correct errors by modeling blending the word sound by sound. ⬤ **RF.1.3a**

REVIEW

Author's Purpose

- Remind children that authors write for different reasons. Ask them to suggest different reasons authors write. Then brainstorm examples of writing that were written for different purposes. Ask questions such as:

  What was written to teach us?
  What was written to make us laugh?
  What was written to make us do something?

- Make a chart to record ideas. As a class, come up with different examples to fill in the chart. Encourage children to offer specific examples, such as a comic book they like, or a specific textbook from class.

To Teach	To Entertain	To Persuade
Dictionary Textbooks (*Sea Animals*)	Comic Books Riddles (*Pup's Bath*)	Advertisements Speeches

- Now say, *Think about the selections we looked at this week. First, we read the story called* Sea Animals. *Then, we read* Pup's Bath. *Think about why these stories were written. Where do you think they fit on our chart?*

Turn and Talk Have children work with a partner to discuss the question. Then ask volunteers to share their responses. First, ask about *Sea Animals*. Have volunteers stand up and point to the spot on the chart where it goes, and ask for reasons why. Then, repeat the process for *Pup's Bath*.

Quick Check **Fluency**

Listen to individual children read aloud *Pup's Bath*. Encourage them to use expression and to pay attention to commas.

RETURN TO THE ANCHOR TEXT

"Be a Reading Detective!"
Student Book pages 15–29
Write-In Reader pages 111A–111B

- Page through "At Home in the Ocean" with children and review important ideas and information. Encourage volunteers to talk about each page.

- Read page 111A of the **Write-In Reader** with children. Remind children that reading detectives find clues in words and pictures to help them understand what they read.

- Discuss the questions with children. Guide them to find clues in the words and photographs that help them answer the questions.

- Have children complete item 1 on page 111B on their own. Then have them share their work with a partner. Encourage them to discuss how they came up with their answer.

- Read item 2 on page 111B. Have children talk with a partner about how the animals in the selection move around. Have them discuss clues that help them answer the question.

DAILY FLUENCY

Read Around the Room Have one child point to words that are on display in the room. Have the group read the words. Give each child a chance to be the pointer.

SHARE OBJECTIVES

- Blend and segment words.
- Read words with *ch* and *tch*.
- Read High-Frequency Words in context.

MATERIALS

Sound/Spelling Card: *chick*

Write-In Reader Vol. 1 pages 112–113

Context Cards: *never, off, own, very*

> **TERMS ABOUT READING/ LANGUAGE ARTS**
>
> order   sequence

COMMON CORE **RF.1.2b** orally produce single-syllable words by blending sounds; **RF.1.2d** segment spoken single-syllable words into their complete sequence of individual sounds; **RF.1.3a** know the spelling-sound correspondences for common consonant digraphs; **RF.1.3g** recognize and read irregularly spelled words; **SL.1.1a** follow rules for discussions

Warm Up

Phonemic Awareness

Blend and Segment

- Say, *First I'll say the sounds in a word, then I will blend the sounds to read the word. Then I'll say the sounds again: /s/ /l/ /ĕ/ /p/ /t/, slept, /s/ /l/ /ĕ/ /p/ /t/.*

- Have children say /s/ /l/ /ĕ/ /p/ /t/, *slept*, /s/ /l/ /ĕ/ /p/ /t/ with you.

- Have children say /s/ /l/ /ĕ/ /p/ /t/, *slept*, /s/ /l/ /ĕ/ /p/ /t/ on their own.

- Continue, using the following words:

/ch/ /ĭ/ /l/	chill	/ch/ /ĭ/ /l/
/t/ /r/ /ĭ/ /k/	trick	/t/ /r/ /ĭ/ /k/
/h/ /ă/ /ch/	hatch	/h/ /ă/ /ch/

- Correct errors by repeating the process. ▬ **RF.1.2b, RF.1.2d**

RETEACH

Phonics: Digraphs *ch, tch*

Sound/Spelling Cards

- Display the **Sound/Spelling Card** for *chick*. Say the word and ask, *What sound do you hear at the beginning of* chick? (/ch/) Point to *ch* and teach that *ch* stands for /ch/. Teach that *tch* also stands for /ch/. Have children say /ch/ several times.

- Write *chip* and *latch* on the board or on a pad. For each word, say the sounds as you point under the letters. Then blend sounds to read the word.

- Write the following words on a board or pad:

| match | chest | rich | chap | chess | chat |

- Point under the *ch* or *tch* having children say the sound. Then point under each letter, having children say the sounds and blend them to read each word.

- Correct errors by repeating the process. ▬ **RF.1.3a**

Talk About It

- Ask children to think about a typical school day. Explain that things happen in a certain order, or sequence, in school. First, they may have reading. Then they may do math, followed by lunch and recess. Have children discuss other things that happen during a school day. Make a flow chart to record children's responses.

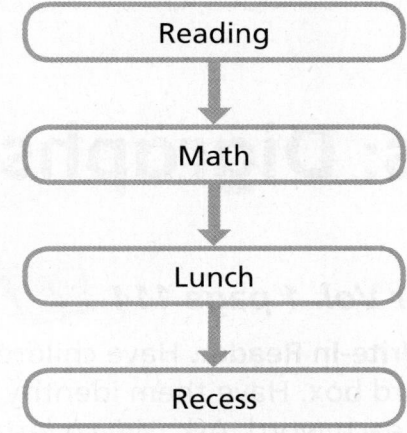

Reading

↓

Math

↓

Lunch

↓

Recess

- Ask, *Why is it important to know the order in which things happen?* (Responses will vary, but children may say that knowing the order in which things happen helps us know what to plan for.) ◼ SL.1.1a

RETEACH

Words to Know

Write-In Reader Vol. 1 pages 112–113

- Introduce *Animal Stories*. Read the heading. Have children look at the photographs and guess what these pages are about.

- Discuss each photograph, asking, *What is the fox (cow, chick, beaver) doing?*

- Read each sentence aloud with children as they point to each word. Ask what the highlighted word in each sentence means. See suggested definitions in the right-hand column. Then have children write the target word.

- Have children take turns rereading each sentence. Then have them choral read the words in the Words to Know box with you. ◼ RF.1.3g

Quick Check | Words to Know

Have children use one of the Words to Know in a sentence.

✓ WORDS TO KNOW

Never means at no time. It means not ever.

Off means away from.

Own means that something belongs to you.

Very means a lot.

DAILY FLUENCY

Build automaticity by using **Context Cards** or word lists on display. Point to the words in any order and have children read them aloud. Continue until children can read all words fluently.

DAY 2

SHARE OBJECTIVES

- Read and use High-Frequency Words.
- Read and write words with *ch* and *tch*.
- Listen to and analyze a story.

MATERIALS

Context Cards: *never, off, own, very*

Write-In Reader Vol. 1 page 114

Leveled Reader: *Peacock's Tail*

TERMS ABOUT READING/
LANGUAGE ARTS

sequence   events

Warm Up

Words to Know

never, off, own, very

Distribute the **Context Cards** to children. Include *never, off, own,* and *very*. Have partners practice reading the words. Then ask each child to use one word in a sentence. For a challenge, ask if anyone can use two words in one sentence.  **RF.1.3g**

REVIEW

Phonics: Digraphs *ch, tch*

Write-In Reader Vol. 1 page 114

- Introduce the **Write-In Reader.** Have children choral read the words in the word box. Have them identify the letters that stand for /ch/ in each word. Ask, *Which letters stand for /ch/ in* chin *(patch, check, chess)?* Then direct their attention to the images in the first row.

- Say, *Look at the pictures in the first row. Point to each one as I name it.* (chin, check) Then have children say the name of each object together.

- Follow the same procedure for the second row. (chess, patch)

- Assign children to work on their own, writing the correct word below each object.

- Check children's work. If any children have written the incorrect word, determine whether the misunderstanding results from being unable to name the pictured objects or from being unable to read the words. **RF.1.3a**

Teacher Read Aloud

Leveled Reader: *Peacock's Tail*

Leveled Reader

- Use the **Think Aloud** to introduce sequence of events. Tell children that you are going to read aloud a story called *Peacock's Tail*.

  Think Aloud *As I read to you, pay attention to the sequence of events. Think about what is happening in the beginning, in the middle, and at the end of the story.*

- Read the story aloud. Ask questions such as:

After page 2: *What do we know about Crow and Peacock at the beginning of the story?* Reread the first paragraph, asking children to listen for clues. (The two birds are friends. They both have plain white feathers.) *What does plain mean?* (ordinary)

After page 3: *What do the friends decide to do?* (paint their feathers)

After page 5: *I just read "Peacock had never seen such a fine display of feathers." What does display mean?* (show) *Peacock started to strut around. What do you think strut means?* (to walk proudly) *What is happening to Peacock?* (Peacock is so proud of his new colors that he only pays attention to himself.)

After page 7: *What does Peacock do when it is Crow's turn to get painted?* (He pours black paint on Crow's head.) *How do you think Crow feels?* (sad, mad) *Where does Peacock go next?* (He travels around the world.)

After page 10: *Why does Peacock come back at the end of the story?* (because he is lonely) *How does Crow feel about Peacock coming home?* (Crow is happy. He missed Peacock.) *What lesson did Peacock learn?* (Pride doesn't make you happy.) **RL.1.2, SL.1.1c, SL.1.2**

Quick Check **Comprehension**

Ask, *Were Crow and Peacock friends in the middle of the story?*

ORAL VOCABULARY

- display   - plain   - strut

DAILY FLUENCY

Build automaticity by using **Context Cards** or word lists on display. Point to the words in any order and have children read them aloud. Continue until children can read all words fluently.

SHARE OBJECTIVES

- Substitute initial phonemes.
- Read words with possessive *'s*.
- Read to apply comprehension skills.

MATERIALS

Write-In Reader Vol. 1 pages 115–120

TERMS ABOUT READING/ LANGUAGE ARTS

sequence   events

Warm Up

Phonemic Awareness

Substitute Initial Phonemes

- Say, *I'll say a word:* sit. *Now I'll change /s/ to /b/ and say the new word:* bit.

- Have children say *sit*. Tell them to change /s/ to /b/ and say the new word with you.

- Have children say *sit*. Tell them to change /s/ to /b/ and say the new word on their own.

- Continue, using the following words:

lean	/l/ to /s/	seen
man	/m/ to /t/	tan
hot	/h/ to /p/	pot

- Correct errors by repeating the process. ◖ **RF.1.2b, RF.1.2c**

RETEACH

Phonics: Possessive 's

- Write *'s* on the board or a pad. Teach that when a word ends in *'s* we find the base word first, then read the word with the ending. Teach that *'s* means ownership.

- Write the following words on a board or pad:

Beth's	man's	Sam's	pig's	block's

- Point under the word *Beth* and say *Beth*. Then point under *Beth's and* say *Beth's*. Have children say *Beth* and *Beth's* with you as you point under each one. Finally, have children read *Beth* and *Beth's* on their own.

- Follow the same procedure with the remaining words, having children say the noun alone and then with the ending.

- Correct errors by repeating the process. ◖ **RF.1.3g**

COMMON CORE **RL.1.1** ask and answer questions about key details; **RL.1.10** read prose and poetry; **RF.1.2b** orally produce single-syllable words by blending sounds; **RF.1.2c** isolate and pronounce sounds in spoken single-syllable words; **RF.1.3g** recognize and read irregularly spelled words

READ

Al and Lop

Write-In Reader Vol. 1 pages 115–120

Preview *Al and Lop* using the **Think Aloud** to reteach
sequence of events.

Think Aloud *In this story, we will read about two animals
named Al and Lop. As we read the story, think about the
sequence of events. This means you should think about what
happens in the beginning, in the middle, and at the end of
the story.*

READ

Have children choral read the story for accuracy. If they
mispronounce or hesitate over a word, stop the reading and tell the
class the correct word. Have all children repeat the word, and then
continue reading from the beginning of the sentence.

REREAD

Reread the story with children. Use the following questions to check
children's understanding of the story.

After page 115: *What kind of animal is Lop?* (a rabbit) *Look at the
picture. Does Lop look like most rabbits?* (No, he has a long tail.)

After page 116: *Who is Lop talking to?* (Al, the alligator) *Why do you
think Lop needs tricks?* (Possible response: Lop doesn't like water,
and he wants to cross the river.)

After page 118: *Why do you think Lop wants Al to set his pals up in
a path?* (Possible response: so he can use them as stepping stones to
cross the water)

After page 119: *What happens after the alligators make a path?*
(Lop runs across them.)

After page 120: *What happens at the end of the story?* (Al bites
Lop's tail and Lop runs away.) ▬ **RL.1.1, RL.1.10**

Quick Check **Comprehension**

Ask, *How does Lop lose his tail?*

DAILY FLUENCY

Build automaticity by using **Context
Cards** or word lists on display. Point to
the words in any order and have children
read them aloud. Continue until children
can read all words fluently.

DAY 4

SHARE OBJECTIVES

- Read and use High-Frequency Words.
- Build words using the phonogram -atch.
- Review decodable story to build fluency and comprehension.

MATERIALS

Context Cards: been, brown, know, never, off, out, own, very

Letter Cards

Write-In Reader Vol. 1 pages 115–121

TERMS ABOUT READING/ LANGUAGE ARTS

rate

☑ WORDS TO KNOW

Been is a word to show that something happened in the past.

Brown is a color. Tree bark and mud are brown.

Know means to understand or know how to do something.

Out means to be away or in another place.

Warm Up

Words to Know

been, brown, know, never, off, out, own, very

- Distribute the **Context Cards** to children. Include *been, brown, know, never, off, out, own,* and *very*.
- Have children practice reading the words. Then challenge children to use as many of these words as possible in one sentence. **RF.1.3g**

Quick Check | **Words to Know**

Ask each child to use one of the week's words in a sentence.

RETEACH

Phonics: Phonogram -atch

Letter Cards

- Create the phonogram -atch with the **Letter Cards**.
- Model using additional **Letter Cards** to create new words by adding one or two letters in front of -atch.
- Challenge children to create as many words as they can by adding one or more letters in front of the phonogram. Record words on the board or on a pad. If children create nonsense words, say, *That's not a real word, but we can read it anyway.*
- Have children read the list of words. **RF.1.3b**

| **a** | **t** | **c** | **h** |

Possible Words

| match | latch | scratch | thatch | snatch |

RETEACH

Fluency: Rate

Write-In Reader Vol. 1 page 115

- Explain that you are going to read page 115 in two different ways. Children will listen and give you some tips after each reading. First, read page 115 very slowly, pausing between each word. Ask, *What do you think about my first reading?* Encourage feedback.

- Next, read the page very quickly, running words together. Ask, *Was this reading better than the last?* Invite feedback. Encourage children to recognize that it is difficult to understand someone who reads too slowly or too quickly.

- Model how to read at an appropriate rate. Have children practice reading the rest of the story aloud at an appropriate rate. ⬤ **RF.1.4b**

Look Back and Respond

Write-In Reader Vol. 1 pages 115–121

Read aloud each question and the answer choices with children. Help children find answers using the suggestions below. Model how to look back at the story to find the answer.

1. Whom do we see first? **(Lop)** *Look at the first page of the story. Whom do you see?* **(Lop, the rabbit)**

2. What happened last? **(Lop ran away.)** *Find the picture that shows Lop running away. On which page is it?* **(page 120)**

3. What happened after Al's pals got mad? **(Al bit Lop's tail.)** *Look at page 120. Which sentence tells us Al's friends were angry?* **(the first sentence)** *What does the next sentence tell us?* **(Al bit Lop.)**

Turn and Talk 4. Have children talk about Lop's trick. Ask, *Was Lop's trick clever? Was it successful?* Have volunteers respond, and write several responses on the board. Then have the children write their responses. ⬤ **RL.1.1**

DAILY FLUENCY

Build automaticity by using **Context Cards** or word lists on display. Point to the words in any order and have children read them aloud. Continue until children can read all words fluently.

SHARE OBJECTIVES

- Substitute initial phonemes.
- Read words with *sh*, *wh*, and *ph*.
- Apply the sequence of events skill to real life and to reading.

MATERIALS

Sound/Spelling Cards: *fish, sheep, whale*

Word Cards: *brush, graph, ship*

Picture Cards: *brush, graph, ship*

Write-In Reader Vol. 1 pages 115–120

TERMS ABOUT READING/ LANGUAGE ARTS

sequence   events

Warm Up

Phonemic Awareness

Substitute Initial Phonemes

- Say, *I'll say a word:* dig. *Now I'll change /d/ to /p/ and say the new word:* pig.
- Have children say *dig*. Tell them to change /d/ to /p/ and say the new word with you.
- Have children say *dig*. Tell them to change /d/ to /p/ and say the new word on their own.
- Continue, using the following words:

hop	/h/ to /sh/	shop
send	/s/ to /l/	lend
hill	/h/ to /f/	Phil

- Correct errors by repeating the process. ■ **RF.1.2b, RF.1.2c**

PRETEACH

Phonics: Digraphs *sh, wh,* and *ph*

Sound/Spelling Cards, Word Cards, Picture Cards

- Display the **Sound/Spelling Card** for *sheep*. Say the word, and ask, *What sound do you hear at the beginning of* sheep? (/sh/) Point to the *sh* and teach that *sh* stands for /sh/.
- Repeat using the **Sound/Spelling Card** for *whale*, teaching that *wh* can stand for /hw/ or /w/.
- Write the name *Phil* on the board. Use the **Sound/Spelling Card** for *fish* to teach that *ph* stands for the sound /f/.
- Show the **Word Card** for *ship*. Point under *sh* and say /sh/. Then say the word. Have children say the sound as you point under *sh* and say the word. Show the **Picture Card** for *ship*.
- Follow the same procedure using the **Word** and **Picture Cards** for *brush* and *graph*, having children sound out and say the words on their own.
- Correct errors by modeling the words sound by sound.
  ■ **RF.1.3a**

COMMON CORE **RL.1.3** describe characters, settings, and major events; **RF.1.2b** orally produce single-syllable words by blending sounds; **RF.1.2c** isolate and pronounce sounds in spoken single-syllable words; **RF.1.3a** know the spelling-sound correspondences for common consonant digraphs

REVIEW

Sequence of Events

- Remind children that when they think about the sequence of events, they think about what happened first, next, and last.

- Have children think of a story, such as *Goldilocks and the Three Bears*. Ask, *What is the sequence of events in this story?*

- Guide the discussion by asking:

  What happened first?
  Then what happened?
  What happened last?

- Draw a simple flow chart on the board or on a sheet of paper, and record children's ideas. If needed, remind children how to use the flow chart to record the events in a story.

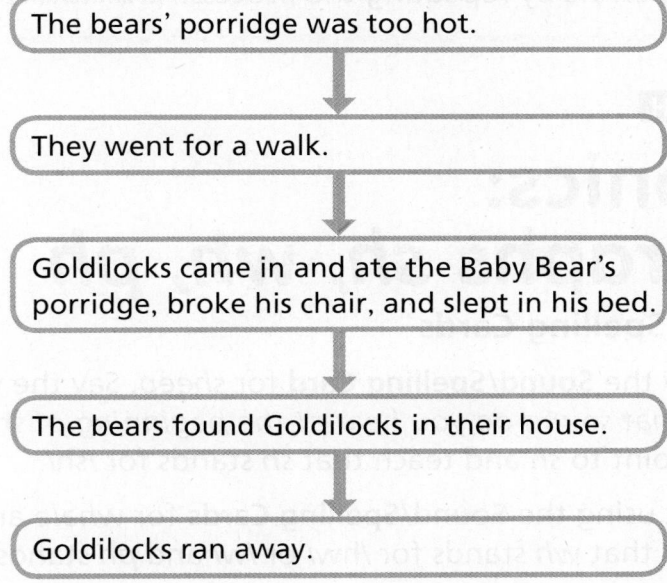

The bears' porridge was too hot.

They went for a walk.

Goldilocks came in and ate the Baby Bear's porridge, broke his chair, and slept in his bed.

The bears found Goldilocks in their house.

Goldilocks ran away.

- Tell children to think about the story *Al and Lop*. Tell them to think about the order in which things happened. Ask, *What happened first? What happened next? What happened last?*

Turn and Talk Have children work with a partner to write or draw what happens first and what happens last in the story *Al and Lop*.

■ RL.1.3

Quick Check Fluency

Listen to individual children read aloud *Al and Lop*. Encourage them to use expression and to pay attention to the rate at which they are reading.

RETURN TO THE ANCHOR TEXT

"Be a Reading Detective!"

Student Book pages 47–63
Write-In Reader pages 121A–121B

- Page through "How Leopard Got His Spots" with children and review the main characters and events. Encourage volunteers to talk about what is happening on each page.

- Read page 121A of the **Write-In Reader** with children. Remind children that reading detectives find clues in the words and pictures of a story.

- Discuss the questions with children. Guide them to find clues in the words and pictures that help them answer the questions.

- Have children complete item 1 on page 121B on their own. Then have them share their work with a partner. Encourage them to discuss how they came up with their answer.

- Read item 2 on page 121B. Have children talk with a partner about how Leopard got his spots. Have them discuss what clues help them answer the question.

DAILY FLUENCY

Read Around the Room Have one child point to words that are on display in the room. Have the group read the words. Give each child a chance to be the pointer.

DAY 1

SHARE OBJECTIVES

- Substitute initial phonemes.
- Read words with digraphs *sh, wh,* and *ph*.
- Read High-Frequency Words in context.

MATERIALS

Sound/Spelling Card: *fish, sheep, whale*

Context Cards: *down, goes, open, yellow*

Write-In Reader Vol. 1 pages 122–123

Warm Up

Phonemic Awareness
Substitute Initial Phonemes

- Say, *I'll say a word:* dip. *Now I'll change /d/ to /sh/ and say the new word:* ship.

- Have children say *dip.* Tell children to change /d/ to /sh/ and say the new word with you.

- Have children say *dip.* Tell children to change /d/ to /sh/ and say the new word on their own.

- Continue, using the following words:

tell	/t/ to /b/	bell
hen	/h/ to /m/	men
thin	/th/ to /ch/	chin

- Correct errors by repeating the process. ⬤ **RF.1.2b, RF.1.2c**

RETEACH

Phonics:
Digraphs *sh, wh, ph*
Sound/Spelling Cards

- Display the **Sound/Spelling Card** for *sheep.* Say the word and ask, *What sound do you hear at the beginning of* sheep? (/sh/) Point to *sh* and teach that *sh* stands for /sh/.

- Repeat using the **Sound/Spelling Cards** for *whale* and *fish.* Explain that *wh* stands for /hw/ or /w/ and *ph* stands for /f/.

- Write on a board or on a pad the following words:

hush	wham	graph	shelf	when

- Point under the *sh, wh,* or *ph,* having children say the sound, then the word.

- Correct errors by modeling sounding out the word, sound by sound. ⬤ **RF.1.3a**

COMMON CORE **RF.1.2b** orally produce single-syllable words by blending sounds; **RF.1.2c** isolate and pronounce sounds in spoken single-syllable words; **RF.1.3a** know the spelling-sound correspondences for common consonant digraphs; **RF.1.3g** recognize and read irregularly spelled words; **SL.1.1a** follow rules for discussions

Talk About It

- Ask children to think about the seasons. Have a volunteer name them. Then ask children to think about what makes each season special. Record notes on the board or on a pad.

- Then say, *Each new season brings changes. Let's think about what makes these changes happen.* Have children help you complete the sentences. ▬ **SL.1.1a**

What Happens	Reason Why
In summer, I stay inside because...	it is hot out.
In spring, there is lots of mud because...	it rains a lot.
In autumn, we have to rake because...	the leaves fall.
In winter, I need to wear a hat because...	it gets cold.

RETEACH

Words to Know

Write-In Reader Vol. 1 pages 122–123

- Introduce *Seasons Changing*. Ask children to look at the photographs and guess what these pages are about.

- Discuss each photograph, asking questions such as: *What is the weather like in this picture? What time of year is it? What else happens in fall/winter/spring/summer?*

- Read each sentence aloud with children as they point to each word. Ask what the highlighted word in each sentence means. See the right-hand column for suggested definitions. Then have children write the target word.

- Have children take turns rereading each sentence. Then have them choral-read the words in the Words to Know box with you. ▬ **RF.1.3g**

Quick Check **Words to Know**

Have children use one of the Words to Know in a sentence.

✓ **WORDS TO KNOW**

Down means to go from a higher place to a lower place.

Goes means that something or someone moves.

Open means not closed or not covered.

Yellow is a color. Lemons are **yellow**.

DAILY FLUENCY

Build automaticity by using **Context Cards** or word lists on display. Point to the words in any order and have children read them aloud. Continue until children can read all words fluently.

DAY 2

SHARE OBJECTIVES

- Read and use High-Frequency Words.
- Read and write words with digraph *sh*.
- Listen to and analyze a story.

MATERIALS

Context Cards: *down, goes, open, yellow*

Write-In Reader Vol. 1 page 124

Leveled Reader: *Seasons Around the World*

TERMS ABOUT READING/ LANGUAGE ARTS

reason   cause

Warm Up

Words to Know

down, goes, open, yellow

Distribute the **Context Cards** to children. Include *down, goes, open,* and *yellow*. Have partners practice reading the words. Then ask each child to use one word in a sentence. For a challenge, ask if anyone can use two of the words in one sentence. 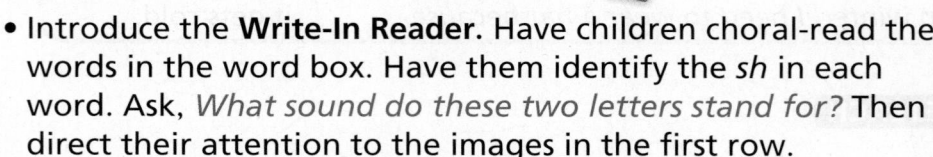 **RF.1.3g**

REVIEW

Phonics: Digraph *sh*

Write-In Reader Vol. 1 page 124

- Introduce the **Write-In Reader.** Have children choral-read the words in the word box. Have them identify the *sh* in each word. Ask, *What sound do these two letters stand for?* Then direct their attention to the images in the first row.

- Say, *Look at the pictures in the first row. Point to each one as I name it.* Then have children say the name of each object together. (shell, ship)

- Follow the same procedure in the second row. (dish, cash)

- Assign children to work on their own, writing the correct word below each object.

- Check children's work. If any children have written the incorrect word, determine whether the misunderstanding results from being unable to name the pictured objects or from being unable to read the words. **RF.1.3a**

COMMON CORE **RF.1.3a** know the spelling-sound correspondences for common consonant digraphs; **RF.1.3g** recognize and read irregularly spelled words; **SL.1.1c** ask questions to clear up confusion about topics and texts under discussion; **SL.1.2** ask and answer questions about details in a text read aloud, information presented orally, or through other media

Teacher Read Aloud

Leveled Reader: *Seasons Around the World*

● **Leveled Reader**

- Use the **Think Aloud** to introduce cause and effect. Tell children that you are going to read aloud a story called *Seasons Around the World*.

> **Think Aloud** *As you listen to this story, think about why things happen. What are the reasons, or causes, why things happen?*

- Read aloud the story. Ask questions such as:

After page 2: *What are the four seasons?* (summer, fall, winter, spring) *What does the word* season *mean?* (the changing weather at different times of the year) *What changes can fall cause?* (The leaves fall. It starts to get cold.) *What changes can spring cause?* (Flowers open up and grass turns green.)

After page 4: *What happens after the wet season?* (the dry season) *Why does this change occur?* (The rain stops and the sun comes out.)

After page 5: *Why do the rain forests need both wet and dry weather?* (so the plants can grow) *What does the word* weather *mean? Name some kinds of weather.* (how it is outside; rainy, snowy, stormy)

After page 6: *What can cause a tornado?* (wind blowing very fast in a circle)

After page 8: *I just read, "This time of year is called Polar Day." What does* polar *mean?* (Something that happens in the North or South Pole is called polar.) *What causes a Polar Day?* (The sun doesn't go down.) ▬ **SL.1.1c, SL.1.2**

Quick Check | **Comprehension**

Ask, *Why are seasons different around the world?*

DAILY FLUENCY

Build automaticity by using **Context Cards** or word lists on display. Point to the words in any order and have children read them aloud. Continue until children can read all words fluently.

DAY 3

SHARE OBJECTIVES

- Substitute initial phonemes.
- Read contractions.
- Read to apply comprehension skills.

MATERIALS

Write-In Reader Vol. 1 pages 125–130

TERMS ABOUT READING/ LANGUAGE ARTS

cause   effect

reason

Phonemic Awareness

Substitute Initial Phonemes

- Say, *I'll say a word: ship. Now I'll change /sh/ to /ch/ and say the new word: chip.*

- Have children say *ship.* Tell children to change /sh/ to /ch/ and say the new word with you.

- Have children say *ship.* Tell children to change /sh/ to /ch/ and say the new word on their own.

- Continue, using the following words:

ship	/sh/ to /l/	lip
lash	/l/ to /s/	sash
hut	/h/ to /b/	but

- Correct errors by repeating the process. ◼ **RF.1.2b, RF.1.2c**

RETEACH

Phonics: Contractions *'s* and *n't*

- Write *he is* and *he's* on the board or on a pad. Teach that *he's* is a short way of writing *he is.* Say, *We read the base word first:* he. *Then we read the word with the ending:* he's. Repeat for *can't.*

- Write on the board or on a pad the following words:

it's	she's	didn't	hasn't	hadn't

- Point under *it.* Say *it,* then say *it's.* Have children blend the sounds and read *it* and *it's* on their own.

- Follow the same procedure with the remaining words.

- Correct errors by repeating the process. ◼ **RF.1.3g**

COMMON CORE

RL.1.1 ask and answer questions about key details; **RL.1.10** read prose and poetry; **RF.1.2b** orally produce single-syllable words by blending sounds; **RF.1.2c** isolate and pronounce sounds in spoken single-syllable words; **RF.1.3g** recognize and read irregularly spelled words

READ

Max Has His Bath

Write-In Reader Vol. 1 pages 125–130

Preview *Max Has His Bath* using the **Think Aloud** to reteach cause and effect.

Think Aloud *Things have certain reasons for happening. For instance, if you eat something, it is because you are hungry. A cause is what makes something happen. Your hunger is the cause for eating. The effect is that you eat something. As you read* Max Has His Bath, *think about cause and effect. In other words, listen for the reasons why things happen.*

READ

Have children choral-read the story for accuracy. If they mispronounce or hesitate over a word, stop the reading and tell the class the correct word. Have all children repeat the word, and then continue reading from the beginning of the sentence.

REREAD

Reread the story with children. Use the following questions to check children's understanding of the story:

After page 125: *Why is the path so muddy?* (because it is raining)

After page 126: *Why does Max need a bath?* (He is muddy.) *Look at Max's expression. Is he happy?* (no) *Why not?* (He doesn't want to take a bath.)

After page 127: *Look at Max in this picture. What made his fur look like that?* (the weather; it is hot and dusty out) *What does he have to do because of his dusty fur?* (take a bath)

After page 129: *What time of year is it now?* (winter) *What is the weather like?* (It is cold and snowy and icy.) *Does it look like Max likes the cold?* (No, he looks unhappy.) 🔊 **RL.1.1, RL.1.10**

Quick Check | **Comprehension**

Ask, *The cold causes Max to do something unusual. What does he do?*

DAILY FLUENCY

Build automaticity by using **Context Cards** or word lists on display. Point to the words in any order and have children read them aloud. Continue until children can read all words fluently.

SHARE OBJECTIVES

- Read and use High-Frequency Words.
- Build words using the phonogram -ash.
- Review decodable story to build fluency and comprehension.

MATERIALS

Context Cards: down, fall, goes, green, grow, new, open, yellow

Letter Cards

Write-In Reader Vol. 1 pages 125–131

TERMS ABOUT READING/ LANGUAGE ARTS

recognize

☑ WORDS TO KNOW

Fall is the season after summer. The leaves on many trees change color.

Green is a color. Grass is **green**.

Grow means to get bigger.

New means never used.

COMMON CORE **RL.1.1** ask and answer questions about key details; **RF.1.3b** decode regularly spelled one-syllable words; **RF.1.3g** recognize and read irregularly spelled words; **RF.1.4b** read on-level text orally with accuracy, appropriate rate, and expression

Warm Up

Words to Know

down, fall, goes, green, grow, new, open, yellow

- Distribute the **Context Cards** to children. Include *down, fall, goes, green, grow, new, open,* and *yellow*.
- Have children practice reading the words. Then challenge children to use as many of these words as possible in one sentence. ▪ **RF.1.3g**

Quick Check | **Words to Know**

Ask each child to use one of the week's words in a sentence.

RETEACH

Phonics: Phonogram -*ash*

Letter Cards

- Create the phonogram -*ash* with the **Letter Cards**.
- Model using additional **Letter Cards** to add one or two letters in front of -*ash* to create words.
- Challenge children to create as many words as they can by adding one or two letters in front of the phonogram. Record words on the board or on a pad. If children create nonsense words, say, *That's not a real word, but we can read it anyway.*
- Have children blend the sounds to read each word. ▪ **RF.1.3b**

a	s	h

Possible Words

lash	rash	flash	splash	crash	dash

RETEACH

Fluency: Word Recognition

Write-In Reader Vol. 1 page 129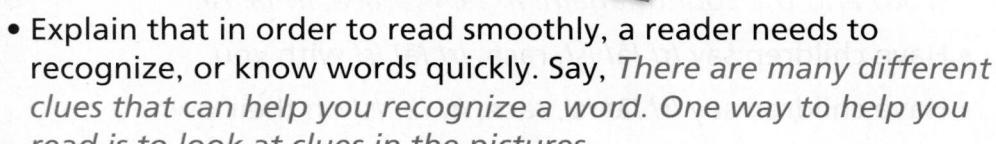

- Explain that in order to read smoothly, a reader needs to recognize, or know words quickly. Say, *There are many different clues that can help you recognize a word. One way to help you read is to look at clues in the pictures.*

- Model using picture clues to figure out a word. Say, *Look at page 129. If I did not know how to read the word* slush, *I could look at the picture. I see a winter scene, so that gives me a clue to what this word means.* ◼ **RF.1.4b**

Look Back and Respond

Write-In Reader Vol. 1 pages 125–131

Read aloud each question and the answer choices with children. Help children find answers using the suggestions below. Model how to look back at the story to find the answer.

1. Why does Max have so many baths? (He is always a mess.) *What happens each time Max needs a bath?* (He goes outside and gets his fur dirty.)

2. Why does the girl pick Max up? (He will not hop into the tub.) *When does she need to pick Max up? Look for the page.* (page 128) *Read this page again. Why does she have to pick Max up?*

3. What happens when Max is cold? (He wants a bath.) *When does Max get cold?* (in winter) *What is his bath like in winter? Do the kids need to force him to take the bath?* (No, he hops in himself.)

Turn and Talk 4. Have children talk about what Max does in winter. Ask, *How is winter different from other seasons? What does Max like to do?* Ask for volunteers and write several responses on the board. Then have the children draw or write their responses. ◼ **RL.1.1**

DAILY FLUENCY

Build automaticity by using **Context Cards** or word lists on display. Point to the words in any order and have children read them aloud. Continue until children can read all words fluently.

DAY 5

SHARE OBJECTIVES

- Blend and segment words.
- Read words with long *a*, soft *c*, and soft *g*.
- Apply the cause-and-effect skill to real life and reading.

MATERIALS

Sound/Spelling Cards: *acorn, jump, seal*

Word Card: *gate*

Picture Card: *gate*

Write-In Reader Vol. 1 pages 125–130

TERMS ABOUT READING/ LANGUAGE ARTS

cause   effect

COMMON CORE **RI.1.3** describe the connection between individuals, events, ideas, or information in a text; **RF.1.2a** distinguish long from short vowel sounds in spoken single-syllable words; **RF.1.2b** orally produce single-syllable words by blending sounds; **RF.1.2d** segment spoken single-syllable words into their complete sequence of individual sounds; **RF.1.3c** know final -e and vowel team conventions for representing long vowel sounds

Warm Up

Phonemic Awareness

Blend and Segment

- Say, *First I'll say the sounds in a word, then I will say the word and the sounds again: /r/ /ā/ /s/, race, /r/ /ā/ /s/.*
- Have children say /r/ /ā/ /s/, race, /r/ /ā/ /s/ with you.
- Have children say /r/ /ā/ /s/, race, /r/ /ā/ /s/ on their own.
- Continue, using the following words:

/s/ /ā/ /l/	sail	/s/ /ā/ /l/
/k/ /ā/ /j/	cage	/k/ /ā/ /j/
/f/ /ā/ /s/	face	/f/ /ā/ /s/

- Correct errors by repeating the process. ▬ **RF.1.2b, RF.1.2d**

PRETEACH

Phonics: Long *a*, Soft *c* and *g*

Sound/Spelling Cards, Word Card, Picture Card

- Display the **Sound/Spelling Card** for *acorn*. Say the word, and ask, *What sound do you hear at the beginning of acorn?* (/ā/) Show the **Picture Card** and then the **Word Card** for *gate*. Point to *ate* and teach that when a word ends in *a*-consonant-*e*, the *a* stands for its long sound and the *e* is silent.
- Repeat using the **Sound/Spelling Card** for *seal*, teaching that *ce* and *ci* stand for /s/. Write *cent* and *circle* on the board or on a pad. Point to and say each word. Repeat for the **Sound/ Spelling Card** for *jump*, teaching that *g* before an *e* or *i* stands for /j/. Write *giant* on the board or on a pad and say the word. ▬ **RF.1.2a, RF.1.3c**

Cause and Effect

Write-In Reader Vol 1 pages 125–130

- Review cause and effect. Remind children that a cause makes something happen, and an effect is what happens because of it.

- Demonstrate some simple examples of cause and effect using classroom objects. Make a chart to record cause and effect. After giving the first two examples, ask children to provide the effect themselves. If students have difficulty, prompt them by asking, *What happens if...*

Cause	Effect
I let go.	*The pencil falls.*
I push the door.	*It closes.*
I turn off the TV.	It stops working.
I knock over the cup.	The pencils spill.
I drop the book.	It makes a noise.

- Then say, *Everything you do has an effect on things around you. For instance, you might say you don't like your friend's shoes. This will probably make your friend feel bad. This action has a negative, or bad, effect. On the other hand, you might tell a classmate that he or she did a great job on a project. This will make your classmate feel good. This is a positive, or good, effect.*

Turn and Talk Have children work in pairs to brainstorm things they could do that would have a positive effect on the world around them. Have them draw or write the cause. Then have them draw or write the effect. ◼ RI.1.3

Quick Check **Fluency**

Listen to individual children read aloud *Max Has His Bath*. Encourage them to use picture clues if they don't know a word.

RETURN TO THE ANCHOR TEXT

"Be a Reading Detective!"

Student Book pages 81–99
Write-In Reader pages 131A–131B

- Page through "Seasons" with children and review important ideas and information. Encourage volunteers to talk about each page.

- Read page 131A of the **Write-In Reader** with children. Remind children that reading detectives find clues in words and pictures to help them understand what they read.

- Discuss the questions with children. Guide them to find clues in the words and photographs that help them answer the questions.

- Have children complete item 1 on page 131B on their own. Then have them share their work with a partner. Encourage them to discuss how they came up with their answer.

- Read item 2 on page 131B. Have children talk with a partner about when the weather gets colder. Have them discuss clues that help them answer the question.

DAILY FLUENCY

Read Around the Room Have one child point to words that are on display in the room. Have the group read the words. Give each child a chance to be the pointer.

SHARE OBJECTIVES

- Identify medial phonemes.
- Read words with long *a*.
- Read High-Frequency Words in context.

MATERIALS

Sound/Spelling Card: *acorn*

Word Cards: *skate, tape, vase, wave, whale*

Picture Cards: *skate, tape, vase, wave, whale*

Write-In Reader Vol. 1 pages 132–133

Context Cards: *over, three, two, watch*

TERMS ABOUT READING/ LANGUAGE ARTS

activities

COMMON CORE **RF.1.2a** distinguish long from short vowel sounds in spoken single-syllable words; **RF.1.2b** orally produce single-syllable words by blending sounds; **RF.1.2c** isolate and pronounce sounds in spoken single-syllable words; **RF.1.3b** decode regularly spelled one-syllable words; **RF.1.3c** know final -e and vowel team conventions for representing long vowel sounds; **RF.1.3g** recognize and read irregularly spelled words; **SL.1.1a** follow rules for discussions

Warm Up

Phonemic Awareness
Identify Medial Phonemes

- Say, *I'll say a word:* save. *Now, I will say the middle sound:* /ā/.
- Have children say *save* and the middle sound with you.
- Have children say *save* and the middle sound on their own.
- Continue, using the following words:

sail	/ā/
leaf	/ē/
rate	/ā/

- Correct errors by repeating the process.

RF.1.2a, RF.1.2b, RF.1.3b

RETEACH

Phonics: Long *a*
Sound/Spelling Card, Word Cards, Picture Cards

- Display the **Sound/Spelling Card** for *acorn*. Say the word and ask, *What sound do you hear at the beginning of* acorn? (/ā/) Write *fame* on the board. Point to *ame* and teach that when a word ends in *a*-consonant-*e*, the *a* stands for its long sound and the *e* is silent.

- Display the **Word Card** for *tape*. Point out that the word ends in *e* and that *a* stands for /ā/. Say the word. Show the **Picture Card** for *tape*.

- Follow the same procedure using the **Word** and **Picture Cards** for *skate, vase, wave,* and *whale*, having children say the long vowel sound and the word on their own.

- Correct errors by saying /ā/ and then the word.

RF.1.2c, RF.1.3b, RF.1.3c

Talk About It

- Ask children to think about things they are good at doing. Have children discuss these activities. Make a chart to record children's ideas. Then ask children how they feel when they are doing activities they do well.

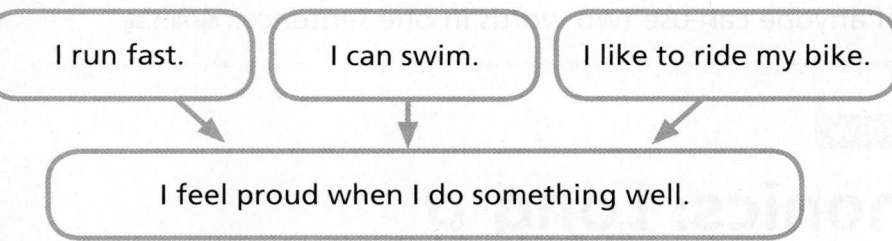

| I run fast. | I can swim. | I like to ride my bike. |

I feel proud when I do something well.

- Ask, *What can we learn about a person from his or her favorite activities?* 🔊 **SL.1.1a**

RETEACH

Words to Know

Write-In Reader Vol. 1 pages 132–133

- Introduce *Races*. Read the heading. Have children look at the photographs and guess what these pages are about.

- Discuss each photograph, asking, *What are the children (people) doing in this picture?*

- Read each sentence aloud with children as they point to each word. Ask what the highlighted word in each sentence means. See suggested definitions in the right-hand column. Then have children write the target word.

- Have children take turns rereading each sentence. Then have them choral-read the words in the Words to Know box with you. 🔊 **RF.1.3g**

Quick Check **Words to Know**

Have children use one of the Words to Know in a sentence.

✓ **WORDS TO KNOW**

Over means above.

Three is a number that is one more than two.

Two is a number. Most animals have **two** eyes.

Watch means to look at.

DAILY FLUENCY

Build automaticity by using **Context Cards** or word lists on display. Point to the words in any order and have children read them aloud. Continue until children can read all words fluently.

SHARE OBJECTIVES

- Read and use High-Frequency Words.
- Read and write words with long *a*.
- Listen to and analyze a story.

MATERIALS

Context Cards: *over, three, two, watch*

Write-In Reader Vol. 1 page 134

Leveled Reader: *Cam the Camel*

TERMS ABOUT READING/ LANGUAGE ARTS

consonant	information
conclude	details

Warm Up

Words to Know

over, three, two, watch

Distribute the **Context Cards** to children. Include *over, three, two,* and *watch*. Have partners practice reading the words. Then ask each child to use one word in a sentence. For a challenge, ask if anyone can use two words in one sentence. ▬ **RF.1.3g**

REVIEW

Phonics: Long *a*

Write-In Reader Vol. 1 page 134

- Introduce the **Write-In Reader**. Have children choral-read the words in the word box. Have them identify the *a*-consonant-*e* pattern in each word. Ask, *What sound does a-consonant-e stand for in this word?* Then direct children's attention to the images in the first row.

- Say, *Look at the pictures in the first row. Point to each one as I name it.* Then have children say the names of each object together. (snake, plane)

- Follow the same procedure for the second row. (tape, game)

- Assign children to work on their own, writing the correct word below each object.

- Check children's work. If any children have written the incorrect word, determine whether the misunderstanding results from being unable to name the pictured objects or from being unable to read the words.
  ▬ **RF.1.2c, RF.1.3b, RF.1.3c**

COMMON CORE **RF.1.2c** isolate and pronounce sounds in spoken single-syllable words; **RF.1.3b** decode regularly spelled one-syllable words; **RF.1.3c** know final -e and vowel team conventions for representing long vowel sounds; **RF.1.3g** recognize and read irregularly spelled words; **SL.1.1c** ask questions to clear up confusion about topics and texts under discussion; **SL.1.2** ask and answer questions about details in a text read aloud, information presented orally, or through other media

Teacher Read Aloud

Leveled Reader: *Cam the Camel*

Leveled Reader

• Use the **Think Aloud** to introduce conclusions. Tell children that you are going to read aloud a story called *Cam the Camel*.

Think Aloud *Using information in a story, we can conclude that characters are feeling a certain way. As I read to you, think about details that will help us figure out how Cam is feeling.*

• Read aloud the story. Ask questions such as:

After page 2: *How does Cam feel about school?* Reread the second paragraph, asking children to listen for clues. (She wants to be a good camel and do well in school.)

After page 3: *How did Cam do in the running lesson?* (She tried her best but came in last.) *How do you think she feels about that?* (Possible responses: sad, frustrated, mad)

After page 4: *I read, "If you are ever in a* sandstorm, *you need to call for help." What do you think a* sandstorm *is?* (a storm that blows sand) *Was Cam good at calling for help?* (no)

After page 6: *What does Cam have to learn now?* (how to walk in the sand) *Is this easy for Cam?* (No; she fell.)

After page 7: *We read that Cam took a bite of* cactus. *What is* cactus? (a desert plant with thorns) *What are* thorns? (sharp points on a plant) *After everything Cam has tried in camel school, how is she feeling?* (like she can't do anything right)

After page 10: *What did Cam do?* (She saved Mr. Camel.) *How do you think she feels now?* (proud of her ability to swim) ▬ **SL.1.1c, SL.1.2**

Quick Check **Comprehension**

Ask, *Cam felt like she couldn't do anything right. What changed her mind?*

DAILY FLUENCY

Build automaticity by using **Context Cards** or word lists on display. Point to the words in any order and have children read them aloud. Continue until children can read all words fluently.

SHARE OBJECTIVES

- Substitute medial phonemes.
- Read words with soft *c*, soft *g*, and *dge*.
- Read to apply comprehension skills.

MATERIALS

Sound/Spelling Cards: *jump, seal*

Write-In Reader Vol. 1 pages 135–140

TERMS ABOUT READING/ LANGUAGE ARTS

details	information
conclusion	

COMMON CORE **RL.1.1** ask and answer questions about key details; **RL.1.10** read prose and poetry; **RF.1.2a** distinguish long from short vowel sounds in spoken single-syllable words; **RF.1.2b** orally produce single-syllable words by blending sounds; **RF.1.2c** isolate and pronounce sounds in spoken single-syllable words; **RF.1.3b** decode regularly spelled one-syllable words; **RF.1.3g** recognize and read irregularly spelled words

Warm Up

Phonemic Awareness

Substitute Medial Phonemes

- Say, *I'll say a word:* hope. *Now, I'll change* /ō/ *to* /ŏ/ *and say the new word:* hop.

- Have children say *hope,* change the sound, and say the new word with you.

- Have children say *hope,* change the sound, and say the new word on their own.

- Continue, using the following words:

sail	/ā/ to /ē/	seal
hat	/ă/ to /ā/	hate
rice	/ī/ to /ā/	race

- Correct errors by repeating the process.
  ▬ **RF.1.2a, RF.1.2b, RF.1.3b**

RETEACH

Phonics: Soft *c*, Soft *g*, and *dge*

Sound/Spelling Cards

- Display **Sound/Spelling Card** *seal.* Say the word, and ask, *What sound do you hear at the beginning of* seal? (/s/) Point to *ce* and *ci.* Teach that *c* before *e* and *i* often stands for /s/.

- Repeat, using **Sound/Spelling Card** *jump,* to teach that *g* before *e* and *i* stands for /j/. Teach that *dge* also stands for /j/.

- Write *judge* on the board or on a pad. Teach that *e* at the end of *dge* does not make the *u* long. Point under *u* and say /ŭ/. Point under *dge* and say /j/. Then say the whole word.

- Write the following words on the board or on a pad:

race	cent	gel	edge	bridge

- For each word, say the sound for the first vowel, the sound for *ce* or *ge,* and then the word. For *dge* words, remind children that the first vowel is short. Have children say the vowel sound, then the sound represented by *ce, ge,* or *dge.* Then have them blend the sounds to read the word on their own.

- Correct errors by modeling the process.
  ▬ **RF.1.2b, RF.1.2c, RF.1.3g**

READ

Jake's Best Race

Write-In Reader Vol. 1 pages 135–140

Preview *Jake's Best Race* using the **Think Aloud** to reteach conclusions.

Think Aloud   In *Jake's Best Race,* the characters are Jake, Kim, and Jane. As we read the story, we will look for details that help us understand the characters. Details are pieces of information that help us draw conclusions about the story.

READ

Have children choral-read the story for accuracy. If they mispronounce or hesitate over a word, stop the reading and tell the class the correct word. Have all children repeat the word, and then continue reading from the beginning of the sentence.

REREAD

Reread the story with children. Use the following questions to check children's understanding of the story.

After page 135: *What does Jake want to do?* (win the race) *Why?* (He thinks he will not have fun otherwise.)

After page 137: *What happens to Jake?* (He runs over a rock and falls.) *How do you think he feels?* (mad, since he wanted to win the race)

After page 138: *Who talks to Jake?* (Kim) *What does she tell him?* (that he won't race) *Is Kim nice?* (not really) *How is Jake feeling now?* (mad, upset)

After page 139: *What does Jane do when she sees Jake?* (She helps him up.) *Who is the better friend, Kim or Jane? Why?* (Jane, because she helps Jake)

After page 140: *At the beginning of the story, Jake thought the race would not be fun if he didn't win. Does he still feel that way?* (no) *Why not?* (He meets Jane. She helps him have fun even though he didn't win.) ⬛ **RL.1.1, RL.1.10**

Quick Check **Comprehension**

Ask, *Do you think Jake will enter any more races? Why?*

DAILY FLUENCY

Build automaticity by using **Context Cards** or word lists on display. Point to the words in any order and have children read them aloud. Continue until children can read all words fluently.

SHARE OBJECTIVES

- Read and use High-Frequency Words.
- Build words using phonograms *-ake* and *-ace*.
- Reread decodable story to build fluency and comprehension.

MATERIALS

Letter Cards

Context Cards: *five, four, into, over, starts, three, two, watch*

Write-In Reader Vol. 1 pages 135–141

TERMS ABOUT READING/ LANGUAGE ARTS

expression

☑ WORDS TO KNOW

Five is a number. People have **five** fingers on each hand.

Four is a number. A dog has **four** legs.

Into means to go inside of something.

Starts means to begin.

RL.1.1 ask and answer questions about key details; **RF.1.3b** decode regularly spelled one-syllable words; **RF.1.3g** recognize and read irregularly spelled words; **RF.1.4a** read on-level text with purpose and understanding; **RF.1.4b** read on-level text orally with accuracy, appropriate rate, and expression

Warm Up

Words to Know

five, four, into, over, starts, three, two, watch

- Distribute the **Context Cards** to children. Include *five, four, into, over, starts, three, two,* and *watch*.
- Have children practice reading the words. Then challenge children to use as many of these words as possible in one sentence. **RF.1.3g**

Quick Check Words to Know

Ask each child to use one of the week's words in a sentence.

RETEACH

Phonics: Phonograms -*ake* and -*ace*

Letter Cards

- Create the phonogram -*ake* with the **Letter Cards**.
- Model adding additional **Letter Cards** in front of the phonogram to create words.
- Challenge children to create as many words as they can by adding one or more letters in front of the phonogram. Record words on the board or on a pad. If children create nonsense words, say, *That's not a real word, but we can read it anyway.*
- Have children read the list of words.
- Repeat using the phonogram -*ace*. **RF.1.3b**

| a | k | e | | a | c | e |

Possible Words

-*ake*			-*ace*		
make	sake	flake	face	grace	pace
rake	cake	Jake	lace	brace	race

RETEACH

Fluency: Expression

Write-In Reader Vol. 1 page 135

• Explain that you are going to read a page in two different ways. Children will listen and give you some tips after each reading. First, read page 135 without expression. Ask, *What do you think about my first reading?* Encourage feedback.

• Point out the exclamation mark in the first sentence. Ask, *How should I read this sentence?* Point out the verb *hissed* in the third sentence. Ask, *How should I read what Jake says?*

• Reread the text on page 135 modeling how to use punctuation and word clues to help you read with expression. Have children echo-read the page, paying attention to their expression. ▬ RF.1.4a, RF.1.4b

Look Back and Respond

Write-In Reader Vol. 1 pages 135–141

Read aloud each question and the answer choices with children. Help them find answers using the suggestions below. Model how to look back at the story to find the answer.

1. Why can't Jake race? (because he fell) *Look at page 136. Read the third sentence. What happened to Jake?* (He ran over a rock.)

2. Why was this Jake's "best" race? (because he met Jane) *Look at page 140. Read the first two sentences. What do they tell us?* (Jake had fun even though he didn't win.)

3. What will happen next? (Jake and Jane will be pals.) *Look at the last page. What sentence on page 140 helps us draw this conclusion?* (The last one: "He had fun with his new pal, Jane.") ▬ RL.1.1

Turn and Talk 4. Have children talk about a race they were in. Ask for volunteers, and write several responses on the board. Then have the children draw or write their responses.

DAILY FLUENCY

Build automaticity by using **Context Cards** or word lists on display. Point to the words in any order and have children read them aloud. Continue until children can read all words fluently.

Warm Up

Phonemic Awareness

Substitute Medial Phonemes

- Say, *I'll say a word:* bite. *Now, I'll change /ī/ to /ĭ/ and say the new word:* bit.
- Have children say *bite*, change the sound, and say the new word with you.
- Have children say *bite*, change the sound, and say the new word on their own.
- Continue, using the following words:

mope	/ō/ to /ŏ/	mop
cap	/ă/ to /ā/	cape
kite	/ī/ to /ĭ/	kit

- Correct errors by repeating the process.

RF.1.2a, RF.1.2b, RF.1.3b

PRETEACH

Phonics: Long *i*, Digraphs *kn, wr, gn,* and *mb*

Sound/Spelling Cards

- Display the **Sound/Spelling Card** for *ice cream*. Say the word, and ask, *What sound do you hear at the beginning of* ice cream? (/ī/) Write *rice* on the board. Point to *ice* and teach that when a word ends in *i*-consonant-*e*, the *i* stands for its long sound and the final *e* is silent.
- Repeat using the **Sound/Spelling Cards** for *noodle, rooster,* and *mouse* to teach that *kn* and *gn* stand for /n/, *wr* stands for /r/, and *mb* stands for /m/.
- Write on a board or pad the following words:

like	mine	wren	gnat	knob	lamb

- Point under the first vowel and say its sound. Point under the newly taught letter combinations and say the sound, then say the word. Then have children repeat the sounds and word with you.
- Correct errors by modeling the process.

RF.1.2b, RF.1.2c, RF.1.3a, RF.1.3c

REVIEW

Conclusions

Write-In Reader Vol. 1 pages 135–140

- Remind children that when they draw conclusions, they use details in a story to come to a decision.

- Hold up a bag with a paper clip inside. Say, *I'm going to give you some details about the object in this bag. Use these details to draw a conclusion about what is inside the bag.*

- Provide details and encourage feedback, asking:

  It is made from metal wire. What do you think it could be?
  It is small and flat. What could it be?
  It is used to hold paper together. What could it be?

- Draw a details map on the board or on a sheet of paper, and record children's responses. If needed, remind children how to use the map to draw conclusions.

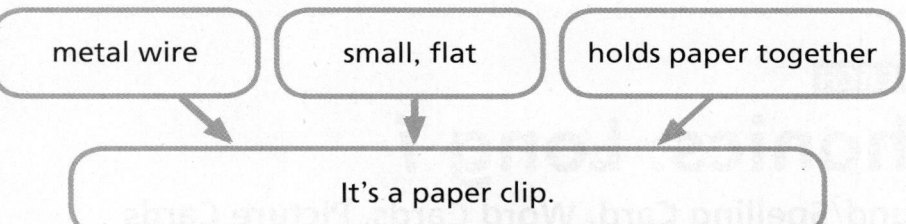

| metal wire | small, flat | holds paper together |

It's a paper clip.

- Tell children to think about *Jake's Best Race*. Remind them that Jake learned something about himself in the race. Tell children to think about themselves. Ask, *What do you like to do most? What are your least favorite things to do? How do you spend your free time?*

Turn and Talk Have children work with a partner to discuss what their descriptions tell them about themselves. Then have them draw a picture of themselves on a piece of paper. At the top of the paper, have them draw or write details from their descriptions. At the bottom, have them draw or write a sentence that draws a conclusion about themselves. ◖ RL.1.7

Quick Check **Fluency**

Listen to individual children read aloud *Jake's Best Race*. Encourage them to use expression when they read.

RETURN TO THE ANCHOR TEXT

"Be a Reading Detective!"
Student Book pages 125–143
Write-In Reader pages 141A–141B

- Page through "The Big Race" with children and review the main characters and events. Encourage volunteers to talk about what is happening on each page.

- Read page 141A of the **Write-In Reader** with children. Remind children that reading detectives find clues in the words and pictures of a story.

- Discuss the questions with children. Guide them to find clues in the words and pictures that help them answer the questions.

- Have children complete item 1 on page 141B on their own. Then have them share their work with a partner. Encourage them to discuss how they came up with their answer.

- Read item 2 on page 141B. Have children talk with a partner about who eats cake at the end of the story. Have them discuss what clues help them understand that Red Lizard shares the cake with all his friends.

DAILY FLUENCY

Read Around the Room Have one child point to words that are on display in the room. Have the group read the words. Give each child a chance to be the pointer.

DAY 1

SHARE OBJECTIVES

- Substitute medial phonemes.
- Read words with long *i*.
- Read High-Frequency Words in context.

MATERIALS

Sound/Spelling Card: *ice cream*
Word Cards: *bike, dime, kite, nine, prize*
Picture Cards: *bike, dime, kite, nine, prize*
Write-In Reader Vol. 1 pages 142–143
Context Cards: *eyes, long, or, walk*

TERMS ABOUT READING/ LANGUAGE ARTS

alike   different

Warm Up

Phonemic Awareness

Substitute Medial Phonemes

- Say, *I'll say a word:* fine. *Now, I'll change* /ī/ *to* /ĭ/ *and say the new word:* fin.
- Have children say *fine,* change the sound, and say the new word with you.
- Have children say *fine,* change the sound, and say the new word on their own.
- Continue, using the following words:

file	/ī/ to /ĭ/	fill
rob	/ŏ/ to /ō/	robe
dome	/ō/ to /ī/	dime

- Correct errors by repeating the process.
  RF.1.2a, RF.1.2b, RF.1.3b

RETEACH

Phonics: Long *i*

Sound/Spelling Card, Word Cards, Picture Cards

- Display the **Sound/Spelling Card** for *ice cream*. Say the word, and ask, *What sound do you hear at the beginning of* ice cream? (/ī/) Write *fine* on the board. Point to *ine* and teach that when a word ends in *i*-consonant-*e*, the *i* stands for its long sound and the final *e* is silent.

- Show the **Word Card** for *bike*. Say, *This word ends in* e. *The* i *stands for* /ī/. *The* e *is silent. This word is* bike. Have children say the vowel sound and then blend the sounds to say the word. Show the **Picture Card** for *bike*.

- Follow the same procedure using the **Word Cards** and **Picture Cards** for *dime, kite, nine,* and *prize*.

- Correct errors by modeling the process.
  RF.1.2b, RF.1.2c, RF.1.3c

COMMON CORE **RF.1.2a** distinguish long from short vowel sounds in spoken single-syllable words; **RF.1.2b** orally produce single-syllable words by blending sounds; **RF.1.2c** isolate and pronounce sounds in spoken single-syllable words; **RF.1.3b** decode regularly spelled one-syllable words; **RF.1.3c** know final -e and vowel team conventions for representing long vowel sounds; **RF.1.3g** recognize and read irregularly spelled words; **SL.1.1a** follow rules for discussions

Talk About It

- Ask children to think about animals they have seen. Explain that there are many different types of animals. Some animals are big, like an elephant. Some animals are small, like an ant. Have children discuss these different types of animals. Make a chart to record children's ideas.

Big Animals	Small Animals
elephant	ant
whale	mouse
rhino	lizard

- Ask, *How are all of these animals alike? How are they different?*
  🔊 SL.1.1a

RETEACH

Words to Know

Write-In Reader Vol. 1 pages 142–143

- Introduce *Animal Groups*. Read the heading. Have students look at the photographs and guess what these pages are about.

- Discuss each photograph, asking, *What animal group does this goldfish (snake, bug, cat) belong to?* (fish, reptile, insect, mammal)

- Read each sentence aloud with children as they point to each word. Ask what the highlighted word in each sentence means. See suggested definitions in the right-hand column. Then have children write the target word.

- Have children take turns rereading each sentence. Then have them choral-read the words in the Words to Know box with you. 🔊 RF.1.3g

Quick Check **Words to Know**

Have children use one of the Words to Know in a sentence.

✓ **WORDS TO KNOW**

Eyes are the parts of a body that are used to see.

Long means not short.

Or is used to join other words when you have a choice between things.

Walk means to move your legs to go somewhere.

DAILY FLUENCY

Build automaticity by using **Context Cards** or word lists on display. Point to the words in any order and have children read them aloud. Continue until children can read all words fluently.

DAY 2

Warm Up

Words to Know

eyes, long, or, walk

Distribute the **Context Cards** to children. Include *eyes, long, or,* and *walk*. Have partners practice reading the words. Then ask each child to use one word in a sentence. For a challenge, ask if anyone can use two words in one sentence. 🔊 **RF.1.3g**

REVIEW

Phonics: Long *i*

Write-In Reader Vol. 1 page 144

- Introduce the **Write-In Reader.** Have children choral-read the words in the word box. Have them identify the *i*-consonant-*e̅* in each word. Ask, *What sound does* i *stand for in this word?* Then direct their attention to the images in the first row.

- Say, *Look at the pictures in the first row. Point to each one as I name it.* Then have children say the name of each object together. (kite, dime)

- Follow the same procedure for the second row. (mice, ice)

- Assign children to work on their own, writing the correct word below each object.

- Check children's work. If any children have written the incorrect word, determine whether the misunderstanding results from being unable to name the pictured objects or from being unable to read the words.

🔊 **RF.1.2b, RF.1.2c, RF.1.3c**

COMMON CORE **RF.1.2b** orally produce single-syllable words by blending sounds; **RF.1.2c** isolate and pronounce sounds in spoken single-syllable words; **RF.1.3c** know final -e and vowel team conventions for representing long vowel sounds; **RF.1.3g** recognize and read irregularly spelled words; **SL.1.1c** ask questions to clear up confusion about topics and texts under discussion; **SL.1.2** ask and answer questions about details in a text read aloud, information presented orally, or through other media

Teacher Read Aloud

Leveled Reader: *Bald Eagles*

Leveled Reader

• Use the **Think Aloud** to introduce compare and contrast. Tell children that you are going to read aloud a story called *Bald Eagles*.

Think Aloud *As I read to you, use what you know to compare bald eagles to other birds. Think about how bald eagles are like other birds and how they are different.*

• Read the story aloud. Ask questions such as:

After page 2: *Describe the bald eagle.* Reread the second paragraph, asking children to listen for details. (It is not bald. It has white feathers on its head and tail. The feathers on its body are brown.)

After page 3: *Think about a hummingbird. How is an eagle like a hummingbird?* (Both have hollow bones. Both can fly.) *How are eagles and hummingbirds different?* (Eagles are big, with long wings. Hummingbirds are very small.)

After page 5: *What do bald eagles eat?* (fish) *What happens if a fish is too heavy?* (The eagle swims with it to shore.)

After page 7: *What is a* nest? (the home a bird lives in) *How are bald eagle nests like other bird nests that you know about?* (They are in trees; they are made of twigs, grass, and feathers.) *How are bald eagle nests different?* (They are very big.)

After page 8: *I read, "The nest is a good shelter from wind and rain." What do you think* shelter *means?* (protection) *Who feeds the baby eagles?* (both parents)

After page 10: *We read that the bald eagle is the* national *bird. What do you think this means?* (It is a symbol of America.) **SL.1.1c, SL.1.2**

Quick Check | **Comprehension**

Ask, *How are bald eagles different from other birds?*

DAILY FLUENCY

Build automaticity by using **Context Cards** or word lists on display. Point to the words in any order and have children read them aloud. Continue until children can read all words fluently.

SHARE OBJECTIVES

- Substitute medial phonemes.
- Read words with *kn, wr, gn,* and *mb*.
- Read to apply comprehension skills.

MATERIALS

Sound/Spelling Cards: *mouse, noodle, rooster*

Write-In Reader Vol. 1 pages 145–150

TERMS ABOUT READING/ LANGUAGE ARTS

compare   contrast

COMMON CORE **RI.1.1** ask and answer questions about key details; **RI.1.10** read informational texts; **RF.1.2a** distinguish long from short vowel sounds in spoken single-syllable words; **RF.1.2b** orally produce single-syllable words by blending sounds; **RF.1.3a** know the spelling-sound correspondences for common consonant digraphs; **RF.1.3b** decode regularly spelled one-syllable words

---

Warm Up

Phonemic Awareness

Substitute Medial Phonemes

- Say, *I'll say a word:* mile. *Now, I'll change /ī/ to /ĭ/ and say the new word:* mill.
- Have children say *mile*, change the sound, and say the new word with you.
- Have children say *mile*, change the sound, and say the new word on their own.
- Continue, using the following words:

night	/ī/ to /ĭ/	knit
zig	/ĭ/ to /ă/	zag
kite	/ī/ to /ĭ/	kit

- Correct errors by repeating the process.

  ◼ **RF.1.2a, RF.1.2b, RF.1.3b**

RETEACH

Phonics: Digraphs *kn, wr, gn,* and *mb*

Sound/Spelling Cards

- Display the **Sound/Spelling Card** for *noodle*. Say the word, and ask, *What sound do you hear at the beginning of* noodles? (/n/) Write *knit* and *gnat* on the board. Point to *kn* and *gn* and teach that *kn* and *gn* stand for /n/.

- Write *limb* and *wren* on the board and use the **Sound/Spelling Cards** for *mouse* and *rooster* to teach that *mb* stands for /m/ and *wr* stands for /r/.

- Write the following words on a board or pad:

knife	gnat	write	wrist	thumb	lamb

- Using the word *knife*, point under the first vowel and say its sound. Point under the newly taught letter combination and say the sound. Blend the sounds to read the word. Then have children repeat the steps with you. Continue with the remaining words, having children blend sounds to read each word.

- Correct errors by modeling the process.

  ◼ **RF.1.2b, RF.1.3a, RF.1.3b**

READ

Cats

Write-In Reader Vol. 1 pages 145–150

Preview *Cats* using the **Think Aloud** to reteach compare and contrast.

Think Aloud *In this story, we will learn about cats. As we read the story, we will compare and contrast different types of cats. Compare means to look for things that are the same. Contrast means to look for things that are different.*

READ

Have children choral-read the story for accuracy. If they mispronounce or hesitate over a word, stop the reading and tell the class the correct word. Have all children repeat the word, and then continue reading from the beginning of the sentence.

REREAD

Reread the story with children. Use the following questions to check children's understanding of the story.

After page 145: *Are all cats the same?* (no) *How can you tell?* (The pictures show many types of cats.)

After page 146: *How are cats alike?* (They can all bite.) *How are they different?* (They are different sizes.)

After page 148: *What does this cat eat?* (other animals)

After page 149: *How is this cat like the cat on page 148?* (They are both spotted.)

After page 150: *How are big cats like pet cats?* (They look similar.) *We just compared big cats and pets. Now contrast them. How are they different?* (Big cats are fierce. They are not cuddly.)

▬ RI.1.1, RI.1.10

Quick Check Comprehension

Ask, *Which animal would you rather learn more about, bald eagles or big cats? Explain why.*

DAILY FLUENCY

Build automaticity by using **Context Cards** or word lists on display. Point to the words in any order and have children read them aloud. Continue until children can read all words fluently.

DAY 4

SHARE OBJECTIVES

- Read and use High-Frequency Words.
- Build words using the phonograms *-ine* and *-ite*.
- Review decodable story to build fluency and comprehension.

MATERIALS

Context Cards: *bird, both, eyes, fly, long, or, those, walk*

Letter Cards

Write-In Reader Vol. 1 pages 145–151

TERMS ABOUT READING/ LANGUAGE ARTS

compare   contrast

☑ WORDS TO KNOW

A **bird** is an animal that has two wings. Most **birds** can fly.

Both means two things together.

Fly means to move through the air by using wings or parts like wings.

Those is a word you use instead of *that* when you are talking about more than one thing.

COMMON CORE **RI.1.1** ask and answer questions about key details; **RF.1.2b** orally produce single-syllable words by blending sounds; **RF.1.3b** decode regularly spelled one-syllable words; **RF.1.3g** recognize and read irregularly spelled words; **RF.1.4b** read on-level text orally with accuracy, appropriate rate, and expression

Warm Up

Words to Know

bird, both, eyes, fly, long, or, those, walk

- Distribute the **Context Cards** to children. Include *bird, both, eyes, fly, long, or, those,* and *walk*.
- Have children practice reading the words. Then challenge children to use as many of these words as possible in one sentence. 🔲 **RF.1.3g**

Quick Check | **Words to Know**

Ask each child to use one of the week's words in a sentence.

RETEACH

Phonics: Phonograms *-ine* and *-ite*

Letter Cards

- Create the phonogram *-ine* with the **Letter Cards**.
- Model using additional **Letter Cards** to create new words by adding one or more letters in front of *-ine*.
- Challenge children to create as many words as they can by adding one or two letters in front of the phonogram. Record words on the board or on a pad. If children create nonsense words, say, *That's not a real word, but we can read it anyway.*
- Have children read the list of words.
- Repeat the process with the phonogram *-ite*.
  🔲 **RF.1.2b, RF.1.3b**

| i | n | e | i | t | e |

Possible Words

-ine			-ite		
whine	mine	line	bite	write	site
pine	fine	spine	kite	white	quite

RETEACH

Fluency: Intonation

Write-In Reader Vol. 1 page 145

- Explain that you are going to read a page in two different ways. Children will listen and give you some tips after each reading. First, read page 145 in a monotone. Ask, *What do you think about my first reading?* Encourage feedback.

- Point out that the first sentence is a statement, and the second is an exclamation. Ask, *Does my voice go up or down at the end of a statement? What does my voice do at the end of an exclamation?* Explain that the tone of your voice changes depending on punctuation. Model natural intonation for a statement and then an exclamation.

- Reread the text on page 145 with natural intonation. Then have children echo-read the page. **RF.1.4b**

Look Back and Respond

Write-In Reader Vol. 1 pages 145–151

Read aloud each question and the answer choices with children. Help children find answers using the suggestions below. Model how to look back at the story to find the answer.

1. How are all cats the same? **(They can all bite.)** *Look at page 146. Which sentence compares all cats?* (the second one)

2. How can big cats differ? **(in color)** *What color can big cats be?* (black, brown, white, orange)

3. If you see a big cat... **(Let it be.)** *Look at page 150. Why should you not walk up to big cats?* (They are not like pets.)

Turn and Talk **4.** Have children talk about cats. Ask for volunteers to respond and write several responses on the board. Then have children write a word that describes cats. **RI.1.1**

DAILY FLUENCY

Build automaticity by using **Context Cards** or word lists on display. Point to the words in any order and have children read them aloud. Continue until children can read all words fluently.

SHARE OBJECTIVES

- Identify medial phonemes.
- Read words with long *o* and *u*.
- Apply the compare and contrast skill to real life and reading.

MATERIALS

Sound/Spelling Cards: *ocean, uniform*

Word Cards: *mule, nose, note, rope, stone*

Picture Cards: *mule, nose, note, rope, stone*

Write-In Reader Vol. 1 pages 145–150

TERMS ABOUT READING/ LANGUAGE ARTS

compare   contrast

Venn diagram

COMMON CORE **RI.1.3** describe the connection between individuals, events, ideas, or information in a text; **RF.1.2a** distinguish long from short vowel sounds in spoken single-syllable words; **RF.1.2b** orally produce single-syllable words by blending sounds; **RF.1.3b** decode regularly spelled one-syllable words; **RF.1.3c** know final -e and vowel team conventions for representing long vowel sounds

Warm Up

Phonemic Awareness

Identify Medial Phonemes

- Say, *I'll say a word:* hole. *Now, I'll say the middle sound:* /ō/.
- Have children say *hole* and the middle sound with you.
- Have children say *hole* and the middle sound on their own.
- Continue, using the following words:

fume	/yo͞o/
hose	/ō/
both	/ō/

- Correct errors by repeating the process.
  RF.1.2a, RF.1.2b, RF.1.3b

PRETEACH

Phonics: Long *o* and *u*

Sound/Spelling Cards, Word Cards, Picture Cards

- Display the **Sound/Spelling Card** for *ocean*. Say the word and ask, *What sound do you hear at the beginning of* ocean? (/ō/) Write *rose* on the board or on a pad. Point to *ose* and teach that the *o*-consonant-*e* pattern stands for /ō/. Point to *o* and teach that when a word ends in *o*, the *o* stands for /ō/. Write *go* on the board or on a pad.

- Repeat using the **Sound/Spelling Card** for *uniform*. Write *cute* on the board and teach that the *u*-consonant-*e* pattern stands for /yo͞o/.

- Show the **Word Card** for *nose*. Say, *This word ends in* e. *The* o *stands for* /ō/. *The* e *is silent. The word is* nose. Tell children to say the first vowel sound and the word. Show the **Picture Card** for *nose*.

- Follow the same procedure using **Word** and **Picture Cards** for *mule, note, rope, stone*.
  RF.1.2a, RF.1.3b, RF.1.3c

REVIEW

Compare and Contrast

Write-In Reader Vol. 1 pages 145–150

- Remind children that when they compare and contrast, they think about how things are alike and how they are different.

- Hold up a paper clip and a rubber band. Ask, *How are a paper clip and a rubber band alike? How are they different?*

- Guide the comparison by asking:

  What do you use them for?
  What are they made of?
  How do they look?

- Draw a simple Venn diagram on the board or on a sheet of paper, and record children's ideas. If needed, remind children how to use the Venn diagram to compare and contrast.

Paper clip	Both	Rubber band
metal spiral	hold things together bendable different sizes	rubber circle

- Tell children to think about the story *Cats*. Have them think about an animal they like. Ask, *How is your animal like a cat? How is it different? What does your animal eat? What do big cats eat? How does your animal move? Does it run, swim, or fly? How do big cats move?*

Turn and Talk Have children work with a partner to discuss the animals they chose. Then have them fold a sheet of paper into quarters. Have them draw or write the label "Big Cats" in one of the top boxes, and the name of their animal in the other top box. In the bottom two boxes, have them draw or write how the animals are alike and how they are different. ◖ RI.1.3

Quick Check | Fluency

Listen to individual children read aloud *Cats*. Encourage them to use expression and to pay attention to intonation.

RETURN TO THE ANCHOR TEXT

"Be a Reading Detective!"
Student Book pages 165–183
Write-In Reader pages 151A–151B

- Page through "Animal Groups" with children and review important ideas and information. Encourage volunteers to talk about each page.

- Read page 151A of the **Write-In Reader** with children. Remind children that reading detectives find clues in words and pictures to help them understand what they read.

- Discuss the questions with children. Guide them to find clues in the words and photographs that help them answer the questions.

- Have children complete item 1 on page 151B on their own. Then have them share their work with a partner. Encourage them to discuss how they came up with their answer.

- Read item 2 on page 151B. Have children talk with a partner about how all fish are the same. Have them discuss clues from the selection that help them answer the question.

DAILY FLUENCY

Read Around the Room Have one child point to words that are on display in the room. Have the group read the words. Give each child a chance to be the pointer.

Lesson 11

At Home in the Ocean

Build Background: What kinds of plants and animals would you find in the ocean?

Comprehension: Author's Purpose; Analyze/Evaluate

Words to Know: blue, cold, far, little, live, their, water, where

High-Utility Words: animals, home, lots, swim

Lesson 12

How Leopard Got His Spots

Build Background: Which animals have stripes and which have spots?

Comprehension: Sequence of Events; Question

Words to Know: been, brown, know, never, off, out, own, very

High-Utility Words: black, spot, stripe

Lesson 13

Seasons

Build Background: How is each season different?

Comprehension: Cause and Effect; Visualize

Words to Know: down, fall, goes, green, grow, new, open, yellow

High-Utility Words: ends, hot, spring, sun, wet

Lesson 14

The Big Race

Build Background: What animals live in a desert?

Comprehension: Conclusions; Infer/Predict

Words to Know: five, four, into, over, starts, three, two, watch

High-Utility Words: chase, hop, race, trip, win

Lesson 15

Animal Groups

Build Background: How are animals different from each other?

Comprehension: Compare and Contrast; Monitor/Clarify

Words to Know: bird, both, eyes, fly, long, or, those, walk

High-Utility Words: body, hair, shape, size, skin

DAY 1

SHARE OBJECTIVES

- Practice using Words to Know orally. **LANGUAGE**
- Listen to and recite a chant. **CONTENT**
- Practice words with digraph *th*. **LANGUAGE**

MATERIALS

Language Support Card 11
Context Cards
Student Book
Sound/Spelling Card *thumb*

☑ WORDS TO KNOW

blue
cold
far
little
live
their
water
where

TERMS ABOUT LANGUAGE

• = *Spanish cognate*

consonant   • *consonante*

Speaking and Listening

USE LANGUAGE SUPPORT CARD
Present **Language Support Card 11.**
Use the activities on the back of the
card to introduce concepts and
vocabulary from *At Home in the Ocean*
and to practice Academic English.

◼ **L.1.6**

Develop Words to Know

USE CONTEXT CARDS Show the **Context Cards** for *live* and *water*.
Present the cards using Steps 1–3 of the Introduce Words to Know
routine on **Teacher's Edition** p. T20.

- Help children use *live* and *water* to discuss animals that live in the
  ocean.

- Encourage children to use high-utility words in their responses.

USE ORAL LANGUAGE CHANT Read the title of the chant below
aloud, and have children repeat. Then read the chant and have
children listen to *A Home in the Sea* once in its entirety. Read each
line again and have children repeat.

A Home in the Sea

Hey, **little** animals,
where can you be?
We **live** in the **water,**
the **cold, blue** sea!

- Help children practice saying the chant with a partner. Then have
  them take turns saying the chant while their partner listens.

THINK-PAIR-SHARE Help partners orally complete the following
sentence frames:

1. Some little animals live in the _____sea_____.

2. Their _____home_____ is cold and blue. ◼ **RF.1.3g**

COMMON CORE **RI.1.5** know and use text features to locate facts or
information; **RF.1.3a** know the spelling-sound
correspondences for common consonant digraphs;
RF.1.3g recognize and spell irregularly spelled words; **L.1.6** use words
and phrases acquired through conversations, reading and being read
to, and responding to texts

Scaffold Comprehension

PREVIEW *AT HOME IN THE OCEAN* Help children scan the photos, captions, and other features of **Student Book** pp. 14–29. Have them predict one thing they may learn by reading the text. ◼ **RI.1.5**

PRETEACH

Digraph *th*

PHONEMIC AWARENESS WARM-UP *I am going to say some words. Listen to the sound at the end. Let's do the first one together:* with, /th/, with, /th/. Have children repeat the word and its ending sound.

- Continue, having children identify the final sound in *bath, bathe, both, breathe, moth, soothe,* and *path,* first with you and then by themselves.

TEACH/MODEL Display the **Sound/Spelling Card** *thumb.* Hold up your thumb as you say the word. Have children repeat after you: /th/, /th/, thumb.

- *What is the beginning sound in* thumb? *The word* thumb *starts with one sound that two* **consonants** *stand for:* /th/. Remind children that consonants are letters that are not *a, e, i, o,* or *u. The consonants* t and h *together stand for the sound* /th/.

- Write and pronounce *this.* Then say This *is my* thumb, /th/, /th/, this. Have children repeat after you.

GUIDED PRACTICE Write *thin, that, with, Beth,* and *them.* Say each word aloud as you point out the letters that represent the two sounds of the digraph *th.* Have children repeat. ◼ **RF.1.3a**

- Offer Corrective Feedback as needed.

CHECK PROGRESS

Do children …

- correctly pronounce and use Words to Know and high-utility words?
- recite a chant with fluency?
- identify and say words with the digraph *th*?

REVIEW TOGETHER

- Have partners use **Context Cards** to review the Words to Know and their meanings. Have them complete the activities on the backs of the cards.
- Help children list and pronounce words with the digraph *th.*

Corrective Feedback

- Review the **Sound/Spelling Card.**
- Point to the image and say *thumb.*
- Touch the letters *th.*
- Have children repeat after you as you pronounce the digraph *th.*
- Have them repeat after you as you pronounce *this, them, thin,* and *with* correctly.

✏️ Scaffolded Practice and Application

Beginning	**Low Intermediate**	**High Intermediate**	**Proficient**
Write *th.* Point to the letters and help children pronounce the sound /th/ after you. Then help them say *this, thin,* and *them.*	Write *this, thin,* and *them.* Help children pronounce each word. Have them circle the letters that stand for the digraph *th* in each word, then help them pronounce each word again.	Have children repeat this sentence: *These are their thin thumbs.* Have them take turns saying the sentence to a partner. Write *thin* and have them circle the letters that stand for the digraph *th.*	Have children list all the words they know with the digraph *th,* then use as many of them as possible in sentences. Have them say their sentences to a partner.

DAY 2

SHARE OBJECTIVES

- Blend and segment phonemes. **LANGUAGE**
- Review and discuss informational texts. **CONTENT**
- Analyze and evaluate information in *At Home in the Ocean*. **CONTENT**
- Identify the author's purpose in *At Home in the Ocean*. **CONTENT**

MATERIALS

Student Book
Student eBook
Language Support Card 11
Context Cards

TERMS ABOUT INFORMATIONAL TEXT

• = *Spanish cognate*

informational text	• *texto informativo*
analyze	• *analizar*
evaluate	• *evaluar*
author's purpose	• *propósito del autor*
topic	

COMMON CORE **RI.1.2** identify the main topic and retell key details; **RI.1.3** describe the connection between individuals, events, ideas or information in a text; **RI.1.5** know and use text features to locate facts or information; **RF.1.2b** orally produce single-syllable words by blending sounds **RF.1.2d** segment spoken single-syllable words into their complete sequence of individual sounds; **L.1.6** use words and phrases acquired through conversations, reading and being read to, and responding to texts;

Phonemic Awareness Warm-Up

BLEND AND SEGMENT PHONEMES *I am going to say some sounds. I can blend the sounds to say a word. Listen: /k/, /r/ /ă/ /b/, crab. What is the word?* (crab) *What are the sounds in the word?* (/k/ /r/ /ă/ /b/)

- Continue with *fish, sea, claw,* and *water.*

- Review the meaning of each word as needed.
  🔲 RF.1.2b, RF.1.2d

Scaffold Comprehension

REVIEW *AT HOME IN THE OCEAN* Use a Think Aloud and the following prompts to lead children on a guided review of *At Home in the Ocean.* Remind children that looking over pictures and key words will help them understand and remember what they read.

Think Aloud **PAGE 15:** Help children read the title aloud. *Fish are not the only animals that live in the ocean. What other animals live in the ocean?* (crabs, penguins, sea stars, whales)

PAGES 18–23: Look at the pictures of the blue whale and the manatee. *How are a blue whale and a manatee alike? How are they different?* (They are both large sea animals that live in the ocean. Blue whales live in cold water, but manatees live in warm water.)

PAGES 24–27: Point to the pictures and labels of sea animals. *What sea animals would you like to learn more about?* (Answers will vary. Some children may want to learn more about turtles; others may want to know more about sea otters.)

PAGES 28–29: Point to the pictures of the fish. *Fish come in many colors. What colors are these fish?* (yellow, purple, orange)

CHECK COMPREHENSION If children need additional support with the main selection, make the **Student eBook** for *At Home in the Ocean* available. Have partners or individuals page through *At Home in the Ocean*, focusing on the photographs as they listen.

1. Which big sea animal is blue? (blue whale)
2. Which sea animal swims slowly and eats lots of plants? (manatee)
3. Penguins have wings. How do their wings help them in the water? (They can swim fast.) 🔲 RI.1.5, L.1.6

PRETEACH

Analyze/Evaluate

INTRODUCE Pronounce and explain *analyze* and *evaluate*. *When we analyze, we tell what we think about a text. When we evaluate, we explain why.*

THINK-PAIR-SHARE Flip through the main selection. Read the captions, and discuss as a group the differences between various animals. Ask children why they think these differences exist. For example, ask *Why do big and little animals live in the ocean?* ▭ **RI.1.3**

RETEACH

Author's Purpose

TEACH/MODEL Remind children that the *author's purpose* is the reason an author writes. *In an informational text, the author often wants to tell facts about a topic.* Use a Think Aloud to model identifying the author's purpose in *At Home in the Ocean*.

> **Think Aloud** *At Home in the Ocean has many facts about animals that live in the ocean. It also has captions that tell the animals' names, like penguins and sea otters. I think the author's purpose is to tell about a topic. The topic is different animals that live in the ocean.*

GUIDED PRACTICE As a class, identify three things you can learn from reading *At Home in the Ocean*. *The author's purpose is to teach, or tell, about sea animals. What kinds of sea animals do we learn about?*

- Review Teach Academic English on **Language Support Card 11**. Remind children to use *what* and *about* to ask and answer questions about the author's purpose.

- Remind children that details in the text support the author's purpose. For example, a sentence telling about penguins' wings helps the author tell about penguins and how they swim. ▭ **RI.1.2**

CHECK PROGRESS

Do children …
- correctly blend and segment phonemes?
- use Words to Know to discuss *At Home in the Ocean*?
- analyze and evaluate information in *At Home in the Ocean*?
- identify the author's purpose in *At Home in the Ocean*?

REVIEW TOGETHER

- Have partners repeat the Phonemic Awareness Warm-Up.
- Provide additional practice with **Context Cards**.
- Have partners take turns analyzing and evaluating the information on one spread of *At Home in the Ocean*.
- Help children reread *At Home in the Ocean* and find details supporting the author's purpose.

✏️ Scaffolded Practice and Application

Beginning	**Low Intermediate**	**High Intermediate**	**Proficient**
Page through *At Home in the Ocean* with children. Help them identify details about fish and other animals. Remind them that the author's purpose is to tell facts about sea animals.	Page through *At Home in the Ocean* with children. Name the author's purpose for them (telling facts about sea animals) and help them find details that support this purpose.	Have partners page through *At Home in the Ocean*. Remind them that the author's purpose for writing is to tell facts about sea animals. Have them find three details that support this purpose.	Have children page through *At Home in the Ocean*. Have them state the author's purpose for writing, then find three details that support this purpose. Have them share their findings with a partner.

SHARE OBJECTIVES

- Blend and segment phonemes. **LANGUAGE**
- Classify and categorize words about colors. **LANGUAGE**
- Identify and use base words (or root words) and *-s, -es, -ed, -ing.* **LANGUAGE**
- Listen to and recite a chant. **CONTENT**

MATERIALS

Student Book

Index Cards/Letter Cards

Context Cards

TERMS ABOUT LANGUAGE

• = *Spanish cognate*

classify	• *clasificar*
category	• *categoría*
base word	• *palabra base*

Phonemic Awareness Warm-Up

BLEND AND SEGMENT PHONEMES *I am going to say some sounds. I can blend the sounds to say a word. Listen: /r/ /ĕ/ /d/,* red. *What is the word?* (red) *What are the sounds in the word?* (/r/ /ĕ/ /d/)

- Continue with *blue, green, pink, yellow,* and *brown.*

  🔲 **RF.1.2b, RF.1.2d**

Practice Words to Know

USE ORAL LANGUAGE CHANT Read the title of the chant aloud. Then read each line aloud and have children repeat.

A Home in the Sea

Hey, **little** animals,
where can you be?
We **live** in the **water**,
the **cold, blue** sea!

- Help children identify Words to Know and high-utility words in the chant. Write and pronounce the Words to Know. Have children read and repeat them. 🔲 **RF.1.3g**

PRACTICE FLUENCY: STRESS Read the chant aloud, modeling how to change the pitch and volume of your voice to stress certain words or syllables.

COMMON CORE **RF.1.2b** orally produce single-syllable words by blending sounds **RF.1.2d** segment spoken single-syllable words into their complete sequence of individual sounds; **RF.1.3g** recognize and read irregularly spelled words; **L.1.4c** identify frequent occurring root words and their inflectional forms; **L.1.5a** sort words into categories to gain a sense of concepts the categories represent

RETEACH

Classify and Categorize: Colors

INTRODUCE *When we sort things into groups, we* classify *them. The groups we make are called* categories.

- Display *At Home in the Ocean.* Point to a picture showing blue water. *The word* blue *tells about color. The ocean is* blue. *Let's look for other words about color. We can classify them into the same category.*

- Help children identify other color words, such as *red, brown, yellow,* and *green.*

THINK-PAIR-SHARE Help children complete these sentences orally:

1. *Blue* and *green* both tell about ___color___.
2. They are in the ___same___ category.
3. We can classify ___red___ together with *blue* and *green.* ⬛ **L.1.5a**

RETEACH

Base Words and *-s, -es, -ed, -ing*

PHONEMIC AWARENESS WARM-UP *I am going to use one word to make two new ones:* cook, cooks, cooking. *What endings did I add to* cook *to make* cooks *and* cooking? *(-s, -ing)*

TEACH/MODEL Explain that many action words, or verbs, have letters added to the end. The added letters tell when the action happens.

- Write *j, u, m, p; s; e, d;* and *i, n, g* on index cards or use **Letter Cards** *j, u, m, p; s; e, d; i, n, g.* Display the cards *j, u, m, p.* Read *jump. Jump is a* **base word**, *a word I can use to make other words.*

- *Listen as I make three new words from* jump: jumps, jumped, jumping. Show the cards for the ending letters as you say them. Have children repeat after you. *I jump. Molly jumps. We are jumping. They jumped.* Repeat with base word *miss.*

GUIDED PRACTICE Write *cracks, cracked, cracking; fills, filled, filling.* Pronounce the sounds in each word slowly. Have children repeat. Use each word in a sentence. ⬛ **L.1.4c**

CHECK PROGRESS

Do children …

- correctly use Words to Know?
- demonstrate fluency as they recite the chant?
- correctly classify and categorize words about color?
- practice using base words (or root words) and *-s, -es, -ed, -ing*?

REVIEW TOGETHER

- Provide additional practice with **Context Cards.**
- Reread *At Home in the Ocean* with children.
- Have partners page through *At Home in the Ocean* and decide if various words belong in the category for words about color.
- Have small groups practice forming new words using base words (or root word) and *-s, -es, -ed, -ing.*

Corrective Feedback

- Review the **Letter Cards.**
- Review that *jump* is a base word (or root word).
- Draw an *s* in the air or hold up the *s* card as you say *jumps.*
- Have children repeat after you as you pronounce *jumps.*
- Have them repeat after you as you pronounce *jumps, jumped,* and *jumping* correctly.

✏️ **Scaffolded Practice and Application**

| **Beginning** Write and say *run.* Have children repeat. Then write *runs* and *running.* Help children circle the base word (or root word) and underline the endings. | **Low Intermediate** Write and say *pack.* Have children repeat. Help them write it three times and add *-es, -ed,* and *-ing.* Have them repeat each new word. | **High Intermediate** Write *pack* and *pass, -s, -es, -ed,* and *-ing.* Have children write *pack* and *pass* three times, then add endings. Have them read the new words. | **Proficient** Have children write *miss.* Have them use the endings *-es, -ed,* and *-ing* to form three new words. Have them use each word in a sentence. |

- Blend and segment phonemes. **LANGUAGE**
- Comprehend and discuss informational texts. **CONTENT**
- Read the Leveled Reader. **CONTENT**
- Review digraph *th* and base words with *-s, -es, -ed, -ing.* **LANGUAGE**
- Identify proper nouns, including names for people and animals, and titles for people. **LANGUAGE**
- Build reading proficiency through supported reading. **LANGUAGE**

MATERIALS

Student Book
Leveled Reader
Sound/Spelling Card *thumb*
Index Cards/Letter Cards
Context Cards

TERMS ABOUT LANGUAGE/ INFORMATIONAL TEXT

• = *Spanish cognate*

informational text	• *texto informativo*
base word	• *palabra base*
proper noun	• *nombre propio*
capital letter	
title	• *título*

COMMON CORE **RI.1.5** know and use text features to locate facts or information; **RI.1.10** read informational texts; **RF.1.2b** orally produce single-syllable words by blending sounds; **RF.1.2d** segment spoken single-syllable words into their complete sequence of individual sounds; **RF.1.3f** read words with inflectional endings; **RF.1.4b** read on-level text orally with accuracy, appropriate rate, and expression; **L.1.1b** use common, proper, and possessive nouns; **L.1.2a** capitalize dates and names of people

Phonemic Awareness Warm-Up

BLEND AND SEGMENT PHONEMES *I am going to say some sounds. I can blend the sounds to say a word. Listen: /d/ /ĭ/ /g/, dig. What is the word?* (dig) *What are the sounds in the word?* (/d/ /ĭ/ /g/)

- Continue with *digs, digging, swim,* and *swims.*
- Review the meaning of each word as needed.
  RF.1.2b, RF.1.2d

Scaffold Informational Text

DISCUSS *WATER* Use the following prompts to lead children on a review of *Water*. Remind them that *Water* is an **informational text**. It gives facts about water.

PAGE 34: Have children point to the title *Water*. *For sea animals, water is their home. They swim in water. Why do people need water?* (for drinking)

- Point to the picture. *Is this water in a glass or in the sea?* (a glass)

PAGE 35: Read the second paragraph aloud. *Is ice made of water that is cold or hot?* (cold)

- Read the final sentence aloud and point to the picture of the snowflakes. *Are pieces of snow little or big?* (little)

PAGE 36: Point to the picture. *This is a polar bear. What is it like where polar bears live?* (cold, icy) **RI.1.5, RI.1.10**

Supported Reading

READ *LIFE IN THE CORAL REEFS* To read more about water and animals that live in it, direct children to the **Leveled Reader**. Help partners or small groups take turns rereading aloud phrases or sentences from the selection.

English Language Learners

BUDDY READING Pair an adult with a struggling reader. Possible pairings include you and a child, or a child and an aide or other adult.

- Have the adult read aloud, clearly and distinctly, while the struggling reader follows along in the text.
- Have the adult help the less proficient reader with any problems understanding the text. For example, adjust the rate of reading to match the struggling reader's proficiency level.
  RI.1.10, RF.1.4b

Digraph *th*
Base Words and *-s, -es, -ed, -ing*

REVIEW Display the **Sound/Spelling Card** *thumb*. Remind children that *thumb* begins with /th/. T *and* h *side by side stand for* /th/.

- Show the index cards or **Letter Cards** for *j, u, m, p; s; e, d; i, n, g.* Display *j, u, m, p.* Read *jump.* Remind children that *jump* is a **base word**, a word used to make other words. Make *jumps, jumped,* and *jumping* out of the cards, and then read each word.

PRACTICE Help children identify words with *th* and add *-s, -es, -ed,* or *-ing* to base words. Have children raise their hands when they hear and see a /th/ word. Say and display *this, then, thump, cloth, bath.* Then write *-s, -es, -ed,* and *-ing.* Have children make new words from the base words, such as *thumped, clothes,* and *bathing.* ◼ **RF.1.3f**

Proper Nouns

TEACH/MODEL Say *proper noun* and have children repeat after you. *Proper nouns name exact people and animals, like* Beth *and* Spot.

- *My dog's name is* Spot, *so* Spot *is a proper noun. It names an exact animal.* Beth *is also a proper noun. It names an exact person.* Write *Spot* and *Beth.* *Proper nouns start with a* **capital letter.**

- *There are also* **titles,** *like* Doctor. Write and say *Dr. Black.* *This is a proper noun with a title.* Dr. *tells the person's job.*

GUIDED PRACTICE Write *rosa, tim,* and *dr. tang.* Help children use capital letters to correct each proper noun. ◼ **L.1.1b, L.1.2a**

Do children …

- correctly blend and segment phonemes?
- use expanding vocabulary and sentence structure to talk about *Water* and *Life in the Coral Reefs?*
- identify and use words with digraph *th* and base words (or root words) with *-s, -es, -ed, -ing?*
- correctly identify and use proper nouns, including names for people and animals and titles for people?

- Have partners repeat the Phonemic Awareness Warm-Up.
- Provide additional practice with **Context Cards.**
- Have partners read Words to Know found in *Water.*
- Have children use words with digraph *th,* and base words (or root words) with *-s, -es, -ed, -ing,* in sentences.
- Have small groups list proper nouns naming people and animals.

Transfer Skills
Using Capital Letters

Children with literacy skills in Cantonese may need practice in starting proper nouns with a capital letter since these conventions exist only in alphabetic systems. Provide practice with starting proper nouns and sentences with a capital letter.

✏️ **Scaffolded Practice and Application**

Beginning Write *fish* and *tom.* Help children read the words after you. Then help them identify the letter that should be capitalized. Help them write a capital *T.*

Low Intermediate Write *fish, tom,* and *mr. lopez.* Help children say the words. Then help them identify the letters that should be capitalized. Help them write *Tom* and *Mr. Lopez.*

High Intermediate Have partners list five proper nouns naming people and animals. Have them circle the places where they used a capital letter. Then have them explain why to one another.

Proficient Have children list five proper nouns, including one title. Have them circle the capital letters and explain why each is capital. Have them read their list to a partner.

DAY 5

SHARE OBJECTIVES

- Blend and segment phonemes. **LANGUAGE**
- Make a chart to compare and contrast texts. **CONTENT**
- Use domain-specific vocabulary words to write sentences that inform about sea animals. **LANGUAGE/CONTENT**
- Build academic sentence structures. **LANGUAGE**

MATERIALS

Student Book

Leveled Reader

Writing Rubric Blackline Master in Grab-and-Go™ Resources

TERMS ABOUT WRITING/ LANGUAGE

• = *Spanish cognate*

sentence

information   • *información*

topic

verb   • *verbo*

adverb   • *adverbio*

capital letter

period

COMMON CORE **RI.1.9** identify similarities in and differences between texts on the same topic; **RF.1.2b** orally produce single-syllable words by blending sounds; **RF.1.2d** segment spoken single-syllable words into their complete sequence of individual sounds; **W.1.2** write informative/explanatory texts

Phonemic Awareness Warm-Up

BLEND AND SEGMENT PHONEMES *I am going to say some sounds. Let's blend the sounds to say a word. Listen: /s/ /ē/. What is the word?* (sea) *What are the sounds in the word?* (/s/ /ē/)

- Continue, having children blend and segment *water*, *sand*, *land*, and *ice*, first with you and then by themselves.
  RF.1.2b, RF.1.2d

Compare Texts

ORGANIZE CONCEPTS Use the model below to help children complete a chart comparing *At Home in the Ocean, Water,* and *Life in the Coral Reefs*. Have children refer to the **Student Book** for specific text evidence and the **Leveled Reader**.

Selection Title	*At Home in the Ocean*	*Water*	*Life in the Coral Reefs*
What is it about?	animals that live in the ocean	different forms of water	animals that live in coral reefs
Does it tell facts?	yes	yes	yes
What can you learn from it?	about different sea animals, like blue whales, penguins, and manatees	about different forms of water, like ice and snow	about animals that live in coral reefs, like fish, coral, and eels

- Help children orally form sentences based on the information in the chart. Provide sentence frames such as the following:

1. *At Home in the Ocean* is _____about_____ animals that live in the ocean.

2. *Water* tells _____true_____ facts.

3. *Life in the Coral Reefs* tells about _____animals_____ like eels.

BUILD ACADEMIC SENTENCE STRUCTURES Use the following sentence frames to help children compare and contrast *At Home in the Ocean, Water,* and *Life in the Coral Reefs*.

4. Both *Sea Animals* and *Life in the Coral Reefs* tell _____facts_____ about fish.

5. *Water* tells about ice and snow, but *Life in the Coral Reefs* _____does not_____.

6. *At Home in the Ocean, Water,* and *Life in the Coral Reefs* all tell _____facts_____. **RI.1.9**

RETEACH

Scaffold Informational Writing

TEACH/MODEL Remind children that *sentences* tell a complete idea about something. Many sentences tell facts, or *information,* about a **topic.** *A good sentence tells an interesting idea.*

- Read and discuss the Writing Traits Checklist on **Student Book** p. 40.

- Read and discuss the Writing Model on **Student Book** pp. 40–41. Point out examples of interesting ideas.

GUIDED PRACTICE Explain that the class will write sentences about an animal that lives in the ocean. As a group, choose a topic, such as an animal, to write about. Display *At Home in the Ocean, Water,* and *Life in the Coral Reefs* to help give children ideas for their writing.

- *What verbs, or action words, can we use to tell what this animal does?* (swims, digs, crawls) Make a list of verbs.

- *What adverbs, or words that describe an action, can tell more detail about the animal?* (fast, far, slowly) Make a list of adverbs.

- Help children write sentences describing an animal that lives in the sea. Have them choose verbs and adverbs from the list and domain-specific vocabulary.

- Remind children that complete sentences begin with a *capital* letter and end with a *period.* As a class, go through the sentences you have written and make sure they are correctly capitalized and punctuated.

- As a class, read aloud the shared writing. Discuss how each sentence tells information about the topic. ▬ **W.1.2**

Domain-Specific Vocabulary
Words About Water

arctic, current, tidal

✏️ **Scaffolded Practice and Application**

| **Beginning** Have children draw a picture of a sea animal. Help them write a few words to describe their picture. | **Low Intermediate** Have children draw a picture of a sea animal. Help them write a short phrase, including a verb, to describe their picture. | **High Intermediate** Have children use words from the list to write an additional sentence that tells about the sea animal the class has written about. | **Proficient** Have children choose another sea animal. Have them write a sentence that tells a fact about the animal, using suitable words from the list. |

DAY 1

SHARE OBJECTIVES

- Say, read, and use Words to Know and high-utility words. **LANGUAGE**
- Listen to and recite a dialogue. **LANGUAGE**
- Practice digraphs *ch* and *tch*. **LANGUAGE**

MATERIALS

Language Support Card 12
Context Cards
Student Book
Sound/Spelling Card *chick*

☑ TARGET VOCABULARY

been
brown
know
never
off
out
own
very

TERMS ABOUT LANGUAGE

	• = *Spanish cognate*
consonant	• *consonante*

COMMON CORE **RF.1.2c** isolate and pronounce sounds in spoken single-syllable words; **RF.1.3a** know the spelling-sound correspondences for common consonant digraphs; **RF.1.3g** recognize and read irregularly spelled words; **L.1.6** use words and phrases acquired through conversations, reading and being read to, and responding to texts

---

Speaking and Listening

USE LANGUAGE SUPPORT CARD

Present **Language Support Card 12**. Use the activities on the back of the card to introduce concepts and vocabulary from *How Leopard Got His Spots* and to practice Academic English.

🔊 **L.1.6**

Develop Words to Know

USE CONTEXT CARDS Show the **Context Cards** for *brown* and *know*. Present the cards using Steps 1–3 of the Introduce Words to Know routine on **Teacher's Edition** p. T118.

- Help children use *brown* and *know* to discuss animals with stripes and spots.
- Encourage children to use high-utility words in their responses.

USE ORAL LANGUAGE DIALOGUE Read the title of the dialogue below aloud, and have children repeat. Then read the dialogue and have children listen to *At the Zoo* once in its entirety. Read each line again and have children repeat.

At the Zoo

Mom: We have **never been** to this zoo.
Dee: No, but I **know** all the animals **very** well.
Mom: What is that animal with **brown** spots?
Dee: It is a giraffe!

- Help children practice saying part of the dialogue with a partner. Then have them repeat the dialogue. Help them substitute the names and descriptions of other animals, like zebras and leopards.

THINK-PAIR-SHARE Help partners orally complete the following sentence frames:

1. What is the animal with brown ___spots___ ?

2. Dee knows all the animals ___very___ well. 🔊 **RF.1.3g**

Scaffold Comprehension

PREVIEW *HOW LEOPARD GOT HIS SPOTS* Help children scan the illustrations, highlighted words, and other features of **Student Book** pp. 47–63. Have them predict one thing they may learn by reading the text.

Digraphs *ch, tch*

PHONEMIC AWARENESS WARM-UP *I am going to say two words that sound almost the same. Listen for one difference:* new, chew. *The first sound in each word is different. Let's change the /n/ in* new *to /ch/:* chew. Briefly pantomime chewing.

- Continue with *check, deck; chin, pin; bag, batch;* and *watch, wall*.

TEACH/MODEL Display the **Sound/Spelling Card** *chick*. Explain that a chick is a baby chicken. Say the sound of the digraph *ch* and have children repeat after you: /ch/, /ch/, chick.

- *What is the beginning sound in* chick? (/ch/) Chick *begins with /ch/. Together, the consonants* c *and* h *stand for the sound /ch/.* Remind children that consonants are letters that are not *a, e, i, o,* or *u*.

- Write and pronounce *catch*. Circle the *tch*. Say *Together, the consonants* t, c, *and* h *also stand for the sound /ch/.* Have children repeat after you: /ch/, /ch/, catch. Pantomime catching a ball.

GUIDED PRACTICE Write *chin, pinch, chip, match, itch,* and *patch*. Say each word aloud as you point out the digraphs *ch* and *tch*. Have children repeat after you. ▬ **RF.1.2c, RF.1.3a**

- Offer Corrective Feedback as needed.

Do children…

- correctly pronounce and use Words to Know and high-utility words?
- recite a dialogue with fluency?
- identify and say words with digraphs *ch* and *tch*?

- Have partners use **Context Cards** to review the Words to Know and their meanings. Have them complete the activities on the backs of the cards.
- Help children list and pronounce words with *ch* and *tch* digraphs. Display the words to note the different spellings.

Corrective Feedback

- Review the **Sound/Spelling Card**.
- Point to the image and say *chick*.
- Touch the letters *ch*.
- Have children repeat after you as you pronounce the sound of the digraph.
- Have them repeat after you as you pronounce *chin, chip, catch,* and *match*.

✏️ Scaffolded Practice and Application

| **Beginning** Write *ch* and *tch*. Point to each group of letters and help children pronounce the sound the digraphs stand for. | **Low Intermediate** Write *chick, chin,* and *itch*. Help children pronounce each word. Have children circle the letters that form the digraphs *ch* or *tch*. | **High Intermediate** Help children pronounce *ch* and *tch* words such as *pinch, catch,* and *chip*. Have them use the words in original sentences. | **Proficient** Have children brainstorm four words with the digraphs *ch* and *tch* and say them aloud. Have them use each word in an original sentence. |

DAY 2

SHARE OBJECTIVES

- Blend and segment phonemes. **LANGUAGE**
- Review and discuss a folktale. **CONTENT**
- Ask questions about *How Leopard Got His Spots*. **CONTENT**
- Identify the sequence of key events in *How Leopard Got His Spots*. **CONTENT**

MATERIALS

Student Book
Student eBook
Language Support Card 12
Context Cards

TERMS ABOUT LITERATURE/ LANGUAGE

folktale
question
sequence of events

COMMON CORE **RL.1.1** ask and answer questions about key details; **RL.1.3** describe characters, settings, and major events; **RL.1.10** read prose and poetry; **RF.1.2b** orally produce single-syllable words by blending sounds; **RF.1.2d** segment spoken single-syllable words into their complete sequence of individual sounds; **L.1.1j** produce and expand simple and compound declarative, interrogative, imperative, and exclamatory sentences

Phonemic Awareness Warm-Up

BLEND AND SEGMENT PHONEMES *I am going to say some sounds. I can blend the sounds to say a word. Listen: /s/ /p/ /ŏ/ /t/ /s/, spots. What is the word?* (spots) *What are the sounds in the word?* (/s/ /p/ /ŏ/ /t/ /s/)

- Continue with *stripes*, *brown*, *black*, and *fur*.
- Review the meaning of each word as needed.

▬ **RF.1.2b, RF.1.2d**

Scaffold Comprehension

REVIEW *HOW LEOPARD GOT HIS SPOTS* Use a Think Aloud and the following prompts to lead children on a guided review of *How Leopard Got His Spots*. Remind children that reviewing and retelling what they read will help them understand and remember new words.

> **Think Aloud** **PAGE 47:** Help children read the title aloud. *In this picture, Len Leopard has spots. When the story begins, Len Leopard doesn't have spots yet. The title of the story tells us that we will learn how Len gets his spots.*

PAGE 51: *Len Leopard ran to help Fred Turtle after Fred got stuck in a plant. Describe Len Leopard. Does Len have spots?* (Len is a big, brown cat. No.)

PAGE 55: *What did Fred paint on Zel Zebra?* (stripes)

PAGES 56–61: *Fred Turtle painted Jill Giraffe and Len Leopard. What did he do to Hal Hyena?* (He splashed Hal with brown paint.)

CHECK COMPREHENSION If children need additional support with the main selection, make the **Student eBook** for *How Leopard Got His Spots* available. Have partners or individuals page through *How Leopard Got His Spots*, focusing on the illustrations as they listen.

1. Who helps Fred Turtle get out of the plants? (Len Leopard)

2. Why does Fred say he has never been so happy? (He got out of the plants. He is dancing with Len.)

3. What does Len get of his very own? (brown spots)

▬ **RL.1.1, RL.1.3, RL.1.10**

Question

INTRODUCE Pronounce and explain *question*. *Good readers ask questions about what they read, so they understand it better.*

- Model asking questions about *How Leopard Got His Spots*. Point to the picture on **Student Book** p. 61. *When I see this picture, I ask myself: Why does Fred splash paint on Hal Hyena? I think it is because Hal tricked Fred first.*

THINK-PAIR-SHARE Flip through the main selection. Write *Who, What, Why, Where, When, Which, How,* and *I wonder. . .* Have partners use the words to ask each other questions about the text.
    RI.1.1, L.1.1j

RETEACH

Sequence of Events

TEACH/MODEL Remind children that a sequence of events is a series of things that happen. It tells about the order in which things happen. Use a Think Aloud to model describing a sequence of events in *How Leopard Got His Spots.*

> *Think Aloud*   *When I read* How Leopard Got His Spots, *I can think about the order in which things happen. First, Len helps Fred get out of the plants. Next, they dance in the sun. I have to read the rest of the story to see what happens last.*

GUIDED PRACTICE As a class, make a list of the events that take place in *How Leopard Got His Spots.* Help children place the events on the list in the correct order.

- Review **Teach Academic English** on **Language Support Card 12**. Remind children to use adverbs of time to describe the sequence of events in *How Leopard Got His Spots.*   RL.1.1, RL.1.3

CHECK PROGRESS

Do children...

- blend and segment phonemes correctly?
- ask questions about *How Leopard Got His Spots?*
- identify the sequence of key events in *How Leopard Got His Spots?*

REVIEW TOGETHER

- Have partners repeat the Phonemic Awareness Warm-Up.
- Provide additional practice with **Context Cards.**
- Have children ask three questions about *How Leopard Got His Spots.*
- Help children reread *How Leopard Got His Spots* and point out what happens first, next, and last.

✏️ Scaffolded Practice and Application

| **Beginning** Page through *How Leopard Got His Spots* with children. Ask what happens first, next, and last. Help children answer by pointing or giving one- or two-word answers. | **Low Intermediate** Page through *How Leopard Got His Spots* with children. Help them form simple sentences that tell what happens first, next, and last in the story. | **High Intermediate** Have partners page through *How Leopard Got His Spots.* Have them take turns telling each other what happens first, next, and last. | **Proficient** Have children page through *How Leopard Got His Spots.* Have them use adverbs of time to describe the sequence of events. Have them share their answers. |

DAY 3

SHARE OBJECTIVES

- Substitute initial phonemes. **LANGUAGE**
- Practice using Words to Know orally. **LANGUAGE**
- Identify and use homophones. **LANGUAGE**
- Practice possessives with *'s*. **LANGUAGE**

MATERIALS

Student Book
Sound/Spelling Cards *seal* and *zebra*
Context Cards

TERMS ABOUT LANGUAGE

• = *Spanish cognate*

homophone	• *homófono*
apostrophe	• *apóstrofe*
possessive	• *posesivo*

Phonemic Awareness Warm-Up

SUBSTITUTE PHONEMES: INITIAL *We are going to change a sound in a word to make a new word. Listen:* pen. *What are the sounds?* (/p/ /ĕ/ /n/) *Change* /p/ *to* /t/, /t/ /ĕ/ /n/. *What is the new word?* (ten)

- Repeat with *know, show; fur, purr; patch, match;* and *zoo, moo.*
  ◼ **RF.1.2c**

Practice Words to Know

USE ORAL LANGUAGE DIALOGUE Read the title of the dialogue aloud. Then read each line aloud and have children repeat.

At the Zoo

Mom: We have **never been** to this zoo.
Dee: No, but I **know** all the animals **very** well.
Mom: What is that animal with **brown** spots?
Dee: It is a giraffe!

- Help children identify Words to Know and high-utility words in the dialogue. Write and pronounce the Words to Know. Have children read and repeat them. ◼ **RF.1.3g**

PRACTICE FLUENCY: PHRASING: PUNCTUATION Choose a child to help you model the dialogue. Emphasize pausing at the comma.

PRETEACH

Homophones

INTRODUCE *Two words that sound the same but look different when you read are called homophones.*

- Write *no* and *know*. Point to *no*. *No is the opposite of* yes. *No, this is not my book.* Point to *know*. *Know means understand. I know how to tell time.* No *and* know *are homophones.*

THINK-PAIR-SHARE Write *to, two; bee, be*. Review each word. Then help partners complete the following sentence frames:

1. I have _____two_____ pairs of shoes.

2. Let's go _____to_____ the zoo.

3. Don't _____be_____ afraid of the _____bee_____!

RETEACH

Possessives with 's

PHONEMIC AWARENESS WARM-UP Write *This is Bill's dog. What are the sounds in* Bill's? *(/b/ /ĭ/ /l/ /z/) What is the sound at the end of* Bill's? *(/z/) Yes,* Bill's *ends with the sound /z/.*

TEACH/MODEL *Sometimes naming words have special endings. The ending letters can tell that someone or something owns something.*

- Display *cat* and *cat's* so children can compare. *The second word has a special mark and the letter* s. Underline the *s* and circle the apostrophe. *The apostrophe and the* s *are a possessive.*

- *Sometimes* 's *stands for /z/, like in* Bill's, *or for /s/, like in* cat's. Use the **Sound/Spelling Cards** *seal* and *zebra* to review /s/ and /z/.

GUIDED PRACTICE Write and say *Ben's, dog's, Mom's,* and *Dad's.* Emphasize the difference between the /s/ and /z/ sounds. Have children repeat after you. 🔊 **L.1.1b**

- Offer Corrective Feedback as needed.

CHECK PROGRESS

Do children…
- correctly substitute initial phonemes?
- use Words to Know to discuss *How Leopard Got His Spots*?
- demonstrate fluency as they recite the dialogue?
- identify and practice homophones?
- correctly pronounce possessives with 's?

REVIEW TOGETHER

- Provide additional practice with **Context Cards.**
- Have partners talk about each other's possessions using 's: *Maria's book, Ling's pencil.*

Corrective Feedback

- Review the possessive word *cat's.*
- Point to the word and say *cat's. A cat's fur is soft.*
- Touch the punctuation and letter *s* that stand for the possessive.
- Have children repeat after you as you pronounce *cat's.*
- Have them repeat after you as you pronounce *dog's, Dutch's* and *Chet's.*

Scaffolded Practice and Application

Beginning	Low Intermediate	High Intermediate	Proficient
Write and say *Bill's* and *cat's*. Have children repeat the words. Help them circle each possessive 's.	Write *Bill's, cat's, Mom's*. Help children pronounce the words. Then write *Dad* and *dog*. Help children copy the words and add the possessive 's to each one.	Have children pronounce possessives with 's, such as *cat's, dog's,* and *Mom's*. Have them write a short phrase using each word, such as *Mom's bag*.	Have children list possessives, such as *cat's, Mom's, dog's, Dad's*. Have them write a complete sentence with each word and circle the possessives.

DAY 4

Phonemic Awareness Warm-Up

BLEND AND SEGMENT PHONEMES *I am going to say some sounds. I can blend the sounds to say a word. Listen: /b/ /l/ /ă/ /k/, black. What is the word?* (black) *What are the sounds in the word?* (/b/ /l/ /ă/ /k/)

- Continue with *brown, spot, stripe,* and *fur.*
- Review the meaning of each word as needed.
  🔲 RF.1.2b, RF.1.2d

Scaffold Informational Text

DISCUSS *THE RAIN FOREST* Use the following prompts to lead children on a review of *The Rain Forest.* Remind them that *The Rain Forest* is an **informational text**. It tells facts about a topic.

PAGE 68: *We are going to read about rain forests. What animals that live in a rain forest do you know?* (Possible answer: monkey)

- Read the first sentence on the page. *The rain forest is very wet. What word in* rain forest *is a clue, or hint, that it is very wet?* (rain)

PAGE 69: *Which animal has brown spots?* (jaguar) *Point to the sloth. Do you think the sloth will fall off the tree? Why or why not?* (Answers will vary.)

PAGE 70: Read the first sentence. *What almost never reaches the rain forest floor?* (sunlight)

- Point to the continents on the map. *Which of these places have you been to?* (Answers will vary.) 🔲 RI.1.1

Supported Reading

READ *BEAR'S LONG, BROWN TAIL* To read more about animals, direct children to the **Leveled Reader.** Help partners or small groups take turns reading target words to one another.

◆ **English Language Learners**

PAIRED READING Pair an adult with a struggling reader. Possible pairings include you and a child, or a child and an aide or another adult. Share the following tips with readers:

1. Sit side by side and partner read each sentence.

2. Take turns reading after you have read a few sentences each.

3. Read at a rate that helps the struggling reader better understand the text.

Do children...

- blend and segment phonemes correctly?
- use expanding vocabulary and sentence structures to talk about *The Rain Forest* and *Bear's Long, Brown Tail*?
- review digraphs *ch* and *tch* and possessives with *'s*?
- identify and use commands?

RETEACH

Digraphs *ch, tch*
Possessives with *'s*

REVIEW Display the **Sound/Spelling Card** *chick*. Remind children that *chick* begins with /ch/, that consonants *c* and *h* side by side stand for.

- Display the **Sound/Spelling Cards** *seal* and *zebra*. Remind children that *'s* can stand for /s/ or /z/. Give examples, such as *Matt's, Ella's*. Remind children that an apostrophe and *s* form a possessive.

PRACTICE Help children recognize digraphs *ch* and *tch* and possessive endings with *'s*. Have them write *ch/tch* and *'s* on separate index cards. *Hold up your /ch/ card when you hear a word with* ch *or* tch. *Hold up your 's card when you hear a word with* /s/ *or* /z/ *at the end.*

- Say and display *match, Matt's, catch, Bill's, chick, Chen's*.
  RF.1.3a, L.1.1b

RETEACH

Commands

TEACH/MODEL Explain, *A sentence that tells someone to do something is a command. A command can end with a period or with an exclamation point. The exclamation point means that the sentence is said with a strong feeling.*

Say, softly and in a polite way, *Have a seat.* Have children repeat with a similar intonation. Then say, showing a strong feeling, *Have a seat!* Have children repeat with a similar intonation. Have children compare both sentences.

GUIDED PRACTICE Model using different kinds of sentences to talk about classroom activities such as *I really loved the story we've just read* and *Choose another story to read on your own.* Have children decide which ones are commands. L.1.2b

- Have partners repeat the Phonemic Awareness Warm-Up.
- Provide additional practice with **Context Cards**.
- Have children form a sentence using words with digraphs *ch* and *tch* and possessives with *'s*, such as *Bill's dog plays catch*.
- Provide additional examples of commands.

Transfer Skills
Commands

Students from a Spanish background may be inclined to use an inverted exclamation point (¡) at the beginning of a command, as that is the norm in their primary language. Provide extra practice with English usage of commands ending with an exclamation point.

Scaffolded Practice and Application

Beginning Write on the board: *Take Joan home, please!* and *I will take her home in a minute.* Have children read both sentences aloud. Then help them decide which one is a command.

Low Intermediate Provide the sentence frame *Please, _____ your books!* Have children provide verbs so that the sentence is a command.

High Intermediate Help children brainstorm different kinds of sentences. Write them on the board. Have other children in the group say which ones are commands.

Proficient Have partners dictate a few command sentences with and without exclamation points. Write them on the board. Have children read each sentence with the appropriate intonation.

SHARE OBJECTIVES

- Substitute initial phonemes. **LANGUAGE**
- Make a chart to compare and contrast texts. **CONTENT**
- Build academic sentence structures. **LANGUAGE**
- Use domain-specific vocabulary words to write an instructional letter. **CONTENT**

MATERIALS

Student Book

Leveled Reader

Writing Rubric Blackline Master in Grab-and-Go™ Resources

TERMS ABOUT WRITING

• = *Spanish cognate*

instructions • *instrucciones*

sequence

letter

COMMON CORE **RL.1.5** explain major differences between story books and informational books; **RF.1.2c** isolate and pronounce sounds in spoken single-syllable words; **W.1.2** write informative/explanatory texts; **L.1.6** use words and phrases acquired through conversations, reading and being read to, and responding to texts

Phonemic Awareness Warm-Up

SUBSTITUTE PHONEMES: INITIAL *We are going to change a sound in a word to make a new word. Listen: off. What are the sounds?* (/ŏ/ /f/) *Change /ŏ/ to /ĭ/: /ĭ/ /f/. What is the new word?* (if)

- Repeat with *how, now; got, hot; tail, pail;* and *rain, pain.*
- Review the meaning of each word as needed. ▭ **RF.1.2c**

Compare Texts

ORGANIZE CONCEPTS Use the model below to help children complete a chart comparing *How Leopard Got His Spots, The Rain Forest,* and *Bear's Long, Brown Tail.* Have children refer to the **Student Book** and the **Leveled Reader** for specific text evidence.

Selection Title	*How Leopard Got His Spots*	*The Rain Forest*	*Bear's Long, Brown Tail*
What animals does it tell about?	leopard, turtle,	monkey, tapir, jaguar, eagle, sloth, toucan	bear, fox
Does it tell true facts?	no	yes	no
Is it a folktale?	yes	no	yes
What is it about?	how some animals got stripes and spots	the rain forest and animals that live in it	how Bear's tail got shorter

- Help children orally form sentences based on the information in the chart. Provide sentence frames such as the following:

1. *How Leopard Got His Spots* _____is_____ a folktale.

2. *The Rain Forest* is _____not_____ a folktale.

3. *Bear's Long, Brown tail* tells how Bear's tail got ____shorter____.

BUILD ACADEMIC SENTENCE STRUCTURES Use the following sentence frames to help children compare and contrast the three selections.

4. *How Leopard Got His Spots, The Rain Forest,* and *Bear's Long, Brown Tail* all tell about ____animals____.

5. *How Leopard Got His Spots* and *Bear's Long, Brown Tail* are ____folktales____.

6. Folktales like *How Leopard Got His Spots* and *Bear's Long, Brown Tail* ____explain____ why things are the way they are.

▭ **RL.1.5, L.1.6**

RETEACH

Scaffold Informative Writing

TEACH/MODEL Remind children that instructions tell someone how to do something, like bake a cake. *Instructions usually have a set of steps, listed in the proper **sequence**, or order.*

- Read and discuss the Writing Traits Checklist on **Student Book** p. 74.

- Read and discuss the Writing Model on **Student Book** pp. 74–75. Point out examples of sentence fluency and the use of order words.

GUIDED PRACTICE Explain that the class will work together to write a letter, or a message, that gives instructions to someone for drawing an animal. Display the **Leveled Reader** and **Student Book** to help give children ideas for their writing.

- Write and read aloud the following frame for a letter.

> **DOMAIN-SPECIFIC VOCABULARY**
> **Jungle Animals**
> predator, primate, jungle

  Dear Mom and Dad,

  You can draw a _____! _____, draw a _____. _____, color the _____. _____, hang up the picture!

  Love,

  _____

- Help children read the frame. Point out that the words *First, Next,* and *Last* will help put the instructions in the correct sequence.

- Help children work together to fill in the blanks in the frame.

- Chorally read the completed letter aloud. ◼ W.1.2

CHECK PROGRESS

Do children...
- correctly substitute initial phonemes?
- correctly identify similarities and differences among texts?
- practice writing instructions?

REVIEW TOGETHER

- Have partners repeat the Phonemic Awareness Warm-Up.
- Help partners or small groups review the comparison chart.
- Help partners check for and include domain-specific vocabulary and order words.
- Have children review **My Writing Rubric** and use it to improve their writing.

✏️ Scaffolded Practice and Application

Beginning Have children draw a picture of an animal. Then help them label parts of their drawing with the words *first, next,* and *last.*	**Low Intermediate** Help children orally fill in words to complete the first two sentences of the letter frame.	**High Intermediate** Have children copy the letter frame and fill in the missing words.	**Proficient** Have children write their own letter with instructions about how to draw another animal, such as a zebra.

DAY 1

- Participate in a discussion about the seasons. **CONTENT/LANGUAGE**
- Practice using Words to Know and high-utility words. **LANGUAGE**
- Listen to and recite a chant. **CONTENT**
- Practice words with *sh*, *wh*, and *ph* digraphs. **LANGUAGE**

MATERIALS

Language Support Card 13
Context Cards
Student Book
Sound/Spelling Cards *sheep, whale, fish*

☑ TARGET VOCABULARY

• = *Spanish cognate*

down
fall
goes
green
grow
new   • *nuevo*
open
yellow

TERMS ABOUT LANGUAGE

• = *Spanish cognate*

consonant   • *consonante*

COMMON CORE **RI.1.5** know and use text features to locate facts or information; **RF.1.3a** know the spelling-sound correspondences for common consonant digraphs; **L.1.6** use words and phrases acquired through conversations, reading and being read to, and responding to texts

Speaking and Listening

USE LANGUAGE SUPPORT CARD
Present **Language Support Card 13**.
Use the activities on the back of the
card to introduce concepts and
vocabulary from *Seasons* and to
practice Academic English. ◼ **L.1.6**

Develop Words to Know

USE CONTEXT CARDS Show the **Context Cards** for *green* and *grow*.
Present the cards using Steps 1–3 of the Introduce Words to Know
routine on **Teacher Edition** p. T218.

- Help children use *green* and *grow* to discuss how each season
  is different.

- Encourage children to use high-utility words in their responses.

USE ORAL LANGUAGE CHANT Read aloud the title of the chant
below, and have children repeat. Then read the chant and have
children listen to *Season Song* once in its entirety. Read each line
again and have children repeat.

Season Song

In summer, **green** leaves **grow**.
In fall, they turn **yellow** and **fall**.
In winter, a sled **down** snowy hills **goes**.
In spring, **new** leaves **open**. That is all!

- Help children practice saying part of the chant with a partner.
  Then have them change roles and say part of the chant again.

THINK-PAIR-SHARE Help partners orally complete the following
sentence frames:

1. Green leaves grow in ___summer___.

2. In the fall, ___leaves___ turn yellow. ◼ **RL.1.3g, L.1.6**

Scaffold Comprehension

PREVIEW SEASONS Help children scan the photographs, headings, and other features of **Student Book** pp. 81–99. Have them predict one thing they may learn by reading the text. ⬤ RI.1.5

PRETEACH

Digraphs *sh, wh, ph*

PHONEMIC AWARENESS WARM-UP *I am going to say some sounds. I can blend the sounds to say a word. Listen: /sh/ /ĕ/ /l/, shell. What is the word?* (shell) *What are the sounds in the word?* (/sh/ /ĕ/ /l/)

• Continue with *shape, when, whip*, and *phone*.

TEACH/MODEL Display the **Sound/Spelling Card** *sheep*. Remind children that a sheep is a farm animal. Have children repeat after you: /sh/, /sh/, sheep. *Together, s and h stand for the sound /sh/.*

• Display the **Sound/Spelling Card** *whale*. Explain that a whale is a very large sea animal. Point to the digraph *wh* as you have children repeat after you: /hw/, /hw/, whale. *The consonants w and h side by side stand for the sound /hw/.*

• Display the **Sound/Spelling Card** *fish*. Remind children that a fish is an animal that lives in water. Have children repeat after you: /f/, /f/, fish.

• Write and say *graph*. Explain that a graph is a line or drawing that shows different information. Underline the digraph *ph*. Graph ends with /f/. *Together, p and h also stand for the sound /f/.* Have children repeat /f/ and *graph*.

GUIDED PRACTICE Write and say *dash, ship, graph, Phil, when*, and *whip*. Point to each digraph as you pronounce the sound it stands for. Then have children repeat each word after you.

• Offer Corrective Feedback as needed. ⬤ RF.1.3a

CHECK PROGRESS

Do children...

• correctly pronounce and use Words to Know and high-utility words?

• recite a chant with fluency?

• identify and say words with digraphs *sh, wh,* and *ph*?

REVIEW TOGETHER

• Have partners use **Context Cards** to review the Words to Know and their meanings. Have them complete the activities on the backs of the cards.

• Help children list and pronounce additional words with digraphs *sh, wh,* and *ph*.

Corrective Feedback

• Review the **Sound/Spelling Card**.

• Point to the image and say *whale*.

• Touch the letters *wh*.

• Have children repeat after you as you pronounce the digraph *wh*.

• Have them repeat after you as you pronounce *fresh, when,* and *graph*.

✏️ Scaffolded Practice and Application

Beginning Write *sh, wh,* and *ph*. Point to each group of letters and help children pronounce the sounds each digraph stands for.

Low Intermediate Write *shut, graph,* and *when*. Help children pronounce each word. Help them circle the letters that form the digraphs *sh, wh,* or *ph*.

High Intermediate Have children pronounce words with digraphs *sh, wh,* and *ph*, such as *dash, when,* and *graph*. Have them use the words in original sentences.

Proficient Have children brainstorm a list of words with the digraphs *sh, wh,* and *ph* and say each word aloud. Have children use each word in an original sentence.

DAY 2

SHARE OBJECTIVES

- Blend and segment phonemes. **LANGUAGE**
- Use Words to Know to discuss informational text. **CONTENT/LANGUAGE**.
- Visualize scenes and events in *Seasons*. **CONTENT**
- Identify causes and effects in *Seasons*. **CONTENT**

MATERIALS

Student Book
Student eBook
Language Support Card 13
Context Cards

TERMS ABOUT INFORMATIONAL TEXT

• = *Spanish cognate*

informational text	• *texto informativo*
visualize	• *visualizar*
cause	• *causa*
effect	• *efecto*

Phonemic Awareness Warm-Up

BLEND AND SEGMENT PHONEMES *I am going to say some sounds. I can blend the sounds to say a word. Listen: /w/ /ĕ/ /t/, wet. What is the word?* (wet) *What are the sounds in the word?* (/w/ /ĕ/ /t/)

- Continue with *dry, hot, cold*, and *sun*.

- Review the meaning of each word as needed.

  ▭ RF.1.2b, RF.1.2d

Scaffold Comprehension

REVIEW *SEASONS* Use a Think Aloud and the following prompts to lead children on a guided review of *Seasons*. Remind children that reviewing what you read and retelling to a partner will help them recall details.

> **Think Aloud** **PAGE 81:** *This selection is about different times of the year. People can do different things at different times of the year. In summer, for example, we can fly kites on the beach.*

PAGE 84: *Baby birds are born in spring. What is the adult bird doing?* (feeding the baby birds)

PAGES 86–93: *How are summer and fall alike? How are they different?* (You can play outside in summer and fall. The leaves are different colors.)

PAGES 98–99: *What is your favorite season? Why?* (Answers will vary.)

CHECK COMPREHENSION If children need additional support with the main selection, make the **Student eBook** for *Seasons* available. Have partners or individuals page through *Seasons*, focusing on the photographs as they listen.

1. In which season do eggs hatch open? (in the spring)

2. What blows leaves down from the trees in fall? (a gust of wind)

3. What do some animals do in winter? (rest)

▭ RI.1.1, RI.1.2, RI.1.3

COMMON CORE **RI.1.1** ask and answer questions about key details; **RI.1.2** identify the main topic and retell key details; **RI.1.3** describe the connection between individuals, events, ideas, or information in a text; **RF.1.2b** orally produce single-syllable words by blending sounds; **RF.1.2d** segment spoken single-syllable words into their complete sequence of individual sounds

Do children...
- correctly blend and segment phonemes?
- visualize scenes and events in *Seasons*?
- identify causes and effects in *Seasons*?

PRETEACH
Visualize

INTRODUCE Pronounce and explain *visualize*. *Good readers picture what they are reading about. When I read about winter, I can see a picture in my mind of snow falling. This is called visualizing.*

THINK-PAIR-SHARE Flip through the main selection. Read the headings and identify key words that describe each season, such as *green, wet, snow*, or *hot*. Have partners take turns telling each other what they are visualizing as they read. ▬ **RI.1.3**

RETEACH
Cause and Effect

TEACH/MODEL Remind children that a cause is why something happens and an **effect** is what happens as a result of a cause. Push a crayon onto the floor. *What happened? The crayon fell. Why? I pushed it. The cause is me pushing the crayon. The effect is the crayon falling.* Use a Think Aloud to model identifying cause and effect in *Seasons*.

> Think Aloud *On page 85 I read that the grass gets wet. I see a picture of a girl with an umbrella standing in the rain. I understand! The grass gets wet because it is raining. The cause is the rain. The effect is the wet grass.*

GUIDED PRACTICE Draw a T-Map with the headings *What Happens?* and *Why?* As a class, flip through *Seasons* and use the photographs and text to answer the questions in the graphic organizer.

- Review **Teach Academic English** on **Language Support Card 13**. Model using verbs and *because* to explain causes and effects in *Seasons*. *The leaves* fall *down* because *the wind blows*. ▬ **RI.1.3**

REVIEW TOGETHER

- Have partners repeat the Phonemic Awareness Warm-Up.
- Provide additional practice with **Context Cards**.
- Have children visualize what they would do on a sunny summer day. Have them share their visualizations with a partner.
- Help children reread *Seasons* and point out two causes and effects.

✏️ **Scaffolded Practice and Application**

| **Beginning** Page through *Seasons* with children. Help them identify causes and effects, such as new plants growing because people planted seeds. Have them repeat the cause and effect after you. | **Low Intermediate** Page through *Seasons* with children. Help them identify and name causes and effects, such as new plants growing because people planted seeds. | **High Intermediate** Have partners page through *Seasons* together. Have them take turns identifying causes and effects. | **Proficient** Have children page through *Seasons* and identify causes and effects. Have them form sentences with *because* to explain what they have found. |

DAY 3

Phonemic Awareness Warm-Up

SUBSTITUTE PHONEMES: INITIAL *We are going to change a sound in a word to make a new word. Listen:* camp. *What are the sounds?* (/k/ /ă/ /m/ /p/) *Let's change* /k/ *to* /d/. *Listen:* /d/ /ă/ /m/ /p/. *What is the new word?* (damp)

- Repeat with *fall, hall; hot, dot; seed, need;* and *goes, knows.* **RF.1.2c**

Practice Words to Know

USE ORAL LANGUAGE CHANT Read the title of the chant aloud. Then read each line aloud and have children repeat.

Season Song

In summer, **green** leaves **grow**.
In fall, they turn **yellow** and **fall**.
In winter, a sled **down** snowy hills **goes**.
In spring, **new** leaves **open**. That is all!

- Help children identify Words to Know and high-utility words in the chant. Have children read and repeat the Words to Know. **RF.1.3g**

PRACTICE FLUENCY: RATE Model reading the chant at an appropriate rate. Have children practice with a partner.

PRETEACH

Words Ending in *-ed, -ing,* or *-s*

INTRODUCE Explain that a word's ending can tell us if it is in the **present tense**, something that is happening now, or the **past tense**, something that already happened.

- Write *opens, opening, opened*. Use gestures to demonstrate: *I am opening the book. The book* opens. *I* opened *the book just now.*

THINK-PAIR-SHARE Help partners use words ending with *-ed, -ing,* or *-s* to complete the following sentence frames orally:

1. The plants are ___growing___.

2. It ___snowed___ a lot last winter.

3. It ___rains___ every spring. ▬ **RF.1.3f, L.1.1e, L.1.4c**

RETEACH

Contractions with *'s, n't*

PHONEMIC AWARENESS WARM-UP *Listen as I change two words into one:* it is, it's. *The sound at the end of* it's *is* /s/. *Repeat:* it is, it's.

- Continue with *there is, there's; that is, that's; what is, what's;* and *let us, let's.*

TEACH/MODEL *Sometimes words have letters* n't *or* 's *added to the ends that are short for* not *or* is. *These are contractions.*

- Use **Large Letter Cards** to form *is not*. Read: *is not.* Model forming a contraction *isn't. This is the contraction* isn't. *It is a shorter way to say* is not. *To make the contraction, I replace the letter* o *in* not *with this special mark called an apostrophe.*

- Repeat with *it is, it's; he is, he's; did not, didn't; has not, hasn't.*

GUIDED PRACTICE Write *she's, hasn't, isn't, what's.* Say each word as you point out the contractions. Have children repeat after you.

- Offer Corrective Feedback as needed. ▬ **L.1.6**

CHECK PROGRESS

Do children…

- correctly substitute initial phonemes?
- use Words to Know to discuss *Seasons.*
- demonstrate fluency as they recite a chant?
- correctly identify and use words ending with *-ing, -ed,* and *-s?*
- correctly identify and use contractions with *'s* and *n't?*

REVIEW TOGETHER

- Provide additional practice with **Context Cards.**
- Have children work with a partner to repeat the Think-Pair-Share activity.
- Have small groups work together to change *let us, it is,* and *do not* into their contracted forms.

Corrective Feedback

- Review the **Letter Cards.**
- Point to them and say *it is, it's.*
- Model replacing the *i* in *is* with an apostrophe to form the contraction.
- Have children repeat after you as you pronounce the contraction.
- Have them repeat after you as you pronounce *can't, it's, she's.*

✏ Scaffolded Practice and Application

| **Beginning** Write *it is, is not, it's,* and *isn't.* Help children match the words to their contractions. Help them point out apostrophes and deleted letters. | **Low Intermediate** Write *it is, is not, has not.* Help children change the words into contractions. Have them say a sentence with each word. | **High Intermediate** Write *it is, is not, has not.* Help partners change the words into contractions. Have children write a short phrase with each, such as *It's hot.* | **Proficient** Have children brainstorm three contractions and say them. Have them write each contraction in a sentence, such as *I don't have a pet.* |

DAY 4

- Blend and segment phonemes. **LANGUAGE**
- Comprehend and discuss informational text. **CONTENT**
- Read the Leveled Reader. **CONTENT**
- Review words with digraphs *sh*, *wh*, *ph*, and contractions with *'s*, *n't*. **LANGUAGE**
- Identify and use subjects and verbs. **LANGUAGE**

MATERIALS

Student Book
Leveled Reader
Sound/Spelling Cards *sheep*, *whale*, *fish*
Letter Cards
Context Cards

TERMS ABOUT LANGUAGE

• = *Spanish cognate*

contraction	• *contracción*
subject	• *sujeto*
verb	• *verbo*
sentence	
present tense	• *tiempo presente*

COMMON CORE **RI.1.5** know and use text features to locate facts or information; **RI.1.10** read informational texts; **RF.1.2b** orally produce single-syllable words by blending sounds; **RF.1.2d** segment spoken single-syllable words into their complete sequence of individual sounds; **RF.1.3a** know the spelling-sound correspondences for common consonant digraphs; **RF.1.3f** read words with inflectional endings; **L.1.1c** use singular and plural nouns with matching verbs in sentences

E28 • Lesson 13

Phonemic Awareness Warm-Up

BLEND AND SEGMENT PHONEMES *I am going to say some sounds. I can blend the sounds to say a word. Listen: /g/ /r/ /ē/ /n/, green. What is the word?* (green) *What are the sounds in the word?* (/g/ /r/ /ē/ /n/)

- Continue with *red*, *yellow*, *brown*, and *leaves*. 🔊 **RF.1.2b, RF.1.2d**

Scaffold Informational Text

DISCUSS *FOUR SEASONS FOR ANIMALS* Use the following prompts to lead children on a review of *Four Seasons for Animals*. Remind them that *Four Seasons for Animals* is **informational text**. Remind them that informational text uses facts to tell about a topic.

PAGE 105: Point to the picture of the bird's nest high in the tree. *In what season are there eggs in a bird's nest?* (spring) *Is spring warm or cold?* (warm)

- Point to the buds on the tree. *When winter ends, new green buds open and grow. What season is it then?* (spring)

PAGE 108: Look at the chicks in the bird's nest. *In summer there are chicks in a bird's nest. What else happens in summer?* (Answers will vary.)

- Look at the insects in the picture. *What insects do you see?* (a bee, a butterfly) *What sound does a bee make?* (buzz)

PAGES 105, 108, 110, 112: Point to the pictures. *How are spring, summer, fall, and winter different?* (Answers will vary.) 🔊 **RI.1.5**

Supported Reading

READ *IN THE FALL* To read more about how seasons are different, direct children to the **Leveled Reader**. Help partners or small groups take turns reading target words to one another.

READING WITH STICKY NOTES Pair an adult with a struggling reader. Possible pairings include you and a child, or a child and an aide or other adult.

◆ English Language Learners

1. Have children read the selection and put sticky notes on pages they have difficulty with or would like to discuss.

2. Have them talk about the sections they marked. 🔊 **RI.1.10**

Digraphs *sh, wh, ph*
Contractions with *'s, n't*

REVIEW Display the **Sound/Spelling Cards** *sheep, whale, fish.* Remind children that *sheep* begins with /sh/, *whale* begins with /hw/, and the letters *ph* stand for /f/, the sound at the beginning of *fish.*

• Review forming **contractions** with **Letter Cards**. Help children use contracted words, such as *it's, what's,* and *isn't* in sentences.

PRACTICE Have children identify *sh, wh, ph* words. Have each child write *sh, wh,* and *ph* on index cards. Say these words, giving children time to raise the correct card: *when, photo, dash, ship, graph, where.*

• Remind children that a contraction is a way of making two words into one. Say *is not, isn't. What is the contraction of* is not? (isn't) Repeat with *it is, it's; has not, hasn't; let us, let's; did not, didn't.*
▭ RF.1.3a

Subjects and Verbs

TEACH/MODEL Write and say *subject* and *verb. A sentence has two parts. The subject names something or someone. The verb tells about an action.*

> **Transfer Skills**
> **Subject-Verb Inversion**
>
> In Cantonese, Hmong, and Tagalog, the order of subject and verb may be the same in both questions and statements. Provide support and extra practice with subject-verb inversion in questions that use helping verbs.

• Display **Student Book** p. 94. *The boy plays in the snow. In this sentence,* the boy *is the subject.* Plays *is the verb.* Explain that a verb in the **present tense** may have an *-s* ending.

GUIDED PRACTICE Write *The cold wind blows.* Underline *the cold wind. This is the subject.* Circle *blows. This is the verb.* Put a square around the *s* in *blows.* Have pairs flip through **Student Book** pp. 83–85 and identify as many subjects and verbs as they can.
▭ RF.1.3f, L.1.1c

CHECK PROGRESS

Do children...
• correctly blend and segment phonemes?
• use expanding vocabulary and sentence structures?
• identify words with *sh, wh,* and *ph* digraphs and contractions with *'s* and *n't*?
• identify and use subjects and verbs?

REVIEW TOGETHER

• Have partners repeat the Phonemic Awareness Warm-Up.
• Provide additional practice with **Context Cards.**
• Have children use words with *sh, wh,* and *ph* digraphs and contractions with *'s* and *n't* in sentences.
• Provide additional sentences for children. Have them work with a partner to name the subject and verb.

✎ Scaffolded Practice and Application

Beginning Write and say *The plant grows. The boy plays.* Help children repeat the subjects and verbs after you.	**Low Intermediate** Write and say *The green plant grows.* The *brown leaves fall.* Help children underline the subject and circle the verb in each sentence.	**High Intermediate** Have children write a simple sentence based on the examples. Have them write *subject* and *verb* under the correct part of each sentence.	**Proficient** Have children write an original complete sentence using at least one noun and verb. Have them write *subject* and *verb* under the correct part of each sentence.

SHARE OBJECTIVES

- Substitute initial phonemes. **LANGUAGE**
- Make a chart to compare and contrast texts about seasons. **CONTENT**
- Build academic sentence structures. **LANGUAGE**
- Use domain-specific vocabulary to write sentences that inform. **LANGUAGE**

MATERIALS

Student Book

Leveled Reader

Writing Rubric Blackline Master in Grab-and-Go™ Resources

TERMS ABOUT WRITING

• = *Spanish cognate*

sentence

inform   • *informar*

facts

topic

main idea   • *idea principal*

Phonemic Awareness Warm-Up

SUBSTITUTE PHONEMES: INITIAL *We will change a sound in a word to make a new word. Listen: dot. What are the sounds? (/d/ /ŏ/ /t/) Change /d/ to /p/: /p/ /ŏ/ /t/. What is the new word?* (pot)

- Repeat with *blow, slow; wet, pet; year, hear;* and *four, more.*
- Review the meaning of each word as needed. 🔊 **RF.1.2c**

Compare Texts

ORGANIZE CONCEPTS Use the model below to help children complete a chart comparing *Seasons, Four Seasons for Animals,* and *In the Fall.* Have children refer to their **Student Book** and the **Leveled Reader** for specific text evidence.

Selection Title	Seasons	Four Seasons for Animals	In the Fall
Does it have photos?	yes	yes	yes
What kind of book is it?	informational text	informational text	informational text
What can you learn from it?	facts about different seasons	what happens to animals during different seasons	all about what it is like in the fall

- Help children orally form sentences based on the information in the chart. Provide sentence frames such as the following:

1. *Seasons* tells facts about the different ____seasons____.

2. *In the Fall* tells us about what it is like in the ____fall____.

BUILD ACADEMIC SENTENCE STRUCTURES Use the following sentence frames to help children compare and contrast *Seasons, Four Seasons for Animals,* and *In the Fall.*

3. *Seasons, Four Seasons for Animals,* and *In the Fall* are all ____informational____ texts.

4. *Four Seasons for Animals* and *Seasons* tell ____facts____ about the different seasons.

5. There are many interesting things to learn about ____seasons____.

🔊 **RI.1.9**

COMMON CORE **RI.1.9** identify similarities in and differences between texts on the same topic; **RF.1.2c** isolate and pronounce sounds in spoken single-syllable words; **W.1.2** write informative/explanatory texts

E30 • Lesson 13

RETEACH

Scaffold Informative Writing

TEACH/MODEL Remind children that a sentence tells a complete idea about something. A sentence that informs is one that tells facts about a **topic**. *All sentences should tell about the topic.*

- Read and discuss the Writing Traits Checklist on **Student Book** p. 118.

- Read and discuss the Writing Model on **Student Book** pp. 118–119. Point out the main idea sentence.

GUIDED PRACTICE Explain that the class will write sentences about a season. As a group, choose a season (e.g., spring) to write about. Display *Seasons, Four Seasons for Animals,* and *In the Fall* to help give children ideas for their writing.

- *What facts do we know about what happens in spring?* (Possible answers: Eggs open. It rains.) Make a list of facts about spring. Then ask *What is the **main idea** we want to tell about spring?* (Everything is green and growing.) Make a list of possible main ideas. Display the lists for children to use later.

> **DOMAIN-SPECIFIC VOCABULARY**
> **Seasons**
> *weather, cycle, sunlight*

- Help children write sentences that inform about spring, using the facts and ideas from the lists, as well as domain-specific words. As a class, go through the sentences you have written and underline the one that tells the main idea.

- Read aloud the shared writing. Discuss how each sentence tells information about the topic. ⬛ **W.1.2**

CHECK PROGRESS

Do children...
- correctly substitute initial phonemes?
- correctly identify similarities and differences among texts?
- use a main idea to write sentences that inform?

REVIEW TOGETHER

- Have partners repeat the Phonemic Awareness Warm-Up.
- Help partners or small groups review the rows and columns of the comparison chart about the seasons.
- Help partners check for and include a main idea in their writing.
- Have children review **My Writing Rubric** and use it to improve their writing.

✏️ Scaffolded Practice and Application

Beginning	**Low Intermediate**	**High Intermediate**	**Proficient**
Have children draw a picture showing one of the seasons. Help them write a few words to describe their picture.	Have children draw a picture of one of the seasons. Help them write a short phrase expressing an important idea about the season.	Have children use the list of facts and ideas to write an additional sentence that informs about the season the class has written about.	Have children choose a different season. Have them write a sentence that tells a fact about the season, using words from the lists as appropriate.

DAY 1

SHARE OBJECTIVES

- Say, read, and use Words to Know and high-utility words. **LANGUAGE**
- Listen to and recite a dialogue. **CONTENT/LANGUAGE**
- Practice words with the long *a* sound. **LANGUAGE**

MATERIALS

Language Support Card 14
Context Cards
Student Book
Sound/Spelling Card *acorn*

☑ WORDS TO KNOW

five
four
into
over
starts
three
two
watch

TERMS ABOUT LANGUAGE

vowel

RF.1.2a distinguish long from short vowel sounds in spoken single-syllable words; **RF.1.3c** know final -e and vowel team conventions for representing long vowel sounds; **RF.1.3g** recognize and read irregularly spelled words; **L.1.6** use words and phrases acquired through conversations, reading and being read to, and responding to texts

Speaking and Listening

USE LANGUAGE SUPPORT CARD
Present **Language Support Card 14**. Use the activities on the back of the card to introduce concepts and vocabulary from *The Big Race* and to practice Academic English. 🔲 **L.1.6**

Develop Words to Know

USE CONTEXT CARDS Show the **Context Cards** for *two* and *watch*. Present the cards using Steps 1–3 of the Introduce Words to Know routine on **Teacher Edition** p. T322.

- Help children use *two* and *watch* to discuss desert animals.

- Encourage children to use high-utility words in their responses.

USE ORAL LANGUAGE DIALOGUE Read aloud the title of the dialogue below, and have children repeat. Then read the dialogue and have children listen to *It's a Race!* once in its entirety. Read each line again and have children repeat.

It's a Race!

Marco: Let's run. We can race **into** the park.
Jill: Okay! Do not trip. Go **over** those rocks.
Marco: I will win. You will clap for me.
Jill: **Five. Four. Three. Two.** One. **Start!**

- Help children act out and say part of the dialogue with a partner. Then have them change roles and say part of the dialogue again.

THINK-PAIR-SHARE Help partners orally complete the following sentence frames:

1. Marco and Jill race into the ____park____.

2. They must go over those ____rocks____. 🔲 **RF.1.3g, L.1.6**

Scaffold Comprehension

PREVIEW *THE BIG RACE* Help children scan the illustrations, highlighted words, and other features of **Student Book** pp. 124–143. Have them predict one thing they may learn by reading the text.

Long *a* (CVCe)

PHONEMIC AWARENESS WARM-UP *Listen for the difference between these two words: at, ate. The first sound in each word is different. Let's change the /ă/ in at to /ā/:* ate. Have children repeat the long *a* sound after you.

• Repeat with *hat, hate; hop, hope; cap, cape;* and *mad, made.*

TEACH/MODEL Display the **Sound/Spelling Card** *acorn.* Explain that an acorn is a nut that grows on trees. Have children repeat after you: /ā/, /ā/, acorn.

• Point to the letter *a. We draw out the* **vowel** *a in acorn to stand for a long sound: /ā/, /ā/, acorn.* Have children repeat. Remind them that vowels are the letters *a, e, i, o, u,* and sometimes *y.*

• Write and pronounce *cake.* Have children repeat after you. Circle the *a.* Say *I like to eat* cake. /ā/, /ā/, cake. Have children repeat after you.

GUIDED PRACTICE Write *rake, lake, gate, wake, plate,* and *shade.* Say each word aloud as you point out the letters that represent the long *a* sound. Have children repeat after you.

• Offer Corrective Feedback as needed. 🔊 **RF.1.2a, RF.1.3c**

Do children…
• correctly pronounce and use Words to Know and high-utility words?
• recite a dialogue with fluency?
• identify and say words with long *a*?

• Have partners use **Context Cards** to review the Words to Know and their meanings. Have them complete the activities on the backs of the cards.
• Help children practice words with long *a.* Display the words to note different spellings.

Corrective Feedback
• Review the **Sound/Spelling Card.**
• Point to the image and say *acorn.*
• Touch the letter *a.*
• Have children repeat after you as you pronounce the long *a* sound.
• Have them repeat after you as you pronounce *acorn, bake,* and *gate* correctly.

Scaffolded Practice and Application

Beginning Write *ake, ate,* and *ade.* Point to each group of letters and help children pronounce them, emphasizing the long a sound.

Low Intermediate Write *ate, bake,* and *gate.* Help children pronounce each word. Help them point to the letters that stand for the long *a* sound.

High Intermediate Have children pronounce long *a* words, such as *lake, plate,* and *shade.* Have children use the words in original phrases.

Proficient Have children brainstorm three words with the long *a* sound and say them aloud. Have them use each word in a sentence.

Phonemic Awareness Warm-Up

IDENTIFY MIDDLE SOUND *I am going to say some words. Listen:* sad, sat. *What is the sound in the middle of* sad? (/ă/) *What is the sound in the middle of* sat? (/ă/) *Is the sound in the middle of* sad *the same as the sound in the middle of* sat? (yes)

- Repeat with *chase, race* (/ā/; /ā/; yes); *hop, stop* (/ŏ/; /ŏ/; yes); *run, sun* (/ŭ/; /ŭ/; yes); and *clap, win* (/ă/; /ĭ/; no).
- Review the meaning of each word as needed. **RF.1.2c**

Scaffold Comprehension

REVIEW *THE BIG RACE* Use a Think Aloud and the following prompts to lead children on a guided review of *The Big Race.* Remind children that reviewing and retelling what they read will help them remember details.

> **Think Aloud**
> **PAGE 125:** Read the title aloud. *This story is about animals that ran in a race. Many different animals ran in this race. I know that this story is a fantasy because different animals would not run together in a race like this in real life.*

PAGES 126–127: Help children read the sign on page 126 aloud. *Why did Red Lizard decide to run in the race?* (He likes cake. He wanted to win the cake.)

PAGES 128–130: *How many animals ran in the race? Who were they?* (five; Cottontail, Rat, Snake, Roadrunner, and Red Lizard)

PAGES 141–143 *Red Lizard won the race and the cake. Why did Red Lizard share his cake?* (because the other animals were his pals)

CHECK COMPREHENSION If children need additional support with the main selection, make the **Student eBook** for *The Big Race* available. Have partners or individuals page through *The Big Race,* focusing on the illustrations as they listen.

1. How many animals run the race? (five)

2. What does Cottontail stop to watch? (a butterfly)

3. What does Roadrunner trip over? (a rake)

RL.1.1, RL.1.3, RL.1.10

PRETEACH

Infer/Predict

INTRODUCE Pronounce and explain *infer* and *predict*. *When you infer, you use clues from the story to figure something out. When you predict, you guess what will happen next.*

THINK-PAIR-SHARE Flip through the main selection. Have partners find clues to make inferences and predictions about which animal will win the race.

RETEACH

Conclusions

TEACH/MODEL Remind children that drawing **conclusions** means making a smart guess about something the author does not say. Remind them that good readers use details to help them draw conclusions. Use a Think Aloud to model drawing conclusions about *The Big Race*.

> Think Aloud *I know from the text and the pictures that the cake is much bigger than Red Lizard. I draw the conclusion that Red Lizard can't eat the whole cake by himself, so he will share it with his friends.*

GUIDED PRACTICE As a class, use details from the text and pictures to draw a conclusion about why Red Lizard was the one to win the race. (He did not get distracted or trip.) *What happened to all the other animals?* (Cottontail watches a butterfly; Rat falls into hay; Snake stops and chases bugs; Roadrunner trips.)

• Review **Teach Academic English** on **Language Support Card 14**. Remind children to use simple present verbs to describe actions as they draw conclusions about the story. 🔲 **RL.1.7**

CHECK PROGRESS

Do children...
• correctly identify middle sounds?
• practice making inferences and predictions about *The Big Race*?
• draw conclusions about *The Big Race*?

REVIEW TOGETHER

• Have partners repeat the Phonemic Awareness Warm-Up.
• Provide additional practice with **Context Cards**.
• Have children make one inference and one prediction about *The Big Race*.
• Help children reread *The Big Race* and draw a conclusion about where the story takes place.

✏️ Scaffolded Practice and Application

Beginning Page through *The Big Race* with children. Point out details from the text and illustrations, such as the cake and animals clapping. Help them draw a conclusion about how the animals feel when the race is over.

Low Intermediate Page through *The Big Race* with children. Help them identify details from the text and illustrations, such as the cake and animals clapping. Help them draw a conclusion about how the animals feel when the race is over.

High Intermediate Have partners page through *The Big Race* and identify details, such as the cake and animals clapping. Have them draw a conclusion about how the animals feel when the race is over.

Proficient Have children page through *The Big Race*, using story details to draw conclusions about how the animals feel when the race is over. Have them share their conclusions with a partner.

SHARE OBJECTIVES

- Substitute medial phonemes. **LANGUAGE**
- Classify and categorize words according to their shades of meaning. **LANGUAGE**
- Practice words with soft *c*, *g*, and *dge*. **LANGUAGE**

MATERIALS

Student Book
Sound/Spelling Card *jump*
Context Cards

TERMS ABOUT LITERATURE/ LANGUAGE

• = *Spanish cognate*

classify	• *clasificar*
category	• *categoría*

Phonemic Awareness Warm-Up

SUBSTITUTE PHONEMES: MEDIAL *We are going to change a sound in a word to make a new word. Listen:* dig. *What are the sounds?* (/d/ /ĭ/ /g/) *Change /ĭ/ to /ŭ/: /d/ /ŭ/ /g/. What is the new word?* (dug)

- Repeat with *rug, rag; pan, pin; mad, mud;* and *tap, tip*.
- Review the meaning of each word as needed. **RF.1.2c**

Practice Words to Know

USE ORAL LANGUAGE DIALOGUE Read the title of the dialogue aloud. Then read each line aloud and have children repeat.

It's a Race!

Marco: Let's run. We can race **into** the park.
Jill: Okay! Do not trip. Go **over** those rocks.
Marco: I will win. You will clap for me.
Jill: **Five. Four. Three. Two.** One. **Start!**

- Help children identify Words to Know and high-utility words in the dialogue. Write and pronounce the Words to Know. Have children read and repeat them. **RF.1.3g**

PRACTICE FLUENCY: ACCURACY: WORD RECOGNITION Choose a child to help you model the dialogue. Emphasize the correct pronunciation of each word.

COMMON CORE **RF.1.2c** isolate and pronounce sounds in spoken single-syllable words; **RF.1.3g** recognize and read irregularly spelled words; **L.1.5d** distinguish shades of meaning among verbs by defining or by acting out the meanings; **L.1.6** use words and phrases acquired through conversations, reading and being read to, and responding to texts

CHECK PROGRESS

Do children…
- correctly substitute medial phonemes?
- use Words to Know to discuss *The Big Race*?
- demonstrate fluency as they recite the chart?
- correctly classify and categorize words according to their shades of meaning?
- practice using words with soft *c*, *g*, and *dge*?

PRETEACH

Shades of Meaning

INTRODUCE Display *The Big Race*. Have children point to the word *watch* on p. 133. *The word* watch *means "to look," but it means something a little bit different from "look." Watch means "to look at to see what happens." Let's look for other words about watching or seeing. We can **classify**, or sort verbs or adjectives that mean almost the same thing, these words into the same **category**, or group.* Page through the book to help children identify other words about watching or seeing *(looks)*. Then have children act out these words (or synonyms) to show their slightly different shades of meaning.

THINK-PAIR-SHARE Help children complete these sentences orally:

1. *Watch* and *look* both mean _____see_____.

2. They are in the _____same_____ category.

3. We can classify _____see_____ together with *watch* and *look*.

◼ L.1.5d, L.1.6

REVIEW TOGETHER

- Provide additional practice with **Context Cards**.
- Have small groups classify and categorize words according to their shades of meaning.
- Have partners think of three words with soft *c*, *g*, and/or *dge* and use them in a phrase or sentence.

RETEACH

Soft *c*, *g*, and *dge*

PHONEMIC AWARENESS WARM-UP *I will say a word and you say the middle sound. Listen:* cage. *The middle sound is /ā/. Let's do some together. Listen:* badge. *The middle sound is /ă/. Listen:* stage. *The middle sound is /ā/. Now let's do more:* mat /ă/, date /ā/, page /ā/.

TEACH/MODEL *Write* mice. *Listen:* mice, /s/. *Now you say it. The letter* c *stands for the sound at the end of* mice. *Read with me:* mice. *Mice ends with /s/. Say it again with me and listen for the sound at the end of* mice. *The letter* c *stands for /s/ at the end of* mice.

- Display the **Sound/Spelling Card** *jump*. Jump or have a child jump once. Point to the *g* and *dge* for /j/ on the card. Explain that these both stand for /j/. Write and read *badge* and *cage*.

GUIDED PRACTICE Write and say *face*, *cell*, *cage*, *lodge*, and *nudge*. Say each word aloud as you point to the letter or letters that stand for the soft *c*, *g*, or *dge* sounds. Have children repeat after you.

- Offer **Corrective Feedback** as needed.

Corrective Feedback
- Review the **Sound/Spelling Card**.
- Point to the image and say *jump*.
- Touch the letters that stand for /j/.
- Have children repeat after you as you pronounce the /j/ sound.
- Have them repeat after you as you pronounce *race*, *cage*, and *badge*.

✏️ **Scaffolded Practice and Application**

| **Beginning** Write *face*, *page*, and *badge*. Point to each word and help children pronounce it correctly, emphasizing the soft *c*, *g*, and *dge*. | **Low Intermediate** Write *face*, *page*, *badge*. Point to the word and help children pronounce each. Help them circle the letters that stand for the soft *c*, *g*, and *dge*. | **High Intermediate** Have children pronounce words with soft *c*, *g*, and *dge*. Help them use the words in original phrases or sentences. | **Proficient** Have children brainstorm three words with soft *c*, *g*, and *dge* and say them aloud. Have them use each word in a sentence. |

SHARE OBJECTIVES

- Identify middle sounds. **LANGUAGE**
- Comprehend and discuss informational text. **CONTENT**
- Read the Leveled Reader. **CONTENT**
- Build reading proficiency through supported reading. **LANGUAGE**
- Review words with long *a* and words with soft *c*, *g*, and *dge*. **LANGUAGE**
- Identify verbs that tell past and present time. **LANGUAGE**

MATERIALS

Student Book

Leveled Reader

Sound/Spelling Cards *acorn, jump, seal*

Index Cards

Context Cards

TERMS ABOUT INFORMATIONAL TEXT/LANGUAGE

	• = *Spanish cognate*
informational text	• *texto informativo*
vowel	
consonant	• *consonante*
verb	• *verbo*
present tense	• *tiempo presente*
past tense	• *tiempo pasado*

COMMON CORE **RL.1.10** read prose and poetry; **RI.1.5** know and use text features to locate facts or information; **RI.1.7** use illustrations and details to describe key ideas; **RI.1.10** read informational texts; **RF.1.2a** distinguish long from short vowel sounds in spoken single-syllable words; **RF.1.2c** isolate and pronounce sounds in spoken single-syllable words; **L.1.1e** use verbs to convey sense of past, present, and future

Phonemic Awareness Warm-Up

IDENTIFY MIDDLE SOUND *I am going to say some words. Listen:* game, same. *What is the sound in the middle of game?* (/ā/) *What is the sound in the middle of same?* (/ā/) *Is the sound in the middle of game the same as the sound in the middle of same?* (yes)

- Repeat with *rat, fat* (/ă/; /ă/; yes); *lane, line* (/ā/; /ī/; no); *win, tin* (/ĭ/; /ĭ/; yes); and *cake, can* (/ā/; /ă/; no).

- Review the meaning of each word as needed. ◼ **RF.1.2a, RF.1.2c**

Scaffold Informational Text

DISCUSS *RULES AND LAWS* Use the following prompts to lead children on a review of *Rules and Laws*. Remind them that *Rules and Laws* is an **informational text.** It gives facts about a topic.

PAGE 148: *We all need to follow rules. Some rules keep us safe and healthy. Other rules help us learn and even have fun.* Have children read the word *Rules*. *What kinds of rules do you know about?* (Answers will vary.)

PAGE 149: Point to the pictures. *What kinds of rules do you see on this page?* (a safety rule, a school rule, and a game rule)

- Ask children to read the labels inside the pictures. *How do the labels tell you more about the pictures?* (They show a safety rule, a school rule, and a game rule.)

PAGE 152: Point to the pictures. *How are the people who are walking and the car at the "Stop" sign obeying the law?* (The people are crossing at the crosswalk. The car is stopped at the "Stop" sign.) (Answers will vary.) ◼ **RI.1.5, RI.1.7, RI.1.10**

Supported Reading

READ *THE MAP AND THE TREASURE* To read more about games, direct children to the **Leveled Reader.** Help partners or small groups point out art and tell one another what happened on that page.

READING WITH STICKY NOTES Pair an adult with a struggling reader. Possible pairings include you and a child, or a child and an aide or other adult.

◆ **English Language Learners**

1. Have children read the selection and put sticky notes on pages they have difficulty with or would like to discuss.

2. Have them talk about the sections they marked. ◼ **RL.1.10**

Long *a* (CVC*e*), Soft *c*, *g*, *dge*

REVIEW Display the **Sound/Spelling Card** *acorn*. Remind children *acorn* starts with the long **vowel** /ā/. *Say it with me: /ā/, /ā/, acorn.*

- Remind children that some **consonants** have soft and hard sounds. Display the **Sound/Spelling Cards** *jump* and *seal*. Review that *g* and *dge* can stand for /j/, as in *page*, *badge*. Review that *c* can stand for /s/, as in *cell*, *nice*.

PRACTICE Help children recognize long *a*, soft *c*, *g*, and *dge*. Have them write *a*, *c*, and *g/dge* on index cards. *Hold up your a card if you hear a word with /ā/, your c card for a word with /s/, and your g/dge card for each word with /j/.*

- Say *race, page, lane, face, cat, ice, lodge, badge.*
  RF.1.2c

Verbs and Time

TEACH/MODEL *A verb is an action word, like* walk *or* hop. Walk a few steps. I walk *is in the* **present tense**. *It is happening now. The ending* -ed *shows an action in the* past tense, *or one that already happened:* I walked.

GUIDED PRACTICE Write *walk, walked, hop, hopped.* Have children repeat. Review meanings and if each is in the present or past tense.

- Page through *The Big Race* with children. As a group, use present and past tense verbs to describe each action.

- Ask questions to prompt children's use of verbs. *What is Cottontail doing now? What happened to Roadrunner?* L.1.1e

CHECK PROGRESS

Do children…
- correctly identify middle sounds?
- use expanding vocabulary and sentence structures to talk about *Rules and Laws* and *The Map and the Treasure*?
- identify and practice words with long *a* and words with soft *c*, *g*, and *dge*?
- correctly use verbs to show past and present tense?

REVIEW TOGETHER

- Have partners repeat the Phonemic Awareness Warm-Up.
- Provide additional practice with **Context Cards.**
- Have children use words with long *a* and soft *c*, *g*, and *dge* in a complete sentence.
- Provide additional practice with past and present verbs.

Transfer Skills
Verb Tense
Children with literacy skills in Cantonese, Hmong, Vietnamese, and Haitian Creole may need help forming the past tense, as verbs in these languages do not change to show tense. Provide additional practice with regular past tense verbs such as *walked*, *started*, and *watched*.

🖍 Scaffolded Practice and Application

Beginning	Low Intermediate	High Intermediate	Proficient
Orally list regular past tense verbs such as *jumped, walked,* and *talked.* Help children circle the *-ed* endings.	Help children write past tense verbs such as *walked, chased,* and *jumped.* Then help them explain the meaning of each word and circle the *-ed* endings.	Have children change *walk, talk,* and *jump* into the past tense by adding the *-ed* ending. Have them write a short phrase using each past tense verb.	Have children change *walk, talk,* and *jump* into the past tense by adding the *-ed* ending. Have them write a complete sentence using each past tense verb.

SHARE OBJECTIVES

- Substitute medial phonemes. **LANGUAGE**
- Make a chart to compare and contrast texts. **CONTENT**
- Build academic sentence structures. **LANGUAGE**
- Use vocabulary to write a report that informs about desert animals. **CONTENT/LANGUAGE**

MATERIALS

Student Book
Leveled Reader

TERMS ABOUT WRITING

• = *Spanish cognate*

report
facts
topic
inform   • *informar*

Phonemic Awareness Warm-Up

SUBSTITUTE PHONEMES: MEDIAL *We are going to change a sound in a word to make a new word. Listen:* trip. *The sounds are /t/ /r/ /ĭ/ /p/. Let's change /ĭ/ to /ă/: /t/ /r/ /ă/ /p/. What is the new word?* (*trap*)

- Repeat, having children substitute medial phonemes for *stop, step; win, won; race, rice;* and *map, mop,* first with you and then by themselves. ⬤ **RF.1.2c**

Compare Texts

ORGANIZE CONCEPTS Use the model below to help children complete a chart comparing *The Big Race, Rules and Laws,* and *The Map and the Treasure.* Have children refer to the **Student Book** and the **Leveled Reader** for specific text evidence.

Selection Title	The Big Race	Rules and Laws	The Map and the Treasure
What is it about?	desert animals having a race	rules and laws people follow	desert animals playing a game
Does it tell true facts about a topic?	no	yes	no
What kind of games does it tell about or show?	racing	racing	finding treasure

- Help children orally form sentences based on the information in the chart. Provide sentence frames such as the following:

1. *The Big Race* is about five animals having a ____race____.

2. *Rules and Laws* tells facts about a ____topic____.

3. *The Map and the Treasure* ____is not____ a true story.

BUILD ACADEMIC SENTENCE STRUCTURES Use the following sentence frames to help children compare and contrast *The Big Race, Rules and Laws,* and *The Map and the Treasure.*

4. *The Big Race* and *The Map and the Treasure* ____both____ are made-up stories.

5. *Rules and Laws* tells true facts, ____but____ *The Map and the Treasure* does not.

6. When you read *Rules and Laws,* think about the ____rules____ you follow in school. ⬤ **RL.1.5, SL.1.1a**

COMMON CORE **RL.1.5** explain major differences between story books and informational books; **RF.1.2c** isolate and pronounce sounds in spoken single-syllable words; **W.1.2** write informative/explanatory texts; **W.1.7** participate in shared research and writing projects; **SL.1.1a** follow rules for discussions

Scaffold Narrative Writing

TEACH/MODEL Remind children that a **report** gives **facts** about a **topic.** *A good report uses interesting ideas and details to **inform** about a person or thing.*

- Read and discuss the Prewriting Checklist on **Student Book** p. 158.

- Read and discuss the Planning Chart on **Student Book** p. 159. Point out the facts.

GUIDED PRACTICE Explain that the class will work together to prewrite a report about a desert animal, such as a snake. Display *The Big Race* and *The Map and the Treasure* to help give children ideas for their prewriting.

- As a group, brainstorm ideas about the kinds of special features the animal has, such as having no legs and smooth skin.

- Draw an Idea-Support Map. Write *What are snakes like?* in the first box. Fill the remaining boxes with details, facts, and ideas about snakes. Prompt children with questions about snakes, such as *Do snakes have legs? How do they move? What do they eat? Is it against the law to have some snakes as pets?*

- Point to different boxes in the completed map and have children use the ideas inside them to orally form sentences that inform about the animal you have chosen. ▬ **W.1.2, W.1.7**

CHECK PROGRESS

Do children…
- correctly substitute medial phonemes?
- correctly identify similarities and differences among texts?
- apply ideas to their report plans?

REVIEW TOGETHER

- Have partners repeat the Phonemic Awareness Warm-Up.
- Help partners or small groups review the comparison chart.
- Help partners check for and include interesting ideas and vocabulary in their prewriting.

Extend Language
Words for Desert Animals
deadly, fast, poisonous, habitat, nocturnal

✏️ Scaffolded Practice and Application

Beginning	**Low Intermediate**	**High Intermediate**	**Proficient**
Have children draw a picture of a desert animal. Help them prewrite words they could use in a report about the animal.	Have children draw a picture of a desert animal. Help them prewrite words and short phrases they could use in a report about the animal.	Have children copy the prewriting Idea-Support Map. Then have them add another two boxes to the map and add their own ideas for a report.	Have children draw a blank Idea-Support Map. Have them choose another desert animal to report on and fill in the boxes with their own prewriting ideas.

✅ WORDS TO KNOW

• = *Spanish cognate*

bird
both
eyes
fly
long
or   • *o*
those
walk

TERMS ABOUT LANGUAGE

• = *Spanish cognate*

vowel
consonant   • *consonante*

COMMON CORE **RI.1.5** know and use text features to locate facts or information; **RF.1.2a** distinguish long from short vowel sounds in spoken single-syllable words; **RF.1.2c** isolate and pronounce sounds in spoken one-syllable words; **RF.1.3b** decode regularly spelled one-syllable words; **RF.1.3g** recognize and read irregularly spelled words; **L.1.6** use words and phrases acquired through conversations, reading and being read to, and responding to texts

Speaking and Listening

USE LANGUAGE SUPPORT CARD
Present **Language Support Card 15**. Use the activities on the back of the card to introduce concepts and vocabulary from *Animal Groups* and to practice Academic English. ◗ **L.1.6**

Develop Words to Know

USE CONTEXT CARDS Show the **Context Cards** for *walk* and *fly*. Present the cards using Steps 1–3 of the Introduce Words to Know routine on **Teacher's Edition** p. T424.

- Help children use *walk* and *fly* to discuss how animals are different from each other.
- Encourage children to use high-utility words in their responses.

USE ORAL LANGUAGE CHANT Read the title of the chant below aloud, and have children repeat. Then read the chant and have children listen to *Cats Can't Fly* once in its entirety. Read each line again and have children repeat.

Cats Can't Fly

Those birds have **eyes**. Those cats have eyes.
They **both** have eyes. They are the same.
Those birds can **fly**. Those cats can't fly!
Cats can't fly. They're not the same.

- Help small groups recite the chant, with each child taking turns to say a line.

THINK-PAIR-SHARE Help partners orally complete the following sentence frames:

1. Both _____birds_____ and cats have eyes.

2. Cats walk, but they don't _____fly_____. ◗ **RF.1.3g**

Scaffold Comprehension

PREVIEW *ANIMAL GROUPS* Help children scan photographs, labels, and other features of **Student Book** pp. 165–183. Have them predict one thing they may learn by reading the text. ⬛ RI.1.5

PRETEACH

Long *i* (CVCe)

PHONEMIC AWARENESS WARM-UP *I am going to change the middle vowel sound in a word. Listen:* bit. *The middle sound is /ĭ/. Listen again:* bite. *The middle sound is /ī/. Now you change the middle sound.*

- Continue with *lick, like; dim, dime; fin, fine;* and *slid, slide.*

TEACH/MODEL Display the **Sound/Spelling Card** *ice cream.* Say *I like to eat* ice cream. Remind children that **vowels** are *a, e, i, o, u,* and sometimes *y.*

- *The vowel sound in* ice *is long* i. Say /ī/, /ī/, ice cream. Have children repeat after you.

- Write and read *bit.* Have children sound out and pronounce the word with you. Then circle the *i. When we add* e *to the end of a word with* i *between two* **consonants***, the way we say the* i *changes. It turns into a long* i *sound.* Add e to the end of *bit.* Say *bit, bite. Bit, bite.* Have children repeat after you.

GUIDED PRACTICE Write *time, line, fine, pine, hide,* and *pipe.* Say each word aloud as you point out the letter pattern that represents the long *i* sound.

- Offer Corrective Feedback as needed.
  ⬛ RF.1.2a, RF.1.2c, RF.1.3b

CHECK PROGRESS

Do children…
- correctly pronounce and use Words to Know and high-utility words?
- recite a chant with fluency?
- identify and say words with long *i*?

REVIEW TOGETHER
- Have partners use **Context Cards** to review the Words to Know and their meanings. Have them complete the activities on the backs of the cards.
- Help children list and pronounce additional words with long *i.*

Corrective Feedback
- Review the **Sound/Spelling Card.**
- Point to the image and say *ice cream.*
- Point out the i_e pattern.
- Have children repeat after you as you pronounce the long *i* sound.
- Have them repeat after you as you pronounce *mine, time,* and *bite* correctly.

✏ Scaffolded Practice and Application

Beginning	**Low Intermediate**	**High Intermediate**	**Proficient**
Write *ice* and *nice.* Point to the letter *i* in each word. Help children pronounce the long *i* sound. Then have them pronounce each word after you, emphasizing the long *i.*	Write *kit, bit, fin, pin.* Help partners take turns saying the words. Then write an *e* on the end of each word and help children pronounce the new words.	Write *kit, bit, fin, pin.* Have partners add an *e* to each word and say it aloud. Then have them say a sentence using each word.	Have children brainstorm and write three words with a long *i.* Have them say a sentence using each word. Then have them repeat their sentences to a partner.

- Identify middle sounds. **LANGUAGE**
- Review and discuss an informational text. **CONTENT**
- Monitor and clarify information in *Animal Groups*. **CONTENT**
- Compare and contrast information from *Animal Groups*. **CONTENT**

MATERIALS

Student Book
Student eBook
Language Support Card 15
Context Cards

TERMS ABOUT INFORMATIONAL TEXT

• = *Spanish cognate*

informational text	• *texto informativo*
monitor	
clarify	• *clarificar*
compare	• *comparar*
contrast	• *contrastar*

Phonemic Awareness Warm-Up

IDENTIFY MIDDLE SOUND *I am going to say some words. Listen:* cat, bad. *What is the sound in the middle of cat?* (/ă/) *What is the sound in the middle of bad?* (/ă/) *Is the sound in the middle of cat the same as the sound in the middle of bad?* (yes)

- Repeat with *kite, size* (/ī/; /ī/; yes); *skin, scan* (/ĭ/; /ă/; no); *frog, dog* (/ŏ/; /ŏ/; yes); and *fins, fans* (/ĭ/; /ă/; no).

- Review the meaning of each word as needed. **RF.1.2c**

Scaffold Comprehension

REVIEW *ANIMAL GROUPS* Use a Think Aloud and the following prompts to lead children on a guided review of *Animal Groups*. Remind children that looking over pictures and key words and explaining what they see will help them better understand what they read.

Think Aloud **PAGES 166–167:** *This selection is about five different animal groups. We learned that bears are mammals. Do mammals live on land or in water?* (Some mammals, like polar bears, live both on land and in water.)

PAGES 168–175: Help children name the animals shown in the photographs. (fish, alligator, turtle, snake, frogs) *Is a frog a reptile or an amphibian?* (amphibian)

PAGES 176–178: *Most birds can fly. Can birds swim?* (Some birds can swim.) *How are some birds like fish?* (They know how to swim.)

PAGES 179–183: *What is your favorite animal group? Why?* (Answers will vary.)

CHECK COMPREHENSION If children need additional support with the main selection, make the **Student eBook** for *Animal Groups* available. Have partners or individuals page through *Animal Groups*, focusing on photos as they listen.

1. What is an animal that can fly? (a bird)

2. Can fish walk, or can they swim? (swim)

3. Which animal lives on both land and water? (amphibians)
   RI.1.3, RI.1.7

COMMON CORE **RI.1.3** describe the connection between individuals, events, ideas, or information in a text; **RI.1.4** ask and answer questions to determine or clarify the meaning of words and phrases; **RI.1.7** use illustrations and details to describe key ideas; **RF.1.2c** isolate and pronounce sounds in spoken single-syllable words

E44 • Lesson 15

PRETEACH

Monitor/Clarify

INTRODUCE Pronounce and explain *monitor* and *clarify*. Monitoring *means noticing when we don't understand something that we are reading.* Clarifying *means finding ways to understand it better.*

THINK-PAIR-SHARE Flip through the main selection. Read the headings, labels, and key phrases from each section. Have children raise their hands when they do not understand something, then pause to clarify their questions. ◼ RI.1.4

RETEACH

Compare and Contrast

TEACH/MODEL Write and say *compare* and *contrast*. Have children repeat. Comparing *means showing how things are the same. We often use* and *when we compare: Bears* and *seals have fur.* Contrasting *means showing how things are different. We often use* but *when we contrast: Bears have hair,* but *birds have feathers.* Use a Think Aloud to model comparing and contrasting in *Animal Groups.*

> Think Aloud   **PAGE 176:** *It says that birds have feathers and wings. I was not sure what feathers and wings were, so I looked at the labels. Now I know that feathers are the soft, colorful things that cover a bird's body. Wings are on the sides of a bird's body, like arms. I can see that the eagle uses wings to fly.*

GUIDED PRACTICE As a class, identify two similarities and two differences between mammals and fish. *Do fish have hair? Do mammals lay eggs?*

- Review Teach Academic English on **Language Support Card 15**. Remind children to use complex sentences with conjunctions to compare and contrast information when they are reading.
  ◼ RI.1.3, RI.1.7

CHECK PROGRESS

Do children...
- correctly identify middle sounds?
- monitor and clarify information in *Animal Groups*?
- compare and contrast information in *Animal Groups*?

REVIEW TOGETHER

- Have partners repeat the Phonemic Awareness Warm-Up.
- Provide additional practice with **Context Cards**.
- Have children work with a partner to monitor and clarify information on a page from *Animal Groups*.
- Have children work with a partner to compare and contrast two animals from *Animal Groups*.

✏️ **Scaffolded Practice and Application**

| **Beginning** Have children draw two animals. Help them use short phrases to tell one way the animals are alike and one way they are different. | **Low Intermediate** Have children draw two animals. Help them use *and* and *but* to tell one way the animals are alike and one way they are different. | **High Intermediate** Have partners page through *Animal Groups* and take turns comparing and contrasting different animals, using *and* and *but* in their sentences. | **Proficient** Have children reread *Animal Groups*. Have them briefly describe how two animal groups are alike and different, using sentences with *and* and *but*. |

DAY 3

SHARE OBJECTIVES

- Substitute medial phonemes. **LANGUAGE**
- Practice using Words to Know orally. **LANGUAGE**
- Identify and use words with suffixes -er and -est. **LANGUAGE**
- Identify and use words with digraphs kn, wr, gn, and mb. **LANGUAGE**

MATERIALS

Student Book
Sound/Spelling Cards noodles, rooster, mouse
Context Cards

ACADEMIC LANGUAGE

• = Spanish cognate

suffix	• sufijo
consonant	• consonante

Phonemic Awareness Warm-Up

SUBSTITUTE PHONEMES: MEDIAL *We are going to change a sound in a word to make a new word. Listen:* cat. *What are the sounds?* (/k/ /ă/ /t/) *Let's change /ă/ to /ŏ/: /k/ /ŏ/ /t/. What is the new word?* (cot)

- Repeat with *bat, bit; pot, pit; wet, wit;* and *fin, fan.* **RF.1.2c**

Practice Words to Know

USE ORAL LANGUAGE CHANT Read the title of the chant aloud. Then read each line aloud and have children repeat.

Cats Can't Fly

Those birds have **eyes**. Those cats have eyes.
They **both** have eyes. They are the same.
Those birds can **fly**. Those cats can't fly!
Cats can't fly. They're not the same.

- Help children identify Words to Know and high-utility words in the chant. Have children read and repeat the Words to Know. **RF.1.3g**

PRACTICE FLUENCY: EXPRESSION Read the chant once with little expression. Then read it a second time, modeling appropriate expression. Have children practice saying the chant with a partner.

COMMON CORE **RF.1.2c** isolate and pronounce sounds in spoken one-syllable words; **RF.1.3a** know the spelling-sound correspondences for common consonant digraphs; **RF.1.3b** decode regularly spelled one-syllable words; **RF.1.3f** read words with inflectional endings; **RF.1.3g** recognize and read irregularly spelled words

PRETEACH

Suffix *-er*, *-est*

INTRODUCE *A suffix is a word ending. The suffix -er means* more. *The suffix -est means* most.

- Draw three snakes of increasing length. Point to the first snake. *This snake is* long. Write *long*. Point to the next snake. *This snake is* longer. Write *longer*. Underline the *-er*. Point to the last snake. *This snake is the* longest. Write *longest*. Underline the *-est*.

THINK-PAIR-SHARE Help children complete these sentences orally:

1. A snake is ____longer____ than a worm.
2. A frog is ____smaller____ than a cat.
3. An elephant is one of the ____biggest____ animals. 🔊 RF.1.3f

REVIEW TOGETHER

- Provide additional practice with **Context Cards**.
- Have small groups think of words with *kn*, *wr*, *gn*, and *mb* digraphs and use them in short phrases.

RETEACH

Digraphs *kn*, *wr*, *gn*, *mb*

PHONEMIC AWARENESS WARM-UP *I will change the beginning sound in a word to make a new word. Listen:* bat, gnat. *What sound is at the beginning of* bat? (/b/) *And* gnat? (/n/)

- Continue with *bee, knee; tap, wrap; raw, gnaw;* and *cot, knot.*

TEACH/MODEL Remind children that two consonants side by side can stand for one sound. Write and read *knock, gnash*. Circle *kn, gn*. *Listen:* knock, /n/. *Now you say it. Listen:* gnash, /n/. *Now you say it.*

- Display the **Sound/Spelling Card** *noodles* to review /n/. *Noodles, /n/.* Then point to *kn* and *gn* on the card. Explain that these letters can also stand for /n/. Reread *knock* and *gnash*.

- Repeat for *wrap*, using the **Sound/Spelling Card** *rooster* to review /r/. Repeat for *thumb*, using the card for *mouse* to review /m/.

GUIDED PRACTICE Write *knot, wrap, numb,* and *gnat*. Say each word and have children repeat. Point out each silent consonant.

- Offer Corrective Feedback as needed. 🔊 RF.1.3a, RF.1.3b

Corrective Feedback

- Review the **Sound/Spelling Cards**.
- Point to the image and say *noodles*.
- Touch the letters *kn* and *gn*.
- Have children repeat after you as you pronounce the sound /n/.
- Have them repeat after you as you pronounce *knit, numb, sign, gnat*.

✏️ **Scaffolded Practice and Application**

| **Beginning** Point to *kn, wr, gn, mb*. Help children say the sound that each digraph stands for. Ask children to point out the silent letter in each. | **Low Intermediate** Write *knit, gnat, write, numb*. Help children pronounce each word. Have them circle the letters that stand for each digraph. | **High Intermediate** Have children pronounce words such as *knit, gnat, write, numb*. Discuss the meanings. Have children use the words in original phrases. | **Proficient** Have children brainstorm words with digraphs *kn, wr, gn,* and *mb*, and say them aloud. Have them use each word in a sentence. |

DAY 4

SHARE OBJECTIVES

- Identify middle sounds. **LANGUAGE**
- Comprehend and discuss a play. **CONTENT**
- Read the Leveled Reader. **CONTENT**
- Review words with long *i* and words with digraphs *kn*, *wr*, *gn*, and *mb*. **LANGUAGE**
- Build proficiency through supported reading. **LANGUAGE**
- Identify and practice the verb *be*. **LANGUAGE**

MATERIALS

Student Book

Leveled Reader

Sound/Spelling Cards *ice cream, noodles, rooster, mouse*

Index Cards

Context Cards

TERMS ABOUT LITERATURE/ LANGUAGE

• = *Spanish cognate*

play	
vowel	• *vocal*
verb	• *verbo*
present (tense)	• *(tiempo) presente*
past (tense)	• *(tiempo) pasado*

COMMON CORE **RF.1.2c** isolate and pronounce sounds in spoken one-syllable words; **RF.1.3a** know the spelling-sound correspondences for common consonant digraphs; **L.1.1c** use singular and plural nouns with matching verbs in sentences; **L.1.1e** use verbs to convey sense of past, present, and future

Phonemic Awareness Warm-Up

IDENTIFY MIDDLE SOUND *I am going to say some words. Listen:* thumb, numb. *What is the sound in the middle of* thumb? (/ŭ/) *What is the sound in the middle of* numb? (/ŭ/) *Is the sound in the middle of* thumb *the same as the sound in the middle of* numb? (yes)

- Repeat with *nice, fine* (/ī/; /ī/; yes); *gnat, not* (/ă/; /ŏ/; no); *write, rat* (/ī/; /ă/; no); and *numb, sum.* (/ŭ/; /ŭ/; yes) **RF.1.2c**

Scaffold Play

DISCUSS ***ANIMAL PICNIC*** Use the following prompts to lead children on a review of *Animal Picnic*. Remind them that *Animal Picnic* is a **play**. Remind them that a play is a story that people act out.

PAGE 188: Read the title. *When you have a picnic, are you eating inside or outside?* (outside)

- *Besides Bird, who are the other two characters in this play?* (Cow and Fox) *How did Cow and Bird get to the picnic?* (Cow walked. Bird flew.)

PAGE 189: Point to the food baskets. Then read the third and fourth lines of dialogue. *What do Cow and Fox both have?* (teeth)

- *What does Fox eat with his long teeth?* (meat)

PAGE 190: Point to Bird. *Bird brought seeds to eat. How does he eat those seeds?* (with his beak)

Supported Reading

READ ***MANY KINDS OF BATS*** To read more about how animals are different from each other, direct children to the **Leveled Reader**. Help partners or small groups take turns rereading phrases or sentences from the selection aloud.

◆ **English Language Learners**

BUDDY READING Pair an adult with a struggling reader. Possible pairings include you and a child, or a child and an aide or other adult.

1. Have the adult read aloud, clearly and distinctly, while the struggling reader follows along in the text.

2. Have the adult help the less proficient reader with any problems understanding the text. For example, adjust the rate of reading to match the struggling reader's proficiency level.

RETEACH

Long *i* (CVCe)
Digraphs *kn, wr, gn, mb*

REVIEW Display the **Sound/Spelling Card** *ice cream*. Remind children that *ice* has the long **vowel** /ī/. Repeat with the cards for *noodles*, *rooster*, and *mouse*, pointing out the digraphs *kn, gn, wr*, and *mb*.

PRACTICE Help children recognize the long *i* sound and the digraphs *kn, wr, gn*, and *mb*. Have them write *i, kn/gn, wr*, and *mb* on index cards. Have them hold up the appropriate card as you say several words, giving children time to raise the correct card.

• Say *fine, fin, size, knot, write, crumb, knit, gnash.* ⬤ **RF.1.3a**

RETEACH

The Verb *be*

TEACH/MODEL *A verb is an action word, like* walk *or* fly. *We use the verb* be *when talking about what is.* Is, are, was, *and* were *are different forms of the verb* be.

GUIDED PRACTICE Write *is, are, was, were*. Have children repeat. *We use* is *and* are *when we speak in the* **present tense**, *what is true now, and* was *and* were *when we speak in the* **past tense**, *what was true before.*

• Page through *Animal Groups* with children. Read the question on p. 142 and have children answer it using *are*. As a group, identify forms of the verb *be* on the pages.

• Ask questions to help children practice using forms of the verb *be* to discuss the main selection. *What is* Animal Groups *about? What groups of animals* are *in the book?* ⬤ **L.1.1c, L.1.1e**

CHECK PROGRESS

Do children...
• correctly identify middle sounds?
• use expanding vocabulary and sentence structure to talk about *Animal Picnic* and *Many Kinds of Bats*?
• practice and review words with long *i* and words with *mb, wr, gn*, and *kn* digraphs?
• identify and practice forms of the verb *be*?

REVIEW TOGETHER

• Have partners repeat the Phonemic Awareness Warm-Up.
• Provide additional practice with **Context Cards**.
• Have children work in small groups to write words with long *i* and words with digraphs *mb, wr, gn*, and *kn*.
• Have children say a sentence using a form of the verb *be*.

Transfer Skills
Verb Tense

The verb *to be* can be left out in Cantonese, Hmong, Vietnamese and Haitian Creole. If children say *I happy* instead of *I am happy*, provide extra practice with forms of *to be*.

✏️ Scaffolded Practice and Application

| **Beginning** Write sentences with forms of the verb *be*. Have children repeat the sentences. Help them underline the verb form of *be* in each sentence. | **Low Intermediate** Write sentences with forms of the verb *be*. Have children repeat the sentences. Help them rewrite the verb form of *be* in each sentence. | **High Intermediate** Write and say *is, are, was, were*. Review the words with children. Have them write phrases using each word, such as *cats are; the bird was.* | **Proficient** Have children write four sentences using the verbs *is, are, was*, and *were*. Have them read their writing aloud to a partner. |

SHARE OBJECTIVES

- Substitute medial phonemes. **LANGUAGE**
- Make a chart to compare and contrast texts. **CONTENT**
- Build academic sentence structures. **LANGUAGE**
- Use domain-specific vocabulary words to write a report that informs about different animals. **CONTENT**

MATERIALS

Student Book
Leveled Reader
Writing Rubric Blackline Master in Grab-and-Go™ Resources

TERMS ABOUT WRITING

• = *Spanish cognate*

report
facts
inform • *informar*
topic

RL.1.5 explain major differences between story books and informational books; **RF.1.2c** isolate and pronounce sounds in spoken single-syllable words; **RF.1.2d** segment spoken single-syllable words into their complete sequence of individual sounds; **W.1.2** write informative/explanatory texts; **L.1.6** use words and phrases acquired through conversations, reading and being read to, and responding to texts

Phonemic Awareness Warm-Up

SUBSTITUTE PHONEMES: MEDIAL *We are going to change a sound in a word to make a new word. Listen: fox. What are the sounds? (/f/ /ŏ/ /ks/) Change /ŏ/ to /ĭ/: /f/ /ĭ/ /ks/. What is the new word? (fix)*

- Repeat with *snake, sneak; shape, ship; land, lined;* and *same, sum.*
  RF.1.2c, RF.1.2d

Compare Texts

ORGANIZE CONCEPTS Use the model below to help children complete a chart comparing *Animal Groups, Animal Picnic,* and *Many Kinds of Bats*. Have children refer to the **Student Book** and the **Leveled Reader** for specific text evidence.

Selection Title	*Animal Groups*	*Animal Picnic*	*Many Kinds of Bats*
What is it about?	fish, birds, reptiles, amphibians, and mammals	a cow, bird, and fox who have a picnic	bats
What kind of book is it?	informational text with facts	play that tells a story	informational text with facts
What can you learn from it?	how different animal groups are different	what cows, birds, and foxes eat	all about bats

- Help children orally form sentences based on the information in the chart. Provide sentence frames such as the following:

1. *Animal Groups* tells true ____facts____.

2. *Animal Picnic* is a story about a cow, a fox, and a ____bird____.

3. *Many Kinds of Bats* tells facts about ____bats____.

BUILD ACADEMIC SENTENCE STRUCTURES Use the following sentence frames to help children compare and contrast *Animal Groups, Animal Picnic,* and *Many Kinds of Bats.*

4. *Animal Picnic* tells a story, ____but____ *Many Kinds of Bats* tells facts.

5. Both *Animal Groups* and *Many Kinds of Bats* tell facts about ____animals____.

6. *Many Kinds of Bats* tells about one kind of animal, but ____Animal Groups____ tells about many kinds of animals.

RL.1.5, L.1.6

RETEACH

Scaffold Informative Writing

TEACH/MODEL Remind children that a report tells facts that inform about a topic. *When we write a report, we tell things about our topic that are true. Whoever reads our report will learn many facts.*

- Read and discuss the Revising Checklist on **Student Book** p. 194.

- Read and discuss the Writing Model on **Student Book** pp. 194–195. Point out examples of word choice.

GUIDED PRACTICE Explain that the class will write a report about different animals. As a group, choose two animals or animal groups, such as fish and birds, to write about. Display *Animal Groups, Animal Picnic*, and *Many Kinds of Bats* to help give children ideas for their writing.

- *What facts do we know about these animals?* (Possible answers: Fish swim. Birds fly.) Make a list of facts about the animals you have chosen. *What words can we use to clearly tell about these animals?* (tail, fins, wings, feathers) Make a list of words that will be helpful for writing the report. Display the lists for later use.

- Help children write sentences that inform about animals, using the facts and words listed. As a class, go through the sentences you have written. Find places where you can use *and* and *but* to compare and contrast. Remind children that comparing and contrasting means telling how things are alike and different.

- Read aloud the shared writing. Discuss how each sentence in the report tells information about the topic. 🔲 **W.1.2**

✏️ Scaffolded Practice and Application

Beginning	**Low Intermediate**	**High Intermediate**	**Proficient**
Have children draw a picture showing two animals. Help them write a few words to describe their picture.	Have children draw a picture showing two animals. Help them write a short phrase expressing an important idea about each animal.	Have children use facts and words from the list to write an additional sentence that informs about the animals the class has written about.	Have children choose two different animals or animal groups. Have them write one or two sentences that could be used to begin a report about the animals. Let them use facts and words from the lists.

Teacher Notes

Resources

Contents

SHARE OBJECTIVE

- Explain the major differences between story books and informational books.
- Find a book in a library.

MATERIALS

- Unit 3 Student Book
- library map

 **RL.1.5** explain major differences between story books and informational books; **W.1.7** participate in shared research and writing projects

Library Research: Find a Book

1 Teach/Model

Remind children that the library provides many reading materials, including books. Discuss ways to find a book in the library, including the following tips:

- Library books are arranged to make it easy for readers to find them. Usually, all fiction books are shelved in one area and nonfiction (informational) books are shelved in another.

- Fiction books, or the made-up stories, may be organized on shelves alphabetically by the author's last name. Sometimes picture books, chapter books, and folktales may be grouped in their own sections.

- Nonfiction, or informational, books about real people, places, and things are grouped together in categories. Numbers are given to the categories and put on the books to make them easier to find.

- Have children explain the major differences between story books and informational books.

- Point out that you can use computers in libraries to find a book's title, author, and location in the library.

2 Guided Practice/Apply

- Have small groups identify key elements of a map of their school or local library and use it to identify where in a library they might find selections listed in the Unit 3 Table of Contents.

- Have children use the library's computer to find the location of their favorite book or a book they have read recently.

SHARE OBJECTIVE

- Identify the title page, the author, and the illustrator.
- Use book parts to find information, including the Glossary.

MATERIALS

- Unit 3 Student Book

Parts of a Book

1 Teach/Model

Display the **Student Book** and explain that books have many parts.

- Display the cover and then page through the **Student Book** and identify the important parts.

- Point out the title page and discuss where to find the author, the illustrator or photographer if there is one, and the publisher.

- Follow a similar procedure with the table of contents, the Glossary, and other parts.

2 Guided Practice/Apply

- Have children look at other textbooks or books in the classroom.

- Ask them to use the cover and the title page to find out the book's title, author, illustrator, and publisher.

- Ask them to find a new word in the Glossary and read the entry to find out its meaning. Have partners take turns looking up each other's new words.

 **RI.1.5** know and use text features to locate facts or information

▶ SHARE OBJECTIVE

- Distinguish true stories from fantasies.
- Explain the major differences between story books and informational books.

MATERIALS

- fantasy books
- informational books
- self-stick notes

RL.1.5 explain major differences between story books and informational books

Distinguish Nonfiction from Fiction

1 Teach/Model

Discuss books that tell about things that might really happen and those that tell about things that are make-believe. Cover these points:

- A book may tell about things that cannot happen in real life, like animals that talk, cook, or drive cars. It has make-believe parts. It is called a **fantasy**.

- Display the fantasy book. Model how to identify some make-believe elements.

- A book may give facts about what happens in the real world. This kind of book tells true ideas about real-life people and things.

- Display the **informational text**. Help children find facts in it.

- Have children explain the major differences between story books and informational books.

- Emphasize that good listeners and good readers think about what happens in a story. They decide what is true or true-to-life and what must be make-believe. They find clues and use what they know to help them decide.

2 Guided Practice/Apply

Look through familiar books with children. Have them help you use self-stick notes to mark parts that could really happen and parts that tell about make-believe things. Ask:

- *Is this part of the story about real things or make-believe things? How do you know?*

- *What can the characters do that real people or animals cannot do?*

- *Does this book give true information?*

Word Lists

	ORAL VOCABULARY		☑ WORDS TO KNOW High-Frequency Words		DOMAIN-SPECIFIC VOCABULARY	SELECTION VOCABULARY		TERMS ABOUT READING/ LANGUAGE ARTS
Lesson 11	companions exchange gracefully	portions practice strict	blue cold far little	live their water where	arctic current tidal	biggest grow ocean sea otters warm	feet manatees penguins turtle whales	author details author's purpose classify categorize
Lesson 12	adventure frisky shivered	spied tumbled view	been brown know never	off out own very	predator primate jungle	flowers giraffe zebra paint	hyena leopard danced	story lesson sequence of events context homophone
Lesson 13	bouquet burst glows	plow shrivel vines	down fall goes green	grow new open yellow	weather cycle sunlight	blow day leaves snow school tall	snowman spring summer winter seeds	cause effect onomatopoeia base word
Lesson 14	cactus habitat mainly	search stems howl	four five into over	starts three two watch	legal rule duty	cottontail hay hooray	lizard race roadrunner	conclusion cause effect categorize classify context
Lesson 15	alert directions scale	sensitive swivel threatened	bird both eyes fly	long or those walk	trait adapt survive	amphibians body breathe feathers hair wings	group mammals reptiles tadpoles tails	text and graphic features compare contrast suffix

LESSON 11

Seth and Beth
Decodable Reader, page 3
Target Skills:
Digraph th

Zeb Yak
Decodable Reader, page 9
Target Skills:
Digraph th

The Duck Nest
Decodable Reader, page 15
Target Skills:
Endings -s, -es, -ed, -ing
Digraph th

Animal Moms
Decodable Reader, page 21
Target Skills:
Endings -s, -es, -ed, -ing
Digraph th

Decodable Words

Target Skill: Digraph *th*
Beth, path, Seth, them, then, this, with

Previously Taught Skills
and, asks, at, Ben, big, Bob, can, cap, Duck, Frog, fun, get, has, hats, help, his, Huck, in, is, it, map, met, pass, pond, quacks, Sam, tip, tips, trip, up, us, will, yells

Decodable Words

Target Skill: Digraph *th*
path, paths, then, this, thud, thump, with

Previously Taught Skills
and, big, can, cut, dad, get, glad, grass, hill, his, is, lots, mom, nap, not, on, sun, up, will, yak, yaks, yet, Zeb

Decodable Words

Target Skill: Endings *-s, -es, -ed, -ing*
asked, cracked, cracks, eggs, filled, its, jumped, jumping, lots, misses

Target Skills: Digraph *th*
Beth, that, then, this, with

Previously Taught Skills
and, Ann, at, back, bet, big, bug, did, duck, egg, get, Gram, has, had, is, it, left, lots, mom, must, nest, not, quit, us, will, yes, yum

Decodable Words

Target Skill: Endings *-s, -es, -ed, -ing*
cubs, ducks, filled, grasses, hunting, jumping, kits, lots, pups, resting, rocks, sticks, twigs

Target Skills: Digraph *th*
that, them, this, with

Previously Taught Skills
and, can, fast, fun, grab, has, hunt, in, is, it, just, mom, mud, on, pond, rest, snack, swim, wet

---

High-Frequency Words

New
blue, far, live, their, where

Previously Taught
a, are, call, does, go, here, play, see, the, they

High-Frequency Words

New
blue, cold, little, live

Previously Taught
a, be, eat, go, like, look, no, of, one, see, the

High-Frequency Words

New
far, little, where

Previously Taught
a, be, come, here, I, look, of, said, she, was

High-Frequency Words

New
cold, little, their, water

Previously Taught
a, animal, are, have, her, like, of, she, the, they, what

LESSON 12

Scratch, Chomp
Decodable Reader, page 27
Target Skills:
Digraphs ch, tch

Decodable Words

Target Skill: Digraphs *ch, tch*
catch, chips, chomp, chomping, chop, Chuck, Finch, pitch, scratch, scratching

Previously Taught Skills
an, and, asks, at, big, but, can, dad, did, fast, has, his, in, is, it, lots, lump, miss, not, off, on, pond, stump, tell, this, trip, went, yes

High-Frequency Words

New
brown, never, off, out

Previously Taught
a, animal, do, find, hear, I, of, played, see, the, what, why, you

Rich Gets a Dog
Decodable Reader, page 33
Target Skills:
Digraphs ch, tch

Decodable Words

Target Skill: Digraphs *ch, tch*
Fletch, much, Rich

Previously Taught Skills
and, asked, bed, big, can, Dad, dog, dogs, fast, fat, get, gets, has, his, Hmmm, hugs, in, is, just, Mom, pals, picks, run, sat, then, thin, tucked, up, will, yes

High-Frequency Words

New
brown, own, very

Previously Taught
a, are, be, called, here, I, like, one, said, see, small, today

Champs
Decodable Reader, page 39
Target Skills:
Possessives with 's
Digraphs ch, tch

Decodable Words

Target Skill: Possessives with *'s*
Bill's, Dutch's, Fran's

Target Skill: Digraphs *ch, tch*
bench, catch, catches, champ, champs, chat, Chet, Dutch, such

Previously Taught Skills
and, Bill, dog, dogs, Fran, fun, get, has, his, is, it, jumps, not, on, pal, rest, set, sits, spot, them, then, tug, up, will, with, yells

High-Frequency Words

New
been, know, own

Previously Taught
a, are, good, here, like, play, the, they, to, too

Kits, Chicks, and Pups
Decodable Reader, page 45
Target Skills:
Possessives with 's
Digraphs ch, tch

Decodable Words

Target Skill: Possessives with *'s*
mom's

Target Skill: Digraphs *ch, tch*
chicks, hatch, such

Previously Taught Skills
and, big, can, cat, cats, dad, dads, dog, dogs, duck, ducks, eggs, fed, get, has, his, in, is, it, kit, mom, moms, must, nap, nest, not, off, pond, pop, pups, run, sit, still, stop, swim, that, then, this, will, with

High-Frequency Words

New
know, off, out

Previously Taught
a, do, eat, good, have, her, in, make, picture, the, they, too

LESSON 13

Phil's New Bat
Decodable Reader, page 51
Target Skills:
Digraphs sh, wh, ph

Decodable Words

Target Skill: Digraphs *sh, wh, ph*
bash, Phil, Phil's, wham, when, wished

Previously Taught Skills
and, bat, bit, can, cannot, catch, dad, did, fell, fun, get, got, had, hands, him, his, hit, hits, if, in, is, it, just, leg, let, mom, not, on, pal, runs, sad, went, will, with, yes

High-Frequency Words

New
down, fall, new

Previously Taught
a, do, for, good, he, many, play, was, what, you

In a Rush
Decodable Reader, page 57
Target Skills:
Digraphs sh, wh, ph

Decodable Words

Target Skill: Digraphs *sh, wh, ph*
bash, cash, dash, mush, Phil's, rush, Shan, shop, slush, splash, splish, wham

Previously Taught Skills
and, at, best, did, fell, felt, fun, get, glad, got, has, in, is, it, just, last, lots, must, not, plod, plop, sat, slip, slop, still, stuff, that, then, up, went, wet, will

High-Frequency Words

New
down, goes, new, open, yellow

Previously Taught
a, all, cold, like, look, now, of, she, the, to, what

Ralph Goes to Camp
Decodable Reader, page 63
Target Skills:
Contractions 's, n't
Digraphs sh, wh, ph

Decodable Words

Target Skill: Contractions *'s, n't*
didn't, isn't, it's

Target Skill: Digraphs *sh, wh, ph*
Ralph, Ralph's, rush, Shep, shocked, splashing, splishing, trash, when

Previously Taught Skills
and, asked, asks, at, bad, bag, bath, big, bins, but, camp, can, dad, did, dog, fun, got, had, hat, his, if, is, it, job, jobs, just, last, mom, spill, that, trip, tug, well, went, wet, yes

High-Frequency Words

New
goes, yellow

Previously Taught
a, do, give, go, he, no, said, some, the, to, today, was, you

Trish's Gift
Decodable Reader, page 69
Target Skills:
Contractions 's, n't
Digraphs sh, wh, ph

Decodable Words

Target Skill: Contractions *'s, n't*
can't, didn't, it's, let's, that's

Target Skill: Digraphs *sh, wh, ph*
shed, Trish, Trish's, when

Previously Taught Skills
and, ask, asked, at, back, bench, big, brass, but, can, cloth, Dad, desk, did, fast, gift, got, Gramps, had, him, his, hunted, in, is, it, just, lifted, Mom, on, ran, sent, sit, ten, that, then, this, trim, up, with, yelled, yes

High-Frequency Words

New
green, grow, new, opened

Previously Taught
a, call, I, know, put, said, see, the, was, we, where

LESSON 14

Tate's Cakes
Decodable Reader, page 75
Target Skills:
Long a (CVCe)

Decodable Words

Target Skill: Long *a* (CVC*e*)
ate, bake, cake, cakes, came, cave, Jade, Jade's, made, make, sale, Tate, Wade

Previously Taught Skills
am, and, ask, big, can, did, glad, got, had, has, hot, if, in, is, it, just, let's, must, on, sand, tell, ten, that, them, this, us, well, went, will, yes

High-Frequency Words

New
five, four, into, over

Previously Taught
a, are, goes, I, know, me, never, said, the, they, to, was, what, you

Dave and the Whales
Decodable Reader, page 81
Target Skills:
Long a (CVCe)

Decodable Words

Target Skill: Long *a* (CVC*e*)
came, chase, Dave, Dave's, Jake, Lane, made, make, name, tape, waves, whale, whales

Previously Taught Skills
am, and, as, asked, big, but, can, can't, catch, did, fast, get, hills, him, his, hit, is, it, let's, not, pals, sad, then, will, with, yelled

High-Frequency Words

New
five, four, three, two, watch

Previously Taught
a, be, I, me, one, play, said, sing, the, to, we, why

A Safe Lodge
Decodable Reader, page 87
Target Skills:
Soft c, g, dge
Long a (CVCe)

Decodable Words

Target Skills: Soft *c, g, dge*
lodge, place, space

Target Skill: Long *a* (CVC*e*)
lake, made, make, makes, place, safe, space

Previously Taught Skills
an, and, back, big, can, cut, cuts, Dad, dam, drag, drags, fix, get, has, help, helps, if, in, is, it, its, kits, Mom, mud, rest, romp, spills, sticks, that, them, this, when, will, with

High-Frequency Words

New
over, starts, watch

Previously Taught
a, animal, for, go, holds, of, out, own, the, their, they, water

The Race
Decodable Reader, page 93
Target Skills:
Soft c, g, dge
Long a (CVCe)

Decodable Words

Target Skills: Soft *c, g, dge*
Ace, badges, Grace, judge, Madge, pace, race, space, Trace

Target Skill: Long *a* (CVC*e*)
Ace, Blake, Dave, gave, Grace, lane, lanes, pace, race, shade, skate, space, take, Trace, trade

Previously Taught Skills
and, as, can, can't, clap, crack, fast, fun, get, got, has, his, in, is, it, jump, last, must, off, past, red, run, set, sit, that, them, this, will, yell

High-Frequency Words

New
four, into, over, starts, two, watch

Previously Taught
a, blue, go, of, off, the, they, to, you

LESSON 15

Mike's Bike
Decodable Reader, page 99
Target Skills:
Long i (CVCe)

The Nest
Decodable Reader, page 105
Target Skills:
Long i (CVCe)

The Nice Vet
Decodable Reader, page 111
Target Skills:
Digraphs wr, mb
Long i (CVCe)

Kite Time
Decodable Reader, page 117
Target Skills:
Digraphs kn, wr
Long i (CVCe)

Decodable Words

Target Skill: Long *i* (CVCe)
bike, bikes, five, life, like, Mike, Mike's, miles, mine, nice, pride, ride, rides, stripes, time, white, wide

Previously Taught Skills
and, at, back, best, big, can, dad, did, end, face, fun, got, grin, had, has, him, his, is, it, its, just, Nell, Nell's, on, path, place, red, six, stop, take, that, this, well, will, with

Decodable Words

Target Skill: Long *i* (CVCe)
dive, fine, glide, like, mice, pile, quite, rise, side, time, vines, white, wide

Previously Taught Skills
and, as, at, big, can, chest, chick, chicks, Dad, dip, eggs, flap, get, grasp, had, has, his, if, in, is, it, its, just, let, make, made, Male, Male's, Mom, name, neck, nest, not, Pale, past, sticks, take, them, then, this, up

Decodable Words

Target Skill: Digraphs *wr, mb*
numb, writes

Target Skill: Long *i* (CVCe)
dime, file, five, nice, price, Spike, Spike's, time, whines, writes

Previously Taught Skills
an, and, at, can, dad, dog, drops, fast, fix, get, hands, has, his, in, is, isn't, it, itch, itching, it's, Kate's, Kate, last, make, mom, not, place, rubs, still, stop, tells, them, vet, vet's, will, with

Decodable Words

Target Skill: Digraphs *kn, wr*
knock, wrap

Target Skill: Long *i* (CVCe)
dives, glide, glides, kite, kite's, kites, like, line, ride, rise, slides, time

Previously Taught Skills
and, back, can, dip, dips, fast, fists, fun, if, in, is, it, it's, let, make, not, on, quit, run, stops, takes, them, then, up, will, wind, with

---

High-Frequency Words

New
both, long, or

Previously Taught
a, for, go, have, I, my, new, of, said, see, the, they, to, too, was

High-Frequency Words

New
bird, both, fly, long, those, walk

Previously Taught
a, down, find, for, go, look, now, of, small, the, they, to, you

High-Frequency Words

New
eyes, long, walk

Previously Taught
a, calls, goes, I, puts, see, the, they, to, who

High-Frequency Words

New
bird, fly, or

Previously Taught
a, do, down, go, hold, play, the, to, too

Scoring Rubrics

RUBRIC

Retelling Fiction

4 Highly Effective	The child describes the plot (problem and solution); retells the beginning, middle, and end, with attention to the sequence of events; describes the characters and the reasons for their actions and feelings; requires little or no prompting.
3 Generally Effective	The child describes most of the plot; retells most of the beginning, middle, and end, with some attention to the sequence of events; describes the characters and may provide some reasons for their actions and feelings; may require some prompting.
2 Somewhat Effective	The child describes some plot details; retells some of the beginning, middle, and end, with some omissions or errors; describes some of the characters; requires some prompting.
1 Ineffective	The child retells few, if any, details about the story elements, possibly with errors; is unable to retell the story without prompting.

RUBRIC

Summarizing Nonfiction

4 Highly Effective	The child restates the main idea; identifies the important facts or details; retells the order of events by referring to the words and/or illustrations; requires little or no prompting.
3 Generally Effective	The child restates the main idea; identifies some important facts or details; retells the order of most events and may refer to the words and/or illustrations; may require some prompting.
2 Somewhat Effective	The child may restate the main idea; identifies some facts or details; retells the order of some events with some omissions or errors; requires some prompting.
1 Ineffective	The child is unable to restate the main idea; identifies some facts or details, possibly with errors; is unable to retell the order of events; is unable to summarize without prompting.

Multipurpose Writing RUBRIC

	Score of 6	Score of 5	Score of 4	Score of 3	Score of 2	Score of 1
FOCUS / SUPPORT	The writer adheres to the topic, is interesting, has a sense of completeness. Develops topic or events with relevant facts or details.	The writer adheres to the topic, is usually interesting, has sense of completeness. Mostly develops topic or events with relevant facts or details.	The writer mostly adheres to the topic, is somewhat interesting, and has some sense of completeness. Adequately develops topic or events with some relevant facts or details.	The writer adheres to the topic somewhat, and has adequate sense of completeness. Develops topic or events with some relevant facts or details.	The writer does not always adhere to the topic, and has limited sense of completeness. Develops topic or events with few relevant facts or details.	The writer does not adhere to the topic, and has no sense of completeness. May not develop topic or events with relevant facts or details.
ORGANIZATION	The writer introduces topic or situation clearly; organizes ideas clearly to support purpose; provides a strong sense of closure.	The writer introduces topic or situation; organizes ideas to support purpose; provides some sense of closure.	The writer introduces topic or situation; organizes ideas somewhat to support purpose; provides adequate sense of closure.	The writer partially introduces topic or situation; organizes some ideas to support purpose; provides minimal sense of closure.	The writer may introduce topic or situation; organizes few ideas to support purpose; provides little sense of closure.	The writer may attempt to introduce topic or situation; may not organize ideas to support purpose; may not provide sense of closure.
WORD CHOICE / VOICE	The writer uses vivid verbs, strong adjectives, and specific nouns. Connects with reader in a unique, personal way.	The writer uses some vivid verbs, strong adjectives, and specific nouns. Connects with reader in a way that is personal and often unique.	The writer uses some specific and descriptive verbs, adjectives, and nouns. Generally connects with reader in a way that is personal and sometimes unique.	The writer uses some specific verbs, adjectives, and nouns. Connects with reader in a way that is somewhat personal but rarely unique.	The writer uses mostly simple nouns and verbs, and may have a few adjectives. Connects with reader in a way that is somewhat personal but not unique.	The writer uses only simple nouns and verbs, some inaccurate. Writing is not descriptive. Does not connect with reader. Does not sound personal or unique.
CONVENTIONS / SENTENCE FLUENCY	The writer demonstrates exemplary command of conventions of grammar, spelling, capitalization, and punctuation. Includes a variety of complete sentences that flow smoothly, naturally.	The writer demonstrates good command of conventions of grammar, spelling, capitalization, and punctuation. Includes some variety of complete sentences. Some parts flow smoothly, naturally.	The writer demonstrates adequate command of grammar, spelling, capitalization, and punctuation. Includes little variety of complete sentences. Few flow smoothly, naturally.	The writer demonstrates some command of grammar, spelling, capitalization, and punctuation, with errors. Includes mostly simple sentences, some of which are incomplete.	The writer demonstrates growing command of grammar, spelling, capitalization, and punctuation. Sentences do not vary. Incomplete sentences hinder meaning.	The writer demonstrates little or no command of grammar, spelling, capitalization, and punctuation. Sentences hinder meaning.

Handwriting

Individual children come to first grade with various levels of handwriting skills, but they all have the desire to communicate effectively. To learn correct letter formation, they must be familiar with concepts of

- position (top, middle, bottom; on, above, below).
- size (tall, short).
- direction (left, right; up, down; over, around, across).
- order (first, next, then, last).
- open and closed.
- spacing.

The lessons in *Journeys* build on these concepts in both formal and informal handwriting lessons so that children develop the skills they need to become independent writers. To assess children's handwriting skills, have them write each capital and lowercase letter of the alphabet. Note whether children use correct formation, appropriate size, and spacing.

Stroke and Letter Formation

The shape and formation of letters taught in *Journeys* are based on the way experienced writers write their letters. Most are formed with a continuous stroke, so children do not often pick up their pencils when writing a single letter. Letter formation is simplified through the use of "letter talk"—an oral description of how the letter is formed. Models for manuscript and D'Nealian Handwriting are used in this program to support different writing systems.

Learning Modes

A visual, kinesthetic, tactile, and auditory approach to handwriting is used throughout *Journeys*. To help children internalize letter forms, each letter is taught in the context of how it looks, the sound it stands for, and how it is formed.

Position for Writing

Establishing the correct posture, pencil grip, and paper position for writing will help prevent handwriting problems later on.

Posture Children should sit with both feet on the floor and with hips to the back of the chair. They can lean forward slightly but should not slouch. The writing surface should be smooth and flat and at a height that allows the upper arms to be perpendicular to the surface and the elbows to be under the shoulders.

Writing Instrument An adult-sized number-two lead pencil is a satisfactory writing tool for most children. However, use your judgment in determining what type of instrument is most suitable for a child, given his or her level of development.

Hand Dominance To determine each child's hand dominance, observe him or her at play and note which hand is the preferred hand. Watching the child turn a doorknob, roll a ball, build a block tower, or turn the pages in a book will help you note hand dominance.

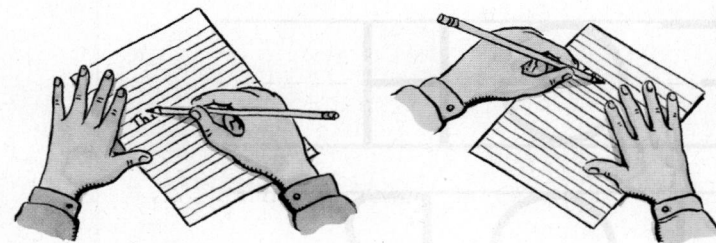

Paper Position and Pencil Grip The paper is slanted along the line of the child's writing arm, and the child uses his or her nonwriting hand to hold the paper in place. The child holds the pencil slightly above the paint line—about 1 inch from the lead tip.

Develop Handwriting

The best instruction builds on what children already know and can do. Given the tremendous range in children's experience with writing materials prior to first grade, a variety of approaches will be needed.

Writing for Different Purposes For children with limited print concepts, one of the first and most important understandings is that print carries meaning and that writing has real purpose. Provide many opportunities for writing in natural settings. For example, children can

- make a class directory listing names and phone numbers of their classmates.
- record observations in science.
- write and illustrate labels for art materials.
- draw and label maps, pictures, graphs, and picture dictionaries.

Meaningful Print Experiences Children should participate in meaningful print experiences. They can

- write signs, name tags, and messages.
- label pictures.
- join in shared writing experiences.

Writing Fluently To ensure the continued rapid advancement of children who come to the first grade already writing, provide

- exposure to a wide range of reading materials.
- opportunities for independent writing on self-selected and assigned topics.
- explicit instruction in print conventions (punctuation, use of capital letters).
- instruction for simple editing marks and encourage children to proofread and edit their own work.

ABCDEFGH
IJKLMNOP
QRSTUVW
XYZ

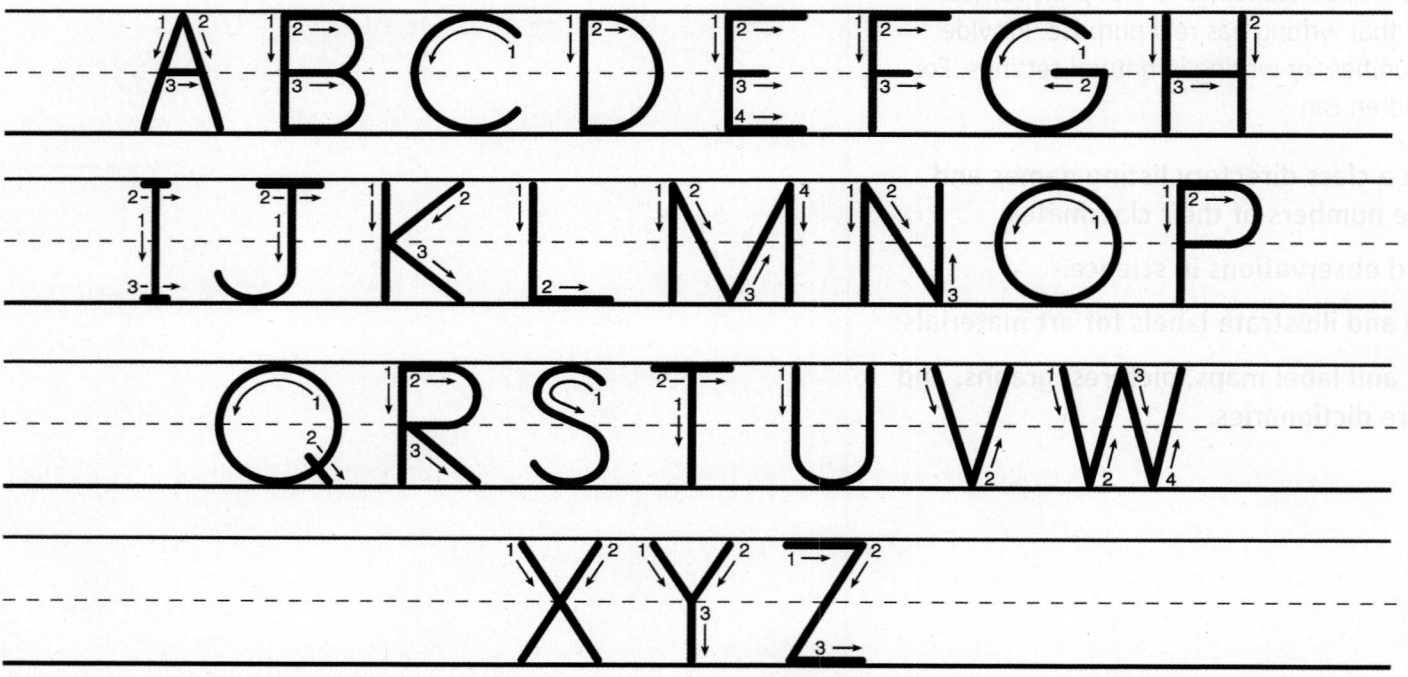

a b c d e f g h
i j k l m n o p
q r s t u v w
x y z

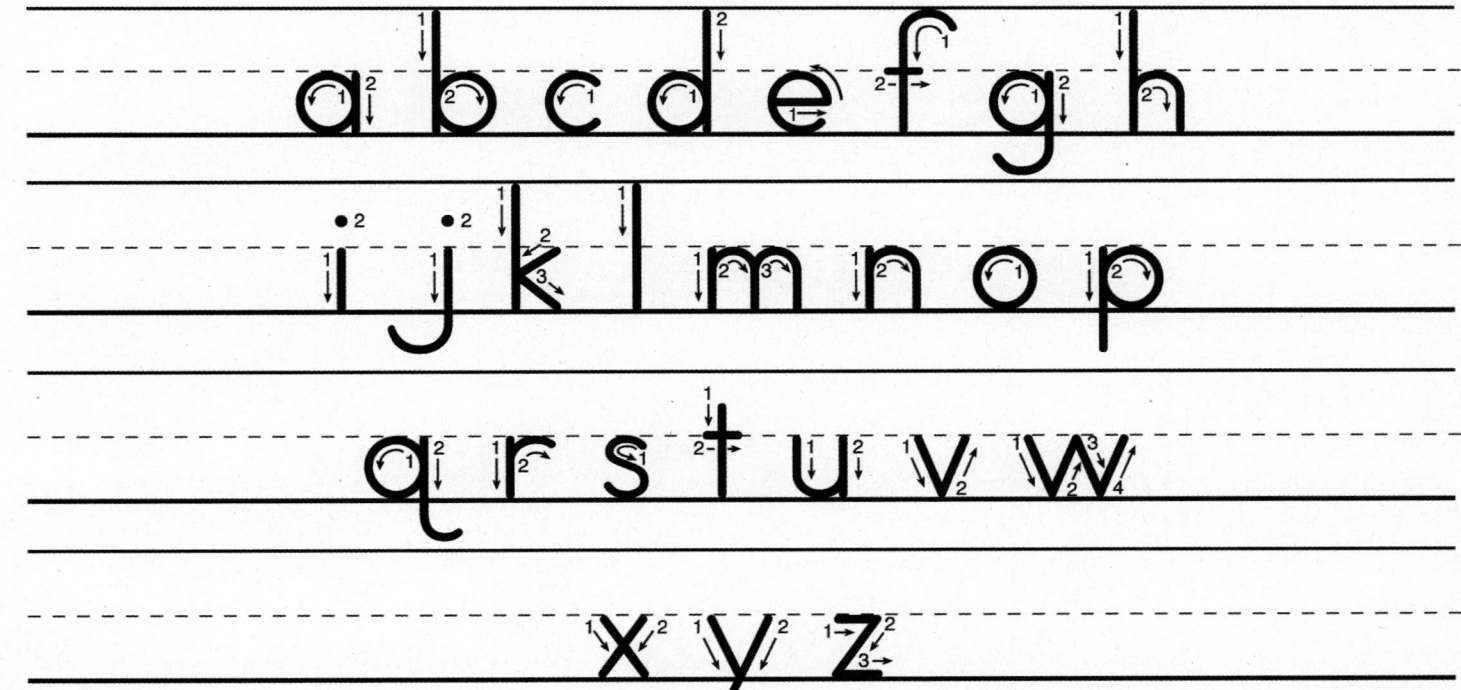

A B C D E F G H
I J K L M N O P
Q R S T U V W
X Y Z

a b c d e f g h

i j k l m n o p

q r s t u v w

x y z

Glossary

Glossary

A

amphibians
An **amphibian** is an animal that lives in water and on land. Frogs are **amphibians**.

B

biggest
Something that is the **biggest** is bigger in size than anything else. The whale is the **biggest** animal in the ocean.

blow
To **blow** means to push air. The winds **blow** the cold air across the land.

body
The **body** of a person or animal is made up of the parts you can see and touch. We are learning about the parts of the **body**.

breathe
To **breathe** is to take in breaths of air. I **breathe** in the fresh air when I am outside.

C

cottontail
A **cottontail** is a kind of rabbit. That **cottontail** has a white fluffy tail.

D

danced
To **dance** means to move to music. We played music and **danced** for hours.

day
A **day** is the time from one morning to the next morning. Tuesday was a sunny **day**.

F

feathers
A **feather** is a part of a bird. The bird had soft **feathers**.

feet
A foot is a measurement that equals 12 inches. **Feet** means more than one foot. Some trees can grow as tall as 100 **feet**.

flowers
A **flower** is a part of a plant. We planted pretty **flowers** in the garden.

G

giraffe
A **giraffe** is a tall spotted animal with a long neck. The **giraffe** ate leaves from the top of the tree.

grow
When plants and animals **grow**, they get bigger and bigger. Kittens **grow** and become cats.

group
A **group** is a number of people or things together. A **group** of us went swimming last Saturday.

H

hair
Hair is what grows on your head. My dad cuts my **hair** when it gets too long.

hay
Hay is a kind of grass that has been cut and dried. My horse likes to eat **hay**.

home
A **home** is a place where people or animals live. Jellyfish make their **home** underwater.

hooray
Hooray is something people shout when they are happy. When I hit a home run, my parents yelled **hooray**!

hyena
A **hyena** is a wild animal that looks like a dog. The **hyena** is found in Africa and Asia.

L

leaves
A **leaf** is a part of a plant. In the fall, the **leaves** turn pretty colors.

leopard
A **leopard** is a wild animal that looks like a cat with spots. The **leopard** paced in its cage.

lions
A **lion** is a large wild animal that looks like a big cat. We saw a movie about **lions** in Africa.

lizard
A **lizard** is a small reptile. The **lizard** lay on the rock in the hot sun.

M

mammals
A **mammal** is a warm-blooded animal. Cats are **mammals**.

G6

manatees
A **manatee** is a plant-eating animal with flippers and a flat tail that lives in warm water. When we visited Florida, we saw **manatees** swimming in the water.

O

ocean
An **ocean** is a large body of salt water. It's fun to sail on the **ocean**.

P

paint
To **paint** means to cover something with color. Aunt Carly likes to **paint** houses.

penguins
A **penguin** is a kind of bird that lives in cold places. **Penguins** keep their chicks warm.

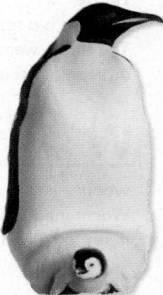

G7

R

race
A **race** is a contest to find out who is the fastest. Selena got to the finish line first and won the **race**.

reptiles
A **reptile** is a cold-blooded animal. Snakes are **reptiles**.

roadrunner
A **roadrunner** is a very fast bird. We saw a **roadrunner** in the Arizona desert.

S

school
A **school** is a place where students learn from teachers. My best friend and I go to the same **school**.

sea otters
Sea otters are mammals with thick, brown fur that live in and by the ocean. After a swim, **sea otters** like to sit in the warm sun.

G8

seeds
A **seed** is a part of a plant. Most plants grow from tiny little **seeds**.

snow
Snow is tiny pieces of frozen water that fall from the clouds. When we woke up, the ground was covered with **snow**.

snowman
A **snowman** looks like a person made of snow. We piled three balls of snow on top of each other and made a **snowman**.

spring
Spring is the season that comes after winter. In the **spring**, the flowers begin to bloom.

summer
Summer is the season that comes after spring. This **summer** my family will go to the beach.

G9

Glossary/Acknowledgments

T

tadpoles
A **tadpole** is a baby frog. I found **tadpoles** swimming in our pond.

tails
A **tail** is a part of some animals' bodies. Rats have long **tails**.

tall
To be **tall** is to stand high above the ground. The giraffe is very **tall**.

turtle
A **turtle** is a reptile with a shell. The **turtle** went inside its shell as soon as I touched it.

W

warm
Warm means not very hot. The tea was still **warm** after it sat for a while.

G10

---

whales
A **whale** is the biggest mammal that lives in the ocean. When we went boating, we saw **whales** as big as our boat!

wings
A **wing** is a part that helps something to fly. The bird flapped its **wings** and flew away.

winter
Winter is a season that comes after fall. Last **winter** was very cold!

Z

zebra
A **zebra** is a striped animal that looks like a horse. My favorite animal is the **zebra**.

G11

G12

G13

Research Bibliography

Achieve, Inc. (2007). *Closing the expectations gap 2007: An annual 50-state progress report on the alignment of high school policies with the demands of college and work.* Washington, DC: Author. http://www.achieve.org/files/50-state-07-Final.pdf.

Achugar, M., Schleppegrell, M., & Oteíza, T. (2007). Engaging teachers in language analysis: A functional linguistics approach to reflective literacy. *English Teaching: Practice and Critique,* 6 (2), 8–24.

ACT, Inc. (2006). *Reading between the lines: What the ACT reveals about college readiness in reading.* Iowa City, IA: Author.

ACT, Inc. (2009). *ACT National Curriculum Survey 2009.* Iowa City, IA: Author.

ACT, Inc. (2009). *The condition of college readiness 2009.* Iowa City, IA: Author.

Adams, M. J. (2009). The challenge of advanced texts: The interdependence of reading and learning. In E. H. Hiebert (Ed.), *Reading more, reading better: Are American students reading enough of the right stuff?* (pp. 163–189). New York, NY: Guilford.

Adams, M. J. (2000). *Beginning to Read: Thinking and Learning About Print.* Cambridge: MIT Press.

Afflerbach, P., Pearson, P. D., & Paris, S. G. (2008). Clarifying differences between reading skills and reading strategies. *The Reading Teacher,* 61, 364–373.

Anderson, Jeff. (2005). *Mechanically Inclined: Building Grammar, Usage, and Style into Writer's Workshop.* Portsmouth, NH: Heinemann.

Angelillo, Janet. (2002). *A Fresh Approach to Teaching Punctuation.* New York: Scholastic.

Armbruster, B., Anderson, T. H., & Ostertag, J. (1987). Does text structure/summarization instruction facilitate learning from expository text? *Reading Research Quarterly,* 22 (3), 331–346.

Armbruster, B., Lehr, F., & Osborn, J. (2001). *Put Reading First: The Research Building Blocks for Teaching Children to Read* (pp. 21–31). Washington, D.C.: National Institute for Literacy.

Askew, B. J. & Fountas, I. C. (1998). Building an early reading process: Active from the start! *The Reading Teacher,* 52 (2), 126–134.

Baker, S. K., Chard, D. J., Ketterlin-Geller, L. R., Apichatabutra, C., & Doabler, C. (in press). The basis of evidence for Self-Regulated Strategy Development for students with or at risk for learning disabilities. *Exceptional Children.*

Ball, E., & Blachman, B. (1991). Does phoneme awareness training in kindergarten make a difference in early word recognition and developmental spelling? *Reading Research Quarterly,* 26 (1), 49–66.

Balmuth, M. (1992). *The roots of phonics: A historical introduction.* Baltimore, MD: York Press.

Bardovi-Harlig, K. (2000). *Tense and aspect in second language acquisition: Form, meaning, and use.* Language Learning Monograph Series. Malden, MA: Blackwell.

Bartholomae, D. (1980). The study of error. *College Composition and Communication,* 31 (3), 253–269.

Baumann, J. F. & Bergeron, B. S. (1993). Story map instruction using children's literature: Effects on first graders' comprehension of central narrative elements. *Journal of Reading Behavior,* 25 (4), 407–437.

Baumann, J. F., & Kame'enui, E. J. (1991). Research on vocabulary instruction: Ode to Voltaire. In J. Flood, J. M. Jensen, D. Lapp, & J. R. Squire (Eds.), *Handbook of research on teaching the English language arts* (pp. 604–632). New York, NY: Macmillan.

Baumann, J. F. & Kame'enui, E. J. (Eds.). (2004). *Vocabulary Instruction: Research to Practice.* New York: Guilford Press.

Baumann, J. F., Seifert-Kessell, N., & Jones, L. A. (1992). Effect of think-aloud instruction on elementary students' comprehension monitoring abilities. *Journal of Reading Behavior,* 24 (2), 143–172.

Bear, D. R. & Templeton, S. (1998). Explorations in developmental spelling: Foundations for learning and teaching phonics, spelling, and vocabulary. *The Reading Teacher,* 52 (3), 222–242.

Beck, I. L. (2006). *Making Sense of Phonics: The Hows and Whys.* New York: Guilford Press.

Beck, I. L. & McKeown, M. (2006). *Improving Comprehension with Questioning the Author: A Fresh and Expanded View of a Powerful Approach (Theory and Practice).* New York, NY: Scholastic.

Beck, I. L., & McKeown, M. G., (2001). Text talk: Capturing the benefits of read-aloud experiences for young children. *The Reading Teacher,* 55 (1), 10–20.

Beck, I. L., McKeown, M., Hamilton, R., & Kucan, L. (1997). *Questioning the Author: An Approach for Enhancing Student Engagement with Text.* Newark, DE: International Reading Association.

Beck, I. L., McKeown, M., Hamilton, R., & Kucan, L. (1998). Getting at the meaning. *American Educator,* Summer, 66–71.

Beck, I. L., McKeown, M. G., & Kucan, L. (2002). *Bringing Words to Life: Robust Vocabulary Instruction.* New York: Guilford Press.

Beck, I. L., McKeown, M. G., & Kucan, L. (2008). *Creating robust vocabulary: Frequently asked questions and extended examples.* New York, NY: Guilford.

Beck, I. L., Perfetti, C. A., & McKeown, M. G. (1982). Effects of long-term vocabulary instruction on lexical access and reading comprehension. *Journal of Educational Psychology,* 74 (4), 506–521.

Becker, W. C. (1977). Teaching reading and language to the disadvantaged—What we have learned from field research. *Harvard Educational Review,* 47, 518–543.

Bereiter, C. & Bird, M. (1985). Use of thinking aloud in identification and teaching of reading comprehension strategies. *Cognition and Instruction,* 2, 131–156.

Bettinger, E., & Long, B. T. (2009). Addressing the needs of underprepared students in higher education: Does college remediation work? *Journal of Human Resources,* 44, 736–771.

Betts, E. A. (1946). *Foundations of reading instruction, with emphasis on differentiated guidance.* New York, NY: American Book Company.

Biber, D. (1991). *Variation across speech and writing.* Cambridge, England: Cambridge University Press.

Biemiller, A. (2001). Teaching vocabulary: Early, direct, and sequential. *American Educator,* 25 (1), 24–28, 47.

Biemiller, A. (2001). Vocabulary development and instruction: A prerequisite for school learning. In D. Dickinson & S. Neuman (Eds.), *Handbook of Early Literacy Research,* (Vol. 2), New York: Guilford Press.

Biemiller, A. (2005). Size and sequence in vocabulary development: Implications for choosing words for primary grade vocabulary. In E. H. Hiebert & M. L. Kamil (Eds.), *Teaching and Learning Vocabulary* (pp. 223–242). Mahwah, NJ: Lawrence Erlbaum.

Research Bibliography

Biemiller, A. & Slonim, N. (2001). Estimating root word vocabulary growth in normative and advantaged populations: Evidence for a common sequence of vocabulary acquisition. *Journal of Educational Psychology,* 93 (3), 498–520.

Blachman, B. (2000). Phonological awareness. In M. Kamil, P. Mosenthal, P. D. Pearson, & R. Barr (Eds.), *Handbook of Reading Research,* (Vol. 3). Mahwah, NJ: Lawrence Erlbaum.

Blachman, B., Ball, E. W., Black, R. S., & Tangel, D. M. (1994). Kindergarten teachers develop phoneme awareness in low-income, inner-city classrooms: Does it make a difference? *Reading and Writing: An Interdisciplinary Journal,* 6 (1), 1–18.

Bowen, G. M., & Roth, W.-M. (1999, March). "Do-able" questions, covariation, and graphical representation: Do we adequately prepare preservice science teachers to teach inquiry? Paper presented at the annual conference of the National Association for Research in Science Teaching, Boston, MA.

Bowen, G. M., Roth, W.-M., & McGinn, M. K. (1999). Interpretations of graphs by university biology students and practicing scientists: Towards a social practice view of scientific re-presentation practices. *Journal of Research in Science Teaching,* 36, 1020–1043.

Bowen, G. M., Roth, W.-M., & McGinn, M. K. (2002). Why students may not learn to interpret scientific inscriptions. *Research in Science Education,* 32, 303–327.

Brown, I. S. & Felton, R. H. (1990). Effects of instruction on beginning reading skills in children at risk for reading disability. *Reading and Writing: An Interdisciplinary Journal,* 2 (3), 223–241.

Bryson, B. (1990). *The mother tongue: English and how it got that way.* New York, NY: Avon Books.

Bus, A. G., Van Ijzendoorn, M. H., & Pellegrini, A. D. (1995). *Joint book reading makes for success in reading: A meta-analysis on intergenerational transmission of literacy.* Review of Educational Research, 65 (5), 1–21.

Carlo, M. (2004). Closing the gap: Addressing the vocabulary needs of English-language learners in bilingual and mainstream classrooms. *Reading Research Quarterly,* 39 (2), 188–215.

Carver, R. P. (1994). Percentage of unknown vocabulary words in text as a function of the relative difficulty of the text: Implications for instruction. *Journal of Reading Behavior,* 26, 413–437.

Catts, H., Adolf, S. M., & Weismer, S. E. (2006). Language deficits in poor comprehenders: A case for the simple view of reading. *Journal of Speech, Language, and Hearing Research,* 49, 278–293.

Chall, J. (1996). *Learning to Read: The Great Debate (revised, with a new foreword).* New York: McGraw-Hill.

Chall, J. S., Conard, S., & Harris, S. (1977). *An analysis of textbooks in relation to declining SAT scores.* Princeton, NJ: College Entrance Examination Board.

Chard, D. J., Ketterlin-Geller, L. R., Baker, S. K., Doabler, C., & Apichatabutra, C. (2009). Repeated reading interventions for students with learning disabilities: Status of the evidence. *Exceptional Children,* 75 (3), 263–281.

Chard, D. J., Stoolmiller, M., Harn, B., Vaughn, S., Wanzek, J., Linan-Thompson, S., & Kame'enui, E. J. (2008). Predicting reading success in a multi-level school-wide reading model: A retrospective analysis. *Journal of Learning Disabilities,* 41 (2), 174–188.

Charity, A. H., Scarborough, H. E., & Griffin, D. M. (2004). Familiarity with school English in African American children and its relation to early reading achievement. *Child Development,* 75 (5), 1340–1356.

Chiappe, P. & Siegel, L. S. (2006). A longitudinal study of reading development of Canadian children from diverse linguistic backgrounds. *Elementary School Journal,* 107 (2), 135–152.

Coyne, M. D., Kame'enui, E. J., & Simmons, D. C. (2004). Improving beginning reading instruction and intervention for students with LD: Reconciling "all" with "each." *Journal of Learning Disabilities,* 37 (3), 231–239.

Coyne, M. D., Kame'enui, E. J., Simmons, D. C., & Harn, B. A. (2004). Beginning reading intervention as inoculation or insulin: First-grade reading performance of strong responders to kindergarten intervention. *Journal of Learning Disabilities,* 37 (2), 90–104.

Coyne, M. D., Zipoli Jr., R. P., Chard, D. J., Faggella-Luby, M., Ruby, M., Santoro, L. E., & Baker, S. (2009). Direct instruction of comprehension: Instructional examples from intervention research on listening and reading comprehension. *Reading & Writing Quarterly,* 25 (2), 221–245.

Coyne, M. D., Zipoli Jr., R. P., & Ruby, M. (2006). Beginning reading instruction for students at risk for reading disabilities: What, how, and when. *Intervention in School and Clinic,* 41 (3), 161–168.

Craig, H. K. & Washington, J. A. (2001). Recent research on the language and literacy skills of African American students in early years. In D. Dickinson & S. Neuman (Eds.), *Handbook of Early Literacy Research,* (Vol. 2), New York: Guilford Press.

Craig, H. K. & Washington, J. A. (2006). *Malik Goes to School: Examining the Language Skills of African American Students From Preschool-5th Grade.* Mahwah, NJ: Lawrence Erlbaum Associates.

Daneman, M, & Green, I. (1986). Individual differences in comprehending and producing words in context. *Journal of Memory and Language,* 25 (1), 1–18.

DeVilliers, J., & DeVilliers, P. (1973). A cross-sectional study of the acquisition of grammatical morphemes in child speech. *Journal of Psycholinguistic Research,* 2, 267–278.

Dickinson, D. K., & Smith, M. W. (1994). Long-term effects of preschool teachers' book readings on low-income children's vocabulary and story comprehension. *Reading Research Quarterly,* 29, 104–123.

Dixon, R. C., Isaacson, S., & Stein, M. (2002). Effective strategies for teaching writing. In E. J. Kame'enui, D. W. Carnine, R. C. Dixon, D. C. Simmons, & M. D. Coyne (Eds.), *Effective Teaching Strategies That Accommodate Diverse Learners* (2nd ed., pp. 93–119). Upper Saddle River, NJ: Merrill Prentice Hall.

Dowhower, S. L. (1987). Effects of repeated reading on second-grade transitional readers' fluency and comprehension. *Reading Research Quarterly,* 22 (4), 389–406.

Duke, N. K. (2000). 3.6 minutes a day: The scarcity of informational text in first grade. *Reading Research Quarterly,* 35 (2), 202–224.

Duke, N. K. & Pearson, P. D. (2002). Effective practices for developing reading comprehension. In A. E. Farstrup & S. J. Samuels (Eds.), *What Research Has to Say About Reading Instruction* (3rd ed., pp. 205–242). Newark, DE: International Reading Association.

Durán, E., Shefelbine, J., Carnine, L., Maldonado-Colón, E., & Gunn, B. (2003). *Systematic Instruction in Reading for Spanish-Speaking Students.* Springfield, IL: Charles C. Thomas.

Durkin, D. (1978). What classroom observations reveal about comprehension instruction. *Reading Research Quarterly,* 14, 481–533.

Edwards Santoro, L., Chard, D. J., Howard, L., & Baker, S. K. (2008). Making the VERY most of classroom read alouds: How to promote comprehension and vocabulary in K-2 classrooms. *The Reading Teacher,* 61 (5), 396–408.

Ehri, L. C. (1998). Grapheme-phoneme knowledge is essential for learning to read words in English. In J. Metsala & L. Ehri (Eds.), *Word Recognition in Beginning Literacy* (pp. 3–40). Hillsdale, NJ: Lawrence Erlbaum Associates.

Ehri, L. & Nunes, S. R. (2002). The role of phonemic awareness in learning to read. In A. E. Farstrup & S. J. Samuels (Eds.), *What Research Has to Say About Reading Instruction* (3rd ed., pp. 110–139). Newark, DE: International Reading Association.

Ehri, L. & Wilce, L. (1987). Does learning to spell help beginners learn to read words? *Reading Research Quarterly,* 22 (1), 48–65.

Erickson, B. L., & Strommer, D. W. (1991). *Teaching college freshmen.* San Francisco, CA: Jossey-Bass.

Farr, R. (1990). Reading. *Educational Leadership,* 47 (5), 82–83.

Farr, R., Lewis, M., Faszholz, J., Pinsky, E., Towle, S., Lipschutz, J. & Faulds, B. P. (1990). Writing in response to reading. *Educational Leadership,* 47 (6), 66–69.

Feitelson, D., Goldstein, Z., Iraqui, J., & Share, D. I. (1993). Effects of listening to story reading on aspects of literacy acquisition in a diglossic situation. *Reading Research Quarterly,* 28, 70–79.

Feitelson, D., Kita, B., & Goldstein, Z. (1986). Effects of listening to series stories on first graders' comprehension and use of language. *Research in the Teaching of English,* 20, 339–356.

Fletcher, J. M. & Lyon, G. R. (1998). Reading: A research-based approach. In Evers, W. M. (Ed.), *What's Gone Wrong in America's Classroom?* Palo Alto, CA: Hoover Institution Press, Stanford University.

Fogel, H., & Ehri, L. C. (2000). Teaching elementary students who speak Black English Vernacular to write in Standard English: Effects of dialect transformation practice. *Contemporary Educational Psychology,* 25, 212–235.

Foorman, B. (Ed.). (2003). *Preventing and Remediating Reading Difficulties.* Baltimore, MD: York Press.

Foorman, B. R., Francis, D. J., Fletcher, J., Schatschneider, C., & Mehta, P. (1998). The role of instruction in learning to read: Preventing reading failure in at-risk children. *Journal of Educational Psychology,* 90 (1), 37–55.

Fountas, Irene & Pinnell, Gay Su. (2001). *Guiding Readers and Writers: Grades 3-6.* Portsmouth, NH: Heinemann.

Francis D. J., Rivera, M., Lesaux, N., Kieffer, M., & Rivera, H. (2006). Practical Guidelines for the Education of English Language Learners: Research-based recommendations for instruction and academic interventions (Book 1). Texas Institute for Measurement, Evaluation, and Statistics. University of Houston for the Center on Instruction.

Francis D. J., Rivera, M., Lesaux, N., Kieffer, M., & Rivera, H. (2006). Practical Guidelines for the Education of English Language Learners: Research-based recommendations for serving adolescent newcomers (Book 2). Texas Institute for Measurement, Evaluation, and Statistics. University of Houston for the Center on Instruction.

Fromkin, V., Rodman, R., & Hyams, N. (2006). *An introduction to language* (8th ed.). Florence, KY: Wadsworth.

Fuchs, L., Fuchs, D., & Hosp, M. (2001). Oral reading fluency as an indicator of reading competence: A theoretical, empirical, and historical analysis. *Scientific Studies of Reading,* 5 (3), 239–256.

Fukkink, R. G. & de Glopper, K. (1998). Effects of instruction in deriving word meaning from context: A meta-analysis. *Review of Educational Research,* 68 (4), 450–469.

Fulkerson, R. (1996). *Teaching the argument in writing.* Urbana, IL: National Council of Teachers of English.

Gambrell, L. B., Morrow, L. M., & Pennington, C. (2002). Early childhood and elementary literature-based instruction: Current perspectives… *Reading Online,* 5 (6), 26–39.

Ganske, K. (2000). *Word journeys.* New York, NY: Guilford.

García, G. G., & Beltrám, D. (2003). Revisioning the blueprint: Building for the academic success of English learners. In G. G. García (Ed.), *English Learners* (pp. 197–226). Newark, DE: International Reading Association.

Gargani, J. (2006). *UC Davis/SCUSD Teaching American History Grant technical memo: Years 1 & 2 essay and CST analysis results.* Unpublished report.

Gersten, R. (2005). Behind the scenes of an intervention research study. *Learning Disabilities Research & Practice,* 20 (4), 200–212.

Gersten, R. & Baker, S. (2000). What we know about effective instructional practices for English learners. *Exceptional Children,* 66 (4), 454–470.

Gersten, R., Baker, S. K., Haager, D., & Graves, A. W. (2005). Exploring the role of teacher quality in predicting reading outcomes for first-grade English learners: An observational study. *Remedial and Special Education,* 26 (4), 197–206.

Gersten, R. & Geva, E. (2003). Teaching reading to early language learners. *Educational Leadership,* 60 (7), 44–49.

Gersten, R. & Jiménez, R. (2002). Modulating instruction for English-language learners. In E. J. Kame'enui, D. W. Carnine, R. C. Dixon, D. C. Simmons, & M. D. Coyne (Eds.), *Effective Teaching Strategies That Accommodate Diverse Learners.* Upper Saddle River, NJ: Merrill Prentice Hall.

Gipe, J. P. & Arnold, R. D. (1979). Teaching vocabulary through familiar associations and contexts. *Journal of Reading Behavior,* 11 (3), 281–285.

Graff, G. (2003). *Clueless in academe.* New Haven, CT: Yale University Press.

Graham, Steve & Hebert, Michael. (2010). *Writing to Read: Evidence for How Writing Can Improve Reading. A Carnegie Corporation Time to Act Report.* Washington, DC: Alliance for Excellent Education.

Griffith, P. L., Klesius, J. P., & Kromrey, J. D. (1992). The effect of phonemic awareness on the literacy development of first grade children in a traditional or a whole language classroom. *Journal of Research in Childhood Education,* 6 (2), 85–92.

Guthrie, J. & Wigfield, A. (2000). Engagement and motivation in reading. In M. Kamil, P. Mosenthal, P. Pearson, & R. Barr, (Eds.), *Handbook of Reading Research, Vol. III,* 403–422.

Guthrie, J. T., Wigfield, A., Barbosa, P., Perencevich, K. C., Taboada, A., Davis, M. H., et al. (2004). Increasing reading comprehension and engagement through concept-oriented reading instruction. *Journal of Educational Psychology,* 96 (3), 403–423.

Hale, Elizabeth. (2008). *Crafting Writers: K-6.* Portsmouth, NH: Heinemann.

Research Bibliography

Hall, S. L. & Moats, L. C. (1999). *Straight Talk About Reading.* Chicago, IL: Contemporary Books.

Hanna, P. R., Hanna, S., Hodges, R. E., & Rudorf, E. H. (1966). *Phoneme-grapheme correspondences as cues to spelling improvement.* Washington, DC: Department of Health, Education, and Welfare.

Harm, M. W., McCandliss, B. D. & Seidenberg, M. S. (2003). Modeling the successes and failures of interventions for disabled readers. *Scientific Studies of Reading,* 7 (2), 155–182.

Harn, B. A., Stoolmiller, M., & Chard, D. (2008). Identifying the dimensions of alphabetic principle on the reading development of first graders: The role of automaticity and unitization. *Journal of Learning disabilities,* 41 (2), 143–157.

Hart, B., & Risley, T. R. (1995). *Meaningful differences in the everyday experience of young American children.* Baltimore, MD: Brookes.

Hasbrouck, J. & Tindal, G. A. (2006). Oral reading fluency norms: A valuable assessment tool for reading teachers. *The Reading Teacher,* 59 (7), 636–644.

Hayes, D., & Ahrens, M. (1988). Vocabulary simplification for children: A special case of "motherese"? *Journal of Child Language,* 15, 395–410.

Hayes, D. P., & Ward, M. (1992, December). *Learning from texts: Effects of similar and dissimilar features of analogies in study guides.* Paper presented at the 42nd Annual Meeting of the National Reading Conference, San Antonio, TX.

Hayes, D. P., Wolfer, L. T., & Wolfe, M. F. (1996). Sourcebook simplification and its relation to the decline in SAT-Verbal scores. *American Educational Research Journal,* 33, 489–508.

Heller, R., & Greenleaf, C. (2007). *Literacy instruction in the content areas: Getting to the core of middle and high school improvement.* Washington, DC: Alliance for Excellent Education.

Henry, M. (2003). *Unlocking literacy: Effective decoding and spelling instruction.* Baltimore, MD: Brookes.

Herman, P. A., Anderson, R. C., Pearson, P. D., & Nagy, W. E. (1987). Incidental acquisition of word meaning from expositions with varied text features. *Reading Research Quarterly,* 22, 263–284.

Hiebert, E. H. & Kamil, M. L. (Eds.). (2005). *Teaching and Learning Vocabulary: Bringing Research to Practice.* Mahwah, NJ: Lawrence Erlbaum Associates.

Hoffman, J., Sabo, D., Bliss, J., & Hoy, W. (1994). Building a culture of trust. *Journal of School Leadership,* 4, 484–501.

Hoover, W. A., & Gough, P. B. (1990). The simple view of reading. *Reading and Writing,* 2, 127–160.

Horn, Martha, & Giacobbe, Mary Ellen. (2007). *Talking, Drawing, Writing: Lessons for Our Youngest Writers.* Portland, ME: Stenhouse.

Hseuh-chao, M. H., & Nation, P. (2000). Unknown vocabulary density and reading comprehension. *Reading in a Foreign Language,* 13 (1), 403–430.

Hudson, R., (2006). Using Repeated Reading and Readers Theater to Increase Fluency. Reading First National Conference. http://www3.ksde.org/sfp/rdgfirst/natl_rdgfirst_conf_2006/hudson_using_repeated_reading_to_increase_fluency.pdf.

Hudson, R., Lane, H., & Pullen, P. (2005). Reading fluency assessment and instruction: What, why, and how? *The Reading Teacher,* 58 (8), 702–714.

Hulit, L. M., Howard, M. R., & Fahey, K. R. (2010). Born to talk: An introduction to speech and language development. Boston, MA: Allyn & Bacon.

Intersegmental Committee of the Academic Senates of the California Community Colleges, the California State University, and the University of California (ICAS). (2002). *Academic literacy: A statement of competencies expected of students entering California's public colleges and universities.* Sacramento, CA: Author.

Juel, C. (1988). Learning to read and write: A longitudinal study of fifty-four children from first through fourth grades. *Journal of Educational Psychology,* 80 (4), 437–447.

Juel, C., & Minden-Cupp, C. (2000). Learning to read words: Linguistic units and instructional strategies. *Reading Research Quarterly,* 35 (4), 458–492.

Kamil, M. L., Mosenthal, P. B., Pearson, P. D., & Barr, R. (2000). *Handbook of Reading Research.* Vol. III. Mahway, NJ: Lawrence Erlbaum Associates.

Kintsch, W. (1998). *Comprehension: A paradigm for cognition.* New York, NY: Cambridge University Press.

Kintsch, W. (2009). Learning and constructivism. In S. Tobias & M. Duffy (Eds.), *Constructivist instruction: Success or failure?* (pp. 223–241). New York, NY: Routledge.

Krauthamer, H. S. (1999). *Spoken language interference patterns in written English.* New York, NY: Peter Lang.

Kutner, M., Greenberg, E., Jin, Y., Boyle, B., Hsu, Y., & Dunleavy, E. (2007). *Literacy in everyday life: Results from the 2003 National Assessment of Adult Literacy* (NCES 2007–480). U.S. Department of Education. Washington, DC: National Center for Education Statistics.

Landauer, T. K., & Dumais, S. T. (1997). A solution to Plato's problem: The latent semantic analysis theory of acquisition, induction, and representation of knowledge. *Psychological Review,* 104, 211–240.

Landauer, T. K., McNamara, D. S., Dennis, S., & Kintsch, W. (Eds.) (2007). *Handbook of latent semantic analysis.* London, England: Psychology Press.

Laufer, B. (1988). What percentage of text-lexis is essential for comprehension? In C. Laurén & M. Nordman (Eds.), *Special language: From humans to thinking machines* (pp. 316–323). Clevedon, England: Multilingual Matters.

Lefstein, A. (2009). Rhetorical grammar and the grammar of schooling: Teaching "powerful verbs" in the English National Literacy Strategy. *Linguistics and Education,* 20, 378–400.

Lehr, F. & Osborn, J. (2005). A Focus on Comprehension. Pacific Resources for Education and Learning (PREL) Monograph. U.S. Department of Education. www.prel.org/programs/rel/rel.asp.

Lehr, F., Osborn, J., & Hiebert, E. H. (2004). A Focus on Vocabulary. Pacific Resources for Education and Learning (PREL) Monograph. U.S. Department of Education. www.prel.org/programs/rel/rel.asp.

Lesaux, N. K., Kieffer, M. J., Faller, S. E., & Kelley, J. G. (2010). The effectiveness and ease of implementation of an academic English vocabulary intervention for linguistically diverse students in urban middle schools. *Reading Research Quarterly,* 45, 196–228.

Lesaux, N. K. & Siegel, L. S. (2003). The development of reading in children who speak English as a second language. *Developmental Psychology,* 39 (6), 1005–1019.

Lipson, M. Y., Mosenthal, J. H., Mekkelsen, J., & Russ, B. (2004). Building knowledge and fashioning success one school at a time. *The Reading Teacher,* 57 (6), 534–542.

Lipson, M. Y. & Wixson, K. K. (2008). New IRA commission will address RTI issues. *Reading Today,* 26 (1), 1, 5.

Lonigan, C. J., Burgess, S. R., & Anthony, J. L. (2000). Development of emergent literacy and early reading skills in preschool children: Evidence from a latent-variable longitudinal study. *Developmental Psychology,* 36 (5), 596–613.

Lundberg, I., Frost, J., & Petersen O. (1988). Effects of an extensive program for stimulating phonological awareness in preschool children. *Reading Research Quarterly,* 23 (3), 263–284.

McCardle, P. & Chhabra, V. (Eds.). (2004). *The Voice of Evidence in Reading Research.* Baltimore: Brooks.

McIntosh, A. S., Graves, A., & Gersten, R. (2007). The effects of response to intervention on literacy development in multiple-language settings. *Learning Disability Quarterly,* 30 (3), 197–212.

McIntosh, K., Chard, D. J., Boland, J. B., & Horner, R. H. (2006). Demonstration of combined efforts in school-wide academic and behavioral systems and incidence of reading and behavior challenges in early elementary grades. *Journal of Positive Behavior Interventions,* 8 (3), 146–154.

McIntosh, K., Horner, R. H., Chard, D. J., Boland, J. B., Good, R. H. (2006). The use of reading and behavior screening measures to predict non-response to school-wide positive behavior support: A longitudinal analysis. *School Psychology Review,* 35 (2), 275–291.

McIntosh, K., Horner, R. H., Chard, D. J., Dickey, C. R., & Braun, D. H. (2008). Reading skills and function of problem behavior in typical school settings. *The Journal of Special Education,* 42 (3), 131–147.

McKenna, M. C. & Stahl, S. A. (2003). *Assessment for Reading Instruction,* New York: Guilford Press.

McKeown, M. G. & Beck, I. L. (2001). Encouraging young children's language interactions with stories. In D. Dickinson & S. Neuman (Eds.), *Handbook of Early Literacy Research* (Vol. 2). New York: Guilford Press.

McKeown, M. G., Beck, I. L., Omanson, R. C., & Pople, M. T. (1985). Some effects of the nature and frequency of vocabulary instruction on the knowledge and use of words. *Reading Research Quarterly,* 20 (5), 522–535.

McNamara, D. S., Graesser, A. C., & Louwerse, M. M. (in press). Sources of text difficulty: Across the ages and genres. In J. P. Sabatini & E. Albro (Eds.), *Assessing reading in the 21st century: Aligning and applying advances in the reading and measurement sciences.* Lanham, MD: R&L Education.

Merino, B. & Scarcella, R. (2005). Teaching science to English learners. *University of California Linguistic Minority Research Institute Newsletter,* 14 (4).

Mesmer, H. A. E. (2008). *Tools for matching readers to texts: Research-based practices.* New York, NY: Guilford.

Milewski, G. B., Johnson, D., Glazer, N., & Kubota, M. (2005). *A survey to evaluate the alignment of the new SAT Writing and Critical Reading sections to curricula and instructional practices* (College Board Research Report No. 2005-1 / ETS RR-05-07). New York, NY: College Entrance Examination Board.

Miller, G. A. (1999). On knowing a word. *Annual Review of Psychology,* 50, 1–19.

Moats, L. (2001). When older students can't read. *Educational Leadership,* 58 (6), 36–46.

Moats, L. (2004). Efficacy of a structured, systematic language curriculum for adolescent poor readers. *Reading & Writing Quarterly,* 20 (2), 145–159.

Moats, L. C. (1998). Teaching decoding. *American Educator,* 22 (1 & 2), 42–49, 95–96.

Moats, L. C. (1999). *Teaching Reading Is Rocket Science.* Washington, DC: American Federation of Teachers.

Moats, L. C. (2000). *Speech to Print: Language Essentials for Teachers.* Baltimore, MD: Paul H. Brookes Publishing Co., Inc.

Moats, L. C. (2008). *Spellography for teachers: How English spelling works.* (LETRS Module 3). Longmont, CO: Sopris West.

Morrow, L. M. (2004). Developmentally appropriate practice in early literacy instruction. *The Reading Teacher,* 58 (1), 88–89.

Morrow, L. M., Kuhn, M. R., & Schwanenflugel, P. J. (2006/2007). The family fluency program. *The Reading Teacher,* 60 (4), 322–333.

Morrow, L. M. & Tracey, D. H. (1997). Strategies used for phonics instruction in early childhood classrooms. *The Reading Teacher,* 50 (8), 644–651.

Morrow, L. M., Tracey, D. H., Woo, D. G., & Pressley, M. (1999). Characteristics of exemplary first-grade literacy instruction. *The Reading Teacher,* 52 (5), 462–476.

Mosenthal, J. H., Lipson, M. Y., Torncello, S., Russ, B., & Mekkelsen, J. (2004). Contexts and practices of six schools successful in obtaining reading achievement. *Elementary School Journal,* 104 (5), 343–367. ABSTRACT ONLY.

Moss, B., & Newton, E. (2002). An examination of the informational text genre in basal readers. *Reading Psychology,* 23 (1), 1–13.

Nagy, W. E., Anderson, R. C., & Herman, P. A. (1987). Learning word meanings from context during normal reading. *American Educational Research Journal,* 24, 237–270.

Nagy, W. E., Herman, P., & Anderson, R. C. (1985). Learning words from context. *Reading Research Quarterly,* 20, 233–253.

Nagy, W. E. & Scott, J. A. (2000). Vocabulary processes. In M. L. Kamil, P. B. Mosenthal, P. D. Pearson, & R. Barr (Eds.), *Handbook of Reading Research,* (Vol. 3, 269–284). Mahwah, NJ: Erlbaum.

National Assessment Governing Board. (2006). *Writing framework and specifications for the 2007 National Assessment of Educational Progress.* Washington, DC: U.S. Government Printing Office.

National Assessment Governing Board. (2007). *Writing framework for the 2011 National Assessment of Educational Progress,* pre-publication edition. Iowa City, IA: ACT, Inc.

National Center to Improve Tools of Educators. NCITE: http://idea.uoregon.edu/~ncite/.

National Commission on Writing. (2004). *Writing: A Ticket to Work…or a Ticket Out.* New York: The College Board.

National Endowment for the Arts. (2004). *Reading at risk: A survey of literary reading in America.* Washington, DC: Author.

National Institute of Child Health and Human Development. (2000). *Report of the National Reading Panel. Teaching children to read: An evidence-based assessment of the scientific research literature on reading and its implications for reading instruction* (NIH Publication No. 00-4769). Washington, DC: U.S. Government Printing Office.

Research Bibliography

National Reading Panel (2000). *Teaching children to read: An evidence-based assessment of the scientific research literature on reading and its implications for reading instruction.* (NIH Publication No. 00-4754). Washington, DC: National Institute of Child Health and Human Development.

Neuman, S. B., & Dickinson, D. K., (Eds.). (2002). *Handbook of Early Literacy Research.* New York: Guilford Press.

O'Connor, R., Jenkins, J. R., & Slocum, T. A. (1995). Transfer among phonological tasks in kindergarten: Essential instructional content. *Journal of Educational Psychology,* 87 (2), 202–217.

Orkwis, R. & McLane, K. (1998, Fall). *A Curriculum Every Student Can Use: Design Principles for Student Access.* ERIC/OSEP Special Project, ERIC Clearinghouse on Disabilities and Gifted Education, Council for Exceptional Children.

Osborn, J. & Lehr, F. (2003). *A Focus on Fluency: Research-Based Practices in Early Reading Series.* Honolulu, HI: Pacific Resources for Education and Learning.

O'Shea, L. J., Sindelar, P. T., & O'Shea, D. J. (1985). The effects of repeated readings and attentional cues on reading fluency and comprehension. *Journal of Reading Behavior,* 17 (2), 129–142.

Paris, S. G., Cross, D. R., & Lipson, M. Y. (1984). Informed strategies for learning: A program to improve children's reading awareness and comprehension. *Journal of Educational Psychology,* 76 (6), 1239–1252.

The Partnership for Reading. (2003). *Put Reading First: The Research Building Blocks for Teaching Children to Read.* (2nd ed.). MD: National Institute for Literacy.

Payne, B. D., & Manning, B. H. (1992). Basal reader instruction: Effects of comprehension monitoring training on reading comprehension, strategy use and attitude. *Reading Research and Instruction,* 32 (1), 29–38.

Pence, K. L., & Justice, L. M. (2007). *Language development from theory to practice.* Upper Saddle River, NJ: Prentice-Hall.

Perfetti, C. A., Landi, N., & Oakhill, J. (2005). The acquisition of reading comprehension skill. In M. J. Snowling & C. Hulme (Eds.), *The science of reading: A handbook* (pp. 227–247). Oxford, England: Blackwell.

Phillips, B. M. & Torgesen, J. K. (2001). Phonemic awareness and reading: Beyond growth of initial reading accuracy. In D. Dickinson & S. Neuman (Eds.), *Handbook of Early Literacy Research* (Vol. 2). New York: Guilford Press.

Pikulski, J. J., (1998). Business we should finish. *Reading Today,* 15 (5), 30.

Pikulski, J. J., & Chard, D. J. (2005). Fluency: Bridge between decoding and reading comprehension. *The Reading Teacher,* 58 (6), 510–519.

Postman, N. (1997). *The end of education.* New York, NY: Knopf.

Pressley, M. (1998). *Reading Instruction That Works: The Case for Balanced Teaching.* New York: The Guilford Press.

Pritchard, M. E., Wilson, G. S., & Yamnitz, B. (2007). What predicts adjustment among college students? A longitudinal panel study. *Journal of American College Health,* 56 (1), 15–22.

RAND Reading Study Group. (2002). *Reading for understanding: Toward an R & D program in reading comprehension.* Santa Monica, CA: RAND.

Rasinski, T. (2003). *The Fluent Reader: Oral Reading Strategies for Building Word Recognition, Fluency and Comprehension.* New York: Scholastic.

Rasinski, T. V., Padak, N., Linek, W., & Sturtevant, E. (1994). Effects of fluency development on urban second-grade readers. *Journal of Educational Research,* 87 (3), 158–165.

Rayner, K., Foorman, B. R., Perfetti, C. A., Pesetsky, D., & Seidenberg, M. S. (2001). How psychological science informs the teaching of reading. *Psychological Science in the Public Interest,* 2 (2), 31–74.

Rayner, K., Foorman, B. R., Perfetti, C. A., Pesetsky, D., & Seidenberg, M. S. (2002) How should reading be taught? *Scientific American,* pp. 85–91.

Report from the National Reading Panel. (2000). *Teaching Children to Read: An Evidence-Based Assessment of the Scientific Research Literature on Reading and its Implications for Reading Instruction.* Bethesda, MD: National Institute of Child Health and Human Development. http://www.nationalreadingpanel.org/Publications/summary.htm.

Rinehart, S. D., Stahl, S. A., & Erickson, L. G. (1986). Some effects of summarization training on reading and studying. *Reading Research Quarterly,* 21 (4), 422–438.

Robbins, C. & Ehri, L. C. (1994). Reading storybooks to kindergartners helps them learn new vocabulary words. *Journal of Educational Psychology,* 86 (1), 54–64.

Rosenshine, B., & Meister, C. (1994). Reciprocal teaching: A review of research. *Review of Educational Research,* 64 (4), 479–530.

Rosenshine, B., Meister, C., & Chapman, S. (1996). Teaching students to generate questions: A review of the intervention studies. *Review of Educational Research,* 66 (2), 181–221.

Routman, R. (2000). *Conversations: Strategies for Teaching, Learning, and Evaluating.* Portsmouth, NH: Heinemann.

Samuels, S., Schermer, N., & Reinking, D. (1992). Reading fluency: Techniques for making decoding automatic. In S. J. Samuels, J. Samuels, & A. E. Farstrup (Eds.), *What Research Has to Say About Reading Instruction* (pp. 124–143). Newark, DE: International Reading Association.

Samuels, S. J. & Farstrup, A. E. (2006). *What Research Has to Say About Fluency Instruction.* Newark, DE: International Reading Association.

Scarcella, R. (2003) Academic English: A conceptual framework. *The University of California Linguistic Minority Research Institute, Technical Report* 2003-1.

Scarcella, R. English learners and writing: Responding to linguistic diversity. http://wps.ablongman.com/wps/media/objects/133/136243/english.pdf.

Scarcella, R. (1990). *Teaching Language Minority Students in the Multicultural Classroom.* Englewood Cliffs, NJ: Prentice Hall Regents.

Scharer, P. L., Pinnell, G. S., Lyons, C., & Fountas, I. (2005). Becoming an engaged reader. *Educational Leadership,* 63 (2), 24–29.

Schleppegrell, M. (2001). Linguistic features of the language of schooling. *Linguistics and Education,* 12, 431–459.

Schleppegrell, M. (2004). *Teaching Academic Writing to English Learners,* 13 (2). Grant Report: University of California Linguistic Minority Research Institute.

Scott, J., & Nagy, W. E. (1997). Understanding the definitions of unfamiliar verbs. *Reading Research Quarterly,* 32, 184–200.

Sénéchal, M. (1997). The differential effect of storybook reading on preschoolers' acquisition of expressive and receptive vocabulary. *Journal of Child Language,* 24 (1), 123–138.

Shanahan, T. (2005). FAQs about Fluency. http://www.springfield.k12.il.us/resources/languagearts/readingwriting/readfluency.html.

Shanahan, T., & Shanahan, C. (2008). Teaching disciplinary literacy to adolescents: Rethinking content-area literacy. *Harvard Educational Review,* 78 (1), 40–59.

Shany, M. T. & Biemiller, A. (1995). Assisted reading practice: Effects on performance for poor readers in grades 3 and 4. *Reading Research Quarterly,* 30 (3), 382–395.

Shaughnessy, M. P. (1979). *Errors and expectations: A guide for the teacher of basic writing.* New York, NY: Oxford University Press.

Shaywitz, S. (2003). *Overcoming Dyslexia.* New York: Alfred A Knopf.

Short, D. J., & Fitzsimmons, S. (2007). *Double the work: Challenges and solutions to acquiring language and academic literacy for adolescent English language learners.* New York, NY: Alliance for Excellent Education.

Simmons, D. C., Kame'enui, E. J, Coyne, M. D. & Chard, D. J. (2002). Effective strategies for teaching beginning reading. In E. J. Kame'enui, D. W. Carnine, R. C. Dixon, D. C. Simmons, & M. D. Coyne (Eds.), *Effective Teaching Strategies That Accommodate Diverse Learners.* Upper Saddle River, NJ: Merrill Prentice Hall.

Sindelar, P. T., Monda, L. E., & O'Shea, L. J. (1990). Effects of repeated readings on instructional- and mastery-level readers. *Journal of Educational Research,* 83 (4), 220–226.

Snow, C., Burns, M., & Griffin, P. (Eds.). (1998). *Preventing Reading Difficulties in Young Children.* Washington, D.C.: National Academy Press.

Stahl, S. A. & Fairbanks, M. M. (1986). The effects of vocabulary instruction: A model-based meta-analysis. *Review of Educational Research,* 56 (1), 72–110.

Stanovich, K. E. (1986). Matthew effects in reading: Some consequences of individual differences in the acquisition of literacy. *Reading Research Quarterly,* 21, 360–407.

Stanovich, K. E. & Stanovich, P. J. (2003). Using research and reason in education: How teachers can use scientifically based research to make curricular & instructional decisions. Jessup, MD: National Institute for Literacy. Retrieved January, 26, 2006, http://www.nifl.gov/partnershipforreading/publications/pdf/Stanovich_Color.pdf.

Stenner, A. J., Koons, H., & Swartz, C. W. (in press). *Text complexity and developing expertise in reading.* Chapel Hill, NC: MetaMetrics, Inc.

Sternberg, R. J., & Powell, J. S. (1983). Comprehending verbal comprehension. *American Psychologist,* 38, 878–893.

Sticht, T. G., & James, J. H. (1984). Listening and reading. In P. D. Pearson, R. Barr, M. L. Kamil, & P. Mosenthal (Eds.), *Handbook of reading research* (Vol. 1) (pp. 293–317). White Plains, NY: Longman.

Strickland, D. S. (2002). The importance of effective early intervention. In A. E. Farstrup & S. J. Samuels (Eds.), *What Research Has to Say About Reading Instruction* (3rd ed., pp. 69–86). Newark, DE: International Reading Association.

Strickland, D. S. & Morrow, L. M. (2000). *Beginning Reading and Writing.* Newark, DE: International Reading Association.

Strickland, D. S., Snow, C., Griffin, P., Burns, S. M. & McNamara, P. (2002). *Preparing Our Teachers: Opportunities for Better Reading Instruction.* Washington, D.C.: Joseph Henry Press.

Stuart, L., Wright, F., Grigor, S., & Howey, A. (2002). *Spoken language difficulties: Practical strategies and activities for teachers and other professionals.* London, England: Fulton.

Tabors, P. O. & Snow, C. E. (2002). Young bilingual children and early literacy development. In S. Neuman & D. K. Dickinson (Eds.), *Handbook of Early Literacy Research* (pp. 159–178). New York: Guilford Press.

Templeton, S. (1986). Synthesis of research on the learning and teaching of spelling. *Educational Leadership,* 43 (6), 73–78.

Templeton, S., Cain, C. T., & Miller, J. O. (1981). Reconceptualizing readability: The relationship between surface and underlying structure analyses in predicting the difficulty of basal reader stories. *Journal of Educational Research,* 74 (6), 382–387.

Torgesen, J., Morgan, S., & Davis, C. (1992). Effects of two types of phonological awareness training on word learning in kindergarten children. *Journal of Educational Psychology,* 84 (3), 364–370.

Torgesen, J., Wagner, R., Rashotte, C., Rose, E., Lindamood, P., Conway, T., & Garvan, C. (1999). Preventing reading failure in young children with phonological processing disabilities: Group and individual responses to instruction. *Journal of Educational Psychology,* 91 (4), 579–593.

Torgesen, J. K. & Hudson, R. (2006). Reading fluency: Critical issues for struggling readers. In S. J. Samuels & A. Farstrup (Eds.), *What Research Has to Say About Fluency Instruction.* Newark, DE: International Reading Association.

Torgesen, J. K., & Mathes, P. (2000). *A Basic Guide to Understanding, Assessing, and Teaching Phonological Awareness.* Austin, TX: PRO-ED.

Torgesen, J. K., Rashotte, C. A., & Alexander, A. (2001). Principles of fluency instruction in reading: Relationships with established empirical outcomes. In M. Wolf (Ed.), *Dyslexia, Fluency, and the Brain.* Parkton, MD: York Press.

Valencia, S. W., Au, K. H., Scheu, J. A., & Kawakami, A. J. (1990). Assessment of students' ownership of literacy. *The Reading Teacher,* 44 (2), 154–156.

Valencia, S. W. & Buly, M. R. (2004). Behind test scores: What struggling readers *really* need. *The Reading Teacher,* 57 (6), 520–531.

Valencia, S. W. & Sulzby, E. (1991). Assessment of emergent literacy: Storybook reading. *The Reading Teacher,* 44 (7), 498–500.

van den Broek, P., Lorch, Jr., R. F., Linderholm, T., & Gustafson, M. (2001). The effects of readers' goals on inference generation and memory for texts. *Memory and Cognition,* 29, 1081–1087.

van den Broek, P., Risden, K., & Husebye-Hartmann, E. (1995). The role of readers' standards for coherence in the generation of inferences during reading. In R. F. Lorch & E. J. O'Brien (Eds.), *Sources of coherence in reading* (pp. 353–373). Hillsdale, NJ: Erlbaum.

Vaughn, S. & Linan-Thompson, S. (2004). *Research-Based Methods of Reading Instruction: Grades K-3.* Alexandria, VA: ASCD.

Research Bibliography

Vaughn, S., Linan-Thompson, S., Pollard-Durodola, S. D., Mathes, P. G. & Hagan, E. C. (2001). Effective interventions for English language learners (Spanish-English) at risk for reading difficulties. In D. Dickinson & S. Neuman (Eds.), *Handbook of Early Literacy Research* (Vol. 2, pp. 185–197). New York: Guilford Press.

Vaughn, S., Moody, S. W., & Shuman, J. S. (1998). Broken promises: Reading instruction in the resource room. *Exceptional Children,* 64 (2), 211–225.

Vellutino, F. R., & Scanlon, D. M. (1987). Phonological coding, phonological awareness, and reading ability: Evidence from a longitudinal and experimental study. *Merrill-Palmer Quarterly,* 33 (3), 321–363.

Venezky, R. (2001). *The American way of spelling.* New York, NY: Guilford.

Vogt, M. (2004/2005). Fitful nights. *Reading Today,* 22 (3), 6.

Vogt, M. & Nagano, P. (2003). Turn it on with light bulb reading!: Sound-switching strategies for struggling readers. *The Reading Teacher,* 57 (3), 214–221.

Washington, J. A. (2001). Early literacy skills in African-American children: Research considerations. *Learning Disabilities Research and Practice,* 16 (4), 213–221.

Weaver, Constance. (2007). *The Grammar Plan Book: A Guide to Smart Teaching.* Portsmouth, NH: Heinemann.

Wheeler, R., & Swords, R. (2004). Code-switching: Tools of language and culture transform the dialectally diverse classroom. *Language Arts,* 81, 470–480.

Whipple, G. (Ed.) (1925). The Twenty-fourth Yearbook of the National Society for the Study of Education: Report of the National Committee on Reading. Bloomington, IL: Public School Publishing Company.

White, T. G., Graves, M. F., & Slater, W. H. (1990). Growth of reading vocabulary in diverse elementary schools: Decoding and word meaning. *Journal of Educational Psychology,* 82 (2), 281–290.

Whitehurst G. J., Falco, F. L., Lonigan, C. J., Fischel, J. E., DeBaryshe, B. D., Valdez-Menchaca, M. C., & Caufield, M. (1988). Accelerating language development through picture book reading. *Developmental Psychology,* 24, 552–558.

Williams, G. (2000). Children's literature, children and uses of language description. In L. Unsworth (Ed.), *Researching Language in Schools and Communities: Functional Linguistic Perspectives* (pp. 111–129). London, England: Cassell.

Williams, G. (2005). Grammatics in schools. In R. Hasan, C. M. I. M. Matthiessen, & J. Webster (Eds.), *Continuing discourse on language* (pp. 281–310). London, England: Equinox.

Williams, J. M., & McEnerney, L. (n.d.). *Writing in college: A short guide to college writing.* http://writing-program.uchicago.edu/resources/collegewriting/index.htm.

Williamson, G. L. (2006). *Aligning the journey with a destination: A model for K–16 reading standards.* Durham, NC: MetaMetrics, Inc.

Wirt, J., Choy, S., Rooney, P., Provasnik, S., Sen, A., & Tobin, R. (2004). The condition of education 2004 (NCES 2004-077). U.S. Department of Education, National Center for Education Statistics. Washington, DC: U.S. Government Printing Office. http://nces.ed.gov/pubs2004/2004077.pdf.

Wixson, K. K. (1986). Vocabulary instruction and children's comprehension of basal stories. *Reading Research Quarterly,* 21 (3), 317–329.

Yopp, H. K., & Yopp, R. H. (2006). Primary students and informational texts. *Science and Children,* 44 (3), 22–25.

Index

Index

Index

Index

Index

Index

6:T146, 6:T150, 6:T154, 6:T166, 6:T174, 6:T176,
6:T182, 6:T185, 6:T187, 6:T195, 6:T197, 6:T207,
6:T213, 6:T216, 6:T220, 6:T226, 6:T230, 6:T234,
6:T240, 6:T242, 6:T244, 6:T247, 6:T248, 6:T254,
6:T256, 6:T264, 6:T266, 6:T269, 6:T272, 6:T274,
6:T280, 6:T282, 6:T285, 6:T293, 6:T305, 6:T314,
6:T318, 6:T324, 6:T328, 6:T330, 6:T336, 6:T342,
6:T344, 6:T346, 6:T349, 6:T350, 6:T351, 6:T354,
6:T358, 6:T366, 6:T368, 6:T376, 6:T382, 6:T385,
6:T407, 6:T416, 6:T420, 6:T436, 6:T446, 6:T450,
6:T454, 6:T458, 6:T466, 6:T471, 6:T474, 6:T476,
6:T486, 6:T489, 6:T491, 6:T499

Lesson Plans, 1:xx–1:xxi, 1:E1–1:E51, 1:T6–1:T7,
1:T20, 1:T26, 1:T38, 1:T40, 1:T50, 1:T62,
1:T102–1:T103, 1:T116, 1:T122, 1:T134,
1:T136, 1:T146, 1:T158, 1:T166, 1:T168,
1:T198–1:T199, 1:T212, 1:T218, 1:T224,
1:T230, 1:T232, 1:T234, 1:T242, 1:T254,
1:T262, 1:T264, 1:T294–1:T295, 1:T308,
1:T316, 1:T320, 1:T326, 1:T330, 1:T338,
1:T350, 1:T390–1:T391, 1:T399, 1:T404,
1:T426, 1:T434, 1:T446, 1:T462, 2:xx–2:xxi,
2:E1–2:E51, 2:E7, 2:E9, 2:E11, 2:E32–2:E39,
2:E41, 2:T6–2:T7, 2:T20, 2:T26, 2:T28, 2:T30,
2:T34, 2:T40, 2:T42, 2:T44, 2:T50, 2:T52,
2:T56, 2:T64, 2:T106–2:T107, 2:T118, 2:T124,
2:T128, 2:T132, 2:T138, 2:T140, 2:T142,
2:T152, 2:T162, 2:T206–2:T207, 2:T216,
2:T222, 2:T224, 2:T236, 2:T240, 2:T248,
2:T252, 2:T260, 2:T262, 2:T304–2:T305,
2:T314, 2:T320, 2:T322, 2:T334, 2:T336,
2:T338, 2:T346, 2:T356, 2:T358, 2:T360,
2:T406–2:T407, 2:T412, 2:T436, 2:T444,
2:T456, 2:T458, 2:T472, 2:T499, 2:T501,
3:xx–3:xxi, 3:E1–3:E51, 3:E11, 3:T6–3:T7,
3:T20, 3:T26, 3:T28–3:T29, 3:T40, 3:T42,
3:T44, 3:T64, 3:T66, 3:T104–3:T105, 3:T118,
3:T144, 3:T164, 3:T166, 3:T204–3:T205,
3:T218, 3:T244, 3:T268, 3:T270, 3:T308–
3:T309, 3:T322, 3:T348, 3:T370, 3:T372,
3:T410–3:T411, 3:T424, 3:T450, 3:T470,
3:T472, 3:T486, 4:xx–4:xxi, 4:E1–4:E51,
4:T6–4:T7, 4:T108–4:T109, 4:T118, 4:T122,
4:T140, 4:T146, 4:T148, 4:T150, 4:T154,
4:T158, 4:T160, 4:T162, 4:T172, 4:T178,
4:T180, 4:T189, 4:T193, 4:T210–4:T211,
4:T211, 4:T215, 4:T220, 4:T224, 4:T230,
4:T236, 4:T238, 4:T242, 4:T248, 4:T250,
4:T252, 4:T260, 4:T264, 4:T272, 4:T280,
4:T282, 4:T291, 4:T294, 4:T303, 4:T312–
4:T313, 4:T410–4:T411, 5:xx–5:xxi,
5:E1–5:E51, 5:T6–5:T7, 5:T7, 5:T20, 5:T34,
5:T44, 5:T52, 5:T56, 5:T64, 5:T72, 5:T74,
5:T104–5:T105, 5:T118, 5:T124, 5:T130,
5:T132, 5:T134, 5:T140, 5:T142, 5:T144,
5:T152, 5:T156, 5:T164, 5:T172, 5:T174,

5:T204–5:T205, 5:T218, 5:T236, 5:T246,
5:T254, 5:T258, 5:T266, 5:T274, 5:T276,
5:T306–5:T307, 5:T320, 5:T340, 5:T358,
5:T362, 5:T370, 5:T410–5:T411, 5:T424,
5:T440, 5:T458, 5:T462, 5:T472, 5:T480,
5:T482, 5:T488, 6:xx–6:xxi, 6:E1–6:E51,
6:T6–6:T7, 6:T7, 6:T20, 6:T36, 6:T46, 6:T54,
6:T58, 6:T66, 6:T74, 6:T76, 6:T106–6:T107,
6:T120, 6:T126, 6:T130, 6:T134, 6:T136,
6:T142, 6:T144, 6:T146, 6:T154, 6:T166,
6:T174, 6:T176, 6:T206–6:T207, 6:T220,
6:T234, 6:T244, 6:T254, 6:T256, 6:T264,
6:T266, 6:T272, 6:T274, 6:T304–6:T305,
6:T318, 6:T336, 6:T346, 6:T354, 6:T358,
6:T366, 6:T368, 6:T376, 6:T406–6:T407,
6:T420, 6:T428, 6:T432, 6:T436, 6:T442,
6:T444, 6:T446, 6:T454, 6:T458, 6:T466,
6:T474, 6:T476, 6:T482

Materials for, 1:xxi, 2:xxi, 2:E1, 2:E3–2:E4,
2:E11, 2:E12–2:E31, 2:E32–2:E37, 2:E41,
3:xxi, 3:E1–3:E5, 3:E7–3:E9, 3:E11, 4:xxi,
4:T118, 4:T148, 4:T154, 4:T160, 4:T189,
4:T193, 4:T211, 4:T220, 4:T230, 4:T236,
4:T238, 4:T250, 4:T291, 4:T294, 5:xxi, 5:T7,
5:T93, 5:T124, 5:T130, 5:T132, 5:T140,
5:T142, 5:T205, 5:T307, 5:T411, 6:xxi, 6:T7,
6:T107, 6:T207, 6:T305, 6:T407

Enrichment. *See* Differentiated Instruction,
Advanced

Essential Question, 1:T25, 1:T40, 1:T121,
1:T217, 1:T232, 1:T313, 1:T409, 2:T25, 2:T123,
2:T221, 2:T319, 2:T417, 2:T434, 2:T497, 2:T502,
3:T25, 3:T123, 3:T142, 3:T223, 3:T242, 3:T327,
3:T346, 3:T429, 3:T448, 4:T25, 4:T46, 4:T82,
4:T127, 4:T148, 4:T229, 4:T250, 4:T331, 4:T348,
4:T429, 4:T448, 5:T25, 5:T42, 5:T123, 5:T142,
5:T223, 5:T244, 5:T325, 5:T348, 5:T429, 5:T448,
6:T25, 6:T44, 6:T125, 6:T144, 6:T225, 6:T242,
6:T323, 6:T344, 6:T425, 6:T444

Evaluating Writing. *See* Writing, Rubrics

Exclamatory Sentences. *See* Grammar,
Sentences

Expository Texts. *See* Genre, Informational Text

Expression. *See* Fluency, Expression

Fables. *See* Genre, Fable

Fairy Tales. *See* Student Book, Genre, Fairy Tale

Family Connections, 1:xxi, 1:T3, 2:xxi, 2:T3,
3:xxi, 3:T3, 4:xxi, 4:T3, 5:xxi, 5:T3, 6:xxi, 6:T3

Fantasy. *See* Genre

Fiction. *See* Genre, Realistic Fiction

Figurative Language. *See* Vocabulary Strategies

Flexible Grouping. *See* Literacy Centers; Small
Group Instuction, Suggested Small Group Plan

Fluency, 1:E26, 1:S33, 1:S35, 1:S37, 1:S39, 1:S41,
1:T3, 1:T49, 1:T86–1:T87, 1:T99, 1:T145, 1:T182–
1:T187, 1:T195, 1:T241, 1:T278–1:T279, 1:T291,
1:T337, 1:T374–1:T375, 1:T387, 1:T433, 1:T474–
1:T475, 2:T3, 2:T51, 2:T86–2:T87, 2:T88–2:T89,
2:T101, 2:T149, 2:T183, 2:T186–2:T187, 2:T199,
2:T247, 2:T284–2:T285, 2:T297, 2:T345, 2:T382–
2:T383, 2:T395, 2:T443, 2:T484–2:T485, 3:T51,
3:T88–3:T89, 3:T101, 3:T151, 3:T188–3:T189,
3:T251, 3:T292–3:T293, 3:T355, 3:T385–3:T386,
3:T394–3:T395, 3:T407, 3:T457, 3:T498–3:T499,
4:T55, 4:T92–4:T93, 4:T110, 4:T157, 4:T185,
4:T194–4:T195, 4:T214, 4:T216, 4:T244, 4:T254,
4:T259, 4:T261, 4:T266, 4:T276, 4:T285, 4:T287,
4:T296–4:T297, 4:T297, 4:T357, 4:T394–4:T395,
4:T457, 4:T498–4:T499, 5:S3, 5:S5, 5:S7, 5:S9,
5:S11, 5:S33, 5:S35, 5:S37, 5:S39, 5:S41, 5:T3,
5:T51, 5:T77, 5:T88–5:T89, 5:T101, 5:T151,
5:T177, 5:T188–5:T189, 5:T201, 5:T253, 5:T277,
5:T290–5:T291, 5:T303, 5:T357, 5:T383, 5:T388–
5:T389, 5:T394–5:T395, 5:T407, 5:T423, 5:T457,
5:T489, 5:T500–5:T501, 6:T3, 6:T53, 6:T90–6:T91,
6:T103, 6:T153, 6:T190–6:T191, 6:T203, 6:T251,
6:T288–6:T289, 6:T301, 6:T353, 6:T390–6:T391,
6:T403, 6:T453, 6:T494–6:T495

Accuracy, 1:T48, 1:T49, 1:T144, 1:T145, 1:T183,
1:T187, 1:T240, 1:T403, 1:T432, 1:T433,
1:T443, 1:T475, 2:E6, 2:E46, 2:S5, 2:S7, 2:S11,
2:S13, 2:S15, 2:S17, 2:S19, 2:S21, 2:S23,
2:S25, 2:S27, 2:S29, 2:S31, 2:S33, 2:S35,
2:S37, 2:S39, 2:S41, 2:S43, 2:S45, 2:S47,
2:S49, 2:S51, 2:T313, 2:T344, 2:T345, 2:T355,
2:T383, 3:E26, 3:E36, 3:T217, 3:T250, 3:T251,
3:T261, 3:T293, 4:S3, 4:S5, 4:S7, 4:S9, 4:S11,
4:S23, 4:S25, 4:S27, 4:S29, 4:S31, 4:S33,
4:S35, 4:S37, 4:S39, 4:S41, 4:S43, 4:S45,
4:S47, 4:S49, 4:S51, 4:T121, 4:T145, 4:T156,
4:T223, 4:T258, 4:T269, 4:T277, 4:T447,
5:E26, 5:T151, 5:T161, 5:T179, 5:T189, 6:T53,
6:T81, 6:T91, 6:T190–6:T191

Adjust Rate to Purpose, 6:S49, 6:T453, 6:T485,
6:T495

Connected Text, 1:E6, 1:E16, 1:S9, 1:T51,
1:T183, 2:E46, 2:S39, 3:E36, 3:S29, 3:T253,
5:E26, 5:S19, 5:T151, 6:T55

Expression, 2:E16, 2:S11, 2:S21, 2:S31, 2:S41,
2:S51, 2:T50, 2:T51, 2:T61, 2:T87, 3:E46,
3:S39, 3:T354, 3:T355, 3:T365, 3:T395, 4:E36,
4:S29, 4:T121, 4:T145, 4:T156, 4:T216,
4:T223, 4:T244, 4:T247, 4:T254, 4:T258,
4:T259, 4:T269, 4:T287, 4:T297, 5:E46, 5:S39,

Index

Index

My Favorite Foods, 4:T292-T293
People in the Town, 4:T390-T391
Reading Together, 2:T378-T379
Reading, 2:T84-T85
Shark, 3:T84-T85
So Many Sounds, 5:T286-T287
Soccer, 6:T490-T491
Spots, 3:T184-T185
Trains, 1: T470-T471
Trees, 5:T84-T85
The Weather, 4:T494-T495
Worms, 5:T390-T391
Write-in Reader, 4:T210
  Ant's Grand Feast, 4:T210
  Bo's Big Space Trip, 4:T6
  Hit It!, 2:S27
  How Do Animals Talk?, 2:S13
  Music Time!, 2:S23
  Run, Run, Run!, 2:S7
  Scott and His Red Pen, 2:S37
  Tell Cat!, 2:S17
  Tree Frog Sings His Song, 4:T410
  Who Can Help A Cat?, 2:S47

Listening and Speaking. *See* Speaking and
Listening

Listening Comprehension, 1:T15, 1:T111,
1:T207, 1:T303, 1:T399, 2:T15, 2:T113, 2:T211,
2:T309, 2:T407, 3:T15, 3:T113, 3:T213, 3:T317,
3:T419, 4:T15, 4:T114, 4:T117, 4:T216, 4:T219,
4:T321, 5:T15, 5:T113, 5:T213, 5:T315, 5:T419,
6:T15, 6:T115, 6:T215, 6:T313, 6:T415

Listening Log, 1:T69, 1:T165, 1:T261, 2:T169,
2:T171, 2:T463, 3:T171, 3:T275, 3:T377, 4:T75,
4:T177, 4:T279, 4:T477, 5:T71, 5:T273, 5:T479,
6:T271, 6:T373, 6:T473

Literacy and Language Guide, 1:xxi, 1:xxiii,
1:T8–1:T9, 1:T52–1:T53, 1:T62–1:T63, 1:T79,
1:T92–1:T93, 1:T104–1:T105, 1:T148–1:T149,
1:T158–1:T159, 1:T175, 1:T188–1:T189, 1:T200–
1:T201, 1:T244–1:T245, 1:T271, 1:T254–1:T255,
1:T284–1:T285, 1:T296–1:T297, 1:T340–1:T341,
1:T350–1:T351, 1:T380–1:T381, 1:T392–1:T393,
1:T436–1:T437, 1:T446–1:T447, 1:T467, 1:T480–
1:T481, 2:xxi, 2:xxiii, 2:T8–2:T9, 2:T54–2:T55,
2:T64–2:T65, 2:T81, 2:T94–2:T95, 2:T106–2:T107,
2:T152–2:T153, 2:T162–2:T163, 2:T192–2:T193,
2:T204–2:T205, 2:T250–2:T251, 2:T260–2:T261,
2:T276, 2:T290–2:T291, 2:T302–2:T303, 2:T348–
2:T349, 2:T358–2:T359, 2:T375, 2:T388–2:T389,
2:T400–2:T401, 2:T446–2:T447, 2:T456–2:T457,
2:T477, 2:T490–2:T491, 3:xxi, 3:xxiii, 3:T8–3:T9,
3:T54–3:T55, 3:T64–T65, 3:T94–3:T95,
3:T106–3:T107, 3:T154–3:T155, 3:T164–3:T165,
3:T194–3:T195, 3:T206–3:T207, 3:T254–3:T255,

3:T268–3:T269, 3:T285, 3:T298–3:T299,
3:T310– 3:T311, 3:T358–3:T359, 3:T370–3:T371,
3:T387, 3:T400–3:T401, 3:T412–3:T413,
3:T460–3:T461, 3:T470–3:T471; 3:T504–3:T505,
4:xxi, 4:xxiii, 4:T8–4:T9, 4:T58–4:T59,
4:T68–4:T69, 4:T83, 4:T98–4:T99, 4:T110–4:T111,
4:T118, 4:T119, 4:T120, 4:T140, 4:T143, 4:T144,
4:T150, 4:T154, 4:T160– 4:T161, 4:T162, 4:T163,
4:T170–4:T171, 4:T173, 4:T185, 4:T188, 4:T200–
4:T201, 4:T212–4:T213, 4:T222, 4:T240, 4:T242,
4:T245, 4:T246, 4:T252, 4:T262–4:T263, 4:T264,
4:T265, 4:T267, 4:T268, 4:T272–4:T273, 4:T277,
4:T282, 4:T287, 4:T290, 4:T291, 4:T296,
4:T302–4:T303, 4:T314–4:T315, 4:T360–4:T361,
4:T370–4:T371, 4:T400–4:T401, 4:T412–4:T413,
4:T460–4:T461, 4:T470–4:T471, 4:T489, 4:T504–
4:T505, 5:xxi, 5:xxiii, 5:T8–5:T9, 5:T54–5:T55,
5:T64–5:T65, 5:T81, 5:T94–5:T95, 5:T106–5:T107,
5:T154–5:T155, 5:T164–5:T165, 5:T179, 5:T181,
5:T194–5:T195, 5:T206–5:T207, 5:T256–5:T257,
5:T266–5:T267, 5:T281, 5:T283, 5:T296–5:T297,
5:T308–5:T309, 5:T360–5:T361, 5:T370–5:T371,
5:T387, 5:T400–5:T401, 5:T412–5:T413,
5:T460–5:T461, 5:T472–5:T473, 5:T491, 5:T493,
5:T506–5:T507, 6:xxi, 6:xxiii, 6:T8–6:T9,
6:T56–6:T57, 6:T66–6:T67, 6:T81, 6:T83,
6:T96–6:T97, 6:T108–6:T109, 6:T156–6:T157,
6:T166–6:T167, 6:T181, 6:T183, 6:T196–6:T197,
6:T208–6:T209, 6:T254–6:T255, 6:T264–6:T265,
6:T279, 6:T281, 6:T294–6:T295, 6:T306–6:T307,
6:T356–6:T357, 6:T366–6:T367, 6:T381,
6:T383, 6:T396–6:T397, 6:T408–6:T409,
6:T456–6:T457, 6:T466–6:T467, 6:T485, 6:T487,
6:T500–6:T501

Literacy Centers, 1:T8–1:T9, 1:T79,
1:T104–1:T105, 1:T175, 1:T200–1:T201, 1:T271,
1:T296–1:T297, 1:T392–1:T393, 1:T467,
2:T8–2:T9, 2:T81, 2:T106–2:T107, 2:T204–2:T205,
2:T276, 2:T302–2:T303, 2:T375, 2:T400–2:T401,
2:T477, 3:T8–3:T9, 3:T106–3:T107,
3:T206–3:T207, 3:T285, 3:T310– 3:T311, 3:T387,
3:T412–3:T413, 4:T8–4:T9, 4:T83, 4:T110–4:T111,
4:T118, 4:T119, 4:T120, 4:T140, 4:T143, 4:T144,
4:T150, 4:T154, 4:T162, 4:T163, 4:T173, 4:T185,
4:T188, 4:T212–4:T213, 4:T222, 4:T240, 4:T242,
4:T245, 4:T246, 4:T252, 4:T264, 4:T265, 4:T267,
4:T268, 4:T277, 4:T282, 4:T287, 4:T290, 4:T291,
4:T296, 4:T314–4:T315, 4:T412–4:T413, 4:T489,
5:T8–5:T9, 5:T81, 5:T106–5:T107, 5:T179,
5:T181, 5:T206–5:T207, 5:T281, 5:T283,
5:T308–5:T309, 5:T387, 5:T412–5:T413, 5:T491,
5:T493, 6:T8–6:T9, 6:T81, 6:T83, 6:T108–6:T109,
6:T181, 6:T183, 6:T208–6:T209, 6:T279, 6:T281,
6:T306–6:T307, 6:T381, 6:T383, 6:T408–6:T409,
6:T485, 6:T487

Literary Forms. *See* Genre

Literary Response. *See* Write About Reading;
Writing, Respond to a Selection

Literature. *See* Leveled Readers; Student Book;
Teacher Read Aloud; Trade Books; Vocabulary,
Reader

Main Idea. *See* Comprehension, Skills, Main
Ideas and Details

Main Selections. *See* Student Book, Anchor
Texts

Mass Media. *See* Digital Resources; Research

Media Literacy. *See* Research, Media

Meeting Individual Needs. *See* Differentiated
Instruction

Model Fluency. *See* Fluency, Modeling

Modeled Writing. *See* Writing, Modeled Writing

Modeling. *See* Fluency, Modeling; Think Aloud;
Writing, Modeled Writing

Monitor/Clarify. *See* Comprehension, Strategies,
Monitor/Clarify

Monitor Comprehension. *See* Comprehension,
Strategies, Monitor/Clarify

Multiple-Meaning Words. *See* Vocabulary
Strategies

Mystery. *See* Genre

Myth. *See* Genre

Narrative Nonfiction. *See* Genre

Narrative Writing. *See* Writing, Forms, Mode

Negatives. *See* Grammar

Nonfiction. *See* Genre; Writing, Forms, Mode

Notes. *See* Research, Taking Notes, Writing,
Prewrite

Nouns. *See* Grammar, Nouns

Ongoing Assessment. *See* Assessment

**Online Teacher Book and Planning
Resources.** *See* Digital Resources, Online TE and
Planning Resources

Index

Index

Photo Cards. *See* English Language Learners, Materials for; Student Book, Vocabulary in Context

Phrasing. *See* Fluency

Planning. *See* Common Core Focus; Digital Resources, Online TE and Planning Resources; Suggested Small Group Plan; Unit Planning and Pacing; Week at a Glance; Weekly Planner

Plot. *See* Comprehension, Skills, Plot

Plural Nouns. *See* Grammar, Nouns, Plural

Poetry. *See* Genre; Writing, Form

Possessive Pronouns. *See* Grammar, Pronouns

Predictions, Make. *See* Comprehension, Skills, Make Predictions

Prefixes. *See* Spelling; Vocabulary Strategies

Prepositional Phrases. *See* Grammar

Prepositions. *See* Grammar

Preview the Topic, 1:T23, 1:T119, 1:T215, 1:T311, 1:T407, 2:T23, 2:T121, 2:T219, 2:T317, 2:T415, 3:T23, 3:T121, 3:T221, 3:T325, 3:T427, 4:T23, 4:T125, 4:T227, 4:T329, 4:T427, 5:T23, 5:T121, 5:T221, 5:T323, 5:T427, 6:T23, 6:T123, 6:T223, 6:T321, 6:T423. *See also* Lesson Topic

Prewriting. *See* Writing, Forms, Prewrite; Writing, Process, Brainstorm; Writing, Traits, Ideas

Prior Knowledge. *See* Preview the Topic

Progress Monitoring. *See* Assessment, Daily Assessment; Assessment, Progress Monitoring

Projects

Pronouns. *See* Grammar, Pronouns

Proofreading. *See* Daily Proofreading Practice; Grammar; Writing, Process, Proofread

Proper Mechanics. *See* Grammar

Proper Nouns. *See* Grammar, Nouns, Proper

Prosody. *See* Fluency, Intonation; Fluency, Stress

Publishing. *See* Writing, Process, Publish

Punctuation. *See* Fluency, Phrasing; Grammar

Purposes for Reading. *See* Set Purpose

Purposes for Writing. *See* Comprehension, Author's Purpose; Writing, Forms, Prewrite

Questions. *See* Analyze the Text; Comprehension, Strategies, Question; Dig Deeper; Essential Question; Grammar; Listening Comprehension; Research; Formulate Questions, Think Through the Text; Writing

Quotation Marks. *See* Grammar, Punctuation

Index

Index

Index

Index

Index

Credits

T12 ©JUPITERIMAGES/Creatas/Alamy Images; **T36** Image Source/Jupiterimages/Getty Images; **T46** Brand X Pictures/Getty Images; **T58** ©HMH; **T68** ©Corbis; **T70** ©Liquidlibrary/Jupiterimages/Getty Images; **T110** ©Digital Vision/Getty Images; **T136** © PhotoDisc/Getty Images; **T158** Tom Brakefield;

T168 Brand X Pictures/Getty Images; **T170** Photodisc/Getty Images; **T210** Corbis; **T236** ©Corbis; **T246** ©Corbis; **T258** Corbis; **T272** OJO Images/Getty Images; **T274** Photodisc/Getty Images; **T362** ©William Leaman/Alamy; **T376** Comstock/Getty Images; **T416** ©Royalty-free/Corbis;

T416 © Westend61/Alamy; **T452** Stockbyte/Getty Images; **T464** Natphotos/Digital Vision/Getty Images; **T474** ©Photodisc/Getty Images; **T474** ©GK Hart/Vikki Hart/Getty Images; **T474** Photodisc; **T476** Photodisc/Getty Images

Correlation to Common Core State Standards

COMMON CORE

Reading Standards for Literature

	Key Citations	Additional Practice and Student Application
Key Ideas and Details		
RL.1.1 Ask and answer questions about key details in a text.	**1-2:** T71 **1-3:** T121, T125, T128 **1-4:** T437	**1-1:** xxiv, T60, T122, T123, T124, T125, T126, T146, T218, T219, T221, T242, T251, T311, T411, T412, T414, T434, T462 **1-2:** xxiv–xxv, T26, T28–T29, T30–T31, T222, T224, T226–T227, T238, T248, T418, T420–T421, T422–T423, T424–T425, T444 **1-3:** T124, T125, T127, T129, T130, T131, T142, T152, T217, T328, T330, T331, T332, T333, T334, T335, T356 **1-4:** xxiv, xxv, T117, T130, T133, T135, T137, T158, T430, T433, T434, T435, T436, T438, T458, R2 **1-5:** xxv, T26, T29, T30, T32, T42, T52, T63, T225, T226, T228, T229, T230, T231, T233, T244, T430, T431, T433, T435, T436, T448, T458, T489 **1-6:** xxv, T23, T26, T28, T30, T32, T44, T54, T226, T228, T230, T231, T242, T252, T325, T326, T327, T328, T329, T331, T332, T334, T344, T354, T482, T508
RL.1.2 Retell stories, including key details, and demonstrate understanding of their central message or lesson.	**1-1:** T223, T348 **1-2:** T23, T27, T31, T33, T40–T41 **1-4:** T437, T446–T447 **1-6:** T164, T335	**1-1:** xxiv, T15, T127, T144, T146, T155, T207, T211, T232, T242, T336, T349, T403, T415, T421, T463 **1-2:** T26, T32, T42–T43, T52, T62–T63, T117, T229, T235, T238, T248, T309, T333, T344, T407, T425, T444, T453 **1-3:** T15, T127, T129, T130, T131, T141, T142, T152, T161, T317, T337, T365, T423, T456 **1-4:** xxiv, T19, T81, T137, T138, T158, T167, T356, T367, T419, T428, T435, T439, T458, T468 **1-5:** T19, T32, T39, T52, T63, T162, T217, T232, T234, T244, T254, T319, T426, T431, T437, T438, T458, T488 **1-6:** T34, T35, T41, T54, T152, T219, T233, T252, T327, T334, T354, T464, T465, R2
RL.1.3 Describe characters, settings, and major events in a story, using key details. .	**1-1:** T406, T411, T422–T423 **1-5:** T22, T29, T40–T41 **1-6:** T222, T227, T240–T241	**1-1:** xxiv, xxv, T118, T122, T123, T124, T125, T126, T127, T135, T136, T146, T214, T218, T220, T221, T222, T223, T229, T231, T232, T240, T242, T403, T410, T412, T413, T414, T415, T421, T424, T434, T443, T463 **1-2:** T22, T26–T27, T28–T29, T30–T31, T41, T42–T43, T50, T52, T55, T71, T219, T222–T223, T224, T226, T229, T233, T237, T238, T246, T248, T414, T418–T419, T420, T422, T433, T434, T444, T464 **1-3:** T39, T120, T124, T126, T127, T128, T129, T130, T131, T141, T152, T163, T171, T328, T330, T331, T332, T333, T334, T335, T336, T337, T345, T423 **1-4:** T124, T128, T129, T131, T133, T134, T136, T147, T158, T235, T426, T428, T430, T431, T432, T433, T435, T437, T439, T446, T447, T448, T458, T468, T469, T483, R2 **1-5:** T26, T28, T29, T30, T31, T32, T42, T52, T61, T162, T163, T220, T224, T225, T226, T227, T230, T231, T232, T233, T234, T243, T244, T254, T263, T265, T367, T426, T430, T433, T434, T435, T437, T447, T448, T458, T488 **1-6:** xxv, T26, T28, T29, T33, T34, T35, T43, T44, T54, T65, T163, T164, T226, T228, T229, T230, T231, T232, T233, T242, T252, T263, T320, T325, T327, T328, T329, T330, T331, T332, T334, T335, T343, T344, T354, T419, T464, T482, T483, T508, T510, T512, T513
Craft and Structure		
RL.1.4 Identify words and phrases in stories or poems that suggest feelings or appeal to the senses.	**1-1:** T60 **1-2:** T62–T63, T356–T357, T454–T455, T463 **1-4:** T477 **1-6:** T26–T27	**1-1:** T61, T137, T219, T231, T348 **1-2:** T434 **1-4:** xxiv, T270, T430, T433, T468, T469 **1-5:** T27, T30, T41, T225, T227, T243, T265 **1-6:** T32, T33, T43, T124, T167, T325, T330, T343, T364, T365, T465, T510

	Key Citations	Additional Practice and Student Application
RL.1.5 Explain major differences between books that tell stories and books that give information, drawing on a wide reading of a range of text types.	**1-1:** T253, T413, T422–T423 **1-2:** T318 **1-3:** T428 **1-4:** T270 **1-5:** T428 **1-6:** T224	**1-1:** T423, T445 **1-2:** T55, T122, T124, T239, T267, T416, T434 **1-3:** xxv, T122, T369, R2, R3 **1-4:** T24, T126 **1-5:** T124, T163, T342, T377, T423 **1-6:** T231, T241, T363, T464, T512
RL.1.6 Identify who is telling the story at various points in a text.	**1-2:** T227, T236–T237 **1-4:** T133, T146–T147 **1-5:** T431, T446–T447	**1-2:** T230, T237, T253, T421, T433, T457 **1-4:** T183 **1-5:** T432
Integration of Knowledge and Ideas		
RL.1.7 Use illustrations and details in a story to describe its characters, setting, or events.	**1-1:** T406, T411, T422–T423 **1-2:** T414, T419, T432–T433 **1-5:** T22, T29, T40–T41	**1-1:** xxiv, xxv, T118, T120, T122, T123, T124, T125, T126, T127, T135, T136, T137, T144, T146, T155, T216, T219, T221, T222, T223, T232, T242, T410, T413, T414, T434, T443 **1-2:** xxiv–xxv, T28–T29, T30, T42, T71, T223, T224–T225, T226, T237, T238, T246, T248, T418, T420–T421, T422–T423, T424, T433, T434, T444 **1-3:** T124, T127, T128, T129, T130, T131, T141, T142, T150, T152, T328, T330, T333, T334, T335, T336, T345, T346, T356 **1-4:** xxiv, T129, T132, T137, T158, T356, T426, T430, T431, T432, T433, T434, T436, T439, T446, T448, T458, T483 **1-5:** T26, T28, T42, T52, T220, T224, T225, T226, T229, T231, T232, T234, T243, T244, T254, T426, T432, T434, T437, T447, T448, T449, T456, T458 **1-6:** T30, T35, T44, T54, T222, T227, T228, T230, T231, T232, T233, T241, T242, T243, T252, T263, T320, T325, T327, T328, T329, T330, T331, T332, T334, T335, T343, T344, T354, T431, T464, T482, T483, T484, T508, T509, T513, T514
RL.1.8 (Not applicable to literature.)		
RL.1.9 Compare and contrast the adventures and experiences of characters in stories.	**1-2:** T62, T455 **1-4:** T124, T129, T146–T147 **1-6:** T22, T33, T42–T43, T271	**1-1:** T125, T349 **1-2:** T63 **1-4:** T128, T131, T136, T169, T183, T436, T437 **1-5:** T163, T265, T435, T489 **1-6:** T27, T29, T30, T34, T44, T263, T334, T484, T511, T513
Range of Reading and Level of Text Complexity		
RL.1.10 With prompting and support, read prose and poetry of appropriate complexity for grade 1.	**1-1:** T216–T222 **1-2:** T356–T357, T454–T455 **1-4:** T468–T469 **1-5:** T24–T32, T222–T233 **1-6:** T224–T232, T322–T334	**1-1:** T60, T121, T146, T242, T348, T408, T409, T434, T462 **1-2:** T25, T221, T236–T237, T248, T417, T444 **1-3:** T152, T327, T356, T468 **1-4:** xxiv, xxv, T127, T158, T429, T446 **1-5:** xxv, T52, T162, T264, T429, T458 **1-6:** xxv, T24, T25, T54, T164, T252, T354, T364, T464, T482

Reading Standards for Informational Text

	Key Citations	Additional Practice and Student Application
Key Ideas and Details		
RI.1.1 Ask and answer questions about key details in a text.	**1-1:** T311, T315, T316 **1-2:** T317, T321, T326 **1-4:** T23, T27, T29, T31 **1-5:** T323, T327, T329	**1-1:** T27, T40, T50, T156, T317, T318, T338, T444 **1-2:** T124, T126, T128, T130, T150, T258–T259, T313, T320, T322, T324, T336, T346 **1-3:** xxiv, xxv, T27, T28, T29, T30, T31, T52, T224, T226–T227, T228, T229, T230–T231, T232, T242, T252, T265, T430, T431, T432, T433, T435, T436, T438, T458, T469, T477, T486, T487, T488 **1-4:** xxv, T22, T28, T30, T32, T33, T34, T46, T230, T232, T234, T235, T236, T237, T238, T260, T332, T333, T334, T338, T348, T358, T487, R2 **1-5:** xxiv, T124, T127, T128, T129, T130, T131, T132, T142, T152, T326, T331, T332, T333, T334, T336, T338, T339, T348, T358, T369, T470, T471, T490 **1-6:** xxiv, xxv, T29, T126, T127, T128, T130, T133, T134, T144, T154, T317, T427, T428, T429, T430, T432, T433, T444, T454, T473, T484
RI.1.2 Identify the main topic and retell key details of a text.	**1-1:** T22, T29, T31, T38–T39 **1-2:** T120, T125, T131, T138–T139, T327 **1-4:** T22, T27, T29, T36–T37, T44–T45 **1-6:** T422, T434, T435, T442–T443	**1-1:** T26, T30, T40, T50, T319, T338 **1-2:** T61, T124, T126, T128, T130, T140, T148, T150, T326, T335, T346, T498–T499, T501, T502 **1-3:** xxiv, xxv, T27, T28, T29, T30, T31, T33, T41, T42, T52, T61, T232, T252, T263, T264, T265, T266, T366, T367, T368, T377, T431, T438, T439, T458 **1-4:** T24, T28, T30, T32, T34, T46, T66, T67, T226, T240, T247, T358, T368, T487, T488 **1-5:** xxiv, xxv, T63, T117, T132, T133, T152, T328, T332, T333, T336, T338, T339, T358, T470, T479, T490 **1-6:** T19, T128, T135, T154, T423, T426, T427, T428, T429, T430, T431, T433, T444, T454, T484
RI.1.3 Describe the connection between two individuals, events, ideas, or pieces of information in a text.	**1-3:** T220, T229, T240–T241, T426, T433, T446–T447 **1-4:** T328, T333, T346–T347 **1-5:** T322, T329, T346–T347	**1-1:** T28 **1-2:** T120, T140, T160, T258–T259, T500–T501, T502 **1-3:** T62, T63, T141, T162, T163, T224, T226–T227, T228, T231, T232, T242, T252, T263, T264, T367, T368, T377, T431, T434, T435, T436, T448, T486, T487 **1-4:** T31, T32, T168, T230, T235, T271, T334, T335, T337, T338, T348, T358, T369, T383, T512, T513, T515, T516, T517 **1-5:** T62, T63, T117, T129, T326, T328, T331, T332, T333, T334, T335, T336, T337, T339, T348, T358, T368, T469, T471, T479, T490 **1-6:** T65, T126, T127, T128, T129, T144, T154, T262, T428, T429, T433, T454, T484
Craft and Structure		
RI.1.4 Ask and answer questions to help determine or clarify the meaning of words and phrases in a text.	**1-3:** T228, T240–T241, T427, T430, T436 **1-4:** T31, T329, T337, T346–T347 **1-5:** T127, T327, T329 **1-6:** T133, T142–T143	**1-1:** T310, T318, T327 **1-3:** xxiv, T225, T266, T434, T488 **1-4:** T238, T332, T333, T334, T383 **1-5:** xxiv, T130, T140, T141, T331, T334, T347 **1-6:** xxiv, T130, T473
RI.1.5 Know and use various text features (e.g., headings, tables of contents, glossaries, electronic menus, icons) to locate key facts or information in a text.	**1-1:** T310, T315, T326–T327, T357 **1-2:** T127, T138–T139, T321 **1-3:** T262–T266, T446 **1-4:** T75 **1-5:** T171, T468, T470	**1-1:** T53, T245, T252, T314, T316, T338, T341, T357, T437, T444 **1-2:** T126, T128–T129, T160, T162–T163, T251, T258, T316, T318, T320, T322–T323, T324, T335, T349, T351, T447 **1-3:** T27, T55, T62, T162, T163, T255, T359, T366, T367, T432, T434, T435, T436, T447, T461, R2 **1-4:** T26, T28, T59, T66, T168, T368, R3 **1-5:** T62, T152, T165, T257, T326, T333, T349, T361, T368, T461, T473, R2 **1-6:** T57, T64, T157, T255, T262, T357, T457

Correlation to Common Core State Standards

	Key Citations	Additional Practice and Student Application
RI.1.6 Distinguish between information provided by pictures or other illustrations and information provided by the words in a text.	**1-1:** T156 **1-2:** T316, T320–T321, T334–T335 **1-3:** T263, T265 **1-4:** T28, T33 **1-5:** T469	**1-1:** T314, T326, R2 **1-2:** T322, T324, T326, T498–T499, T500 **1-3:** T31 **1-4:** T169, T234, T368, T512 **1-5:** T358 **1-6:** T126, T128, T130, T131

Integration of Knowledge and Ideas

	Key Citations	Additional Practice and Student Application
RI.1.7 Use the illustrations and details in a text to describe its key ideas.	**1-1:** T156 **1-2:** T316, T320–T321, T334–T335 **1-3:** T263, T265, T446–T447 **1-4:** T235, T248–T249 **1-5:** T125, T469	**1-1:** T26, T27, T28, T29, T30, T39, T133, T328, T338, T406 **1-2:** T52, T124–T125, T127, T128, T139, T140, T258, T316, T321, T322–T323, T324, T336, T498–T499, T500 **1-3:** xxiv, xxv, T26, T27, T28, T29, T41, T42, T43, T63, T230, T252, T264, T266, T366, T368, T430, T432, T433, T434, T435, T436, T438, T439, T445, T448, T458, T467 **1-4:** T168, T230, T232, T233, T234, T236, T237, T238, T250, T260, T285, T336, T337, T338, T487, T488, T512, T513, T514, T515, T517 **1-5:** xxiv, T120, T126, T128, T130, T131, T132, T133, T141, T142, T152, T334, T335, T337, T339, T348, T349, T369, T490 **1-6:** xxiv, T127, T131, T132, T133, T135, T135, T144, T154, T262, T426, T427, T429, T433, T434, T444, T454, T484
RI.1.8 Identify the reasons an author gives to support points in a text.	**1-3:** T22, T27, T29, T40–T41 **1-4:** T27, T28, T29, T44–T45, T226, T237, T248–T249 **1-6:** T122, T127, T142–T143	**1-1:** T50, T338 **1-2:** T150, T336, T346 **1-3:** T28, T31, T42, T52, T227, T230, T367, T488 **1-4:** T34, T35, T81, T230, T232, T234, T236, T239, T250, T285, T369, T487, T513 **1-5:** T124, T126, T131 **1-6:** T126, T128, T129, T131, T132, T133, T422, T426, T428, T430, T433, T434, T443, T444
RI.1.9 Identify basic similarities in and differences between two texts on the same topic (e.g., in illustrations, descriptions, or procedures).	**1-2:** T160, T161, T169 **1-3:** T267, T275 **1-5:** T368, T369	**1-1:** T61, T157, T349 **1-2:** T357 **1-3:** T63, T264, T469 **1-4:** T67, T169, T488 **1-6:** T65, T165, T484

Range of Reading and Level of Text Complexity

	Key Citations	Additional Practice and Student Application
RI.1.10 With prompting and support, read informational texts appropriately complex for grade 1.	**1-2:** T318–T326 **1-3:** T24–T32, T428–T438 **1-4:** T228–T239 **1-5:** T62–T63, T324–T338	**1-1:** T25, T50, T156, T252, T312, T313, T338, T444 **1-2:** T52, T62, T122–123, T150, T160, T258, T346 **1-3:** xxiv, xxv, T52, T62, T162, T223, T252, T262, T366, T458 **1-4:** T25, T168, T260, T331, T358, T486 **1-5:** xxiv, xxv, T123, T152, T355, T368, T468, T490 **1-6:** xxiv, xxv, T64, T125, T154, T262, T424, T425, T454, T482

Reading Standards Foundational Skills

	Key Citations	Additional Practice and Student Application
Print Concepts		
RF.1.1 Demonstrate understanding of the organization and basic features of print.		
RF.1.1a Recognize the distinguishing features of a sentence (e.g., first word, capitalization, ending punctuation).	**1-1:** BTS8, T12, T225, T235, T257	**1-1:** xxiv, xxv, T321, T325, T331 **1-2:** xxiv, T12, T44, T56, T72, T134, T230–T231, T240, T252–T253, T263, T268, T330, T360 **1-3:** xxiv **1-4:** xxiv, xxv, T48, T60 **1-5:** xxiv, xxv, T58 **1-6:** xxv, T46, T58

Phonological Awareness

RF.1.2 Demonstrate understanding of spoken words, syllables, and sounds (phonemes).		
RF.1.2a Distinguish long from short vowel sounds in spoken single-syllable words.	**1-4:** T16, T52, T118, T344 **1-6:** T350	**1-3:** T315, T341, T351, T363, T375 **1-6:** T13
RF.1.2b Orally produce single-syllable words by blending sounds (phonemes), including consonant blends.	**1-1:** T16, T57, T141, T142, T153, T237 **1-3:** T13, T47	**1-1:** BTS9, T36, T46, T112, T142, T163, T208, T228, T238, T249, T259, T304, T324, T345, T355, T400, T420 **1-2:** T38, T69, T115, T146, T166, T234, T310, T343, T352, T409, T430, T441 **1-3:** T16, T17, T38, T48, T60, T69, T111, T114, T137, T138, T211, T214, T215, T237, T238, T248–T249, T319, T353, T421, T455 **1-4:** T17, T50, T53, T144, T155, T164, T221, T257, T323, T355, T455 **1-5:** T17, T49, T149, T215, T317, T355, T421, T455 **1-6:** T17, T51, T217, T249, T360
RF.1.2c Isolate and pronounce initial, medial vowel, and final sounds (phonemes) in spoken single-syllable words.	**1-1:** T13, T35, T109, T163, T397, T419, T451 **1-2:** T233, T243, T265	**1-1:** BTS11, T16, T46, T112, T131, T153, T205, T227, T250, T259, T300, T306, T323, T330, T333, T402, T419, T430 **1-2:** T16, T18, T37, T47, T48, T60, T167, T212, T244, T256, T310, T336, T342, T353, T354, T363, T408, T430, T439, T440, T451, T452, T461 **1-3:** T60, T160, T260, T315, T318, T342, T352, T364, T417, T420, T443, T444, T453, T465, T466, T475 **1-4:** T42, T115, T143, T153, T154, T165, T217, T220, T245, T255, T256, T319, T322, T343 **1-5:** T37, T47, T137, T160, T169, T211, T239, T261, T262, T271, T313, T353, T366, T417, T443, T466 **1-6:** T39, T62, T216, T237, T259, T350, T361
RF.1.2d Segment spoken single-syllable words into their complete sequence of individual sounds (phonemes).	**1-2:** T111, T135, T145, T331 **1-3:** T37, T59, T69	**1-1:** BTS15, T54, T150, T246, T342, T346, T429, T438, T441, T451 **1-2:** T13, T56, T59, T114, T146, T154, T157, T209, T252, T255, T307, T310, T342, T350, T354, T405, T429, T440, T448, T461 **1-3:** T16, T48, T56, T60, T111, T114, T137, T156, T211, T214, T237, T248, T256, T360, T462 **1-4:** T60, T162, T166, T264, T268, T362 **1-5:** T13, T56, T156, T258, T362, T462 **1-6:** T58, T256

Phonics and Word Recognition

RF.1.3 Know and apply grade-level phonics and word analysis skills in decoding words.		
RF.1.3a Know the spelling-sound correspondences for common consonant digraphs.	**1-3:** T17, T38, T115, T138, T215, T238, T455	**1-2:** T17, T19, T29, T30–T31, T38, T49, T50, T60–T61 **1-3:** T17, T19, T38, T39, T115, T117, T138, T139, T149, T160, T161, T215, T217, T238–T239, T455, T456 **1-5:** T355

RF.1.3b Decode regularly spelled one-syllable words.	**1-1:** T17, T47, T113, T143, T209, T239, T305, T335, T401, T431	**1-1:** BTS5, BTS9, BTS11, BTS15, BTS17, T19, T26–T30, T36, T48, T59, T115, T122–T126, T132, T133, T144, T147, T154, T155, T211, T218–T222, T228, T229, T240, T250, T300, T307, T314–T318, T324, T325, T334, T336, T346, T347, T403, T410–T414, T420, T421, T432, T442, T443 **1-2:** T17, T19, T26–T32, T38–T39, T49, T50, T60–T61, T115, T117, T124–T130, T136–T137, T147, T148, T158–T159, T213, T215, T222–T228, T234–T235, T244, T246, T256–T257, T310, T313, T320–T326, T332–333, T343, T344, T355, T409, T411, T418–T424, T430–T431, T441, T442, T452–T453 **1-3:** T19, T26–T32, T39, T49, T50, T60, T61, T117, T124–T131, T149, T150, T161, T217, T224–T232, T239, T249, T250, T260–T261, T319, T321, T328–T336, T342, T343, T353, T354, T364, T365, T421, T423, T430¬–T438, T444, T445, T466, T467 **1-4:** T17, T19, T34, T42, T43, T53, T54, T64, T65, T119, T121, T135, T145, T155, T156, T221, T223, T234, T246, T257, T258, T269, T323, T325, T336, T345, T355, T367, T455, T456, T466, T467, T482 **1-5:** T17, T19, T26–T33, T38, T39, T49, T50, T61, T115, T117, T128–T132, T138, T139, T149, T150, T153, T160, T161, T215, T217, T240, T241, T251, T252, T263, T317, T319, T326–T338, T344, T345, T355, T356, T366, T367, T421, T422, T423, T430–T437, T444, T445, T456, T466, T467, T480 **1-6:** T17, T19, T41, T51, T52, T53, T62, T63, T119, T141, T163, T217, T219, T226–T232, T239, T250, T261, T317, T341, T351, T352, T362, T363, T463
RF.1.3c Know final -e and common vowel team conventions for representing long vowel sounds.	**1-3:** T319, T342, T364, T421,T444 **1-4:** T17, T42, T53, T119,T144 **1-6:** T51, T217, T238	**1-3:** T318, T321, T334, T343, T352, T353, T354, T365, T423, T437, T442, T445, T456, T466, T467 **1-4:** T19, T43, T54, T64, T65, T72, T121, T145, T156, T164, T182, T221, T223, T246, T268, T269, T284, T323, T325, T344, T345, T355, T364, T366, T367, T382, T416, T421, T423, T466, T467 **1-6:** T52, T62, T63, T219, T239, T260, T261
RF.1.3d Use knowledge that every syllable must have a vowel sound to determine the number of syllables in a printed word.	**1-5:** T250–T251, T262 **1-6:** T150–T151, T162, T416–T417	**1-4:** T420 **1-5:** T114, T312, T417 **1-6:** T315, T462
RF.1.3e Decode two-syllable words following basic patterns by breaking the words into syllables.	**1-5:** T250–T251,T262 **1-6:** T150–T151, T162, T416–T417	**1-4:** T421, T423, T445, T470, T474, T482 **1-5:** T60, T252, T263 **1-6:** T152, T163, T315, T324, T340, T419, T432, T440, T441, T451, T452, T460, T462, T463
RF.1.3f Read words with inflectional endings.	**1-1:** T239 **1-6:** T117, T140, T249, T260	**1-1:** T240, T251 **1-2:** T338 **1-3:** T37, T49, T50, T60, T61, T149, T269 **1-4:** T161 **1-5:** T118, T320, T365 **1-6:** T17, T19, T20, T26–T34, T40, T41, T51, T52, T53, T60, T62, T63, T119, T126¬–T134, T141, T163, T220, T250, T261, T420

RF.1.3g Recognize and read grade-appropriate irregularly spelled words.

1-1: T20–T21
1-2: T20–T21
1-3: T118–T119
1-4: T122–T123
1-5: T218–T219
1-6: T220–T221

1-1: BTS5, BTS9, BTS11, BTS15, BTS17, T13, T17, T19, T26–T30, T35, T37, T45, T47, T48, T57, T67, T109, T113, T115, T116, T122, T126, T131, T132, T133, T141, T143, T144, T153, T155, T205, T209, T211, T212, T218–T222, T227, T229, T237, T239, T240, T249, T251, T259, T300, T307, T308, T314–T318, T323, T324, T325, T333, T335, T336, T345, T347, T355, T397, T401, T403, T404, T410–T414, T419, T421, T429, T431, T432, T441, T443, T451

1-2: T13, T17, T19, T26–T32, T37, T39, T47, T49, T56, T59, T61, T69, T111, T117, T118, T135, T137, T145, T147, T148, T157, T159, T167, T209, T213, T215, T216, T233, T235, T236–T237, T243, T245, T246, T255, T257, T265, T307, T310, T313, T314, T331, T333, T341, T343, T344, T353, T355, T363, T405, T409, T411, T412–T413, T418–T424, T429, T431, T439, T441, T442, T451, T453, T461

1-3: T13, T17, T19, T20, T26–T32, T39, T47, T49, T50, T60, T61, T69, T111, T115, T117, T124–T131, T137, T139, T147, T150, T158, T161, T169, T211, T214, T215, T217, T218–T219, T224–T232, T237, T239, T247, T249, T250, T259, T261, T273, T315, T319, T321, T322, T328–T336, T341, T343, T351, T353, T354, T363, T365, T375, T417, T421, T423, T424, T430–T438, T443, T445, T453, T455, T456, T465, T467, T475

1-4: xxv, T13, T19, T20, T41, T43, T51, T53, T54, T63, T65, T80, T119, T121, T143, T145, T153, T155, T156, T175, T182, T217, T221, T223, T224, T245, T246, T255, T257, T258, T267, T269, T277, T284, T319, T323, T325, T326, T343, T345, T353, T355, T367, T375, T382, T417, T421, T423, T424, T443, T453, T456, T465, T467, T475, T482

1-5: xxv, T13, T17, T19, T20, T26–T33, T37, T39, T47, T49, T50, T59, T61, T111, T115, T117, T118, T137, T139, T147, T149, T159, T161, T169, T211, T215, T217, T224–T233, T239, T241, T249, T251, T252, T261, T263, T271, T313, T317, T319, T320, T326–T338, T343, T345, T353, T355, T356, T366, T367, T375, T417, T422, T423, T424, T430–T437, T443, T445, T453, T455, T456, T465, T467, T477

1-6: xxv, T13, T17, T19, T20, T26–T34, T39, T41, T49, T51, T52, T61, T63, T71, T113, T117, T119, T120, T126–T134, T139, T141, T149, T151, T152, T161, T163, T171, T213, T217, T219, T226–T232, T239, T247, T249, T250, T259, T261, T269, T311, T315, T317, T318, T324–T334, T339, T341, T349, T351, T352, T361, T363, T371, T413, T417, T419, T420, T426–T434, T439, T441, T449, T452, T461, T463, T471

Fluency

RF.1.4 Read with sufficient accuracy and fluency to support comprehension.

RF.1.4a Read on-level text with purpose and understanding.

1-1: T25, T241
1-2: T25, T247
1-3: T123, T250
1-4: T54, T229
1-5: T25, T456
1-6: T153, T323

1-1: xxv, T19, T49, T59, T121, T145, T217, T313, T337, T339, T409, T432
1-2: T51, T52, T117, T123, T137, T159, T221, T313, T318–T319, T333, T355, T411, T417, T431, T442, T453
1-3: T19, T25, T39, T50, T61, T151, T217, T223, T239, T250, T261, T321, T327, T343, T354, T365, T423, T429, T445, T456, T467
1-4: xxv, T19, T25, T43, T65, T121, T127, T145, T156, T158, T223, T258, T260, T261, T269, T325, T331, T345, T367, T423, T429, T456, T467
1-5: xxv, T19, T39, T50, T61, T117, T123, T139, T150, T161, T217, T223, T241, T252, T263, T319, T325, T345, T356, T367, T423, T429, T445, T467
1-6: T19, T41, T52, T63, T119, T125, T141, T152, T163, T219, T225, T239, T250, T261, T317, T341, T352, T363, T419, T425, T441, T452, T463

Correlation to Common Core State Standards

	Key Citations	Additional Practice and Student Application
RF.1.4b Read on-level text orally with accuracy, appropriate rate, and expression on successive readings.	**1-1:** T49, T145 **1-2:** T51, T149, T345 **1-3:** T151, T251, T355 **1-4:** T259, T457 **1-6:** T353, T453	**1-1:** T19, T37, T48, T59, T115, T133, T144, T147, T155, T211, T229, T240, T241, T243, T251, T307, T325, T336, T337, T347, T403, T421, T433, T443 **1-2:** T19, T39, T50, T52, T61, T117, T137, T148, T151, T159, T247, T249, T344, T355, T411, T431, T442–T443, T445 **1-3:** xxiv, xxv, T19, T50, T51, T53, T61, T152, T153, T161, T217, T239, T250, T253, T261, T321, T343, T357, T365, T423, T445, T457, T459, T467, T468 **1-4:** xxiv, xxv, T43, T55, T57, T65, T121, T156, T157, T159, T167, T223, T247, T258, T261, T269, T325, T345, T357, T359, T367, T423, T445, T459, T467, T468 **1-5:** xxiv, xxv, T19, T39, T50, T51, T53, T61, T117, T139, T150, T151, T153, T161, T217, T252, T253, T255, T319, T345, T356, T357, T359, T367, T423, T445, T456, T457, T459, T467 **1-6:** xxiv, xxv, T19, T41, T52, T55, T119, T141, T153, T155, T163, T164, T219, T239, T251, T253, T261, T317, T341, T355, T363, T419, T441, T452, T455, T463
RF.1.4c Use context to confirm or self-correct word recognition and understanding, rereading as necessary.	**1-1:** T51, T433, T435 **1-3:** T253, T459 **1-6:** T53	**1-1:** xxiv, xxv, T13 **1-2:** xxiv, T111, T347, T405 **1-4:** T417, T459 **1-5:** T13, T228, T459 **1-6:** T52, T55, T155, T413

Writing

	Key Citations	Additional Practice and Student Application
Text Types and Purposes		
W.1.1 Write opinion pieces in which they introduce the topic or name the book they are writing about, state an opinion, supply a reason for the opinion, and provide some sense of closure.	**1-6:** T37, T47, T59, T69, T137, T147, T169, T176–T177, T245, T359, T369, T459, T469, T476–T477	**1-1:** T233 **1-2:** T143, T239, T249, T434 **1-3:** T243, T347 **1-4:** T149, T159, T251, T377, T518, R2 **1-5:** T43, T143, T255, T449 **1-6:** T76, T159, T235, T257, T267, T274, T337, T345, T347, T376, T437, T447
W.1.2 Write informative/explanatory texts in which they name a topic, supply some facts about the topic, and provide some sense of closure.	**1-2:** T35, T45, T57, T67, T339, T351, T361, T368–T369 **1-3:** T235, T257, T278–T279,T339, T380–T381, T441,T480–T481	**1-1:** xxvi–xxvii **1-2:** xxvi–xxvii, T67, T133, T155, T165, T172, T231, T253, T263, T270, T329, T351, T427, T437, T449, T459, T466 **1-3:** xxvi–xxvii, T35, T42, T45, T57, T67, T71, T74, T135, T145, T157, T167, T174, T245, T271, T349, T361, T369, T373, T451, T463, T473 **1-4:** xxvi, xxvi–xxvii, T75, T349 **1-5:** xxvi–xxvii, T377, R4 **1-6:** xxvi–xxvii, T145, T165, T173, R3
W.1.3 Write narratives in which they recount two or more appropriately sequenced events, include some details regarding what happened, use temporal words to signal event order, and provide some sense of closure.	**1-1:** T321, T331, T343, T353,T360–T361 **1-5:** T167, T174–T175, T259, T276–T277, T380–T381, T463, T482–T483	**1-1:** T72, T168, T247, T257, T264, T425, T439, T445, T449, T456 **1-3:** T143, T163 **1-4:** T39, T49, T61, T71, T78, T141, T151, T163, T169, T173, T180, T243, T253, T265, T275, T282, T341, T351, T363, T373, T380, T441, T466, T467, T473, T480 **1-5:** T35, T45, T57, T67, T74, T135, T145, T157, T237, T245, T247, T269, T296, T341, T351, T363, T369, T373, T441, T451, T475 **1-6:** T514
Production and Distribution of Writing		
W.1.4 (Begins in Grade 3)		

W.1.5 With guidance and support from adults, focus on a topic, respond to questions and suggestions from peers, and add details to strengthen writing as needed.	**1-1:** T331, T343, T353, T360–T361 **1-2:** T35, T57 **1-3:** T473 **1-4:** T141, T151, T173 **1-5:** T475 **1-6:** T37, T69, T137	**1-1:** T41, T43, T55, T72, T129, T139, T151, T161, T168, T247, T257, T264, T321, T417, T427, T439, T449, T456 **1-2:** T67, T74, T143, T155, T165, T231, T253, T263, T270, T329, T339, T351, T361, T368–T369, T459, T466, R2 **1-3:** T35, T42, T57, T67, T74, T135, T157, T167, T174, T235, T245, T255, T257, T271, T278, T339, T373, T380, T441, T463, T480 **1-4:** T39, T49, T61, T71, T78, T163, T180, T243, T265, T275, T282, T341, T351, T363, T373, T380, T441, T449, T464, T473, T480 **1-5:** T45, T57, T67, T135, T143, T145, T157, T167, T174, T237, T259, T269, T276, T341, T351, T363, T373, T380, T441, T463, T482, R5 **1-6:** T45, T47, T59, T76, T147, T159, T169, T176, T235, T243, T245, T257, T267, T274, T337, T347, T359, T369, T376, T437, T445, T447, T459, T469, T476
W.1.6 With guidance and support from adults, use a variety of digital tools to produce and publish writing, including in collaboration with peers.	**1-3:** T441, T451, T463, T480–T481 **1-4:** T463, T480 **1-5:** T373, T463, T482 **1-6:** T437, T476–T477	**1-2:** T172, T427, T449, T459, T466 **1-3:** T35, T74, T373, T380 **1-4:** T373, T380, T441, T464, T473, R5 **1-5:** T377, T380, T451, R5 **1-6:** T173, T447, T459, T469

Research to Build and Present Knowledge

W.1.7 Participate in shared research and writing projects (e.g., explore a number of "how–to" books on a given topic and use them to write a sequence of instructions).	**1-1:** T453 **1-2:** T267 **1-3:** T71 **1-5:** T377 **1-6:** T173	**1-1:** T357, R2 **1-2:** R2 **1-3:** xxvi–xxvii, R2 **1-4:** xxvi, xxvi–xxvii, T377, T469, R3, R4 **1-5:** xxvi–xxvii, T265, T369, R3 **1-6:** xxvi–xxvii, T365, R3
W.1.8 With guidance and support from adults, recall information from experiences or gather information from provided sources to answer a question.	**1-1:** T453 **1-2:** T267 **1-3:** T71, T245, T257, T441 **1-5:** T377 **1-6:** T173	**1-1:** xxvi–xxvii, T157, T253, T349, T357, T445, R2 **1-2:** xxvi–xxvii, T63, T337, R3 **1-3:** xxvi–xxvii, T71, T349, T361, T373, T380, T449, T451, T463, T469, T473, T480 **1-4:** xxvi, xxvi–xxvii, T271, T377, T469, R4 **1-5:** xxvi–xxvii, T63, T163, T349, T471 **1-6:** xxvi–xxvii, T73, T145
W.1.9 (Begins in Grade 4)		

Range of Writing

W.1.10 (Begins in Grade 3)		

Speaking and Listening

	Key Citations	Additional Practice and Student Application
Comprehension and Collaboration		
SL.1.1 Participate in collaborative conversations with diverse partners about *grade 1 topics and texts* with peers and adults in small and larger groups.		

SL.1.1a Follow agreed-upon rules for discussions (e.g., listening to others with care, speaking one at a time about the topics and texts under discussion).	**1-1:** T165, T328 **1-2:** T15, T165, T169, T211,T365, T463 **1-3:** T377 **1-4:** T177 **1-6:** T373	**1-1:** xxiv, xxv, T13, T40, T50, T57, T69, T108, T111, T141, T153, T157, T165, T204, T207, T232, T237, T249, T300, T301, T303, T333, T345, T399, T424, T429, T441 **1-2:** xxiv, T42, T46, T111, T140, T145, T150, T157, T161, T208, T238, T243, T255, T259, T306, T341, T346, T353, T405, T407, T428, T439, T451, T458, T502 **1-3:** T12, T47, T59, T110, T113, T142, T147, T152, T159, T210, T213, T242, T247, T252, T314, T351, T363, T369, T417, T419, T453, T458, T465, T469 **1-4:** T13, T51, T63, T114, T115, T117, T148, T153, T165, T217, T219, T255, T267, T319, T321, T353, T365, T369, T417, T419, T465 **1-5:** T15, T42, T47, T59, T63, T113, T147, T152, T159, T211, T213, T238, T244, T249, T261, T313, T315, T353, T365, T416, T419, T448, T453 **1-6:** xxvi–xxvii, T12, T13, T15, T38, T49, T61, T65, T112, T113, T144, T161, T212, T213, T215, T247, T259, T271, T310, T311, T313, T338, T344, T349, T413, T415, T444, T449, T461
SL.1.1b Build on others' talk in conversations by responding to the comments of others through multiple exchanges.	**1-1:** T69 **1-2:** T169, T365 **1-3:** T275, T377 **1-4:** T177 **1-6:** T271	**1-1:** T40, T50, T140, T232, T399, T424 **1-2:** xxiv, T42, T110, T113, T140, T150, T211, T232, T306, T328, T346, T463 **1-3:** T15, T42, T46, T113, T142, T152, T242, T252, T346, T351, T363, T369, T419, T448, T453, T458, T465, T469 **1-4:** T15, T63, T115, T148, T165, T255, T266, T267, T321, T342, T348, T353, T365, T416, T453 **1-5:** T59, T146, T152, T159, T244, T248, T261, T348, T353, T365, T417, T465, T471 **1-6:** T44, T61, T115, T144, T161, T259, T415, T444, T461
SL.1.1c Ask questions to clear up any confusion about the topics and texts under discussion.	**1-1:** T69, T165, T261 **1-2:** T169, T365 **1-3:** T171, T377 **1-6:** T271	**1-1:** T15, T50, T111, T207, T303, T399 **1-2:** T15, T71, T113, T150, T211, T309, T328, T346, T407 **1-3:** T15, T52, T71, T213, T275, T317, T448, T469, T477 **1-4:** T15, T117, T177, T216, T219, T321, T363, T377, T419 **1-5:** T15, T59, T71, T113, T171, T213, T273, T315, T419, T479 **1-6:** T15, T73, T115, T173, T215, T313, T415, T473
SL.1.2 Ask and answer questions about key details in a text read aloud or information presented orally or through other media.	**1-1:** T15, T165, T261 **1-2:** T15, T169, T211, T365 **1-3:** T377, T477 **1-4:** T279 **1-6:** T73, T271	**1-1:** T40, T111, T207, T303, T399, R2 **1-2:** T71, T113, T238, T309, T336–T337, T407 **1-3:** T15, T113, T171, T213, T317, T419 **1-4:** xxv, T15, T117, T219, T250, T321, T377, T419 **1-5:** xxv, T15, T71, T113, T213, T315, T419, T479 **1-6:** T15, T115, T215, T313, T415, T473
SL.1.3 Ask and answer questions about what a speaker says in order to gather additional information or clarify something that is not understood.	**1-1:** T165 **1-3:** T171, T377 **1-4:** T75	**1-1:** T61, T130, T261, T300 **1-2:** T15, T110, T211 **1-3:** T15, T213, T275, T317, T448, T477 **1-4:** T15, T117, T177, T219, T253, T321 **1-5:** T15, T71, T113, T142, T171, T213, T273, T315, T419, T479 **1-6:** T15, T73, T115, T215, T310, T313, T415

Presentation of Knowledge and Ideas

SL.1.4 Describe people, places, things, and events with relevant details, expressing ideas and feelings clearly.	**1-1:** T165, T328 **1-3:** T171 **1-4:** T177, T477 **1-5:** T71, T273 **1-6:** T271, T373	**1-1:** T43, T152, T232, T344, T349, T445, R2, R3 **1-2:** T161, T259, T352, T357 **1-3:** xxv, T42, T63, T267, T346 **1-4:** T40, T46, T67, T148, T253, T271, T448, T488, T518, R4, R5 **1-5:** T42, T142, T145, T237, T241, T244, T246, T247, T265, T348, T448, T471, R5 **1-6:** xxv, T44, T65, T115, T147, T242, T263, T344, T465, R2

SL.1.5 Add drawings or other visual displays to descriptions when appropriate to clarify ideas, thoughts, and feelings.	**1-1:** T165, T261, T328, T424 **1-4:** T279 **1-6:** T373	**1-1:** T157, R2 **1-2:** T215, R2–R3 **1-3:** T63, T142, T145, T150 **1-4:** T271 **1-5:** T248, R4 **1-6:** T19, T465, T514
SL.1.6 Produce complete sentences when appropriate to task and situation.	**1-1:** T55, T69, T328, T424 **1-3:** T257 **1-5:** T341	**1-1:** T17, T33, T40, T47, T59, T113, T138, T143, T160, T209, T225, T234, T239, T241, T258, T305, T330, T332, T335, T342, T352, T401, T426, T428, T431, T438, R3 **1-2:** T17, T34, T66–T67, T72, T115, T133, T140. T144, T154, T166, T169, T213, T232, T263, T310. T328, T340, T352, T360, T363, T365, T366, T368, T404, T409, T438 **1-3:** T17, T35, T45, T46, T52, T68, T110, T115, T145, T158, T168, T213, T215, T234–T235, T244, T272, T319, T338, T346, T362, T421, T440, T462, T472 **1-4:** T17, T38, T40, T46, T69, T119, T140, T150, T162, T174, T221, T242, T323, T340, T366, T374, T421, T440, T462, T475 **1-5:** T17, T34, T47, T57, T58, T71, T111, T115, T144, T147, T158, T166, T211, T215, T236, T238, T248, T249, T258, T260, T262, T313, T317, T340, T348, T350, T351, T352, T364, T372, T375, T417, T421, T440, T450, T453, T464, T474, T476, T477 **1-6:** T13, T17, T36, T49, T113, T117, T136, T137, T149, T158, T159, T162, T170, T171, T213, T217, T234, T247, T265, T268, T269, T311, T315, T336, T346, T358, T359, T360, T370, T371, T374, T413, T417, T436, T448, T449, T451, T460, T471, R2

Language Standards

	Key Citations	Additional Practice and Student Application
Conventions of Standard English		
L.1.1 Demonstrate command of the conventions of standard English grammar and usage when writing or speaking.		
L.1.1a Print all upper- and lowercase letters.	**1-1:** BTS4, BTS8, BTS10,BTS14, BTS16, T42 **1-2:** T44 **1-3:** T44	**1-1:** T138, T264, T330, T352, T426 **1-2:** T66, T141, T142, T164, T262, T358, T436 **1-3:** T166, T244, T270, T348, T372, T450 **1-4:** T48, T252, T450 **1-5:** T44, T166, T246, T350, T450, T474 **1-6:** T46, T146, T346
L.1.1b Use common, proper, and possessive nouns.	**1-1:** T32, T42, T54, T64, T70–T71, T128, T150, T166–T167, T256 **1-2:** T164 **1-3:** T34, T44, T56, T66, T72–T73 **1-4:** T70	**1-1:** T33, T72, T129, T151, T160, T168, T235, T321, T360, R3 **1-2:** T154, T338, T350, T366, T368 **1-3:** T72, T372 **1-4:** T242, T252, T264, T280
L.1.1c Use singular and plural nouns with matching verbs in basic sentences (e.g., *He hops*; *We hop*).	**1-2:** T338, T366–T367 **1-3:** T244, T256, T276–T277, T440, T450, T462, T478–T479 **1-4:** T274	**1-2:** T350, T368, R3 **1-3:** T166, T234, T270, T278, T372, T419 **1-6:** T235, T257
L.1.1d Use personal, possessive, and indefinite pronouns (e.g., *I, me, my; they, them, their, anyone, everything*).	**1-5:** T134, T144, T156, T172–T173, T236, T246, T258,T274–T275, T340, T350, T362,T378–T379 **1-6:** T168, T266, T368	**1-2:** T19, T136, T256, T366 **1-3:** T116 **1-5:** T34, T35, T44, T56, T72, T166, T172, T216, T251, T276, T363, T480 **1-6:** T37, T68, T337, T468

L.1.1e Use verbs to convey a sense of past, present, and future (e.g., *Yesterday I walked home; Today I walk home; Tomorrow I will walk home*).	**1-1:** T224, T234, T246, T262–T263, T352 **1-3:** T338, T348, T360, T378–T379, T440, T462, T478–T479 **1-4:** T340, T350, T362, T372, T378–T379 **1-5:** T372	**1-1:** T225, T247, T264, T343, T417 **1-2:** T133, T155 **1-3:** T35, T116, T361, T441, T450 **1-4:** T222, T341, T383 **1-5:** T174, T216, T251
L.1.1f Use frequently occurring adjectives.	**1-1:** T320, T330, T342, T358–T359, T416, T448, T454–T455 **1-2:** T66 **1-6:** T234, T244, T256, T272–T273	**1-1:** T360, T417, T426, T427, T438, T439, T456 **1-2:** T35, T43, T45, T57, T58, T74, T143, T155, T156, T172, T239, T241, T253, T270, T339, T361, T368, T427, T436, T458, T502 **1-3:** xxv, T135, T321, T451 **1-4:** T61, T442, T450, T451 **1-5:** T161, T463 **1-6:** T165, T267, T436, T438, T446, T458, T459, T465, T469, T474
L.1.1g Use frequently occurring conjunctions (e.g., *and, but, or, so, because*).	**1-4:** T140, T150, T162, T178–T179 **1-5:** T166 **1-6:** T158, T174–T175	**1-2:** T154, T170–T171 **1-3:** T158 **1-4:** T13, T150 **1-5:** T146 **1-6:** T58, T176, T243
L.1.1h Use determiners (e.g., articles, demonstratives).	**1-2:** T426, T448, T464–T465 **1-3:** T144, T156, T172–T173,T472	**1-2:** T436, T466 **1-3:** T172–T173 **1-6:** T58, T74
L1.1i Use frequently occurring prepositions (e.g., *during, beyond, toward*).	**1-4:** T440, T462, T478–T479 **1-5:** T474	**1-3:** T339 **1-4:** T180, T265, T450, T472, T483 **1-5:** T66, T482
L.1.1j Produce and expand complete simple and compound declarative, interrogative, imperative, and exclamatory sentences in response to prompts.	**1-2:** T240, T252, T268–T269 **1-3:** T134, T144, T156, T270 **1-4:** T38, T48, T60, T76–T77, T140, T150, T162, T172, T178–T179 **1-5:** T66, T166 **1-6:** T46, T58, T74–T75, T136, T146	**1-1:** T139, T161, T168, T225, T235, T256, T257, T264, T321, T331, T353, T360, T417, T427, T449, T456, R3 **1-2:** T34–T35, T44–T45, T66–T67, T72, T74, T137, T154, T170, T172, 230, T241, T262–263, T270, T337, T350, T360, T458 **1-3:** T67, T74, T139, T166, T172, T234, T244, T256–T257, T276, T321, T348, T360, T372, T378, T440, T450, T451, T462, T478 **1-4:** T39, T47, T81, T141, T151, T183, T252, T253, T274, T275, T280, T282, T341, T350, T362, T372, T378, T441, T450, T451, T462, T473, T478 **1-5:** T44, T56, T72, T172, T237, T246, T247, T258, T351, T362, T372, T378, T440, T441, T450, T451, T462, T463, T474, T475 **1-6:** T36, T45, T47, T68, T76, T158, T165, T168, T169, T174, T234, T244, T266, T272, T274, T336, T358, T365, T368, T374, T436, T445, T446, T458, T474
L.1.2 Demonstrate command of the conventions of standard English capitalization, punctuation, and spelling when writing.		
L.1.2a Capitalize dates and names of people.	**1-3:** T34, T44, T56, T72–T73 **1-4:** T70, T242, T252, T264, T280–T281 **1-5:** T268	**1-1:** T64, T306 **1-2:** xxvi–xxvii **1-3:** T66 **1-4:** T243, T275, T282, T285
L.1.2b Use end punctuation for sentences.	**1-1:** T235, T257 **1-2:** T252, T268–T269 **1-4:** T48, T60, T76–T77	**1-1:** T18, T250 **1-2:** T270, T332, T360 **1-3:** T66, T172, T270, T449, T480 **1-4:** T47, T78, T81, T178, T180 **1-5:** T66 **1-6:** T46, T47, T58, T74, T76, T136, T158, T174, T176, T218, T316, T418, T469

L.1.2c Use commas in dates and to separate single words in a series.	**1-2:** T132, T142, T154, T170–T171 **1-4:** T264, T280–T281 **1-5:** T268	**1-2:** T164 **1-4:** T243, T253, T275, T282, T285 **1-6:** T244, T256
L.1.2d Use conventional spelling for words with common spelling patterns and for frequently occurring irregular words.	**1-1:** T18, T54, T131, T150, T227 **1-2:** T59, T312	**1-1:** T32, T42, T64, T70, T114, T132, T138, T154, T160, T163, T166, T210, T228, T234, T246, T256, T262, T306, T323, T324, T330, T342, T345, T346, T358, T402, T419, T420, T429, T438, T442, T448, T454 **1-2:** T18, T38, T47, T49, T56, T60, T66, T72, T74, T116, T132, T135, T142, T147, T154, T158, T164, T170, T214, T234, T240, T252, T262, T265, T268, T312, T328, T328, T332, T338, T350, T360, T410, T436, T441, T448, T458, T464 **1-3:** T18, T34, T44, T56, T72, T137, T138, T144, T156, T160, T169, T172, T216, T244, T249, T256, T276, T320, T348, T360, T364, T372, T378, T422, T444, T450, T455, T462, T472, T478, T480 **1-4:** T18, T42, T48, T53, T60, T70, T76, T120, T150, T162, T172, T178, T221, T222, T246, T252, T257, T264, T274, T280, T324, T350, T355, T362, T372, T378, T423, T444, T455, T472, T478 **1-5:** T18, T44, T49, T56, T66, T72, T116, T138, T144, T149, T156, T166, T172, T246, T258, T262, T268, T274, T318, T350, T362, T372, T378, T422, T444, T450, T455, T462, T474, T480 **1-6:** T18, T40, T46, T58, T62, T68, T74, T118, T140, T146, T158, T168, T174, T176, T218, T238, T244, T256, T266, T272, T274, T316, T340, T346, T358, T368, T374, T418, T440, T446, T451, T458, T468, T474
L.1.2e Spell untaught words phonetically, drawing on phonemic awareness and spelling conventions.	**1-1:** T18, T32, T306, T320 **1-2:** T312, T328	**1-1:** T36, T54, T58, T128, T132, T224, T228, T324, T416, T420 **1-2:** T18, T34, T38, T49, T116, T133, T147, T214, T230, T234, T245, T343, T410, T426, T430 **1-3:** T18, T34, T38, T44, T49, T56, T138, T149, T216, T234, T238, T320, T338, T342, T353, T422, T440, T455 **1-4:** T38, T42, T53, T119, T140, T144, T242, T246, T257, T323, T324, T340, T344, T355, T421, T440, T455 **1-5:** T18, T34, T38, T49, T115, T116, T134, T138, T149, T236, T240, T318, T340, T344, T355, T422, T440, T444, T455 **1-6:** T18, T36, T51, T118, T136, T140, T151, T218, T234, T238, T249, T316, T336, T340, T351, T417, T418, T436, T440

Knowledge of Language

L.1.3 (Begins in Grade 2)		

Vocabulary Acquisition and Use

L.1.4 Determine or clarify the meaning of unknown and multiple-meaning words and phrases based on *grade 1 reading and content*, choosing flexibly from an array of strategies.		
L.1.4a Use sentence-level context as a clue to the meaning of a word or phrase.	**1-1:** T158–T159, T254–T255, T446–T447 **1-3:** T164–T165 **1-6:** T66–T67, T142–T143	**1-1:** xxiv, xxv, T162, T300 **1-2:** xxv, T359, T457 **1-3:** T228, T241, T488 **1-4:** T74, T135, T238, T273, T284, T332, T337, T347, T383, T459 **1-5:** T126, T127, T130, T140, T141, T225, T227, T243, T329, T334, T371, T374 **1-6:** T70, T133, T143, T148, T265, T268
L.1.4b Use frequently occurring affixes as a clue to the meaning of a word.	**1-3:** T470–T471 **1-4:** T68–T69 **1-5:** T64–T65 **1-6:** T366–T367	**1-4:** T80 **1-5:** T460 **1-6:** T315, T317, T341, T352, T363, T436, T446, T451, T452, T458, T462, T463, T467, T474

Standard		
L.1.4c Identify frequently occurring root words (e.g., *look*) and their inflectional forms (e.g., *looks*, *looked*, *looking*).	**1-3:** T268–T269, T338–T339, T360–T361, T378	**1-4:** T160, T276 **1-5:** T256, T257 **1-6:** T249
L.1.5 With guidance and support from adults, demonstrate understanding of word relationships and nuances in word meanings.		
L.1.5a Sort words into categories (e.g., colors, clothing) to gain a sense of the concepts the categories represent.	**1-1:** T62–T63 **1-3:** T64–T65 **1-6:** T166–T167	**1-1:** T56, T66, T108, T226, T260, T322, T396, T440 **1-3:** T58, T136, T246, T338, T452, T460 **1-4:** T12, T62, T142, T152, T244, T254, T352, T442 **1-5:** T46, T136, T168, T210, T342, T442 **1-6:** T38, T48, T170, T236, T246, T348, T412
L.1.5b Define words by category and by one or more key attributes (e.g., a *duck* is a bird that swims; a *tiger* is a large cat with stripes).	**1-2:** T260–T261 **1-4:** T170–T171 **1-5:** T266–T267	**1-2:** T12, T264 **1-3:** T154 **1-4:** T182 **1-5:** T154, T270 **1-6:** T338
L.1.5c Identify real-life connections between words and their use (e.g., note places at home that are *cozy*).	**1-1:** T45, T52, T141, T148, T237, T244, T333, T340, T429, T436	**1-1:** T35, T57, T68, T149, T153, T164, T205, T245, T249, T260, T356, T397, T437, T441, T452 **1-2:** xxv, T47, T54, T70, T135, T145, T152, T157, T168, T243, T250, T255, T266, T307, T331, T341, T348, T364, T439, T446, T451, T462 **1-3:** T13, T37, T47, T54, T59, T68, T69, T70, T147, T159, T170, T211, T247, T254, T255, T259, T274, T351, T358, T376, T443, T460, T461, T465, T476 **1-4:** T13, T41, T47, T51, T63, T74, T143, T153, T160, T245, T255, T262, T267, T278, T343, T353, T361, T365, T376, T443, T460, T476 **1-5:** T37, T54, T55, T59, T70, T154, T170, T239, T256, T261, T272, T343, T360, T361, T365, T376, T453, T460, T478 **1-6:** T56, T57, T61, T72, T149, T156, T172, T237, T254, T255, T259, T270, T356, T357, T372, T439, T449, T456, T457, T461, T472
L.1.5d Distinguish shades of meaning among verbs differing in manner (e.g., *look, peek, glance, stare, glare, scowl*) and adjectives differing in intensity (e.g., *large, gigantic*) by defining or choosing them or by acting out the meanings.	**1-2:** T64–T65, T456–T457 **1-3:** T370–T371 **1-4:** T370–T371 **1-5:** T472–T473	**1-1:** T136 **1-2:** xxiv, T68, T331 **1-4:** T382
L.1.6 Use words and phrases acquired through conversations, reading and being read to, and responding to texts, including using frequently occurring conjunctions to signal simple relationships (e.g., *because*).	**1-1:** T35, T227 **1-3:** T377 **1-4:** T177, T477 **1-5:** T13, T111, T137, T465 **1-6:** T271	**1-1:** T13, T53, T67, T68, T109, T131, T141, T148, T153, T163, T164, T165, T205, T237, T245, T249, T259, T260, T300, T323, T333, T341, T345, T355, T356, T397, T419, T429, T441, T451, T452 **1-2:** T13, T37, T47, T55, T63, T69, T70, T153, T167, T168, T209, T233, T243, T250, T255, T265, T266, T307, T341, T348–T349, T353, T357, T363, T364, T405, T429, T438–T349, T446–T447, T451, T461, T462–T463 **1-3:** T13, T47, T54, T69, T70, T137, T155, T159, T169, T170, T211, T237, T247, T254, T259, T271, T273, T274, T315, T341, T347, T351, T359, T362, T363, T375, T376, T417, T443, T453, T460, T465, T475 **1-4:** T41, T46, T51, T63, T73, T74, T115, T143, T149, T153, T160, T165, T175, T176, T217, T245, T255, T262, T263, T267, T277, T278, T319, T353, T365, T375, T376, T377, T460, T464 **1-5:** T13, T37, T47, T54, T69, T70, T111, T137, T147, T155, T158, T159, T162, T169, T170, T211, T244, T257, T261, T264, T265, T271, T272, T273, T313, T343, T353, T360, T365, T375, T376, T417, T443, T451, T453, T461, T463, T465, T477, T478 **1-6:** xxv, T13, T39, T49, T56, T61, T67, T71, T72, T113, T137, T139, T147, T149, T156, T159, T161, T171, T172, T176, T213, T247, T254, T269, T270, T311, T339, T349, T356, T361, T364, T365, T371, T372, T439, T449, T456, T459, T469, T471, T472